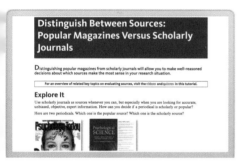

The Call to Write

The Call to Write

SIXTH EDITION

John Trimbur

EMERSON COLLEGE

WADSWORTH
CENGAGE Learning

Australia • Brazil • Japan • Korea • Mexico • Singapore • Spain • United Kingdom • United States

WADSWORTH
CENGAGE Learning·

The Call to Write, Sixth Edition
John Trimbur

Publisher: Monica Eckman

Acquisitions Editor: Margaret Leslie

Senior Development Editor: Leslie Taggart

Development Editor: Margaret Manos

Assistant Editor: Sarah Turner

Editorial Assistant: Cailin Barrett-Bressack

Media Editor: Janine Tangney

Brand Manager: Lydia Lestar

Senior Content Project Manager: Corinna Dibble

Senior Art Director: Marissa Falco

Manufacturing Planner: Betsy Donaghey

Rights Acquisition Specialist: Ann Hoffman

Production Service and Compositor: MPS Limited

Text Designer: Liz Harasymczuk

Cover Designer: Wing Ngan

Cover Image: Nycretoucher/Workbook Stock/Getty Images

For product information and technology assistance, contact us at
Cengage Learning Customer & Sales Support, 1-800-354-9706

For permission to use material from this text or product, submit all requests online at **www.cengage.com/permissions**. Further permissions questions can be emailed to **permissionrequest@cengage.com**.

Library of Congress Control Number: 2012935642

Student Edition:
ISBN-13: 978-1-133-31114-0
ISBN-10: 1-133-31114-8

Wadsworth
20 Channel Center Street
Boston, MA 02210
USA

Cengage Learning is a leading provider of customized learning solutions with office locations around the globe, including Singapore, the United Kingdom, Australia, Mexico, Brazil and Japan. Locate your local office at **international.cengage.com/region**

Cengage Learning products are represented in Canada by Nelson Education, Ltd.

For your course and learning solutions, visit **www.cengage.com**.

Purchase any of our products at your local college store or at our preferred online store **www.cengagebrain.com**.

Instructors: Please visit **login.cengage.com** and log in to access instructor-specific resources.

Printed in the United States of America
1 2 3 4 5 6 7 16 15 14 13 12

Brief Contents

Contents

PART 2   WRITING PROJECTS 123

CHAPTER 5   Memoirs 125

PART 3   WRITING AND RESEARCH PROJECTS 393

CHAPTER 13   Doing Research: Critical Essays, Research Papers, and Magazine Articles 395

CHAPTER 15 A Guide to Print, Electronic, and Other Sources 465

CHAPTER 22   Writing Portfolios 576

Guide to Visual Design

Preface

The Call to Write, Sixth Edition, offers students a broad introduction to writing so that they can learn to write with flexibility and influence in a variety of settings. Many of the assignments in the following chapters are typical of the writing college students are called on to do. A central aim of this book is to help students become effective writers in their college coursework. At the same time, *The Call to Write* takes as its starting point the view that writing is much more than a school subject. Writing is an activity individuals and groups rely on to communicate with others, organize their social lives, get work done, entertain themselves, and voice their needs and aspirations. Accordingly, this textbook presents a wide range of situations that call on people to write—in everyday life, in school, in the workplace, and in the public sphere.

Just as the situations that give rise to writing differ, so do the tools available to writers. Writing can no longer refer simply to the traditional forms of print literacy. It also involves the visual design of the page and screen and the new digital media that enable the integration of text, graphics, sound, and video. Although *The Call to Write* cannot teach many of the skills needed to operate the new writing technologies, it takes into account how writers use these new means of communication and how many forms of writing combine words and graphics to deliver a message.

One of the main premises of the book is that writing should belong to everyone in the various roles people play. *The Call to Write* offers students an education in writing, with the goal of enabling them to see how writing connects individuals to others and to the cultural practices and social institutions that shape their lives. In this regard, the call to write—the felt sense that something needs to be said—presents writing not just as a skill to master but as a means to participate meaningfully in the common life and to influence its direction.

DISTINCTIVE FEATURES OF *THE CALL TO WRITE*

The goal of *The Call to Write* is to offer teachers and students a range of activities that are grounded in rhetorical traditions and the accumulated experience of successful writing instruction. It has been enormously gratifying that teachers and students who used the first five editions of *The Call to Write* have confirmed the practical value of its approach. The sixth edition builds on—and seeks to refine—the basic features that give *The Call to Write* its distinctive character:

▶ **An emphasis on the rhetorical situation.** *The Call to Write* begins with the idea that writing doesn't just happen but instead takes place in particular social contexts. Throughout the textbook, students are provided with opportunities to analyze how rhetorical situations give rise to the call to write. A wide array of writing—from news stories, reports, op-ed pieces, and music reviews to posters, graffiti, ads, and flyers, as well as academic articles, literary essays, and student work—illustrates the range and richness of situations that call on people to write.

▶ **Genre-based writing assignments.** To help students understand the choices available to them when they respond to the call to write, the "Writing Projects" in Part Two use the notion of genre as the basis for guided writing assignments. Each chapter includes individual and collaborative writing assignments based on familiar genres; extensive treatment of invention, planning, peer commentary, and revision; samples of student writing; and an opportunity for students to reflect on the process of writing.

▶ **Integration of reading and writing through rhetorical analysis.** Chapter 2, "The Choices Writers Make: Writing a Rhetorical Analysis," introduces students to rhetorical analysis, with an emphasis on the way writers craft a rhetorical stance in response to the call to write. This focus continues in Part Two, with For Critical Inquiry questions that ask students to read closely and carefully, to understand their response as readers and the decisions writers make when they take up the call to write. The Further Exploration section in each chapter in Part Two includes Rhetorical Awareness and Genre Choice questions that explore rhetorical situations and strategies across genres and media.

▶ **A focus on visual design and delivery.** *The Call to Write* emphasizes not only how many types of writing integrate text and graphics but that writing itself is a form of visible language designed to deliver messages to readers. Chapter 17, "Visual Design," explores how visual design is used for purposes of identification, information, and persuasion; the chapter also provides instruction in effective page design. Chapter 18, "Web Design," considers how Web pages integrate word and image, and Chapter 19, "PowerPoint Presentations," includes guidelines on designing PowerPoint slides.

▶ **An emphasis on ethics and the writer's responsibilities.** *The Call to Write* presents boxes on the ethics of writing that raise issues concerning writers' responsibilities toward their readers and their subjects. Chapter 3, "Persuasion and Responsibility: Writing a Position Paper," includes extensive coverage of how writers can deal responsibly with disagreements and negotiate their differences with others.

▶ **An emphasis on collaborative learning.** *The Call to Write* includes many opportunities for group discussions, as well as guidelines for peer commentaries in each of the chapters in Part Two. Chapter 20, "Case Study of a Writing Assignment," traces how a student used peer response to write an academic paper, and Chapter 21, "Working Together: Collaborative Writing Projects," offers information and advice about group writing projects.

NEW TO THE SIXTH EDITION

The sixth edition includes new and revised features to help students understand and respond to the call to write. These additions come in large part from discussions with writing teachers who used the first five editions of *The Call to Write*.

▶ **A new emphasis on multimodal composition.** *The Call to Write* emphasis on multimodality comes from the recognition that the tools, media, and platforms of writing have expanded the possibility of composition to include images, color, movement, and sound. Multimodal design in print and new media appears in Chapter 1. Each of the chapters in Part Two, "Genres of Writing," features two examples of multimodal composition, with suggestions for analyzing them.

▶ **The Occupy Wall Street presence.** The Occupy Wall Street movement, with its now famous slogan "We Are the 99%," spread like wildfire across the United States and internationally in the fall of 2011. At the time this edition of *The Call to Write* is published, it is hard to predict what will become of the Occupy movement. But no matter what its fate may be, the Occupy movement provides an interesting opportunity to examine how writing and graphics are tied into public life and the ongoing struggle to influence opinion and shape the social future. *The Call to Write* presents a variety of writing and graphics from or about Occupy, including posters, a letter-writing campaign, and essays by Robert Hass and Paul Krugman.

▶ **A new chapter on the essay.** Chapter 4, "The Shape of the Essay: How Form Embodies Purpose," is designed to explore the particular possibilities of the essay as an instrument of inquiry, exploration, observation, and reflection. This chapter builds on the rhetorical analysis of Jerald Walker's personal essay "Before Grief" in Chapter 2 to examine the craft of essay writing, how essayists engage their readers' attention, and the forms they use.

▶ **A new chapter on multigenre writing projects.** Chapter 12, "Multigenre Writing: Publicity, Advocacy Campaigns, and Social Movements," presents a capstone writing assignment at the end of Part Two, "Genres of Writing." The chapter investigates publicity for a film series, press kits, social media, and manifestos. The chapter offers students the opportunity to examine how these and other genres in Part Two fit together in public writing, and to design their own multigenre writing projects.

▶ **Updated MLA and APA guidelines for citation and formatting,** based on the seventh edition of the *MLA Handbook for Writers of Research Papers* (2009) and the sixth edition, second printing of the *Publication Manual of the American Psychological Association* (2009), appear in Chapter 14, "Working with Sources."

USING THE CALL TO WRITE

The Call to Write is meant to be used flexibly, to fit the goals and local needs of teachers, courses, and writing programs. Although there is no single path to follow in teaching *The Call to Write*, for most teachers the core of the book will be the Writing Projects in Part Two—the guided writing assignments based on common genres.

Teachers can choose from among these genres and assign them in the order that best suits their course design.

A rich array of material appears in the other sections of *The Call to Write*, and teachers may draw on the various chapters to introduce key concepts and deepen students' understanding of reading and writing. It can be helpful to think of the organization of the book as a modular one that enables teachers to combine chapters in ways that emphasize their own interests and priorities.

The following overview of the organization of *The Call to Write* describes the six main parts of the book.

▶ **Part One, "Writing and the Rhetorical Situation,"** introduces students to the notion of the call to write, offers strategies for critical reading and rhetorical analysis, and presents methods for identifying disputed issues, planning responsible arguments, and negotiating differences with others. These chapters can serve to introduce central themes at the beginning of a course, or they can be integrated throughout the course.

▶ **Part Two, "Writing Projects,"** presents familiar genres of writing, with examples, For Critical Inquiry questions, and individual and collaborative writing assignments. Assignments call on students to write for a number of different audiences and in a number of different settings, ranging from everyday life to the academic world, to public forums. These chapters form the core of *The Call to Write*.

▶ **Part Three, "Writing and Research Projects,"** explores the genres of the critical essay, the research paper, and the fieldwork report. It considers what calls on people to do research, how they formulate meaningful questions, and the sources they typically use. Part Three provides an overview of the research process, introduces students to library and online research, and includes information about research projects that use observation, interviews, and questionnaires. This section is particularly appropriate for writing courses that emphasize writing from sources and research-based writing.

▶ **Part Four, "Delivery: Presenting Your Work,"** looks at how writers communicate the results of their work to readers. It includes chapters on visual design, Web design, and PowerPoint presentations. These chapters can be integrated into a course at many points, depending on the teacher's goals.

▶ **Part Five, "Writers at Work,"** presents a case study of a student using peer commentary to complete an academic writing assignment, looks at how writers work together on collaborative writing projects, and examines how writers assembly portfolios to represent their work. These chapters can be integrated into a course at a number of points—to initiate discussion of how writers manage individual writing projects, to enhance student understanding of peer commentary, to prepare students for collaborative writing projects, and to plan an end-of-term writing portfolio.

▶ **Part Six, "Guide to Editing"**

ADDITIONAL RESOURCES FOR *THE CALL TO WRITE*

The Call to Write, Sixth Edition, is accompanied by many helpful supplements for both teachers and students.

Interactive eBook for *The Call to Write*

Students can choose to do all of their reading online and use the eBook as a handy reference while completing their coursework. The eBook includes the full text of the print version and gives students the ability to search, highlight, and take notes.

Enhanced InSite™ for *The Call to Write*

Easily create, assign, and grade writing assignments with Enhanced InSite™ for *The Call to Write*. From a single, easy-to-navigate site, you and your students can manage the flow of papers online, check for originality, and conduct peer reviews. This course includes YouBook, a fully customizable, interactive, and true-to-page eBook. YouBook gives instructors the option to reorder chapters and sections of the book to match their syllabus, embed YouTube videos directly on eBook pages, and also includes a discussion board. Through Enhanced InSite™, students can also access private tutoring options, and resources for writers that include anti-plagiarism tutorials and downloadable grammar podcasts. Enhanced InSite™ provides the tools and resources you and your students need plus the training and support you want. Learn more at http://www.cengage.com/insite.

Online Instructor's Manual for *The Call to Write*

Available for download on the Book Companion Web site, this manual contains valuable resources to help instructors maximize their class preparation efforts. It includes sample syllabi and teaching tips for each chapter in the sixth edition.

ACKNOWLEDGMENTS

Preparing *The Call to Write* has made me acutely aware of the intellectual, professional, and personal debts I have accumulated over the years teaching writing, training writing teachers and peer tutors, and administering writing programs and writing centers. I want to acknowledge the contributions so many rhetoricians and composition specialists have made to my thinking about the study and teaching of writing, and I hope they will recognize—and perhaps approve of—the way their work has influenced the design of this book.

The unifying theme of the "call to write," as many will note immediately, comes from Lloyd Bitzer's notion of "exigence" and the "rhetorical situation." The influence of Carolyn Miller's seminal work on genre as "social action," along with explorations of genre theory by Charles Bazerman, Anis Bawarshi, and Amy Devitt, should be apparent at every turn. The emphasis on multimodal composition in this edition of *The Call to Write* is indebted to Gunther Kress, the indispensable source of thinking about the design of print and new media. I learned to teach writing from two great mentors, Ken Bruffee and Peter Elbow, and their mark is everywhere in the book.

I want to thank the lecturers and graduate instructors in the First-Year Writing Program at Emerson College for the work they've done redesigning the first-year writing curriculum and turning what had become a more or less moribund second-semester term paper class into an exciting and innovative genre-based research writing course. Their teaching, the writing assignments they developed, and their students' work shaped many of the changes that appear in the sixth edition of *The Call to Write*. Working with these wonderful colleagues since 2007 has been one of the best experiences in my professional life, and I am happy to note in particular the contribution that Aaron Block made to this edition, helping to invent the Emerson undergraduate Stacy Yi and her writing. I also want to note the writing from real Emerson students and from students at Brown University and Worcester Polytechnic Institute, where I developed and taught early versions of *The Call to Write*. Some of the student writing has been edited for this book.

Margaret Manos was the development editor for *The Call to Write*, Sixth Edition, and Margaret Leslie was the acquisitions editor; I want to acknowledge their hard work, careful attention, good senses of humor, and loyalty to this project.

To the many reviewers who provided valuable feedback at many points, my thanks: Vivian Adzaku, University of Arkansas, Pine Bluff; Susanne Bentley, Great Basin College; Candace Boeck, San Diego State University; Nancie Burns-McCoy, University of Idaho; Mary Ann Dietiker, Hill College; Marie Fitzwilliam, College of Charleston; Kimberly Halpern, Rose State College; Michael Hill, Henry Ford Community College; Colin Innes, Saddleback College; Katherine Judd, Volunteer State Community College; Noreen Lace, California State University, Northridge; Quincy Lieskse, Craven Community College; Molly Lingenfelter, Truckee Meadows Community College; Marilyn Metzcher-Smith, Florida State College, Jacksonville; Sally Nielsen, Florida State College, Jacksonville; Steven Pauley, Marshall University; Arnetra Pleas, Holmes Community College; Douglas Robillard, University of Arkansas, Pine Bluff; Susan Swetnam, Idaho State University; Katherine Tracy, Nicholls State University; Wendy Vergoz, Marian University; Theresa Walther, Rose State College; Carol Warren, Georgia Perimeter College; and Brett Wiley, Mount Vernon Nazarene University.

Finally I want to acknowledge the contributions to *The Call to Write* made by Lundy Braun, Lucia Trimbur, and Martha Catherine Trimbur. They not only provided emotional support; they were coworkers, contributing samples of their writing, suggesting readings and assignments, and locating Web sites and other resources. This has been, in many respects, a joint venture, and I am gratified by their presence in the book.

John Trimbur

Writing and the Rhetorical Situation

INTRODUCTION: THE CALL TO WRITE

The call to write may come from a teacher who assigns a paper, someone who wants to friend you on Facebook, or a supervisor at work. Maybe you keep a journal or write short stories. Maybe you go to poetry slams. You may feel called to write an email to your congressman or sign a petition. Or you belong to a campus organization or community group and want to publicize its aims and activities. In any case, as you will see throughout this book, people who write typically experience a felt sense that some need can be met by writing. This feeling is the call to write, the urge to put thoughts and emotions into words to make something happen.

By analyzing occasions that give rise to the impulse to write, you can deepen awareness of your own and other people's writing, expand your writing repertoire, and develop a flexible and persuasive approach to a range of writing genres.

The three chapters in Part One look at why and how people respond to the call to write:

▶ Chapter 1: "What Is Writing Today? Analyzing Literacy Events and Practices" examines writing in the digital age—in both print texts and new media.

▶ Chapter 2: "Understanding the Rhetorical Situation. The Choices Writers Make. Writing a Rhetorical Analysis" investigates how writers identify and respond to the call to write.

▶ Chapter 3: "Persuasion and Responsibility. Writing a Position Paper" considers what makes writing persuasive and how to construct a responsible argument.

⇨ REFLECTING ON YOUR WRITING |||||||||||||||||||||||||||||||||||||||||||||||||||||||||||||

The Call to Write

1. Choose a piece of writing you've done at some time in the past. Think of something other than a writing assignment you did in school. The piece of writing could be an email to a friend, a blog, a Web page, something you wrote at work, a diary entry, a letter, an article for a student newspaper or community newsletter, a petition, a flyer, or a leaflet for an organization you belong to. Whatever the writing happens to be, write a page or two in which you describe what called on you to write and how you responded.

   • What was the situation that made you feel a need to respond in writing?

   • Why did you decide to respond in writing instead of taking some other action or not responding at all?

   • What was your purpose in responding to the call to write? Who was your audience? What relationship to your readers did you want to establish? What tone of voice did you use? How did you make these decisions?

2. With two or three other students, take turns reading aloud what you have written. Compare the situations that gave rise to the call to write and the way each of you responded. What, if anything, is similar about the ways you identified and responded to the call to write? What was different? How would you account for the differences and similarities?

CHAPTER 1

What Is Writing Today?

Analyzing Literacy Events and Practices

Learning to write involves an understanding of your experience as a writer and a knowledge of the forms and media of writing. The purpose of this chapter is to analyze how writing actually takes place in the world, to examine how it circulates in contemporary society—in the design and production of texts, in print and electronic networks of distribution and reception, and in the institutions and values that writing is part of.

The writing assignment at the end of the chapter "Analyzing Literacy Events and Practices" calls on you to analyze a particular occasion or type of writing—an event or a practice—to understand how writing shapes people's identities, interests, and interactions. The aim of the assignment is to examine how people use writing to participate in social life, to inscribe their presence in the written record and give voice to their own and others' needs and aspirations. The assignment asks you to identify social roles and identities linked to writing, such as student, intellectual, literary artist, visual designer, citizen, worker, knowledge manufacturer, culture jammer—sign makers of all sorts.

Exploring literacy events and practices, drawn from your own and your classmates' experience, is meant to survey a broad range of writing occasions—to generate data, evidence, and subject matter for writing about the role of writing in people's lives. It starts a course on writing by locating ourselves as writers in the context of our times, with all the resources of representation available. This chapter asks you to investigate writing across social domains, genres, and media.

A GALLERY OF SIGNS

We live in a world that is saturated by writing. As you walk around campus or the streets of a city, notice how written the built environment is, how signs of all sorts compose your field of vision. Imagine the signs are voices contending for your attention. Which ones stick out for you? Why? What relation do these signs have to each other and to the places where they appear?

Here is a gallery of signs you might encounter in any urban landscape. Consider the purposes the signs serve. On whose behalf do the signs speak? What sort of relationship do these signs seek to establish with the people who read them?

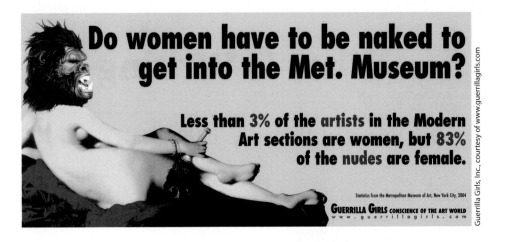

Do women have to be naked to get into the Met. Museum?

Less than 3% of the artists in the Modern Art sections are women, but 83% of the nudes are female.

Statistics from the Metropolitan Museum of Art, New York City, 2004

GUERRILLA GIRLS CONSCIENCE OF THE ART WORLD
w w w . g u e r r i l l a g i r l s . c o m

Guerrilla Girls, Inc., courtesy of www.guerrillagirls.com

DIVORCE FROM $250

Charles Gullung /Getty Images

WEDDING CHAPEL
MARRIAGE INFORMATION
OPEN 7 DAYS
TIL MIDNIGHT

Digital Vision/Photodisc/Jupiterimages

DANGER
ASBESTOS
CANCER AND LUNG DISEASE HAZARD
AUTHORIZED PERSONNEL ONLY

iStockphoto.com/Dan Moore

© Bruno Medley/Alamy

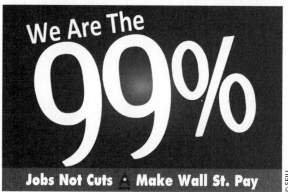

© SEIU

LUCY NICHOLSON/Reuters /Landov

ETHICS OF WRITING

Graffiti has become an omnipresent feature of contemporary urban life. Spray-painted or otherwise pasted on walls and subway cars, graffiti can perform a number of functions: marking a gang's turf, putting forth political messages, expressing the individual writer's identity, expressing grief for someone killed or

©Martha Cooper

Martha Cooper

anger at an enemy. Reactions to graffiti differ dramatically. Some see it simply as a crime—an antisocial act of vandalism—whereas others see it as a form of artistic expression and political statement by the disenfranchised. What ethical issues are raised for you? Do you consider graffiti a justified form of writing even though it is illegal? Why or why not?

Frank Mullin

KEEPING A LITERACY LOG

To get a sense of how writing saturates everyday life, keep a literacy log for 8 hours. Carry a notebook with you so you can record every time you read or write something. Note time, place, and type of written text involved. Here's an example of the first couple of hours.

MARCIE CHAMBERS, DECEMBER 2, 2011

8:02 a.m.	Dorm room	Checked email and Facebook. Wrote email to my sister Lucille.
8:25 a.m.	Walking from dorm to classroom	Noticed sign about stopping gentrification in Olneyville. Text message from Dave (really sexist).
8:30–9:45 a.m.	Sociology 121 lecture	Took notes on lecture. Doodled on handout (is that writing?).
9:52 a.m.	Walking from class-room to Starbucks	Passed homeless man with a sign.
9:54 a.m.	Starbucks	Looked at menu. Took free MP3 download card. Text-messaged Sean to meet in library.

Meet with two or three classmates to analyze your logs. Group types of writing into categories according to their purposes. What patterns emerge from your analysis?

Text message

Stuart Key/Dreamstime.com

Sign from homeless person

Joe Drivas/Getty Images

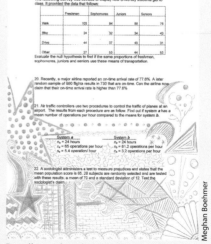

Doodles on handout, Sociology 121

Meghan Boehmer

DOMAINS OF WRITING: PRINT TEXTS AND NEW MEDIA

The Call to Write includes examples of writing from various social domains—everyday life; schooling; the workplace; advertising; social marketing; media outlets; the academic, literary, and intellectual networks of the public sphere; the partisan world of civic engagement; social movements; and advocacy campaigns. The forms of writing that result can be divided into **print texts**, which you can hold and turn the pages, and new media, which appear to exist weightlessly in the digital signals on computer screens.

Print texts date back to the fifteenth-century invention of the printing press. They continue to maintain a powerful hold in contemporary society as the most authoritative source of information, knowledge, and public influence. Legal documents; government records; archival collections in museums, libraries, and research institutes; textbooks; dictionaries and encyclopedias; scholarly and trade publishing; journals of opinion, editorials in the leading national newspapers—all these print texts retain great cultural prestige and authority.

One change over the past decades is that print texts are now for the most part composed, designed, produced, and distributed digitally from networked computers. The difference between word processing today and the typewriter of the past is similar to that between vinyl phonograph recordings and an MP3 file—everything recent is digital rather than analogical, expanding dramatically writers' ability to lay out page designs and insert files of images and visual displays of information into print texts. Writers are now, in effect, graphic designers and desktop publishers as well as the composers of print texts.

New media expand the channels and outlets for writing, as well as the capacity to store and share information. In the era of digital communication, texting, instant messenger, phone apps, email, the blog-o-sphere, informational Web sites, Twitter, LinkedIn, and Facebook all involve new formats and platforms for writing and disseminating messages. Any investigation of writing today must take these new media into account to examine how they operate, how they structure communication, and the role they play in people's interactions.

Eviction Memories

Molly Osberg and Tim Fitzgerald

....

Molly Osberg and Tim Fitzgerald recall the night of November 15, 2011, when New York police raided Zuccotti Park and evicted Occupy Wall Street. Notice how new media shape access to information and communication with others. Circle every time there is some reference to new media—its platforms and devices—to examine how connectivity operates at this moment in the Occupy movement. DICEY (A.K.A. TIM): The first sign of trouble was a Tweet:

[at]mcduh: [at]questlove sayin he saw hundreds of riot cops on South St, Manhattan bout 1hr ago. #occupywallst [at]DiceyTroop are yall aware of anything?

I immediately crossed Broadway on the south side of Liberty, side-stepping dormant traces of ongoing street maintenance and responding: [at]mcduh [at]questlove all quiet at the Park. What did you see questo? Maybe Batman stuff?

As I neared Pearl Street, bad omens rounded the corner, driving back the way I came and toward Liberty Square: ten NYPD trucks towing the kind of lighting rigs often seen illuminating nocturnal construction projects. I'd been thinking about the Spokes Council meeting I'd just left, and my heart and mind bickered the way they do when confronted by disruptive truths. I was far from ready to admit that everything was about to change.

MOLLY: Tim's text woke me. Before I got into bed I had checked my phone and scrolled through what was later dubbed Questlove's "Paul Revere Moment." I'd thought: another false alarm. We'd rushed down to the park maybe two weeks before, practically jumping up and down on the 4 train platform, only to find our friends at Zuccotti shrugging and bedding down for another night. It was a testament to how routine the extremes of life in the park had become. That night, we had found the comfort station sorting blankets, had helped a friend carry jail support supplies to the crosstown subway, had planned a half-baked theatrical action somewhere along the way, and had enjoyed a short—and really, shockingly civil—argument with a twentysomething far to the right of us politically . . . Normalcy. That night, it had been enough to soothe all our fears.

DICEY: As I reached Water Street, the whole police phalanx suddenly emerged from the flat block between Water and South Street. NYPD van after NYPD van rolled through the intersection in a single-file bumper-to-bumper line. Running up Pine to Nassau to Cedar, I recognized several members of Liberty Square's non-activist homeless population moving away from the park. Well, that's a bad sign. At Cedar and Broadway, fifty riot police were already assembled next to the red cube, backed by those enormous and shockingly bright klieg lights.

On the other side of the street, I pulled out my phone and snapped a shot of an equally large and well-lit deployment staring into our park from the top of the steps. I tweeted it with the words: Red alert at Liberty Square!

The biggest group of our people was at the kitchen. I reached them and realized I wasn't sure what to do with myself. What was my role here, right now? I went with what I knew and managed to assemble 140 characters of coherent thought: NOT A DRILL. SHIT IS GOING DOWN. PARK DEFENSE IN PROGRESS. If you want to save #occupywallstreet, come to park NOW.

MOLLY: Tim wrote: Eviction happening. Sound the Alarm. But what alarm did we have? I woke my roommates. We turned on the Livestream around the same time the second text came in from Occupy's emergency alert system. My laptop was still on the bed, and the three of us stood around it in various states of undress, staring.

MULTIMODAL COMPOSITIONS

Print and New Media

New media have made readers and writers alike more conscious of the visual design of writing. New software and online digital resources make multimodal composition more widely possible, enabling writers to design compositions that integrate a number of modalities, such as writing, typography, layout, still images, color, sound, music, moving pictures, quality of paper, gestures, and even smell.

In a sense, there is nothing new about multimodal compositions. They go back to earlier forms of writing, such as the illuminated manuscripts of the Middle Ages—Christian and Muslim alike—that combined word and image by hand in literary activity that was simultaneously an act of devotion.

By the nineteenth century, page design in the illustrated magazines of the print era combined words, wood engravings, and lithographic images to document social life and political upheavals in the modern world.

Photojournalism flourished in the twentieth century, combining words and photos in asymmetrical patterns across two pages. Contemporary news, popular science, music, fashion, travel, food, home, and sports magazines continue to use the double-page spread as a field of reading and seeing that integrates text and images in highly imaginative groupings.

Leemage/Universal Images Group/Getty Images

© Sonia Halliday Photographs/Alamy

Muhammed listening to a weeping doe. Turkey. 18th century.

Annunciation to the Shepherds. The Book of Hours. France. 14th century.

Scribner's was one of the leading magazines of its era, combining literary writing, investigative journalism, and essays of opinion and reflection on richly illustrated pages. This cover was done in the art nouveau style of the time. To see how lithography produced realistic images before the era of photojournalism, you can find articles from *Scribner's* in the 1890s at http://catalog.hathitrust.org/Record00505912.

This double-page spread appeared in *Life* magazine on August 16, 1937, as a tribute to the photographer Gerda Taro, who was killed during the Spanish Civil War—according to the magazine, "Probably the first woman photographer ever killed in action." She was the partner of Robert Capa, whose famous photo of a falling Loyalist militiaman can be seen at the top of the page.

NEW ORLEANS: A PERILOUS FUTURE

Protected only by dwindling wetlands and flawed levees, New Orleans is sinking further below rising seas and facing stronger hurricanes. Some experts say that the question isn't whether another disaster on the scale of Hurricane Katrina will hit New Orleans, but when. Even so, people are returning to the city they call home, and rebuilding yet again. At what cost?

As you read "New Orleans: A Perilous Future," you should consider the following questions:

- How would you feel if your home was devastated? Can you empathize with the residents of New Orleans?
- As you read the article below, keep the topic of insurance in mind, not only as a practical consideration but also as a concept, along with any questions that arise.

Struggling with debt and red tape as he rebuilt his cottage in the Gentilly neighborhood, Eric Martin nearly pulled it down in protest and moved to Chicago. Now he's raising the structure for flood protection and staying put. "Every time I think of leaving," he says, "I bump into somebody I know."

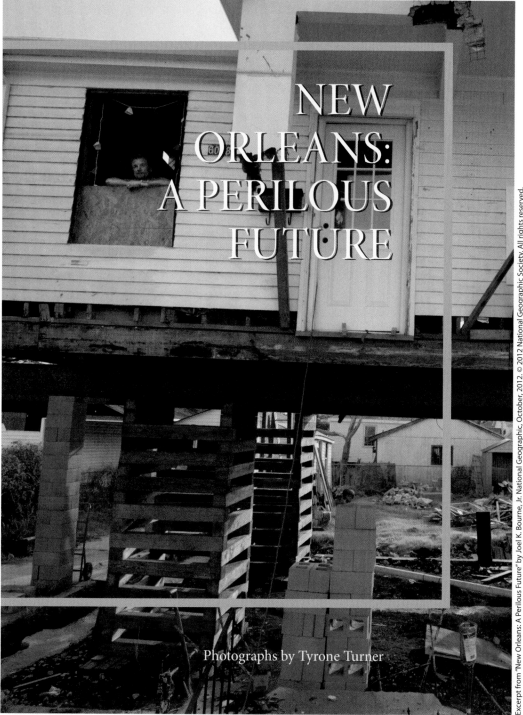

NEW ORLEANS: A PERILOUS FUTURE

Photographs by Tyrone Turner

⟶ FOR CRITICAL INQUIRY ||||||||||||||||||||||||||||||||||||||||||||||||||||||||||||||||||||||||||||||||||||||||||

Double-Page Spread

Compare the visual design of the double-page spreads in *Life*'s tribute to Gerda Taro and in *National Geographic*'s "New Orleans: A Perilous Future." Notice, for example, how the graphic designer at *Life* used the grid as the underlying matrix of composition and varied the size and distribution of the photographs to create asymmetrical patterns across the two pages. Blocks of written text are used as separate design elements that further define the space of the page. On the other hand, the designer at *National Geographic* uses one image to span both pages, with text and questions to the left of the photo. Consider the reading path your eyes take across these pages and how the page design influences you, as the reader/viewer, in connecting the images to each other and to the written text.

Technology, Dining, and Social Interactions

Ryan Catalani

··

New media has expanded the design possibilities of multimodal composition. Ryan Catalani wrote "Technology, Dining, and Social Interactions" for a first-year research writing class at Emerson College using the social storytelling site Storify to assemble text, photos, and links to scholarly journals, newspapers, blogs, Twitter, Flickr, and YouTube. By embedding links in his research essay, Ryan was able to create a hypertext where readers can connect immediately to his sources—to read newspaper, magazine, and scholarly journal articles and watch video clips. Notice in these two passages how the links provide access to sources of information in a way that is unimaginable in print texts. You can read the complete version of "Technology, Dining, and Social Interaction" at http://storify.com/ryancatalani/technology-dining-and-social-interactions.

Technology, dining, and social interactions

How does technology help and hurt social interactions? Can technology make dining and other group experiences better, or does it only detract from the user's participation in the "real life" event?

1.

The table was set and everyone was sitting around, chatting, laughing, and trying to distract themselves from the smells of the completely filled kitchen – yes, competely filled, cutting boards and baking sheets and various spatterings of flour and tomato sauce blanketed every counter and each burner on the stove held a pot or skillet or saucepan – which were wafting, unstoppable and delicious, into our noses, teasing us with the promise of equally-delicious food, which we could eat as soon as the water started boiling and Danny and I could cook the pasta. I looked at the big pot, then back at Danny and shrugged. He understood. Everyone was patient.

Photo by Ryan Catalani

rc-20120211-124

•• **ryancatalani** 3 months ago

Ryan Catalani, "Technology, Dining, and Social Interaction." http://storify.com/ryancatalani /technology-dining-and-social-interactions. Reprinted by permission of the author.

Ironically, Danny and I had been the first to arrive at Tamera's house that afternoon. Tamera, our research writing professor, told us we were the first group to ever show up on time for the cooking project, let alone five minutes early. We had some tea and got to work on our recipe, a Greek meat sauce composed not only of beef, but also pork and veal. The sauce was pleasantly bubbling away by the time the other two groups arrived and started to make their arepas and alfajores.

It was a uniquely exciting experience to cook with seven of my peers in our professor's kitchen, as our elbows bumped and we asked each other to please pass the salt or that spatula. We watched each other knead, chop, and stir, sweat beading on our foreheads and determination pouring from our hearts into those raw ingredients at our hands. The mixer whirred, the butter sizzled, and occassionally, the fire alarm blared.

The water, so impertinent, finally decided to boil. We cooked the spaghetti in a snap, and soon everyone's plates were replete with our evening's labors. Nothing was absent from the table — not an unfilled glass, misplaced fork, or glum face — well, except for our cellphones. Yes, our phones, which were out throughout the cooking process, suddenly disappeared from our hands when we started eating. This certainly wasn't unexpected; it's commonly considered impolite to use technology around the dinner table.

But why? It is perfectly acceptable to use technology in most social settings, except for, of course, dining. Laptops and iPads are becoming more prevalent in schools. Blackberries and, more recently, iPhones, are staples of corporate communication. On busses, trains, and airplanes, you're more than likely to find people staring at the shiny glass screens of their smartphones, perhaps playing Angry Birds, checking Facebook, or listening to music on Spotify. What makes the dinner table such a sacred space, when in pratically every other social situation, using mobile devices is okay? Or should dinner enjoy such a unique status, when technology has become so pervasive in otherwise everyday situations?

Dining isn't going to be any worse without the use of technology – somehow we've managed to live without Facebook for the past thousand years or so – but nor is it necessarily going to be any better by forcing people to keep their phones in their pockets. I'm eager to integrate technology into real-life experiences. I'll "check in" to locations using Foursquare and broadcast that check-in using Twitter and Facebook. I'll post photos of events with Instagram and upload videos with the iMovie app for iPhone. I'll look up answers to inane questions in conversation with Wikipedia, Wolfram Alpha, and of course, Google. I'll pay for drinks at Starbucks and the Apple Store with their respective iPhone apps, and use LevelUp to pay wherever I can.

Yet when I'm with others and it's time to eat, I won't hesitate to put my phone away (well, after I take a picture of the food). The Internet will be okay without you for a few hours. Why waste your time socializing with your list of Close Friends on Facebook when you can interact with your close friends right in front of you? Have a memorable dinner with the people around the table – only then can you tweet about it afterwards.

Photo by Ryan Catalani

rc-20120211-141

ryancatalani   3 months ago

Multimodal Composition and New Media

As you read "Technology, Dining, and Social Interactions," notice you have choices to click on the links or follow the line of analysis without interruption (http://storify.com/ryancatalani/technology-dining-and-social-interactions). Read the research essay twice. The first time, read straight through; the second time, click on all the links. Compare the reading experiences. What are the main differences? What are the advantages or disadvantages of the two ways of reading? How does the connectivity of hypertext change the nature of reading print texts?

ANALYZING LITERACY EVENTS AND PRACTICES

The terms *literacy events* and *literacy practices* give us a way to think about how reading and writing enter our lives and shape our interactions with others. Consider, for example, the following two written texts, the first from a third-grade classroom and the second from the Chicago Title Company office in Providence, Rhode Island. Explain how the texts cue us to the identities and social relations in the event.

> I will not get out of my seat
>
> I will not get out of my seat
>
> I will not get out of my seat
>
> I will not get out of my seat
>
> I will not get out of my seat
>
> I will not get out of my seat
>
> I will not get out of my seat

Memo to a Thief

. . . .

memorandum

To: The thief that has been stealing pens from the IBM.

From: A very angry phone receptionist who is constantly putting more pens near the IBM and who is perpetually frustrated with the fact that whenever he/she goes to use them they are missing.

Re: A way to remedy this situation.

Date: The summer

Over the course of the summer it has come to my attention that pens were mysteriously vanishing from the IBM computer. The action causes significant trouble when one tries to take a PHONE MESSAGE or attempts to take a START and commit it to memory. Instead of philosophizing about the possible criminals who insist on making my life harder (I know who you are!), I simply ask that if you, per chance, notice the absence of a pen or pencil near the IBM that you take it upon yourself to correct this mishap and replace one immediately.

I thank you for your time and efforts in this matter.

Analyzing literacy events and practices amounts to examining how writing, whether in the form of print texts or new media, is woven into people's lives and their relations to others. You can focus on a particular moment—a literacy *event*—in which writing plays a telling role in your interactions with others and the way participants interpret the event. Or you can focus on a particular use or type of writing—a literacy *practice*—that takes place routinely for a particular social purpose.

THREE LITERACY NARRATIVES, THREE EVENTS

These literacy narratives tell stories in which reading and writing are centrally involved in social interactions and power relations. As narratives, they have plots that tell of conflicts between characters and moments of revelation when the meaning of the event comes into focus.

From *Narrative of the Life of Frederick Douglass*
Frederick Douglass
....

This is a famous passage from Frederick Douglass's first autobiography in 1841 about his life as a slave and his escape from slavery.

Very soon after I went to live with Mr. and Mrs. Auld, she very kindly commenced to teach me the A, B, C. After I had learned this, she assisted me in learning to spell words of three or four letters. Just at this point of my progress, Mr. Auld found out what was going on, and at once forbade Mrs. Auld to instruct me further, telling her, among

---

other things, that it was unlawful, as well as unsafe, to teach a slave to read. To use his own words, further, he said, "If you give a nigger an inch, he will take an ell. A nigger should know nothing but to obey his master—to do as he is told to do. Learning would spoil the best nigger in the world. Now," said he, "if you teach that nigger (speaking of myself) how to read, there would be no keeping him. It would forever unfit him to be a slave. He would at once become unmanageable, and of no value to his master. As to himself, it could do him no good, but a great deal of harm. It would make him discontented and unhappy." These words sank deep into my heart, stirred up sentiments within that lay slumbering, and called into existence an entirely new train of thought. It was a new and special revelation, explaining dark and mysterious things, with which my youthful understanding had struggled, but struggled in vain. I now understood what had been to me a most perplexing difficulty—to wit, the white man's power to enslave the black man. It was a grand achievement, and I prized it highly. From that moment, I understood the pathway from slavery to freedom. It was just what I wanted, and I got it at a time when I the least expected it. Whilst I was saddened by the thought of losing the aid of my kind mistress, I was gladdened by the invaluable instruction which, by the merest accident, I had gained from my master. Though conscious of the difficulty of learning without a teacher, I set out with high hope, and a fixed purpose, at whatever cost of trouble, to learn how to read. The very decided manner with which he spoke, and strove to impress his wife with the evil consequences of giving me instruction, served to convince me that he was deeply sensible of the truths he was uttering. It gave me the best assurance that I might rely with the utmost confidence on the results which, he said, would flow from teaching me to read. What he most dreaded, that I most desired. What he most loved, that I most hated. That which to him was a great evil, to be carefully shunned, was to me a great good, to be diligently sought; and the argument which he so warmly urged, against my learning to read, only served to inspire me with a desire and determination to learn. In learning to read, I owe almost as much to the bitter opposition of my master, as to the kindly aid of my mistress. I acknowledge the benefit of both.

Petitioning the Powers
Russell Cruz

This literacy narrative was written in 1997 in a first-year writing course about an event that took place five years before when the writer was in junior high.

I think I really started to understand something about how writing actually works in the world when I was in the eighth grade. If you can remember what eighth grade is like, you might recall what hot shits kids think they are at that age. They've left childhood and are briefly at the top of the world before they go to high school and begin all over again as freshmen. That's how we were. And one of the things we got into was knowing our rights. This was a combination of what we heard on Clash and Rage Against the Machine albums and what we learned in American history. We knew that grownups couldn't just walk all over us. We knew we had rights and could petition the powers that be to change things.

Along with my friend Mike, I was a member of our junior high chorus. This was a big deal because the chorus director, Mr. DeSouza, was a legendary figure in our community. Every year for the past fifteen years or so, he took the chorus on a trip to an international competition, held in places like San Francisco, Toronto, Miami, and once in London. Every year the chorus won a gold medal. But Mike and I thought Mr. DeSouza was getting out of step with the times and that our repertoire of songs needed some updating. We mentioned this to him but he was not responsive. So, naturally, knowing our rights, we took the logical next step.

We went over to Mike's house after school and wrote a petition that asked Mr. DeSouza to add a few contemporary songs to the chorus's repertoire. We printed the petition and circulated it the next day among chorus members and other students as well to sign, figuring the chorus belonged to the school and the added names would make us look good.

We thought that Mr. DeSouza would see the numbers and meet right away to negotiate a settlement. We weren't asking for all that much, so we didn't think it would be a hassle. Wrong. The day after we left the petition in Mr. DeSouza's box, Mike and I got called into the principal's office. Mr. Boisvert, the principal, said we had a big problem. Mr. DeSouza was totally offended and insulted by the petition and had threatened to quit as chorus director, which would be a disaster because he was one of the most successful chorus directors in the country. And it was all our fault. We had "gone too far this time." When Mike and I said it was our right—and the American way—to petition for change peacefully, Mr. Boisvert looked right through us and said we weren't being fair to Mr. DeSouza, to the chorus, or to the school. We could write petitions later, when we were adults and could "accept responsibility for our actions" (whatever that meant). We had a choice: we could either apologize and stay in the chorus or quit. No deals.

The fact that Mike and I quit, missing a great trip the chorus took that year to Puerto Rico, isn't exactly the point of this literacy tale. Looking back on it, I'm interested in how writing a petition created such a crisis. Neither Mike nor I had imagined that Mr. DeSouza would react as he did. We certainly didn't intend to hurt his feelings or insult him. We thought we were just acting on our rights. But more important, the principal showed us that in fact we didn't have any rights. To him, we were still little kids and while we were expected to learn all about the Declaration of Independence and the Bill of Rights, we were really dependents. Knowing your rights, he said, was "for later."

Who Is Stacy Yi?

Stacy Yi is an imaginary student at Emerson College who graduates with a BA in Writing, Literature & Publishing in 2013, when she is moving to New York to work as a graphic designer on a small independent press that publishes mostly poetry and translation. Then maybe she will go to law school and concentrate in artistic and intellectual property. Stacy is a little bit of a hipster, loves 'zines, riot grrrls, and Wata the guitarist-vocalist in the Japanese drone metal band Boris. She participated in Occupy Boston in 2011 but doesn't consider herself a far-out anarchist. She is active in a community writing project that tutors high school students.

She is a composite of many students we have known and taught. Samples of her writing appear in *The Call to Write*, representing the kind of work we have seen students do at Emerson and elsewhere. The range of print and new media texts we attribute to Stacy provides the opportunity for her and us to reflect on her development as a writer—to make sense of what happened when she came to college and encountered new writing tasks, genres of writing, and modes of representation. In Chapter 22 "Writing Portfolios," Stacy pulls together examples of her writing and reflects on her work.

Here is a list of Stacy's writing:

▶ "Blogs Are Not Pseudo-Diaries" (literacy narrative), p. 23

▶ Revising Somali Pirates: A Rhetorical Analysis of 'You Are Being Lied to About Pirates' by Johann Hari", p. 58

▶ "iComics" (position paper), p. 84

▶ "A Very Edgy Ad: Phonak Hearing Aids" (rhetorical analysis), p. 238

▶ "Vinyl Underground: Boston's In Your Ear Records Turns 30" (PowerPoint presentation), p. 279

▶ "'Where More Americans Get Their News . . . Than Probably Should': *The Daily Show*" (rhetorical analysis), p. 308

▶ "Training Fighters, Making Men: A Study of Amateur Boxers and Trainers" (research proposal), p. 319

▶ "More Than Just Burnouts: Book Review of Donna Gaines' Teenage Wasteland," p. 372

▶ "Jigsaw Falling Into Place?: Radiohead and the Tip-Jar Model" (critical research essay), p. 397

▶ Stacy's portfolio, p. 578

Blogs Are Not Pseudo-Diaries
Stacy Yi

....

Stacy Yi wrote this literacy narrative for her first-year writing course at Emerson College in spring 2010.

Though it was not the first time I'd traveled outside of the United States, the summer I spent in the Dominican Republic after I graduated high school still presented me with a number of surprises. Discovering that after three years of Spanish classes I could only barely make conversation was one, and coping with the change in climate was another. Those were relatively minor obstacles, both of which I soon overcame. Far more interesting, though, was my hands-on education in the possibilities of travel journalism, and the freedom that comes with disregarding expectations.

Before I left home I set up a blog dedicated entirely to my trip–a kind of public travel journal. My list of people who wanted to hear from me while I was gone was growing quite long, so I figured a blog was the best way to make sure I wouldn't leave anyone out. And the comment section meant any responses I received would be organized right there on the page, eliminating the stuffed-full inbox that I would inevitably just delete in frustration. The morning of my departure I wrote my first post, about expectations and nerves, clicked "publish" and set off for the airport.

For the first week or so I updated diligently. My posts were fairly generic, the kind of stuff you'd expect to read from someone living abroad for the first time–I'm having fun, life here is different, here's a few pictures, I sure miss home–but I thought that's what you were supposed to say when you traveled, and what my readers would want to know. But fairly quickly my regimen fell away. My posts grew shorter and less frequent as I became bored with that kind of writing. And also, I noticed the number of views for each post dropping steadily. Apparently my audience was as bored with my writing as I was.

That was the end of my blog for a while–I didn't update it, didn't look for comments. For all intents and purposes, I forgot about it. But one afternoon after a long conversation with Lorena, the eldest daughter of my host family, I decided to write about her, and turned once again to the blog. That kicked off a series of posts in which I profiled each member of the family, writing about what I felt made them tick, the things we shared and disagreements we had. Very suddenly I was re-engaged with the blog, and began making daily posts–not about myself, or boring pseudo-diary entries, but reviews of restaurants I ate at, recaps of soccer games at the school nearby, even an opinion piece about the organization I'd traveled with. My page views didn't exactly go up, but I felt much more satisfied with my written work.

I realized that creating just another day-by-day diary might collect a lot of information, but wouldn't capture the feel of being in Santo Domingo for those three months. To make a record of my trip I needed to write in ways that fit the experiences I had, just like a professional travel writer would.

⟩⟩ FOR CRITICAL INQUIRY ‖‖‖

Analyzing Literacy Narratives

1. Use the following questions to examine each narrative:

   • What social interaction takes place? Who is involved? Who has power? How is power related to writing?

   • What is the plot? Is there a central conflict? How is it resolved?

   • How do the participants make sense of the event? Do they see the event the same way or do they differ in their interpretations?

2. What are the main differences and similarities between the three narratives? What is the significance of the differences and similarities?

3. Shirley Brice Heath defines a literacy event as "any occasion in which a piece of writing is integral to the nature of the participants' interactions and their interpretive practices." Use this definition as a conceptual framework to apply to the literacy narratives. What does it bring to light about the event? Exactly how is writing "integral"?

ANALYZING LITERACY PRACTICES

The term *literacy practices* refers to patterns in the way people use reading and writing to meet social needs—to form identities and social groupings, to include and exclude, to maintain status hierarchies or contest the unequal distribution of social power. Literacy events are singular, one-of-a-kind happenings that have a narrative structure, whereas literacy practices emphasize recurring uses of writing, in print texts and new media, that call for a slightly different attention and analysis to explain their ongoing function.

The following excerpt is a good example of how to analyze a literacy practice, to explain how a particular type of writing—in this case note-passing in junior high—operates in maintaining the status of a particular group—the social queens.

Note-Passing: Struggles for Status

Margaret J. Finders

....

This is taken from Just Girls: Hidden Literacies and Life in Junior High *(1997), Finders' study of how junior high girls used literacy outside the official school curriculum—signing yearbooks, passing notes, writing bathroom graffiti, and reading teen magazines.*

Note-writing as a genre did not allow for much individual expression or originality. The girls all protested indignantly whenever I suggested such a notion: "You can write whatever you want." Yet the following notes illustrate the standards required for the genre of note-writing.

LAUREN: Yo! What's up? Not much here. I'm in math and it is BORING. Did you know that I like Nate a lot. But he'd probably never go out with me caz I'm too ugly. AND FAT. Oh, well though. I'm still going to try and get him to go with me caz I like him. I hope he goes with me before the football game Friday. I want to be going with him at the game. Are you and Ricky going to the game? I want to go somewhere after that. Maybe you could come over or I could come to your house. Don't show this to anyone. W-B [Write Back] Maggie

LAUREN: Hey. What's up? You don't need to ask Bill for me cause he won't go and he's just that way I guess. You can try but I know he's not going to go. Well I'm almost positive. I'm in social studies and I just got busted caz I had none of my homework done. Fun. My handwriting majorly Sucks. I hate it. Go to *Body Guard* at the mall and I'll say you need a ride home. Then you can spend the night at my house. Call me tonight. I will be at my mom's. SS [Stay Sweet or Stay Sexy] Carrie.

Notes regularly began with a common salutation, "Hey, what's up?" followed by a reference to where the note was written—"I'm in math." "I'm in social studies." Because notes were always written in school, this move positioned the queen in opposition to the institutional power by boldly announcing an act of defiance during one particular class and then adding a condemning judgment such as, "It's so boring." In this move, queens perceived themselves as powerful by defying authority. Yet that power was somewhat diffused as they often embedded in the body of the note a reference to themselves as inadequate: too fat, too ugly, my handwriting sucks. Often in notes, messages closed with "Sorry So Sloppy," which were sometimes shortened to SSS. For the most part, extreme care was taken to write neatly, at times dotting the i's with circles or hearts.

The content of notes was generally about making social arrangements for after-school activities and for requesting help in making romantic contacts. The notes carried highly coded messages such as NMH. (not much here) that limited the readership to those who were inside the circle of friends. The closing, as well, was most often highly coded—BFF (best friends forever) W-B (write back)—to provide an insider quality to those who knew the codes. Britton (1970), noting the "with-it" language of adolescents, argues for the necessity of "drawing together members of a group or the set, and keeping outsiders out" (p. 235). The meaning behind SSS evolved over time. At first it meant "Sorry So Sloppy," but over the course of the seventh-grade year, it came to carry a completely different meaning: "Stay Sweet and Sexy." The evolution of this one code illustrates the demands embedded within shifting social roles from girl to adolescent.

Although notes generally followed a standard format, a few did contain important unknown information such as the appropriate time to receive a call, an apology for flirting with a boyfriend, or guarded information about family problems. The queens attempted to control the circulation of their notes and regularly added to their messages, "Don't show this to anyone." For the most part, notes created boundaries around a group of friends. By creating a tangible document, girls created proof of their memberships.

As stated previously, girls all voiced the opinion that "you just write whatever you want," yet when someone outside the intimate circle of friends wrote a note to one of the most popular girls, she was criticized. As one girl described it, "Look at that. She doesn't even know how to write right." These teens were criticized for not recognizing or following the rules and rituals on note-writing, a primary rule being that notes could be passed only to friends of equal social status. The unstated rules of adhering to established social hierarchies were clearly enforced. If, for example, a girl did not know her place in the social hierarchy and wrote a note to a more popular girl, she became the object of ridicule and laughter within the higher circle.

This need for social sorting at the junior high was visible to teachers. Debra Zmoleck described the practice in this way:

> I think part of the way junior high kids feel good about themselves is they've got to have that ego, you know, it's a pecking order. They've got to have somebody that's down there that all the other chickens peck at, you know. And I don't know why, I guess it's just part of junior high.

The "pecking order" to which Debra referred was often documented in literate practices. Literacy was a tool used to document and maintain social position. In private interviews, Angie and Lauren both made statements in accord with Tiffany's own self-assessment.

> I don't write notes much so now I don't get 'em. Lauren gets the most because she writes the most. She's the most popular. Me, not so much.

Tiffany lost status because she didn't write as many notes as other girls and slowly over time received fewer and fewer, marking her less popular. On the other hand, Lauren was perceived to be the most popular girl among her network of friends because "she has the most notes." She also received more notes from boys, which further served to document her high status among her friends.

In the fall of seventh grade, the number of notes passed increased until mid-November, when a plateau was reached; January saw a sharp decline. When asked about this decline, the queens all relayed the fact that there just wasn't as much to write about; yet the events that they had written about all year—social arrangements, sports, and boys—had not decreased in their interest or in their activity. I contend that note-passing had served its purpose—to sort and select a hierarchy among the queens who had just entered a new arena in the fall. Arriving from different sixth-grade classrooms, the queens used literacies in the new school context to negotiate entry into new friendship networks. Through print sources, they maintained familiar ties in this strange new world, connecting at first with old sixth-grade friends and then negotiating their ways into other social groups. By January, new social positions were securely established, and note-passing decreased because jockeying for position was no longer an option for gaining status or entry into the social queens' network.

Note-passing was clearly a gendered activity. It functioned to control male voices and to try out women's voices. Circulation of notes was controlled exclusively by girls. Girls decided who was entitled to see, receive, or write a note. Boys did not write notes to boys, and they wrote to girls only when they were invited or instructed to do so by a girl directly or through a channeling system, where one girl wrote to another girl who would then write to a boy, thereby granting him permission to write to the first girl. This act of literacy bestowed power and control of romantic interactions exclusively to females. The hierarchical arrangement placed power firmly in the hands of the social queens, who controlled and regulated which boys wrote or received notes.

To guard the circulation of messages, the queens informed me that learning to fold a note properly was vital to ensure that it would not open if it were dropped. Notes were folded into small triangles or squares with edges tucked in, serving as a lock to protect messages from unauthorized eyes. Such skill in intricate folding was also used to gain status within the inner circle. One's knowledge of elaborate folds signaled one as a member in good standing. Again, literacy served to document status within the circle of friends. If one queen learned a new and extremely complex fold, she received high praise and then attained the honored position of teacher, instructing others in how to fold.

Note-folding was a crucial skill because passing the note was a fine game that required a small, streamlined object. A note could have no rough edges to catch in a pocket lining, and it must be easily manipulated in the palm of one hand in order to avoid detection as it slipped from hand to hand boldly under the nose of a teacher. Passing notes from one of the social queens to another under the sharp scrutiny of a teacher was seen by these girls as an act of defiance and a behavior to be admired. Girls wrote, circulated, and responded to notes while reading aloud, participating in classroom discussions, and completing written work. A girl, for instance, could participate in a large-group discussion while writing and then passing notes without skipping a beat as she actively engaged in the classroom discussion. Designed to fool the teacher into thinking one was paying attention, such a game documented allegiance to peers. Ironically, a queen had to pay extremely close attention to keep the game going in her favor, yet this game was played to make the teacher appear foolish and the teen powerful.

Whenever the risk became heightened by a teacher's reprimands or threats of posting notes on classroom walls, notes became a greater avenue of status-building. When the risks were greatest, girls began lacing their texts with obscene language to up the ante, for to have one such note confiscated would mean not only a disruption at school but disruption at home as well.

More often than not, the content of the note was inconsequential; meaning was conveyed in the passing of the note rather than within the text itself. The act of passing the note during class relayed the message, an act of defiance of adult authority. The message was modified not through words but through the creative manipulation of the passing. The closer one was to the teacher physically when the note was written or delivered, the more powerful the message. By mid-November, after the girls had grown to trust me, they would often dig into their pockets and notebooks and hand me unopened notes. They did not need to read the notes because the message was implicit in the process of passing: in clues such as who sent, who received, who was present during the passing, and how the note was transported.

After I examined note-passing as a ritualized event, several themes emerged: (1) Writing is a social event; (2) special status is ascribed to the girl who receives the most notes, especially from boys; and (3) meaning often resides in the act of passing a note. Note-passing was a tool used to document and maintain social position. For the most part, notes were used to bestow power and patrol boundaries around a group of friends.

⟫ FOR CRITICAL INQUIRY

Examining Literacy Practices

Margaret J. Finders examines note-passing by junior high girls as a "literate practice" that documents the "pecking order" of friendship hierarchies where the most "popular" girl gets the most notes. Notice the organization of this passage from her book *Just Girls: Hidden Literacies and Life in Junior High:*

- This section begins (¶ 1–5) with a definition of the genre of note-writing and its conventions.

- Then (¶ 5–10) Finders explains how note-passing is a "gendered activity" that defies adult authority and maintains social position among girls in junior high.

- Next (¶ 11–14) Finders looks at note-folding as a "crucial skill" and the relation of risk to status-building in note-passing.

- Finally (¶ 15) Finders summarizes, listing three main themes.

Take Finders' approach to a literate practice that you have participated in or know about. Define the genre of writing and its conventions. Consider how the literate practice documents social position. To what extent does the literate practice maintain the status quo? To what extent does it challenge authority?

WRITING ASSIGNMENT

Analyzing Literacy Events and Practices

Now it's your turn to analyze a literacy event or a literacy practice. Your task is to identify a meaningful encounter with writing (an event) or a significant pattern in the use of writing (a practice) and explain what that event or practice reveals about how the people involved made sense of the situation and the role that writing played in their interactions.

Directions

1. Select an encounter with writing or a type of writing. Look for events that reveal powerful feelings or strong responses on the part of the people involved, where there are interesting conflicts, misunderstandings, resolutions, or alliances formed in which writing plays a key role. Or look for literate practices that have shaped people's sense of themselves as individuals or as part of a group, where there are patterns and regularities in how people use literacy. If you have time, discuss with a partner three or four literacy events or practices that you are considering for this assignment. See what seems most interesting to another person. Use this information to help you make a decision about the literacy event you want to analyze.

2. Analyze the literacy event or practice. Here are some questions to take into account:

   ▶ For events: Describe what happened. What is the social context of the encounter with writing? Who is involved? What did they do? Is there conflict? What is the plot?

   ▶ For practices: What type of writing is involved? What are the specific features of the writing? What is its purpose? How does the writing articulate identities and social networks?

   ▶ How is the writing produced? What form does it take—print text or new media? How does it circulate—hand to hand or virtually? What is the significance?

   ▶ How do the participants make sense of the literacy event or practice? Do they share the same perspective or differ? How would you account for these differences or similarities?

3. Choose a genre of writing to present your investigation of the literacy event or practice. Consider the two sample student essays. There is an academic essay, Valery Sheridan's "'Please, order whatever you want. I insist': Ordering Meals at the Burning Spear Country Club as a Literacy Event," which presents results and interpretations in a conventional way; and a personal essay, Conor Boyland's "Confessions of an Instant Messenger," which relies on anecdotes

to reflect on the writer's experience plugged in to new media. Both are print texts. Other possibilities for this assignment include multimodal compositions such as video interviews, podcasts, and PowerPoint presentations.

WRITERS' WORKSHOP

The two student essays offer different ways of addressing this writing assignment. The first, Valery Sheridan's "'Please, order whatever you want. I insist': Ordering Meals at the Burning Spear Country Club as a Literacy Event," is an academic essay designed to present research that Valery wrote in her writing studies minor as a junior. The second, Conor Boyland's "Confessions of an Instant Messenger," is a personal essay written when he was a sophomore at Northeastern University and published in the *Boston Globe*.

As you read, notice the different writing strategies employed—differences in the writer's persona and stance toward readers, the level of formality or informality in the writing, and whether the writer cites the work of others. How does each writer frame the investigation of the literacy event or practice and draw out its implications? To what extent is the analysis presented explicitly? To what extent embedded in a narrative?

Valery Sheridan

Professor Wheeler

WR101

October 6, 2008

"Please, order whatever you want. I insist": Ordering Meals at the Burning Spear Country Club as a Literacy Event

Literacy events are often so embedded in everyday social life that they are hidden from plain sight, even when they happen right in front of us. A good example of this is how members of the Burning Spear Country Club order meals when they are hosting guests. At first glance, it may be hard to see how reading or writing is involved. But if we think of a "literacy event," in Shirley Brice Heath's words, as "any occasion in which a piece of writing is integral to the nature of the participants' interactions and their interpretive processes" ("Protean Shapes" 93), then the literacy involved in ordering meals starts to come into view. The "piece of writing" in this case is the menu. In my experience as a waitress at the Burning Spear Country Club for the last two years, I have witnessed literally hundreds of instances of members and their guests reading the menu, making their choices, and ordering meals. Heath puts particular emphasis on talk as a "necessary component" in analyzing literacy events (*Ways with Words* 196). In this paper, I will examine the talk between members and guests that takes place once the menu appears and what these social interactions reveal about relationships and identities.

When taking guests to dinner at Burning Spear, the club member is often concerned that guests will make an entrée choice based on price, as a courtesy to their host, rather than on their actual preference. In order to deter this from happening, at Burning Spear, as well as at other country clubs where I've waitressed, two different menus are used. The menus look identical, including the supposedly elegant embossed cover, the tacky gold tassel peeking out of the menu's binding, and the typical restaurant prose (e.g., "hand-torn lettuce," "our chef's secret demi-glaze"). The difference is that the member menu lists the prices, while the guest menu does not. Many hosts apparently feel, however, that even hiding the price is not enough. I've heard it happen so many times, after a dinner party has been seated and served cocktails, as guests are starting to read the menu, the host will say, "Please, order whatever you want. I insist."

Such statements are often followed by further talk on the part of the member host, addressed to guests, about their dinner order:

> "No, don't get the baked haddock. It's usually not fresh here."
> "The Catch of the Week was excellent. I had it last night."
> "Get an appetizer, too."
> "You're going to get a salad, right?"

As talk that revolves around a "piece of writing," the menu, the member's statements serve a number of purposes, establishing his identity as a discriminating food connoisseur and a generous host for whom the prices on the menu are of no concern. And such statements also reinforce his standing and sense of belongingness, as an insider, at Burning Spear Country Club, in comparison to his guests, who are identified, in turn, as visitors invited by the host member.

As the moment of ordering approaches, I've often overheard conversations like this one:

> GUEST: "Ooh, the chicken piccata sounds good . . . but I don't care for capers."
> MEMBER: "Oh! Well, they can make it any way you want!"

Members often encourage guests not just to order what they want but to feel free to include alterations and special orders. If guests seem reluctant to make a special order, members will typically say something like:

MEMBER: "Don't worry. I have special orders made for me all the time."

What the member is asserting here is that having "special orders made for me all the time" means the member is a special person, to whom the restaurant staff extends special courtesies and considerations. It enhances the member's social status in relation to other members who don't get "special orders" and underlines the member's personal relationship to the restaurant staff, who supposedly want to take good care of him and pamper him with "special orders." Of course, this is amusing to us, as staff, because the reality is that all the members act similarly, requesting special orders, and all are accommodated by the kitchen.

In conclusion, we see that the talk in ordering meals by member hosts at Burning Spear functions similarly to the note-passing of the "social queens" in Margaret J. Finders's study of hidden literacies in junior high—"to document and maintain social position." Like the notes, this talk serves "to bestow power" on the host and "patrol boundaries" between members and guests (69).

Works Cited

Finders, Margaret J. *Just Girls: Hidden Literacies and Life in Junior High*. New York: Teachers College P., 1997. Print.

Heath, Shirley Brice. "Protean Shapes in Literacy Events: Ever-Shifting Oral and Literate Traditions." *Spoken and Written Language: Exploring Orality and Literacy*. Ed.

_____. *Ways with Words: Language, Life, and Work in Communities and Classrooms*. Cambridge: Cambridge UP, 1983. Print.

Confessions of an Instant Messenger
Conor Boyland

I was sitting at my computer, and I realized something: I spend way too much time sitting at my computer. Granted, I'm a college student, and my options on where to sit in my room are limited, but that just makes it easier to justify the time I waste every day online, mostly instant messaging. Admit it: You do it too. We all do, to different degrees. It's just one of the most commonly accepted things to do when you have a computer; "I think, therefore IM."

It seems fairly harmless, but it snowballs, and before you know it, you can't stop or you'll go into withdrawal. When you get to the point where you can't take a shower without putting up that witty away message that says, "I'm all hot and steamy," you're officially addicted—welcome to the club. You're also really sick.

One of the lamest aspects of addiction to AIM, America Online's instant messaging system, is that even if you have people on your buddy list you haven't talked to in years, you can still keep up on their day-to-day activities by checking their away messages when you're bored. Or when you're doing homework. Or when you're supposed to be in class. The funny thing is, some of them are probably doing it to you too, but it doesn't matter. Next thing you know, you're fiending for recent pictures of them, who they're dating, where they're living, and who their favorite movies are.

Enter: The Facebook. If AIM is a gateway drug, the Facebook is Internet crack. If you're in college, you know the deal: upload your picture, add in some interests, list every single band you've ever listened to, girls write down your favorite "I love shopping and my best friends" quote from "Sex and the City," and guys write down that you like "Scarface" and "The Da Vinci Code." Then you browse through different profiles and compile a list of friends, some of whom you know and some of whom you've (maybe) met once but never talked to after that. You can even hunt down people from your hometown that now go to other colleges. That way you can ignore over the Internet the same people you used to ignore in high school!

If you're one of those people who like to stay up on the latest trends, like striped shirts and quoting Napoleon Dynamite, you're probably thinking, "Idiot! Facebook is so last semester, gosh!" Well, there's a new friend-making site for you folks called Catch27, which is basically the Facebook with attitude. You actually trade friends here based on how hot they are, and if you can't get hot friends on your own you can even pay money for them. "99 ¢ for a Wax Pack of 3: just like real life, only cheaper," writes the site's creator, E. Jean Carroll, who is either really desperate for friends or is laughing all the way to the bank. Now, don't get me wrong here, if you want to spend money to create an online list of "friends" you've never actually met, that's your own business. Just remember (and I quote my roommate on this one), "FBI agents make the sexiest cyber babes."

I don't have a problem with gimmicky websites, but I do take issue with the rapidly growing trend of communicating online rather than in person. I hate it, but I find the temptation increasingly hard to resist. When it comes down to it, reading someone's profile is so much easier than actually talking to them, and it carries no risk of them not liking you. Therein lies the problem: Online directories like the Facebook make it possible to find out quite a lot about a person without ever speaking to them, which not only appeals to stalkers but ruins your social skills as well. Actually, I shouldn't speak for anybody else, but I admit that mine have certainly suffered.

On top of that, browsing the Facebook can quickly go from being fun to becoming a compulsion, just like with AIM. It's not that we don't know this compulsive behavior is unhealthy; it's just another one of those guilty pleasures you know is bad for you but that you don't care enough about to stop doing. The Internet is so addicting that in many ways it has now become the most popular way to contact new people. A friend of mine met a cute girl at a party recently, and as he was leaving he told her to look him up on the Facebook, no joke. I waited until he left and then got her *phone number*.

If drug addiction damages your mental capacities, then Internet addiction damages your social ones (Do you really think my friend has any chance with that girl?), and as with any addiction, admitting that you have a problem is only the first step. I'm just as guilty as the next guy, so I'm not going to say something preachy like "seize the day," or "get out and live life to the fullest," but I will say this: We need to sign off AIM and Facebook and get up off our asses a little more often. Go run around outside, read a book, or—God forbid—talk to a stranger. Practice the dying art of conversation.

Communicating online is convenient, but no amount of smileys or pokes can substitute for real human connection, which is far more worthy of our time than anonymous Facebook connections (of which I have 2,137 by the way). As for the compulsive behavior, I'm quitting cold turkey. I just have to put one more witty away message up, one last fix, and then I'm done. TTYL.

CHAPTER 2

The Choices Writers Make

Writing a Rhetorical Analysis

A major theme of this book is that writing doesn't just happen. It occurs when people encounter a situation that calls on them to write, when they experience the sense that something is lacking, something needs to be paid attention to, something needs to be said. This can happen in a relatively simple and straightforward manner—when you realize, for example, that you should send a note of condolence to the family when a friend or relative dies, or a text message to your best friend at another college to congratulate her on being chosen for a great summer internship program. In these cases, the situation seems to determine the appropriate response. You can buy cards for these types of occasions—births, christenings, bar mitzvahs, graduations, anniversaries, and so on. New media, like texting, email, instant messaging, and Skype, provide additional options to design and send messages.

Other situations are more complicated. Take, for instance, the situation following the financial collapse of 2008, when banks and Wall Street investment firms were bailed out by the government while ordinary people faced foreclosures, layoffs, rising student debt, declining wages, threatened cuts to pensions, and an uncertain future for themselves and their families. Everything seemed to be rigged against the average citizen, who was facing economic insecurity unknown since the Great Depression of the 1930s.

Occupy Wall Street was a response to this situation that spread spontaneously in the fall of 2011, across the country and very quickly around the world. Part of the impact of the movement—and the source of its appeal—was how the slogan "We are the 99%" brought the post-2008 economic situation into focus for millions of Americans as a problem of economic and social inequality where concentrations of wealth and power threatened democracy.

Unlike situations where the response is dictated by convention, Occupy Wall Street activists and supporters had to define the rhetorical situation to give it a meaning that people could rally around. The slogan "We are the 99%" put into words the sense of grievance and discontent people were feeling about economic and social inequality, giving the majority a positive identity and reminding everyone that the people are the basis of democracy.

The purpose of this chapter is to investigate what calls on people to write—or, for that matter, to produce other forms of communication, whether signs, posters, graffiti, websites—to have their say, to influence the course of events, to exchange ideas and feelings with others. This is where the motivation to write takes place, in what we call the *rhetorical situation*.

This chapter is an introduction to analyzing rhetorical situations to understand the choices made by writers—and sign makers—when they respond to the call to write. We will explore three factors that work together in shaping and responding to rhetorical situations:

1. How writers *interpret the rhetorical situation* to which they're responding
2. How writers *choose genres* to respond to the rhetorical situation
3. How writers *craft rhetorical stances* to respond to the rhetorical situation

The chapter presents some conceptual tools and a series of steps to analyze rhetorical situations. The aim is to promote rhetorical awareness by highlighting how writers can respond flexibly and creatively to the call to write.

The chapter closes with a writing assignment that calls on you to write your own rhetorical analysis, and includes a sample student paper.

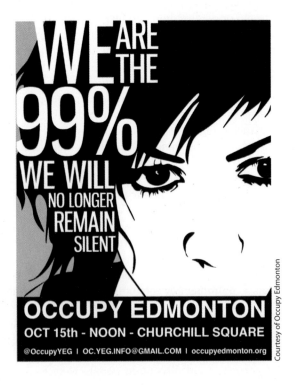

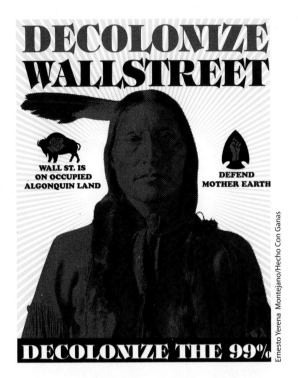

Ernesto Yerena Montejano/Hecho Con Ganas

The first two Occupy posters use the slogan "We are the 99%" to urge people to come to demonstrations in Edmonton, Canada, and Fargo, North Dakota. The third is a variation on the 99% theme. Consider the visual rhetoric of each poster. What do the images, color, and design highlight about the Occupy movement? What is the style of each poster? How does that style put across Occupy's message?

ANALYZING THE RHETORICAL SITUATION

Jerald Walker is the author of the memoir *Street Shadows: A Memoir of Race, Rebellion, and Redemption*, which won the 2011 PEN New England/L.L. Winship Award for Nonfiction. He is currently Chair of the Writing, Literature & Publishing Department at Emerson College and an essayist whose work has been published three times in *Best American Essays* and twice in *Best African American Essays*, where "Before Grief" appeared in 2010.

In an introductory note, one of the *Best African American Essays* editors Gerald Early explains the rhetorical situation that gave birth to this essay. He says that his co-editor Randall Kennedy had already sent their selections for the 2009 book to press when important events occurred that they wanted to acknowledge and find essayists to write about. One of these events was Michael Jackson's untimely death. Early notes that he was not particularly moved by any of the commentary that was published in the wake of Jackson's death—much of it shallow and sensationalistic media buzz, focusing on Jackson as a freakish celebrity and failing to come to terms with the meaning of Jackson's life and music. This is where Jerald Walker comes in, as someone who wanted very much to write about Jackson—to make sense of what Michael Jackson's career signified to him personally, as an essayist, and to the wider culture.

There is a stop-the-presses urgency here, to hold up publication until Jerald Walker could write something on short notice. The tight deadline seems to have produced an intense sense of immediacy in the essay, a nearness to Jackson's death and the possible meanings of his life. As Early notes, Jackson was an important figure to Walker, and a depth of feeling comes across in the essay, a close connection between the writer and his subject.

These are the circumstances surrounding Walker's essay. They are meant to provide background for the rhetorical analysis that follows the essay, where we present a series of steps to reconstruct Walker's response to the call to write.

AN INTERVIEW WITH JERALD WALKER

Photo by Brenda Molife

1. **What called on you to write about Michael Jackson at the time of his death? What was at stake for you? What sense of exigency did you feel?** A few days after Jackson's death, I saw a post on Facebook by one of my twenty-something-year-old students in which she complained about the attention Michael Jackson was getting when he was "only a freak." I didn't take issue with the word *freak*, but I did take issue with the word *only*. It occurred to me that people of her generation had little or no sense of Jackson's true legacy, of the historical impact he and his family had on the culture generally and race-relations specifically. To dismiss him as "only a freak" was to dismiss what was in essence a heroic figure in the black community.

2. **What relationship to your readers were you thinking about as you wrote the essay? How did you want readers to understand what you were saying? How did you want them to respond to the essay?** I was trying to get readers to look beyond Jackson's largely self-created caricature to see what else was there. For some readers, I knew that would be nearly impossible—one mention of Michael Jackson and the talk turns to trials and plastic surgeons—and so I used my "normal" family to draw readers into the story and to show not only what Jackson's appeal was, but also how that appeal, by virtue of its emotional and historical components, cannot be so easily undone.

3. **How did you work out the form of "Before Grief"?** I knew that I had to acknowledge Jackson's peculiarities and scandals early and often, so the reader could see I wasn't trying to sugarcoat important aspects of his life. It was my way of earning the readers' trust. In other words, I was saying, "Yes, I see your point. Now, let me show you mine."

4. **Thinking about "Before Grief" and other short essays you've written, what does the genre of the personal essay enable you to do? How does it compare to other genres of writing?** I was devastated by the news of Jackson's death, but at the time I didn't fully understand why. It wasn't until I'd written the essay— in fact, the final sentence of the essay—that I realized I wasn't grieving the loss of a single life so much as the loss of a family bond. And that's the power of the personal essay—its ability to teach us about ourselves. And usually what we learn teaches us about each other.

Before Grief

Jerald Walker

Before the glove; before the anorexia and addictions; before the moonwalk and crotch grabs and Fred Astaire's admiration and envy; before his color faded and his nose shriveled; before he stunned and confused me, entwining one arm with Brooke Shields's and nestling Emmanuel Lewis with the other; before he was said to be spending some nights with Lisa Marie and other nights alone in an oxygen chamber; before Bubbles and the boa constrictor and the rest of the menagerie that he'd come to trust more than people; before the people he *did* finally trust mentioned "Jesus juice" and sleepovers and gave me reason not to trust *him*, another reason to wonder if now was the time for my disavowal, the moment when I'd say, at last, I've had enough, even though I knew I never could, because yes, before all of this there was the dazzling child vocalist with a pink gangster hat slicing toward one eye, his four brothers dancing at his side, while the Walker Six—that's what we called ourselves—mimicked their act, imagined that it was us up on Ed Sullivan's stage, blowing people's minds.

Though my siblings and I were only having fun, just messing around, for Michael this was serious business, this was *work*—like performing was work for James Brown, the man whose style he had already mastered, like performing was work for Smokey Robinson, the man whose soul he had already cloned. The fact that Michael was less than half their age was part of his appeal, because implicit in his youth was the promise of more, the hope that there'd be years and then decades of watching his legend unfold. But for now it was still 1969, a blustery December evening, bringing to a close a blustery American decade, assassinations and race riots at our heels, and the Walker Six, dumbstruck to see a black family on TV, was bantering over who should sing lead.

Jimmy's case was strong. Like Michael, he was the youngest of the group, having departed our mother's womb a full twelve minutes after me. But I owned a pink gangster hat (really a brown skullcap, but still . . .), Mary could reach those high notes, Linda could carry a tune, Tommy was the best dancer, while Timmy, by his own estimation, was the cutest. All of these points were argued compellingly but a little too loudly, prompting our father to threaten corporal punishment, ending a debate that would erupt again the next morning when we heard "I Want You Back" on the living-room console. I don't remember how or if the matter was resolved—perhaps we were *all* Michael—only that the volume was cranked up and we fell into our clumsy choreography, dipping in time to our off-key voices, our arms open wide as we implored six loves to return.

Meanwhile, just as we were being Michael, our parents were being his parents—stern, loving, optimistic, highly religious, and always on the lookout for an escape hatch, some elusive portal that would lead us to better opportunities. They would find that portal in 1970, issuing out into a middle-class community on Chicago's South Side. Until then we lived in a ghetto not unlike the Jacksons' in Gary, Indiana, a mere thirty miles away. But that night in 1969, it was clear that their family would be leaving soon, carried off to the good life—not by talent, our parents stressed, but by the values that had seen it to fruition. No loitering in the streets for Michael and his brothers, no slacking in school, no messing around with drugs and gangs, and certainly no being spared the rod, because this was before belts and the backs of hands were considered cruel weapons, before parents' desire to instill discipline and respect in their children by any means necessary was considered wrong. "Hard *work*," our father said that night, over the applause of the Ed Sullivan studio audience, "is what got those boys to where they are." To which our mother added, "Hard work *and*, of course, God."

Theirs was named Jehovah. In the eyes of some black folk, that made the Jacksons a little strange. But at least most people had *heard* of the Jehovah's Witnesses, whereas very few had heard of our religion, the Worldwide Church of God, and that made the Walkers even stranger. Like the Jacksons' faith, ours forbade celebrating Christmas, Halloween, birthdays, and Easter, and we were also discouraged from socializing with nonmembers, resulting in siblings being not just siblings but also best friends. And so I understood that the childhood bond between Michael and his brothers and sisters was both strong and vital, exactly like the bond between my brothers and sisters and me. But this was before the Walker Six grew up and then apart, slowly establishing and tending to separate lives, just as the Jackson Five became the Jacksons, and then the Jacksons became Michael Jackson, and then Michael Jackson became the King.

Now the King is dead. I write this more than three weeks after he passed away, at a time when the media's preoccupation with him is still going strong. Many feel this is justified, a sensible response to his unparalleled fame. Others disagree. "I've seen so many good people the last few days," said one New York politician, "who aren't going to get credit for anything, and then I see this guy, who's really a lowlife, and he's being treated like a hero of civilization." A reporter at *The Washington Post* echoed this theme: "The coverage is out of control, and it's becoming an embarrassment to the news business." Another reporter commented in his blog, "This country has misplaced priorities and a lack of moral values. We celebrate the lives of freaks, yet neglect real heroes."

But back in 1971, no one held this view; that was the year the Walker Six was allowed to turn on the television on a Saturday, our Sabbath, because the first episode of the *Jackson 5ive* cartoon was on. Breaking the Sabbath was a violation of God's law, pretty significant stuff, but then so, too, was an all-Negro cartoon. Something important was happening in our country, our parents understood, a new level of racial tolerance and acceptance, being brought about by a family that looked and behaved like our own. And so my parents sanctioned those Saturday morning viewings, and it was okay for us to spend our allowances on the Jackson Five albums, T-shirts, and posters. It was okay to stay up late after their television specials in 1971 and 1972 to practice our routine. And in 1976, when the Jacksons launched their variety show, the first black family to have one, it was okay to say that Donny and Marie Osmond were lame.

Two years later, the Jacksons were also lame. Michael must have thought so too, because he was already busy on his first solo album, *Off the Wall*, which debuted in 1979, when I was fifteen and seeking, like Michael, my own way. I'd found it by 1982 when *Thriller* was released, and by some bizarre fate it was as if the portal I'd entered this time led me directly to the music video of his title song, a world of ghouls and goblins, otherwise known as pushers and pimps. This was during a terrible period of chaos and wrong choices for me, when the only family I was close to was two of my brothers, who'd climbed through portals similar to mine. While I do not know if this is true, I have a vague memory that the three of us, in 1983, watched the *Motown 25* television special together, and maybe we rose at some point to attempt Michael's moonwalk before collapsing back into our seats, succumbing to the dope coursing through our veins, much as dope would course through Michael's, nearly three decades later, and stop his heart.

Mine stopped, for a moment, when I heard the news. And in that pause before grief, I had a vision of the Walker Six, dancing and singing . . . and then it was gone.

RECONSTRUCTING JERALD WALKER'S RESPONSE TO THE CALL TO WRITE

To reconstruct how Jerald Walker responded to the rhetorical situation of Michael Jackson's death, we begin by describing the formal organization of the essay and how it embodies Walker's purposes. Then we turn to analyzing Walker's interpretation of the rhetorical situation, his choice of genre, and the rhetorical stance he crafted.

▶ **Describe how the formal organization of the essay embodies the writer's purposes.** The first step in rhetorical analysis is to suspend judgment for a moment about the writer's ideas or the quality of the writing in order to examine the writer's purposes and the formal organization of the essay. The emphasis at this stage is on description and analysis rather than evaluation, to read closely in order to identify how the parts of an essay—individual paragraphs or sections of paragraphs—function in the piece of writing as a whole.

It's helpful to think of formal organization not as a set of containers or prescribed sections to fill with writing, as the laboratory report or the five-paragraph theme might make forms of writing appear to be. A better way of thinking about form is in terms of how writing arouses and fulfills readers' expectations.

A good question to ask is "How does a piece of writing cue readers to its purposes and seek to involve them in grasping and responding to its main themes?"

In personal essays like Jerald Walker's "Before Grief," form can be quite fluid, not so much prescribed in advance as invented for the occasion. Form in the essay is more a matter of improvisation that draws on motifs and patterns from a common stock of rhetorical moves. The job of the essayist is to design a pattern for the essay that gives readers a scaffolding to follow the essayist's train of thought and perceptions.

As the outline of "Before Grief" shows, one of the main patterns in the essay is the alternation of past (the "before" part) and present (the "grief" at hearing of Michael Jackson's death). Jerald Walker uses this back and forth movement to unpack particular moments—in 1969, 1971, 1976, and 1979–1983—to examine what linked the Walker and Jackson families at times in the past in order to come to terms with Michael Jackson's death in the present.

PARAGRAPH	TIME FRAME	DESCRIPTION
¶ 1	Present	Presents main theme. Sequence of "before" phrases details Michael Jackson in the present and establishes a past before Jackson became a celebrity freak, when he was a "dazzling child vocalist" that Walker and his siblings mimicked, when the Jackson Five were "blowing people's minds." Establishes the writer's personal connection to Jackson.
¶ 2–5	Past	Presents a sequence of memories to link the Walker and Jackson families and provide evidence of the Jacksons' cultural significance.
¶ 2	1969	Characterizes Jackson as a hard-working musical performer, combining aspects of James Brown and Smokey Robinson. Notes cultural significance: Walker Six in 1969 were "dumbstruck to see a black family on TV."
¶ 3		Anecdote shows how Walker Six argued about singing lead, illustrating intensity of personal connection to Michael Jackson.
¶ 4		Compares Walker and Jackson families, in terms of value of hard work, echoing the theme of work in ¶ 2 and end of ¶ 3.
¶ 5		Compares Walker and Jackson families in terms of religion as the basis of social isolation and "strong and vital" sibling bonds.
¶ 6	Present	Locates Jackson's death in present, at a moment in which "media's preoccupation with him is still going strong." Describes media controversy, but doesn't take sides.
¶ 7–8	Past 1971 1976	¶ 7: Cuts back to 1971, when he was allowed to watch Jackson Five cartoons on the Sabbath. Describes cartoons as "new level of racial tolerance" and notes appearance in 1976 of the Jacksons' first black television variety show, extending the idea of cultural significance introduced in ¶ 2.
	1979–1983	¶ 8: Presents the late 1970s–early 1980s period as a "terrible period of chaos and wrong choices." Links the "ghouls and goblins" in the *Thriller* music video to "pushers and pimps."
¶ 9	Present	Describes the moment Walker heard the news of Jackson's death as a "pause before grief" and a "vision of the Walker Six." In the closing phrase—"and then it was gone"—the past vanishes and at least for now we are returned to the present.

▶ **Interpreting the rhetorical situation.** When someone dies, a conventional response is the newspaper obituary, which presents the details of the person's life, generally without much commentary, to notify the community about the passing of one of its members and perhaps to inform people about a wake or funeral or where to send contributions on behalf of the deceased. In the case of celebrities and prominent individuals, there is often more involved than just informing the public of a person's death—there is, in addition, a felt need to come to terms with the person's life and legacy.

This was certainly the case with Michael Jackson, and there was an outpouring of columnists and TV pundits on the meaning of Jackson's life and death. Still, *Best African American Essays of 2010* editor Gerald Early notes that he "was not especially taken with any of the voluminous commentary on Jackson that appeared in the days and weeks following his death." Walker appears to feel the same way, as he distances himself in the essay from the "media's preoccupation" with Jackson and the debate about fixating on the lives of freak celebrities. For Walker, as we have just seen, to understand Michael Jackson's death in the present, we have to go back earlier, before all his weirdness, to the past, to the late 1960s, when he was "the dazzling child vocalist with a pink gangster hat slicing toward one eye" and the inspiration for the Walker Six; or to 1976, when the Jacksons had the first black variety show on television.

As Walker defines the rhetorical situation, it calls on him to remember, to bring the past to light in order to capture the cultural significance of Michael Jackson that is missing in many of commentaries on his later freakishness that appeared at the time of his death. In this sense, Walker constructs a rhetorical situation that calls for a more complicated understanding of Michael Jackson's life and times, a version that makes it possible to mourn Jackson and to feel grief.

▶ **Choosing a genre.** The term *genre* refers to the various types of writing people draw on to respond to the call to write. An understanding of how various genres of writing work and when they are appropriate is an essential component of any writer's repertoire, giving writers a range of choices so that they can respond flexibly to the call to write.

The personal essay—the genre that Walker has chosen—is a familiar type of writing that puts the reflective consciousness of the writer at the center of the text, as he or she renders events and experiences with presence and personality, enabling readers to feel a connection to the writer and an involvement with the writer's materials. As just noted, compared to other genres, the personal essay is flexible in form, with room for a good deal of creativity on the writer's part. In "Before Grief," the personal essay offers Walker the means to juxtapose past and present, to respond to a rhetorical situation that he sees as calling on him to complicate readers' understanding of Michael Jackson's life and significance so as to give readers a fuller, more generous portrayal of Jackson than the picture of a freak celebrity that was circulating in the media right after his death.

▶ **Crafting a rhetorical stance**. The term *rhetorical stance* refers to the way writers coordinate presentation of self, their readers' interests and emotions, and the message they want to deliver as interrelated components in designing a piece of writing.

The idea of a rhetorical stance as a response to the rhetorical situation derives from the *appeals* of classical rhetoric—*ethos, pathos,* and *logos.* The appeals are the available means of persuasion available in any given rhetorical situation, the resources that representation writers—and sign makers more generally—rely on to put their version of reality across.

The idea of persuasion is explored more fully in the next chapter, "Persuasion and Responsibility." For now, it is sufficient to think of persuasion not just as defeating opponents in debate or winning converts to a cause, but as something subtler and more civil in temperament, a matter of persuading readers to take you seriously as a writer, to consider your ideas and perceptions in an open-minded way. Persuasion is marked by readers' willingness to engage print texts and new media, the meeting of minds that takes place when readers join with writers in conversation.

Ethos has to do with the writer's character as it is projected to readers through the written text (or other kinds of sign making). The modern terms *personality, attitude,* and *tone* capture some of the meaning of ethos in classical rhetoric. Ethos refers to the persona the writer constructs and the impression of the writer's character that readers take from the text. It involves judgments about how credible, fair, reliable, and authoritative the writer appears to be. See Tone and Rhetorical Distance for more on how writers' tone positions them in relation to readers.

Pathos refers to the reader's emotions and the responses a piece of writing arouses in them. It offers a way to think about readers' state of mind and the intensity with which they hold various beliefs and values. The notion of pathos enables writers to consider what emotional responses they want to evoke on the part of their readers. It does not counterpose emotion and intellect, but rather links them in the investments readers make in various ideas, positions, and points of view.

Logos refers to what is said or written. Its original meaning was "voice" or "message," though the term later took on an association with logic and reasoning. For our purposes, the term offers a way to focus on the writer's message and how it is developed and delivered.

As noted, Jerald Walker positions himself in "Before Grief" at the intersection of past and present. From the very first (and very long) masterfully controlled sentence that comprises the opening paragraph, we encounter Walker's *ethos* as someone who knows and cares about Michael Jackson, who was close to disavowing him, but never did. The tone is warm, and the sentiment in the essay is generous.

Later, in ¶ 6, Walker doesn't want to get involved in media arguments. He doesn't have an ax to grind, we feel, but rather is trying to come to terms with the connections between Michael Jackson and his own life. And he is honest and unsparing of himself in ¶ 8, when he describes the "terrible period of chaos and wrong choices" he went through and its connection to Jackson. Most of all, Walker is capable of feeling grief

TONE AND RHETORICAL DISTANCE

A writer's tone of voice is one key way of establishing his or her relationship to readers. Notice how the following examples of informal, standard, and official tone put the writers into quite different relationships to readers:

- **Informal:** Writing that speaks in the first person singular, addresses readers as "you" or tries to include them in collective "we," uses colloquialisms and contractions, poses rhetorical questions, and generally strives to sound like spoken language that creates an informal tone and reduces the distance between the writer and readers. Notice the informal tone of the opening two sentences in Johann Hari's newspaper column "You Are Being Lied to About Pirates":

  > Who imagined that in 2009, the world's governments would be declaring a new War on Pirates? As you read this, the British Royal Navy—backed by the ships of more than two dozen nations, from the US to China—is sailing into Somalian waters to take on men we still picture as parrot-on-the-shoulder pantomime villains.

- **Standard:** The tone of voice readers hear in many instances of professional communication, journalism, textbooks, and other forms of nonfiction prose can be characterized as "standard" because it relies on a plain, relatively formal (but not elevated or pretentious) style. This tone does not usually call attention to the writer's personality, as is often the case with an informal tone, or address readers intimately as "you." Instead, it seeks to establish a relationship with readers based on shared interests and the mutual respect of reasonable persons exchanging views. The first three paragraphs of Amnesty International's "Call on Kenya to Ease the Suffering of Nairobi's 2 Million Slum Dwellers" is a good example:

  > More than half of Nairobi's population—some two million people—live in slums and informal settlements. Crammed into makeshift shacks on just one per cent of the city's usable land, people live without adequate access to water, hospitals, schools and other essential public services.

  > Up to a million people live in Kiberia, Nairobi's largest slum, crowded onto just 550 acres of sodden land that straddles the main railway line. Most earn barely enough to rent a mud-floored, tin-roofed wooden shack with no toilet or running water.

  > Slum Dwellers are under the constant threat of forced evictions, which are illegal under international human rights law. These evictions are often carried out with brutality and victims are not compensated despite losing their homes, businesses and possessions.

- **Official:** An official tone creates the most distance between the written document and readers. The voice that readers hear is not that of an individual writer, but of an institution or collective body speaking. The style of writing tends to have a certain bureaucratic or legalistic tone. The controversial Proposition 215 to legalize medical uses of marijuana that appeared on the California state ballot in 1996 is a typical example:

  > The people of the State of California hereby find and declare that the purposes of the Compassionate Use Act of 1996 are as follows:

  > To ensure that seriously ill Californians have the right to obtain and use marijuana for medical purposes where that medical use is deemed appropriate and has been recommended by a physician. ...

  > This measure amends state law to allow persons to grow or possess marijuana for medical use when recommended by a physician.

Petition "Call on Kenya to ease the suffering of Nairobi's 2 million slum dwellers," June 9, 2009, Amnesty International. All rights reserved. Reproduced by permission.

and finding grounds for mourning Jackson that are lost in the media's fascination with his freakishness and his sad decline.

In terms of *pathos*, Walker invites readers to join him in sidestepping the contentiousness and sensationalism of the media and recalling, through anecdotal accounts of Walker's own family, the sheer joyfulness of the Jackson Five and their cultural significance as African American trailblazers on television. At the same time, Walker wants to make sure that readers do not evade the direction things took in Jackson's life. The emotions he evokes from readers, accordingly, are complex, a sober recognition of both the exhilaration of the past and the tragic state of affairs that led to Jackson's death.

The *logos* of the essay follows. The message cannot be found in a single thesis statement, as in school-based genres such as the five-paragraph theme and term paper. The central theme rather is contained in the tension already noted between past and present, as Walker cuts back and forth to bring Michael Jackson, in life and death, into focus.

⚡ ETHICS OF READING ‖‖‖

Boredom and Persistence

Going to college means that you will encounter a wide range of academic and professional writing, some of which may be specialized and technical. You may find at times that the reading you're assigned is intimidating and hard to follow. You may wonder what the writer is trying to prove, or you may think the writer is splitting hairs. The writing may seem abstract, detached from the real world. These are all symptoms of boredom, and the danger is that you will give up at this point and say you weren't really interested in the first place. What is often the case, though, is not that you aren't interested, but rather that you are unfamiliar with the particular type of writing, its forms, specialized vocabularies, and ways of reasoning. To act responsibly in college, the workplace, and the public domain, you need to read writing that is pertinent and carries weight. An ethics of reading holds that readers need to give difficult material a chance. It's not simply a matter of being fair to the writer. By working on new and difficult material, you also, in effect, refuse to be alienated from it. In this regard, you avoid the threat of boredom leading to the premature closure of communication.

CRAFTING AN APPROPRIATE RHETORICAL STANCE

Experienced writers know that to influence their readers they need to construct a persuasive rhetorical stance. And they also know that this means finding the right balance between ethos, pathos, and logos, coordinating the three appeals in a way that is appropriate to the rhetorical situation. Too much emphasis on ethos or presentation of self, for example, can make readers feel the writer is self-absorbed or overly preoccupied with his or her own thoughts and feelings. On the other hand, too much emphasis on pathos or readers' emotions can make them feel pandered to or manipulated by the writer. And too much emphasis on logos—the message of the writing—can make the writing seem dry or pedantic. The craft of writing involves finding a relationship between the three components of the rhetorical stance that works in the circumstances.

Let's take what seems to be a pretty straightforward rhetorical situation: Greater Worcester Media Cable Company has advertised a summer internship program, and sophomore communication major Lucy Brown has decided to apply. Lucy sees the internship as a step toward her professional goals and understands she needs to make an effective case for herself to the director of the program. The genre in which to respond is obviously a letter of application, sent along with the student's résumé. The rhetorical situation calls on Lucy to present herself as fitting for the internship—to give reasons why she is qualified and to explain how the internship fits in her professional goals.

Consider the following two letters. It is evident in each letter that Lucy wants Greater Worcester Media Cable Company to hire her. The question is whether the rhetorical stance she develops is appropriate to the occasion.

Sample Letters of Application

Letter 1

Hugh McDonald, Director of Summer Intern Program

Greater Worcester Media Cable Company

1025 Transit Blvd.

Worcester, MA 01609

Dear Mr. McDonald:

I would like to apply for a summer internship at Greater Worcester Media Cable Company. I've just switched my major from pre-med to mass communication, and I'm really excited about getting out of those boring science classes and into something that interests me. I just finished this great video production class and made a short documentary called "Road Kill," about all the animals that get run over on Highway 61. It was pretty arty and punk, with a sound track dubbed from Sonic Youth.

I want to learn everything I can about television. I'd love to eventually have my own show like Rachel Maddow. I've always known that television is one of the most influential parts of American life, and I think it would be awesome to be seen nightly by millions of viewers. Think of all the influence—and fun—you could have with everyone watching you.

Of course, if I do get the internship, I won't be able to go home this summer, and that will be kind of a bummer because my parents and boyfriend are counting on me being around. But still, it would be worth it to get into television because that's where I see myself going long term.

Sincerely,

Lucy Brown

Letter 2

Hugh McDonald, Director of Summer Intern Program

Greater Worcester Media Cable Company

1025 Transit Blvd.

Worcester, MA 01609

Dear Mr. McDonald:

I would like to apply for a summer internship at Greater Worcester Media Cable Company. As my résumé indicates, I am a Mass Communication major in my sophomore year, with course work in video production, mass communication theory, and the history of television. In addition, I have a strong background in the natural sciences.

I believe that my studies in Mass Communication have given me skills and experience that would be valuable in a summer internship. In my video production class, I filmed and edited a short documentary, and I am eager to gain more experience in production and editing.

A summer internship would be a wonderful opportunity for me to learn how the day-to-day world of cable television works. This kind of practical experience would be an invaluable complement to my coursework in the history and theory of the media.

Sincerely,

Lucy Brown

▷ WORKING TOGETHER

Rhetorical Stance

You have probably concluded that the first letter is inappropriate as a letter of application to Greater Worcester Media Cable Company and that the second letter is more suitable. Your task now is to explore the uses and limits of the two letters and the way Lucy Brown has crafted a rhetorical stance in each of them. Work together with two or three other students. Follow these directions:

1. Compare the two letters in terms of the rhetorical stance the writer has constructed in each case. Be specific here, and point to words, phrases, and passages that reveal how the writer coordinates ethos, logos, and pathos.

2. Think of a situation in which the first letter would be appropriate to the writer's purposes and the interests of readers. It may be inappropriate when applying for a summer internship, but that doesn't mean it is not as well written as the second. Notice that in certain respects it has more life, more telling details, and more of a sense of the writer's personality than the second letter.

3. The second letter is clearly better suited to apply for a summer internship, but that doesn't mean that it crafts the most effective rhetorical stance. What, if anything, do you think is lacking in this letter? What, if anything, could be done to strengthen its appeal to Greater Worcester Media Cable Company?

ANALYZING MULTIMODAL COMPOSITIONS: OCCUPY WALL STREET POSTER

You can analyze multimodal compositions in much the same way we just analyzed an essay, adapting the steps from a print text to designs that combine words, images, moving pictures, sound, music, gesture, and so on. To continue the exploration of Occupy Wall Street, we use a poster from New York City where the movement began.

The Rhetorical Situation

This poster was designed by the graphic artist R. Black. (You can see other work he has done for indie bands and music shows at www.rblack.org.) It appeared right after New York City police raided Occupy Wall Street at Zuccotti Park, the original site of the movement. At the time, there was considerable sentiment among Occupy supporters that city officials had authorized an overreaction on the part of the police, coming in the middle of night, in an intimidating display of force with riot gear, klieg lights, and loudspeakers, to trash the Occupy encampment and arrest anyone who did not flee. In response, Occupy Wall Street called for nonviolent direct actions on November 17: day-long demonstrations on Wall Street; Occupy activists engaging other New Yorkers on subways across the city; and a culminating rally at Foley Square. Perhaps the greatest sense of urgency on Occupy's part was to make the movement's presence known across the city, to show Mayor Bloomberg and other New Yorkers that it could not be driven out of the city.

© R. Black

▶ **Describing the visual design of the poster.** We begin with a description of the visual design of the poster, just as we began above with the formal organization of the essay. A big difference, of course, is that essays unfold in time, and outlining them offers a way to identify patterns of development. A poster, on the other hand, is taken in all at once, as viewers identify the location of words and images in space. Let's look at how the verbal and visual components are arranged.

The poster is organized in panels that slant from left to right, the angle giving it a sense of dynamism and forward motion. In the center of the poster is a rendering of the famous photograph of the individual figure confronting tanks in Tiannamen Square in Beijing, during the 1989 pro-democracy protests in China.

© Stuart Franklin/Magnum Photos

The figures in the poster and photo are dressed identically and carry a bag in each hand. Beyond that, the differences are revealing.

For one thing, in the Occupy poster, the tanks are arranged left to right instead of front to back, each standing for a place of direct action targeted by Occupy, with the times of the actions included. In this sense, the military force of the state so evident in the Tiannamen Square photo is transformed into signs of political gatherings in New York City—Wall Street, the Five Boroughs, and Foley Square.

Second, the individual facing the tanks is not alone in the Occupy poster, as he is in the photo; in keeping with the "Occupy together" slogan of the movement, he is backed up by rows of fellow Occupy supporters, reinforcing the poster's call for *mass* nonviolent direct action and projecting a sense of collective strength in the Occupy poster that is not present in the photo.

The words on the poster give voice to the dynamism of the poster, as the words "direct action" grow larger from left to right and are accented by an exclamation point. There is a sense of militancy in the verbs that animate the three imperative phrases calling for direct action—"*shut down* Wall Street," "*occupy* the subways," and "*take* the square."

Lower down on the poster, three political demands of the movement appear in a panel as another series of imperative phrases—"*resist* austerity," "*reclaim* the economy," and "*recreate* our democracy"—with the verbs echoing as a "*re-*" sound.

▶ **Interpreting the rhetorical situation.** Occupy Wall Street had choices to make interpreting and responding to the rhetorical situation they faced after the police raid on Zuccotti Park dismantled its encampment and base of operations. The key decision was to opt for direct action. This wasn't the only choice. Occupy could have focused on presenting its case to the courts or media outlets such as the press, television, Facebook, and Twitter. Instead, the movement decided it was crucial under the circumstances to make its physical presence felt across New York, to let Occupy supporters and the city at large know it was not going away just because of the police raid.

▶ **Choosing a genre.** Organizing direct actions like those on November 17, 2011, typically involves a multigenre approach, such as posters to rally people, signs and banners to carry at demonstrations and marches, informational flyers to hand out to passersby and participants, and press releases—not to mention the speeches at rallies, slogans to chant, songs to sing, and so on.

▶ **Crafting a rhetorical stance.** The appeals ethos, pathos, and logos are just as applicable to visual designs and multimodal compositions as they are to print texts.

In the case of the Occupy poster, the appeals are organized by a central image that invokes widely known and widely admired pro-democracy demonstrations in China. In the case of both poster and photo, the *ethos* involves a confrontation with a powerful state, where justice is clearly on the side of the individual. As noted, the Occupy poster, unlike the photo, links the individual to the collective strength of mass action and a strong attitude of unity and militancy—to resist the illegitimate authority that raided Occupy Wall Street's encampment.

The *pathos* of the poster is designed to invoke a sense of injustice on the part of readers and a feeling of solidarity with the Occupy movement. The *logos* of the poster makes the simple and compelling case that the struggles of Occupy Wall Street supporters in 2011 and pro-democracy demonstrators in 1989 China are similar, based on resistance to illegitimate power.

The overall appeal of the poster—on emotional and intellectual grounds—relies on the validity of this comparison, of persuading the public that if they supported the pro-democracy movement in China, they should also support Occupy Wall Street.

⋙ WORKING TOGETHER

Analyzing Multimodal Compositions

Work together in a group of three or four on a rhetorical analysis of a multimodal composition. This could be anything from an advertisement in a magazine to a public service announcement on television, to the website of a college or nonprofit organization, a billboard for a movie or a poster for a band, a slide show at the *New York Times* online, or a double-page spread in a history textbook. Use your imagination in choosing a visual design or multimodal composition to analyze. Then follow the steps outlined above. Depending on your teacher's directions, prepare a PowerPoint or Prezi presentation of your analysis.

WRITING ASSIGNMENT

Writing a Rhetorical Analysis

The chapter's culminating assignment is to write your own rhetorical analysis. Here are a series of steps to help you organize this writing project:

1. *Choose something to analyze.* What you analyze can range from print texts to new media and multimodal compositions. Op-ed pieces, columns, and other short commentaries in newspapers and magazines are good sources for this assignment, as you can see in the sample student paper, Stacy Yi's rhetorical analysis of Johann Hari's "You Are Being Lied to About Pirates," which appeared originally in *The Independent* in Britain. Other equally likely possibilities for this assignment go beyond print texts to include posters, print and television ads, music videos, podcasts, and other multimodal compositions.

2. *Describe the formal organization or visual design of what you are analyzing.* Outlining an essay or describing the visual design of a poster is the first step in rhetorical analysis, to begin with a close reading that identifies the writer's purpose and rhetorical strategies. You can see Stacy Yi's outline of Hari's commentary right before her rhetorical analysis.

3. *Design the sections of your rhetorical analysis.* The focus of rhetorical analysis may vary, depending on whether you are analyzing a print text or a multimodal composition. Still, the design of the analysis is often similar, with sections that typically accomplish the following purposes:

   ▶ **Introduction.** Presents the topic and purpose of the analysis. Establishes main themes and focus of attention.

   ▶ **Background.** Provides information on the context of issues, the writer or designer, the publication or place (museum, gallery, street) in which the work appears, and the audience. See Background: First Questions to Ask, pp. 54–55.

   ▶ **Description.** Summarizes print texts and/or describes their patterns of development. Describes the various components of multimodal compositions and how they are organized.

   ▶ **Analysis of rhetorical situation.** Explains how writer or designer defined the rhetorical situation and decided how to respond to its call to write.

   ▶ **Analysis of genre choice.** Explains why the writer or designer chose a particular genre and the expectations genres call up on the readers' part.

   ▶ **Analysis of rhetorical stance.** Explains how the writer or designer coordinated the rhetorical appeals—ethos, pathos, and logos. Considers style and tone in writing and visual design. See Tone and Rhetorical Distance, p. 46.

   ▶ **Ending.** Provides a qualified sense of closure by pointing out implications and wider significance of the main themes, connecting themes to wider contexts of issues, and reevaluating themes in light of the rhetorical analysis.

4. *Plan the visual design of your rhetorical analysis.* Writing software makes it easy to insert images from the Internet, digital cameras, or scanners into print texts. You can also take screen shots of websites. Many computers have programs that enable you to crop images. For rhetorical analysis that appears online, you can put links in your text that will take readers to a written text, a podcast, YouTube, or other site. You might think of this aspect of your analysis as similar to including quotes from print texts. Both need to be integrated into the analysis with commentary from the writer—and both should be cited at the end of the paper.

BACKGROUND: FIRST QUESTIONS TO ASK

Background information about the context of issues, the writer, the publication or location where the work appeared, and the audience is useful in understanding how the writer or designer identifies the call to write.

Context of Issues

- What do you know about the particular topic the writer or designer is treating?
- If your knowledge is limited, where can you get reliable background information?
- What have people been saying about the topic?
- What do they think the main issues are?
- What seems to be at stake in these discussions?
- Do people seem divided over these issues? If so, what positions have they taken?

The Writer or Designer

- What do you know about the writer or designer?
- What authority and credibility can you attribute to the writer or designer?
- Is there reason to believe that the writer or designer will provide informed accounts and responsible arguments, whether you agree with them or not?
- What political, cultural, social, or other commitments is the writer or designer known for? How are these commitments likely to influence the argument or design?
- How do these commitments relate to your own views?

- How is this relationship likely to influence your evaluation of the work?

Publication or Location

- If you are analyzing a print text, what do you know about the publication?
- Who is the publisher?
- Is it a commercial publication?
- Does it have an institutional affiliation—to a college or university, an academic field of study, a professional organization, a church?
- Does it espouse an identifiable political, social, cultural, economic, or religious ideology?
- If the publication is a periodical—a magazine or journal—what other writers and types of writing and topics appear in the issue?
- Who would be likely to read the publication?
- If the site of publication is the web, consider whether the site is .edu (educational), .org (nonprofit), .gov (government), or .com (commercial). What is the purpose of the website? When was it last updated? Does it have links to other websites?
- If the work you are analyzing appears on television or radio, consider the network, sponsors, and programming. If the work is in a museum or gallery,

consider how it is presented. If it appears in public, explain the circumstances.

Audience

- Who is the intended audience?
- Is the writer addressing one group of readers or more than one?

- Is the writer trying to bring an audience into being?
- What kind of relationship is the writer trying to establish with readers?
- What assumptions about readers does the writer seem to make?

FOR RHETORICAL ANALYSIS

This commentary appeared on January 5, 2009 in Britian's *The Independent,* where Johann Hari has been a columnist. As you will see, Stacy Yi used it for her rhetorical analysis assignment, the sample student essay which follows the column.

You Are Being Lied to About Pirates

Johann Hari

Who imagined that in 2009, the world's governments would be declaring a new War on Pirates? As you read this, the British Royal Navy— backed by the ships of more than two dozen nations, from the US to China—is sailing into Somalian waters to take on men we still picture as parrot-on-the-shoulder pantomime villains. They will soon be fighting Somalian ships and even chasing the pirates onto land, into one of the most broken countries on earth. But behind the arrr-me-hearties oddness of this tale, there is an untold scandal. The people our governments are labelling as "one of the great menaces of our times" have an extraordinary story to tell—and some justice on their side.

Pirates have never been quite who we think they are. In the "golden age of piracy"— from 1650 to 1730—the idea of the pirate as the senseless, savage Bluebeard that lingers today was created by the British government in a great propaganda heave. Many ordinary people believed it was false: pirates were often saved from the gallows by supportive crowds. Why? What did they see that we can't? In his book *Villains Of All Nations,* the historian Marcus Rediker pores through the evidence.

If you became a merchant or navy sailor then—plucked from the docks of London's East End, young and hungry—you ended up in a floating wooden Hell. You worked all

---

hours on a cramped, half-starved ship, and if you slacked off, the all-powerful captain would whip you with the Cat O' Nine Tails. If you slacked often, you could be thrown overboard. And at the end of months or years of this, you were often cheated of your wages.

Pirates were the first people to rebel against this world. They mutinied—and created a different way of working on the seas. Once they had a ship, the pirates elected their captains, and made all their decisions collectively, without torture. They shared their bounty out in what Rediker calls "one of the most egalitarian plans for the disposition of resources to be found anywhere in the eighteenth century."

They even took in escaped African slaves and lived with them as equals.

The pirates showed "quite clearly—and subversively—that ships did not have to be run in the brutal and oppressive ways of the merchant service and the Royal Navy." This is why they were romantic heroes, despite being unproductive thieves.

The words of one pirate from that lost age, a young British man called William Scott, should echo into this new age of piracy. Just before he was hanged in Charleston, South Carolina, he said: "What I did was to keep me from perishing. I was forced to go a-pirateing to live." In 1991, the government of Somalia collapsed. Its nine million people have been teetering on starvation ever since—and the ugliest forces in the Western world have seen this as a great opportunity to steal the country's food supply and dump our nuclear waste in their seas.

Yes: nuclear waste. As soon as the government was gone, mysterious European ships started appearing off the coast of Somalia, dumping vast barrels into the ocean. The coastal population began to sicken. At first they suffered strange rashes, nausea and malformed babies. Then, after the 2005 tsunami, hundreds of the dumped and leaking barrels washed up on shore. People began to suffer from radiation sickness, and more than 300 died.

Ahmedou Ould-Abdallah, the UN envoy to Somalia, tells me: "Somebody is dumping nuclear material here. There is also lead, and heavy metals such as cadmium and mercury—you name it." Much of it can be traced back to European hospitals and factories, who seem to be passing it on to the Italian mafia to "dispose" of cheaply. When I asked Mr Ould-Abdallah what European governments were doing about it, he said with a sigh: "Nothing. There has been no clean-up, no compensation, and no prevention."

At the same time, other European ships have been looting Somalia's seas of their greatest resource: seafood. We have destroyed our own fish stocks by overexploitation—and now we have moved on to theirs. More than $300m-worth of tuna, shrimp, and lobster are being stolen every year by illegal trawlers. The local fishermen are now starving. Mohammed Hussein, a fisherman in the town of Marka 100km south of Mogadishu, told Reuters: "If nothing is done, there soon won't be much fish left in our coastal waters."

This is the context in which the "pirates" have emerged. Somalian fishermen took speedboats to try to dissuade the dumpers and trawlers, or at least levy a "tax" on them. They call themselves the Volunteer Coastguard of Somalia—and ordinary Somalis agree. The independent Somalian news site WardheerNews found 70 per cent "strongly supported the piracy as a form of national defence."

No, this doesn't make hostage-taking justifiable, and yes, some are clearly just gangsters—especially those who have held up World Food Programme supplies. But in a telephone interview, one of the pirate leaders, Sugule Ali: "We don't consider ourselves sea bandits. We consider sea bandits [to be] those who illegally fish and dump in our seas." William Scott would understand.

Did we expect starving Somalians to stand passively on their beaches, paddling in our toxic waste, and watch us snatch their fish to eat in restaurants in London and Paris and Rome? We won't act on those crimes—the only sane solution to this problem—but when some of the fishermen responded by disrupting the transit-corridor for 20 per cent of the world's oil supply, we swiftly send in the gunboats.

The story of the 2009 war on piracy was best summarised by another pirate, who lived and died in the fourth century BC. He was captured and brought to Alexander the Great, who demanded to know "what he meant by keeping possession of the sea." The pirate smiled, and responded: "What you mean by seizing the whole earth; but because I do it with a petty ship, I am called a robber, while you, who do it with a great fleet, are called emperor." Once again, our great imperial fleets sail—but who is the robber?

WRITERS' WORKSHOP

Stacy Yi. "Revising Somali Pirates: A Rhetorical Analysis of 'You Are Being Lied to About Pirates' by Johann Hari."

The first step Stacy Yi took to prepare a rhetorical analysis of Johann Hari's column was describing its formal organization.

Description of the Formal Organization of "You Are Being Lied to About Pirates"

¶1: Gives background information on the British Royal Navy's campaign against Somali pirates. Redefines the situation as an "untold scandal" and presents the writer's position that the Somali pirates have "an extraordinary story to tell—and some justice on their side."

¶2–4: Presents a revised view of pirates in history. Cites historian Marcus Rediker to portray pirates as egalitarian rebels.

¶5: Makes transition from pirates of the past to Somali pirates of today, emphasizing common point that both sought to secure a livelihood in a world of starvation and political collapse.

¶6–9: Presents details on nuclear dumping (¶ 6–7) and illegal fishing (¶ 8) by European ships as context for organization of Somali fishermen to patrol the coast (¶ 9).

¶10: Includes hostage taking as a qualification to positive image of pirates but then turns paragraph back to question of who the real bandits are.

¶11–12: Ending. Uses rhetorical question to justify pirates and proposes a different approach (¶ 11). Uses quote from a fourth-century BC pirate to pose again in closing (¶ 12) the question of who the real bandits are.

Stacy Yi

Professor Rumney

College Writing

January 5, 2012

Revising Somali Pirates:

A Rhetorical Analysis of "You Are Being Lied to About Pirates" by Johann Hari

By early 2009, when the columnist Johann Hari published "You Are Being Lied to About Pirates" in the British newspaper *The Independent*, Somali pirates had become a hot news item in the press for high-jacking ships in the Gulf of Aden and holding them for ransom. Pirate activity was a growing source of concern to governments and multinational corporations who depend on the 20,000 or more cargo ships that pass each year through the Gulf of Aden on their way to the Suez Canal. In 2008, Somali pirates attacked 111 ships and successfully highjacked 42 of them. The number of attacks increased dramatically in early 2009, and the British Royal Navy joined ships from other nations to pursue the highjackers. It looked like a new war on pirates was breaking out when Hari wrote his column, calling on readers to stop and reconsider their image of the Somali pirates and what a war on them might mean. Hari's column offers a frankly revisionist account of the Somali pirates and their motives.

Hari identifies the rhetorical situation as one that has kept the truth about the Somali pirates—the "untold scandal"—from readers. While the British government pictures the Somali pirates as "one of the great menaces of our time," Hari argues that pirates past and present have been misunderstood as "senseless" and "savage," misrepresented by government propaganda both in the present and the past, in the "golden age of piracy" from 1650 to 1730. What seems to call on Hari to write about the pirates is his desire to correct the historical record and the current representation of Somali pirates—to turn things around by revising our understanding as readers. The newspaper column is an excellent means to do this because it allows the writer to address readers directly, in an informal voice that seems to take readers into the writer's confidence, to join Hari in looking behind the myths about pirates.

Part of the appeal of the column is how Hari has crafted a rhetorical stance that projects a certain intimacy with the reader, an ethos that presents Hari as a knowing and reliable commentator, much like a trusted friend. At key points, moreover, Hari's credibility and reasonableness are reinforced, when he cites the academic authority Marcus Rediker in the section on the history of pirates or, later in the column, when Hari concedes that hostage taking is not justifiable. Hari approaches his readers as people who are interested in getting the story behind the news and the government's representations of the Somali pirates as a "great menace." There is a good deal of research in Hari's commentary, but he doesn't come off as pedantic. His tone rather is informal, treating readers as people who can think for themselves, inviting them to join him in examining piracy, past and present.

The reassurance readers may feel about Hari's motives does not totally hide the fact that another source of the column's appeal is the pleasure of overturning conventional wisdom, the pathos or emotional charge for the reader of bringing an "untold scandal" to light by seeing that pirates "have never been quite who we think they are." This sense of cutting through the layers of propaganda and historical misrepresentation to get to the truth about pirates sets up the logos of the column, the line of reasoning that calls into question who the real bandits are—the Somali pirates or the European ships dumping nuclear waste and overfishing in Somalian waters. The emotional satisfaction of challenging authority and imagining oneself on the pirates' side, as part of the crowd who saved pirates from the gallows, is linked to the intellectual pleasure of revising our understanding of pirates past and present and what they stand for.

There are times in the column where Hari uses rhetorical questions that assume readers agree with him, such as the next to last paragraph that begins "Did we expect starving Somalians to stand passively on their beaches, paddling in our toxic waste, and watch us snatch their fish to eat in restaurants in London and Paris and Rome?" For the most part, however, Hari is quite skilled at leading readers to revise their picture of pirates, to see them as "romantic heroes" who have at least "some justice on their side."

CHAPTER 3

Persuasion and Responsibility

Writing a Position Paper

Imagine you are taking a walk and encounter an elderly man whose car has broken down. His request, "Can you give me a hand?" requires no explanation. What makes it persuasive is the shared belief that people should help each other in times of need.

Persuasion amounts to a meeting of the minds. It takes place on a casual everyday level, often spontaneously and without discussion. A friend suggests that you go to the basketball game together on Friday night, and you agree. Neighbors ask whether you can feed their cat when they are away for the weekend. Woven into the fabric of social life, persuasion refers to moments when people reach agreements and join together on common purposes.

Moments such as these require no elaborate explanation. In other instances, however, we do need to make explicit arguments—to give reasons and explanations—to persuade others. Persuasion of this type appears everywhere in the public sphere—attorneys' arguments in court, the president's state of the union address, newspaper editorials, or commentary from a TV anchorperson. You can find persuasion in multimodal form in advertising and advocacy campaigns where the reasoning appears visually as much as verbally. In movements such as Occupy Wall Street or the popular uprisings of Arab Spring, persuasion is a matter of banding together to take action through new social identities, to have influence as a political force.

There are academic, literary, and intellectual worlds within the public sphere where persuasion means gaining your readers' attention and getting them to engage your ideas and perceptions. Persuasion in such circumstances is the willingness to enter into a conversation with the writer. Many of the readings in *The Call to Write* come from this world of scholarly publication, popular books, journalism, and literary nonfiction. Learning how to get into these conversations is the primary purpose of this chapter.

Writing a position paper—the assignment at the end of the chapter—is a good way to begin because it calls on writers to locate themselves in relation to what others have said in order to create their own rhetorical stance in relation to positions that have already been staked out.

ETHICS OF WRITING: UNDERSTANDING ARGUMENT

People often think of arguments as heated moments when tempers flare and discussion degenerates into a shouting match. There is no question such arguments can be found in the political arena and the media, on radio and television talk shows, and in the blogosphere.

For our purposes, such images of argument are not very useful. Part of the problem is that arguments in politics and the media are often cast in simplistic, pro or con, liberal or conservative terms, where polarized speakers or writers are trying to defeat each other. This winner-take-all mentality is hardly conducive to the responsible investigation of complicated issues, where there may be more than just two positions and the task is to identify the range of options and how and why people differ in their views of what to do.

Another problem is that restricted adversarial notions of argument can lead people to give up altogether on the hope of negotiating their differences with others. Some just say, "What's the point? Everyone has their own ideas, and there's nothing you can do about it." Although such a statement does, in an important sense, acknowledge the validity of others' perspectives, it is often based on a sense of powerlessness in the face of differences and can end up leading to a refusal to take others seriously enough to engage with them about issues facing us all.

Genuine argument (as opposed to a shouting match) is devoted to understanding the reasonable differences that divide people and using this understanding to clarify the issues. This view of argument does not mean that you can't hold strong positions or find weaknesses in the views of people who differ with you. It means that you need to take others seriously—to see them not as obstacles to your views but as reasonable human beings. In this sense, arguments involve working with as much as against others. Exploring and negotiating reasonable disagreements through argument amounts to a collective effort to understand what divides people and what the best course of action may be.

⊃ FOR CRITICAL INQUIRY

Looking at Polarized Arguments

Write an account or prepare an oral presentation of an argument you witnessed or took part in that polarized into opposing sides. Describe what happened, and explain why the polarization took place. The point of this exercise is not to condemn the people involved but to understand what happened and why. Remember, polarization is not necessarily a bad thing. It may be unavoidable as people begin to identify their differences or invoke a matter of principle, where a person finds no alternative but to make a counterargument and take a stand. Your task here is to analyze what took place and to consider whether the polarization was inevitable or could have been avoided.

What Is Argument? Dealing with Reasonable Differences

Some disagreements among people are not, properly speaking, reasonable ones. Two people might disagree, for example, about the driving distance between New York City and Buffalo, New York, or about the chemical composition of dioxin. These are not reasonable disagreements because they can be resolved by consulting a road atlas or a chemistry book. There are well-established sources available to settle the matter, so there's really no point in arguing.

On the other hand, people might reasonably disagree about the best route to drive to Buffalo or about the best policy concerning the production and use of dioxin. In disagreements such as these, there are no final, definitive answers available. One person may prefer a certain route to Buffalo because of the scenery, while another wants only the fastest way possible. By the same token, some may argue that policy on dioxin needs above all to take environmental and health risks into account, while for others the effect of policy on the economy and workers' jobs must also be a prime consideration.

Exchange of Letters

D. Peters and Marcus Boldt

Following is an exchange of letters between D. Peters, a homemaker from Camas, Washington, and her representative in the state legislature, Marcus Boldt, a recently elected Republican. As you will see, Peters wrote to Boldt, asking him to oppose a plan to eliminate the state's Readiness to Learn program, which supported the Family Learning Center, an adult education and preschool program that Peters and her three sons attended in Camas. Included here are Peters's letter and the response from Representative Boldt.

Representative Marcus Boldt:

Please do not cancel funding for the Readiness to Learn Family Learning Center.

Our family came to the learning center frustrated. Barely self-supportive, we were struggling but living with no outside assistance. My husband was frequently laid off from work, and I was a full-time mother, not working outside the home. With four-year-old twins and another child, age three, we couldn't afford to pay for a preschool program. When I went to the Head Start program, I was told that we were ineligible because we made too much money. I felt like a victim of the system.

I was thrilled to find out we were eligible for the Readiness to Learn program. My children could all attend, and so could I. My sons have learned so much at the center. They constantly surprise me with skills I didn't even know they had. I am so proud of their success. I myself have learned a great deal as well. Being challenged academically has sparked a thirst for learning that I never knew existed in me. I have seen the world open up before me, and I feel capable of meeting any academic challenge. Furthermore, using one of the agencies I learned of at the center, my husband is making a career change, having decided to leave the construction business to become an electrician.

This has been such a valuable experience that I hope many other families are able to attend the center. Abolishing Readiness to Learn might rob another family of the chance to improve itself and reach its long-term goals. We need this program in our area.

Sincerely,

D. Peters

From "The New Right Writes Back," by D. Peters and M. Boldt. *Harper's Magazine*, July 1995.

Dear Ms. Peters:

Thank you for writing to me about your concerns regarding funding for the Family Learning Center. Your letter goes to the heart of the matter in the area of budgetary reform. My positions on budget expenditures are well-known and served in large measure to assure my election to this office.

I see that you have three children, ages three and four. You wrote that your husband is subject to frequent layoffs. You indicate that you are a "full-time mother, not working outside the home."

The concerns expressed by the taxpayers over your situation are as follows:

a. If your situation was subject to so much financial instability, then why did you have three children?

b. Why is your husband in a line of work that subjects him to "frequent layoffs"?

c. Why, in the face of your husband's ability to parent as a result of his frequent layoffs, are you refusing to work outside the home?

d. Because there is no state or federally mandated requirement that children attend these programs, why should the taxpayer foot the bill for them?

e. Because your family apparently makes too much money for assistance, why should you receive subsidies of any kind?

f. How much of the situation outlined in your letter should be the responsibility of the people of this state?

g. What arrangements have you made to repay this program at some future date?

I do not necessarily agree with all of these perspectives. But I must contend with the expectations of a constituency that is tired of paying for so many programs without any discernible return.

The voters have made it clear that, in this era of personal responsibility, life must become a more "pay-as-you-go" proposition. To put it bluntly, the taxpayers' perspective says, "This program is something that D. Peters wants to have, and not something that she must have."

Thank you for your time.

Marcus Boldt
State Representative

⤳ FOR CRITICAL INQUIRY

1. What argument is D. Peters making? What differences are at issue in the two letters? Do they seem to be reasonable ones? On whose behalf is she writing? How does she seem to imagine her relationship to Representative Boldt? How can you tell?

2. How does Boldt seem to identify differences? On whose behalf is he writing? How does he seem to imagine his relationship to Peters? How can you tell?

3. Peters's letter clearly did not persuade Boldt or lead to a meeting of the minds. By the same token, it is not likely that Boldt's letter persuaded Peters either. Here, then, is a

situation in which arguments have failed to achieve their intended aims. How would you explain this failure? Does the exchange clarify the differences that divide the two? Can you imagine some common ground on which agreement might take place? Why or why not?

WHAT DO READERS EXPECT FROM ARGUMENTS?

In high school and college courses, you've probably been assigned papers that call on you to take a position and back it up. Thesis and support are common features of written academic work. This is also true of persuasive writing in everyday life, in the workplace, and in the public sphere. But whether the writing is for a class assignment or a petition circulated to increase state funding for the arts, readers expect arguments to take certain predictable forms.

Readers justifiably expect that the writer's line of thinking will be easy to identify and to follow. Otherwise, they will have a hard time engaging the writer's thinking, and that defeats the whole purpose of taking a position on matters where there are reasonable differences and asking readers to consider the writer's perspective.

Accordingly, arguments are persuasive that elicit reader involvement by providing four things that readers expect:

▶ A clear statement of the context of issues and the writer's position on the issue at hand. This statement is the writer's central claim (or *thesis*) in the argument.

▶ Evidence that supports the claim, such as statistics, research, expert testimony, and examples.

▶ Clear explanations of how this evidence actually supports the main claim. These explanations are the reasons in the argument—the statements that show how the writer's evidence is linked to the claim.

▶ A sense of the larger implications of the main claim.

⟫ FOR CRITICAL INQUIRY

The order in which the four reader expectations appear in a piece of writing is less important than whether they appear in a convincing way. Consider the two print texts in Chapter 2, Jerald Walker's "Before Grief" and Johann Hari's "You Are Being Lied to About Pirates," in terms of how they meet the four reader expectations. In what ways are they similar? What are the main differences? What is the significance of the similarities and differences in how the two pieces of writing—a personal essay from the world of literary nonfiction and an op-ed commentary by a newspaper columnist—define and respond to the call to write?

ENTERING A CONTROVERSY

The idea that argument takes place when there are reasonable disagreements among people means that writers do not just start arguments from scratch. Rather, they enter a field of debate—or a controversy—where some positions have already been staked out and people are already arguing.

Entering a controversy is like coming into a room where a heated conversation is taking place. You may know some of the people talking, but not all of them. You need to listen for a while to find out what the various speakers are saying and what the issues seem to be. You may find yourself drawn toward some of the views argued and skeptical about others. Some speakers may be throwing out facts and figures, but you may not be quite sure what they are trying to prove. Some may be taking jabs at other speakers' reasoning.

Gradually, as you listen, you find you agree with some of the speakers' views but oppose others. The controversy begins to make sense to you, and you start to speak.

Entering a controversy, as this scenario reveals, is a matter of coming into the middle of something, and it takes some time to learn your way around and figure out what is going on. It might well be considered rude or presumptuous if you started arguing the moment you entered the room. You need to listen first to see how you can fit your own views into the stream of debate.

A second point this scenario illustrates is that people enter controversies through their relations to others. As the scenario reveals, your sense of what the debate is about depends on what others have said, what they value, what they propose to do. For this reason, when you do step forward to speak, you are also articulating your relationship to others—whether it is agreement, qualified support, or counterargument. Entering a controversy inevitably draws a person into alliances with some people and differences with others.

Analyzing the Context of Issues

Listening to and reflecting on the conversation going on around you amounts to analyzing the context of issues—the set of terms, the tone, and the emotional and intellectual investments that have shaped the discussion, the sense of why talking about the subject is important at all. To take part in a controversy—to have your say—you need to first understand why speakers disagree and what they have at stake. This can be complicated—and sometimes confusing—because people do not always agree on what they are arguing about.

Take the following argument about baseball superstar Manny Ramirez's suspension in 2009 for taking performance-enhancing drugs:

▶ One person says that now we know why Manny Ramirez was such a productive home run hitter with the Boston Red Sox and Los Angeles Dodgers.

▶ A second person responds that the Ramirez incident just goes to show how corrupt all sports have become, that athletes will do anything to be successful, whether in pro sports or the Olympics.

▶ A third person chimes in, claiming the real point is that Major League Baseball has for years failed its fans and its players by not developing and enforcing a league-wide policy on steroids and other performance-enhancing drugs.

These people might argue all night long, but their argument will be fruitless and unproductive unless they can agree on what they are arguing about. In fact, one person could hold all three of these views and agree with each of the speakers, though we sense that some real differences divide them. The problem is they have not sufficiently clarified the nature of the disagreement.

To enter a controversy and argue responsibly, your arguments must respond to the issues already posed in dispute. Otherwise, you cannot possibly engage with others. You will simply be left with personal opinions but little productive debate about how and why people differ.

But let's not give up on the three people in our example. They may still be able to engage each other and find out where and how they differ. But first they need to agree on what the issues are. They need to do some work, some sorting out, to understand what is at stake in the various claims they have made.

TYPES OF ISSUES

Issues are arguable points that people make when reasonable differences exist. For example, the statement "Jimmy Carter was elected president in 1976" isn't an issue because no one would dispute it. Instead, most people would agree that the statement is an established fact. On the other hand, the statement "The shortcomings of the Carter presidency paved the way for Ronald Reagan's conservative revolution in 1980" raises a point of interpretation, a debatable issue about the relation between the two presidencies that could be looked at from a number of positions.

To return to our three speakers, we can see that there are three different and distinct types of issues in their argument about the case of Manny Ramirez's suspension—issues of substantiation, evaluation, and policy. Each of these issues offers a place to begin a productive argument.

Issues of Substantiation

Issues of substantiation are questions of disputed facts, definitions, causes, and consequences. The argument that failures of the Carter administration resulted in the triumph of Reagan conservatism involves a cause-and-effect relationship. The connection cannot be proven in any absolute sense, but it can be substantiated according to the evidence available.

The first speaker raises an issue that can be substantiated by asserting that performance-enhancing drugs gave Manny Ramirez extra strength and an edge in hitting. This is an issue that asks us to look at the available evidence to establish the properties of the drugs, how they work, and what their effects are.

Issues that call for substantiation occur regularly in ongoing arguments:

▶ How widely are amateur and professional athletes using steroids? (question of disputed fact)

▶ What kinds of actions amount to sexual harassment? (question of definition)

▶ Are environmental carcinogenics responsible for the increase in breast cancer? (question of cause)

▶ Has expansion of pro football into new cities increased the league's profits? (question of consequences)

Issues of Evaluation

Issues of evaluation are questions about whether something is good or bad, right or wrong, desirable or undesirable, effective or ineffective, valuable or worthless. The second speaker addresses an issue of evaluation when he focuses not so much on the effects of performance-enhancing drugs (in running faster times or hitting more home runs) but on a moral judgment about athletes' decision to use drugs.

Issues of evaluation appear routinely in all spheres of life:

▶ Is a Macintosh or a PC computer system best suited to your computing needs?

▶ Is *American Idol* a cruel display of untalented performers or an old-fashioned talent show that everyone can enjoy?

▶ Why is diversity important in higher education?

▶ What novels should be included in an American literature course?

Issues of Policy

Issues of policy are questions about what we should do and how we should implement our aims. The third speaker takes on a policy issue when he finds fault with how Major League Baseball has handled its drug problem. Support or refutation of policy issues will typically focus on how well the policy solves an existing problem or addresses a demonstrable need.

Issues about policy are pervasive in public discussions. Typically, they use the terms *should, ought*, or *must* to signal the courses of action they recommend:

▶ Should the federal government ban late-term abortions?

▶ Ought students be required to take a first-year writing course?

▶ Should there be a moratorium on capital punishment?

▶ Must schools provide bilingual education?

Identifying what type of issue is at stake in a speaker's claim offers a way to cut into an ongoing controversy and get oriented. This does not mean, however, that controversies come neatly packaged according to type of issue. The three types of issues are tools of analysis to help you identify how and why people disagree. As you prepare to enter an ongoing controversy, you are likely to find that the three types of issues are intertwined and lead from one to the next.

Here is an example of how the three types of issues can be used to explore a controversy and invent arguments.

Sample Exploration of a Controversy

Should High Schools Abolish Tracking and Assign Students to Mixed-Ability Classrooms Instead?

1. **Issues that can be substantiated:** How widespread is the practice of tracking? When did it begin? Why was tracking instituted in the first place? What purposes was it designed for? What are the effects of tracking on students? What experiments have taken place to use mixed-ability groupings instead of tracking? What are the results?

2. **Issues that require evaluation:** What educational values are put into practice in tracking? Are these values worthy? Is tracking fair to all students? Does it benefit some students more than others? What values are embodied in mixed-ability classrooms? How do these compare to the values of tracking?

3. **Issues of policy:** What should we do? What are the reasons for maintaining tracking? What are the reasons for implementing mixed-ability groupings? Can mixed-ability classrooms succeed? What changes would be required? What would the long-term consequences be?

TAKING A POSITION: FROM ISSUES TO CLAIMS

The point of analyzing the issues in any ongoing controversy is to clarify your own thinking and determine where you stand. Taking a position amounts to entering into the debate to have your own say. Determining your position means you have an arguable claim to make—an informed opinion, belief, recommendation, or call to action you want your readers to consider.

Look at the following two statements:

Tracking was recently dismantled in a local school district.

Tracking has become a very heated issue.

As you can see, these sentences simply describe a situation. They aren't really arguable claims because no one would reasonably disagree with them. They don't tell readers what the writer believes or thinks should be done. Now take a look at these two statements:

For the dismantling of tracking to be successful, our local school district should provide teachers with in-service training in working with mixed-ability groups.

Tracking has become such a heated issue because parents of honors students worry unnecessarily that their children won't get into the best colleges.

Notice that in each statement you can see the writer's stand on the issue right away. The first writer treats an issue of policy, whereas the second is trying to substantiate the cause of the tracking controversy. What makes each claim arguable is that there can be differing views regarding the issue. Readers could respond that in-service training is a waste of money because teachers already know how to teach different levels of students, or that the real reason tracking is so controversial is because it holds back the brightest students. To make sure a claim is arguable, ask yourself whether someone could reasonably disagree with it—whether there could be at least two differing views on the issue on which you've taken a position.

Both writers have successfully cued readers to their positions, in part by using key words that typically appear in position statements. Notice that in the first sentence, the writer uses *should* (but could have used similar terms such as *must, ought to, needs to,* or *has to*) to signal a proposed solution. In the second, the writer uses a *because* statement to indicate to readers that there is evidence available to back up the claim. Writers also use terms such as *therefore, consequently, thus, it follows that,* and *the point is* to signal their positions.

▷ WRITING EXERCISE

Notes toward a Tentative Position

Take a current controversy you know something about or are interested in learning about, where reasonable differences divide people. It could be anti-immigrant legislation in Alabama or Arizona, drug testing for high school or college athletes, the argument against gay marriage from within the gay movement, or the effects of social media. The main consideration is that the controversy interests you and that you believe it is important. Write some notes to map out the controversy and see where you fit in.

1. State the controversy in its most general terms in the form of a question: "Should colleges routinely conduct drug tests on varsity athletes?" "Do we need a rating system for television shows similar to the one used for movies?"

2. Use the three types of issues—substantiation, evaluation, and policy—to generate a list of questions: How do drug tests work? What's wrong with performance-enhancing drugs? Does drug testing violate the right to privacy? Are drug tests reliable?

3. Consider how the issues and the questions are interrelated. What are the connections? If drug tests are not reliable, for example, then it is hard to argue for them as policy. On the other hand, if performing-enhancing drugs have serious medical consequences, then it's easier to consider abridging rights to privacy on public health grounds.

   Revise as needed the question you began with, narrowing it down or rephrasing as you see fit. Then write a sentence or two that states a tentative position in response to the question. Test whether this is an arguable claim by trying to write a sentence or two that takes the opposite position.

4. Consider to what extent your tentative position is an informed claim. Write a paragraph or two that states what you know about the issue and what further information and analysis you need to explain the issues responsibly and develop an arguable claim with sufficient evidence.

MAKING AN ARGUMENT

Good arguments aren't found ready to use. They have to be made. To make a persuasive argument, you need to develop an effective line of reasoning. To do that, it is helpful to look at the parts that go into making an argument. In this section, we draw on a model of argument developed by the philosopher Stephen Toulmin, although we use somewhat different terms.

What Are the Parts of an Argument?

Here is a quick sketch of the parts of an argument that we'll be considering in more detail in this section:

Claim	Your position, the basic point you want readers to accept
Evidence	The supporting material for the claim
Enabling assumption	The line of reasoning that explains how the evidence supports the claim
Differing views	Disagreements with all or part of your argument
Qualifiers	Words that modify or limit the claim

Claims, Evidence, and Enabling Assumptions

As you have seen, you can't have a responsible argument unless you have an arguable claim, and you've looked at some ways to develop claims by analyzing issues and constructing an appropriate rhetorical stance. In this section, we look in detail at the three basic parts of an argument—claims, evidence, and enabling assumptions. Taken together, these terms give us a way to think about the line of reasoning in an argument. Readers justifiably expect writers to provide evidence for the claims they make. Moreover, they expect the evidence a writer offers to have a clear connection to the claim. As you will see, enabling assumptions are explanations of how the evidence supports a writer's claim.

To see how these connections work, take a look at the following two evaluations that students wrote of their composition instructor.

Sample Evaluations

Student 1

Ms. Smith is probably the worst teacher I've had so far in college. I've never been so frustrated. I could never figure out what the teacher wanted us to do. She didn't grade the papers we turned in but instead just wrote comments on them. Then we had to evaluate each other's writings. How are students qualified to judge each other's writing? This is the teacher's job. We had to revise some of our writing to put in a portfolio at the end of the term. How were we supposed to know which papers were any good?

Student 2

Ms. Smith is probably the best teacher I've had so far in college. I really liked how she organized the work. By not grading our papers, she gave us the opportunity to select our best writing and revise it for a portfolio at the end of the term. The comments she offered on drafts and the evaluations we did of each other's papers really helped. I found this freed me to experiment with my writing in new ways and not worry about getting low grades. This system made me realize how important revision is.

In one sense, both evaluations are persuasive. It's hard not to be convinced, at the level of lived experience, that the first student did not like the class, whereas the second student did. But what are we to make of these differences? What do they tell us about the teacher and her way of teaching writing?

In this case, to understand why the two students differ, it will help to see *how* they differ. Each has made an argument, and we can analyze how the arguments have been made. Each consists of the same basic parts.

Claims

In the two student evaluations, the competing claims are easy to find: Ms. Smith is either the best or the worst teacher in the student's experience. Each claim, moreover, meets the test for writing arguable claims.

▶ **Reasonable differences:** Both claims are matters of judgment that can't be decided by referring to an established, authoritative source. The question of whether Ms. Smith is a good teacher is worth arguing about.

▶ **Plausibility:** Both claims could be true. Each has a certain credibility that a claim like "An invasion of flying saucers will take place next week" doesn't have.

▶ **Sharable claims:** Both claims can be argued on terms that can be shared by others. In contrast, there's no reason to argue that blue is your favorite color or that you love the feel of velvet. Such a claim refers to a personal preference based on subjective experience and can't really be shared by others.

Evidence

Evidence is all the information available in a particular situation. Like detectives in the investigation of a crime, writers begin with the available evidence—data, information, facts, observations, personal testimony, statistics, common knowledge, or any other relevant material.

Writers use this evidence to construct a sense of what happened and what the unresolved issues are. Notice in the two evaluations of Ms. Smith that the students

QUESTIONS TO ASK ABOUT EVIDENCE

To make a persuasive argument, you need evidence for your claim—and you also need some guidelines to evaluate whether the evidence you turn up will work for your argument. Here are some questions to ask yourself:

1. **Is the evidence clearly related to the claim?** As you plan an argument, you are likely to come up with lots of interesting material. Not all of it, however, will necessarily be relevant to the claim you want to support. For example, if you are arguing about how Darwin's theory of evolution influenced fiction writers in the nineteenth century, it doesn't make sense to give a lot of biographical details on Darwin. They may be interesting, but it's unlikely that they will help you explain the influence of his theory.

2. **Do you have enough evidence?** Basing a claim on one or two facts is hardly likely to persuade your readers. They are likely to dismiss your argument as hasty and unjustifiable because of insufficient evidence. The fact that two people in your neighborhood were laid off recently from their construction jobs is not enough evidence for claiming that the construction industry is in crisis. You would need to establish a pattern by showing, say, a decline in housing starts, the postponement of many major building projects, layoffs across the country, or bankruptcies of construction companies.

3. **Is your evidence verifiable?** Readers are likely to be suspicious of your argument unless they can check out the evidence for themselves. For instance, to support an argument for campaign finance reform, you might use examples of how corporate donations influenced politicians' voting, but if you don't tell readers who the politicians and corporations are, they will have no way to verify your evidence.

4. **Is your evidence up to date?** Readers expect you to do your homework and provide them with the latest information available. If your evidence is dated, readers may well suspect that newer information has supplanted it, and may therefore find your argument unpersuasive. If you are arguing for gender equity in medical education, citing figures on the enrollment of women in medical schools in the 1960s (around 10 percent) will be quickly dismissed because women currently represent around 50 percent of students entering medical school classes. (You might build a better case for gender equity by looking at possible patterns of discrimination in residency assignments or at the specializations women go into.)

5. **Does your evidence come from reliable sources?** You would probably not make an argument based on the *Weekly World News*'s latest Elvis sighting—although it is perfectly respectable to write an analysis of the tabloid press and the cult of celebrity in the United States in a writing or mass media course. Scientific studies, government reports, research by academics, professional associations, and independent research institutes, the writing of reporters, intellectuals, and literary artists in respectable newspapers, magazines, and journals are likely to carry authority for readers. Partisan sources—magazines such as the conservative *National Review* or the liberal *Nation*—often contain important evidence and arguments you can use persuasively by acknowledging the slant and asking readers to consider their merits in the context of your argument.

do not seem to differ about what happened in class. Both describe the same teaching strategies: students wrote papers that were not graded; they received comments from the teacher and from other students; they were required to revise a number of the papers for a final portfolio. The difference is in how each uses this evidence.

Enabling Assumptions

Consider how the two students move from the available evidence—the facts that neither disputes—to their differing claims. This is a crucial move that each argument relies on. For an argument to be persuasive, readers need to know how and why the evidence cited by the writer entitles him or her to make a claim. This link—the connection in an argument between the evidence and the writer's claim—is called the *enabling assumption* because it refers to the line of reasoning that explains how the evidence supports the claim. Such assumptions are often implied rather than stated explicitly.

Notice that the enabling assumptions in the two student evaluations are implied but not directly stated. To find out how the two students connect the evidence to their claims, let's imagine we could interview them, to push them to articulate this missing link in their arguments.

Sample Interviews

Interview with Student 1

Q. How was your writing teacher?

A. She was the worst teacher I've had so far. [*claim*]

Q. What makes you say that?

A. The teacher never graded our papers. We had to evaluate each other's papers and then revise a few and put them in a portfolio. [*evidence*]

Q. So why was that so bad?

A. Well, because good teachers give you lots of graded evaluations so you know exactly where you stand in a class. [*enabling assumption*]

Interview with Student 2

Q. How was your writing teacher?

A. She was great, the best I've had so far. [*claim*]

Q. What makes you say that?

A. The teacher never graded our papers. We had to evaluate each other's papers and then revise a few and put them in a portfolio. [*evidence*]

Q. So, why was that so good?

A. Well, because good teachers help you develop your own judgment by experimenting without worrying about grades. [*enabling assumption*]

Of course, we could push each writer further to explore the assumptions that underlie the one he or she has articulated. If we push far enough, we are likely to find fundamental beliefs that each holds about the nature of education and learning. For example, in the case of the second student, an exploration of assumptions might look like this:

Assumption 1: Good teaching helps students develop judgment by enabling them to experiment without having to worry about grades.

Assumption 2: Too much emphasis on grades can get in the way of developing judgment through trial and error.

Assumption 3: Education should emphasize the development of individual judgment as much as or more than the learning of subject material.

Assumption 4: Students naturally want to learn and will do so if given the chance.

This process could continue indefinitely, and exploring the assumptions underlying assumptions can be a useful exercise. The practical question in making an argument is to decide which of these assumptions—or some combination of them—are likely to be shared by your readers and which ones can best clarify differences you have with others.

⮞ FOR CRITICAL INQUIRY

Analyzing Claims, Evidence, and Enabling Assumptions

To master the terms introduced here, work with a group of students to analyze the statements that appear below. Identify the claim each statement makes. Identify the evidence that each statement relies on. Finally, explain how an enabling assumption, which may or may not be stated explicitly, connects the evidence to the claim.

1. Ultraviolent video games will inevitably lead to more school shootings.

2. The current increase in cases of tuberculosis can be attributed to new strains of the disease that are resistant to treatment by antibiotics.

3. The fact that both parents have to work just to make ends meet is destroying the American family.

4. It is reasonable that the CEOs of American corporations make over one hundred times in salary and bonuses what the average worker in the company earns, no matter whether the company performs well or not.

Differing Views

To argue responsibly, you can't pretend that no one disagrees with you or that there are no alternative perspectives. To note these differences does not, as students sometimes think, undermine your own argument. In fact, it can strengthen it by showing that you are willing to take all sides into account, that you can refute objections to your argument, and, when necessary, that you can concede the validity of differing views.

Summarize Differing Views Fairly and Accurately

Readers often detect when writers handle differing views in a distorted way. In fact, their impressions of a writer's credibility and good character—the writer's ethos—depend in part on how reasonably the writer deals with differences. For that reason, the ability to summarize fairly and accurately is quite important to the success of your argument. By summarizing fairly and accurately, you can show readers that you have anticipated reasonable differences and intend to deal with them responsibly.

This can help avoid having your readers jump into your argument with objections you've overlooked—"Sure, the government creating jobs for people on welfare sounds like a good idea, but what about the cost? And what about personal responsibility? Doesn't this just make people dependent in a different way?"—or rushing to the defense of people you have characterized unfairly—"Not all conservative Christians believe women should be barefoot and pregnant."

Refuting Differing Views

For views that differ from yours, summarize them briefly, fairly, and accurately. Then explain what's wrong with them. Your best chance of persuading readers that your position is preferable to others is to clarify the differences that divide you and explain what you see as the weaknesses in other lines of reasoning.

Refuting differing views can involve a number of rhetorical moves: showing factual inaccuracies, presenting counterevidence, identifying differences in assumptions and values, pointing out a differing view's limits in explaining the current situation and anticipating its consequences, and emphasizing what is preferable in the writer's position, what it makes possible or sheds light on that the differing view doesn't.

Conceding Differing Views

When differing views have merit, don't avoid them. Remember that your readers will likely think of these objections, so you're better off taking them head on. Summarize the view and explain what you concede. Such concessions are often signaled by words and phrases such as *admittedly, granted, although it may be true, despite the fact,* and *of course she is right to say.*

The purpose of concession is not to give up on your argument but to explain how it relates to differing views. In this sense, it's another means of clarifying differences and explaining your position in the fullest possible way. To concede effectively, follow it up right away with an explanation of how your position relates to the point you have conceded. Otherwise, you may give readers the impression that you endorse the point.

In the case of the student evaluations, the first student could make good use of concession. For example, he or she might concede the second student's point that an important goal of education is developing independent judgment. The student then could go on to show that in practice the teacher's methods don't really lead to independent judgment but instead leave students to flounder on their own. In fact, conceding the point offers the student a line of reasoning he or she could pursue to strengthen the argument by explaining how the development of independent judgment depends on constant interaction with and regular evaluation from a more experienced and knowledgeable person.

Finding Viable Alternatives

Finding viable alternatives means identifying possible points of agreement in differing views. Once again, your purpose is not to abandon your views but to see whether you can find any common ground with those who hold differing positions. Think of it as combining elements in reasonable differences in order to come up with new solutions and perspectives. Sometimes this is possible, but not always. Still, it's worth trying because offering viable alternatives can strengthen your argument by broadening its appeal and demonstrating your desire to take into account as many views as possible.

Back to the student evaluations. The first student might concede that the teacher's portfolio system of evaluation has some merit because it bases grades on student improvement. But from this student's perspective, it still has the problem of not providing enough evaluation and information on the teacher's expectations. To propose a viable alternative, the student might propose that the teacher grade, but not count, the first writing assignment so that students can see the teacher's evaluative standards in practice. The student might also suggest that the teacher give students a midterm progress report on where they stand in the class, and again grade but not count one paper between midterm and the end of class.

Such a solution may not satisfy everyone, but it is likely to enhance the reader's impression of the student as someone who doesn't just criticize but tries to deal with differences constructively.

Qualifiers

Qualifiers modify or limit the claim in an argument by making it less sweeping, global, and categorical. For most claims, after all, there are exceptions that don't necessarily disprove the claim but need to be noted. Otherwise, you will needlessly open your claim to attack and disbelief. In many instances, a qualifier is as simple as saying "Many students at Warehouse State drink to excess" instead of "The students at my school get drunk all the time." Qualifiers admit exceptions without undermining your point, and they make statements harder to refute with a counterexample—"I know students who never drink" or "Some students drink only occasionally" or "My friends drink moderately."

You can qualify your claim with words and phrases such as *in many cases, often, frequently, probably, perhaps, may* or *might, maybe, likely,* or *usually*. In some instances, you will want to use a qualifying clause that begins with *unless* to limit the conditions in which the claim will hold true: "Unless the DNA evidence proves negative, everything points to the accused as the murderer."

Putting the Parts Together

To see how the various parts of argument we've just discussed can help you make an argument, let's look at the notes a student wrote to plan an argument opposing a recent proposal to the local school committee that would require students to wear uniforms at Middlebrook High School. No one contests that there are real problems at Middlebrook—declining test scores, drug use, racial tensions, lack of school spirit, a growing sense of student alienation. But, as you will see, the student doesn't think school uniforms can really address these problems.

Claim

Middlebrook High School should not require students to wear uniforms.

Evidence

School uniforms don't have the intended effects. I could use examples from schools that require uniforms to show they don't increase discipline, improve self-esteem, or alleviate social tensions.

Teachers oppose requiring uniforms because it would make them into cops. I could get some good quotes from teachers.

Even if they are required to wear uniforms, students will figure out other ways to show what group they are in. Jewelry, hairstyles, shoes, jackets, body piercing, tattoos, and so on will just become all the more important.

Uniforms violate students' right to self-expression. I could call the American Civil Liberties Union to see whether they have any information I could use.

Requiring uniforms will make students hate school. I could get more on this by talking to students.

Enabling Assumptions

The uniform proposal is based on a faulty view of what influences student behavior. More rules will just lead to more alienation from school.

To address Middlebrook's problems, students must be given more responsibility, instead of given regulations from above. They need to be brought into the decision-making process so they can develop a stake in what happens at school.

The proposal to require uniforms is based on the desire to return to some mythic age in Middlebrook's past when students were orderly, disciplined, filled with school spirit—namely, all the same kind of white, middle-class students. Middlebrook has changed, and the proposal doesn't deal with these changes.

Differing Views

Some uniform supporters claim that the success of Catholic and private schools is based on the fact students are required to wear uniforms. I need to show the causes of success are not uniforms but other factors.

I'll concede that there are real problems at Middlebrook but maintain my position that uniforms aren't the way to deal with them.

I could also concede that what students wear sometimes gets out of hand but argue that the best way to deal with this is to get students involved, along with teachers and parents, in writing a new dress code. In fact, I could extend this argument to say that the way to deal with some of the problems is for the school to get the different groups—whites, Latinos, blacks, and Cambodians—together to look at the problems and propose some solutions.

Qualifiers

My position is set. I'm against uniforms, period. But maybe I should state my claim in a way that takes uniform supporters' views into account. For example, I could say, "Admittedly there are a number of problems at Middlebrook that need attention, but requiring uniforms will not solve these problems."

As you can see, using the parts of argument has given this student a lot of material to work with and some leads about where to get more. Just as important, using the parts of argument offers a way to see the connections among the available material and how they might fit together in developing the writer's line of reasoning. Not all of this material will necessarily turn up in the final version of the student's argument, of course. This can only be determined through the process of drafting and revising. In fact, she might turn up new material and new arguments as she composes.

ANALYZING A POSITION PAPER

Andrew Gelman is a professor of statistics and political science at Columbia University. "Do We Hate the Rich or Don't We?" was published in the online *New York Times* on December 22, 2011, following the apparently contradictory results of public opinion polls by Gallup and Pew and the quite different advice for Obama's reelection campaign derived by two writers, William Galston in *New Republic* and Matthew Yglesias at *Slate.com*. As you read, notice that Gelman spends a lot of time positioning his own thinking in relation to the poll results and the commentaries by Galston and Yglesias. His own position comes out only gradually, and we don't fully grasp it until the final paragraph.

We present Gelman's position paper for analysis in anticipation of writing your own position paper. The aim to become familiar with the genre—to see how writers use position papers to define and respond to rhetorical situations by locating their

Andrew Gelman, "Do We Hate the Rich or Don't We?" In *The New York Times* on December 22, 2011. Copyright © 2011 The New York Times. Reprinted by permission.

own thinking in relation to what others have said—aligning themselves with writers whose views they share, refuting or conceding points by other writers, negotiating differences, and finding viable alternatives.

Do We Hate the Rich or Don't We?

Andrew Gelman

Here's an example of how the results of polls taken at the same time can be given exactly opposite interpretations.

The Danger of the New Populism

William Galston, a senior fellow at the Brookings Institution and a former adviser to President Clinton, writes in the New Republic about "Why Obama's New Populism May Sink His Campaign."

> President Obama's much-heralded speech in Osawatomie, Kan., focused on inequality, which, he argued, is undermining our prosperity, weakening our democracy, and shrinking our middle class. While there's a serious data-based argument to be made in favor of that view, recent surveys suggest that most Americans don't share it.

Galston went on to cite a Gallup survey released on Dec. 15, "Fewer Americans See U.S. Divided Into 'Haves,' 'Have Nots', which showed not only that the number of Americans who see American society as divided into haves and have-nots has decreased significantly since the 2008 election, but that the majority of Americans continue to consider themselves among the haves.

Galston also wrote about another Gallup survey, "Americans Prioritize Growing Economy Over Reducing Wealth Gap," which was released the next day. Galston pointed out that:

> When Gallup asked a sample of Americans in 1998 whether the gap between the rich and the poor was a problem that needed to be fixed, 52 percent said yes, while 45 percent regarded it as an acceptable part of the economic system. Today, those numbers are reversed: Only 45 percent see the gap as in need of fixing, while 52 percent don't.

Galston convincingly supports his summary with this table from Gallup.

Taking it all in, Galston concludes that "none of this is to say" that Obama is doomed to one term:

> Indeed, if the economy grows a bit more quickly and unemployment falls farther than the standard forecasts predict, he may well prevail. It is to say that a campaign emphasizing growth and opportunity is more likely to yield a Democratic victory than is a campaign focused on inequality.

The Promise of the New Populism

Now, here's Matthew Yglesias, Slate's business and economics correspondent, on "A Nation of Class Warriors":

> The latest Pew poll on Occupy Wall Street finds some decidedly mixed feelings out there, with Americans generally expressing much more sympathy with the concerns of the movement than with its tactics. But when Pew moved a bit away from the focus on O.W.S. and asked some more general questions about wealth and power, they revealed what more or less looks like a nation of hardened class warriors. Huge majorities of self-identified Democrats and clear majorities of self-identified independents say that there's too much power in the hands of a few rich people, that the country's economic system unfairly favors the wealthy, and that Wall Street does more to hurt the economy than to help it.

Yglesias convincingly supports his summary with this graph from the Pew data. His conclusion?

> Under the circumstances, we should expect to see Democrats continue to double down on "tax the rich" themes and populist messages.

Putting It All Together

Let's summarize. A vast majority of Americans—including half of all self-identified Republicans—think there is "too much power in the hands of a few rich people and large corporations." And a solid majority believes that "the country's economic system unfairly favors the wealthy." On the other hand, close to 60 percent of Americans do not see the country as "divided into haves and have-nots" and over 60 percent see "big government" as the biggest threat to the country in the future. What gives?

I think it's fair to say that there's enough here to support different political themes. A supporter of higher taxes for higher incomes can focus on the "too much power in the hands of the rich" angle, whereas a supporter of cuts in low-income and middle-income entitlement programs can focus on the lack of resonance of the haves and have-nots argument.

The ambiguity revealed in these polls actually makes sense: if there were a clear and unambiguous majority in favor of some policy and all its ramifications, we would expect it would have already passed and there would be no remaining political dispute. Democrats and Republicans are no longer arguing about laws against racial discrimination or child labor (with rare exceptions). The very fact that an issue is politically live suggests some flexibility on opinions and helps us understand what otherwise seems contradictory about these poll results.

What does this say about candidates' optimal political strategies? As the political scientist Lynn Vavreck has shown, presidential campaigns typically turn on the economy, and candidates adapt their messages to suit economic conditions. I agree with Galston that "a campaign emphasizing growth and opportunity" would probably be Obama's best choice—but he may not have that choice, if the economy does not seem to be doing better next year. Given the current persistent slowdown, Yglesias may well be right that Democrats will push a "tax the rich" message and attempt to frame the conversation that way.

In a way, the poll findings cited by Galston and Yglesias are not that contradictory. They give a sense of how the debate might go, with liberals focusing on the power of the rich and big business, and conservatives reminding voters that taxes taken from the rich will go straight to the federal government.

Suppose for a moment that the responses captured in these polls went in the opposite direction, with a majority having a positive feeling about the government and an increasing concern about inequality, but with most Americans not thinking the rich have too much power. In that case, one might expect a very different sort of debate.

As the political scientists Lawrence Jacobs and Robert Shapiro have demonstrated, politicians don't just see public opinion as a constraint; they also use it as a tool to achieve their policy goals. Conflicting majority attitudes—for example, a belief that the economic system unfairly favors the wealthy, juxtaposed with a relative lack of concern for income inequality—represent an opportunity for smart politicians to reshape public opinion their way.

⊏⟩ FOR CRITICAL INQUIRY ||||||||||||||||||||||||||||||||||||||||||||||||||||||||||||||||||||||||||||||||||||

1. Notice that Andrew Gelman has organized "Do We Hate the Rich or Don't We?" into three sections, after a very brief, one-sentence introduction. Write an outline that describes the formal organization of the position paper, the function of each section, and the role each section plays, developing Gelman's line of reasoning and establishing the grounds for the position he takes at the very end.

2. Consider how Gelman deals with the differing views of William Galston and Matthew Yglesias and the differing advice they give to the Obama reelection campaign. How does he deal with ambiguous evidence from the Gallup and Pew public opinion polls? What rhetorical moves does he emphasize—refutation, concession, finding viable alternatives? How does he distinguish his own views? What is the significance of Gelman's differences with Galston and Yglesias?

3. As an online publication, Gelman's position paper has links that can take readers to other places, to the *New Republic* Web site where Galston's essay originally appeared or to a key graph from the Pew survey. How does reading a position paper with links differ from reading a print text? Is it useful to click links? Is it distracting? Is it a little of both?

WRITING ASSIGNMENT

Writing a Position Paper

The chapter's culminating assignment is to write your own position paper. Here is a series of steps to help you organize this writing project:

1. **Identify a controversy, debate, or discussion where there are differing views.** Begin by noticing, as Gelman does, some interesting and significant differences in writing about a particular topic—in Gelman's case about the meaning of poll results for Obama's reelection strategy. For this assignment, you will need to find good examples of differing views—for example, about how good a recent CD by Kanye West is, whether students should be able to have laptops open in class, or what proposals will work to increase employment. You will likely need to do some research to come up with writing you can use in your position paper. Gelman plays off two differing views in his position paper, but it is perfectly possible that one good source is enough for you to engage to make your own position clear.

2. **Design the sections of your position paper.** There are various ways to organize position papers. Here are two standard formats.

    The first is similar to how Gelman organizes his position paper:

    ▶ Introduces the issue being considered. Notice Gelman is very brief here. You might want to be more expansive in identifying sides or major differences and more explicit in stating your perspective as the claim of your paper.

    ▶ Summarizes differing views fairly and accurately. It is almost certain that it will be a good idea here to quote, even if it is only a key term or short phrase, so that the writer with a differing view has some real presence in your position paper.

    ▶ Explains your relation to these differing views by refuting, conceding, or posing viable alternatives.

    ▶ Presents your own position and its reasons. Here you want to clearly distinguish your position from others and provide evidence and explanations in support of your perspective.

    ▶ Ends by pointing out wider significance of the differences you have just treated and/or the position you have taken.

    The second is a variation on the first that works point by point, where differing views and the writer's perspective alternate:

    ▶ Introduces the issue being considered, the terms of the debate or controversy, and your perspective.

> ▶ Presents one point of difference and your strategy for dealing with it (by refuting, conceding, or finding a viable alternative).

> ▶ Presents a second point of difference and your strategy for dealing with it.

> ▶ Presents a third point of difference, etc. The number of points will differ depending on the debate or controversy.

> ▶ Presents you own position and its reasons.

3. **Plan the visual design of your position paper.** Depending on your topic, you might add photos or other illustrations or graphs, diagrams, tables, or charts. Or you could design your position paper to be online, like Gelman's, and include links to other sites.

WRITERS' WORKSHOP

Stacy Yi wrote this position paper for a Media & Culture class that asked students to examine a controversy involving some aspect of the media or popular culture and to stake out their own position. Here is Stacy's paper, followed by a peer review from one of her classmates, Michael Brody, and Stacy's writer's response.

Stacy Yi

Professor Watkins

Media & Culture

February 26, 2013

iComics

For many comic book readers, the weekly ritual of heading to the local shop to pick up new releases is just as important and satisfying as actually reading the books. Making the trip every Wednesday (when new titles are released)—whether just to flip through new or unfamiliar issues and scan shelves well stocked with graphic novels and trade paperbacks, or argue the merits of a favorite writer or artist with other customers and the store's employees—gives comic fans a sense of community, a real place to share their interests with a diverse crowd and have their passion for the medium recognized and appreciated. Considering that the comic book market shifted away from newsstands and spinner racks in drugstores and toward specialty shops in the early 70s, it's safe to assume that a substantial portion of readers have never bought their comics anywhere but their local store.

But that's likely to change with the recent emergence of digital comics, sold through online retailers like Comixology or Graphic.ly and read on e-readers and tablets. In fact, some fans and retailers, and even some industry professionals, worry that digital sales will eventually make comic book stores an endangered species, like independent record stores before them. The ease of purchase and minimal storage requirements offered by digital comics could, they fear, lure readers away from stores, further taxing an already wounded marketplace. Mark Millar, writer of *Kick-Ass* and *The Ultimates*, has argued that releasing digital comics on the same day as their print equivalents go on sale "is a disastrous idea and makes no economic sense at all to comics as a business. It's potentially ruinous for comic stores, and in the long term it's not going to do publishers any favors either…they think they're cutting out the middlemen and all the guys taking a piece of their gross, but there's an equivalent number of hidden costs in digital too, and it's short term thinking to obliterate the life-blood of the medium."

However, digital sales doesn't have to be the either/or scenario that Millar and others make it out to be. While I share the critics' concern for the health of the direct market, and the comic industry as a whole, I think they overestimate the likelihood that established readers will convert to digital only en masse. In fact, it seems more likely that readers who first bought comics from a brick and mortar shop will continue to do the same, or perhaps divide their purchasing between the shop and the online store. Furthermore, digital critics seem to discount the range of product available at comic stores—digital sales might be competitive when it comes to individual issues, but less so with graphic novels, collected and oversized editions, not to mention local and underground comics, which are largely ignored in the digital conversation. Until publishers digitize their entire print catalogs, including archival material, comic shops will always have something to offer both established and new readers.

In fact, I think a healthy future for comics will depend on existing retailers working with digital outlets to construct a new, more responsive marketplace. Neither party can afford to ignore, or even attack, the other—the digital marketplace isn't capable of completely replacing the brick and mortar experience, and shop owners who say that digital comics are a fad that will pass in years to come are deluding themselves. Looking carefully at each market reveals that their strengths and weaknesses are actually complementary. The streamlined reading experience offered by digital comics could attract those readers who would never otherwise set foot in a comic shop, and the shop provides the community and social experience that they can't get from one-click downloads and comment boards.

That comics will change substantially in the coming years, both in format and the ways we buy them, is inevitable. What those changes will look like, however, is far from certain. The old weekly ritual will likely disappear, but will it be replaced by a new one? Though publishers openly state their reliance on the direct market, they have nonetheless embraced digital outlets as a means of reaching new and/or lapsed readers, and hopefully recouping some of the income lost to online piracy. The transition will be difficult, and businesses (particularly those in smaller cities and towns) may close. But I believe retailers who are creative and flexible in finding ways to incorporate digital sales into their business models will thrive.

PEER REVIEW OF "iCOMICS"

Dear Stacy,

You've got a great topic for a position paper. I'm not a big comics person, but you made this interesting and you gave enough background information so I could understand the issues. It's also very clear where you stand. That's another plus. My main suggestion is to include quotes from someone who doesn't think digital sales will ruin comics stores. In this draft, it's just you refuting Mark Millar, so it doesn't seem like there's a debate or controversy already going on. If you set up two sides—or more—then you could enter into the debate and align yourself with the people who don't think online comics will be the end of comics stores. That would give more authority and credibility to your position by showing that you've done the research needed to understand the issues. You could probably use most or all of the arguments you present here, but there might be some new ones too.

This is a great start and just needs a little more research to make it a great paper.

—Michael Brody

WRITER'S RESPONSE

Michael—

Thank you for reading my paper, and for the compliments. I definitely wanted it to be easy to understand for a reader who isn't into comics, but still relevant for someone who follows the industry, reads the blogs, etc.

I agree with your suggestion that I should include another voice in the argument in favor of digital. Sometimes its easy to take a position in a paper and imagine it's only you against whoever is making the counter-argument, but you're right that finding another professional who thinks digital comics won't hurt stores will give my points more credibility. There are plenty of people, from all over the field, talking about this issue so it shouldn't be too hard to find that kind of source and integrate it into my paper.

Thanks again!

Stacy

CHAPTER 4

The Shape of the Essay

How Form Embodies Purpose

*E*ssay comes from the French word *essai,* which means to try or test out. The meaning of the term *essay* has been debated by scholars in literary studies, rhetoric, and composition. Some think of it as a particular type of creative nonfiction that uses a literary sensibility to fashion experience and observation into writing. Others use it more broadly to refer to writing where the form is open and flexible. In this chapter, we use elements of both senses, to see the essay as a catchall category for short pieces of prose that in one way or another place the essayist's consciousness at the center of the writing. For our purposes, the defining feature of the essay is the openness and the flexibility it gives essayists to work out an active presence in the reader's attention by shaping thoughts, feelings, and experiences into written forms.

This chapter examines what the essay makes possible for writers to put into words—what you might call the rhetorical work of the essay as a genre of writing. The work of the essay is to try out various ways of setting the personal and the public, the literary and the civic, in relation to each other—to find the appropriate form to bring the writer's experience to consciousness. You can distinguish the essay from other genres of writing by the intersection of individual consciousness and the historical present it makes available. The essay is an open and flexible approach to writing that tries to occupy the reader's attention by making nonfiction creative. The essay is an attempt to engage the reader in the shared pleasures—the sociability and common enjoyment—of language by articulating some corner of the world we're living in. Its rhetorical task is to involve the reader on multiple levels, in word and feeling, in deliberating on the fate of us all.

The goal of this chapter is to help you understand how the essay establishes a framework for writers to come to terms with their experience and connect to their readers. This chapter has two main parts. First, we examine what the essay makes possible and what options it presents to writers by looking at essays by three distinguished writers—Robert Hass, George Orwell, and Joan Didion. Then we look at how writers arrange the overall shape of the essay, write introductions and endings, design paragraphs, and connect the parts of an essay. The chapter closes with a final essay, "Terrorflu" by Joshua Clover, for additional inquiry and analysis.

WHAT DOES THE ESSAY MAKE POSSIBLE?

If there is one thing that unites the various forms the essay takes, it must be that the essay provides writers with a means of coming to terms with their experience and their observations of life. Think of "coming to terms" here in the double sense of (1) finding the words, the adequate terms, to represent the events, people, places, and things writers encounter and feel compelled to write about; and (2) deciding what is at stake for the writer as a person. Essayists help us take the world seriously (or laugh at it) by making things matter—by showing how things work and what their consequences are from the writer's point of view.

This work of coming to terms with the writer's experience often gives essays an exploratory character. The essayist often appears as someone still very much in the process of shaping an understanding, still very close to the source of the writing. This is one of the essay's great attractions, the sense of immediacy it creates in the essayist's encounters with whatever is happening in the essay. These moments make readers feel they too are present at the formation of experience, where the meaning of the essay begins in the writer's consciousness. The openness and flexibility of the essay give writers the means to recreate these moments in words, as an active presence on the page.

The terms that the essayist chooses to give meaning to events, people, places, and things are links to the wider social world in which the essay takes place, where the essayist, as a person, lives. The terms that essayists use to give shape to experience have their own histories and social allegiances, aligning essayists with particular social interests and historical aspirations and distancing them from others. Giving voice to experience holds the essayist accountable to the contending forces of history—to those represented in the essay, to be sure, but also to ghosts of the past and readers in the present.

The essay is a unit of attention and a span of time that writers and readers spend together. There is the presence of the writer's voice, directly addressing the reader. At the same time, the essay invokes audiences that did not exist before, calling readers and formerly unimagined ways of reading into being. The duration of the essay is meant to be one sitting. The essayist's approach is to borrow the reader's attention briefly in order to make a concentrated impression. One of the essay's greatest resources is its capacity to join concentration and exploration in a single reading. The openness and flexibility of the essay enable writers to hold distinct realities together in written compositions that are genuinely complicated and that call on readers to recognize the variety and disparities of human existence.

More so perhaps than other genres of writing, the essay is the language of consciousness coming to terms with the complexity of the world. The writer's voice, which is so prominent in the essay, is not exactly the speaking voice but instead the voice in the visible letters that encode reality on the page, creating an intimate space of reading, where the sensation is that of minds interacting, as though they were conversing and could hear each other. But there is no sound, just the words on the page that create this effect. This manner of speaking, the presence of the essayist occupying the page and engaging the reader's attention, is what people loosely call the essayist's style.

The following three essays provide examples of how essayists come to terms with moments of human experience. The aim is to examine how essayists articulate the intersection of the personal and the public, how they imagine their presence on the page as the events of the world impinge on them, and how they connect to their readers' attention.

Poet-Bashing Police
Robert Hass

....

Robert Hass is former poet laureate of the United States and professor of poetry and poetics at the University of California, Berkeley, where the events in this essay took place in November 2011 during the Occupy movement. "Poet-Bashing Police" appeared as an op-ed column in the New York Times on November 19, 2011.

LIFE, I found myself thinking as a line of Alameda County deputy sheriffs in Darth Vader riot gear formed a cordon in front of me on a recent night on the campus of the University of California, Berkeley, is full of strange contingencies. The deputy sheriffs, all white men, except for one young woman, perhaps Filipino, who was trying to look severe but looked terrified, had black truncheons in their gloved hands that reporters later called batons and that were known, in the movies of my childhood, as billy clubs.

The first contingency that came to mind was the quick spread of the Occupy movement. The idea of occupying public space was so appealing that people in almost every large city in the country had begun to stake them out, including students at Berkeley, who, on that November night, occupied the public space in front of Sproul Hall, a gray granite Beaux-Arts edifice that houses the registrar's offices and, in the basement, the campus police department.

It is also the place where students almost 50 years ago touched off the Free Speech Movement, which transformed the life of American universities by guaranteeing students freedom of speech and self-governance. The steps are named for Mario Savio, the eloquent undergraduate student who was the symbolic face of the movement. There is even a Free Speech Movement Cafe on campus where some of Mr. Savio's words are prominently displayed: "There is a time ... when the operation of the machine becomes so odious, makes you so sick at heart, that you can't take part. You can't even passively take part."

Earlier that day a colleague had written to say that the campus police had moved in to take down the Occupy tents and that students had been "beaten viciously." I didn't believe it. In broad daylight? And without provocation? So when we heard that the police had returned, my wife, Brenda Hillman, and I hurried to the campus. I wanted to see what was going to happen and how the police behaved, and how the students behaved. If there was trouble, we wanted to be there to do what we could to protect the students.

Once the cordon formed, the deputy sheriffs pointed their truncheons toward the crowd. It looked like the oldest of military maneuvers, a phalanx out of the Trojan War, but with billy clubs instead of spears. The students were wearing scarves for the first time that year, their cheeks rosy with the first bite of real cold after the long Californian Indian summer. The billy clubs were about the size of a boy's Little League baseball bat. My wife was speaking to the young deputies about the importance of nonviolence and explaining why they should be at home reading to their children, when one of the deputies reached out, shoved my wife in the chest and knocked her down.

Another of the contingencies that came to my mind was a moment 30 years ago when Ronald Reagan's administration made it a priority to see to it that people like themselves, the talented, hardworking people who ran the country, got to keep the money they earned. Roosevelt's New Deal had to be undealt once and for all. A few years earlier, California voters had passed an amendment freezing the property taxes that finance public education and installing a rule that required a two-thirds majority in both houses of the Legislature to raise tax revenues. My father-in-law said to me at the time, "It's going to take them 50 years to really see the damage they've done." But it took far fewer than 50 years.

My wife bounced nimbly to her feet. I tripped and almost fell over her trying to help her up, and at that moment the deputies in the cordon surged forward and, using their clubs as battering rams, began to hammer at the bodies of the line of students. It was stunning to see. They swung hard into their chests and bellies. Particularly shocking to me—it must be a generational reaction—was that they assaulted both the young men and the young women with the same indiscriminate force. If the students turned away, they pounded their ribs. If they turned further away to escape, they hit them on their spines.

NONE of the police officers invited us to disperse or gave any warning. We couldn't have dispersed if we'd wanted to because the crowd behind us was pushing forward to see what was going on. The descriptor for what I tried to do is "remonstrate." I screamed at the deputy who had knocked down my wife, "You just knocked down my wife, for Christ's sake!" A couple of students had pushed forward in the excitement and the deputies grabbed them, pulled them to the ground and cudgeled them, raising the clubs above their heads and swinging. The line surged. I got whacked hard in the ribs twice and once across the forearm. Some of the deputies used their truncheons as bars and seemed to be trying to use minimum force to get people to move. And then, suddenly, they stopped, on some signal, and reformed their line. Apparently a group of deputies had beaten their way to the Occupy tents and taken them down. They stood, again immobile, clubs held across their chests, eyes carefully meeting no one's eyes, faces impassive. I imagined that their adrenaline was surging as much as mine.

My ribs didn't hurt very badly until the next day and then it hurt to laugh, so I skipped the gym for a couple of mornings, and I was a little disappointed that the bruises weren't slightly more dramatic. It argued either for a kind of restraint or a kind of low cunning in the training of the police. They had hit me hard enough so that I was sore for days, but not hard enough to leave much of a mark. I wasn't so badly off. One of my colleagues, also a poet, Geoffrey O'Brien, had a broken rib. Another colleague, Celeste Langan, a Wordsworth scholar, got dragged across the grass by her hair when she presented herself for arrest.

I won't recite the statistics, but the entire university system in California is under great stress and the State Legislature is paralyzed by a minority of legislators whose only idea is that they don't want to pay one more cent in taxes. Meanwhile, students at Berkeley are graduating with an average indebtedness of something like $16,000. It is no wonder that the real estate industry started inventing loans for people who couldn't pay them back.

"Whose university?" the students had chanted. Well, it is theirs, and it ought to be everyone else's in California. It also belongs to the future, and to the dead who paid taxes to build one of the greatest systems of public education in the world.

The next night the students put the tents back up. Students filled the plaza again with a festive atmosphere. And lots of signs. (The one from the English Department contingent read "Beat Poets, not beat poets.") A week later, at 3:30 a.m., the police officers returned in force, a hundred of them, and told the campers to leave or they would be arrested. All but two moved. The two who stayed were arrested, and the tents were removed. On Thursday afternoon when I returned toward sundown to the steps to see how the students had responded, the air was full of balloons, helium balloons to which tents had been attached, and attached to the tents was kite string. And they hovered over the plaza, large and awkward, almost lyrical, occupying the air.

Balloons carrying miniature tents. Sproul Plaza, University of California, Berkeley. November 2011.

⇒ **FOR CRITICAL INQUIRY** ||||||||||||||||||||||||||||||||||||||||||||||||||||||||||||||||||||||

Life ... Is Full of Strange Contingencies

"The Poet-Bashing Police" is a good example of how essays connect disparate realities in complex compositions. In the opening line, Robert Hass says, "Life ... is full of strange contingencies"—the strange ways that events take place as a result of prior events. Consider the contingencies that Hass identifies: "the quick spread of the Occupy movement"; the scene at Sproul Hall where the Free Speech Movement had once occurred; the Reagan administration's dismantling of the New Deal and the effect on public higher education. Hass clearly wants to tell the story of what happened to him and his wife, Brenda Hillman, when police attacked Occupy demonstrators on the UC, Berkeley campus. But he also interrupts and complicates the narrative by interjecting a sense of the contingency of the events he recounts—and the connections they form between past and present. What is the effect of the two levels in the essay? How do the "contingencies" make the Occupy events meaningful? How does the movement back and forth between narrative and reflection define Hass's presence in the essay? How does it position him in the history of the past and present? What are we to make, at the end of essay, of the lyrical image of the balloons with tents attached "occupying the air"?

A Hanging

George Orwell

···

George Orwell is the pen name of Eric Blair (1903–1950), who is widely considered one of great essayists and nonfiction writers of the twentieth century. He is known as well, of course, for his novels 1984 and Animal Farm. "A Hanging" is based on Orwell's experience in the British Imperial Police in Burma from 1922 to 1927.

It was in Burma, a sodden morning of the rains. A sickly light, like yellow tinfoil, was slanting over the high walls into the jail yard. We were waiting outside the condemned cells, a row of sheds fronted with double bars, like small animal cages. Each cell measured about ten feet by ten and was quite bare within except for a plank bed and a pot of drinking water. In some of them brown silent men were squatting at the inner bars, with their blankets draped round them. These were the condemned men, due to be hanged within the next week or two.

One prisoner had been brought out of his cell. He was a Hindu, a puny wisp of a man, with a shaven head and vague liquid eyes. He had a thick, sprouting moustache, absurdly too big for his body, rather like the moustache of a comic man on the films. Six tall Indian warders were guarding him and getting him ready for the gallows. Two of them stood by with rifles and fixed bayonets, while the others handcuffed him, passed a chain through his handcuffs and fixed it to their belts, and lashed his arms tight to his sides. They crowded very close about him, with their hands always on him in a careful, caressing grip, as though all the while feeling him to make sure he was there. It was like men handling a fish which is still alive and may jump back into the water. But he stood quite unresisting, yielding his arms limply to the ropes, as though he hardly noticed what was happening.

Eight o'clock struck and a bugle call, desolately thin in the wet air, floated from the distant barracks. The superintendent of the jail, who was standing apart from the rest of us, moodily prodding the gravel with his stick, raised his head at the sound. He was an army doctor, with a grey toothbrush moustache and a gruff voice. 'For God's sake hurry up, Francis,' he said irritably. 'The man ought to have been dead by this time. Aren't you ready yet?'

Francis, the head jailer, a fat Dravidian in a white drill suit and gold spectacles, waved his black hand. 'Yes sir, yes sir,' he bubbled. 'All iss satisfactorily prepared. The hangman iss waiting. We shall proceed.'

'Well, quick march, then. The prisoners can't get their breakfast till this job's over.'

We set out for the gallows. Two warders marched on either side of the prisoner, with their rifles at the slope; two others marched close against him, gripping him by arm and shoulder, as though at once pushing and supporting him. The rest of us, magistrates and the like, followed behind. Suddenly, when we had gone ten yards, the procession stopped short without any order or warning. A dreadful thing had happened—a dog, come goodness knows whence, had appeared in the yard. It came bounding among us with a loud volley of barks, and leapt round us wagging its whole body, wild with glee at finding so many human beings together. It was a large woolly dog, half Airedale, half pariah. For a moment it pranced round us, and then, before anyone could stop it, it had made a dash for the prisoner, and jumping up tried to lick his face. Everyone stood aghast, too taken aback even to grab at the dog.

'Who let that bloody brute in here?' said the superintendent angrily. 'Catch it, someone!'

A warder, detached from the escort, charged clumsily after the dog, but it danced and gambolled just out of his reach, taking everything as part of the game. A young Eurasian jailer picked up a handful of gravel and tried to stone the dog away, but it dodged the stones and came after us again. Its yaps echoed from the jail wails. The prisoner, in the grasp of the two warders, looked on incuriously, as though this was another formality of the hanging. It was several minutes before someone managed to catch the dog. Then we put my handkerchief through its collar and moved off once more, with the dog still straining and whimpering.

It was about forty yards to the gallows. I watched the bare brown back of the prisoner marching in front of me. He walked clumsily with his bound arms, but quite steadily, with that bobbing gait of the Indian who never straightens his knees. At each step his muscles slid neatly into place, the lock of hair on his scalp danced up and down, his feet printed themselves on the wet gravel. And once, in spite of the men who gripped him by each shoulder, he stepped slightly aside to avoid a puddle on the path.

It is curious, but till that moment I had never realized what it means to destroy a healthy, conscious man. When I saw the prisoner step aside to avoid the puddle, I saw the mystery, the unspeakable wrongness, of cutting a life short when it is in full tide. This man was not dying, he was alive just as we were alive. All the organs of his body were working—bowels digesting food, skin renewing itself, nails growing, tissues forming—all toiling away in solemn foolery. His nails would still be growing when he stood on the drop, when he was falling through the air with a tenth of a second to live. His eyes saw the yellow gravel and the grey walls, and his brain still remembered, foresaw, reasoned—reasoned even about puddles. He and we were a party of men walking together, seeing, hearing, feeling, understanding the same world; and in two minutes, with a sudden snap, one of us would be gone—one mind less, one world less.

The gallows stood in a small yard, separate from the main grounds of the prison, and overgrown with tall prickly weeds. It was a brick erection like three sides of a shed, with planking on top, and above that two beams and a crossbar with the rope dangling. The hangman, a grey-haired convict in the white uniform of the prison, was waiting beside his machine. He greeted us with a servile crouch as we entered. At a word from Francis the two warders, gripping the prisoner more closely than ever, half led, half pushed him to the gallows and helped him clumsily up the ladder. Then the hangman climbed up and fixed the rope round the prisoner's neck.

We stood waiting, five yards away. The warders had formed in a rough circle round the gallows. And then, when the noose was fixed, the prisoner began crying out on his god. It was a high, reiterated cry of 'Ram! Ram! Ram! Ram!', not urgent and fearful like a prayer or a cry for help, but steady, rhythmical, almost like the tolling of a bell. The dog answered the sound with a whine. The hangman, still standing on the gallows, produced a small cotton bag like a flour bag and drew it down over the prisoner's face. But the sound, muffled by the cloth, still persisted, over and over again: 'Ram! Ram! Ram! Ram! Ram!'

The hangman climbed down and stood ready, holding the lever. Minutes seemed to pass. The steady, muffled crying from the prisoner went on and on, 'Ram! Ram! Ram!' never faltering for an instant. The superintendent, his head on his chest, was slowly poking the ground with his stick; perhaps he was counting the cries, allowing the prisoner a fixed number—fifty, perhaps, or a hundred. Everyone had changed colour. The Indians had gone grey like bad coffee, and one or two of the bayonets were wavering. We looked at the lashed, hooded man on the drop, and listened to his cries—each cry another second of life; the same thought was in all our minds: oh, kill him quickly, get it over, stop that abominable noise!

Suddenly the superintendent made up his mind. Throwing up his head he made a swift motion with his stick. 'Chalo!' he shouted almost fiercely.

There was a clanking noise, and then dead silence. The prisoner had vanished, and the rope was twisting on itself. I let go of the dog, and it galloped immediately to the back of the gallows; but when it got there it stopped short, barked, and then retreated into a corner of the yard, where it stood among the weeds, looking timorously out at us. We went round the gallows to inspect the prisoner's body. He was dangling with his toes pointed straight downwards, very slowly revolving, as dead as a stone.

The superintendent reached out with his stick and poked the bare body; it oscillated, slightly. 'He's all right,' said the superintendent. He backed out from under the gallows, and blew out a deep breath. The moody look had gone out of his face quite suddenly. He glanced at his wrist-watch. 'Eight minutes past eight. Well, that's all for this morning, thank God.'

The warders unfixed bayonets and marched away. The dog, sobered and conscious of having misbehaved itself, slipped after them. We walked out of the gallows yard, past the condemned cells with their waiting prisoners, into the big central yard of the prison. The convicts, under the command of warders armed with lathis, were already receiving their breakfast. They squatted in long rows, each man holding a tin pannikin, while two warders with buckets marched round ladling out rice; it seemed quite a homely, jolly scene, after the hanging. An enormous relief had come upon us now that the job was done. One felt an impulse to sing, to break into a run, to snigger. All at once everyone began chattering gaily.

The Eurasian boy walking beside me nodded towards the way we had come, with a knowing smile: 'Do you know, sir, our friend (he meant the dead man), when he heard his appeal had been dismissed, he pissed on the floor of his cell. From fright.—Kindly take one of my cigarettes, sir. Do you not admire my new silver case, sir? From the boxwallah, two rupees eight annas. Classy European style.'

Several people laughed—at what, nobody seemed certain.

Francis was walking by the superintendent, talking garrulously. 'Well, sir, all hass passed off with the utmost satisfactoriness. It wass all finished—flick! like that. It iss not always so—oah, no! I have known cases where the doctor wass obliged to go beneath the gallows and pull the prisoner's legs to ensure decease. Most disagreeable!'

'Wriggling about, eh? That's bad,' said the superintendent.

'Ach, sir, it iss worse when they become refractory! One man, I recall, clung to the bars of hiss cage when we went to take him out. You will scarcely credit, sir, that it took six warders to dislodge him, three pulling at each leg. We reasoned with him. "My dear fellow," we said, "think of all the pain and trouble you are causing to us!" But no, he would not listen! Ach, he wass very troublesome!'

I found that I was laughing quite loudly. Everyone was laughing. Even the superintendent grinned in a tolerant way. 'You'd better all come out and have a drink,' he said quite genially. 'I've got a bottle of whisky in the car. We could do with it.'

We went through the big double gates of the prison, into the road. 'Pulling at his legs!' exclaimed a Burmese magistrate suddenly, and burst into a loud chuckling. We all began laughing again. At that moment Francis's anecdote seemed extraordinarily funny. We all had a drink together, native and European alike, quite amicably. The dead man was a hundred yards away.

⇨ FOR CRITICAL INQUIRY

Narrative Essays

Orwell's essay is organized as a narrative with a plotline that has a bit of exposition to set the scene in the opening two paragraphs, the rising action from the moment the condemned prisoner is taken from his cell and brought to the gallows, the climax (in two paragraphs) when the hanging occurs, and finally the falling action of the uneasy laughter and talk after the execution. Orwell doesn't depart from the narrative or suspend the movement of time, as Robert Hass does in "Poet-Bashing Police," to reflect on events. In this sense, "A Hanging" seems to be a prime instance of the advice to "show, not tell." The only direct presence of Orwell's consciousness occurs in the tenth paragraph, almost in the middle of the essay, where he watches the condemned prisoner sidestep a puddle and realizes the "unspeakable wrongness" of executing other human beings. Aside from that moment, when Orwell's consciousness breaks through to the surface, the unfolding of events is meant to carry meanings that readers are expected to identify without commentary from the writer. What are these meanings? What meaning do you infer, for example, from the nine paragraphs after the hanging takes place? What does Orwell reveal about the relations between the English colonizers and the Burmese colonized? What is the effect of the fact that Orwell presents but does not explain?

Los Angeles Notebook

Joan Didion

....

Joan Didion is an American novelist and essayist associated with the New Journalism of the 1960s, a movement to write nonfiction with the narrative storytelling and literary techniques of novels. "Los Angeles Notebook" appeared in Didion's collection of essays Slouching Toward Bethlehem *(1968).*

There is something uneasy in the Los Angeles air this afternoon, some unnatural stillness, some tension. What it means is that tonight a Santa Ana will begin to blow, a hot wind from the northeast whining down through the Cajon and San Gorgonio Passes, blowing up sandstorms out along Route 66, drying the hills and the nerves to the flash point. For a few days now we will see smoke back in the canyons, and hear sirens in the night. I have neither heard nor read that a Santa Ana is due, but I know it, and almost everyone I have seen today knows it too. We know it because we feel it. The baby frets. The maid sulks. I rekindle a waning argument with the telephone company, then cut my losses and lie down, given over to whatever it is in the air. To live with the Santa Ana is to accept, consciously or unconsciously, a deeply mechanistic view of human behavior.

I recall being told, when I first moved to Los Angeles and was living on an isolated beach, that the Indians would throw themselves into the sea when the bad wind blew. I could see why. The Pacific turned ominously glossy during a Santa Ana period, and one woke in the night troubled not only by the peacocks screaming in the olive trees but by the eerie absence of surf. The heat was surreal. The sky had a yellow cast, the kind of light sometimes called "earthquake weather." My only neighbor would not come out of her house for days, and there were no lights at night, and her husband roamed the place with a machete. One day he would tell me that he had heard a trespasser, the next a rattlesnake.

"On nights like that," Raymond Chandler once wrote about the Santa Ana, "every booze party ends in a fight. Meek little wives feel the edge of the carving knife and study their husbands' necks. Anything can happen." That was the kind of wind it was. I did not know then that there was any basis for the effect it had on all of us, but it turns out to be another of those cases in which science bears out folk wisdom. The Santa Ana, which is named for one of the canyons it rushes through, is a *foehn* wind, like the *foehn* of Austria and Switzerland and the *hamsin* of Israel. There are a number of persistent malevolent winds, perhaps the best known of which are the mistral of France and the Mediterranean sirocco, but a *foehn* wind has distinct characteristics: it occurs on the leeward slope of a mountain range and, although the air begins as a cold mass, it is warmed as it comes down the mountain and appears finally as a hot dry wind. Whenever and wherever a *foehn* blows, doctors hear about headaches and nausea and allergies, about "nervousness," about "depression." In Los Angeles some teachers do not attempt to conduct formal classes during a Santa Ana, because the children become unmanageable. In Switzerland the suicide rate goes up during the *foehn*, and in the courts of some Swiss cantons the wind is considered a mitigating circumstance for crime. Surgeons are said to watch the wind, because blood does not clot normally during a *foehn*. A few years ago an Israeli physicist discovered that not only during such winds, but for the ten or twelve hours which precede them, the air carries an unusually high ratio of positive to negative ions. No one seems to know exactly why that should be; some talk about friction and others suggest solar disturbances. In any case the positive ions are there, and what an excess of positive ions does, in the simplest terms, is make people unhappy. One cannot get much more mechanistic than that.

Easterners commonly complain that there is no "weather" at all in Southern California, that the days and the seasons slip by relentlessly, numbingly bland. That is quite misleading. In fact the climate is characterized by infrequent but violent extremes: two periods of torrential subtropical rains which continue for weeks and wash out the hills and send subdivisions sliding toward the sea; about twenty scattered days a year of the Santa Ana, which, with its incendiary dryness, invariably means fire. At the first prediction of a Santa Ana, the Forest Service flies men and equipment from northern California into the southern forests, and the Los Angeles Fire Department cancels its ordinary non-firefighting routines. The Santa Ana caused Malibu to burn the way it did in 1956, and Bel Air in 1961, and Santa Barbara in 1964. In the winter of 1966–67 eleven men were killed fighting a Santa Ana fire that spread through the San Gabriel Mountains.

Just to watch the front-page news out of Los Angeles during a Santa Ana is to get very close to what it is about the place. The longest single Santa Ana period in recent years was in 1957, and it lasted not the usual three or four days but fourteen days, from November 21 until December 4. On the first day 25,000 acres of the San Gabriel Mountains were burning, with gusts reaching 100 miles an hour. In town, the wind reached Force 12, or hurricane force, on the Beaufort Scale; oil derricks were toppled and people ordered off the downtown streets to avoid injury from flying objects. On November 22 the fire in the San Gabriels was out of control. On November 24 six people were killed in automobile accidents, and by the end of the week the *Los Angeles Times* was keeping a box score of traffic deaths. On November 26 a prominent Pasadena attorney, depressed about money, shot and killed his wife, their two sons, and himself. On November 27 a South Gate divorcee, twenty-two, was murdered and thrown from a moving car. On November 30 the San Gabriel fire was still out of control, and the wind in town was blowing eighty miles an hour. On the first day of December four people died violently, and on the third the wind began to break.

It is hard for people who have not lived in Los Angeles to realize how radically the Santa Ana figures in the local imagination. The city burning is Los Angeles's deepest image of itself: Nathanael West perceived that, in *The Day of the Locust*; and at the time of the 1965 Watts riots what struck the imagination most indelibly were the fires. For days one could drive the Harbor Freeway and see the city on fire, just as we had always known it would be in the end. Los Angeles weather is the weather of catastrophe, of apocalypse, and, just as the reliably long and bitter winters of New England determine the way life is lived there, so the violence and the unpredictability of the Santa Ana affect the entire quality of life in Los Angeles, accentuate its impermanence, its unreliability. The wind shows us how close to the edge we are.

2

"Here's why I'm on the beeper, Ron," said the telephone voice on the all-night radio show. "I just want to say that this *Sex for the Secretary* creature—whatever her name is—certainly isn't contributing anything to the morals in this country. It's pathetic. Statistics *show*."

"It's *Sex and the Office*, honey," the disc jockey said. "That's the title. By Helen Gurley Brown. Statistics show what?"

"I haven't got them right here at my fingertips, naturally. But they *show*."

"I'd be interested in hearing them. Be constructive, you Night Owls."

"All right, let's take one statistic," the voice said, truculent now. "Maybe I haven't read the book, but what's this business she recommends about *going out with married men for lunch?*"

So it went, from midnight until 5 a.m., interrupted by records and by occasional calls debating whether or not a rattlesnake can swim. Misinformation about rattlesnakes is a leitmotiv of the insomniac imagination in Los Angeles. Toward 2 a.m. a man from "out Tarzana way" called to protest. "The Night Owls who called earlier must have been thinking about, uh, *The Man in the Gray Flannel Suit* or some other book," he said, "because Helen's one of the few authors trying to tell us what's really going *on*. Hefner's another, and he's also controversial, working in, uh, another area."

An old man, after testifying that he "personally" had seen a swimming rattlesnake, in the Delta-Mendota Canal, urged "moderation" on the Helen Gurley Brown question. "We shouldn't get on the beeper to call things pornographic before we've read them," he complained, pronouncing it porn-ee-oh-graphic. "I say, get the book. Give it a chance." The original provocateur called back to agree that she would get the book. "And then I'll burn it," she added.

"Book burner, eh?" laughed the disc jockey good-naturedly.

"I wish they still burned witches," she hissed.

3

It is three o'clock on a Sunday afternoon and 105 and the air so thick with smog that the dusty palm trees loom up with a sudden and rather attractive mystery. I have been playing in the sprinklers with the baby and I get in the car and go to Ralph's Market on the corner of Sunset and Fuller wearing an old bikini bathing suit. That is not a very good thing to wear to the market but neither is it, at Ralph's on the corner of Sunset and Fuller, an unusual costume. Nonetheless a large woman in a cotton muumuu jams her cart into mine at the butcher counter. "*What a thing to wear to the market*," she says in a loud but strangled voice. Everyone looks the other way and I study a plastic package of rib lamb chops and she repeats it. She follows me all over the store, to the Junior Foods, to the Dairy Products, to the Mexican Delicacies, jamming my cart whenever she can. Her husband plucks at her sleeve. As I leave the check-out counter she raises her voice one last time: "*What a thing to wear to the Ralph's*," she says.

4

A party at someone's house in Beverly Hills: a pink tent, two orchestras, a couple of French Communist directors in Cardin evening jackets, chili and hamburgers from Chasen's. The wife of an English actor sits at a table alone; she visits California rarely although her husband works here a good deal. An American who knows her slightly comes over to the table.

"Marvelous to see you here," he says.

"Is it," she says.

"How long have you been here?"

"Too long."

She takes a fresh drink from a passing waiter and smiles at her husband, who is dancing. The American tries again. He mentions her husband.

"I hear he's marvelous in this picture."

She looks at the American for the first time. When she finally speaks she enunciates every word very clearly. "He . . . is . . . also . . . a . . . fag," she says pleasantly.

5

The oral history of Los Angeles is written in piano bars. "Moon River," the piano player always plays, and "Mountain Greenery." "There's a Small Hotel" and "This Is Not the First Time." People talk to each other, tell each other about their first wives and last husbands. "Stay funny," they tell each other, and "This is to die over." A construction man talks to an unemployed screenwriter who is celebrating, alone, his tenth wedding anniversary. The construction man is on a job in Montecito: "Up in Montecito," he says, "they got one square mile with 135 millionaires."

"Putrescence," the writer says.

"That's all you got to say about it?"

"Don't read me wrong, I think Santa Barbara's one of the most—Christ, the most—beautiful places in the world, but it's a beautiful place that contains a . . . *putrescence*. They just live on their putrescent millions."

"So give me putrescent."

"No, no," the writer says. "I just happen to think millionaires have some sort of lacking in their . . . in their elasticity."

A drunk requests "The Sweetheart of Sigma Chi." The piano player says he doesn't know it. "Where'd you learn to play the piano?" the drunk asks. "I got two degrees," the piano player says. "One in musical education." I go to a coin telephone and call a friend in New York. "Where are you?" he says. "In a piano bar in Encino," I say. "Why?" he says. "Why not," I say.

1965–67

▷ FOR CRITICAL INQUIRY |||||||||||||||||||||||||||||||||||||||||||||||||||||||||||||||||||

The Essay as a Mosaic

Joan Didion designed this essay as a sequence of five notebook entries, composing a mosaic of vignettes about Los Angeles, in some of which she appears; in others, she is an observer and commentator. There is no overarching statement of purpose to frame the essay or culminating moment of revelation. Instead, readers are asked to put the sections together associatively, to find an implied logic that unifies the sections. Re-read Didion's essay. Annotate each section according to its content and the role it plays in the essay overall. Then write a one-sentence description of the dominant impression the sections of the essay create. Compare your annotations and one-sentence description to those of classmates. What are main differences and similarities? What do these differences and similarities bring to light about the essay?

COMING TO TERMS WITH THE ESSAY

The final task of this section is to put the three essays together, to compare your experience reading Robert Hass's "Poet-Bashing Police," George Orwell's "A Hanging," and Joan Didion's "Los Angeles Notebook." The aim is to use the three essays to come to terms with the genre and how it positions writers in relation to readers and to what takes place in the essay.

▶ Recall how you organized mentally the presentation of material in the three essays. What patterns of organization did you recognize? When did you first recognize them? What cues did you find in the essays to guide your reading? How does the form of the essay engage your attention as a reader?

▶ Recall how you became aware of the point of view of each essay. Toward what understanding does each essay seem to direct its readers? How does the presence of the writer's consciousness occupy your attention as a reader? How does each writer's consciousness intersect the wider social world? How do the essays connect the personal and the public? What social alignments do the essays offer to readers?

Use these questions as the basis of a discussion to identify the particular traits and characteristic features of the essay. Based on your reading of the three essays—as well as other essays you've read in the past—what does the essay make possible as a genre of writing? What does its rhetorical work seem to be?

THINKING ABOUT THE CRAFT OF THE ESSAY

Understanding how the writer's craft works in essays, as well as in other genres of writing, is in part a matter of understanding how the arrangement and style of an essay enable readers to engage the writer's thoughts and purposes.

In some genres of writing, writers and readers alike rely heavily on formal conventions. You can tell, for example, that a piece of writing is a letter simply by looking at it. The same is true for certain kinds of academic writing, such as lab reports and scientific articles, with their fixed sections—introduction, materials and methods, results, discussion. Public documents such as wills, contracts, laws, and resolutions have highly predictable features that make them immediately recognizable. Consider also how readers expect news reports to be written in the form of an inverted pyramid, to front load the most salient information in the opening paragraph.

With the essay, however, writers cannot turn to a single standardized form to shape their material. Instead they must devise a form adequate for their purposes from a repertoire of possibilities. Essay writing is making something new out of a stock of familiar rhetorical moves and possibilities. In the essay, form embodies the writer's purposes, taking shape as a presence that is simultaneously novel and yet recognizable to the reader.

Form in writing has two key dimensions—the visual and the psychological.

▶ **The visual dimension** refers to the way written texts are laid out on a page. Writing materializes people's thoughts and purposes in visible form, and written texts take on a particular look as they occupy the space of a page. Paragraph breaks, headings and subheadings, the use of bullets and illustrations, the size and style of fonts, the layout of the page—these aspects of writing provide readers with visual cues to decode a piece of writing.

▶ **The psychological dimension** of form enables readers to anticipate the writer's purposes and where a piece of writing is going. Form in writing arouses readers' expectations that something significant is at stake and provides the scaffolding for readers to follow the writer's train of thought. In fiction, the arousal of desire to know the outcome of the plot can involve readers so deeply they talk about "getting lost" in a novel or short story. In other genres of writing, form likewise cues readers to the appropriate participation in the text. In the case of the essay, reader involvement is often imagined as entering into a conversation with the writer, to work toward mutual understanding, if not necessarily mutual agreement. This is what is meant by a "meeting of the minds" in writing, the exchange of perspectives that the essay makes possible.

Looking at how the visual and psychological dimensions of form work together can help you see that organizing a piece of writing is not simply filling the blank space of the page with your thoughts—at the rate, say, of one main point per essay and one idea per paragraph. The function of form is to produce common expectations and shared understandings between writers and readers.

SEEING PATTERNS OF ARRANGEMENT: HOW FORM EMBODIES PURPOSE

Let's look at some of the familiar forms in which essays appear to readers—the patterns of arrangement in which essays appear on the page. In this section, we examine four common patterns of arrangement: (1) narrative; (2) top-down order; (3) culminating order; and (4) open, or nonlinear, form.

Narrative

There are many ways to handle chronology and the flow of time in essays, to involve readers in the unfolding of events and their consequences. We have just seen two variations on the use of narrative as a principle of arrangement. George Orwell casts a narrative line to present an unadorned account of events that takes readers close to the formation of experience, giving "A Hanging" an immediacy and nearly visceral presence. Robert Hass, on the other hand, makes a bid for the reader's attention by framing the narrative at the outset and interrupting the arc of the story periodically to involve the reader in moments of analysis and reflection.

In "Los Angeles Notebook," Joan Didion departs from the single narrative to present a multiplicity of events, dispensing with chronology as the organizing principle of the essay as a whole. The overall design of the essay is spatial rather than a narrative line, a nonlinear composition of vignettes that moves readers from place to place.

Top-down Order

This pattern of organization is perhaps the most familiar to school-based writing assignments, as well as many types of public writing. Writers tell readers at the outset what their main point is and then go on to develop and support it. This is the way Robert Hass handles the narrative in "Poet-Bashing Police," by offering a conceptual framework ("life . . . is full of strange contingencies") to understand the events that take place. This pattern of organization enables readers to hold in mind the writer's point of view and to evaluate its appeal based on the evidence and analysis that follow.

Johann Hari's "You Are Being Lied To About Pirates" (pp. 53–55) is another example of top-down order, as this outline reveals:

¶1: Introduction. Presents main idea: "The people our governments are labelling as 'one of the great menaces of our times' have an extraordinary story to tell— and some justice on their side."

¶2–4: Refers to historical record to correct the popular understanding of who pirates were.

¶5: Links past pirates to present pirates in Somalia.

¶6–9: Establishes the context in which the Somali pirates emerged.

¶10–12: Ending. Makes a concession about hostage taking. Asks who the bandits really are. Closes with a quote from a fourth century BCE pirate.

Culminating Order

This form delays the presentation of the writer's central claim or insight until late in the piece of writing. Instead of announcing a position early on and then using the rest of the writing to support it, here the writing is organized so that the writer reviews various perspectives on an issue before drawing conclusions.

Andrew Gelman's "Do We Hate the Rich" is a good example of how a writer examines two different positions before articulating his own.

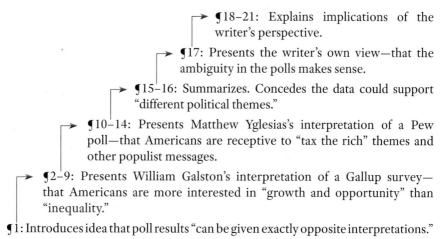

¶18–21: Explains implications of the writer's perspective.

¶17: Presents the writer's own view—that the ambiguity in the polls makes sense.

¶15–16: Summarizes. Concedes the data could support "different political themes."

¶10–14: Presents Matthew Yglesias's interpretation of a Pew poll—that Americans are receptive to "tax the rich" themes and other populist messages.

¶2–9: Presents William Galston's interpretation of a Gallup survey—that Americans are more interested in "growth and opportunity" than "inequality."

¶1: Introduces idea that poll results "can be given exactly opposite interpretations."

Open Form

Open form gives readers less guidance than narrative, top-down, or culminating order. Instead of explicitly pointing out the connections among the parts, open form leaves it to the readers to provide these links. If top-down and culminating order operate logically, open form operates associatively, and the parts of the writing take on meaning implicitly by how they are juxtaposed to each other.

This can be seen in Joan Didion's "Los Angeles Notebook." The five sections are separate units of attention; yet the fact that they appear under one title sets us to work as readers to see how they resonate with each other and what the unstated connections might be.

LOS ANGELES

(implied focus of essay)

Section 1	Section 2	Section 3	Section 4	Section 5
Santa Ana wind	Late-night talk show	Wearing bikini to supermarket	Beverly Hills party	Piano bars

PUTTING THE PARTS TOGETHER

We have looked at the overall arrangement of some short essays. Now we need to look a little more closely at how writers combine the parts of an essay to form a whole. In the following sections, we look at how writers organize introductions and endings and then at how they connect the parts of an essay.

Introductions

The purpose of an introduction is obvious—to let the reader know what the writing is about and how the writer is going to approach the topic.

Sometimes, depending on the situation and the genre, writers just outright tell readers: "This report summarizes the results of the pilot project and makes recommendations for the second stage of implementation" or "This proposal requests funding for a day-care center to serve students, faculty, and staff." In the case of essays, however, introductions do more work in establishing a central issue and explaining what is at stake.

Introductions work when they produce a certain meeting of the minds between the writer and reader. This is not to say that they necessarily agree about anything, only that they are mutually engaged in thinking about an issue, problem, or experience. Effective introductions are able to produce this kind of engagement because they identify something that the reader recognizes as interesting, important, controversial, amusing, urgent, whatever—a shareable concern whose relevance is evident.

In other words, writers need to frame their issues in a way that connects to what readers know and care about. Such a framework, then, can become the base from which the writer ventures his or her own views on the matter. The following are some common strategies writers use to establish a common framework and to explain how their own perspective connects to it.

- ▶ Describe an existing situation.

- ▶ Tell an anecdote.

- ▶ Raise a question to answer or problem to solve.

- ▶ Use a striking fact, statistic, or other background information.

- ▶ Define terms.

- ▶ Provide historical background.

- ▶ Describe a place, person, or object.

- ▶ State a common view and replace it with an alternative perspective.

- ▶ Forecast what your writing is designed to do.

▷▷ FOR CRITICAL INQUIRY

Analyzing Introductions

Bring to class three pieces of writing (or draw on readings in this book) that use different strategies in their introductions. Work in a group with three or four other students. Take turns explaining the strategies you have found. Consider the differences and similarities among the examples you have found. What generalizations can you draw about how introductions work?

Endings

In terms of the psychological dimensions of form, endings are key moments in writing. Writers know that endings need to provide readers with a sense of closure by resolving their expectations. Without a satisfying sense of an ending, readers are likely to feel let down. Writing that ends abruptly or fails to deliver at the end is going to leave readers up in the air, frustrated, and perhaps annoyed at the writer.

Perhaps the most important thing writers can learn about endings is that they perform a function no other part of an essay can perform: they address a question that it doesn't make sense to raise until the writer has developed his or her line of inquiry. This question can be phrased rather bluntly as "So what?" Where are we now? What are we as readers invited to conclude after the writer has explained what is at stake in the event or issue featured in the essay? What are the wider implications or consequences?"

Here are some techniques writers commonly use to write endings that provide a satisfying sense of resolution and closure.

▶ Point out consequences or the wider significance of the main point.

▶ Refine the main point in light of the material presented in the piece of writing.

▶ Offer a recommendation or a solution.

▶ Consider alternatives.

▶ Create an echo effect by looping back to something you presented in the introduction.

▶ Offer a final judgment.

▶ Provide a telling image.

▷ FOR CRITICAL INQUIRY

Analyzing Endings

Compare the endings in three pieces of writing in this book or that you have found elsewhere. First identify where the ending begins in each piece. What cues does the writer give? Next, explain the strategy it uses. How does this strategy embody the writer's purposes?

Connecting the Parts: Keeping Your Purposes Visible

If introductions help readers anticipate what is to come and endings explore the consequences or wider implications of the writer's ideas, the middle section (or main body) is where writers unfold their thinking and develop their ideas. The success of the middle section partly depends on readers being able to see how the reasons, events, evidence, and other materials connect to the main idea presented or implied in the introduction. Writing that is easy to follow, even if the ideas are complex, will use various devices to keep the writer's purposes visible so that readers can stay oriented, identify the relevance of the writer's discussion, and connect it to expectations set up in the introduction.

Here are three standard techniques for connecting the parts.

Use Reasons to Explain

A common way of connecting the parts is to use reasons to explain how the discussion in the middle section develops the main point. In the following sequence of paragraphs, notice how Laurie Ouellette's "Building the New Wave" uses reasons to explain why "young women have shunned feminism."

[W]hat can explain why so many young women have shunned feminism? In her survey of young women, *Feminist Fatale: Voices from the Twentysomething Generation Explore the Future of the Women's Movement*, Paula Kamen found that media-fueled stereotypes of feminists as "man-bashers" and "radical extremists" were behind the fact that many young women don't identify with the women's movement.

But these are not the only reasons. Kamen also points to the lack of young feminist role models as an important factor. The failure of a major feminist organization such as NOW to reach out to a wider spectrum of women, including young women, must be acknowledged as a part of this problem. While individual chapters do have young feminist committees and sometimes officers, they and the national office are led and staffed primarily by older women, and consequently often fail to reflect the interests and needs of a complex generation of young women.

Yet another reason young women have turned away from feminism may lie within its history. If the young women who have gained the most from feminism—that is, white, middle-class women who took advantage of increased accessibility to higher education and professional employment—have been reluctant to associate themselves with feminism, it is hardly surprising that most economically disadvantaged women and women of color, who have seen fewer of those gains, have not been eager to embrace feminism either. The women's movement of the seventies has been called an upper-middle-class white women's movement, and to a large degree I believe that is true. More than a few young feminists—many influenced by feminists of color such as Flo Kennedy, Audre Lorde, and bell hooks—have realized that feminism must also acknowledge issues of race and class to reach out to those women whose concerns have been overlooked by the women's movement of the past. Indeed, numerous statistics, including a poll by the *New York Times*, have noted that young African-American women are more likely than white women to acknowledge many of the concerns conducive to a feminist agenda, including a need for job training and equal earning power outside the professional sector. But for them, feminism has not provided the only answer. Only by making issues of class and race a priority can feminism hope to influence the lives of the millions of women for whom the daily struggle to survive, not feminist activism, is a priority. Will ours be the first generation of feminists to give priority to fighting cuts in Aid to

Families with Dependent Children, establishing the right to national health care, day care, and parental leave, and bringing to the forefront other issues pertinent to the daily struggle of many women's lives? If there is to be a third wave of feminism, they must.

We can diagram the pattern of development in the three paragraphs to make visible how it embodies Ouellette's purposes. Notice how the form creates a hierarchy of levels—the main point, the reasons, and the supporting evidence.

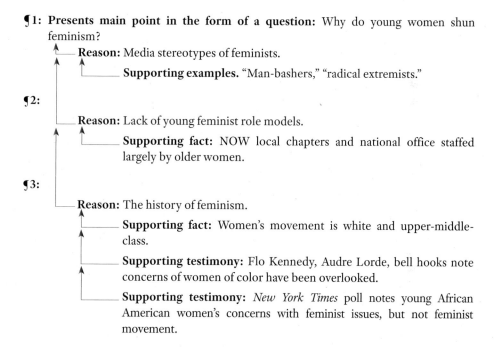

¶1: **Presents main point in the form of a question:** Why do young women shun feminism?
    Reason: Media stereotypes of feminists.
        Supporting examples. "Man-bashers," "radical extremists."

¶2:
    Reason: Lack of young feminist role models.
        Supporting fact: NOW local chapters and national office staffed largely by older women.

¶3:
    Reason: The history of feminism.
        Supporting fact: Women's movement is white and upper-middle-class.
        Supporting testimony: Flo Kennedy, Audre Lorde, bell hooks note concerns of women of color have been overlooked.
        Supporting testimony: *New York Times* poll notes young African American women's concerns with feminist issues, but not feminist movement.

Create Topic Chains

Topic chains help readers establish links between the parts of a piece of writing and allow them to feel that they know where the writer is going. Writers create topic chains by repeating key words, using pronouns and synonyms, and restating main points.

Consider the topic chain Robert Hass establishes in "Poet-Bashing Police":

¶1: Life . . . is full of strange **contingencies**.

¶2: The first **contingency** that came to mind . . . .

¶6: Another of the **contingencies** that came to my mind was a moment 30 years ago . . . .

Use Transitions to Create Patterns

The beginnings of paragraphs are key places to show readers how one statement, paragraph, or section in a piece of writing connects to the next. Writers use transitional words, phrases, and sentences to emphasize patterns of arrangement in essays.

Temporal transitions, for example, indicate the sequence of events that takes place and the passage of time. In the memoir "Black Hair," Gary Soto begins a number of paragraphs with temporal transitions to help readers see the chronological order in his narrative account of work:

¶5: *The next morning,* I arrived early at work.

¶7: I worked carefully *that day.* . . .

¶8: *At five,* the workers scattered. . . .

¶9: From the backyard I walked dully through a residential street, and *as evening came on.* . . .

Logical transitions help readers understand how ideas are related to one another. Henry Jenkins, in "Lessons from Littleton," uses three types of logical transition to establish connections between paragraphs: (1) numbered points separate topics, breaking them down into individual items of scrutiny and analysis; (2) parallel phrases establish a topic chain that enables the reader to see variations on the main theme; and (3) the consequences of the four points are emphasized by the transitional phrase "In short":

First, violent entertainment *offers teens a fantasy* of empowerment. . . .

Second, violent entertainment *offers teens a fantasy* of transgression. . . .

Third, violent entertainment *offers teens an acknowledgement* that the world is not all sweetness and light. . . .

Fourth, violent entertainment *offers teens an intensification* of emotional experience. . . .

In short, teens aren't drawn to *Quake* or *Scream* because they are bloodthirsty. . . .

COMMON TYPES OF TRANSITIONS

To mark sequence and passage of time:	next, later, after, before, earlier, meanwhile, immediately, soon, shortly, often, frequently, again, during, finally, at last
To locate spatially:	near, next to, alongside, facing, adjacent, far beyond, away, off in the distance, between, through, up, down, across, above, below, inside, outside
To give examples:	for example, for instance, namely, specifically, that is
To add further points:	and, in addition, also, furthermore, moreover
To show consequences:	thus, therefore, so, consequently, hence, as a result, for this reason
To compare:	similarly, likewise, also
To contrast:	however, in contrast, but, yet, nevertheless, nonetheless
To compare and contrast:	not only/but also, on the one hand/on the other
To make a concession:	although, even though, granted that

DESIGNING PARAGRAPHS

Paragraphs are the building blocks writers use to assemble larger pieces of writing. That does not mean, of course, that paragraphs come ready-made in standard, prefabricated forms. They need to be designed to perform particular functions depending on the kind of writing and where the paragraph takes place in the larger piece of writing.

Seeing Paragraphs: The Visual Dimension

As mentioned earlier, form in writing has both a visual and a psychological dimension, and this is true as well of paragraphs. Visually, paragraphs are graphic units that mark units of attention for readers by indenting. Paragraph breaks help readers see where a related sequence of ideas begins and ends. In turn, paragraphs provide writers with a means to establish the reader's focus of attention for a period of time.

Experienced writers have learned that the beginning and ending of paragraphs are the points at which readers are most attentive. When a paragraph begins, readers look for cues to tell them what the paragraph is going to be about so that they can concentrate on that particular point and how the writer develops it. When the paragraph ends, readers often pause briefly, to catch their breath and consolidate their sense of what they have just read, before going on to the next paragraph.

In newspaper writing, in part because of the narrow columns in the page layout, paragraphs tend to be short. One of their functions is to make the experience of reading as easy as possible so that readers can get the gist of an article by scanning it quickly. The same thing applies to many kinds of writing in the workplace and the public sphere, where writers and readers alike put a premium on making the information in memos, reports, proposals, news briefings, and brochures concise and easy to process.

In other genres of writing, however, paragraphs have a very different look on the page. Essays, academic writing, and magazine articles often use longer paragraphs, and readers expect that writers will develop their points in greater depth and detail.

The length of a paragraph, in other words, depends on the kind of writing in which it appears and the function it serves.

⊳ FOR CRITICAL INQUIRY

Analyzing Paragraphs

Following is a passage from Lundy Braun's commentary "How to Fight the New Epidemics," without paragraph indentation. You will probably notice right away how dense and forbidding the passage seems. It looks like a lot of extra work to get through it. Your task here is to provide paragraphing to make the passage easier for readers. Follow these steps:

1. On your own, read through the passage and insert paragraph breaks where you think they are most useful.

2. Now work with two or three classmates and compare how each of you has divided the passage into paragraphs. To what extent are the paragraphs alike? To what extent do they differ? In the case of differences, does the effect on readers differ? If so, how? Working together, see whether you can come up with one version that everyone in the group can live with. If you can't agree, explain what your differences are and what seems to be at stake.

One of the hottest topics in the news these days seems to be "killer" viruses. With the outbreak of swine flu and worries about a global pandemic, not to mention the popular accounts of epidemics of virus infection in feature films, made-for-television movies and best-selling nonfiction over the past ten years or so, the public has been captivated by the apparent power of microorganisms to sweep through towns and villages unfettered. But hidden behind our fascination with these real and fictional epidemics is a profound feeling of betrayal, stemming from the widely held view that science had won the war against microbial infections. The recent outbreaks have taken us by surprise, threatening our carefully nurtured sense of health and well-being. We diet, consume vitamins and exercise vigorously to ward off heart disease and cancer. But infectious diseases strike in a seemingly unpredictable pattern, leaving us feeling unprotected and vulnerable. With the re-emergence of tuberculosis as a significant public health problem in the United States, cholera in Latin America, the plague epidemic in India last year and the Ebola virus infection in Zaire, HIV infection, formerly considered an isolated occurrence confined to marginalized populations, now seems a harbinger of ever more terrifying microbial agents. Yet, the reasons for the re-emergence of infectious diseases are not particularly mysterious. In reality, infectious diseases never were conquered, and the recent epidemics are quite predictable. For centuries, infectious diseases have been the major cause of death in the developing world. Moreover, even in the developed world, successful management relies on active disease surveillance and public health policies. In 1966, the eminent Australian immunologist Sir MacFarlane Burnet declared, "In many ways one can think of the middle of the 20th Century as the end of one of the most important social revolutions in history, the virtual elimination of infectious disease as a significant factor in social life." Shared by most of the scientific community, this view is rooted in the rise of the germ theory in the late 19th and early 20th centuries that associated specific microbial agents with particular diseases. The germ theory took hold not only because of the spectacular technical achievements represented by the isolation of the microorganisms, but also because infectious disease, once seen as divine retribution for past sins, now appeared potentially controllable. The discovery of antibiotics and the development of vaccines lent further support to this notion of control. Thus, the germ theory effectively replaced disease prevention policies based on sanitary reforms, including improvement in sewage systems and better housing conditions, which were primarily responsible for the dramatic decline in the death rates from infectious disease.

Unity and Coherence: The Psychological Dimension

Unity and *coherence* are workshop terms referring to the psychological dimension of writing and to how writing arouses the reader's expectations and then goes on to fulfill them. Unity means that a piece of writing has some central point, focus, or center of gravity that readers can readily identify. They don't wonder what the writer is getting at or try to figure out the main point on their own.

Coherence means that the ideas in the writing seem to come in the right order, leading logically from one point to the next. Readers don't feel that the writing rambles or jumps around from point to point, but instead feel that it moves along purposefully.

Often, readers are not even aware that well-crafted writing is unified and coherent. They simply experience the writing as easy to read. The writer's ideas seem to be where they belong, and readers can easily follow the writer's thoughts from point to point. The writing just seems to flow, and readers don't feel confused about its direction. Moreover, when this happens, readers believe they are in good hands—and, as a result, are likely to invest a certain amount of confidence and credibility in what the writer is saying. Whether they agree with the ideas or not, they at least think that the writer knows what he or she is doing and that the ideas are therefore worth considering. In short, unity and coherence are devices for making a meeting of minds possible.

To see how paragraphs use unity and coherence to enhance readability, look at the following paragraph:

> Public toilets ... have become the real frontline of the city's war on the homeless. Los Angeles, as a matter of deliberate policy, has fewer public toilets than any other major North American city. On the advice of the Los Angeles police, who now sit on the "design board of at least one major Downtown project, the redevelopment agency bulldozed the few remaining public toilets on Skid Row." Agency planners then considered whether to include a "free-standing public toilet" in their design for the upscale South Park residential development; agency chairman Jim Wood later admitted that the decision not to build the toilet was a "policy decision and not a design decision." The agency preferred the alternative of "quasi-public restrooms"—toilets in restaurants, art galleries, and office buildings—which can be made available selectively to tourists and white-collar workers while being denied to vagrants and other unsuitables. The same logic has inspired the city's transportation planners to exclude toilets from their designs for Los Angeles's new subway system.
>
> Mike Davis, from City of Quartz

Topic Sentences and Discussion: Unity and Coherence

Notice how Davis's paragraph can be divided into a topic sentence ("Public toilets ... have become the real frontline on the city's war on the homeless") and discussion that explains and amplifies the meaning of the topic sentence.

Topic sentences typically focus on a single idea or on a sequence of related ideas that will be developed in the paragraph. After the first sentence, readers are likely to expect Davis to devote the rest of the paragraph to explaining how public toilets figure into Los Angeles's "war on the homeless." And, as you can see, the rest of the paragraph, or the discussion, is indeed devoted to explaining how planners eliminated the availability of public toilets; it thereby contributes to the unity of the paragraph and to fulfilling readers' expectations. Notice, furthermore, how the order of sentences seems coherent. Each sentence not only follows from the topic sentence but also picks up on the sentence that precedes it. The way one sentence leads to the next can be analyzed by imagining that each sentence answers a question in the reader's mind raised by the preceding sentence or sentences:

Topic Sentence

Public toilets … have become the real frontline in the city's war on the homeless.

(*Question: What is this "war"?*)

Discussion

Los Angeles, as a matter of deliberate policy, has fewer public toilets than any other major North American city.

(*Answers question and raises another about how "policy" was made*)

On the advice of the Los Angeles police, who now sit on the "design board of at least one major Downtown project, the redevelopment agency bulldozed the few remaining public toilets on Skid Row."

(*Answers question about how "policy" was made*)

Agency planners then considered whether to include a "free-standing public toilet" in their design for the upscale South Park residential development; agency chairman Jim Wood later admitted that the decision not to build the toilet was a "policy decision and not a design decision."

(*Amplifies answer about how "policy" was made by giving another example*)

The agency preferred the alternative of "quasi-public restrooms"—toilets in restaurants, art galleries, and office buildings—which can be made available selectively to tourists and white-collar workers while being denied to vagrants and other unsuitables.

(*Answers question about how "policy" amounts to "war on the homeless"*)

The same logic has inspired the city's transportation planners to exclude toilets from their designs for Los Angeles's new subway system.

(*Gives a final example of how "policy" makes "war on the homeless"*)

|||||||||||||||||||||||||||||||||||||||||||||||||||||||||||||||||||||||||||

Analyzing Paragraph Unity and Coherence

Work together in a group of four or five. Read the following passage aloud. Then answer the questions.

I have always wanted to be a high school American history teacher. Many teachers are now feeling the pressure to teach the test rather than educate their students in historical understanding. There are certainly skills and knowledge that high school students should acquire in their American history classes. Historical understanding gives students a way to see how the past shapes the present. In American history courses, students have too often memorized facts and dates rather than learning to understand why historical events took place and how they affect the present. I realize that many students are not interested in the past, but my desire is to help students think about American history and the unresolved questions it raises about the legacy of slavery, the American belief in individualism and free enterprise, and the Vietnam War. The current trend to make high schools more accountable emphasizes testing at the expense of genuine learning. Historical understanding is crucial if we want to have an informed citizenry who can make decisions about the complex issues that face us as a nation.

1. What question does the first sentence raise?

2. How is this question answered?

3. Are there other questions that the paragraph seems to raise?

4. How are these questions answered?

5. How would you revise this paragraph for unity and coherence?

FOR FINAL CONSIDERATION

Terrorflu

Joshua Clover

· ·

Joshua Clover is a poet and critic. He is professor of English literature and critical theory at the University of California, Davis. "Terrorflu" originally appeared in Lana Turner: A Journal of Poetry and Opinion and was chosen for Best Music Writing 2009, edited by Greil Marcus.

RING ROAD

("Roadrunner," Jonathan Richman and the Modern Lovers, original version [1976 release], 4'06")

We begin on Route 128 when it's late at night. That's where the Modern Lovers begin, and the greatest American song of that era. The Modern Lovers are from Massachusetts. Joni Mitchell is from Canada and Bob Dylan is from myth.

Joshua Clover, "Terrorflu" from *Lana Turner: A Journal of Poetry and Opinion*. No. 1, Fall 2008: 42-49. Reprinted by permission.

Route 128 is a beltway around Boston. Such roads are less common in the United States than in Europe, Asia, South America. They tend to encircle dense cities of the older style, giving them a sense of order, of boundedness, or at least the promise that one might navigate around their labyrinthine cores. Younger typologies like grid cities have less use for such designs; sprawl cities almost none at all.

Boston has the road originally called the *Circumferential Highway*, the first of its kind in the U.S., now a curving high-tech run, a silicon rally optimistically dubbed "America's Technology Highway"—but in 1972, when "Roadrunner" was first recorded, it was a scungy corridor of doughnut shops and furniture stores, déclassé towns like Dedham and Lynnfield, nicer burbs like Newton and Milton, and then Natick, where Jonathan Richman was born. I used to take the bus to play miniature golf in Natick, and on the way you passed a butcher called Mr. Meat. That pretty much sums it up.

1972 matters. 1972 matters because it is almost 1973, the year of the oil crisis and gas rationing. It is almost 1973 but not quite and Jonathan Richman is driving the suburban ring road, faster miles an hour, and the price of gas is the farthest thing from his mind, he has the radio on and he's going around and around, the guitar is going around and around, the lyrics are going nowhere and that's the point, there's no particular place to go, just around and around, and he passes the spirit of 1956. 1956 is the commanding heights of the postwar boom, and the homely suburbs are in full bloom, and though it's *close* to the birth of rock'n'roll, it's the *exact* year of the largest public works project in American history, which is of course the *Federal Highway Act*, all 25 billion if it, the birth of the Interstate System, *fucking infrastructure* just like the Stop'n'Shop and the Howard Johnson's and the radio towers are fading remnants from the world of *stuff*, and this is why it's the greatest song of the era, because rock'n'roll is the last great invention of industrial capitalism and "Roadrunner" is a love song for industrial capitalism when it's late at night, and then Jonathan passes the spirit of 1957, he turns around in the night and is consumed by neon.

THE MAIN STREETS AND THE CINEMA AISLES
("Brimful of Asha," Cornershop, Norman Cook Remix Single Version, 1998,4'04")

And then it's 1972 again, leaking into 1973: the tilt from the long boom to the long bust, from the ascent to the decline of the American age, modernity to postmodernity, industrial to finance capital. There's a red thread that runs from 1973 through 1979's conservative counterrevolution. The thread runs through to 1989, year of the "Washington Consensus," when the collapse of the Second World briefly promised a respite from the narrative of decline. That same thread runs through 1997–98 when the global financial crisis known as the Asian Flu spread its contagion from Thailand to Malaysia to Singapore, the Philippines, Indonesia, Hong Kong, South Korea, Russia, Brazil, Argentina, landing on

U.S. shores with the collapse of Long Term Capital Management, a hedge fund so heavy that it has to be bailed out to stem the global crisis, or so we're told. Long Term Capital Management was founded by the guys who developed the mathematical model that made the trading of *non-stuff* a viable and lucrative market. Derivatives, mutual funds, arbitrage, the whole sea-change known as "financialization": these guys brought that to life. Their instrument was called the Black-Scholes Equation, a mechanism so powerful that economic historians have called it an "epistemological rupture," and it was published in 1973, so maybe it's not a red thread but a ring road that runs through history, going around and around.

This is not to argue for something like just desserts, or karma, or other moralizing ideas of the *what-comes-around-goes-around* variety. This is just to name a fact about circulation. When you build the ring road, or the global economy, it becomes possible that something tossed out into the traffic will come back your way again, almost unrecognizable, monstrous, beautiful, who knows? In fact it becomes increasingly likely this will happen, because the circuits are more closely connected, faster, less regulated, the kind of thing that makes Thomas Friedman stain his khakis, and if you toss something catchy out there it's coming back around like the Roadrunner. It feels like freedom but it cuts both ways, sometimes it's the freedom of Jonathan going around and around in his car, and sometimes the Asian Flu going around and around in the markets. And the song itself is not just wheeling through its chord changes but through global culture, and it circulates through the relays of Sex Pistols and Greg Kahn, the Feelies and Yo La Tengo and Joan Jett, and inevitably something really interesting happens: it lands on the second track of an album by a British South Asian band except it's a little hard to recognize because it has different words and a different melody and isn't about the radio and Massachusetts, but about vinyl 45s and "playback singers" and especially Asha Bhosle, who recorded over 12,000 songs for Bollywood cinema. For all these reasons it's a little hard at first to hear that "Brimful of Asha" is Tjinder Singh's version of "Roadrunner" come back around as a global idea, the main streets are cinema aisles and Route 128 is the cultural circuit from Hollywood to South Asia to London and back again, and he suggests "we don't care . . . about the dams they're building," those IMF-mandated building blocks of globalization tearing India apart, and of course it turns out to be Cornershop's first global hit, but it doesn't really accelerate until the next year, as the Asian Flu is spreading to Russia and South America, when the song is remixed by Norman Cook and this is surely one of the greatest remixes in history, because it brings out the genius of the song without fucking it up, shows how the song is infinitely deep, it goes around and around like a 45, a repetitive structure filled with endless possibility, "from the morning past the evening to the end of the light"— and at the same time Norman Cook makes a *critical reading* of the song, he speeds up the crude jangle and pushes it forward, and he extends the final breakdown into the middle of the night, until you can hear, it's *obvious*, that *"forty-five"* is *"radio on!"* and that Cornershop is the Postmodern Lovers and the guitar goes around and around and the remix goes to #1.

FINANCE CAPITAL POP

("Galang," M.I.A., 2003 Showbiz Records version, 3'34")

So you have these songs making circular sounds and it turns out they are trying to think about circulation, about records on turntables and cars on ring roads and sounds in the transnational flow of culture: the relaying of sonic contagions through the system and around the globe and often returning to where they began but different, mutated. There's probably no better example than Rihanna's Stargate's Michael Jackson's Quincy Jones' Manu Dibango's "Soul Makossa," which is from 1972. And influence and pastiche and the import-export business are nothing new but such contagions and mutations intensify and accelerate within the regimes of mobile capital and mobile labor and globalization, until they become inseparable from the *very idea* of pop music: *finance capital pop*. But these conditions are not just the history of pop, they are the *history of history*, they are conjoined with the development of what we now call "the world-system," and *this*—not what anyone says in a song—is why pop music is political.

So it is only to be expected that some of the most interesting pop musicians would take this as pop's *representational problem*, the way the 19th century novel took the social order of industrial urbanization as its representation problem, its *formal* problem. And I am telling you that M.I.A. is a great pop artist, because this is her project: the same way that we work on music and literature and history and dance, M.I.A. works on circulation and she gets around. She's crafty.

Somewhere on *Arular* she seems to be talking back to the song actually called "Pop Muzik," by M, "London Paris New York Munich everybody talk about pop music," but M.I.A. says "London, quieten down, I need to make a sound. New York, quieten down, I need to make a sound." And Kingston and Brazil: hip-hop, grime, reggae, baile funk, but these aren't her *sounds*, they're what's going around on the big ring road; her sound is the big ring road itself. She is in no particular place. Her sound is globalization. But even before then, her very first release begins "London calling" and tosses the hook right into the space of flows and the song starts circling, sinister and joyous, West Indian slang and the chorus-chant going around like jump rope and someone is driving around London and M.I.A. is around London sort of like Tjinder Singh except this time by way of Sri Lanka and you can hear that too, and you know her father is a Tamil freedom fighter slash terrorist in a civil war that goes around and around, twenty-five years during which they perfect the craft of suicide bombing which shortly goes around the world like a contagion, and maybe you know that Sri Lanka was once Ceylon and that the war is much older than 25 years, that the local is the global, that the island has been divided for centuries, and was occupied by the Portuguese and conquered by the United Provinces because it was of interest to the Dutch East India Company, and then the British because it was of interest to their cover version, the *British* East India Company—what you might call *Double Dutch*—and the companies go around and around the globe and we learn to call this geopolitics and now we circle back around to London and *who the hell is hunting you in your BMW* and the song goes around and around, galang-a-lang-a-lang. It is 2003.

BALM ON GILEAD

("Bird Flu," M.I.A., 2007, 3'24")

2003 matters, and by now you hear the pattern. 2003 matters because of the re-emergence of Influenza A virus subtype H5N1. I say "re-emergence" because it first leapt from waterfowl to humans, killing six in Hong Kong, in 1997, the year of the Asian Flu economic crisis. H5N1 is often called "avian influenza," or more commonly, "bird flu." Among many contagions, contagion itself.

Bird flu is pure pop; it goes *around* the world. In 2004, Shigeru Omi, Regional Director of the World Health Organization, forecast "at least seven million deaths, but maybe more—10 million, 20 million, and in the worst case, 100 million." This is still in the future, but is not unlikely; it is perhaps the most predictable of epidemics. It's predictable because we built the situation ourselves: "Human-induced shocks—overseas tourism, wetland destruction, a corporate "Livestock Revolution," and the Third World urbanization with the attendant growth of mega slums," lists Mike Davis in *Monster at Our Door*, putting oarticular emphasis on the last, which has the effect of "shifting the burden of global poverty from the countryside to the slum peripheries of new megacities. Ninety-five percent of future world population growth will be in the poor cities of the South, with immense consequences for the ecology of disease." These are the cities in M.I.A.'s song "World Town," places in which particularity fights a losing battle against the role of the relay, part of the condition, the situation, in which contagions circulate.

It is this that loops through the song "Bird Flu," a disturbing sound that goes around and around, the loop self-produced and mesmerizing and comparable to nothing in pop music except maybe Timbaland's gurgling-baby loop in "Are You That Somebody": it's an ominous bird squawk against an even more ominous clatter of drums, but it's also the whole situation of pop music, in which cars and sounds and economic disasters and epidemics circulate, and the song is terrifying like pop songs rarely go out of their way to be.

It is very hard to say where bird flu comes from. The 2003 outbreak isolated in Hong Kong flared a month earlier in China, where "a strange contagious disease had killed more than a hundred people in Guangdong in a single week." No one is surprised that the radical industrialization of South China might prove an incubator for a pandemic. But the global driver of the "Livestock Revolution" is Tyson Foods, which kills 2.2 billion chickens annually and is, in Davis's words, "globally synonymous with scaled-up, vertically integrated production; exploitation of contract growers; visceral antiunionism; rampant industrial injury; downstream environmental dumping; and political corruption." The Legoes of neoliberalism; Global Fried Chicken with an Arkansas accent. When bird flu arrives in Little Rock, it will be very hard to say it came from somewhere else.

As it happens, there is a single effective treatment for avian influenza: trade name Tamiflu. There is not very much of it; the patent-holder, Gilead Sciences, has gone to great lengths to prevent its inexpensive reproduction in the World Towns. Between George W. Bush's inauguration and 2007, Gilead stock increased in value more than 800 percent. And as it happens, the former chairman and still major stakeholder of Gilead is also signatory to the neoliberal Magna Carta, the "Statement of Principles" of the Project for a New American Century. The document is from 1997. The former Gilead chair is Donald Rumsfeld; you may know him as an apostle of the War on Terror. And M.I.A. writes, "I CALLED THIS BIRD FLU BECAUSE THIS BEAT GON KILL EVERYONE!!"

WELCOME TO THE TERRORFLU
("Bamboo Banger," M.I.A., 2007, 4'58")

So this is one thing you can say about *Kala*: M.I.A. is talking to Donald Rumsfeld. They are talking about blowback, and chickens coming home to roost; they are talking about circulation and contagion and neoliberalism. They are talking about bird flu and about terror: "Hands up—guns out—represent now world town." And the conversation goes around and around the globe, but it doesn't begin in some war zone or some necrojungle but on Route 128 when it's late at night. "Roadrunner Roadrunner, going hundred miles per hour" are her first words and she has the radio on and she's banging on the door of his Hummer Hummer, and we can assume she's listening to Modern Lovers except the beat is from a Tamil movie soundtrack, it's by a guy named Ilaiyaraaja, a prolific Indian film composer whose songs tend to be very difficult to sing and as a result fall to the best playback singers, foremost among them Asha Bhosle. *Forty-five*. Small world. No, it's a big world but M.I.A. gets around, everything gets around, because we have built the world that way. And the song has some hilarious moments, she's "hungry like the wolves" and instantly we remember the Duran Duran video with the beautiful pale boys in their South Asian fantasia, and isn't Duran Duran originally from that movie with the 50-foot Terrorist, *Barbarella?* . . . and it isn't ten seconds before Maya says "Barbarella look like she my dead ringer" as if to make sure *we* know *she* knows, knows she is riding this incredibly elaborate circuit, and she says "I'm a Roadrunner, a world runner" just to clarify things, she is in your system and she is trying to *become* the system like Wintermute at the end of *Neuromancer* except it's not the future it's now, represent now world town, and already she has said "now I'm *sit*ting down *chill*in' on *gun* powder, *strike* match *light* fire, *who's* that girl *called* Maya?" and then the refrain, "M.I.A. coming back with power power."

People like to worry about whether or not M.I.A. advocates political violence, and whether she has a right or a capacity to do so in any real way. The figure of the "terrorist pop star" is, for a certain kind of person, impossibly sexy; for another, entirely offensive; and for a third, conceptually impossible. But any of this is to miss the point almost entirely. The indexing of M.I.A. to the romanticized figure of the lone terrorist, even one draped in Third World nobility, tells us much more about the listener than the singer. Much more about habits of thought than about the music. There are always stories to be told about individuals, and about particular places, and these are stories we like to tell. But what would it mean to really *think* "the local is the global," and to fold the idea that "the personal is the political" back into the awful, exhausting, thrilling knowledge that *the political is the political*? What would it mean to find a sound for the situation?

That is exactly the thing that M.I.A. is trying to grasp, the representational problem for pop music, pop music which is not *in* London, Paris, New York, Munich any more than bird flu is *in* Hong Kong or Guangdong, economic contagion is *in* Thailand or Brazil, terrorism is *in* Baghdad or Colombo or Beirut. All of these things are in a *situation*, all of these things have *conditions of possibility* and they are the same conditions, and the structures that carry pop music around and around carry the others as well, they are riders in the space of flows that was built by people, in history, the great ring road that we built for reasons, that profit some and not others, all of these things are Roadrunners and it is very hard to say where they come from or where they are going, faster miles an hour, and they go around and around in the night.

⤷ FOR CRITICAL INQUIRY

The Connecting Thread

Joshua Clover has organized "Terrorflu" in five sections of two to five paragraphs, with each section marked by a subtitle and the name and recording information of a particular song, starting with Jonathan Richman and the Modern Lovers' 1972 car song, "Roadrunner," then moving to a 1998 remix of the London South Asian group Cornershop's "Brimful of Asha" and three tracks from M.I.A.: "Galang" (2003), "Bird Flu," and "Bamboo Banger" (2007). Each song presents an instance for Clover to reflect on the circulation of pop music, from the beltway around Boston in the 1970s to the global "ring road" that today carries finance capital, bird flu, people, and pop songs around the world. The essay is not rock criticism in the conventional sense of the term, but instead uses songs to identify patterns and themes in a globalized world, following a thread of thought to weave seemingly disparate things together.

Your task is to examine what Clover is trying to accomplish with this design, to make sense of how the form of the essay embodies Clover's purposes. You may need to do background research on the songs highlighted in each section and the events and processes of globalization the essay examines. It's important for you to know something about the material in Clover's essay in order to come to terms with what he is trying to do.

- Reread the essay, keeping the idea of circulation and globalization in mind. Consider how Clover establishes the theme of the essay in the first section. As you read the following sections, write a short note explaining how each one uses a song to extend Clover's line of thinking from section to section.

- Once you've completed this rereading, step back and consider how the sections fit together. What does Clover's purpose seem to be? What is he trying to show and explain? How does the form of the essay—the sequence of sections and the movement from song to song—enable Clover to realize his purpose?

PART 2

Writing Projects

INTRODUCTION: GENRES OF WRITING

The term *genre* refers to different types of writing in print and new media—and the actions, interests, and identities they enable writers to perform. We recognize genres in part by their recurring features, such as the opening line "Once upon a time . . . "in fairy tales, the predictable parts of a laboratory report (Introduction, Methods, Results, Discussion), or the typical design of a Wikipedia entry. But we also recognize genres according to the characteristic way they respond to a rhetorical situation, when, for example, commentators feel called upon to come to terms with the legacy of a complicated life and death, as in the case of Michael Jackson (see discussion of Jerald Walker's "Beyond Grief" in Chapter 2), or when Amnesty International circulates a petition to free a political prisoner. Based on past experience with written texts, people fit what they read into patterns that provide them with information about how to understand and respond to the various genres that circulate in contemporary society.

Writing and Genre Knowledge

Similarly, writers draw on genre knowledge to make sense of the situations that call on them to write. As writers identify a call to write, they typically review past experience to help them determine the genre best suited to the current occasion. To do this, they look for recurring patterns:

▶ How is this writing situation similar to ones I've encountered in the past?

▶ How well do genres of writing I've used in the past match the demands of the present?

▶ Are there genres I haven't used before that fit this situation?

▶ What genre best fits my purposes, given the situation and the intended readers?

In the following chapters, you'll see how writers use various genres to respond to recurring writing situations. You'll see how writers' choice of genre takes into account the occasion that calls for writing, the writer's purposes, and the relationship the writer seeks to establish with readers.

While writing teachers do not always agree on how best to classify genres of writing, the eight chapters in Part Two offer practical examples of how writers use some of the most familiar genres. These chapters are by no means a comprehensive account of all genres of writing. Nor are the genres of writing fixed once and for all. New genres are always emerging in response to new conditions, as you can see in the proliferation of email, instant messaging, message boards, blogs, and Web sites. In the following chapters, some of the most common genres illustrate how writers respond to the call to write. You will find these genres helpful when you are called on to write in college, in the workplace, and in public life.

CHAPTER 5

Memoirs

Writing a *memoir,* as the word itself suggests, involves memory work. Memoirists draw on their pasts to re-create moments of lived experience. This re-creation of particular experiences distinguishes memoir from the genre of autobiography, which seeks to encompass an entire life.

The call to write memoirs comes in part from the desire people have to keep track of the past and to see how their lives have intersected with the world around them. This impulse to remember is what leads people to take photographs, compile scrapbooks, and save letters and keepsakes of all sorts. Long after a particular experience is over, these objects help remind us of how things were at that moment. They also help remind us of how we were.

This sense of connection between present and past is at the center of memoir writing. By re-creating experiences from the past and exploring their significance from the perspective of the present, memoirists identify the continuities and discontinuities in their own lives. In this sense, the memoir writer is both a participant and an observer. On the one hand, the writer appears as a character in the memoir, a participant in the events that unfold. On the other hand, the writer is also an observer—the first-person narrator who comments on and interprets the unfolding events, giving them a shape and meaning for the present.

Memoir writers typically focus on details and incidents that reveal deeper meanings to themselves and to readers. Memoirist Patricia Hampl records details such as a "black boxy Ford" in a photograph, a "hat worn in 1952," an aunt polishing her toenails, and the "booths of the Gopher Grill" at the University of Minnesota. Such details can move writers to recover and convey to readers what might otherwise be overlooked in their pasts—what Hampl calls the "intimate fragments . . . that bind even obscure lives to history."

As Hampl notes, memoirists often put their experiences into a historical or cultural context. They present their pasts in part as exemplifying and shedding light on a larger moment—what it meant, say, to grow up during the 1960s; to experience the attacks on September 11, 2001; to witness the election of the first African American president; or to live through the economic fallout of the 2008 crash. The point here is that as detailed, specific, and filled with sensory impressions as successful memoirs are, it is the larger context that gives these details their significance.

Ultimately, people are called on to write memoirs not only to establish a connection to the past and to inform and entertain readers but also from a sense of responsibility, to bear witness to things that might otherwise be overlooked or forgotten. In many respects, memoirs derive their unique power to move readers from the way writers position themselves in the present in order to bear witness to the past by inventing a first-person narrator who reveals the secrets and unsuspected meanings of ordinary lives that turn out to be not so ordinary after all.

WRITING FROM EXPERIENCE

Consider Patricia Hampl's point that memories are stored in the details of photos, a particular hat, and the booths at a campus hangout. Write a list of things that somehow capture an important moment or period in your life—such as photos, popular songs, hairstyles, articles of clothing, movies, posters, stuffed animals, toys, letters, cards, newspaper clippings, school or team uniforms, art objects, or souvenirs. Compare your list with your classmates' lists. What generalizations can you make about the capacity of things to hold and evoke memories?

READINGS

From *One Writer's Beginnings*

Eudora Welty

Eudora Welty (1909–2001) is a celebrated author of short stories and novels about her native Mississippi, a photographer in One Time, One Place *(1971) and* Photographs *(1989), and a memoirist. Her novel* The Optimist's Daughter *won the Pulitzer Prize in 1973. This excerpt comes from her memoir* One Writer's Beginnings *(1983), which itself is based on the three Massey Lectures in the History of American Civilization she delivered in 1983.*

Sets the scene

Jackson's Carnegie Library was on the same street where our house was, on the other side of the State Capitol. "Through the Capitol" was the way to go to the Library. You could glide through it on your bicycle or even coast through on roller skates, though without family permission.

Introduces Mrs. Calloway. Uses details

I never knew anyone who'd grown up in Jackson without being afraid of Mrs. Calloway, our librarian. She ran the Library absolutely by herself, from the desk where she sat with her back to the books and facing the stairs, her dragon eye on the front door, where who knew what kind of person might come in from the public? SILENCE in big

Reprinted by permission of the publisher and the author's Estate from ONE WRITER'S BEGINNINGS by Eudora Welty, pp. 29–30, Cambridge, Mass.: Harvard University Press, Copyright © 1983, 1984 by Eudora Welty.

black letters was on signs tacked up everywhere. She herself spoke in her normally commanding voice; every word could be heard all over the Library above a steady seething sound coming from her electric fan; it was the only fan in the Library and stood on her desk, turned directly onto her streaming face.

Explains Mrs. Calloway's policy

As you came in from the bright outside, if you were a girl, she sent her strong eyes down the stairway to test you; if she could see through your skirt she sent you straight back home; you could just put on another petticoat if you wanted a book that badly from the public library. I was willing; I would do anything to read.

Anecdote of mother's encounter with Mrs. Calloway

My mother was not afraid of Mrs. Calloway. She wished me to have my own library card to check out books for myself. She took me in to introduce me and I saw I had met a witch. "Eudora is nine years old and has my permission to read any book she wants from the shelves, children or adult," Mother said. "With the exception of *Elsie Dinsmore*," she added. Later she explained to me that she'd made this rule because Elsie the heroine, being made by her father to practice too long and hard at the piano, fainted and fell off the piano stool. "You're too impressionable, dear," she told me. "You'd read that and the very first thing you'd do, you'd fall off the piano stool." "Impressionable" was a new word. I never hear it yet without the image that comes with it of falling straight off the piano stool.

Explains Eudora's response to Mrs. Calloway

Mrs. Calloway made her own rules about books. You could not take back a book to the Library on the same day you'd taken it out; it made no difference to her that you'd read every word in it and needed another to start. You could take out two books at a time and two only; this applied as long as you were a child and also for the rest of your life, to my mother as severely as to me. So, two by two, I read library books as fast as I could go, rushing them home in the basket of my bicycle. From the minute I reached our house, I started to read. Every book I seized on, from *Bunny Brown and His Sister Sue at Camp Rest-a-While* to *Twenty Thousand Leagues under the Sea,* stood for the devouring wish to read being instantly granted. I knew this was bliss, I knew it at the time. Taste isn't nearly so important; it comes in its own time. I wanted to read *immediately.* The only fear was that of books coming to an end.

Analysis: Capturing a Moment in the Past

One of the striking features of this excerpt from *One Writer's Beginnings* is how Eudora Welty uses a few telling details to bring to life the encounter in the Jackson library when Welty's mother introduces her to Mrs. Calloway and explains what Eudora as a nine-year-old will be permitted to read. The interaction has the immediacy of an event involving three characters in a short story or novel. Notice how Welty sketches the scene in the opening paragraph and portrays Mrs. Calloway in the second and third paragraphs, setting the stage for the entrance of Welty's presence as the witness and narrator at the end of paragraph three.

⇨ FOR CRITICAL INQUIRY ||||||||||||||||||||||||||||||||||||||||||||||||||||||||||||||||||||||||||||

1. Notice how this excerpt from *One Writer's Beginnings* takes place almost entirely in the past tense. As readers, we see things for the most part from the perspective of Eudora Welty experiencing events as a nine-year-old. There are points, however, where Welty's perspective as witness and narrator seems to shift to the present looking back on the past. Identify where such moments take place. What is the effect of these shifts from past to present on us as readers?

2. In addition to the immediacy of events in this excerpt, there is also a certain intimacy assumed on the author's part as Welty addresses readers routinely as "you." Consider exactly who that "you" is meant to be. Notice that Welty is not exactly addressing you or me or any other reader as our individual and separate selves. Instead she has something else in mind when she writes of a "you" who "came in from the bright outside" and who "could not take back a book to the Library on the same day you'd taken it out." Consider exactly who and what the "you" is that Welty has invented for us to inhabit as readers.

3. This short excerpt could be read along with the selections from Frederick Douglass, Russell Cruz, and Stacy Yi in Chapter 1 as a literacy narrative. Use the three parts of Question 1 in the For Critical Inquiry section, p. 24, to analyze what happens as a literacy event. What does this bring to light about the excerpt?

Fortunate Son

Dave Marsh

....

Dave Marsh is a rock-and-roll critic and DJ on two Sirius music shows, "Kick Out the Jams" and "Live from E Street Nation," and political talk show host of "Land of Hopes and Dreams," also on Sirius. He has published books on Bruce Springsteen, Elvis Presley, George Clinton and Parliament-Funkadelic, and the Beatles, among others. This memoir appeared as the introduction to a collection of Marsh's shorter critical essays and reviews, Fortunate Son *(1983).*

Introduction

I

> *This old town is where I learned about lovin'*
> *This old town is where I learned to hate*
> *This town, buddy, has done its share of shoveling*
> *This town taught me that it's never too late*
> —*Michael Stanley, "My Town"*

When I was a boy, my family lived on East Beverly Street in Pontiac, Michigan, in a two-bedroom house with blue-white asphalt shingles that cracked at the edges when a

---

ball was thrown against them and left a powder like talc on fingers rubbed across their shallow grooves. East Beverly ascended a slowly rising hill. At the very top, a block and a half from our place, Pontiac Motors Assembly Line 16 sprawled for a mile or so behind a fenced-in parking lot.

Rust-red dust collected on our windowsills. It piled up no matter how often the place was dusted or cleaned. Fifteen minutes after my mother was through with a room, that dust seemed thick enough for a finger to trace pointless, ashy patterns in it.

The dust came from the foundry on the other side of the assembly line, the foundry that spat angry cinders into the sky all night long. When people talked about hell, I imagined driving past the foundry at night. From the street below, you could see the fires, red-hot flames shaping glowing metal.

Pontiac was a company town, nothing less. General Motors owned most of the land, and in one way or another held mortgages on the rest. Its holdings included not only the assembly line and the foundry but also a Fisher Body plant and on the outskirts, General Motors Truck and Coach. For a while, some pieces of Frigidaires may even have been put together in our town, but that might just be a trick of my memory, which often confuses the tentacles of institutions that monstrous.

In any case, of the hundred thousand or so who lived in Pontiac, fully half must have been employed either by GM or one of the tool-and-die shops and steel warehouses and the like that supplied it. And anybody who earned his living locally in some less directly auto-related fashion was only fooling himself if he thought of independence.

My father worked without illusions, as a railroad brakeman on freight trains that shunted boxcars through the innards of the plants, hauled grain from up north, transported the finished Pontiacs on the first leg of the route to almost anywhere Bonnevilles, Catalinas, and GTOs were sold.

Our baseball and football ground lay in the shadow of another General Motors building. That building was of uncertain purpose, at least to me. What I can recall of it now is a seemingly reckless height—five or six stories is a lot in the flatlands around the Great Lakes—and endless walls of dark greenish glass that must have run from floor to ceiling in the rooms inside. Perhaps this building was an engineering facility. We didn't know anyone who worked there, at any rate.

Like most other GM facilities, the green glass building was surrounded by a chain link fence with barbed wire. If a ball happened to land on the other side of it, this fence was insurmountable. But only very strong boys could hit a ball that high, that far, anyhow.

Or maybe it just wasn't worth climbing that particular fence. Each August, a few weeks before the new models were officially presented in the press, the finished Pontiacs were set out in the assembly-line parking lot at the top of our street. They were covered by tarpaulins to keep their design changes secret—these were the years when the appearance of American cars changed radically each year. Climbing *that* fence was a neighborhood sport because that was how you discovered what the new cars looked like, whether fins were shrinking or growing, if the new hoods were pointed or flat, how much thinner the strips of whitewall on the tires had grown. A weird game, since everyone knew people who could have told us, given us exact descriptions, having built those cars with their own hands. But climbing that fence added a hint of danger, made us feel we shared a secret, turned gossip into information.

The main drag in our part of town was Joslyn Road. It was where the stoplight and crossing guard were stationed, where the gas station with the condom machine stood alongside a short-order restaurant, drugstore, dairy store, small groceries and a bakery. A few blocks down, past the green glass building, was a low brick building set back behind a wide, lush lawn. This building, identified by a discreet roadside sign, occupied a long block or two. It was the Administration Building for all of Pontiac Motors—a building for executives, clerks, white-collar types. This building couldn't have been more than three-quarters of a mile from my house, yet even though I lived on East Beverly Street from the time I was two until I was past fourteen, I knew only one person who worked there.

In the spring of 1964, when I was fourteen and finishing eighth grade, rumors started going around at Madison Junior High. All the buildings on our side of Joslyn Road (possibly east or west of Joslyn, but I didn't know directions then—there was only "our" side and everywhere else) were about to be bought up and torn down by GM. This was worrisome, but it seemed to me that our parents would never allow that perfectly functioning neighborhood to be broken up for no good purpose.

One sunny weekday afternoon a man came to our door. He wore a coat and tie and a white shirt, which meant something serious in our part of town. My father greeted him at the door, but I don't know whether the businessman had an appointment. Dad was working the extra board in those years, which meant he was called to work erratically—four or five times a week, when business was good—each time his nameplate came to the top of the big duty-roster board down at the yard office. (My father didn't get a regular train of his own to work until 1966; he spent almost twenty years on that extra board, which meant guessing whether it was safe to answer the phone every time he actually wanted a day off—refuse a call and your name went back to the bottom of the list.)

At any rate, the stranger was shown to the couch in our front room. He perched on that old gray davenport with its wiry fabric that bristled and stung against my cheek, and spoke quite earnestly to my parents. I recall nothing of his features or of the precise words he used or even of the tone of his speech. But the dust motes that hung in the air that day are still in my memory, and I can remember his folded hands between his spread knees as he leaned forward in a gesture of complicity. He didn't seem to be selling anything; he was simply stating facts.

He told my father that Pontiac Motors was buying up all the houses in our community from Tennyson Street, across from the green glass building, to Baldwin Avenue—exactly the boundaries of what I'd have described as our neighborhood. GM's price was more than fair; it doubled what little money my father had paid in the early fifties. The number was a little over ten thousand dollars. All the other houses were going, too; some had already been sold. The entire process of tearing our neighborhood down would take about six months, once all the details were settled.

The stranger put down his coffee cup, shook hands with my parents and left. As far as I know, he never darkened our doorstep again. In the back of my mind, I can still see him through the front window cutting across the grass to go next door.

"Well, *we're* not gonna move, right, Dad?" I said. Cheeky as I was, it didn't occur to me this wasn't really a matter for adult decision-making—or rather, that the real adults, over at the Administration Building, had already made the only decision that counted. Nor did it occur to me that GM's offer might seem to my father an opportunity to sell at a nice profit, enabling us to move some place "better."

My father did not say much. No surprise. In a good mood, he was the least taciturn man alive, but on the farm where he was raised, not many words were needed to get a serious job done. What he did say that evening indicated that we might stall awhile— perhaps there would be a slightly better offer if we did. But he exhibited no doubt that we would sell. And move.

I was shocked. There was no room in my plans for this . . . rupture. Was the demolition of our home and neighborhood—that is, my life—truly inevitable? Was there really no way we could avert it, cancel it, *delay* it? What if we just plain *refused to sell*?

Twenty years later, my mother told me that she could still remember my face on that day. It must have reflected extraordinary distress and confusion, for my folks were patient. If anyone refused to sell, they told me, GM would simply build its parking lot—for that was what would replace my world—around him. If we didn't sell, we'd have access privi- leges, enough space to get into our driveway and that was it. No room to play, and no one there to play with if there had been. And if you got caught in such a situation and didn't like it, then you'd really be in a fix, for the company wouldn't keep its double-your-money offer open forever. If we held out too long, who knew if the house would be worth any- thing at all. (I don't imagine that my parents attempted to explain to me the political proc- ess of condemnation, but if they had, I would have been outraged, for in a way, I still am.)

My dreams always pictured us as holdouts, living in a little house surrounded by asphalt and automobiles. I always imagined nighttime with the high, white-light towers that illuminated all the other GM parking lots shining down upon our house—and the little guardhouse that the company would have to build and man next door to prevent me from escaping our lot to run playfully among the parked cars of the multitudinous employees. Anyone reading this must find it absurd, or the details heavily derivative of bad concentration-camp literature or maybe too influenced by the Berlin Wall, which had been up only a short time. But it would be a mistake to dismiss its romanticism, which was for many months more real to me than the ridiculous reality—moving to accommodate a *parking lot*—which confronted my family and all my friends' families.

If this story were set in the Bronx or in the late sixties, or if it were fiction, the next scenes would be of pickets and protests, meaningful victories and defeats. But this isn't fiction—everything set out here is as unexaggerated as I know how to make it—and the time and the place were wrong for any serious uproar. In this docile Midwestern company town, where Walter Reuther's trip to Russia was as inexplicable as the parting of the Red Sea (or as forgotten as the Ark of the Covenant), the idea that a neighborhood might have rights that superseded those of General Motors' Pontiac division would have been regarded as extraordinary, bizarre and subversive. Presuming anyone had had such an idea, which they didn't—none of my friends seemed particularly disturbed about moving, it was just what they would *do*.

So we moved, and what was worse, to the suburbs. This was catastrophic to me. I loved the city, its pavement and the mobility it offered even to kids too young to drive. (Some attitude for a Motor City kid, I know.) In Pontiac, feet or a bicycle could get you anywhere. Everyone had cars, but you weren't immobilized without them, as everyone under sixteen was in the suburbs. In the suburb to which we adjourned, cars were *the* fundamental of life—many of the streets in our new subdivision (not really a neighborhood) didn't even have sidewalks.

Even though I'd never been certain of fitting in, in the city I'd felt close to figuring out how to. Not that I was that weird. But I was no jock and certainly neither suave nor graceful. Still, toward the end of eighth grade, I'd managed to talk to a few girls, no small feat. The last thing I needed was new goals to fathom, new rules to learn, new friends to make.

So that summer was spent in dread. When school opened in the autumn, I was already in a sort of cocoon, confused by the Beatles with their paltry imitations of soul music and the bizarre emotions they stirred in girls.

Meeting my classmates was easy enough, but then it always is. Making new friends was another matter. For one thing, the kids in my new locale weren't the same as the kids in my classes. I was an exceptionally good student (quite by accident—I just read a lot) and my neighbors were classic underachievers. The kids in my classes were hardly creeps, but they weren't as interesting or as accessible as the people I'd known in my old neighborhood or the ones I met at the school bus stop. So I kept to myself.

In our new house, I shared a room with my brother at first. We had bunk beds, and late that August I was lying sweatily in the upper one, listening to the radio (WPON-AM, 1460) while my mother and my aunt droned away in the kitchen.

Suddenly my attention was riveted by a record. I listened for two or three minutes more intently than I have ever listened and learned something that remains all but indescribable. It wasn't a new awareness of music. I liked rock and roll already, had since I first saw Elvis when I was six, and I'd been reasonably passionate about the Ronettes, Gary

Bonds, Del Shannon, the Crystals, Jackie Wilson, Sam Cooke, the Beach Boys and those first rough but sweet notes from Motown: the Miracles, the Temptations, Eddie Holland's "Jamie." I can remember a rainy night when I tuned in a faraway station and first heard the end of the Philadelphia Warriors' game in which Wilt Chamberlain scored a hundred points and then found "Let's Twist Again" on another part of the dial. And I can remember not knowing which experience was more splendid.

But the song I heard that night wasn't a new one. "You Really Got a Hold on Me" had been a hit in 1963, and I already loved Smokey Robinson's voice, the way it twined around impossibly sugary lines and made rhymes within the rhythms of ordinary conversation, within the limits of everyday vocabulary.

But if I'd heard those tricks before, I'd never understood them. And if I'd enjoyed rock and roll music previously, certainly it had never grabbed me in quite this way: as a lifeline that suggested—no, insisted—that these singers spoke *for* me as well as to me, and that what they felt and were able to cope with, the deep sorrow, remorse, anger, lust and compassion that bubbled beneath the music, I would also be able to feel and contain. This intimate revelation was what I gleaned form those three minutes of music, and when they were finished and I climbed out of that bunk and walked out the door, the world looked different. No longer did I feel quite so powerless, and if I still felt cheated, I felt capable of getting my own back, some day, some way.

Trapped

II

That last year in Pontiac, we listened to the radio a lot. My parents always had. One of my most shattering early memories is of the radio blasting when they got up—my mother around four-thirty, my father at five. All of my life I've hated early rising, and for years I couldn't listen to country music without being reminded almost painfully of those days.

But in 1963 and 1964, we also listened to WPON in the evening for its live coverage of city council meetings. Pontiac was beginning a decade of racial crisis, of integration pressure and white resistance, the typical scenario. From what was left of our old neighborhood came the outspokenly racist militant anti-school busing movement.

The town had a hard time keeping the shabby secret of its bigotry even in 1964. Pontiac had mushroomed as a result of massive migration during and after World War II. Some of the new residents, including my father, came from nearby rural areas where blacks were all but unknown and even the local Polish Catholics were looked upon as aliens potentially subversive to the community's Methodist piety.

Many more of the new residents of Pontiac came from the South, out of the dead ends of Appalachia and the border states. As many must have been black as white, though it was hard for me to tell that as a kid. There were lines one didn't cross in Michigan, and if I was shocked, when visiting Florida, to see separate facilities labeled "White" and "Colored," as children we never paid much mind to the segregated schools, the lily-white suburbs, the way that jobs in the plants were divided up along race lines. The ignorance and superstition about blacks in my neighborhood were as desperate and crazed in their own way as the feelings in any kudzu-covered parish of Louisiana.

As blacks began to assert their rights, the animosity was not less, either. The polarization was fueled and fanned by the fact that so many displaced Southerners, all with the poor white's investment in racism, were living in our community. But it would be foolish to pretend that the situation would have been any more civilized if only the natives had been around. In fact the Southerners were often regarded with nearly as much condescension and antipathy as blacks—race may have been one of the few areas in which my parents found themselves completely in sympathy with the "hillbillies."

Racism was the great trap of such men's lives, for almost everything could be explained by it, from unemployment to the deterioration of community itself. Casting racial blame did much more than poison these people's entire concept of humanity, which would have been plenty bad enough. It immobilized the racist, preventing folks like my father from ever realizing the real forces that kept their lives tawdry and painful and forced them to fight every day to find any meaning at all in their existence. It did this to Michigan factory workers as effectively as it ever did it to dirt farmers in Dixie.

The great psychological syndrome of American males is said to be passive aggression, and racism perfectly fit this mold. To the racist, hatred of blacks gave a great feeling of power and superiority. At the same time, it allowed him the luxury of wallowing in self-pity at the great conspiracy of rich bastards and vile niggers that enforced workaday misery and let the rest of the world go to hell. In short, racism explained everything. There was no need to look any further than the cant of redneck populism, exploited as effectively in the orange clay of the Great Lakes as in the red dirt of Georgia, to find an answer to why it was always the *next* generation that was going to get up and out.

Some time around 1963, a local attorney named Milton Henry, a black man, was elected to Pontiac's city council. Henry was smart and bold—he would later become an ally of Martin Luther King, Jr., of Malcolm X, a principal in the doomed Republic of New Africa. The goals for which Henry was campaigning seem extremely tame now, until you realize the extent to which they *haven't* been realized in twenty years: desegregated schools, integrated housing, a chance at decent jobs.

Remember that Martin Luther King would not take his movement for equality into the North for nearly five more years, and that when he did, Dr. King there faced the most strident and violent opposition he'd ever met, and you will understand how inflammatory the mere presence of Milton Henry on the city council was. Those council sessions, broadcast live on WPON, invested the radio with a vibrancy and vitality that television could never have had. Those hours of imprecations, shouts and clamor are unforgettable. I can't recall specific words or phrases, though, just Henry's eloquence and the pandemonium that greeted each of his speeches.

So our whole neighborhood gathered round its radios in the evenings, family by family, as if during wartime. Which in a way I guess it was—surely that's how the situation was presented to the children, and not only in the city. My Pontiac junior high school was lightly integrated, and kids in my new suburban town had the same reaction as my Floridian cousins: shocked that I'd "gone to school with niggers," they vowed they would die—or kill—before letting the same thing happen to them.

This cycle of hatred didn't immediately elude me. Thirteen-year-olds are built to buck the system only up to a point. So even though I didn't dislike any of the blacks I met (it could hardly be said that I was given the opportunity to *know* any), it was taken for granted that the epithets were essentially correct. After all, anyone could see the grave poverty in which most blacks existed, and the only reason ever given for it was that they liked living that way.

But listening to the radio gave free play to one's imagination. Listening to music, that most abstract of human creations, unleashed it all the more. And not in a vacuum. Semiotics, the New Criticism, and other formalist approaches have never had much appeal to me, not because I don't recognize their validity in describing certain creative structures but because they emphasize those structural questions without much consideration of content: And that simply doesn't jibe with my experience of culture, especially popular culture.

The best example is the radio of the early 1960s. As I've noted, there was no absence of rock and roll in those years betwixt the outbreaks of Presley and Beatles. Rock and roll was a constant for me, the best music around, and I had loved it ever since I first heard it, which was about as soon as I could remember hearing anything.

In part, I just loved the sound—the great mystery one could hear welling up from "Duke of Earl," "Up on the Roof," "Party Lights"; that pit of loneliness and despair that lay barely concealed beneath the superficial bright spirits of a record like Bruce Channel's "Hey Baby"; the nonspecific terror hidden away in Del Shannon's "Runaway." But if that was all there was to it, then rock and roll records would have been as much an end in themselves—that is, as much a dead end—as TV shows like *Leave It to Beaver* (also mysterious, also—thanks to Eddie Haskell—a bit terrifying).

To me, however, TV was clearly an alien device, controlled by the men with shirts and ties. Nobody on television dressed or talked as the people in my neighborhood did. In rock and roll, however, the language spoken was recognizably my own. And since one of the givens of life in the outlands was that we were barbarians, who produced no culture and basically consumed only garbage and trash, the thrill of discovering depths within rock and roll, the very part that was most often and explicitly degraded by teachers and pundits, was not only marvelously refreshing and exhilarating but also in essence liberating—once you'd made the necessary connections.

It was just at this time that pop music was being revolutionized—not by the Beatles, arriving from England, a locale of certifiable cultural superiority, but by Motown, arriving from Detroit, a place without even a hint of cultural respectability. Produced by Berry Gordy, not only a young man but a *black* man. And in that spirit of solidarity with which hometown boys (however unalike) have always identified with one another, Motown was mine in a way that no other music up to that point had been. Surely no one spoke my language as effectively as Smokey Robinson, able to string together the most humdrum phrases and effortlessly make them sing.

That's the context in which "You Really Got a Hold on Me" created my epiphany. You can look at this coldly—structurally—and see nothing more than a naked marketing mechanism, a clear-cut case of a teenager swaddled in and swindled by pop culture. Smokey Robinson wrote and sang the song as much to make a buck as to express himself; there was nothing of the purity of the mythical artist about his endeavor. In any case, the emotion he expressed was unfashionably sentimental. In releasing the record, Berry Gordy was mercenary in both instinct and motivation. The radio station certainly hoped for nothing more from playing it than that its listeners would hang in through the succeeding block of commercials. None of these people and institutions had any intention of elevating their audience, in the way that Leonard Bernstein hoped to do in his *Young People's Concerts* on television. Cultural indoctrination was far from their minds. Indeed, it's unlikely that anyone involved in the process thought much about the kids on the other end of the line except as an amorphous mass of ears and wallets. The pride Gordy and Robinson had in the quality of their work was private pleasure, not public.

Smokey Robinson was not singing of the perils of being a black man in this world (though there were other rock and soul songs that spoke in guarded metaphors about such matters). Robinson was not expressing an experience as alien to my own as a country blues singer's would have been. Instead, he was putting his finger firmly upon a crucial feeling of vulnerability and longing. It's hard to think of two emotions that a fourteen-year-old might feel more deeply (well, there's lust . . .), and yet in my hometown expressing them was all but absolutely forbidden to men. This doubled the shock of Smokey Robinson's voice, which for years I've thought of as falsetto, even though it really isn't exceptionally high-pitched compared to the spectacular male sopranos of rock and gospel lore.

"You Really Got a Hold on Me" is not by any means the greatest song Smokey Robinson ever wrote or sang, not even the best he had done up to that point. The singing on "Who's Loving You," the lyrics of "I'll Try Something New," the yearning of "What's So Good About Goodbye" are all at least as worthy. Nor is there anything especially new-fangled about the song. Its trembling blues guitar, sturdy drum pattern, walking bass and call-and-response voice arrangement are not very different from many of the other Miracles records of that period. If there is a single instant in the record which is unforgettable by itself, it's probably the opening lines: "I don't like you/But I love you . . ."

The contingency and ambiguity expressed in those two lines and Robinson's singing of them was also forbidden in the neighborhood of my youth, and forbidden as part and parcel of the same philosophy that propounded racism. Merely calling the bigot's certainty into question was revolutionary—not merely rebellious. The depth of feeling in that Miracles record, which could have been purchased for 69¢ at any K-Mart, overthrew the premise of racism, which was that blacks were not as human as we, that they could not feel—much less express their feelings—as deeply as we did.

When the veil of racism was torn from my eyes, everything else that I knew or had been told was true for fourteen years was necessarily called into question. For if racism explained everything, then without racism, not a single commonplace explanation made any sense. *Nothing* else could be taken at face value. And that meant asking every question once again, including the banal and obvious ones.

For those who've never been raised under the weight of such addled philosophy, the power inherent in having the burden lifted is barely imaginable. Understanding that blacks weren't worthless meant that maybe the rest of the culture in which I was raised was also valuable. If you've never been told that you and your community are worthless—that a parking lot takes precedence over your needs—perhaps that moment of insight seems trivial or rather easily won. For anyone who was never led to expect a life any more difficult than one spent behind a typewriter, maybe the whole incident verges on being something too banal for repetition (though in that case, I'd like to know where the other expressions of this story can be read). But looking over my shoulder, seeing the consequences to my life had I not begun questioning not just racism but all of the other presumptions that ruled our lives, I know for certain how and how much I got over.

That doesn't make me better than those on the other side of the line. On the other hand, I won't trivialize the tale by insisting upon how fortunate I was. What was left for me was a raging passion to explain things in the hope that others would not be trapped and to keep the way clear so that others from the trashy outskirts of barbarous America still had a place to stand—if not in the culture at large, at least in rock and roll.

Of course it's not so difficult to dismiss this entire account. Great revelations and insights aren't supposed to emerge from listening to rock and roll records. They're meant to emerge only from encounters with art. (My encounters with Western art music were unavailing, of course, because every one of them was prefaced by a lecture on the insipid and worthless nature of the music that I preferred to hear.) Left with the fact that what happened to me did take place, and that it was something that was supposed to come only out of art, I reached the obvious conclusion. You are welcome to your own.

Analysis: Setting Up a Moment of Revelation

Dave Marsh divides this piece of writing into two parts. Part I tells the story of why Marsh's family moved from Pontiac to the suburbs, but Part II returns to Pontiac before the move took place, to dwell there a little longer so that Marsh can draw out the meaning of the place in the fateful years 1963 and 1964. Notice how Marsh's return to Pontiac amounts to a reframing of his experience growing up in Pontiac that depends on what we've learned in Part I but that sets the stage for the memoir's moment of revelation—"the context," as Marsh says, "in which 'You Really Got a Hold on Me' created my epiphany."

⇨ FOR CRITICAL INQUIRY

1. Dave Marsh uses the Smokey Robinson and the Miracles song "You Really Got a Hold on Me" to anchor his memoir and to provide the grounds for the "intimate revelation" or "epiphany" that Marsh sets up in Part I and then explains more fully in Part II. What exactly is this revelation and how does it emerge from Marsh's experience of listening to rock and roll?

2. Consider the shift in perspective that takes place as the memoir moves from Part I to Part II. How does Marsh position himself in relation to his experience growing up in Pontiac in each of the sections? How would you describe the relationship between these two perspectives?

3. At the end of the memoir, Marsh says, "I reached the obvious conclusion. You are welcome to your own." What is Marsh's conclusion? How does telling readers they are welcome to their own indicate the kind of relationship he is seeking to establish with his audience? Is he really suggesting that any conclusion is valid?

Teenage Angst in Texas

Gail Caldwell

Gail Caldwell was formerly the chief book critic at the Boston Globe *and won the Pulitzer Prize for Criticism in 2001. "Teenage Angst in Texas," which appeared in the* New York Times Magazine, *is adapted from her memoir* A Strong West Wind *(2006). She published a second memoir,* Let's Take the Long Way Home, *in 2010.*

In the mid-1960's, the wind-swept plains of the Texas Panhandle could be a languid prison for an adolescent girl with a wild spirit and no place to go. I buried myself in Philip Roth novels and little acts of outrage, and on lonesome afternoons, I would drive my mother's Chevrolet out onto the freeway and take it up to 90 m.p.h., smoking endless cigarettes and aching with ennui. I was bored by the idea of mainstream success and alienated from what the world seemed to offer—one of my poems from those days weighs heavily on the themes of coffins, societal hypocrisy and godlessness. And yet I cannot locate the precise source of my anger. For years I thought all teenagers were fueled by a high-octane mix of intensity and rage; I only know that what sent me onto the highways and into my own corridors of gloom was inexplicable to others and confusing to me.

Around this time my father began what I dismally thought of as our Sunday drives. As kids, my sister and I were bored but tolerant when we had to tag along on his treks, which were always aimless. But now his itinerary was to chart the path of my dereliction, and that meant getting me alone in the car so that we could "talk": about my imminent doom, about my mother's high blood pressure. Thus incarcerated, slouched in the shotgun seat with my arms folded against my chest, I responded to his every effort by either staring out the window or yelling back. I don't remember a word I said. What I still feel is the boulder on my heart—the amorphous gray of the world outside the car window, signaling how trapped I felt, by him and by the hopeless unawareness of my age.

My father, far more than I, seemed to sense that the country was raging, that it was a bad time to surrender your daughters to strange lands. But these things—a war somewhere far away, a civil rights movement over in the Deep South—belonged to the evening news, not to the more intimate treacheries of car rides and deceits and disappointments, and so were rarely addressed on any personal level, not yet. Instead we fought about curfews or bad boyfriends; we fought about straightening up and flying right. We fought about everything but the truth, which was that I would be leaving soon.

I had already seen two casualties claimed by history, men who were lighting out for the territory to avoid the 1-A draft notices they had just received. The first was a boy who stopped by the house to say goodbye a few days before leaving for Toronto. When the other young man disappeared, the federal authorities came sniffing around my high school, and I covered for him without a shred of hesitation. I told them I thought he went east, to his mother's in Missouri, when I knew it was the one place he would never go.

These losses and the lies they demanded frightened me, in vague and then inarticulable ways, about just who was in charge—about the dangers posed by the institutions that were supposed to keep you safe. It was difficult in those days to care much about the College Boards, or to think that the path in front of me would hold the traditional landscapes of marriage and family. In some ways the tempests of my adolescence had set me against myself; I'd found that introspection couldn't buy you love, that poetry helped only momentarily, that straight A's and spelling bees were no guarantee of knowing where to turn. Worse and more pervasive, I was maturing under the assumption that you should never let men know how smart you were, or how mouthy—a girl's intelligence, brazenly displayed, was seen as impolite, unfeminine and even threatening.

So I kept quiet; when I dated a boy who liked George Wallace, I rolled my eyes and looked out the window. The smarter you were, the more subversive you had to be. Girls could excel in English, say, or languages, as long as they didn't flaunt it or pretend to be superior to males. But God forbid they should try to carve a life out of such achievements. God forbid they display a pitcher's arm, or an affinity for chemistry or analytic prowess in an argument with a man.

In the end, my own revisionism was unconscious but thorough. I neglected anymore to mention the mysterious test, taken at age 7, that resulted in my skipping second grade. Toward the end of high school, I began lying to my peers about my high scores on placement exams, and I blew admission, with half-intention and private relief, into the National Honor Society. The summer before college, in 1968, I had to declare a major; I took a deep breath and wrote "mathematics" on my admission forms. And when friends asked me what I'd chosen, I lied about that too.

Analysis: Using Episodes

Instead of telling a story from her past in chronological order, from start to finish, Gail Caldwell brings together a series of episodes to re-create a sense of what her life was like as a teenager in the Texas Panhandle during the mid-1960s. Notice how she moves from one episode to another—driving 90 miles an hour, the rides with her father, the two young men fleeing the military draft, how she lied about the major she wrote on her college admissions forms. Notice also how the episodes are arranged to work together, creating a moment in time that enables readers to see an individual life in the midst of historical events (the Vietnam War, the civil rights movement, the presidential campaign in 1968 of the segregationist George Wallace) and the cultural realities of the day (parent–child relations, pressures on young women).

⊃ FOR CRITICAL INQUIRY

1. How does Gail Caldwell establish her situation in the opening paragraph? Notice she says it was "inexplicable to others and confusing to me." By the time you get to the end of this brief memoir, what light has been shed on this confusion? How would you describe the arc of the memoir, from where it begins to where it ends?

2. How do the various episodes contribute to the memoir? How does Caldwell put them together? Examine the order she uses and the amount of explanation.

3. As is typical of memoirs, the writer is very much in the present looking at the past. What does Caldwell's attitude toward her past seem to be? How does this attitude compare to her state of mind in the past? How do these past and present perspectives shape the reader's experience of Caldwell's memoir?

The Ninth Letter of The Alphabet:
First-Person Strategies in Nonfiction

Richard Hoffman

....

Richard Hoffman is writer in residence at Emerson College and the author of Half the House: A Memoir *(2005),* Interference & Other Stories *(2009), and the poetry collections* Without Paradise *(2002),* Gold Star Road *(2007), and* Emblem *(2011).*

Even setting aside the naïve reader who believes that the process of writing a memoir is 1. having an interesting life, and 2. writing it down (that's what they always say to me after a reading or a panel: "One day I'm going to write it down"), there are many otherwise sophisticated readers who choose to believe that the memoir is a species of journalism, albeit gussied up with some techniques borrowed from fiction writers. It seem to me more accurate to see the memoir, as it has evolved, as a subgenre of the novel, a kind of first-person historical novel, a dramatic work that agrees to be bound by fact. What is being explored is not only what happened, but how one has remembered what happened, including the gaps in the story and one's lapses of memory. The contract with the reader one makes, by calling a work a memoir, i.e. nonfiction, is that you honor what actually took place and write about it, and about the process of remembering it, with honesty.

Although readers want the same pleasures (what Aristotle called delight and instruction) from a memoir as from a work of fiction, they approach the two very differently. I am more than willing to suspend my disbelief in order to be entranced by a work of fiction, but I approach a memoir, because it claims to be nonfiction, with a certain skepticism. A novel need only be consistent with its own imagined world. A memoir needs to be consistent with the world of facts and events that we share.

One more thing remains to be said before we begin a consideration of who or what is represented by the ninth letter of the alphabet. Here I want to issue a disclaimer, cautioning you to hold what I say here in a kind of suspension. The terms I'll be using, terms like, "the engaged I," "the reconstructed I," "the reminiscent I," are provisional terms of my own. There may be better names and, more to the point, other *kinds* of "I"s. We're not trying to create a filing system for ourselves as readers; rather we're trying, as readers, to look at the full potential of this most important and basic component of first-person narrative. It's better to think of these terms as refractions through a prism; besides, these various "I"s shade off into one another as we move from one part of a text to another. In most authors you'll find a tendency to shift through these different first-person strategies like moving through so many gears as the story's changing terrain makes different demands. Many authors primarily toggle back and forth between a couple of the possibilities while others use the full array. Let's have a look.

The engaged I: I want to start with a use of the first-person pronoun I call the "engaged I" because so many memoirists also start with it, and not because it is a primary kind of narration. It does have certain virtues, as we'll see in a moment, that are especially suitable for beginnings.

The "engaged I" makes overt editorial or political statements on behalf of a worldview, belief system, or social/political agenda. We see what the author is engaging in the work: injustice, ignorance, heresy, misunderstanding, life-threatening illness. It is often a bold statement of the reason for the work. Here, for example, is Maxim Gorky expressing his moral indignation and engagement with the issue of childhood poverty and cruelty:

> Sometimes when I recall the abominations of that barbarous Russian life I ask myself whether it is worthwhile to speak of them. And, with renewed conviction, I answer—yes, it is; for they are the vicious, tenacious truth, which has not been exterminated to this very day. They represent the truth which must be exposed to its roots and torn out of our grim and shameful life—torn out of the very soul and memory of man.
>
> Maxim Gorky, *Childhood*

Another kind of engagement is that of the writer with his material, with the labor to translate the vision to the page:

> Not long after our arrival, we went to a bookshop; she asked for an English-German grammar, bought the first book they showed her, took me home immediately, and began instruction. How can I depict that instruction believably? I know how it went—how could I forget?—but still I can't believe it myself.
>
> Elias Canetti, *The Tongue Set Free*

What's more, because every memoir, on one level, is also about the act of remembering, this "engaged I" sometimes struggles with memory itself:

> I am sorry to be so vague, especially because I am proud of my good memory, and many have remarked upon it, but all I can remember is sitting on my one suitcase (I travel light) and waiting for hours to get going. Anywhere.
> Neither can I remember how I got to the pier, although obviously it was on the boat from Paris.
>
> Mary Cantwell, *Speaking with Strangers*

So, what I'm calling "the engaged I" appears most often early in the story, in the first chapter or even the prologue to a memoir, and then gives up its place to "the reminiscent

I," "the reconstructed I," and others we'll talk about in a moment. Because "the engaged I" is often didactic, a little of its use goes a long way. Too much or too often and you're haranguing your reader who, even if he or she agrees with your view, is no longer in the thrall of your storytelling.

The reminiscent I invites us to accompany the narrator in her remembering. The simplest form of this is a sentence that begins, "I remember . . . ," or, "I recall . . . ." Here the narrator views the past at least mostly from the vantage of the present. In any case, this "reminiscent I" straddles two time frames—one foot in the present, one in the past. It is the most usual, probably because it is the most natural, form of the first-person that memoirists use.

> When I first sat down in that great sea of tedium I thought somebody at the *Times* was trying to make me feel humble about working for the paper that printed all the news that was fit to print. Everything seemed aimed at making me feel like the smallest fish in the biggest pond on earth.
>
> Russell Baker, *The Good Times*

The reconstructed I is often introduced by "the reminiscent I," as a way of establishing the time, place, and particulars needed in order to enter into the reconstructed consciousness of the narrator in an earlier time.

Almost all of Frank McCourt's *Angela's Ashes* is written from the reconstructed vantage of a young boy. Nothing young Frankie could not know is recorded, whether because he couldn't have seen it or because he couldn't have understood it; though, as we'll see, much that the boy could not know is nonetheless communicated. When we narrate in the reconstructed voice and consciousness of a child, accepting those bounds, we rely on the reader to interpret and or interpolate things in a way the child cannot. This gap between what the child experiences but cannot understand, or misunderstands, and what the reader, once a child himself, *now* understands can be, in skillful hands, an irresistible invitation to empathy, whether with joy or suffering.

Even when "the reconstructed I" is not the remembered/imagined voice of a child, but the representation of the self in an earlier period, it gives the writer the opportunity to play a scene from the past against some knowledge of what has happened since then, thus involving the reader by engaging her own historical experience. Take, for example, the holocaust memoir of Primo Levi, which derives at least some of its power from the fact that both "the reminiscent I" and the reader know full well the horrors to come that "the reconstructed I," the younger first-person narrator, speaking from within an earlier time-frame, cannot.

> Now another German comes and tells us to put the shoes in a certain corner, and we put them there, because now it is all over and we feel outside the world and the only thing is to obey. Someone comes with a broom and sweeps away all the shoes,

outside the door in a heap. He is crazy, he is mixing them all together, ninety-six pairs, they will all be unmatchable.

Primo Levi, *Survival in Auschwitz*

The self-regarding I is the I interrogating and exploring itself within a specific time-frame. A memoir that doesn't catch the first-person narrator, at whatever age, being self-conscious, hesitant, unsure, is not being honest about the complexity of the self. In other words, if I am to trust the narrator in the present, I need to see him being honest about his or her motives and mistakes and confusions and shortcoming, perhaps even at some cost to our estimation of him.

I hate to say it, but hearing Frank's stories, I became grateful my father died when I was still young before my own hopes got in his way. I say it in part because I'm glad I never had to fight with him, never got stepped on in the way my brothers did. I also say it because I know the range of my own anger and determination, and my own awful, unswerving stubbornness.

Mikal Gilmore, *Shot in the Heart*

The imagining I is fairly straightforward in announcing itself; usually it's heralded by the simple phrase, "I imagine," or "I imagined," although sometimes, for effect, the writer may prefer to let this realization sneak up on the reader.

This is a simple and useful tool for filling in gaps in the story. You either remember what you imagined to be the case when you were a certain age, or you announce "I imagine . . . now," meaning that you acknowledge the limits of your knowledge as a writer, and that you're going to give us the following scene courtesy of your imagination.

In the hospital room as my father told it all to me I could see the journey through his eyes: Mrs. Macek moving before him, her shoulders resolute, and before her the tall figure of Dr. Macek and more distantly, the moving shadow of Pisa. The forest floor and the mountain fields were a combination of snow, puddles and mud, and it was cold and raw. Sometimes at the edge of the snowy meadows, they could see footprints where the border patrol had just been.

Joseph Hurka, *Fields of Light*

The documentary I is an EYE, really, and not much else. This may be the eye, view, or vantage of a "reconstructed I" but it is different in the intensity of its connection to what is going on. This is a narrator who is at one remove from the scene, watching, and not filtering what's seen through any feelings or interpretations. It is as if the camera is on the shoulder of the narrator, merely recording what is visible as she walks on the street, stands in a room, watches and listens. What the reader gets is the place, the events, the other people. The "documentary I" gets its power from the complete lack of commentary, and from a tight focus and careful selection of what's being shown to us.

Afghan rugs. In the 1980s, Afghan rugs, which had drawn their designs from age-old tradition, developed new patterns: helicopters and tanks.

Adam Zagajewski, Another Beauty

The men are drinking stout from bottles again and the women are sipping sherry from jam jars. Uncle Pat Sheehan tells everyone, This is my stout, this is my stout, and Grandma says, 'Tis all right, Pat. No one will take your stout. Then he says he wants to sing "The Road to Rasheen" till Pa Keating says, No, Pat, you can't sing on the day of the funeral. You can sing the night before. But Uncle Pat keeps saying. This is my stout and I want to sing "The Road to Rasheen," and everyone knows he talks like that because he was dropped on his head. He starts to sing his song but stops when Grandma takes the lid off the coffin and Mam sobs, Oh Jesus, oh, Jesus, will it ever stop? Will I be left with one child?

Frank McCourt, Angela's Ashes

Any first-person narrative, but particularly memoir with its insistence on at least the subjective veracity (i.e. *honesty*) of the tale it tells must engage the reader on several levels to be successful. The memoirist, like the novelist, must take pains to create a multifaceted, emotionally three-dimensional character whose name is I. He or she must be continually aware of the gap between what the narrator knows, what the reader knows, and what the character—I—knows, and how to make use of those understandings to create trust and empathy in the reader. Making use of a number of first-person strategies gives a story complexity, texture, and authenticity, and results in a dramatic work that will satisfy even the most sophisticated reader.

Analysis: First-Person Strategies

Richard Hoffman's catalog of first-person strategies in memoir writing offers insight into the variety of ways memoirists present their own experience through acts of remembering. These are not simply tricks of the trade but figure more consequentially, as Hoffman notes, in determining the relationship between the memoirist and readers, in eliciting empathy, trust, and identification. In this sense, Hoffman's "provisional" categories enable us to see how the "contract with the reader one makes" takes shape in memoirs.

▷ FOR CRITICAL INQUIRY

1. Consider the memoirs that appear in this chapter in terms of the first-person strategies employed. You may not find examples of all the categories Hoffman presents, but see whether you can identify a number of them. What functions do they perform in the context of specific memoirs?

2. Hoffman makes the point that memoirs depend, at least in part, on gaining the trust of readers. Pick one or two memoirs in this chapter and explain how the memoirist seeks to gain the reader's trust and the extent to which you think he or she is successful.

3. Consider Hoffman's idea that there are actually three kinds of knowledge in memoirs— "what the narrator knows, what the reader knows, and what the character—I—knows." Pick one of the memoirs that illustrates the three types of knowledge and explain why and how there is a gap between them.

MULTIMODAL COMPOSITION

Audio Memoirs: StoryCorps

StoryCorps is a nonprofit public service project to record the stories of ordinary people. Since it began in 2003, over ten thousand people have recorded interviews of family and friends through StoryCorps. Those interviewed get a free CD, and their stories also appear regularly on National Public Radio and are archived at the Library of Congress, creating what has become a vast oral history of everyday Americans recalling important moments in their lives. In this sense, StoryCorps is a kind of audio memoir project, to encourage people to record their memories as part of a collective portrait. Visit the StoryCorps Web site www.storycorps.org to listen to some of the stories. Consider to what extent they resemble written memoirs in terms of looking at the past from the perspective of the present. Is there a sense that those interviewed invent a first-person narrator, as memoirists typically do? Is there a moment of revelation?

Graphic Memoirs: Harvey Pekar, *American Splendor*

Graphic memoirs go back to 1976 and the appearance of Harvey Pekar's *American Splendor* comic books, which he wrote and comic artists such as R. Crumb, Joe Sacco, Greg Budgett, and Gary Dumm illustrated. Art Spiegelman's *Maus: A Survivor's Tale* appeared in two volumes, *My Father Bleeds History* (1986) and *Here My Troubles*

StoryBooth in Grand Central Station, New York City, where StoryCorps began in 2003.

MobileBooths have recorded stories in more than 100 cities in 48 states.

Begin (1991), combining memoir, biography, and history. Since then, there has been a proliferation of graphic memoirs, including Marjane Satrapi's *Persepolis* (2003) and *Persepolis 2* (2004) and Parsua Bashi's *Nylon Road* (2009) about growing up in Iran; Alison Bechdel's *Fun Home: A Family Tragicomic* (2006); G.B Tran's *Vietnamerica* (2011); and Chester Brown's controversial *Paying for It: A Comic Strip Memoir About Being a John* (2011). Graphic memoirs offer interesting multimodal compositions that draw on the comic strip format to integrate word and image into what the comic theorist Scott McCloud calls "deliberate sequence." As you read the panels from *American Splendor,* notice how you participate in creating the narrative meaning by connecting the panels. Consider the effect of the two panels with no words. How would you describe the ethos of the Harvey Pekar character in *American Splendor*? Compare his persona to that of another main figure in a graphic memoir.

American Splendor, by Harvey Pekar, Ballantine Books, published by Random House © 1984

American Splendor, by Harvey Pekar, Ballantine Books, published by Random House © 1984

ETHICS OF WRITING

BEARING WITNESS

Part of a memoirist's authority derives from the fact of his or her having been an eyewitness to the events recounted. Memoirists are participants as well as observers. For these reasons, memoirists face some important ethical issues concerning their responsibility as witnesses to the past. How does the memoirist represent the other people involved? What are the memoirist's responsibilities to these people? What is the memoirist entitled to divulge about his or her private life? What are the memoirist's loyalties to those he or she writes about? Might such loyalties conflict with obligations to readers? What impact will the memoir have on the writer's relationship with others in the present, and does this potential impact affect the retelling? In cases where the memoirist feels hurt, angry, or offended by what took place, can he or she nonetheless be fair?

These are questions that memoirists invariably struggle with, and there are no easy answers, especially when a memoir treats situations that are difficult or painful. The memoir, don't forget, is an act of self-discovery, and yet memoirs are written for the public to read. As witnesses to the past, memoirists can handle their responsibility to others in an ethical way by seeking to understand the motives and character of those involved, including themselves.

FURTHER EXPLORATIONS

Rhetorical Analysis

Consider the writers' ethos in the memoirs you've just read. See "The Ninth Letter of the Alphabet: First-Person Strategies in Nonfiction" (pp. 140–144) for ideas about the various "I" speakers that appear in memoir. You can focus on one memoir or compare two or more. You might consider audio or graphic memoirs as well as print memoirs. In any case, how do the writers, speakers, or artists construct themselves as characters and as first-person narrators? Does the writer set up the relationship between herself as the memoir's narrator in the present and herself as a character in recollected experience from the past? How have the writers handled their ethical responsibility to others involved in the memoir? What kind of relationship do they want to establish with their readers?

Genre Awareness

Imagine you are going to turn one of the print memoirs in this chapter into a graphic memoir. Turn the opening three paragraphs into panels. How many would you need? What drawings and words would you put in them? How would you set up the transition from one panel to the next? Consider what this exercise reveals about the two types of memoir. What does the reliance on written text in the print memoir make possible? What does the combination of words and images in the graphic memoir make possible? What can each do that the other can't?

WRITING ASSIGNMENT

Memoir

Your task is to write a memoir, to bring to life a moment in the past in order to explore the meanings it has for the present. Because memoirs enable both writers and their readers to understand the past, this assignment can be a good time for you to probe significant times in your life, revisiting them now that you have some distance from them.

▶ Focus on an encounter with an authority figure, like the librarian Mrs. Calloway in Eudora Welty's memoir, or another revealing incident from your childhood, to create your own perspective as a younger person in the past, as well as your perspective as the narrator in the present.

▶ Use a pop song, as Dave Marsh does, to write a memoir about a time and place. Or use a TV show, film, video game, dance craze, clothes or hairstyle, or other aspect of the media or popular culture to focus your memoir in a time and place.

▶ Consider the tensions or conflicts you experienced in high school, as Gail Caldwell does.

▶ Pick a photograph that holds memories and emotional associations. Focus on a particular detail that recalls a particular moment in the past, to explore how your family's history intersects larger social and historical forces.

▶ Recall a particular family ritual, such as visits to grandparents, Sunday dinners, summer vacations, holiday celebrations, weddings, and so on, as a way to focus on an event or a person that is especially significant to you.

▶ Consider some aspect of your own cultural ancestry—whether it is the language your ancestors spoke, a kind of food or music, a family tradition, or an heirloom that has been passed down from generation to generation—to explain how the past has entered your life and what it reveals about your relationship to the culture of your ancestors.

▶ Look through an old diary or journal, if you have kept one. Look for moments when you faced an occasion that challenged your values or where you had a difficult decision to make, experienced a situation that turned out unexpectedly, or were keenly disappointed.

Multimodal Composition

▶ Write a short memoir that focuses on a single incident, and translate it into a graphic memoir. You do not need artistic talent for this assignment; you can draw stick figures if you wish. The purpose is to explore the differences between composing for word-only print texts and for comic book panels that use word and image. Then write a reflection on how the two compare in terms of what they enable you to do in bringing that moment from the past to light.

▶ Use StoryCorps as a model to record audio memoirs for a 15-minute radio broadcast. Consider the main theme of the program. It might focus, for example, on individual memories of life in a small town, being part of a particular generation (such as millennials, Generation X, baby boomers), or having lived through major historical events (such as the Vietnam War, 9/11, the election of Barack Obama). Design a radio broadcast that introduces the theme. Consider how you might use spoken word and music in an introduction that frames the memoirs.

Invention

Past and Present Perspectives

To clarify the purpose of your memoir and what you want it to mean to readers, consider what your feelings were at the moment things were taking place in the past and what they are now as you look back from the perspective of the present.

Considering the memory you're writing about from past and present perspectives can help you to clarify the double role of the memoir writer—as a participant and as an observer—and to decide what relative emphasis each of the two perspectives will take on in your memoir.

▷ EXERCISE

Exploring Past and Present Perspectives

Past perspective: Recall in as much detail as possible what your feelings were at the time you are writing about in your memoir. Spend five minutes or so responding to these questions in writing:

1. What was your initial reaction to the moment in the past you're writing about? What did you think at the time? How did you feel? What did other people seem to think and feel?

2. Did your initial reaction persist or did it change? If it changed, what set of feelings replaced it? What caused the change? Were other people involved in this change?

Present perspective: Now think about your present perspective. Write for another five minutes or so in response to these questions:

1. Looking back on the moment in the past, how do the feelings you experienced at the time appear to you today? Do they seem reasonable? Why or why not?

2. Have your feelings changed? Do things look different from the perspective of the present? If so, how would you explain the change?

3. As you compare your feelings from the past and your feelings in the present, what conclusions can you draw about the significance the memory has for you? Are your feelings resolved, or do they seem unsettled and changing? In either case, what do you think has shaped your current perspective?

Review the two writings: Use them to write a third statement that defines what you **see** as the significance of the memory you're writing about and what your purpose is in re-creating it for your readers. What does the memory reveal about the past? How do you want to present yourself in relation to what happened in the past? If there is conflict or crisis, what are your loyalties toward the people and the events?

Background Research: Putting Events in Context

As the memoirs by Dave Marsh and Gail Caldwell show, placing your memories and experiences in a larger cultural and historical context can add layers of meaning to the event or events you are telling. In this way, you can link your life with social trends and political events happening around you at the time.

You may want (or need) to look in the library and on the Internet for more help in responding to these questions. Check, for example, the *New York Times Index* for that particular year, or the *Facts on File Yearbook.* Weekly periodicals such as *Time, Newsweek,* and *U.S. News & World Report* have an end-of-year issue that can help provide cultural and historical perspectives.

Isolate the year in which your chosen event happened. In answering the following questions, you might need to ask family members or friends for their impressions, insights, and suggestions.

1. Was there anything remarkable about that year in the context of national and world events? Is that year "famous" for anything?

2. What was the "news story" of the year? What was the "success story" of the year? Who were the "heroes" that year?

3. What were the major social conflicts that year? Were there important political demonstrations or social movements in any part of the country? If so, what were they about? Were there any natural disasters that captured national attention that year?

4. Is there a generation associated with that year (World War II veterans, baby boomers, Generation X, millennials)?

5. What kind of music was most popular? What TV shows and movies?

Review your responses. What links, if any, can connect your own experience and the experiences of others at the historical moment you are considering? What cultural and historical contexts might be illuminating in your memoir?

Planning

Arranging Your Material

Memoir writers sometimes use chronology to tell their stories, going from start to finish in a linear way, using the passage of time as the ordering principle of the narrative. In other cases, such as Dave Marsh's "Fortunate Son," the narrative loops back on itself, as Marsh treats his experience growing up in Pontiac from more than one angle, returning in Part II to the last year in Pontiac that he has already described in Part I. Likewise, Gail Caldwell chooses not to use chronology but to present a sequence of episodes that work together, like a mosaic, to create a dominant impression of her teenage years in Texas:

¶1: Driving mother's car 90 miles an hour.

¶2–3: Rides with her father and "talks."

¶4: Two young men Caldwell knows flee to Canada to avoid the military draft.

¶6: Caldwell keeps quiet about George Wallace.

¶7: Caldwell blows admission to National Honor Society and lies about her major.

Here are some questions to help you design a working draft:

▶ **How will you begin?** Do you want to ease into the moment from the past or state it outright? How can you capture your readers' interest? Do you need to establish background information? How will you present yourself—as a participant in the past or as an observer from the perspective of the present? Consider the first-person strategies Richard Hoffman describes in "The Ninth Letter of the Alphabet."

▶ **What arrangement best suits your material?** If you are telling a single story, how can you keep the narrative crisp and moving? Do you need to interrupt the chronology with commentary, description, interpretation, or asides? If you are using selected incidents, what order best conveys the point you want them to make? Do the separate incidents create a dominant impression?

▶ **How will you set up the moment of revelation that gives your memoir its meaning and significance?** Do you want to anticipate this moment by foreshadowing, which gives readers a hint of the revelation that is to come? Or do you want it to appear suddenly?

▶ **How will you end your memoir?** Do you want to surprise readers with an unsuspected meaning? Or do you want to step back from what has taken place to reflect on its significance? Is there a way in which you can echo the opening of the memoir to make your readers feel they have come full circle?

Based on your answers to these questions, make a working outline of your memoir. If you're planning to tell a story from start to finish, indicate the key incidents in the event you're remembering. If you're planning to use a sequence of memories, block out the separate events. Then you can consider the best order to present them.

Selecting Detail

Memoirists often use techniques you can find in fiction: scene setting and description of people, action, and dialogue. These techniques enable memoirists (like fiction writers) to re-create the past in vivid and convincing detail. Designing a memoir (like fiction writing) involves decisions about the type and amount of detail you need to make your re-creation of the past memorable to readers.

▶ **Scene setting:** Use vivid and specific description to set the scene; name particular objects; give details about places and things; use description and detail to establish mood.

▶ **Description of people:** Use descriptions of people's appearances to highlight their personalities in your memoir; describe the clothes they are wearing; give details about a person's physical presence, gestures, facial features, and hairstyle; notice personal habits; use description and detail to establish character.

▶ **Dialogue:** Put words in your characters' mouths that reveal their personalities; invent dialogue that is faithful to people's ways of speaking (even if you don't use their exact words); use dialogue to establish relationships among characters.

▶ **Action:** Put the characters in your memoir in motion; use narrative to tell about something that happened; use narrative to develop characters and reveal the theme of your memoir.

Working Draft

Review the writing you have done so far. Consider the tentative decisions you've made about how to arrange your material—in chronological order or as a related sequence of events. As you begin composing a working draft of your memoir, you'll need to think about how you can best bring out the significance of your memories.

Beginnings and Endings: Locating Your Memoir

Location is a key component of memoirs. Notice how the three examples in this chapter don't simply set the scene where the memoir is going to take place but invest it with a mood:

▶ As the place—the public library—where "you" the reader and everybody who grows up in Jackson confront the fearsome presence of the librarian Mrs. Calloway in the excerpt from Eudora Welty's *One Writer's Beginnings*.

▶ As Pontiac, the company town, where the "rust-red dust" from the foundry that "spat angry cinders into the sky" signifies the presence of General Motors and how its "tentacles" seem to reach everywhere, in Dave Marsh's introduction to *Fortune Son*.

▶ And finally, how Gail Caldwell uses details from the "wind-swept plains of the Texas Panhandle" to create the psychological space of her memoir as a "high octane mix of intensity and rage" that sent her out onto the highway and into "my own corridors of gloom."

Peer Commentary

Once you've written a working draft, you are ready to get feedback from others. Before exchanging papers, work through the following exercise. Then, you can guide your partner or group members in how to best help you.

⤳ EXERCISE |||||||||||||||||||||||||||||||||||||||||||||||||||||||||||||||||||||||||||||||||||||||||||||||

Analyzing Your Draft

1. Write an account of your working draft.

   a. What made you want to write this memoir? Describe what you experienced as the call to write.

   b. What is your purpose in the working draft? What are you trying to reveal about the moment in the past? What significance does this moment hold for you?

   c. What problems or uncertainties do you see in your working draft? Ask your readers about particular passages in the draft so that you can get specific feedback.

2. Your readers can offer you feedback, either oral or written, based on your working draft and the commentary you have written. Here are some questions for your readers to take into account:

   ▶ Does the writer's purpose come across clearly? Are you able to see and understand the significance of the moment in the writer's past? Are the writer's first-person strategies effective in capturing the meaning of the past from the perspective of the present? If the significance of the moment is not revealed clearly enough, what suggestions can you offer?

   ▶ Is the memoir organized effectively? Does the moment of revelation appear in the best place? Does the essay begin with sufficient background information and scene setting? Comment on the ending of the memoir. Does the writer pull things together in a way that is satisfying to the reader?

   ▶ Is the writing vivid and concrete in re-creating particular scenes and moments from the past? Point to passages that are particularly vivid. Are there passages that are too vague, obscure, or abstract? Do the narrative passages move along crisply or do they seem to drag?

Revising

Use the commentary you have received to plan a revision.

1. Do you re-create the experience you're remembering, as opposed to just telling your readers what happened?

2. Can readers easily follow what you're remembering? Are there first-person strategies that you could use to revise?

3. Will readers be able to see clearly how you experienced the events in the past and how you think about them now? Is there a moment of revelation that gives the memoir significance?

4. Are the events and people in the memoir vivid? Do you need more detail?

5. What, if anything, should you cut? What do you need to add?

From Telling to Showing

Jennifer Plante revised the opening paragraphs of her memoir (a complete draft of the memoir is included in the Writers' Workshop on the next page), to move from a summary of Sunday afternoons at her grandparents' house to a much fuller scene setting. Her revision is a good example of the difference between telling and showing. Plante said she wanted to begin by just telling about these family gatherings. Telling about them helped her to bring her memories to consciousness. At the same time, however, she wasn't satisfied that the first version really captured the feeling of those afternoons. There's more she wanted to show about what those afternoons were really like. Notice how the memories in one paragraph of the early draft generate two paragraphs.

Early Draft

When I was ten years old, my family used to go to my grandparents' house every Sunday for dinner. It was a kind of ritual. My grandmother would cook a pot roast—I should say she overcooked it—and at the dinner table, my grandfather would carry forth on his political views. He was an intimidating, opinionated man. Nonetheless, this was a special time for me. As a ten-year-old, I didn't really understand the politics, but I did know I was a special granddaughter.

After dinner, my grandfather and I would watch the New England Patriots if they were on TV that week. He was the kind of hardcore fan who shouted at the Patriots players as if he were the coach, and I imitated him.

Revised Version

The smell of over-cooked pot roast still magically carries me back to Sunday afternoons at my grandparents' house. I was all of ten years old; a tomboyish, pig-tailed girl who worshiped the ground that her elders walked on. Back then, my grandfather seemed like an enormous man, every bit as intimidating as he was loving. He knew what he wanted, what he believed in; he thought that President Reagan was a demigod, and he thought that his only granddaughter was one of the biggest joys of his life. I remember that every time my family went over to my grandparents' humble home, I would run into my grandfather's warm arms and get swallowed up in a loving hug. Then, he'd sweep me off my feet and twirl me around in the air until I was giggling so hard that I could no longer breathe.

After we ate the charcoaled roast, I would follow my grandfather into the living room. Light always seemed to radiate from the huge picture window spreading warmth into the living room; it never seemed to rain while I was at my grandparents' house. I would proceed to sit on my grandfather's lap while he stretched out in his La-Z-Boy and flipped through the TV channels to find the New England Patriots' football game. He would often shout at the players as if he were their coach, and trying to emulate him, I would shout equally as loud, not knowing what the hell I was talking about (face-masking means nothing to a ten-year-old girl). This is how every Sunday afternoon of my childhood was spent; the sequence of events was very ritualistic, and the only thing distinguishing one Sunday from another was which meal my grandmother would decide to burn.

WRITERS' WORKSHOP

Jennifer Plante wrote the following two pieces in response to an assignment in her composition class that called on students to write a memoir. The first piece is Plante's commentary on an early working draft of a short memoir based on her recollections of Sunday afternoon visits to her grandparents' house. In this commentary, she describes the call to write that got her started on the piece in the first place and her own sense of both the potential and the problems of her work in progress. You'll notice that she wrote her commentary as a kind of interim report—to explain what she was trying to do and to request feedback, constructive criticism, and suggestions from her readers.

The second piece of writing is the working draft itself, before Jennifer went on to revise it. As you read, remember that Jennifer's memoir is a work in progress. Try to read it through her commentary, to see what advice or suggestions you would give her concerning revision.

JENNIFER PLANTE'S COMMENTARY

What got me started on this piece of writing is exactly what I begin with—the smell of over-cooked pot roast. For some reason, when I was thinking about a memoir I might write, this smell suddenly seemed to leap out at me and bring me back to the Sunday afternoons we spent at my grandparents. In one way, I wanted to remember these days because I loved them so much. I felt so safe and secure and loved, with not only my parents but my grandparents surrounding me. I tried to find images of warmth, light, and enclosure to re-create this feeling. I wanted the opening to have a Norman Rockwell-like, almost sentimental feel to it—of the "typical" American family living out the American dream of family gatherings. A ritualistic feel.

But I also wanted the paragraphs to serve as a set-up for what was to come, which is really the point of the memoir. It was on a typical Sunday when I was ten that my father and grandfather argued, and my grandfather made these incredibly racist and homophobic comments. I didn't understand at the time exactly what my grandfather meant but I did understand the look on my father's face—and that something had happened that was going to change things.

I think I've done a decent job of setting this scene up, but I don't think it fully conveys what I want it to. So I had to add the final section reflecting back on it and how I now feel betrayed by my grandfather. I think this last part is probably too obvious and maybe even a little bit preachy or self-righteous, though I try to explain how my grandfather is a product of his upbringing. I want readers to understand how my feelings toward my grandfather went from completely adoring to totally mixed and contradictory ones. I don't think this is coming out clearly enough, and I would appreciate any suggestions about how to do it or to improve any other parts of the essay.

JENNIFER PLANTE, SUNDAY AFTERNOONS

The smell of over-cooked pot roast still magically carries me back to Sunday afternoons at my grandparents' house. I was all of ten years old; a tomboyish, pig-tailed girl who worshiped the ground that her elders walked on. Back then, my grandfather seemed like an enormous man, every bit as intimidating as he was loving. He knew what he wanted, what he believed in; he thought that President Reagan was a demigod, and he thought that his only granddaughter was one of the biggest joys of his life. I remember that every time my family went over to my grandparents' humble home, I would run into my grandfather's warm arms and get swallowed up in a loving hug. Then, he'd sweep me off of my feet and twirl me around in the air until I was giggling so hard that I could no longer breathe.

After we ate the charcoaled roast, I would follow my grandfather into the living room. Light always seemed to radiate from the huge picture window spreading warmth into the living room; it never seemed to rain while I was at my grandparents' house. I would proceed to sit on my grandfather's lap while he stretched out in his

La-Z-Boy and flipped through the TV channels to find the New England Patriots' football game. He would often shout at the players as if he were their coach, and trying to emulate him, I would shout equally as loud not knowing what the hell I was talking about (face-masking means nothing to a ten-year-old girl). This is how every Sunday afternoon of my childhood was spent; the sequence of events was very ritualistic, and the only thing distinguishing one Sunday from another was which meal my grandmother would decide to burn.

One Sunday afternoon, my grandfather and I had assumed our normal positions on the brown, beat-up chair and found our Patriots losing to some random team. I'm not exactly sure how the subject came up, but my grandfather and my dad began discussing politics and our society. My grandfather and my dad held different opinions about both topics, so as usual, the debate had gotten pretty heated. I began feeling a bit uncomfortable as the discussion wore on; they talked for what seemed like hours and they must have discussed every issue that was of importance to our society. To numb my discomfort, I became focused on the TV screen—Steve Grogan had just completed a 30-yard touchdown pass, but the referee had called that "face-masking" thing on the offense, sending Patriot fans into a frenzy. Then, just as quickly as it had started, the debate ended in dead silence. My father sat, open-mouthed, in disbelief at what he'd just heard; my grandfather had finally spoken his mind.

"What is this interracial marriage garbage? Decent white people shouldn't be marrying those blacks. And what is this perverted gay business? All the gays should go back into the closet where they belong!"

I didn't understand what my grandfather had said at the time, but I did notice the look on my father's face. It was as if my grandfather had just slapped him, only I somehow knew that what he'd said had hurt my father much more than any slap ever could have. And I did notice that, for the first time ever, a hard rain began to fall outside.

I look back on that day now and I understand why my father looked so hurt. I also understand now what my grandfather had said, and can't help but feel betrayed that a man that I admired so much had managed to insult over half of the population in one breath. I do feel bitter toward my grandfather, but I can't really blame him for his ignorance; he is a product of his time, and they were taught to hate difference. But ever since that day, I have vowed that, when my grandchildren come to visit me on Sunday afternoons, they will never see a hard rain falling outside of my picture window.

▷ WORKSHOP QUESTIONS |||||||||||||||||||||||||||||||||||||||||||||||||||||||||||||||||||||||||

1. Do you agree with Jennifer Plante that she has done a "decent" job of scene setting in the opening sections of her memoir? Does the memoir's opening effectively re-create the "ritualistic feel" of family gatherings? Does it become too sentimental? Explain your responses to these questions, and make any suggestions you might have for strengthening the opening.

2. Plante's memoir relies on a moment of revelation—when her grandfather makes racist and homophobic remarks and these remarks have an effect on her father. Does this moment have the dramatic value and emotional force it needs as the pivotal point in the memoir—the moment that "changed things"? What suggestions, if any, would you offer to strengthen this crucial point in the memoir?

3. Plante seems dissatisfied with the final section of the memoir, in which she writes from the perspective of the present, reflecting back on a moment in the past. She worries about seeming "obvious," "preachy," and "self-righteous" in describing her sense of betrayal. Do you think this is a problem in the draft? What advice would you offer to strengthen this section of the memoir?

REFLECTING ON YOUR WRITING

Write an account that explains how you handled the dual role of the memoir writer as a participant and as an observer. How did you re-create yourself as a character in your memoir? What is the relationship between your self in the past and the perspective of your present self? If memoirs are in part acts of writing that bear witness to and thereby take responsibility for the past, how do the selves you have created and re-created express loyalties and social allegiances?

CHAPTER 6

Letters

Letters are easy to recognize. They have a predictable format that usually includes the date of writing, a salutation ("Dear Jim"), a message, a closing (such as "Sincerely" or "Yours truly"), and a signature. There are many occasions for letter writing, and the genre of letters can be divided into a number of subgenres, such as personal letters, business letters, open letters, letters to the editor, letters of appeal, email, text messages, and so on. Nonetheless, letters are easy to identify because of the way they appear on the page, computer screen, or cell phone.

But it's not only the visual form that makes letters a distinct genre. Just as important is the way letters—along with their digital extension as email, IM, Twitter, texting, and so on—address readers and establish a relationship between the writer and the reader. In a sense, the letter is the genre that comes closest to conversation between people. When you read a letter, you can almost hear the voice of the person writing to you. Letters are also like conversation in that they have the capacity to engage the reader in an interaction, to call for a response whether it's to RSVP a party invitation, attend a meeting, donate to a worthy cause, support an advocacy campaign, pay an overdue bill, or just write back.

One way that letters differ from conversation is that the person you're writing to can't talk back, at least not immediately. (Instant messaging is an interesting exception.) As a writer, you therefore have certain advantages. In a letter, you can talk directly to someone without being interrupted. And you know that the reader can return several times to your letter and reflect on its message before responding to you.

Thus, permanence is also a difference between letters and conversation. Once you've sent a letter, you can't take your words back as easily as you can in conversation. By expressing thoughts and feelings in a letter and sending it to someone, the letter writer may be taking a greater risk than by talking face to face or on the phone.

G. K. Chesterton once described the mailbox as "a sanctuary of the human heart" and the letter as "one of the few things left entirely romantic, for to be entirely romantic, a thing must be irrevocable." Many people save the letters they receive from relatives, friends, lovers, and other correspondents as a record of what their life was like at a particular time. There is a long tradition of letters in which writers reveal their deepest, most intimate thoughts to readers in a language that would be unimaginable in conversation—love letters, letters of advice, letters of friendship, letters of condolence, letters of despair, and letters written on the eve of death.

Other kinds of letters play just as important a role as personal letters in maintaining the social networks that link people together. In this chapter, we explore some familiar types of public letters—open letters, letters to the editor, and letters of appeal—as well as newer digital variations on the letter such as text messaging.

WRITING FROM EXPERIENCE

List the kinds of letters you write and receive, including email, instant messaging, and text messaging. Classify the letters according to the relationship they are based on and the purpose they serve. Are there particular letters you wrote or received that are especially important to you? What makes these letters important? Do you save letters? If so, what kinds of letters, and why? Compare your answers with those of your classmates.

READINGS

Open Letters

We begin with open letters, a form of public writing addressed to a broad audience. The "open" part is that the writer wishes the letter to circulate extensively, in print forms and electronically, to reach a wide cross-section of readers. The aim of an open letter is to influence public opinion, and open letters, accordingly, are typically distributed to the media, public officials, trendsetters, professionals in various roles, and policy makers of all sorts.

The two open letters in this section come from academics. As you will see, they are similar in that each makes a strong case for change:

▶ "Meth Science Not Stigma" calls on the media to end sensationalistic accounts of "meth" or "ice" babies. Circulated widely on the Internet by David C. Lewis of Brown University, this open letter was signed by 92 researchers and clinicians who study the effects of prenatal exposure to drugs.

▶ "Open Letter to Chancellor Linda P. B. Katehi" was written by Nathan Brown, an assistant professor at the University of California, Davis, calling on the chancellor to resign following the use of pepper gas spray on peaceful student demonstrators by police the chancellor had ordered to campus.

There are also interesting differences to examine: in terms of the rhetorical stance in each open letter, the tone and style of writing, and the fact that "Meth Science Not Stigma" is a collective letter, while "Open Letter to Chancellor Linda P. B. Katehi" was written by a single author.

Meth Science Not Stigma: Open Letter to the Media
David C. Lewis

....

July 25, 2005

Contact: David C. Lewis, M.D.

Professor of Community Health and Medicine

Donald G. Millar Distinguished Professor of Alcohol & Addiction Studies

Brown University

Phone: 401-444-1818

E-Mail: David_Lewis@brown.edu

To Whom It May Concern:

Opening establishes credentials of open-letter signers and purpose of letter

As medical and psychological researchers, with many years of experience studying prenatal exposure to psychoactive substances, and as medical researchers, treatment providers and specialists with many years of experience studying addictions and addiction treatment, we are writing to request that policies addressing prenatal exposure to methamphetamines and media coverage of this issue be based on science, not presumption or prejudice.

Explains problem of stigmatizing labels

Uses comparison as evidence

The use of stigmatizing terms, such as "ice babies" and "meth babies," lacks scientific validity and should not be used. *Experience with similar labels* applied to children exposed prenatally to cocaine demonstrates that such labels harm the children to which they are applied, lowering expectations for their academic and life achievements, discouraging investigation into other causes for physical and social problems the child might encounter, and leading to policies that ignore factors, including poverty, that may play a much more significant role in their lives. The suggestion that treatment will not work for people dependent upon methamphetamines, particularly mothers, also lacks any scientific basis.

Despite the lack of a medical or scientific basis for the use of such terms as "ice" and "meth" babies, these pejorative and stigmatizing labels are increasingly being used in the popular media, in a wide variety of contexts across the country. Even when articles themselves acknowledge that the effects of prenatal exposure to

Lewis, David C., M.D. "Meth Science Not Stigma: Open Letter to the Media," July 25, 2005. Reprinted by permission of the author.

methamphetamine are still unknown, headlines across the country are using alarm-
ist and unjustified labels such as "meth babies."

Just a few examples come from both local and national media:

▶ CBS NATIONAL NEWS, "Generation of Meth Babies" (April 28, 2005) at
CBSNews.com

*Gives
examples of
stigmatizing
labels*

▶ ARKANSAS NEWS BUREAU, Doug Thompson, "Meth Baby Bill Survives
Amendment Vote" (Mar. 5, 2005)

▶ CHICAGO TRIBUNE, Judith Graham, "Only Future Will Tell Full Damage
Speed Wreaks on Kids" ("At birth, meth babies are like 'dishrags'") (Mar. 7, 2004)

▶ THE LOS ANGELES TIMES, Lance Pugmire, "Meth Baby Murder Trial Winds
Up" (Sept. 5, 2003 at B3)

▶ THE SUNDAY OKLAHOMAN, "Meth Babies" (Oklahoma City, OK; May 23,
2004 at 8A)

▶ APBNEWS.COM, "Meth Infants Called the New 'Crack Babies' (June 23, 2000).

Other examples include an article about methamphetamine use in the
MINNEAPOLIS STAR TRIBUNE that lists a litany of medical problems allegedly caused
by methamphetamine use during pregnancy, using sensationalized language that
appears intended to shock and appall rather than inform, "… babies can be born
with missing and misplaced body parts. She heard of a meth baby born with an
arm growing out of the neck and another who was missing a femur." Sarah McCann,
"Meth ravages lives in northern counties" (Nov. 17, 2004, at N1). In May, one Fox News
station warned that "meth babies" "could make the crack baby look like a walk in the
nursery." Cited in "The Damage Done: Crack Babies Talk Back," Mariah Blake, COLUMBIA
JOURNALISM REVIEW Oct/Nov 2004.

Concession

*Appeal to
experience
and expertise*

Although research on the medical and developmental effects of prenatal
methamphetamine exposure is still in its early stages, *our experience with almost
20 years of research* on the chemically related drug, cocaine, has not identified a
recognizable condition, syndrome or disorder that should be termed "crack baby"
nor found the degree of harm reported in the media and then used to justify numerous punitive legislative proposals.

*Gives
definition of
"addiction"*

The term "meth addicted baby" is no less defensible. Addiction is a technical term that refers to compulsive behavior that continues in spite of adverse

consequences. By definition, babies cannot be "addicted" to methamphetamines or anything else. The news media continues to ignore this fact.

Further examples

- A CNN report was aired repeatedly over the span of a month, showing a picture of a baby who had allegedly been exposed to methamphetamines prenatally and stating: "This is what a meth baby looks like, premature, hooked on meth and suffering the pangs of withdrawal. They don't want to eat or sleep and the simplest things cause great pain." CNN, "The Methamphetamine Epidemic in the United States," Randi Kaye. (Aired Feb. 3, 2005–Mar. 10, 2005).
- One local National Public Radio station claims that "In one Minnesota County, there is a baby born addicted to meth each week." (Found at news. minnesota.publicradio.org from June 14, 2004).

Provides research findings

In utero physiologic dependence on opiates (not addiction), known as Neonatal Narcotic Abstinence Syndrome, is readily diagnosable and treatable, but no such symptoms have been found to occur following prenatal cocaine or meth-amphetamine exposure.

Similarly, claims that methamphetamine users are virtually untreatable with small recovery rates lack foundation in medical research. Analysis of dropout, retention in treatment and re-incarceration rates and other measures of outcome, in several recent studies indicate that methamphetamine users respond in an equivalent manner as individuals admitted for other drug abuse problems. Research also suggests the need to improve and expand treatment offered to methamphetamine users.

Questions media sources

Too often, media and policymakers rely on people who lack any scientific experience or expertise for their information about the effects of prenatal exposure to meth-amphetamine and about the efficacy of treatment. For example, a NEW YORK TIMES story about methamphetamine labs and children relies on a law enforcement official rather than a medical expert to describe the effects of methamphetamine exposure on children. A police captain is quoted stating: "Meth makes crack look like child's play, both in terms of what it does to the body and how hard it is to get off." (Fox Butterfield, Home Drug-Making Laboratories Expose Children to Toxic Fallout, Feb. 23, 2004 A1)

We are deeply disappointed that American and international media as well as some policymakers continue to use stigmatizing terms and unfounded assumptions that not only lack any scientific basis but also endanger and disenfranchise the

Points out policy implications

children to whom these labels and claims are applied. Similarly, we are concerned that policies based on false assumptions will result in punitive civil and child welfare interventions that are harmful to women, children and families rather than in the ongoing research and improvement and provision of treatment services that are so clearly needed.

How to access signers of open letter

Please click here for a pdf version of the open letter with the complete list of signatures.

Offers further assistance

We would be happy to furnish additional information if requested or to send representatives to meet with policy advisors, staff or editorial boards to provide more detailed technical information. Please feel free to contact David C. Lewis, M.D., 401-444-1818, David_Lewis@brown.edu, Professor of Community Health and Medicine, Brown University, who has agreed to coordinate such requests on our behalf.

Open Letter to Chancellor Linda P. B. Katehi
Nathan Brown

18 November 2011

Linda P. B. Katehi,

I am a junior faculty member at UC Davis. I am an Assistant Professor in the Department of English, and I teach in the Program in Critical Theory and in Science & Technology Studies. I have a strong record of research, teaching, and service. I am currently a Board Member of the Davis Faculty Association. I have also taken an active role in supporting the student movement to defend public education on our campus and throughout the UC system. In a word: I am the sort of young faculty member, like many of my colleagues, this campus needs. I am an asset to the University of California at Davis.

You are not.

I write to you and to my colleagues for three reasons:

1. to express my outrage at the police brutality which occurred against students engaged in peaceful protest on the UC Davis campus today
2. to hold you accountable for this police brutality
3. to demand your immediate resignation

Nathan Brown. "Open Letter to Chancellor Linda P.B. Katehi." Reprinted by permission of the author.

Today you ordered police onto our campus to clear student protesters from the quad. These were protesters who participated in a rally speaking out against tuition increases and police brutality on UC campuses on Tuesday—a rally that I organized, and which was endorsed by the Davis Faculty Association. These students attended that rally in response to a call for solidarity from students and faculty who were bludgeoned with batons, hospitalized, and arrested at UC Berkeley last week. In the highest tradition of non-violent civil disobedience, those protesters had linked arms and held their ground in defense of tents they set up beside Sproul Hall. In a gesture of solidarity with those students and faculty, and in solidarity with the national Occupy movement, students at UC Davis set up tents on the main quad. When you ordered police outfitted with riot helmets, brandishing batons and teargas guns to remove their tents today, those students sat down on the ground in a circle and linked arms to protect them.

What happened next?

Without any provocation whatsoever, other than the bodies of these students sitting where they were on the ground, with their arms linked, police pepper-sprayed students. Students remained on the ground, now writhing in pain, with their arms linked.

What happened next?

Police used batons to try to push the students apart. Those they could separate, they arrested, kneeling on their bodies and pushing their heads into the ground. Those they could not separate, they pepper-sprayed directly in the face, holding these students as they did so. When students covered their eyes with their clothing, police forced open their mouths and pepper-sprayed down their throats. Several of these students were hospitalized. Others are seriously injured. One of them, forty-five minutes after being pepper-sprayed down his throat, was still coughing up blood.

This is what happened. You are responsible for it.

You are responsible for it because this is what happens when UC Chancellors order police onto our campuses to disperse peaceful protesters through the use of force: students get hurt. Faculty get hurt. One of the most inspiring things (inspiring for those of us who care about students who assert their rights to free speech and peaceful assembly) about the demonstration in Berkeley on November 9 is that UC Berkeley faculty stood together with students, their arms linked together. Associate Professor of English Celeste Langan was grabbed by her hair, thrown on the ground, and arrested. Associate Professor Geoffrey O'Brien was injured by baton blows. Professor Robert Hass, former Poet Laureate of the United States, National Book Award and Pulitzer Prize winner, was also struck with a baton. These faculty stood together with students in solidarity, and they too were beaten and arrested by the police. In writing this letter, I stand together with those faculty and with the students they supported.

One week after this happened at UC Berkeley, you ordered police to clear tents from the quad at UC Davis. When students responded in the same way—linking arms and holding their ground—police also responded in the same way: with violent force. The fact is: the administration of UC campuses systematically uses police brutality to terrorize students and faculty, to crush political dissent on our campuses, and to suppress free speech and peaceful assembly. Many people know this. Many more people are learning it very quickly.

You are responsible for the police violence directed against students on the UC Davis quad on November 18, 2011. As I said, I am writing to hold you responsible and to demand your immediate resignation on these grounds.

On Wednesday November 16, you issued a letter by email to the campus community. In this letter, you discussed a hate crime which occurred at UC Davis on Sunday November 13. In this letter, you express concern about the safety of our students. You write, "it is particularly disturbing that such an act of intolerance should occur at a time when the campus community is working to create a safe and inviting space for all our students." You write, "while these are turbulent economic times, as a campus community, we must all be committed to a safe, welcoming environment that advances our efforts to diversity and excellence at UC Davis."

I will leave it to my colleagues and every reader of this letter to decide what poses a greater threat to "a safe and inviting space for all our students" or "a safe, welcoming environment" at UC Davis: 1) Setting up tents on the quad in solidarity with faculty and students brutalized by police at UC Berkeley? or 2) Sending in riot police to disperse students with batons, pepper-spray, and tear-gas guns, while those students sit peacefully on the ground with their arms linked? Is this what you have in mind when you refer to creating "a safe and inviting space?" Is this what you have in mind when you express commitment to "a safe, welcoming environment?"

I am writing to tell you in no uncertain terms that there must be space for protest on our campus. There must be space for political dissent on our campus. There must be space for civil disobedience on our campus. There must be space for students to assert their right to decide on the form of their protest, their dissent, and their civil disobedience—including the simple act of setting up tents in solidarity with other students who have done so. There must be space for protest and dissent, especially, when the object of protest and dissent is police brutality itself. *You may not* order police to forcefully disperse student protesters peacefully protesting police brutality. You may not do so. It is not an option available to you as the Chancellor of a UC campus. That is why I am calling for your immediate resignation.

Your *words* express concern for the safety of our students. Your *actions* express no concern whatsoever for the safety of our students. I deduce from this discrepancy that you are not, in fact, concerned about the safety of our students. Your actions directly threaten the safety of our students. And I want you to know that this is clear. It is clear to anyone who reads your campus emails concerning our "Principles of Community" and who also takes the time to inform themselves about your actions. You should bear in mind that when you send emails to the UC Davis community, you address a body of faculty and students who are well trained to see through rhetoric that evinces care for students while implicitly threatening them. I see through your rhetoric very clearly. You also write to a campus community that knows how to speak truth to power. That is what I am doing.

I call for your resignation because you are unfit to do your job. You are unfit to ensure the safety of students at UC Davis. In fact: you are the primary threat to the safety of students at UC Davis. As such, I call upon you to resign immediately.

Sincerely,

Nathan Brown

Assistant Professor

Department of English

Program in Critical Theory

University of California at Davis

Analysis: Establishing the Context of Issues

These two open letters show interesting differences in the context of issues they set up in their response to the call to write. Establishing the context of issues involves deciding the terms that specify what type of issue the open letter addresses and the general approach it takes. Notice, for example, how "Meth Science Not Stigma: Open Letter to the Media" responds to a shared sense of urgency on the part of leading medical and psychological researchers by focusing to a great extent on issues of substantiation where scientific evidence can be persuasively used, to correct sensationalistic media accounts and to guarantee sound policy toward children. Nathan Brown's "Open Letter to Chancellor Linda P. B. Katehi," on the other hand, begins by examining issues of substantiation—to establish what happened and why Chancellor Katehi was to blame—but shifts later in the letter to issues of evaluation, emphasizing that dissent should be respected as a core value in the university, and policy, arguing that the use of police to forcibly disperse peaceful student protestors should not be an option available to chancellors on UC campuses.

▷ FOR CRITICAL INQUIRY

1. Annotate "Open Letter to Chancellor Linda P. B. Katehi," as has been done already for "Meth Science Not Stigma," breaking the letter into sections and identifying the rhetorical function each section performs within the letter as a whole. Using these analyses of the parts of the two open letters, consider the overall plan of each letter. What does the general rhetorical strategy of the letter seem to be? To what extent do the letters use similar rhetorical strategies? How do they differ?

2. Describe the ethos of each open letter. How does it establish credibility? Consider the tone of the letter. What kind of relationship does the letter seek to establish with readers? How do the two letters differ in designing the writer's or signers' rhetorical stance?

3. "Meth Science Not Stigma" is addressed "To Whom It May Concern," whereas Nathan Brown's open letter is addressed personally to UC Davis Chancellor Linda P. B. Katehi. Consider to whom the letter is addressed and who the intended readers actually are. If they are not the same, what is the significance? How does ostensibly addressing one audience at the same time speak to another?

4. Examine how each letter uses claims and evidence. Identify key claims and the evidence presented in the argument. What assumptions enable the connection of claims and evidence? Are these assumptions made clear or implied? How does each letter develop the larger consequences of its key claims?

Reprinted by permission of Mark Patinkin, Providence Journal

THE COLUMN

Commit a crime, suffer the consequences

Mark Patinkin

At their best, columnists are supposed to leave people thinking, "That's just how I feel and didn't know it until reading that." Well, it took reading a column by an 18-year-old student to crystallize my own feelings about an issue I've been perusing day to day.

The Singapore caning case: The American teenager who's about to be flogged because he spray-painted several cars. From the start, I'd viewed it as a barbaric punishment for a poor kid who just did a little mischief. Then I read a column by an 18-year-old telling Michael Fay, the convicted American, to take it like a man, and learn from it.

Something in me instantly said, "She's right."

Yes, I know caning is harsh, but am I the only one who's tired of Michael Fay's whining? Am I the only one who feels President Clinton has better things to do than to write letters appealing for leniency?

Singaporeans get caned all the time for vandalism. Are we Americans supposed to be exempt when we break their laws? What are we — princes?

I'll tell you what else I'm tired of: Michael Fay's father — his biological father here in America — traveling the country insisting his precious boy didn't do it.

It's a setup, the father says. Supposedly, he says, Michael only pleaded guilty as a bargain with the police — after the local cops leaned on him — with the promise of little punishment.

But suddenly the judge sentenced him to six strikes with a cane.

Not once have I read Michael's parents saying their child was out of line. They just make excuses. Gee, I wonder if a life of such excuse-making is part of why he's so troubled.

See, that's the other line here. First, the father says he didn't do it. Then he says, well, Michael also has personal problems, like Attention Deficit Disorder. I happen to think that's a legitimate syndrome, but not for excusing crimes like vandalizing cars.

All this is just part of the new American game of always saying, "It's not my fault." No one, when caught, seems ready to admit having done wrong anymore. They just whine and appeal. As in: "Your honor, the stabbing was not my client's fault. He had a bad childhood. And was caught up in a riot at the time. In fact, he's not a criminal at all, he's one of society's victims."

That's Michael Fay. All those cars he spray-painted? Not his fault. He's had a hard life.

I might have had sympathy for him if he'd only said, "I admit it. I did a dumb thing. I was with the wrong crowd and crossed the line into criminality. I deserve to pay. And I'm truly sorry for the victims."

But we're not hearing that.

There's another thing. Many articles on this — including a paragraph in a column I wrote — have referred to what Michael Fay did as "mischief."

Well, it's not. It's hardcore vandalism. He spray-painted a bunch of cars.

Michael Fay might want to think about what it feels like to the car owners. Anyone whose car has been vandalized knows. Personally, I've had about four car stereos stolen. I still remember the shock — each time — of seeing the broken window and the damage. I remember having to take a good half day out of work to deal with it. And during the times I had little money, I remember how badly it pinched to have to pay the deductible on the insurance.

Finally, I remember how creepy and unnerving it was. It took weeks before I could approach my car again without feeling nervous. It erodes your trust in the world. And it's worse for women, I think, who feel a heightened vulnerability to crime in the first place.

In short, it's beyond mischief, beyond obnoxious — it's vandalism. A violation. And it's downright mean-spirited.

But after he was caught, Michael Fay and his family have been telling the world that he — not the car owners but HE — is the victim.

Sorry, Michael, you're not the victim. You're the criminal. Caning may well be rough.

But if you do the crime, you've got to pay the price.

Mark Patinkin is a Journal-Bulletin columnist. His column appears in Lifebeat each Tuesday and Thursday, and in the Metro section each Sunday.

Patinkin, Mark. "Commit a crime, suffer the consequences," in *The Providence Journal-Bulletin*, April 19, 1994. Reprinted by permission.

Letters to the Editor
Kristin Tardiff and John N. Taylor, Jr.

....

The column and letters to the editor presented in this section follow a cycle of writing that is common in newspapers and magazines—a pattern of call and response where the writers respond to the views of those who wrote before them. First, Mark Patinkin, a regular columnist at the Providence Journal, *wrote on an item in the news: the authorities in Singapore had just recently sentenced Michael Fay, an American teenager who lived there, to be caned as a punishment for spray-painting cars. Next, Kristin Tardiff wrote a letter to the editor in response to Patinkin's column. Then, John N. Taylor Jr. wrote a letter to the editor that responds to Tardiff's response and to Patinkin's column.*

To the Editor,

I wonder why I continue to read Mark Patinkin's columns. At best they bore me, at worst they anger me. I've thought before of responding to his maudlin whining or self-righteous hypocrisy, but this time I really had to put pen to paper.

Mr. Patinkin has chosen this time to attack Michael Fay, the 18-year-old boy who has been accused of spray-painting some cars in Singapore. Mark, jury of one, has decided that Fay is unequivocally guilty, and that his sentence of jail term, fine, and caning is fitting punishment. "Stop whining, take it like a man," he says.

I find it interesting that Mr. Patinkin has completely ignored the statements of those who may have a little more experience with the Singaporean police than he does. What about the Navy officer who said that our military police were under order to immediately take into custody any American soldier who was going to be arrested by the Singaporean police to protect them? Did he make that up? What about those who have had the experience of being detained in Singapore and tell of torture and forced confessions? Are they just wimpy bleeding hearts in Mark's eyes?

Perhaps as a teenager Mr. Patinkin never made a mistake, never did anything considered wrong in the eyes of the law. Hard to believe, but I'll give him the benefit of the doubt. Had he, however, ever been caught and punished for some infraction, that punishment certainly would not have involved being tied up with his pants around his ankles while someone split his cheeks the opposite way with a water-soaked cane. Nor do I think he would have considered that just. The punishment should fit the crime.

Michael Fay is willing to serve his time in jail and make restitution. He has already suffered physically and psychologically, and has, I'm sure, seen the error of his ways. Is this not enough punishment? Have we become so warped by the violence of our society

---

Tardiff, Kristin. "Letter to the Editor," *The Providence Journal-Bulletin*, May 3, 1994. Reprinted by permission of the author.

that we now see justice as incomplete without the imposition of physical pain? Do we really want to see the young graffiti artist in our neighborhood caned? (I hear some saying yes, but what if it turns out to be your child? Think about it.) Is this really the way we want society to turn? What comes next? Amputation for thieves and maybe prolonged torture and death for drug dealers? Should we just kill all the "bad" people? Why can't we for once work on the causes instead of lashing out blindly at the symptoms?

Just one more thing. Regarding Mr. Patinkin's criticism of Fay's parents' pleas for leniency for their son, as a parent he should have more empathy. What else can parents do when they truly feel that their child is being unjustly treated?

I hope Mark's children all turn out as perfect as their dad. Maybe he should send to Singapore for a cane. Just in case.

Kristin Tardiff
Providence

To the Editor,

The letters . . . denouncing Mark Patinkin's support for caning Michael Fay ("Patinkin should know better than to advocate caning," 5/3) are no different from any of the other whiny, moralizing claptrap we hear from those mawkish people who fear more for Mr. Fay's buttocks than for those who are victimized everyday by the crimes of young punks like Fay. The arguments . . . are laden with the rancid, canting self-righteousness common to all opposing Fay's caning, and evince concern only for the criminal while telling crime victims to go eat cake.

From Ms. Tardiff, we get a lot of sarcasm, a lot of questions, and no answers. If she can't propose any semblance of an idea for controlling crime, then neither she (nor anyone else) has the moral authority to condemn a nation which has come up with its own means of dealing with criminals. . . .

Singapore has in recent years carried out canings of 14 of its own citizens who were convicted of offenses similar in nature to those of Mr. Fay. Why should Fay be treated any differently from these people? Just because Fay is an affluent white American with many powerful supporters in America (like President Clinton) doesn't mean he should be above the law of the nation where he resides. To let Fay out of the caning simply because he has the support of powerful leaders is an affront to the people of Singapore, who have abided by the law or taken their lumps for violating same. Clemency for Fay would effectively divide Americans and Singaporeans into separate, unequal classes, whereby the former avoid punishment because of America's political and economic clout while the latter, who do not enjoy such powerful connections, suffer the consequences.

Taylor, John N. "Letter to the Editor," *The Providence Journal-Bulletin*, May 9, 1994. Reprinted by permission of the author.

The caning of Fay is simply an affirmation of the principle that all people, whether they are wealthy white Americans or poor Chinese Singaporeans, are equal in the eyes of the law. . . . It has much to do with upholding Singaporean mores and nothing to do with Fay being American or U.S. political traditions; these sanctions, as applied to crimes like vandalism and other non-political offenses, are designed to discourage repetition of criminal behavior. And they succeed in this goal. How many drive-by shootings go down in Singapore?

Like American authorities, the Singaporeans perceive crimes to be the individual act and choice of the perpetrator.

There is no doubt Singapore is a non-democratic nation which punishes even peaceable political dissent, and there is no doubt that Singapore's criminal laws are harsh. But Michael Fay knew what the laws were like and freely assumed the risks of getting punished when he engaged in his spree of vandalism. It is the height of arrogance and folly for Americans living or traveling abroad to expect to be protected by the Bill of Rights when they break other nations' laws.

Americans have no right demanding a blanket exemption from foreign laws they violate, or that foreign governments give them easier treatment than they would give their own people under similar circumstances.

And if caning is immoral, is not the American criminal justice system itself laden with unfairness? Where is the morality in releasing quadruple murderer Craig Price into the community after only four years? Is it right that in the U.S., a murderer draws an average sentence of only about six years? Is it right that dangerous criminals are dumped onto communities simply because the prisons don't meet the standards of some soft-headed judge? We in America sacrifice the lives of innocent people in the name of criminals' civil rights, and then have the gall to denounce Singapore as harsh and oppressive! If anyone's justice is extremist, it is America's.

America's approach to crime is to do nothing and let the community be damned, while Singapore has opted to let the offender be damned. What the Michael Fay fan club here in America conveniently forgets while moaning about Singaporean tyranny is the everyday tyranny of violence and fear imposed on millions of Americans by violent criminals in our inner cities and suburbs. These people are oppressed by a dictatorship of criminals and their rights are violated on a massive scale every day. Yet I see more concern for Michael Fay's rear end than I do for people who bear the scars of bullets and knives of criminals.

My heart will not bleed if Fay's rear end does. Given the carnage on America's streets, and in Rwanda, Bosnia and Haiti, the supporters of Michael Fay will just have to excuse me if I fail to shed a tear.

John N. Taylor Jr.
North Providence

Analysis: A Public Forum

Like a lot of newspaper columnists, Mark Patinkin uses short paragraphs, an informal, conversational tone, and a commonsense man-in-the-street approach to his readers. Notice that he speaks to his readers as an equal, not as someone who is more knowledgeable or somehow above them. This approach in effect positions the column as something that readers can and should respond to. The controversial nature of the topic—and of some of Patinkin's comments about the topic—make it all the more likely that readers will respond.

In the letters to the editor, the writers argue a position in response to what they've read. The letters to the editor reveal an intensity of feeling, and at times they resort to logical fallacies and other questionable tactics. These tactics include name-calling: Kristin Tardiff refers to Patinkin's "maudlin whining" and "self-righteous hypocrisy." By the same token, John N. Taylor Jr. says Tardiff's letter contains the "whiny, moralizing claptrap" of "mawkish people." The writers use exaggeration: "What comes next? Amputation for thieves and maybe prolonged torture and death for drug dealers?" (Tardiff). They are not always completely accurate: ". . . in the U.S., a murderer draws an average sentence of only about six years" (Taylor Jr.). At times, they beg the question instead of explaining the point: "What else can parents do?" (Tardiff) and make questionable comparisons: "If caning is immoral, is not the American justice system laden with unfairness?" (Taylor Jr.). The letters are definitely opinionated, and finally that is the point: letters to the editor give people the chance to talk back, to take strong positions, to have their say in a public forum.

☞ FOR CRITICAL INQUIRY

1. Reread Tardiff's letter to the editor. What is it about Patinkin's column that seems to call on her to respond? How does she define her own position in relation to what Patinkin has written? To what extent does her letter respond directly to Patinkin's column? To what extent does it introduce other issues?

2. Reread the letter from Taylor Jr. How would you describe his response to the call to write? How does he define his own position in relation to Patinkin and Tardiff?

3. What is this exchange of letters really about? Although the letters are ostensibly about Michael Fay, his punishment doesn't exactly seem to be the main issue. Try to distill the main issues that emerge and explain how the letters relate to these issues and to each other. What is at stake for these writers?

Letter-Writing Campaign

Occupy the Boardroom

Mark Greif

....

Mark Greif teaches literary studies at the New School in New York City and is cofounder and coeditor of the journal n + 1, as well as a contributor to other journals and magazines

Mark Greif, "Occupy the Boardroom." *From Occupy! #2: An OWS-Inspired Gazette* published by n + 1. www.occupytheboardroom.org. Reprinted by permission.

on culture, literature, and politics. "Occupy the Boardroom" appeared in Occupy! #2: An OWS-Inspired Gazette *published by n + 1. Greif describes Occupy the Boardroom's letter-writing campaign to prominent Wall Street bankers and traders. You can find out more about it at* www.occupytheboardroom.org/.

On the night that police attacked the Occupy protesters in Oakland, Tuesday, October 25, "non-lethally" fired on them and gassed them and threw stun grenades, and shot in the head an Iraq veteran named Scott Olsen, it looked like our Cub Scout stormtroopers were out to murder American citizens. They aimed high with shotguns at soft-looking Californians in T-shirts and shorts. The organized violence was carried live on KCBS. In the black ant farm chambers of YouTube, I tunneled from one protester video to the next, following morbid links, lying awake in bed in New York. If they were going to destroy the encampments, as was happening simultaneously in Atlanta, and be brutal, as also in Denver and Chicago, then there needed to be new fields opening to occupy. Powerlessness and rage arise from watching suffering at a distance, as in the Age of Television. In an age of the internet, links led me back to Occupy the Boardroom, a site that had launched twelve days earlier, and I started writing letters. The website lists the names of executives and trustees for the big six banks in America: Goldman Sachs, Morgan Stanley, Citigroup, Bank of America, JPMorgan Chase, and Wells Fargo. There are no addresses, not even mailing addresses. But the site is organized to allow you to type a long letter to an individual by name. The service routes your letter to the addressee's email address. It also posts it to a roll of previous letters—more than 6,000, when I first visited—so you learn what other letter-writers know and believe.

To: John G Stumpf, Wells Fargo
Thank you for the years of service. But, I am now going to move my money to a Credit Union
until I see an effort by the 1 percent to help the country that gave them their chance.
Mr. & Mrs. Anthony Zayas
75234 [Dallas, TX]

Occupy the Boardroom represents bourgeois protest. I say that as a compliment. I think it's a necessity now, and will be in months to come as mayors try to paint the occupations in the colors of homelessness. Bourgeois protest uses the values of people who hold a stake, who are part of the vast middle class, who are small property owners, or were. The best of America, since Jefferson's vision of yeoman democracy, includes a society of equals in which everyone is an owner of a little bit of the earth to stand on. Occupy Wall Street has, very often, courageously spoken for have-nots, immigrants, and the dispossessed. They're part of America, too. Occupy the Boardroom allows 99 percent of us to speak from principles from which we can never be dispossessed, and from those that, peculiarly, the executives and trustees of banks supposedly share: honesty, probity, contract, politeness, property, savings, professionalism, "customer service," responsibility, citizenship, patriotism. It also lets us speak from everywhere.

To: William R Rhodes, Citigroup
Hello Mr. Rhodes,
I am not poor. In fact, I own a sizeable piece of real estate on the border of Tribeca
and the Financial District. I have even paid my mortgage off already. I am fiscally very conserva-
tive. That is why I have no patience for your company's shenanigans. I have been wanting to leave
Citibank for years now. Moving my account from Citi on Nov. 4th is my message to you, and the
U.S. Government (1 year out from the election) along with this message here and now.
I am not alone, by the way.
Here's hoping you develop a sense of balance, fairness and a conscience.
Fair [sic] thee well,

Heide
[New York, NY]

This matches a new technology to one of the oldest forms enabled by widespread literacy. The individual letter, person to person, secret and intimate or public and formal, but to be read by the recipient in the place appropriate to that communication, on his or her own time, is one of our most protected forms of direct address. Because it is there for the addressee to encounter in calm and security, it is never a trespass if it is a polite. Every one of us is entitled to be heard in this way by anyone else. It may be a legal offense to tamper with the mail, but it's equally a moral crime to read somebody else's sealed missive or tear open an envelope not addressed to you. What goes unsaid, too, is that not reading a personal letter written directly to you is a trespass that leaves us uneasy, an offense against everyone as uncomfortable as tearing up paper money. It suggests fear, or contempt. To do that, you are putting yourself in the wrong.

To: Heidi Miller, JPMorgan Chase
Dear Ms. Miller,
I selected your name from the list of Chase executives listed by the Occupy Wall Street move-ment because my oldest daughter shares her first name with you and also because I have an account with Chase.

You could say that my wife and I are the lucky ones who are financially secure because we are both retired, have secure retirement Social Security, pensions, and have nest eggs that will survive us both. Our children are also lucky to have relatively secure jobs. But if the decline of our country continues, I am afraid for my grandchildren, perhaps yours too.

But what about the rest of the other 99%? What about our country? Isn't our People the nation for whom our heroes died?

I hope you could be one of the small voices who could also help turn our country around.

Sincera,
Enrique C. Cubarrubia

It becomes a way to draw the 1 percent into the movement, odd as that sounds. It neither tries to coopt them or vilify them. It addresses them. Politeness may be the most essential thing. "Remember, be polite!" are the words you find in the text box when you type your letter. "Be sure to" write "in a constructive manner that helps build the movement for a better world. . . . Think funny!" Not many letters are funny. But they are extraordinarily articulate. The politeness is key not because of subservience, and not to charm, but because it assumes community.

To: Ellen V. Futter, JPMorgan Chase
I'm a carpenter, work has been very light since the crash, my wife works in a small factory earning 17 an hour, no insurance. We signed up for "make your home affordable[.]" They reduced our mor[t]gage buy 400 a month[,] why we went th[r]ough the process[.] we were not behind in our payments, we just had a hard time making ends meet. 9 months into the process they said we were not eligable [sic], that they were going to start [to] for[e]close if we could not come up with the 400 that we did not pay or we could refi[n]ance at a lower rate[,] saveing[sic] us from losing our house and in the process taking all the interest we had paid up to that point. . . . 10 years 120,000 dollars[.] i know that no one will read this letter but [it] makes me feel better what make[s] you feel better madame.

Michael G Anderson
98070 [Vashon, WA]

I confess that I hate it when people's letters are just insults, as some are. Or promises of justice. I do respect it, though—I admire the notes of defiance.

To: Diana Taylor, Citigroup
Hi Ms. Taylor:
I have an MBA and work for a large non-profit on the west coast. I'm involved only recently in politics, and I have learned a bit since 2008.

Consider what you could do instead with all the money your company currently contributes to various political campaigns & lobbying groups.

You could make more small business loans, and create jobs and help local economies. You could maintain your profits without having to layoff [sic] people.

You could take your chances competing without stacking the deck by influencing favorable legislation.

Flavia Franco
94403 [San Mateo, CA]

"But none of the bankers are going to read the letters!" one of my family members said. I'm reading them, I said. Other letter-writers are reading mine. Now we all see each other. "But the letters are never even going to be opened by the people to whom they're written!" I'm not sure of that, I said. Mightn't they be?

Needless to say, I was pretty excited when I read that Occupy the Boardroom would be rallying on the steps of the New York Public Library on Friday, October 28 to deliver the letters to banks. On Fridays I don't teach, either.

The familiar techniques of the people's mic were used to let people tell stories about debt to school, hospital bills, and tiny loans that ballooned as jobs were lost. I went with the group that marched to Bank of America, since that's my bank. I have been with them for more than a decade, ever since they bought the bank that bought the bank that sits on a corner in my hometown.

We marched down 42nd Street. The plan was to go to Wells Fargo, after we had a media moment at the Bank of America headquarters on Sixth Avenue, and then Chase. The organizers had asked if anyone wanted to carry the letters personally, and I did—hoping this would mean I'd get to go inside, and see how they planned to get these to people's desks. I had a box filled with several hundred printed letters. I wondered if I'd get to say something noble as I handed them over. I imagined myself like one of the Founders, in a periwig, and I was mentally rehearsing: "You, sir—" and polite but Jacobin remarks, and appeals to humility. We were encouraged to hand out individual letters to people who passed by, and I had to stop to explain what was happening, first to an oddball with a microphone and then to a schoolkid doing a report.

That made me late, crossing the avenue, and left out. There were pirates up front—representing corporate pirates?—and group chanting. The avalanche of police, a hundred or more, for protesters who didn't number more than 300, and then the fact that the police had set up inside the Bank of America Tower perimeter, behind barriers they had set out on the pavement, such that they had made themselves the house security of the bank, seemed to mean we wouldn't be hand-delivering letters, nor even leaving them all in a sack in the lobby. Bank employees stared from inside the glass. It was a sunny day, cold, and very peaceful. Because I was at the back, I saw that close to where I was standing was an opening in the barricade, where the NYPD was talking to folks in a line. I thought I'd give them letters. My logic was that standers on line are more likely to accept reading material than folks you interrupt as they're moving. My patter was: "Can I offer you a letter from an individual American citizen to employees of Bank of America?" starting at the end of the line.

"No," said my first try.

"OK, "I said. Moving on, "Can I offer you a letter?" From an individual American citizen, etc.

This man was completely silent. He and I were standing still, at a distance of social comfort, had calm voices, relaxed postures. He was avoiding my eye. An offer in that situation just about always dictates a spoken "no," unless there's some reason to perceive a threat.

Oh! A dim light dawned. "Are you guys by any chance employees of Bank of America?"

"No," the first man said. Which provoked a reaction like a slap in the face of the second one, because it meant that his comrade had outright lied.

They were all employees, reentering the bank. At the head of the line were uniformed NYPD, working for the in-house B. of A. security, checking ID. So I started working the line. "Sir, can I offer you these letters from fellow American citizens? They're addressed to you."

The people waiting reflected the usual breakdown of decency, shyness, and bad personalities. The surprise was a knot of eager Columbia Business School students. They refused to take letters, until one did, and then they all did.

Meanwhile, I missed the formal protest. On the other side of the police barrier stood a line of thirty or forty blue-uniformed police, backs against the glass front of the Bank of America Tower as if guarding a jewelry exhibit, with thirty feet of barricaded-off open pavement . . . which the protest now filled with a flotilla of paper planes. The original idea had been to write new letters and launch them as a publicity stunt. Absent time to write these, and with no way now to deliver the real letters, people had started using the printouts to make the planes. Everyone then picked up the ones that had blown back onto their side, brushed off any dirt, and moved down 42nd Street to head for Wells Fargo, where the next round of boxes was due for delivery. My trouble was, I still had so many letters. So I went back quickly to try to hand them out to people at the police gate.

With most people gone, I saw that in-house security called out a team of janitors, to sweep up the letters, lying there in the form of paper planes, and dump them in a big gray trash can. I went to the security—five men in suits, who were not bankers—and leaned over the barricade for the one was giving orders. "Hey, these are letters, from individual American citizens, and you're treating them like trash." Nothing doing. "Listen, let me pick up the letters, I'll do it for your guys. Then I'll have the letters, and nobody's letter has to be thrown out."

"YOU CAN'T COME IN HERE!" So he heard me.

"How about this—you have your guys, can they just give them to me—I'll stay on this side—dump them with me, instead of the trash, and I'll clean them up?" Back to pretending. "How come you can't talk to me?" I said. "Is it a legal thing, or are you afraid to? Or do you just not like me?"

"I don't like you!" a banker jeered as he passed through the barricade.

"That's OK, I'm your customer," I said.

It was depressing. The janitors came and did the public sidewalk around me, all three Latino, workers for sub-contracting companies, by the patches on their shirts, presumably so the bank wouldn't have to employ them and pay benefits.

"I'm with you, man, hey, sorry, man. I got to keep my job, if I was off work, I'd be out here with you."

I felt fake, because, in class and privileges, I have plenty in common with those people standing in line to go to their jobs in the bank. I'm a college teacher, well-employed. Any of us employed has it easier than the unemployed, whose stories were in these letters that I kept glancing down at, each one different. My father works for a bank, in Boston, developing their computer systems. I have health benefits, and also the arrogance that comes from fancy degrees, the feeling of comfort and ownership at the library and the museum, that nobody ranks above me except the super-rich (and great artists and writers).

And surely I know how we think—and how the people who work in banks, like my father and his coworkers, think—and school friends, and friends' spouses, who work in the banks, in finance, how they think, and, yes, some of us are assholes, but mostly it's still people with a moral core. The agenda of normalcy and reputation just happens to be what's current with the folks around us. If you spend all your time with bankers, you will think that some things that are wrong are actually OK. We live in bubbles. If a message can get across that barrier, just to say what is coming from your work is not what you believe in, it's a national horror, people will surely change. Won't they?

Analysis: Delivering the Message

Mark Greif divides this report on Occupy the Boardroom into two parts. The first contains background on the emergence of the Web site and letter-writing campaign as part of the larger Occupy Wall Street movement, some examples of letters, and Greif's reflections on how this initiative "matches a new technology to one of the oldest forms enabled by widespread literacy." Then in the second part, Greif describes what happened when Occupy the Boardroom attempted to deliver letters to bank executives at Bank of America and Wells Fargo. As an essay, there is a revealing dramatic tension between the two parts—the desire on the part of ordinary Americans to address those who hold financial and political power in the first part and the police barricades, intimidation, and fear that divide people in the second. As the letters turn into paper planes that Occupy the Boardroom demonstrators launch across police barriers, Greif raises questions about the circulation of messages and their capacity to change people's perspectives.

▷ FOR CRITICAL INQUIRY

1. Mark Greif suggests that the genre of the "individual letter, person to person" is "one of our most protected forms of direct address." Consider what special capacities Greif ascribes to the individual letter and what it might be able to do in addressing others, even as a "way to draw the 1% into the movement." Explain how the examples Greif presents are meant to reveal what is unique about letters.

2. By the end of the essay, Greif seems less certain about the effects of the letter-writing campaign. The essay ends on a querulous note, when Greif speculates that if only messages can get across barriers, then "people will surely change. Won't they?" To develop your own understanding of Occupy the Boardroom, visit the Web site www.occupytheboardroom.org. Notice the two options—Pen Pals and Best Friends Forever—and how they differ. Identify the goals of the campaign. To what extent does the campaign assume that the letters it sends to the bankers' email accounts will actually influence them? To what extent does it aim at something else? What is your sense of the value and effectiveness of the campaign?

3. Just as Occupy the Boardroom emerged with the Occupy Wall Street movement, letter-writing campaigns have become a part of many larger advocacy campaigns. Amnesty International is well-known for its letter-writing campaigns. Investigate how Amnesty International organizes these campaigns. Consider how its campaigns are similar to and differ from Occupy the Boardroom.

Letter as Essay

My Dungeon Shook: Letter to My Nephew
James Baldwin

James Baldwin (1924–1987) was a novelist, playwright, and essayist, whose works include the essays Notes of a Native Son *(1955), the novels* Go Tell It on the Mountain *(1953) and* Another Country *(1962), and the play* Blues for Mister Charlie *(1964). This letter from Baldwin to his nephew was published in* The Fire Next Time *(1962).*

Dear James:

I have begun this letter five times and torn it up five times. I keep seeing your face, which is also the face of your father and my brother. Like him, you are tough, dark, vulnerable, moody—with a very definite tendency to sound truculent because you want no one to think you are soft. You may be like your grandfather in this, I don't know, but certainly both you and your father resemble him very much physically. Well, he is dead, he never saw you, and he had a terrible life; he was defeated long before he died because, at the bottom of his heart, he really believed what white people said about him. This is one of the reasons that he became so holy. I am sure that your father has told you something about all that. Neither you nor your father exhibit any tendency towards holiness: you really are of another era, part of what happened when the Negro left the land and came into what the late E. Franklin Frazier called "the cities of destruction." You can only be destroyed by believing that you really are what the white world calls a *nigger*. I tell you this because I love you, and please don't you forget it.

I have known both of you all your lives, have carried your Daddy in my arms and on my shoulders, kissed and spanked him and watched him learn to walk. I don't know if you've known anybody from that far back; if you've loved anybody that long, first as an infant, then as a child, then as a man, you gain a strange perspective on time and human pain and effort. Other people cannot see what I see whenever I look into your father's face, for behind your father's face as it is today are all those other faces which were his. Let him laugh and I see a cellar your father does not remember and a house he does not remember and I hear in his present laughter his laughter as a child. Let him curse and I remember him falling down the cellar steps, and howling, and I remember, with pain, his tears, which my hand or your grandmother's so easily wiped away. But no one's hand can wipe away those tears he sheds invisibly today, which one hears in his laughter and in his speech and in his songs. I know what the world has done to my brother and how narrowly he has survived it. And I know, which is much worse, and this is the crime of which I accuse my country and my countrymen, and for which neither I nor time nor history will ever forgive them, that they have destroyed and are destroying hundreds of thousands of lives and do not know it and do not want to know it. One can be, indeed one must strive to become, tough and philosophical concerning destruction and death, for this is what most of mankind has been best at since we have heard of man. (But remember: most of mankind is not all of mankind.) But it is not permissible that the authors of devastation should also be innocent. It is the innocence which constitutes the crime.

Now, my dear namesake, these innocent and well-meaning people, your countrymen, have caused you to be born under conditions not very far removed from those described for us by Charles Dickens in the London of more than a hundred years ago. (I hear the chorus of the innocents screaming, "No! This is not true! How *bitter* you are!"—but I am writing this letter to *you,* to try to tell you something about how to handle *them,* for most of them do not really know that you exist. I *know* the conditions under which you were born, for I was there. Your countrymen were *not* there, and haven't made it yet. Your grandmother was also there, and no one has ever accused her of being bitter. I suggest that the innocents check with her. She isn't hard to find. Your countrymen don't know that *she* exists, either, though she has been working for them all their lives.)

Well, you were born, here you came, something like fourteen years ago; and though your father and mother and grandmother, looking about the streets through which they were carrying you, staring at the walls into which they brought you, had every reason to be heavy-hearted, yet they were not. For here you were, Big James, named for me—you were a big baby. I was not—here you were: to be loved. To be loved, baby, hard, at once, and forever, to strengthen you against the loveless world. Remember that: I know how black it looks today, for you. It looked bad that day, too, yes, we were trembling. We have not stopped trembling yet, but if we had not loved each other none of us would have survived. And now you must survive because we love you, and for the sake of your children and your children's children.

This innocent country set you down in a ghetto in which, in fact, it intended that you should perish. Let me spell out precisely what I mean by that, for the heart of the matter is here, and the root of my dispute with my country. You were born where you were born and faced the future that you faced because you were black and *for no other reason.* The limits of your ambition were, thus, expected to be set forever. You were born into a society which spelled out with brutal clarity, and in as many ways as possible, that you were a worthless human being. You were not expected to aspire to excellence: you were expected to make peace with mediocrity. Wherever you have turned, James, in your short time on this earth, you have been told where you could go and what you could do (and *how* you could do it) and where you could live and whom you could marry. I know your countrymen do not agree with me about this, and I hear them saying, "You exaggerate." They do not know Harlem, and I do. So do you. Take no one's word for anything, including mine—but trust your experience. Know whence you came. If you know whence you came, there is really no limit to where you can go. The details and symbols of your life have been deliberately constructed to make you believe what white people say about you. Please try to remember that what they believe, as well as what they do and cause you to endure, does not testify to your inferiority but to their inhumanity and fear. Please try to be clear, dear James, through the storm which rages about your youthful head today, about the reality which lies behind the words *acceptance* and *integration.* There is no reason for you to try to become like white people and there is no basis whatever for their impertinent assumption that *they* must accept *you.* The really terrible thing, old buddy, is that *you* must accept *them.* And I mean that very seriously. You must accept them and accept them with love. For these innocent people have no other hope. They are, in effect, still trapped in a history which they do not understand; and until they understand it, they cannot be released from it. They have had to believe for many years, and for innumerable reasons, that black men are inferior to white men. Many of them, indeed, know better, but, as you will discover, people find it very difficult to act on what they know. To act is to be committed, and to be committed is to be in danger. In this case, the danger, in the minds of most white Americans, is the loss of their identity. Try to imagine how you would feel if you woke up one morning to find the sun shining and all the stars aflame. You would be frightened because it is out of the order of nature. Any upheaval in the universe is terrifying because it so profoundly attacks one's sense of one's own reality. Well, the black man has functioned in the white man's world as a fixed star, as an immovable pillar: and as he moves out of his place, heaven and earth are shaken to their foundations. You, don't be afraid. I said that it was intended that you should perish in the ghetto, perish by never being allowed to go behind the white man's definitions, by never being allowed to spell your proper name. You have, and many of us have, defeated this intention; and, by a terrible law, a terrible paradox, those innocents who believed that your imprisonment made them safe are losing their grasp of reality. But these men are your brothers—your lost, younger brothers. And if the word *integration* means anything, that is what it means: that we, with love, shall force our brothers to see themselves as they are, to cease fleeing from reality and begin to change it. For this is your home, my friend, do not be driven from it, great men have done great things here, and will again, and we can make America what America must become. It will be hard, James, but you come from sturdy, peasant stock, men who picked cotton and dammed rivers and built railroads, and, in the teeth of the most terrifying odds, achieved an unassailable and monumental dignity. You come from a long line of great poets, some of the greatest poets since Homer. One of them said, *The very time I thought I was lost, My dungeon shook and my chains fell off.*

You know, and I know, that the country is celebrating one hundred years of freedom one hundred years too soon. We cannot be free until they are free. God bless you, James, and Godspeed.

Your Uncle,
James

Analysis: Private and Public Audiences

Of all the genres of writing gathered in this book, letter writing may appear to be the most personal and the most intimate. As James Baldwin writes to his nephew, "I keep seeing your face." But as the opening lines of Baldwin's letter indicate—"I have begun this letter five times and torn it up five times"—writing on such intimate terms can bring with it certain complications, especially in this case, because Baldwin actually has two audiences, his nephew and a public audience of readers.

On the one hand, Baldwin represents himself as a concerned and loving uncle writing a letter of advice to his namesake nephew, thereby invoking the sacred institution of the family as the ground to speak. On the other hand, the advice he offers his nephew—to accept white people without accepting their definitions of him—is meant to be overheard by Baldwin's other audience. When Baldwin explains to his nephew that white people are trapped in a history of race relations they don't understand and can't escape, he is also explaining to his white readers how their own identities have been based on a belief in the inferiority of African Americans. By using the form of a letter of advice from one family member to another, Baldwin is simultaneously offering his white readers a way to reposition themselves in relation to their own history and identities.

⏵ FOR CRITICAL INQUIRY

1. Where in the letter does Baldwin first indicate his main point and reason for writing to his nephew? Mark this passage and explain why you think he locates his main point here. How does this passage connect what comes before and what follows?

2. A good deal of the long fifth paragraph involves Baldwin's admonition to his nephew "to be clear ... about the reality that lies behind the words *acceptance* and *integration*." What is the reality Baldwin alludes to here? What does he see as the relation between "acceptance" and "integration"? What assumptions have led him to this view?

3. Baldwin wrote a number of essays concerning race relations in the United States. In this instance, however, he has chosen the more personal form of a family letter addressed directly to his nephew but published for all to read. How does this traditional letter of advice from an older family member to a younger one influence the way you read the letter? What advantages do you see in Baldwin's strategy of addressing his nephew instead of the more anonymous audience of people who read *The Fire Next Time*, in which "My Dungeon Shook: Letter to My Nephew" appeared? Are there things Baldwin can say to his nephew that he can't say directly to this audience?

MULTIMODAL COMPOSITION

Letter of Appeal: Doctors Without Borders/ Medecins Sans Frontières (MSF)

Doctors Without Borders/Medecins Sans Frontières (MSF) delivers emergency medical care to people in crisis in nearly eighty countries worldwide. An independent, international humanitarian organization, MSF was awarded the Nobel Peace Prize in 1999. This letter from Doctors Without Borders, along with an accompanying report on the medical costs of war in the Democratic Republic of Congo, is typical of the letters of appeal that humanitarian and advocacy groups rely on to bring their work to public attention. The letter includes such standard features as the organization name and logo on the letterhead, a salutation (the familiar "Dear Friend"), a signature, and a P.S. Notice also how selective underlining adds a sense of urgency to the letter. The accompanying report describes how Doctors Without Borders provides medical care to victims of the war.

As you read, consider the location of the letter's appeal toward the end. Why do you think it is located there? Explain how the writing that precedes it sets up the appeal. What sort of relationship does this letter want to establish with readers? What assumptions about intended readers does the letter seem to make? How does the enclosed report support the letter's appeal?

	333 Seventh Avenue, 2nd Floor New York, NY 10001
Awarded the 1999 *Nobel Peace Prize*	Tel: (212) 679-6800 Fax: (212) 679-7016
	Web: www.doctorswithoutborders.org

Dear Friend,

In September 2008, I was checking on a clinic in the town of Sake in North Kivu province in the eastern Democratic Republic of Congo. Violent fighting had recently broken out close to the town—and it was getting worse. As head of logistics for Doctors Without Borders/ Médecins Sans Frontières (MSF), I was there to see if the roads around the town were still passable and to see if the clinic needed help caring for the war-wounded.

I will never forget that day. Entire families stood anxiously in the doorways of their homes, listening to the rumble of artillery explosions in the hills to the west of town and hoping they wouldn't have to run and leave everything behind. Suddenly, something changed–and thousands of women, children, and men were flooding the streets in panic. With straw mats, blankets, and water jugs in hand, they fled for their lives.

With no choice but to flee with them, we made room in our car for as many people as we could–including three pregnant women and their young children. For just that brief moment, I experienced what daily life is like for literally hundreds of thousands of people who have known nothing but violence, displacement, and terror for the past 15 years.

Thanks to your support, Doctors Without Borders has been a consistent provider of urgently needed medical care throughout the war. And as the fighting continues to escalate, we need your continued support more than ever.

We have treated thousands of children and women who have been wounded, beaten, or raped in a war that has trapped the most vulnerable in a chaos of lawlessness and violence. We work in overstretched hospitals and clinics and send teams by car, motorcycle, bicycle, and even on foot to bring medical care to families in remote villages and to those uprooted from their homes who have found shelter with generous local families or in overcrowded camps.

In June, four children came down with measles in a huge camp of recently displaced people on the outskirts of Kitchanga in North Kivu province. We immediately ordered more than 100,000 doses of the vaccine and all the supplies and equipment needed to mount a mass vaccination campaign. We hired local community members to tell people when and where to bring their children. Meanwhile, the disease was spreading–80 cases on day two, 140 on day three. By day four, were vaccinating children: 7,000 one day, 10,000 the next.

With your support, our medical teams vaccinated 80,000 children against measles–the vast majority in just six weeks. In doing so, we averted what could have been a devastating measles epidemic.

Andre Heller, "Letter of Appeal: Medecins Sans Frontières/Doctors Without Borders." Reprinted by permission of Medecins Sans Frontières/Doctors Without Borders.

Meanwhile, the war goes on. Year after year everyone waits, and waits, to see if the latest round of violence will bring a period of calm. Year after year people are disappointed. I stayed long enough to live through two of these cycles. The already displaced are displaced again, and then again. Another agricultural season is missed. Another school year is missed. Another relative is lost to violence or preventable illness.

As the front lines move, so the people move, and so must Doctors Without Borders move to find them. In Masisi province, we discovered 10,000 people who had fled to a region so insecure that they were completely cut off from any kind of assistance, trapped between different front lines of fighting. After intense negotiations with militia leaders on all sides of the conflict, our mobile clinic team of five nurses, a doctor, and two logisticians finally made it. And we went back every week, as security allowed, to make sure they had access to primary medical care.

Each time we went back, hundreds of people were there to greet us. They were so appreciative that we had made the effort to find them—and to know that they had not been forgotten. That someone was there to listen to their stories.

Doctors Without Borders is the only international organization delivering medical care to some of the most insecure parts of North Kivu. Our neutrality, our medical work, and our reputation allow us to work on all sides of the front lines—thanks to your generosity. It is your financial support that gives us the independence to provide humanitarian assistance that is neutral and impartial, that is based on need alone.

I originally signed up to work in the Congo for three months. But I was so moved by the constant fighting, displacement, and human suffering that are as much a part of the landscape as the volcanoes in this beautiful terrain that I stayed 14 months. And despite the distance, a part of me is still out there with those who are not lucky enough to be able to make the decision to leave.

As I write, I know from colleagues in the region that the situation has worsened even further. Please give generously so that we can continue to deliver medical care to those who need it the most.

Sincerely,

Andre Heller

Andre Heller
Logistics Coordinator
North Kivu, Democratic Republic of Congo

P.S. The day after 35,000 people fled Sake, I returned to find a ghost town where once a bustling market town stood. The nurse in charge of the clinic was locking its doors, on his way to join those who had fled to camps. This is what war does. What we do at Doctors Without Borders is to make sure that as many children, women, and men as possible survive—thanks to the support of people like you.

DRC:
TREATING VICTIMS OF WAR

In August 2008, after 10 years of simmering conflict, tensions in the North Kivu province of the Democratic Republic of Congo (DRC) exploded into outright war.

Fighting between government forces and rebel groups has displaced some 250,000 people since August. The violence has turned an already disastrous situation into a humanitarian catastrophe as people weakened by years of fighting are forced to flee again and again. Cholera, measles, and other deadly diseases are rampant.

Doctors Without Borders/Médecins Sans Frontières (MSF) is in the midst of this volatile situation that changes from hour to hour. Currently 778 staff are delivering critical medial care throughout North Kivu.

Read this report to see how our teams near the embattled eastern towns of Kitchanga, Rushuru, and the provincial capital, Goma, are treating war-wounded victims, battling contagious outbreaks, and providing essential medial aid to internally displaced people (IDP) who are desperate and exhausted from constantly running for their lives.

MÉDECINS SANS FRONTIERES
DOCTORS WITHOUT BORDERS

© Dominic Nahr/Magnum Photos

"Fighting broke out as we were assessing the situation at a health center and 35,000 people ran for their lives. My driver and I were caught in the middle of this group. We picked up the few who couldn't run and brought them with us. For every 1 we picked up, 20 more couldn't fit in."

"People are literally fleeing into the wild..."

© Dominic Nahr/Magnum Photos

After years of displacement, people are struggling with fragile health. Doctors Without Borders runs medical clinics at two camps for internally displaced people (IDP) in Kitchanga which have about 42,000 people, where our teams treat respiratory infections, cholera, and measles.

"Conditions are desperate," said Annie Desilets, Doctors Without Borders project coordinator. "Kitchanga is at a high altitude, so it rains and it's cold. A lot of people don't have blankets or plastic sheeting to get away from the rain. They get food when they can, but it's not enough to sustain a family of seven or eight people. **We're providing water and health care but basic survival is difficult.**

"A lot of families are fleeing into the bush. They are vulnerable to the elements and the fighting. In the Kitchanga and Mweso areas, we have set up mobile clinics to reach people who cannot reach us.

"**It's not always easy to find displaced people. We go to an area one week where there is a village and we go back the next week and it's empty.** Are they in a camp where we can provide health care? Or are they hiding in the bush where we cannot access them? We don't know."

Together, we can save more lives.

ETHICS OF WRITING

USING THE INTERNET

One of the most exciting aspects of the Internet is its capacity to open up new public forums for the exchange of ideas. A posting from an individual to a mailing list or message board can connect him or her to people all over the world with an immediacy that promotes rapid feedback and response. But precisely because email offers such exciting possibilities for transmitting information and ideas, it is important to use it properly—to understand what can be sent to whom under what conditions.

- **Author's permission:** Communicating on the Internet requires the same attention to copyright and intellectual property as print communication. In other words, you need to cite your sources, and if you want to forward a message written by someone else, you need to secure permission first.

- **Reader's permission:** Don't just assume that people will want to be added to a regular mailing list or newsgroup. You need to secure people's permission before adding their names. Readers are likely to resent unsolicited email and feel imposed upon. Be careful not to flood cyberspace with junk email.

FURTHER EXPLORATION

Rhetorical Analysis

Analyze the writer's argument in one of the letters included in this chapter. Pay particular attention to how the writer establishes a rhetorical stance that combines the persuasive appeals of ethos, pathos, and logos. See guidelines and a sample rhetorical analysis of an argument in Chapter 3.

Genre Awareness

Email, chat rooms, newsgroups, and Listservs are, like letters, forms of correspondence that enable writers to stay in touch and exchange views. Despite this similarity, there are also significant differences between letters and these new electronic genres. Draw on your own experience to examine the similarities and differences between print letters and electronic correspondence. Take into account the occasions when it makes sense to use one or the other. When, for example, is it better to write a letter than email? Or, given something urgent to say, when would you write a letter to the editor, to a politician, or to an organization, and when would you post your views online?

WRITING ASSIGNMENT

Letters

For this writing assignment, compose a letter. Here are some possibilities:

▶ An open letter to a public official, organization, or company that calls for change. Consider how the public is part of the intended readers.

▶ A letter to the editor of a newspaper or magazine responding to a news story, feature article, editorial, or column that particularly moved you. Or you might raise an issue that's important to you but hasn't yet appeared in the press.

▶ A letter to a younger relative or student. You can use James Baldwin's letter to his nephew as a model here—to speak directly to the younger person but include a public audience as your intended readers as well. You might explain what it takes to survive in college or how to handle particular kinds of peer-group pressures such as drinking, drugs, and sex. Or you might explain what it's like to be a scholarship athlete, a woman, an African American, a gay or lesbian, a Latino, or a working-class student in a middle-class college.

▶ A letter to your parents or to a friend explaining the impact of a public event on you personally, how you make sense of it, and, if appropriate, what you have done or plan to do.

Multimodal Composition

▶ Design a letter of appeal and accompanying literature, such as a flyer, fact sheet, petition, or report, that calls on readers to support an organization or cause by making a contribution. This could be for an existing organization like Doctors Without Borders or one that you make up.

▶ Design an online letter as a routine update for supporters of a particular politician, an organization, or a cause. Consider how to embed links in the letter, to take readers to other pages and Web sites.

Invention

Identifying the Call to Write

Identify something that moves you to write.

▶ Has a particular subject been making you curious or angry?

▶ Are you learning something in one of your courses that you want to tell someone about?

▶ Have you recently read something in a newspaper or magazine that you'd like to respond to?

▶ Is there a public issue in your community, on campus, at home, or on the national or international scene that has captured your interest?

▷ EXERCISE

Writing a Statement of Purpose

Write a statement of purpose, using these questions to guide you:

1. What calls on you to write?

2. What do you want to accomplish in your letter? What are you going to say?

3. To whom are you writing? How do you want your reader to respond?

Understanding Your Readers

How successful you will be in eliciting the response you want from your readers depends in part on how well you understand them and your relationship to them. To gather ideas about how you can most effectively address your reader, respond to these questions:

1. On what terms do you know your reader: family, personal, institutional? Describe your relationship to the person. How does this relationship affect what you can and cannot say in your letter? If you are writing online, how does the electronic forum of the Internet affect your relationship to your reader?

2. What is an effective way to present yourself to your reader? What will it take to establish the credibility and authority of what you have to say? What kind of personality or attitude is your reader likely to respond to?

3. What attitude is your reader likely to have toward your letter? What is your reader's interest in what you have to say? Will your reader care personally or read your letter as part of work?

4. What is your reader likely to know about the message you are sending? How much shared information is involved? How much do you need to explain?

5. What values and beliefs do you think your reader might hold about the subject of your letter? What common ground can you establish? What shared values can you appeal to?

Background Research: Finding Models

To determine how to communicate with your readers, find some models of the type of letter you want to write.

1. What is the occasion that calls on people to write the letters?

2. How do writers define the rhetorical situation? How do they develop a rhetorical stance? Consider here especially the ethos of the letter—the attitude and personality that it projects.

3. Consider the formal features of the letter. Do paragraphs tend to be short or long or vary? What is the tone of voice—how formal or informal? Are there any notable ways the letter uses language?

Planning

Establishing the Occasion

Letters often begin by establishing their timeliness: why they're written at that moment, to what person or people, on the basis of what relationship. Notice the ways in which writers establish the occasion in the reading selections:

- ▶ Explaining the writers' professional credentials ("Meth Science Not Stigma")
- ▶ Establishing authority to speak and familiarity with the topic (Kristin Tardiff, regular reader of Mark Patinkin's column)
- ▶ Characterizing an opponent's position, expressing sense of outrage (John N. Taylor, Jr., "whiny, moralizing claptrap")
- ▶ Locating the writer in a scene (Doctors Without Borders, "In September 2008, I was checking on a clinic in the town of Sake")
- ▶ Invoking family ties as the right to speak (James Baldwin)

In your letter, you need to design an opening that treats the occasion of the letter and your relationship to the reader. How explicitly you do this will depend on what your reader needs to hear. Politicians, businesspeople, government officials, and newspaper editors all appreciate letters that get right to the point. In letters home and other personal letters, staying in touch (as much as or more than the letter's content) may be the main point of writing.

Arranging Your Material

List the points you want to make and the information you want to include in your letter. Arrange the material in an outline that consists of three sections:

1. **Opening:** To establish occasion, relationship, and the point of the letter.
2. **Main body:** To explain and develop the point of the letter, whether that means concentrating on one main topic or including a number of separate topics.
3. **Closing:** To reiterate the main point of the letter, whether that involves calling for action, firing a final salvo, reaffirming your relationship to the reader, sending regards, or thanking the reader for his or her time.

Working Draft

Once you have listed main points, write a working draft. As you write, new ideas may occur to you. Don't censor them by trying rigidly to follow your list of points. Instead, try to incorporate new points by connecting them to the ones you have already listed. If you can connect them, the new points probably belong in the letter. If you can't, then you'll need to think carefully about whether they really fit your letter. As you write your working draft, keep in mind the overall movement you want in your letter—from an opening that sets the occasion, to a main body that explains your key points, to a closing that wraps things up for the reader.

Beginnings and Endings: Using an Echo Effect

One effective way to begin and end your letter may be to use an echo effect by looping back in the ending to issues raised in your opening. This echo effect can provide a satisfying sense of closure because it reminds readers of the major themes you introduced earlier.

Andre Heller uses an echo effect in his letter on behalf of Doctors Without Borders. In the opening paragraph, he describes the situation in the town where he was working, "Sake in North Kivu province in the eastern Democratic Republic of the Congo":

> Violent fighting had recently broken out close to the town—and it was getting worse. As head of logistics for Doctors Without Borders/Medecins Sans Frontiére (MSF), I was there to see if the roads around the town were still passable and to see if the clinic needed help caring for the war-wounded.

Then, after detailing the work of Doctors Without Borders in North Kivu province, Heller returns to his own situation: "I originally signed up to work in the Congo for three months. But I was so moved by the constant fighting, displacement, and human suffering that are as much a part of the landscape as the volcanoes in this beautiful terrain, that I stayed 14 months." Using this testimony of personal commitment to close the letter, Heller creates a heightened sense of urgency about donating to MSF by noting "that the situation has worsened even further."

You may want to try this echo effect in your own writing. Take a look at your opening and see whether you find a theme that you would like to have recur in your closing. Or think about adding a theme to your introduction that you will return to at the end of your letter.

Using Topic Sentences

Topic sentences help to guide readers by establishing a paragraph's focus and by explaining how the paragraph is linked to earlier ones. The most common type of topic sentence appears at the beginning of a paragraph and thereby enables readers to anticipate what is to come. Notice how Mark Patinkin uses a topic sentence in the following paragraph from his column about the Michael Fay caning. The first sentence (which we have italicized in the example) establishes the focus of the paragraph; then the rest of the sentences explain it more fully:

> *All of this is just part of the new American game of always saying, "It's not my fault."* No one, when caught, seems ready to admit having done anything wrong anymore. They just whine and appeal. As in: "Your honor, the stabbing was not my client's fault. He had a bad childhood. And was caught up in a riot at the time. In fact, he's not a criminal at all, he's one of society's victims."

Topic sentences also link paragraphs together. To keep readers oriented to the train of thought as it moves from paragraph to paragraph, writers often show how a particular paragraph's focus is linked to the paragraphs that precede and follow.

Sometimes topic sentences appear at the end of a paragraph instead of the beginning. Building toward the topic sentence can give a paragraph a powerful dramatic structure. James Baldwin uses this type of dramatic structure in the second paragraph of his letter by moving from the personal toward a general point about the "crime of which I accuse my country and my countrymen":

> I have known both of you all your lives, . . . I know what the world has done to my brother and how narrowly he has survived it. And . . . this is the crime of which I accuse my country and my countrymen, and for which neither I nor time nor history will ever forgive them, that they have destroyed and are destroying hundreds of thousands of lives and do not know it and do not want to know it. One can be, indeed one must strive to become, tough and philosophical concerning destruction and death, for this is what most of mankind has been best at since we have heard about man. (But remember: most of mankind is not all of mankind.) But it is not permissible that the authors of devastation should also be innocent. *It is the innocence which constitutes the crime.*

By the end of this paragraph, Baldwin has worked his way from a loving tribute about his brother to a painful critique of society's destruction. The topic sentence at the end of the paragraph (italicized here for emphasis) sets Baldwin up to make a transition that links his "countrymen's" crime of innocence to the next paragraph:

> Now, my dear namesake, these *innocent and well-meaning people,* your countrymen, have caused you to be born under conditions not very far removed from those described for us by Charles Dickens in the London of more than a hundred years ago.

Peer Commentary

Exchange working drafts with a classmate and respond to the following questions:

1. What is the occasion of the letter? Where in the letter did you become aware of how the writer defined the rhetorical situation? Be specific—is there a particular phrase, sentence, or passage that alerted you to the writer's purpose?

2. Whom is the writer addressing? What kind of relationship does the writer want to establish with the reader? How does the writer seem to want the reader to respond? How can you tell? Are there places where you think the writer should make the relationship or the desired response more explicit?

3. Does the writer address the reader in a way that makes a positive response likely or possible? Explain your answer. What could the writer do to improve the chances of making the impression he or she wants?

4. Describe the tone of the letter. What kind of personality seems to come through in the letter? What identity does the writer take on in the letter? Do you think the intended reader will respond well to it? If not, what might the writer change?

Revising

Review the peer commentary you received about your letter. Based on the response to your working draft, consider the following points to plan a revision:

▶ Have you clearly defined the occasion and your purpose?

▶ Does the letter establish the kind of relationship with your reader that you want?

► Do you think your reader will respond well to the way you present yourself?

► Do you think you accomplished your purpose with your letter?

Once you are satisfied with the overall appeal of your letter, you can fine-tune your writing. You might look, for example, at your topic sentences to see whether they establish focus and help the reader see how ideas are linked in your letter.

Strengthening Topic Sentences for Focus and Transition

The following two paragraph excerpts show how one student, Michael Brody, worked on his letter to the editor (the final version appears below in Writers' Workshop). Notice how he clarifies the focus of the third paragraph by rewriting the topic sentence so that it emphasizes what "readers need to understand" about the Singapore government's use of the Michael Fay case. Clarifying the focus in the topic sentence of paragraph 3 also strengthens the transition between paragraphs and makes it easier for readers to see how the ideas in the two paragraphs are linked.

---

2   . . . As readers point out, the crime rate in Singapore is low, the streets are

safe, and there are no drive-by shootings. While this picture of Singapore may

appear to be reassuring to some readers, it hides the fact that beneath a

polished, secure, and business-like facade Singapore is ruled by a brutal

dictatorship that keeps its people in fear by punishing not only vandalism and

spraypainting but chewing gum as antisocial crimes.

Readers need to understand how the

3   . . . Michael Fay's actions were [admittedly immature and illegal], calling for

Michael Fay case is being used by the Singapore government as

some official response. But this should not blind us to the problems in

a lesson to its own people about the decadence of American ways

Singapore and how the government is using the Michael Fay case. The leaders

of Singapore are portraying Michael Fay as a living illustration of all that's

flawed about American values of freedom and individual rights. ᴀand his admittedly

immature and illegal actions are held up as a

direct consequences of the American way of life.

Mark Patinkin and his supporters have failed to see . . .

WRITERS' WORKSHOP

Michael Brody wrote the following letter to the editor in a first-year writing class after he read Mark Patinkin's column "Commit a Crime, Suffer the Consequences" and the Letters to the Editor from Kristin Tardiff and John N. Taylor, Jr. As you will see, entering the caning debate at this point enables Brody to summarize positions people have already taken as a way to set up his own main point. The letter to the editor is followed by a commentary Brody wrote to explain his approach to the issue.

MICHAEL BRODY, LETTER TO THE EDITOR

To the Editor:

Mark Patinkin's column "Commit a crime, suffer the consequences" has generated heated responses from readers and understandably so. For some, the sentence of six strokes of the cane, at least by American standards, does indeed seem to be "cruel and unusual punishment," no matter what Patinkin writes about Michael Fay's "whining." On the other hand, Patinkin and those readers who side with him are right that Michael Fay is the criminal in this case, not the victim, and that he deserves to suffer the consequences of his actions.

I happen to agree with readers who argue for leniency. Let Michael Fay pay for his crime by fines and a jail sentence. It worries me that some readers are willing to tolerate or even endorse caning. Obviously, these sentiments show how fed up Americans are with the problem of crime in our society. But there is a tendency in some of the pro-Patinkin letters to idealize Singapore's strong measures as a successful get-tough solution to crime. As readers point out, the crime rate in Singapore is low, the streets are safe, and there are no drive-by shootings. While this picture of Singapore may appear to be reassuring to some readers, it hides the fact that beneath a polished, secure, and business-like facade Singapore is ruled by a brutal dictatorship that keeps its people in fear by punishing not only vandalism and spraypainting but chewing gum as antisocial crimes.

Readers need to understand how the Michael Fay case is being used by the Singapore government as a lesson to its own people about the decadence of American ways. The leaders of Singapore are portraying Michael Fay as a living illustration of all that's flawed about American values of freedom and individual rights, and his admittedly immature and illegal actions are held up as direct consequences of the American way of life. Mark Patinkin and his supporters have failed to see how the Michael Fay incident is more than a matter of whether America, unlike Singapore, is soft on crime, coddles law breakers, and ignores the true victims. For the Singapore government, the caning of Michael Fay is a stern warning to the people of Singapore against the dangers of American democracy.

What is ironic about this attempt to use Michael Fay for anti-American purposes is the fact that caning is itself not a traditional Singapore means of punishment. It's tempting to think of caning as the barbaric practice of cruel Asian despots, but in reality Singapore learned about caning from the British colonial powers who once ruled the country. The British Empire, as I'm sure Mark Patinkin is well aware, took a tough stand on law and order in the colonies and routinely crushed native movements for freedom and independence. I wish Mark Patinkin and others who are properly concerned about crime would consider the lessons Singapore leaders learned from their former masters about how to control and intimidate those they rule. Caning is not a matter of different national customs, as some people make it out to be. Nor is it an extreme but understandable response to crime in the streets. In Singapore, caning is part of both a repressive judicial system and a calculated propaganda campaign to discredit democratic countries and silence dissent.

Michael Brody
Worcester, MA

MICHAEL BRODY'S COMMENTARY

When I read Mark Patinkin's column, I got angry and wanted to denounce him as a fascist. Then I read the letters readers had written opposing or supporting Patinkin's point of view, and they made me realize that I didn't want to follow them because they all seemed to be too emotional, just gut responses. I wanted to find a different approach to the whole caning incident so that I could raise an issue that was different or had been overlooked.

Now I must admit that when I first heard about the sentence of caning, I thought it was barbaric, probably something typical of Asian dictatorships. I thought of the massacre at Tiananmen Square, and I dimly recalled what I had heard when I was young about how the Chinese Communists tortured Catholic missionaries, stuff like bamboo slivers under the fingernails. Then I read somewhere that caning was brought to Singapore by the British in colonial days, and I started to think along new lines. It occurred to me that maybe the caning wasn't just about crime but had something to do with how governments ruled their people.

As I read more in the newspapers, *Time,* and *Newsweek* about the incident, I was shocked to discover how Michael Fay was being used by Singapore leaders to build up anti-American sentiment, to paint America as a permissive society that coddled its criminals. I decided that I'd try to write something that looked at how the case was being used by Singapore's rulers. The more I thought about it, this seemed to give me an angle to go beyond agreeing or disagreeing with Patinkin's column and still have something interesting to say.

When I was getting ready to write, I made a quick outline of my points. I wanted to sound reasonable so I decided to concede that both sides, for or against caning, had some valid points. I decided to show this in my opening and wait until the second paragraph to indicate where I was coming from. I wanted to create the effect that there's this debate going on, which I figured readers would know about and already have their own opinions about, but that I had an angle people maybe hadn't thought about. So I tried to get this point to emerge in the second paragraph and then drive it home at the beginning of the third paragraph with the sentence that starts "Readers need to understand . . . "

That sentence set me up to give my own analysis of the incident and of how Patinkin and the pro-caning people failed to see the full political picture. I decided to leave the idea that caning came from British colonial powers until the end as my clincher. I figured this would do two things. First, it would surprise people, who like me thought caning was a barbaric Asian punishment. Second, it would have an emotional charge because I assumed most people would be against colonialism, especially British colonialism, given that America had to fight England for our independence. Besides I'm Irish, and I know a lot of people where I live are against the British in Ireland, and I knew they'd be against anything associated with the British empire.

I'm not totally sure the irony I talk about in the opening line of the last paragraph works. I remember learning about irony in English class in high school, and how funny or odd it is when things don't turn out the way you expected. So I wanted to throw that in, to make readers feel, well I thought it was one way but when you look at it again, it's another way. I thought this might work in the very end to show that caning is not just this (a barbaric national custom) or that (an extreme form of punishment) but also a form of political intimidation.

⇨ WORKSHOP QUESTIONS

1. When you first read Michael Brody's letter to the editor, at what point did you become aware of his perspective on the caning debate? Is it just a matter of being for or against caning? Note the sentence or passage that enabled you to see where Brody defines his orientation toward the caning debate.

2. Brody devotes considerable space in the first two paragraphs to presenting positions people have already taken on the caning debate. What kind of relationship does he seem to want to establish with his readers by doing so?

3. Describe the tone Brody uses in the letter. How does it compare to the tone in Mark Patinkin's column and in the letters to the editor from Kristin Tardiff and John N. Taylor, Jr.? Do you think Brody's tone works well? Explain your response.

4. Reread Brody's commentary. If you could talk to him, how would you respond to what he says about composing his letter?

REFLECTING ON YOUR WRITING

Use the commentary Michael Brody wrote as a model for writing your own account of how you planned and composed the letter you wrote. Explain how you defined the call to write and how you positioned yourself in relation to your readers, your topic, and what others had already said about your topic (if that applies to your letter). Notice that Brody explains how he developed his own position by considering what others had said and reading newspapers and magazines on the Michael Fay incident. Explain, as Brody does, in a step-by-step way how you composed your letter, what effects you were trying to achieve, and what problems or issues emerged for you along the way. Indicate any aspects of the letter that you're not certain about. Add anything else you'd like to say.

CHAPTER 7

Profiles

Talking about people and places amounts to a sizeable component of conversation—whether you're telling friends what your new roommate is like or describing the neighborhood where you grew up. This impulse to describe, analyze, and understand people and places seems to grow out of a genuine need to come to terms with social experience, where we live, the groups we are part of, and our relationships with others.

It's not surprising, then, that a genre of writing—the profile—is devoted to describing and analyzing people and places. Profiles are a regular feature in magazines such as *Rolling Stone, Sports Illustrated, Ebony*, and *The New Yorker*, as well as in newspapers. Many profiles are of well-known people, and the allure of such profiles is that they promise a behind-the-scenes look at celebrities.

But profiles also focus on ordinary people. When an issue moves to the forefront of the public's attention, ordinary people often become the subject of profiles that describe, say, the lives of undocumented workers or the plight of a corporate executive laid off in the economic downturn. Sometimes profiles focus on groups of people rather than single individuals—profiles, for example, of a community group trying to decrease gang violence in the West End of Providence, Rhode Island; a Japanese drone metal band; or a night in the life of an emergency medical team. Likewise, there are profiles of places that focus, say, on the fate of the Ninth Ward in New Orleans nearly ten years after Katrina or an old industrial city in the rust-belt Midwest that has a new arts district.

Such profiles of people and places supplement statistical and analytical treatments of issues, making concrete and personal what would otherwise remain abstract and remote. These profiles can take readers beyond their preconceptions to explore the remarkable variety of people, backgrounds, lifestyles, and experiences that are frequently reduced to a single category such as "the elderly" or "blue-collar workers." And they look at social processes as well, giving readers a sense of what it's like to live through the collapse of manufacturing or how musical movements like punk or hip-hop embody larger subcultural identities.

Sometimes, profiles seem to take place in real time. They may tell what a person does over the course of a day, what a place is like at a moment in time, or how a group performs its characteristic activities. Such profiles create a sense of immediacy and intimacy, as though the reader were there on the spot, watching and listening to what's going on. Readers of profiles have come to expect that they will be able to visualize people and places, to hear what people sound like, and to witness revealing incidents.

To convey this sense of immediacy and intimacy, writers of profiles often rely on interviewing and observation. This doesn't mean that library and online research isn't involved. Consulting print and electronic sources is a usual step in preparing for interviews and observations, to get some needed background in order to start to identify themes and issues.

In any case, no matter how immediate a profile seems to be, it's helpful to remember we are not seeing a person or a place or a group directly, but rather through the eyes of the writer. A profile—and the impact it has on readers—depends as much on the writer as on the subject profiled. Profiles express, explicitly or implicitly, the author's point of view. No profile will really work for its readers unless it creates a dominant impression—a sharply defined perspective on the subject of the profile.

WRITING FROM EXPERIENCE

We talk about other people and places all the time. Think about the conversations you have with others—friends, relatives, coworkers, neighbors, acquaintances, or strangers. In these conversations, what kinds of stories and comments come up? List four or five occasions when you or someone else told a story or made a comment about another person, a place, or an organization. What was the purpose?

Compare your list with the lists of your classmates and see whether any patterns emerge. Are there, for example, any differences between men's and women's stories and comments? Can you classify these examples—by purpose or by who is speaking or whom the stories or comments are about?

READINGS

Insurgent Images: Mike Alewitz, Muralist
Paul Buhle

....

Paul Buhle is a retired historian of labor, the Left, and popular arts at Brown University; he has written or edited more than thirty books, including The New Left Revisited *(2003),* Tender Comrades: A Backstory of the Hollywood Blacklist *(1999), and* C.L.R. James'

Mike Alewitz

Si Se Puede, Oxnard, California, 1993

Caribbean *(1992). The following profile is of Mike Alewitz, one of the most prominent American muralists in the last twenty years, an art teacher at Central Connecticut State, and a noted social activist. Buhle and Alewitz collaborated on the book* Insurgent Images: The Agitprop Murals of Mike Alewitz *(2002), which features examples of Alewitz's murals, including those that appear here.*

A large outside wall of Cesar Chavez High School in Oxnard, California, carries the portrait of the famed Latino labor leader and social visionary, "the Chicano Martin Luther King, Jr.," against a background of grape fields and a foreground of the message "Si se puede! Yes! It can be done!" Chavez is seen holding up a book, open to facing pages in English and Spanish, with the text: "We need a meaningful education, not just about the union, but about the whole idea of the cause. The whole idea of sacrificing for other people . . . " Not himself Chicano, not even a Californian, muralist Mike Alewitz was (as actor Martin Sheen pronounced at the 1993 dedication ceremony) the natural choice of artists.

Opening paragraph describes an Alewitz mural

Puts Alewitz and murals in historical context

Alewitz is happiest in a small crowd of amateur painters and community members who meet to discuss with him what kind of mural would best suit the purposes of the community and the building. Artistic choices are important, but this is public art, its role in some ways better understood in the past than today: art that becomes part of the daily life of ordinary people by picturing their aspirations and struggles in cartoons, murals,

Mike Alewitz

Monument to the Workers of Chernobyl, right panel, 1996

posters, and banners. Beginning with the tumultuous labor conflicts in the decades after the Civil War, a public art grew out of union-organizing, agitation against war, and the radical dreams of the American left for women's liberation, racial equality, and social justice. Like many of his artistic predecessors, Alewitz was a factory or office worker for most of his working life, until he became a full-time painter.

Gives biographical details

Born in 1951 and growing up in Wilmington, Delaware, and Cleveland, Alewitz was barely aware that his Cleveland neighborhood had produced the creators of Superman, and was about to bring forth such noted popular artist-creators as Harvey Pekar (subject of an award-winning 2003 film, *American Splendor*) and Peter Kuper (current artist of *Mad* magazine's feature, "Spy Versus Spy"). These artists all shared a sense for the vernacular: the art that almost never reaches gallery walls, but captures the attention of young people in particular. He almost didn't make it to college, and dropped out after a year. That college was Kent State.

By an accident of fate, he had landed on the most explosive campus in North America. At President Richard Nixon's announcement of the US invasion of Cambodia in May 1970, enlarging the Vietnam War dramatically, peace demonstrators took over the grounds of universities and colleges for days, and police and National Guardsmen moved in to halt the demonstrations. At Kent State, guardsmen shot into the crowd, killing students and prompting the most provocative rock music hit of the season, "Four Dead in Ohio" by Crosby, Stills, Nash and Young. Alewitz, a central leader of the Kent antiwar movement, dropped out of school to coordinate the Committee of Kent State Eyewitnesses and to help explain the events and their importance to the national student strike then in progress.

Mike Alewitz found a second home in the college town and state capital, Austin, Texas, where he ran for local office as a peace candidate. He began painting signs again,

Mike Alewitz

Monument to the Workers of Chernobyl, left panel, 1996

for the growing antiwar activity among GIs in basic training at nearby Fort Killeen. He was locally famous (or notorious) for his visual sense of humor, aimed at the clichés of activists, politicians and the military alike.

Describes some of Alewitz's murals

For most of the next twenty years, he worked on railroad lines, at print shops, and most happily as a billboard and sign painter. He painted his first murals in Central America, during the regional conflicts of the 1980s, but received his first major commission almost accidentally in 1984 while visiting a historic packinghouse not far from the twin cities of St. Paul/Minneapolis, in Austin, Minnesota. There, a committee of strikers in local P-9, United Food and Commercial Workers (UFCW) asked him to paint a large wall on the side of their union hall. With the help of strikers and local sympathizers, Alewitz created a panorama of labor dignity, assaulted by corporate mismanagement. The mural was dedicated to Nelson Mandela, then-imprisoned leader of the African National Congress and destined to be the black president of a future South Africa. Widely recognized as one of labor's most important artistic statements in decades, it was destroyed at the orders of national union officials who had decided to end the strike and take control of the union local.

Many similar adventures followed in strikes, Labor Day parades, demonstrations for the rights of working people, women, immigrants and minorities. Alewitz became a widely-recognized artist for unions like the Oil, Chemical and Atomic Workers and the United Brotherhood of Carpenters, the movement for a Labor Party (for which he served as Chair of the Cultural Workers and Artists Caucus), but also for many local causes in his adopted New Jersey, and for school buildings. He also traveled abroad, painting for the endangered atomic-plant workers in Chernobyl, Ukraine, site of the world's worst nuclear energy disaster, to the Middle East and to Mexico.

Explains how Alewitz's style emerged

The last was very much like coming home in an artistic sense. The foremost muralists of the Americas in the twentieth century, along with the Works Progress Administration public artists during the 1930s, were the giants of Mexican muralism, especially Diego Rivera, David Alfaro Siqueiros, Jose Clemente Orozco. These artists, with some of their outstanding 1930s work painted in the U.S., more than anyone else restored painting to its public role in conjunction with social movements whose participants best understood what art might become once again. From them, Alewitz learned purpose. But he had to develop his own style.

Everything under the sun is suitable for reworking as an Alewitz image. From comic strips to earth-shaking events like revolutions and wars, labor leaders and ordinary workers, social heroes and martyrs, nature scenes, factories and neighborhoods, funny and tragic lessons alike. Perhaps most continuous and vividly expressed, though, is the reality of working for a living in hundreds of different ways, old style factories to new style computer terminals—and the overwhelming importance of education.

Explains how Alewitz works

All this goes into the making of the mural. Painters and assorted volunteers help to procure materials, erect scaffolding, repair and prime walls for painting, and often block in large areas of color as well. He has also developed methods of providing space for casual or symbolic contributions to the painting by a larger group of supporters. Artists, poets, musicians and activists of all sorts are invited to create work around the project, at concerts, dedication ceremonies and other public events.

Alewitz himself meanwhile takes strong and direct control of the imagery. He does not believe that his role is to attempt to paint "as if" someone else might, but rather to express those events, struggles and personalities through his own experiences as worker, artist and activist. He has learned that art by committee usually fails because art cannot be negotiated without being homogenized. That said, he works out a final design after thorough discussion. He prefers, for the most part, to work with young assistants who will go through the experience and learn skills that will help them create mural art of their own.

Ending uses a particular mural to make closing point

One of Alewitz's most revealing murals stands on the Highlander Center in New Market, Tennessee, a historic center of civil rights activity and craft training. On one side, leading to a loaf of bread and sumptuous tomatoes (because Highlander is famous for its own produce), is Dr. Martin Luther King, Jr., and on the other side, Highlander's founder, the late Myles Horton, with multiracial working people marching underneath, and the banner-message, "Sin accion, no hay conocimiento/Without action, there is no knowledge."

Democracy, Alewitz's paintings boldly insist, demands active citizens, proud of themselves for what they produce, educated to take responsibility for their history and the better future that America may hold.

Analysis: Using Cultural and Historical Background

Rather than focusing on a particular time and place, Paul Buhle's profile of Mike Alewitz looks at his work in a number of locations, from Cesar Chavez High School, where the profile opens, to Austin, Minnesota, where Alewitz painted one of his most important murals, to Alewitz's travels to Chernobyl, the Middle East, and Mexico, to the closing scene at the Highlander Center in Tennessee. To create a dominant impression that conveys the significance of Alewitz's wide-ranging work, Buhle provides crucial cultural and historical background.

Notice how Buhle skillfully integrates information and commentary into his profile at a number of key points: by defining the function of public art in the second paragraph; by describing in the third paragraph Alewitz's Cleveland neighborhood as the home of Superman's creators and other popular artists; by recounting the events of May 1970 at Kent State in the fourth paragraph; and by explaining in the eighth paragraph the muralist traditions of Mexican painters and public artists of the Works Progress Administration in the 1930s.

⅀⋗ FOR CRITICAL INQUIRY

1. In the last sentence of the opening paragraph, Paul Buhle says that Mike Alewitz was the "natural choice of artists" to paint the mural at Cesar Chavez High School, but he doesn't explain why this is so. Consider whether a satisfactory answer emerges for readers by the end of the profile. What is the effect of letting the question of why Alewitz was the "natural choice" float throughout the profile? Do you think it's a good opening strategy?

2. Use the annotations to consider how (or whether) the profile creates a dominant impression of Mike Alewitz. Trace how this impression develops from the opening scene to the end of the profile. List some of the words, phrases, and sentences that are central to conveying a dominant impression.

3. The single-sentence final paragraph is an eloquent commentary on what "Alewitz's paintings boldly insist." What exactly is Buhle's evaluation of Alewitz's work? Do you think the profile has prepared readers to understand and perhaps to share the sentiments of the last sentence? Why or why not?

Photo Essay

Cancer Alley: The Poisoning of The American South

Richard Misrach and Jason Berry

....

Richard Misrach is a photographer whose work has often focused on the American desert, including studies of former nuclear testing sites and bombing ranges. Jason Berry is a writer, investigative reporter, and documentarian who lives in New Orleans. The photo essay originally appeared in Aperture *(Winter 2001).*

Jason Berry "Cancer Alley: The Poisoning of the American South," photos by Richard Misrach, essay by Jason Berry, from *Aperture* 162 (Winter 2001). Text reprinted by permission of Jason Berry.

CANCER ALLEY

THE POISONING OF THE AMERICAN SOUTH

PHOTOGRAPHS / RICHARD MISRACH

ESSAY / JASON BERRY

"Baton Rouge was clothed in flowers, like a bride—no, much more so; like a greenhouse. For we were in the absolute South now," wrote Mark Twain of the vistas from a riverboat in his 1883 classic *Life on the Mississippi*. "From Baton Rouge to New Orleans," he continued, "the great sugar-plantations border both sides of the river all the way, and stretch their league-wide levels back to the dim forest of bearded cypress in the rear. The broad river lying between the two rows becomes a sort of spacious street."

Twain caught the ninety-mile river corridor between the old Capitol and New Orleans at a poignant moment. Plantations still harvested profits in cotton and sugarcane; the black field workers, no longer slaves, were sharecroppers or virtual serfs. The river flowed through a land riddled with injustice. Yet there was beauty in the waterway and surrounding landscape, and beauty—although burdened with an unsavory history—in those old houses of "the absolute South," with their porticoes and pillared balconies.

By the 1940s, when Clarence John Laughlin trained his lens upon the area, some of the mansions had been torn down and others lay in ruins. The wrecked buildings riveted his eye as much as the several dozen that were still preserved (then starting to shift from farming to tourist sites, which most remain today). A haunting sense of loss suffuses the black-and-white surrealism in Laughlin's remarkable book *Ghosts Along the Mississippi*.

Between the time of Twain's reportage and Laughlin's elegiac photographs from the mid-twentieth century, oil and petrochemical

ABANDONED TRAILER HOME

West Bank Mississippi River, near Dow Chemical plant, Plaquemine, Louisiana, 1998

no. 162 Aperture / 31

Richard Misrach, Courtesy Fraenkel Gallery, SF, Marc Selwyn Fine Art, LA and Pace/MacGill Gallery, NY producers bought up vast pieces of land along the river and began grafting an industrial economy over the old agricultural estates. The refineries and plants—like the derricks that dot the Cajun prairie and the oil-production platforms in Louisiana coastal waters off the Gulf of Mexico—boosted the economies of communities once mired in poverty. The downside has been a political mentality blind to the ravages of pollution.

ORIGINS OF CANCER ALLEY

Standard Oil opened a refinery in 1909 on the fringes of Baton Rouge. In 1929 Governor Huey P. Long erected the new Capitol, a thirty-four-story Art Deco tower near the Standard plant. Today that political temple stands out in high relief from the expanded grid of pumping stacks and smoke clouds where Exxon (Standard's successor) functions like a city-within-the-city. The Capitol and the massive oil complex issuing pungent clouds have melded into an awesome symbol of Louisiana politics: pollution as the price of power.

Providence Plantation, which dated to the 1720s, was in the river town of Des Allemands, and on its grounds was a massive tree known as the Locke Breaux Live Oak, which was 36 feet around and 101 feet high, with a limb span of 172 feet. That majestic tree, estimated to be over three hundred years old, died from exposure to pollution in 1968: the new owner of its site, Hooker Chemical, had it cut up and removed.

The human toll has been even more harsh.

By the 1980s, according to the Louisiana Office of Conservation, thousands of oil-waste pits, many leaching toxic chemicals, were scattered across Louisiana; hundreds of them were seeping into areas of the fertile rice belt in Cajun country. As awareness spread about groundwater contamination and diseases in communities along the river's industrial corridor, activists began calling the area "Cancer Alley."

Although Louisiana ranks in the top 10 percent of states in terms of its cancer mortality rate, petrochemical interests dismiss the term "Cancer Alley" as factually unsupported, a provocation. Black irony coats their charge.

The Louisiana Chemical Association provided base funding for the state Tumor Registry, which assembles the data on cancers. The registry is undertaken by a division of the Louisiana State University Medical Center, which is a beneficiary of donations from polluting industries. Louisiana's Tumor Registry, unlike those in most other states, offers no reliable data on incidences of childhood cancer, or incidences by parish (county), or incidences on a yearly basis. It reports trends only in larger geographic groupings; as a result, disease clusters cannot be pinpointed. Rare forms of cancer can't be tracked geographically. Much information gathered by physicians who treat cancer patients is anecdotal.

And that, in the opinion of Dr. Patricia Williams, is just the way business and petrochemical lobbyists want it. "Without reliable data, no one can link disease patterns to pollution," says Williams, who is herself a professor at the LSU Medical School, and is at the forefront of attempts to change the system.

"We're being denied the raw data and it's unconscionable," says Williams. "Embryonic tumors are not being reported as they are diagnosed. Raw data, by parish, would allow prevention programs. If you see a particular trend of brain cancers, you could begin to sort out what's going on. . . . The same [holds true] with cancer clusters."

Despite the state's history of being at or near the top of statistical lists in categories of toxic emissions, plaintiff attorneys have a great deal of trouble getting medical data to prove the impact of pollution in a given community.

Like Clarence John Laughlin before him, Richard Misrach captures the tones of a culture in spiritual twilight—clinging to a past beauty in the old mansions and icons of Catholicism—now facing a darkness brought about by big oil. Misrach's use of color sets him apart from Laughlin stylistically, as does his striking sense of juxtapositions: the petrochemical specters shadowing fields, ponds, buildings, cemeteries, and basketball courts. Misrach's commitment to discovering the ravaged landscape, while conceptually similar to Laughlin's, is rooted in the land itself. His longterm exploration of the American West and its defilement, the epic "Desert Cantos," are relentlessly straightforward. The "Bravo 20" series of the late 1980s—photographs of Nevada's disturbingly stunning bombing ranges—allow the terrain to create its own dark metaphors. Misrach's work reveals the primary emblems and moods of these frightening landscapes; the Louisiana images are thus as mysterious as they are horrific.

CITIZENS TAKE A STAND

Clarence Laughlin was a romantic who saw industry in symbolic terms—machine against man. In 1980, he took a firm stand at a news conference in New Orleans, lashing out against a plan to put the world's largest toxic-waste incinerator next to the historic Houmas House plantation, in Ascension Parish, midway along the river corridor south of Baton Rouge. A California-based company called Industrial Tank (I.T.) had begun with a $350,000 grant from the state government in Baton Rouge for a site feasibility study. I.T. recommended the construction of a massive disposal complex on a piece of land that was a proven flood plain, below sea level, in an already congested industrial road fronting the Mississippi River. In a move that reeked of corrupt politics, state officials then awarded I.T. the necessary permits to build the complex—whose feasibility I.T. had just been paid to assess. (In fact, the company had put money down on the land before it even got the permits.)

Reports soon surfaced that I.T. had pollution problems at its California sites, and was utterly inexperienced in managing a project of the scope envisioned in Louisiana. A citizens' group filed suit against I.T. and the state. In 1984, the state Supreme Court threw out the permits, killing the project. By then, activists were challenging industry over other conflicts.

DYNAMICS OF CHANGE

Amos Favorite, a seventy-eight-year-old black man, is now retired after many years in the union at Ormet Aluminum. Favorite grew up speaking the Creole French patois in the town of Vacherie, where Fats Domino was born. He remembers when ponds were blue. As a teenager he moved to nearby Geismar, where he has lived ever since.

"This was a good place to live at one time," says Favorite. "All the meat was wild game. I was raised on rabbits, squirrels, and deer." He hated work in the fields, however, and when he came home from infantry in World War II, Favorite bought a dozen acres of Geismar plantation, which was being sold off at thirty-five dollars an acre. The town is named for the family that owned the estate. Favorite's nine children grew up on his acreage; one of his sons was building a handsome two-story house next door to Amos Favorite's this past August.

One of his daughters, artist Malika Favorite, was the first black child to desegregate the local white school. Because of that, two KKK members tried to dynamite the family home. Before they could set the charge, Amos Favorite took his shotgun and started blasting. "I gave 'em the red ass, yes I did," he laughs. "They went runnin' to the sheriff, but that sheriff didn't do nothin' to me."

That was in 1968. A few years later, Favorite began to realize that people were getting sick from wells that drew water from the local aquifer, and he started speaking out against Ascension Parish's sacred cow: industry. BASF, the largest chemical company in the world, and Vulcan, which produces perchloroethylene (the chemical that goes into dry cleaning fluid) have plants in the area.

Despite opposition from management at thirteen major plants in Geismar, including BASF and Vulcan, Favorite won support from union members in those industries for his attempt to establish a public water system and separate district for Geismar. Favorite found a valuable ally in Willie Fontenot, the environmental investigator in the state attorney general's office. Fontenot has made a career of helping communities organize and gather research against polluters and unresponsive state agencies.

"The local government in Ascension had failed to provide adequate water," says Fontenot. "Amos Favorite and the Labor Neighbor project [a cross section of activists from various walks of life] broke the impasse and got the Baton Rouge water company to extend piping and set up a distribution system in Ascension to supplant the old private wells. . . . It was a pretty big victory for a ragtag citizens' group."

The most recent "ragtag" victory came in the town of Convent, where a company called Shintech wanted to build a huge chemical plant in an area of low-income black residents. Tulane University's Environmental Law Clinic helped the citizens challenge the state's operating permits, citing new EPA standards to guard against environmental racism. Shintech pulled out, and found another site, rather than risk being the first major test case of EPA's guidelines. The law clinic took a pounding from Governor Mike Foster and the State Supreme Court, which issued a ruling that severely restricts law students from working with community groups on environmental cases.

The people who live and work in this region of the Mississippi take a long view of their struggle. "The pendulum is going to swing," says Dr. Williams, who lives in LaPlace, twenty miles upriver from New Orleans. "Pollution is such a problem that people are becoming aware of cancers in their friends. They're becoming suspicious. Ten or fifteen years from now, what has happened to big tobacco companies is going to happen to industries that are polluting here." A surge of civil-damage suits against industry is inevitable, she predicts, "because there has been such a concerted effort to conceal what's happened."

HOLY ROSARY CEMETERY AND UNION CARBIDE COMPLEX

Taft, Louisiana, 1998. The Union Carbide Corporation purchased the property of the Holy Rosary Church, built circa
1866. A replacement church was constructed in the 1960s
in nearby Hahnville, but the cemetery was left behind.

38 / Aperture no. 162

Richard Misrach, Courtesy Fraenkel Gallery, San Francisco, Marc Selwyn Fine Art, Los Angeles, and Pace/MacGill Gallery, New York

REVETMENT SIGN AND HALE-BOGGS BRIDGE, WEST BANK, MISSISSIPPI RIVER

Luling, Louisiana, 1998. The Mississippi is the dominant river basin in North America and drains more than 1.2 million square miles, or about 40 percent of the continental United States. It provides 18 million people with drinking water, 1.5 million in Louisiana alone. In a recent study of pollutants discovered in the drinking water of a single Louisiana parish, over 75 toxins were found, including the carcinogens carbon tetrachroride, chloroform, O-chloronitrobenzene, p-chloronitrobenzene, 1,4-dichlorobenzene, DDT, DDE, and DDD, dichloromethane, alachlor, atrazine, dieldrin, heptachlor epoxide, hexachlorobenzene, and pentachlorobenzene. The thirteen Louisiana parishes that depend on the Mississippi as a source of drinking water have some of the highest mortality rates in the United States from several forms of cancer.

NORCO CUMULUS CLOUD, SHELL OIL REFINERY

Norco, Louisiana, 1998. Norco, twenty-five miles upriver from New Orleans, is the site of a massive Shell Oil Refinery. Throughout the day, natural-looking clouds, nicknamed "Norco cumulus," hover over the site, created by the comingling of moisture and volatile hydrocarbons originating in the refinery process of gasoline, jet fuel, cooking oil, and other products. Louisiana ranks second in the nation, behind Texas, in the amount of toxic substances released into the air and water: 183 million tons of toxic chemicals were emitted in 1997.

no. 162 Aperture / 41

Analysis: How Photographs and Texts Go Together

Photo essays consist of a series of photographs that work with a written text to tell a story, describe a place, or portray individuals or group. They have the advantage of using images as well as words to create dominant impressions, to enable readers to visualize people and places. In "Cancer Alley," you can see two common features of the photo essay—the double-page spread and the use of captions—that join words and images together. Notice in "Cancer Alley" that the photographs do not simply illustrate ideas in the written text, nor does the written text simply explain what the photographs are showing. Instead, the relationship between photographs and text is dynamic and reciprocal.

⤞ FOR CRITICAL INQUIRY

1. Consider how the double-page spread opens the photo essay. How does Richard Misrach's photograph of the abandoned trailer establish the mood of the photo essay? What terms would you use to describe the dominant impression the photo essay makes in the opening? How is this impression sustained (or is it) in the rest of the photo essay?

2. Jason Berry says that Misrach's photos of "Cancer Alley" are "geography, autobiography, and metaphor." Explain how each of the three terms might be applied to the photos.

3. How do the essay and photos go together? What is the perspective on "Cancer Alley" developed in Berry's essay? What does it say that the photos can't? What do the photos show that the essay can't?

4. As you can see, Misrach's photographs of pollution and environmental devastation are quite beautiful. What is the relationship between this beauty and the damage the photos document?

Interview

A Conversation with Pauline Wiessner: Where Gifts and Stories Are Crucial to Survival

Claudia Dreifus

Claudia Dreifus writes the "Conversation with . . ." feature in the science section of the New York Times. *A collection of these interviews appears in* Scientific Conversations: Interviews on Science from the *New York Times (2002). This conversation was published on May 26, 2009.*

The anthropologist Pauline Wiessner, at the University of Utah, studies the value of social networks among hunter-gatherers like the !Kung of South Africa (the exclamation point represents a click sound characteristic of their language). I spoke with Dr. Wiessner, who is 61 and goes by the name Polly, during a break at last month's "Origins" symposium at Arizona State University and later in an interview in New York City. An edited version of the conversations follows.

Q.   One of the groups you study, the !Kung people of Southern Africa's Kalahari Desert, are native to one of the most unforgiving corners of the planet. How do they survive in a place of frequent droughts, floods, and famine?

A.   They have an intricate system of banking their social relationships and calling on them when times get rough. The system is maintained through gift-giving, storytelling and visiting. It works like insurance does in our culture.

Nicholas Wiessner

Pauline Wiessner eating a lizard in the Australian desert.

I first arrived in the Kalahari in the early 1970s, when the !Kung were still primarily hunter-gatherers. My question then was: how do people without meat on the hoof, grain in the larder and money in the bank survive hard times?

When I was there for about a year, some answers came. There was a heavy rain. The desert plants died and the wild game dispersed. As people grew hungrier, they began telling vivid stories about loved ones who lived as far as 200 kilometers away. They spoke about how they much missed them. Soon people were busily crafting beautiful objects—gifts. Finally, when push came to shove, 150 !Kung began trekking to the encampments of the people they'd been remembering. There they stayed until conditions in their home area improved.

What I'd witnessed was a structured system at play. The Bushmen used the storytelling to keep feelings for distant persons alive. The gifts are their way of telling the receiver, "I've held you in my heart." Over the years, I saw this repeated many, many times. It would turn out that the !Kung spent as much as three months a year visiting "exchange partners," and this was the key to their survival.

Q.   Were there any special messages in the gifts?

A.   That the relationship was alive and well, and to remind the exchange partner that they had a kind of contract to call on each other in times of need.

Actually, in the Kalahari, people send gifts to their exchange partners even when there isn't a crisis. Like Christmas cards and presents, these objects are information on the status of the relationship. We may not particularly want Aunt Sally's holiday fruit cake, but we'd be troubled if it didn't arrive every year. In the Kalahari, if gifts aren't sent, it means the relationship is in poor repair. People know their networks are crucial to how they get past the hard times, and they tend them with loving care.

Q.   Why are these networks worth studying?

A.   I think they are a clue to how modern humans moved out of Africa around 45,000 years ago. Unless these migrants had support systems in a founding group and could maintain ties with them, it probably wouldn't have been possible to keep pushing into unknown territory.

It only took modern humans some 5,000 years to move out of Africa, cross Eurasia and end up in Australia. I think that the invention of social networks—the storing of relationships for a time when you will need them—is what facilitated this expansion.

It may also have played a role in the development of culture. People who made exquisite gifts and told enthralling stories would have been more successful in maintaining relationships. They might have been the ones who would have had better opportunities for survival and to pass their genes onto the next generation.

Q.   Do you see any contemporary examples of this behavior?

A.   Facebook. People who use it say it keeps memories of distant friends alive and it sometimes brings long-lost relationships back home.

We all know of people who've been "friended" by old pals from college and former neighbors they've lost touch with. When they see pictures of them and read "sharings" from their Facebook partners, they are reminded of their presence in their lives.

One constantly hears stories of people finding jobs and business opportunities through these sites. Hey, and what does a blogger do? Tell stories! The videos and snapshots that people post echo the exchange gifts of the !Kung. They are a kind of token that says, "I've kept you in my heart."

Q. Do your Bushmen friends keep you in their networks when you're back in Utah?

A. There are signs they do. About five years ago, my phone in Salt Lake City rang in the middle of the night. Some of my friends managed to gain access to a satellite telephone left untended by a safari tour operator. They'd even found someone who knew how to work the thing. They said they'd just rung up a well-known American who'd been to the Kalahari a few years earlier making a documentary. He had, according to the !Kung, promised to send their soccer team some athletic shoes. Would I, they asked, purchase them in Utah and then send him the bill? He'd agreed to this, they claimed. I could bring the shoes next time I traveled to Namibia.

Q. Were you annoyed?

A. No. I frequently worried about how the !Kung could survive the modern world. Just that day I had worked with data showing that in the 30 years since they'd moved to permanent settlements, their caloric intake had declined from what it had been when they were hunting and gathering.

This call showed that the !Kung could combine new technologies with age-old strategies to get things they needed.

These Bushmen had survived for millennia by maintaining ties of mutual support with people outside their immediate group. By accessing this satellite phone and devising this complex strategy to get the shoes, they'd extended the range of their support network from 200 to 15,000 kilometers.

Analysis: Doing an Interview

Interviews are a type of profile in which we come to know the subject in his or her own words. Interviews can be wide ranging and cover many topics, as in book-length interviews of such notable figures as Pope Benedict XVI or the legendary filmmaker Alfred Hitchcock (interviewed by the equally legendary filmmaker Francois Truffaut) or the complete John Lennon *Rolling Stone* interview of 1970. Interviews that appear in newspapers and magazines, on the other hand, can be relatively short and highly focused, as in "A Conversation with Pauline Wiessner." As part of the weekly Science Times section in the *New York Times*, Claudia Dreifus's questions tend to concentrate on Wiessner's research. We get some sense of Wiessner's personal side, to be sure, but the main emphasis is on her scholarly work.

To get the 1,000 words or so that make up this interview, Dreifus spoke to Wiessner (and no doubt taped the conversation) on two occasions. The result is an edited version that gives a selective profile of some main themes in Wiessner's research. Part of the work on Dreifus's part was doing this editing, to make Wiessner's specialized research accessible to readers. Just as important was Dreifus's preparation for the interview, to become familiar with the research and to develop a series of questions that would guide Wiessner in explaining her work for readers who may be interested but are unlikely to know a good deal about the !Kung. In this sense, we can see the task of the interviewer as a go-between who can bridge the gap between specialized researchers and the reading public.

▷ FOR CRITICAL INQUIRY

1. Consider the sequence of questions that Claudia Dreifus asks of Pauline Wiessner. How do they progress in terms of describing and explaining the significance of Wiessner's research? How does the sequence expand the reader's understanding of her research? What is the dominant impression that is left with the reader?

2. Here is the abstract of Pauline Wiessner's scholarly article "The Vines of Complexity: Egalitarian Structures and the Institutionalization of Inequality among the Enga," which appeared in the journal *Current Anthropology*.

   The initial stages of the institutionalization of hierarchical social inequalities remain poorly understood. Recent models have added important perspectives to "adaptationist" approaches by centering on the agency of "aggrandizers" who alter egalitarian institutions to suit their own ends through debt, coercion, or marginalization. However, such approaches often fail to take the recursive interaction between agents and egalitarian structure seriously, regarding egalitarian structures as the products of simplicity or blank slates on which aggrandizers can make their marks. The approach here, drawing on insights from the work of Douglass North, views egalitarian structures as complex institutions which, together with their accompanying ideologies, have arisen to reduce the transaction costs of exchange in small-scale societies. It will be argued that egalitarian structures and the coalitions that maintain them vary as greatly in configuration, scope, and nature as do hierarchical structures of power, presenting a variety of obstacles on the path to institutionalized inequality. Data from the precolonial historical traditions of 110 Enga tribes, covering a time span of some 250 years in which vast exchange networks developed and hierarchical inequalities began to be institutionalized, will be used to examine (1) the nature of egalitarian structures and coalitions in Enga at the outset, (2) how these steered the perceptions, motivations, and strategies of agents, and (3) the outcomes of different courses of action. By exploring egalitarian structures in this way it should be possible to depart from neoevolutionary models of political "evolution" without abandoning a more encompassing theoretical framework.

Polly Wiessner, "The Vines of Complexity: Egalitarian Structures and the Institutionalization of Inequality among the Enga." *Current Anthropology*, 43(2) April 2002, pp. 233–269.

Consider the style of Wiessner's scholarly writing in the abstract. Notice, for example, the discipline-based terminology she uses in the abstract and how she talks about "recent models" in the second sentence. Identify other features of the abstract that reveal her as a professional anthropologist. Compare the rhetorical stance she takes in the abstract to that in the interview.

3. Compare this interview to the previous profiles in this chapter. How are interviews alike or different from the profiles?

Arkansas Boys
Paul Clemens

....

Paul Clemens is a writer whose first book Made in Detroit *(2006) is about growing up in Detroit as the auto industry collapsed. "Arkansas Boys" is an excerpt from his second book,* Punching Out: One Year in a Closing Auto Plant *(2011), which profiles a group of riggers taking down heavy equipment in an auto plant that is being disassembled.*

There were still places in Detroit that respected working-class culture. The Arkansas Boys' pickups could be seen, most lunchtimes, in the parking lot of the Texas Bar, about a mile southeast of the Budd plant on Kercheval. The bar's demographics contrasted strongly with those of the surrounding area. In one of the bar's front windows, near the door, was a handwritten cardboard sign:

> **No Public Restroom or Telephone's.**
> **No—Bum's.**
> **No—Hooker's.**
> **No—Thieve's.**
> **No—Selling of Anything.**
> **We Do Call the *Police*.**

The lunch special at the Texas was a cheeseburger, fries, and beer for $5.50. I asked the barmaid, on a snowy Friday in February, to substitute a Coke for the beer. I might well have asked for water instead of wine at Canaan. Despite its being a Friday during Lent, I ate the burger, having already forgone the beer. I was waiting on the arrival of the Arkansas Boys—whom, despite months of observing, I'd spoken to only in small snatches. Our dialogues had been nothing to write home about, or even write in my notebook about.

There was honky-tonk on the stereo. A woman down at the end of the bar was holding court. She was in her forties and fat, with a terrific memory for song lyrics. In between laments, she sang along. "I know my kids are bad," she said, "but I don't need no one to tell me they're bad. I don't like my children sometimes, but I love 'em. I had my first child at nineteen. I'm going to get drunk," she said, for some reason employing the future tense.

Behind the bar were stickers: "Union Roofers Local 149." "Proud to Be a Union Sheet Metal Worker." St. Patrick's Day was six weeks away, and behind the bar, too, were one-dollar shamrocks that had been sold on behalf of Jerry's Kids. After purchase, the donor signed his name or that of his organization, and the shamrock was taped up. "From the Heart of _____ Comes a Shamrock to Help Fight Muscular Dystrophy." Local 58 had bought a shamrock. Local 299 had bought a shamrock. So had several individuals, though some used pseudonyms. I doubted the existence of Dr. Felter Snatch.

By the time the Arkansas Boys had walked into the bar and seated themselves at a table, I'd lost my nerve to approach them. This was their habitat, not mine, and I was out of my depth, sipping my Coke. I continued to observe their work from a distance, as I had for months.

My next close brush with the Razorbacks came a couple weeks later, when Arkansas Dave pulled up on the scale alongside Eddie's shack. It was nowhere near quitting time, but Arkansas Dave said that they were going home to the motel "to do laundry and shit." Dave said that they'd come in around 10:00 the next day, a Sunday, to drop the side columns in 9-line. After they'd pulled away, Eddie said that they were angry that they didn't have any lights down in the pits. "Bring a flashlight," Eddie said he'd told them.

"'Do what you have to do to get the job done.' They know we have no electricity. I don't have a charge card. I can't just send them out for whatever they want."

The majority of the plant's power had gone out in mid-January. Generators and flood-lights had been brought in, and Eddie and Guy, as management, would often go around at lunchtime, turning off the lights to keep down costs—parents following after forgetful kids. The lights would click off in this part of the plant, then that, with Budd looking more and more like a movie studio where filming had stopped.

I arrived at the plant around 11:30 on Sunday, hoping to see the Arkansans. When I walked into the press shop, I didn't see a soul. The fire in the basket above 2-line was nearly out—a clue in itself as to how many people might be about. The Budd plant must have been one of the few places on earth where fire's presence or absence was still a pre-dictor of human habitation. In the absence of people, the barrel and basket fires resem-bled the smoldering remains of a sacked village.

In the distance, down by the base of 9-line, I saw the flames of a fire barrel that was serving as the furnace for the Arkansas Boys—who, good as their word, were working to drop the side columns of the line's fourth press. Three fire extinguishers were by the fire barrel to prevent freezing. Their pickups—a 2005 Chevy, a silver Ford F-150, and a white Ford F-150—were parked nearby. Shafts of sunlight came in from the coated windows above, producing something of the effect of stained glass.

Their task for the day wasn't a big deal, rigging-wise, which was just as well, since it gave us time to talk. They were at the rough midpoint of what Matt Sanders called "unstacking" the press. Its crown and ram had been removed. They were, now, working on the columns. After that, they'd pull the bolster, then the base, and that'd be that: another press down.

Jeremy was atop the left column of 9-4. Dave and Josh were down in the pit, the darkness of which Dave had complained about the day before, where Dave was torching off a nut. Terry senior and Terry junior controlled the P&H overhead crane, above us in Bay 5, with the pendant controller that dangled down. I stood next to them. Father and son had a habit of sticking their gloved hands into the barrel fire, both to warm their hands up and to burn the grease from their gloves.

"They heated it," Terry senior said, explaining their problems with the stubborn nut. Heating it had caused it to expand, and "they" were some guys on the crew who weren't from Arkansas and who, as a result, didn't have the slightest idea what the hell they were doing. Dave knew damn well what he was doing down there. I asked the two Terrys how big the nut was that Dave was cutting. They both extended their arms in a circle, as if making to pick up a big dog. They figured it weighed three hundred pounds.

As we waited, Terry junior provided me quick biographical sketches of the Razorback crew. He himself was 18, from Atkins, Arkansas, and was sending some of the money he earned in Detroit back home to his grandfather. With the money he kept, he wanted to buy a truck or a "crotch rocket"—a motorcycle. I said a truck was more practical. "A bike is cheaper on gas," he said.

So far, he'd gotten a thousand dollars' worth of tattoos done in Detroit; he showed me a picture on his cell phone of the tattoo he had done on his upper back. He'd also bought a TV/DVD player for his dad's Ford F-150. He considered this an investment in the future, as he thought that he might want to buy the truck from his father. He'd started at Budd back in September or October—couldn't recall exactly. At the moment, he was waiting on Dave to cut the nut so that, with the overhead crane, he and his dad could pull the tie-rods that ran the length of the press's columns.

Jeremy, atop the columns to handle the hookup between rod and crane, was 20 and from Fort Smith, Arkansas. Dave, in his forties, was from Cabot, Arkansas, but now lived in Indiana. Josh, down below, was 21, looked 12, and was also from Fort Smith. The women in the plant, if there'd been any, would have considered him "cute." He laughed the most, was the quickest to smile, and had curly hair. Terry junior and Jeremy were more withdrawn, intent to learn a craft and draw a check. All three of the kids had started rigging at 18, Terry junior told me.

"After high school?" I asked.

"None of us graduated high school," Terry junior said. "My old man did, and Dave." He said he had dropped out in the ninth grade.

"Aren't you supposed to stay in longer?" I asked.

"Supposed to, I guess, until you're 16, or whatever." His main concern was staying in school long enough to get his driver's license, which somehow he secured. His youth freed him from concerns about future employment. He said his dad "knows everyone in Arkansas. If this goes south, he can always get a job in Arkansas."

Terry senior, who stood with us near the barrel, didn't like the weather in Detroit and wanted to go south in the literal sense. He said that it didn't get this cold in Arkansas—down to the single digits—and that it didn't stay this cold this long. There might be some freezing rain in Arkansas, he said, but there was nearly no snow. Terry senior had graduated from high school in 1980. When I talked to him up close, it looked as if he had more teeth missing than remaining. He was even leaner than he looked, with prominent cheekbones and a bit of gray in his beard. On his head he always wore a green hood, which looked to be the lining from a racing helmet. None of the Arkansas Boys ever wore hard hats—another of their distinctions.

"This is scrapping," Terry senior said of the work that they were doing. I said that 9-line wasn't getting scrapped, but had in fact been bought by Gestamp, the same Spanish auto supplier that had bought 16-line for Mexico. Terry just laughed.

Uli, the German engineer from Müller Weingarten who was overseeing the 16-line and 9-line dismantlings for Gestamp, had been around the plant earlier in the day. Uli—short for Ulrich—had been in Budd since May 2007, back when work on 16-line began. He spent November and December back home, outside Mexico City. "We call Uli 'Schultz,'" Terry senior said. "Sergeant Schultz. Hogan's Heroes." For Christmas, he said, "We got Uli a quart of moonshine."

We looked down into the pit where Dave, an American flag bandanna on his head, was finishing torching the nut off. Josh stood with him in the smoke, oil, and water. When Dave came up from the pit, job done, he explained his technique. "I cussed it more than I cut it," he said. The nut sat smoking in the grease of the pit, cut in three equal pieces. Dave's glasses were covered in grease. He wiped them, and said something I couldn't quite catch about having "the biggest rod and nuts around."

A week or so after Dave's assertion of rod-and-nut supremacy, he and Jeremy got into a fight in their Macomb County motel. It was probably bound to happen: five grown men living in close proximity in lousy conditions for months on end. Guy Betts told me that Jeremy had gone to jail, but was out now. Whatever the story, Dave's left eye, swollen and discolored from a right hand, told it.

"How you doing?" I asked him when I saw his shiner.

"Could be better," he said. "I'm going home. Fuck it."

By home, Dave meant home, not a Macomb County motel. Terry senior would be dropping Dave off in Indiana while on his own way to Arkansas. This was just a quick vacation, Terry senior told me, not a permanent departure. I was greatly relieved: a Budd plant without the senior Arkansas Boys would be a badly diminished thing.

It was early March. "This might be the ugliest I've ever seen the plant look," I said to Guy. It was cloudy and smoky inside the plant, with fog all over the press shop. I could actually see a cloud line above the pits to 3- and 4-lines. "Be careful walking around," Guy warned. "Pipes are bursting right and left." Though it wasn't a Friday, Terry and Dave were waiting on their paychecks to arrive from the rigging company before departing Detroit on their trip.

While they waited, there was some excitement: the plant was invaded. Two crew members, working by the light of a fire in an area outside the press shop, said they spotted the wannabe crooks sneak past them wearing parkas. Once they knew they'd been spotted, the crooks began to run, and the crew members came into the press shop to sound the alarm.

I asked if the invaders might not have just been guys on the crew.

"No guys on the crew run that fast," I was told.

Crew members picked up whatever tools were to hand—crowbars, heavy rods, wood boards, big wrenches—and tore ass thataway, into the plant's darkness. Eddie, who'd been summoned from outside, walked in with a shotgun over his shoulder. I stood by a fire barrel at the base of 8-line with Terry senior and Terry junior. The other two Arkansas youngsters, Jeremy and Josh, had joined the chase, only to return soon thereafter.

"Here comes one dumb ass," Terry junior said, seeing Jeremy reemerge from the darkness, rod in hand. Behind him was Josh, also carrying a rod.

"I stabbed his ass right through the heart," Jeremy said, jokingly.

As the manhunt continued, Guy Betts came over for a chat. "See what people will do for scrap metal?" he said. "They figured we wouldn't be able to hear them during the day, with all this noise."

The search turned up nothing, though later that afternoon, two guys were seen running out of the plant onto Conner Avenue. Eddie, for one, wasn't the least bit surprised that the guys hadn't been caught.

"There's lots of places to hide in here," he said.

I talked to the Arkansas Boys every chance I had from then on. Arkansas Dave's good cheer was a constant. When he'd returned from vacation, I asked him how it had gone.

"What vacation?" he asked. His black eye was healing but still showed traces of trouble. "That was no goddamned vacation. And then I gotta come back to this goddamned place." He yelled at the boys among the Arkansas Boys, who were using a crane. "They don't listen, they don't learn, I'm getting goddamned sick," Dave said.

Around the fire basket a month later, I chatted him up again. His eye had long since healed. "How much longer you here?" I asked.

"Until they're kind enough to tell me to go the fuck home."

I had nothing against Arkansas and wanted to hear from the boys some kindness about the city of my birth. I asked Josh, since he was the sunniest of the Arkansans, if he'd miss Detroit when the Budd job was done.

"No."

"Won't you miss the Texas Bar?" "No," he said. "I don't even drink." He considered the dubious accuracy of this, then added: "I drank thirty-two beers the other night, between six o'clock and one in the morning, but that was the first time in a long time." He wasn't entirely sure how he got back to the motel, but said, "I remember pissing on a Dumpster on 9 Mile Road."

I asked Josh if his real name was Joshua. "Naw, it's just Josh. I mean, it might say Joshua on my Social Security card, or something. I don't know." He asked about the pictures he'd seen me taking around the plant. I said that I could email them to him. "Hell, I don't even know what email is," Josh said. "I think my girlfriend's got a computer, though."

Now that we knew each other, Terry senior had his own way of greeting me. "Asshole of the earth," he said whenever he saw me.

"It's my hometown," I said, defending Detroit.

"It's my hometown, too, last five or six months, and I fucking hate it."

"Where you going after this?" He shrugged. "Unemployment office, probably."

Analysis: Representative Figures

From the opening line, where Paul Clemens locates the Texas Bar as a remaining outpost of working-class culture in Detroit, we realize we are meant to take the Arkansas Boys as representative figures, with their pickups, drinking and fighting, and an "intuitive genius," as Clemens earlier calls it, for their work as expert riggers who travel from one job disassembling plants to another. Like all the workers involved in closing the Budd stamping plant in Detroit, the Arkansas Boys give us a personal look at a larger historical process. The appeal of Clemens's profiles of the Arkansas Boys is how individualized they are, at the same time they represent a moment in the history of the American working class. They come to life on their own, not just as illustrations of the writer's theme, through Clemens's observations of them at work and the use of dialogue as he gets to know them. One of the challenges of writing profiles of ordinary people is how to give their lives and work broader significance, without reducing them to stereotypes of a social group, such as "hillbillies" or "rednecks" or "hardhats."

⤳ FOR CRITICAL INQUIRY

1. We might think of this profile as a series of scenes in which the Arkansas Boys appear. To see how this works, divide the profile into sections. How does Paul Clemens cluster the information and observation he presents? What order does he use? What effects does he achieve by organizing the profile as he does?

2. What is the dominant impression the profile creates? Clemens uses the label "Arkansas Boys" to refer to the five riggers. How are readers meant to understand them as a group? What gives the group its particular identity?

3. Unlike earlier profiles, such as Paul Buhle's profile of Mike Alewitz or Jason Berry's of "Cancer Alley," where the writers don't have a physical presence, Clemens appears in person in "The Arkansas Boys." How does his presence affect the profile, compared to the other two profiles? On the other hand, consider how his words and the interactions he has with the Arkansas Boys differ from those of an interviewer, such as Claudia Dreifus in "Conversation with Pauline Wiessner." How do the relationships differ? What effect overall does this have on the two profiles?

MULTIMODAL COMPOSITION

Soundmap: Folk Songs for the Five Points

This audio archive was created by Alastair Dant, Tom Davis, Victor Gama, and David Gunn for the Lower East Side Tenement Museum's Digital Artists in Residence Program in response to an invitation for "works that explore contemporary immigrant experience in New York City." You can visit Folk Songs for the Five Points at www .tenement.org/folksongs/. Listen to the audio samples on the soundmap. Compare this soundmap of the Lower East Side to the photo essay "Cancer Alley." What does each bring to light about the place it is profiling?

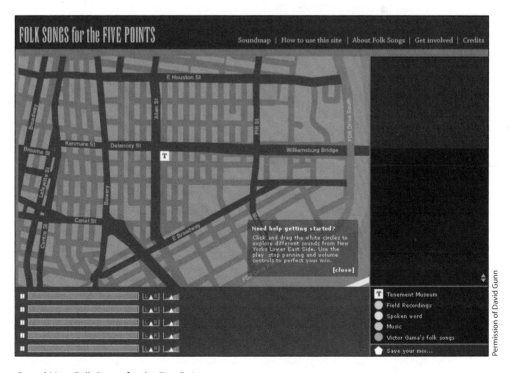

Sound Map: Folk Songs for the Five Points.

Radio Interview: Patti Smith, Interviewed on Amy Goodman's Democracy Now

Patti Smith is sometimes called the "godmother of punk." She was inducted into the Rock and Roll Hall of Fame in 2007 and won the National Book Award in 2010 for her memoir *Just Kids*. Amy Goodman, the host of *Democracy Now* on the Pacific Radio network, interviewed Patti Smith on the April 29, 2010, show. You can listen to the interview and download a transcript of it at http://www.democracynow.org/2010/4/29 /punk_rock_legend_patti_smith_on.

Here are excerpts from the opening minutes:

AMY GOODMAN: Punk rock legend Patti Smith, singing an a capella version of her best-known song "Because the Night" here in our studios. She did it just a few months ago, when we dedicated our new broadcast studios, the greenest in the country. She was with us with hundreds of people celebrating.

Well, on Wednesday, Patti Smith was awarded the National Book Award in the nonfiction category for her memoir *Just Kids*. The book tells the story of Smith's coming of age in New York and her lifelong friendship and creative collaboration with the renowned photographer Robert Mapplethorpe. Patti Smith's influential debut album *Horses* came out in 1975 to critical acclaim.

Her best-known song "Because the Night" was co-written with Bruce Springsteen. More recently, Patti has performed in numerous antiwar rallies. She's written songs about American peace activist Rachel Corrie, the Israeli assault on the Lebanese village of Qana, and Murat Kurnaz, a Turkish citizen of Germany who was imprisoned at Guantánamo for five years.

Well, Patti Smith joined us in the studio and spoke with Anjali Kamat and I about her life, her art, her activism and the focus of her memoir, her friendship with Robert Mapplethorpe.

PATTI SMITH: Well, I met Robert in 1967. Again, you know, I came to New York with nothing. I had a lot of bravado. I had a few dollars in my pocket, but I had a good work ethic. I knew I wanted a job, and that's what I was looking for. And I also didn't feel any fear in New York City. I really loved New York. I was brought up in a very rural community, and we didn't have cars. The roads were dark. There was nowhere to go. You'd have to walk like four or five miles to, you know, go to a pizza place. And, you know, New York, where everything was right there, there was all kinds of places to get coffee, you could sleep on the subway. You know, it seemed like the safest place in the world.

So, and in the middle of this atmosphere, I met Robert, quite accidentally. And we were both quite—we were more alike than not. We were the same age, both wanted to be artists, both had nothing, and both sort of on the fringe of things. You

Amy Goodman, "Interview with Patti Smith." From *Democracy Now* show, Pacifica Radio. April 29, 2010. Reprinted by permission.

know, both of us were more the late bloomer type. And, you know, despite the fact that Robert was—you know, had a very engaging face, he was still sort of a wall-flower, a person on the fringe, even in an art school. So we gravitated toward each other and supported each other and evolved together and went through all kinds of things, you know, from Robert discovering or coming to terms with his evolving sexual identity to becoming a photographer, me evolving from poetry into rock-and-roll. And we evolved together.

ANJALI KAMAT: And he took the iconic photograph of you on the cover of your first album?

PATTI SMITH: Yeah, he did. He did. And we did that just like we did everything else. Our relationship was built on trust. And, you know, sometimes people ask me about how we took this picture, like it was some big drama. Like now, you get your picture taken and the photo shoot, that you'd think they were doing a movie. There's like catering and, you know, four monitors and a bunch of people running around. It's like a Peter Sellers movie, you know. Really, it was just me and Robert, you know, in a white room and with natural light. In fact, his light meter was broken, so he took twelve shots, and we got it.

. . . .

AMY GOODMAN: So talk about 1969 and you and Robert going [to live in the Chelsea Hotel in New York City].

PATTI SMITH: Well, . . . Robert and I were both—we went through a lot of different things. And in 1969, we were a bit down on our luck, and we had heard that if you went to the Chelsea Hotel, they would often trade art for a room. And we went to the Chelsea Hotel, and I checked out the lobby, and the stuff was pretty bad, and I thought, oh, we won't have any problem. But Mr. Bard was not really interested in our work, but he was interested in the fact that I had employment, which was something that probably 70 percent of the people of the hotel did not have, so—

AMY GOODMAN: Who was there?

PATTI SMITH: Who was there at the time? Well, the first person we met in the lobby was Harry Smith, who was definitely not employed. But we saw all kinds of people there. I mean, there was a lot of artists and writers. Virgil Thomson lived there. I'd say Shirley Clarke. I saw Jonas Mekus there a lot and Allen Ginsberg and just about—I mean, we could go on and on with lists of people. Even Arthur C. Clarke lived there.

So I talked Mr. Bard into, you know, letting us have a room based on the fact that I had a job. We had the smallest room in the hotel, which doesn't even exist anymore. It had no bathroom. It was $55 a week, and I made $65 at Scribner's Bookstore. So that pretty much could say what our living situation was. But it was really a great stroke of luck to move at the Chelsea, because the people that we met there—Gregory Corso and William Burroughs and Allen Ginsberg. I met Bobby

ETHICS OF WRITING

RESPONSIBILITY TO THE WRITER'S SUBJECT

What is a writer's responsibility to his or her subject? How does this responsibility interact with the writer's responsibility to readers? What potential conflicts are there between the two responsibilities? These are questions profile writers invariably grapple with.

Profiles, after all, are meant to inform readers and offer them the writer's honest perspective—not to serve as publicity or public relations for the person, place, or organization profiled. If profile writers are to have an independent voice and fulfill their responsibilities to readers, they must be able to make their own judgments about what is fit to print. But an important basis for these judgments is a sense of responsibility toward the subject.

Neuwirth and so many musicians, people you never heard of and people who, you know, we all revere. And I think I said it in the book, but it's true, it became my new university. I couldn't think of a better place to be at the time, because I learned so much about everything, about painting and poetry, performance, activism, all in this one hotel.

This is an unedited transcript of what was broadcast on the air. What we can't reproduce here is Patti Smith singing "Because the Night," her most famous song, which she wrote with Bruce Springsteen and which opens Amy Goodman's interview. Likewise, while we can imagine the voices of Patti Smith and Amy Goodman as we read, we still miss the personal texture of the voice we hear when Smith and Goodman speak. Notice how the unedited voices of Smith and Goodman compare, say, to Pauline Wiessner's voice, as it was edited for print by Claudia Dreifus. Consider the differences and similarities of listening and reading. Listen to the radio interview and consider what audio does in broadcasting the voice as spoken compared to the voice as edited to read in print texts. What do radio interviews do that print interviews can't do? By the same token, what does print do that radio can't?

FURTHER EXPLORATION

Rhetorical Analysis

Profiles and biographies are both genres of writing that inform readers about people, but they do so in different ways. To understand what distinguishes profiles and biographies, read one or two short biographies in a standard reference source, such as an encyclopedia, the *Dictionary of American Biography,* or *Current Biography,* to compare to one of the profiles that appear in this chapter. How do the profile and the biographical entry differ in terms of the type and arrangement of information? What differences do you see in the writers' relationship to the subject of the profile or biography and to their readers? What do the differences in rhetorical stance tell you about the two genres?

Genre Awareness

Profiles and interviews appear on radio (e.g. *Democracy Now, Fresh Air, On Point,* and *World Café*), television (e.g. *The Daily Show, Charlie Rose,* and *60 Minutes*) and in documentary films such as *Crumb*, about the comic artist; *Tupac: The Resurrection,* about the rapper Tupac Shakur; *Fog of War*, about Robert McNamara, Secretary of Defense during the Vietnam War; Werner Herzog's *Grizzly Man*; Wim Wender's profile of the dancer Pia Busch in *Pia*; and Frederick Wiseman's portraits of institutions in *Boxing Gym, Public Housing, High School,* and many others. In a group of three or four, identify a radio or television program or a film that profiles an individual, a group, or a place. Develop an oral presentation that analyzes the profile or interview. Use audio or video clips to illustrate the attitude of the profile and how it wants the audience to see the subject being profiled. Consider what audio or video makes possible that differs from print profiles. What can print profiles do that audio or video ones can't?

WRITING ASSIGNMENT

Profile

Choose a person, a group, or a place to write a profile about. The point of this assignment is to bring your subject to life in writing so that you can help your readers see and understand what makes your subject worth reading about.

Here are some possibilities to help you think about whom you might profile:

▶ Pick an individual, like Mike Alewitz, whose life and work are notable, whether the person is an artist, a worker, a politician, a community activist, a priest or rabbi, doctor or lawyer, and so on. Or focus on an ordinary person whose profile somehow illuminates the common experience of the time—a representative figure of what was happening in the broader society.

▶ Pick a place to profile. It could be somewhere you hang out; a neighborhood; a park; or, as in "Cancer Alley," an industrial site. You could do this as a photo essay.

▶ Pick a group of people. It could be ordinary people like "The Arkansas Boys" or a social or artistic movement locally or nationally.

▶ Do an interview with a scholar, an administrator, or a distinguished teacher at your college or university, with the focus on the person's academic work, as in the interview with Pauline Wiessner.

Multimodal Composition

▶ Design a soundmap like Folk Songs for the Five Points that provides an audio profile of a place. Use sound you have recorded, spoken word, interviews, music, and so on to capture the place. You don't have to turn this into a Web site, like Folk Songs for the Five Points. You can do it on paper as a design prototype, indicating where the sounds you're using would appear on an interactive map.

▶ Plan a radio interview with a local musician or writer that includes live musical performance or reading.

Invention

Finding a Subject

Take some time to decide on the person, place, organization, or artistic or social movement you want to profile.

➪ EXERCISE

Developing Your Topic

1. **Make a list:** Make a list of individual people, types of people, or particular places that, for one reason or another, interest you. Try to come up with at least ten to give you some choices.

2. **Talk to others:** Meet with two or three other students in your class and share the lists each of you has developed for feedback and advice about the most promising subjects. Ask the other students to tell you which are most interesting, why, and what they would like to know about them.

3. **Decide tentatively on a subject:** Use the feedback you have received to help you make a tentative decision about which subject you will profile. Take into account your partners' reasons for being interested.

4. **Contact your subject:** If you are planning an interview, you will need to contact your subject. Explain that you're a student working on an assignment in a writing course. You'll be amazed—and reassured—by how helpful and gracious most people usually are. If they don't have time, they'll tell you so, and then you can go back to your list and try your second choice. Most likely, however, you'll be able to schedule a time to meet and talk with the person. Ask whether he or she can suggest anything you might read or research as background information before the interview to help you prepare for it.

At this point it may also be helpful for you to sketch out a schedule for yourself. To write this profile, you will need to allow time for the several stages of both research and writing.

Clarifying Your Purpose

Write a brief statement of purpose. This can be helpful preparation for an interview or as exploratory writing for a profile from memory or based on research.

➪ EXERCISE

Developing a Statement of Purpose

Take fifteen minutes to answer the following questions:

▶ Why are you interested in the particular person, place, group, or organization you're profiling? What is your attitude toward the subject?

▶ What do you already know? What do you need to find out? How can you get this information?

▶ What do other people think? Do you share these views? What makes your perspective unique?

▶ What do you expect to find out by interviewing or observing ? What background reading do you need to do? What do you need to find out?

▶ What is your purpose in profiling your subject?

Background Research: Deciding What Information You Need

Whether you're planning an interview with people or observing a place, you'll need to determine the type of information called for by your profile. The nature of this research, of course, will vary depending on whom you're profiling and what your purpose is. Here are some questions to help you make appropriate decisions.

For more information about interviews, see the "interviewing" section in Chapter 16, pp. 486–490.

1. What information do you need? What background information do you need on a person's life or the history of a place, an organization, or an artistic or social movement? How is this information pertinent to your profile? Is this information readily available, or do you need to find ways to get it?

2. What, if anything, about your subject has already been written? What would be useful to read? If you're doing an interview, can your subject suggest things you could read before you meet?

3. Are there relevant social, cultural, artistic, or political issues you need to know about for the profile? If so, what's important to understand?

Planning

Deciding on the Dominant Impression

As you have seen from the reading selections in this chapter, the purpose of a profile is to capture your subject at a particular moment in time and to offer readers a dominant impression—a way of seeing and understanding the significance of the person, place, or organization being profiled.

Here are some questions to help you determine the point of view you want to establish and the dominant impression you want to create:

► What is the most interesting, unusual, or important thing you have discovered about your subject?

► What are your own feelings about your subject?

► What do others say about your subject? Are these responses to your subject consistent, or do people differ?

► Can you think of two or more dominant impressions you could create to give readers a way of understanding your subject?

Use your answers to these questions to refine your sense of purpose. It may help at this point to talk to a friend or classmate. Explain the different ways in which you might portray your subject. Ask how the dominant impressions you are considering affect the way your classmate or friend understands your subject.

Arranging Your Material

Inventory the material you have to work with. Look over your notes and notice how many separate items about your subject you have. These are the building blocks of your profile, the raw material that you will put together to construct it. Label each item according to the kind of information it contains—such as physical description, biographical background, historical or cultural context, observed actions and procedures, revealing incidents or anecdotes, direct quotes, and things other people have told you.

Once you have inventoried your material, your task is to sketch a tentative plan for your profile. Consider two options illustrated by the readings in this chapter—open form and claims and evidence.

Notice that Paul Buhle's profile of Mike Alewitz is organized in clusters of information that create a web of meaning with a dominant impression. The point or main claim of the profile is implied rather than stated explicitly. The form is open and works through the connections readers make between the information clusters. Buhle's profile can be represented by this chart:

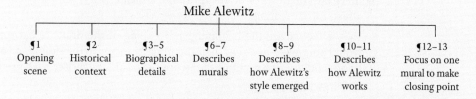

Mike Alewitz

¶1	¶2	¶3–5	¶6–7	¶8–9	¶10–11	¶12–13
Opening scene	Historical context	Biographical details	Describes murals	Describes how Alewitz's style emerged	Describes how Alewitz works	Focus on one mural to make closing point

Experiment with the clusters of information you have. Consider whether open form or a claims and evidence arrangement is better suited. Try a couple different arrangements of the order of information, to determine what's most effective for your purposes and the dominant impression you want to create.

Working Draft

By this time you have organized a lot of material from your research. In fact, you are likely to have more material than you can use, so don't worry if you can't fit everything in as you write a working draft. Consider drafting by clusters of information, with the idea that you might change the order of arrangement when you revise.

Beginnings and Endings: Letting Your Subject Have the Last Word

A standard way to end profiles of people is to give them the final word. This is what happens at the end of "The Arkansas Boys," when the riggers' job is almost finished and Paul Clemens asks Terry senior:

"Where are you going after this?"

He shrugged. "Unemployment office, probably."

Paul Buhle does a variation on giving the subject the final word. However, this time it's not the subject of the profile, Mike Alewitz, who speaks but rather, in a metaphorical way, his paintings. Buhle gives them voice by writing that "Alewitz's paintings boldly insist" that democracy "demands active citizens, proud of themselves for what they produce, educated to take responsibility for their history and the better future that America may hold."

Peer Commentary

Exchange drafts with a partner. Respond in writing to these questions about your partner's draft:

1. Describe what you see as the writer's purposes. Does the working draft create a dominant impression? Does it imply or state a main point? Explain how and where the draft develops a dominant impression (and main point, if pertinent).

2. Describe the arrangement of the working draft. Divide the draft into sections by grouping related paragraphs together. Explain how each section contributes to the overall impression the profile creates. Do you find the arrangement easy to follow? Does the arrangement seem to suit the writer's purposes? If there are rough spots or abrupt shifts, indicate where they are and how they affected your reading.

3. How effective are the beginning and ending of the draft? What suggestions would you make to strengthen the impact, increase the drama, or otherwise improve these two sections of the draft? Should the writer have used a different strategy?

4. Do you have other suggestions about how the writer could enhance the profile? Are there details, reported speech, descriptions, or incidents that the writer could emphasize? Are there elements the writer should cut?

Revising

Use the peer commentary to do a critical reading of your draft.

1. Consider first how your reader has analyzed the arrangement of your profile. Notice in particular how the commentary has divided the draft into sections. Do these sections correspond to the way you wanted to arrange the profile? Are there ways to rearrange material to improve its overall effect?

2. If you are using open form, are the clusters of information clear to your reader? Are there ways to enhance the presentation?

3. If you are presenting a claim and evidence, was this pattern of organization clear to your reader? Are there ways to enhance its presentation?

4. Does the draft create the kind of dominant impression you intended?

5. What did your writing partner suggest? Evaluate specific suggestions.

Establishing Perspective from the Beginning

The beginning of your profile is a particularly important place to establish a perspective on the person, place, or group you're writing about. The strategy you use to design an opening will depend both on your material and on the attitude you want your readers to have toward your subject. Notice how Stacy Yi revised the opening paragraph of her profile of the lawyer and anti-smoking activist Edward Sweda. The early draft reads more like a paragraph from a biography of Edward Sweda, whereas the revised version takes us into Sweda's world.

Early Draft of "A Lawyer's Crusade Against Tobacco"

Edward Sweda began his career as an anti-smoking activist over twenty years ago, when he became involved as a volunteer in a campaign to provide non-smoking sections in restaurants. He is currently the senior staff attorney for the Tobacco Product Liability Project (TPLP) at Northeastern University. Since 1984, when TPLP was established, Sweda and his associates have battled the powerful tobacco interests.

Revised Version of "A Lawyer's Crusade Against Tobacco"

The office of the Tobacco Product Liability Project (TPLP) at Northeastern University in Boston is decorated with anti-smoking propaganda. One poster shows the damage that smoking has done to someone's lungs. The office secretary sat at her desk and typed busily, while Edward Sweda, senior attorney of the TPLP, conversed on the phone with Stanton Glantz, author of the well-known exposé of the tobacco industry Cigarette Papers.

Here is a list of techniques for establishing perspective at the beginning of a profile:

- ▶ **Set the scene:** Describe the place where you encounter your subject; give details about the physical space; describe other people who are there; explain what the people are doing; set the stage for your subject's entrance.

- ▶ **Tell an anecdote:** Narrate an incident that involves your subject; describe how your subject acts in a revealing situation.

- ▶ **Use a quotation:** Begin with your subject's own words; use a particularly revealing, provocative, or characteristic statement.

- ▶ **Describe your subject:** Use description and detail about your subject's appearance as an opening clue to the person's character.

- ▶ **Describe a procedure:** Follow your subject through a characteristic routine or procedure at work; explain the purpose and technical details; use them to establish your subject's expertise.

- ▶ **State your controlling theme:** Establish perspective by stating in your own words a key theme that will be developed in the profile.

WRITERS' WORKSHOP

Stacy Yi. Rhetorical Analysis of a Profile

This is the prompt Stacy Yi got from her teacher to do a short rhetorical analysis of a profile used in advertising or an advocacy campaign:

> Single-page profiles that combine text and image are a staple of advertising, public relations, and advocacy campaigns that personalize the publicity. Here are three examples. The first two come from the organization Jewish Voice for Peace and its campaign for an end to the Israeli occupation of the West Bank, Gaza, and East Jerusalem and a just solution to the conflict between Israel and the Palestinians. The print-ad profile of the hedge fund manager was designed by the Swiss hearing technology company Phonak, in what it has called "the edgiest campaign in the company's (and probably the industry's) history," to overcome the stigma of using hearing aids on the part of "younger baby-boomers." Explain how the ad creates the publicity campaign's rhetorical stance.

Courtesy of Jewish Voice for Peace, www.jvp.org

Courtesy of Jewish Voice for Peace, www.jvp.org

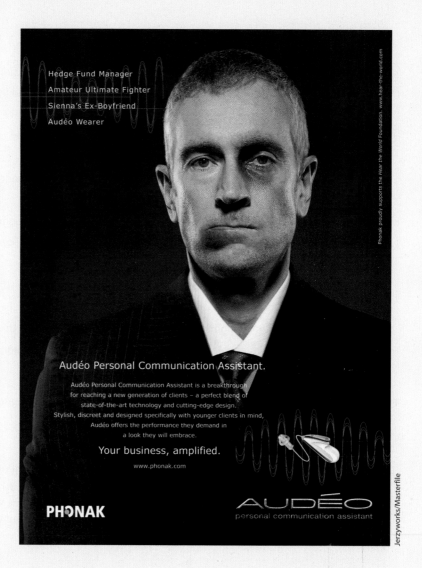

Hedge Fund Manager
Amateur Ultimate Fighter
Sienna's Ex-Boyfriend
Audéo Wearer

Audéo Personal Communication Assistant.

Audéo Personal Communication Assistant is a breakthrough
for reaching a new generation of clients – a perfect blend of
state-of-the-art technology and cutting-edge design.
Stylish, discreet and designed specifically with younger clients in mind,
Audéo offers the performance they demand in
a look they will embrace.

Your business, amplified.

www.phonak.com

PHONAK

AUDÉO
personal communication assistant

Phonak proudly supports the *Hear the World* Foundation. www.hear-the-world.com

Jerzyworks/Masterfile

A Very Edgy Ad: Phonak Hearing Aids

The first thing that sticks out in the Phonak ad is the hedge-fund manager's
bruised and swollen face. The idea that he is an ultimate fighter gives the ethos of
this ad a very edgy feel, like the movie *Fight Club*. There is something cool and bold
and really hip about a businessman being an ultimate fighter. If he is willing to take
this beating, then he deserves a certain stature and credibility.

When I read and looked at the ad, my response was that I respected and slightly feared this guy. He's a little bit dangerous. (Why is he Sienna's ex-boyfriend?) I think that's the main part of the pathos of the ad and fits very well with Phonak's campaign to change people's feelings and perspective on hearing aids. Here's a person that's not old and is super well-dressed, trendy, and slightly weird that wears a hearing aid.

The message or logos of the ad comes out in the text about "reaching a new generation of clients." Terms such as "state-of-the-art" and "cutting-edge" reinforce this point. The logo is meant to sound very dynamic, almost aggressive, like in the Phonak slogan "Your business, amplified." There is a sense of power here that is reflected in the image of an ultimate fighter.

Overall, I think the rhetorical stance this ad takes is successful in capturing readers' attention and giving them something to think about. Personally, I do not support ultimate fighting but it is a daring move that pushes the line. It creates a powerful dominant impression that fits with Phonak's campaign to de-stigmatize hearing aids.

REFLECTING ON YOUR WRITING

Write an account of how you put your profile together. Explain why you selected your subject. Then describe the interview, if you did one. Explain whether your final version confirmed or modified your initial preconceptions about your subject. Finally, explain how writing a profile differs from other kinds of writing you have done. What demands and satisfactions are there to writing profiles?

CHAPTER 8

Reports

Report writers typically begin by identifying a need to know on the part of the public at large or a specific group about events, trends, and ideas. Reports can range from something as simple as the morning weather report to something as complex as state-of-the-art scientific research on nanotechnology.

The forms that reports take vary tremendously, depending on the writer's situation and purposes. News reports and feature articles in newspapers and magazines, scholarly articles in academic journals, briefings and fact sheets, brochures, informational Web sites, studies from government agencies, research institutes, foundations, and advocacy groups, community newsletters, corporations' annual reports—all these are instances of report writing that informs and explains.

The focus in a report tends to be placed on the subject matter rather than on the writer's experience and perceptions. Unlike, say, a memoir, where the reader is asked to share an important moment of revelation with the writer, a report writer's relationship is normally less personal and more concerned with the topic at hand.

Likewise, reports differ from genres such as commentary, proposals, and reviews, where the writer's point of view figures prominently and readers sense they are in the realm of opinion, interpretation, and advocacy. Reports do have a point of view, which is typically expressed in a neutral tone that makes readers feel the key points come from the evidence and not from the writer's intentions. Reports are just as involved in the world as other genres, but the stance of the writer is that of an impartial observer who appears to examine all sides from a nonaligned point of view.

Report writers understand the important role that persuasion plays in informative writing—a persuasion that works when readers feel they are not being persuaded at all but rather that the facts are speaking for themselves. Report writers also know there is a creative part to crafting such a rhetorical stance—creating the grounds for the report, giving it a sense of significance and timeliness, explaining what the key questions are, emphasizing the main themes, designing the display of information.

Reports use the voice of an impartial observer as part of their appeal for readers' attention, to focus the public's interest on pressing issues. This is evident, for example, in the first major anti-smoking report *Smoking and Health: Report of the Advisory*

Committee to the Surgeon General in 1964 or the sense of educational crisis prompted by *A Nation at Risk* in 1983. Or in investigative journalism, such as Bob Woodward and Carl Bernstein's reports in the *Washington Post* on the Watergate scandal, which led to President Nixon's resignation in 1974, or Seymour M. Hersh's exposé in *The New Yorker* of the abuse of detainees by American troops in Iraq's Abu Ghraib prison in 2004. In these instances, reports can have a noteworthy impact, shaping popular consciousness and setting the agenda for public deliberation and policymaking.

WRITING FROM EXPERIENCE

When you need to know something, where do you turn? What are your main sources of information, both in and out of school, and what are your purposes in using them? Make a list of information sources to compare to those of your classmates. Next, pick three or four information sources to analyze in some detail, choosing sources that differ from each other. Analyze the way each source makes information available. What is the purpose of the information source? How does the source select information to include? How does the source organize the information? What uses do people make of the information?

READINGS

News Reports

Mentally Ill People Aren't More Violent, Study Finds

The Associated Press

Studies of Mental Illness Show Links to Violence

Fox Butterfield

....

The following two news reports on the relationship between mental illness and violence appeared on the same day in 1995. The first comes from the Associated Press and was published in many local newspapers. The second was written for the New York Times *by Fox Butterfield, one of its staff reporters at the time. Both provide accurate reports of the findings published in* The Archives of General Psychiatry *by a team of researchers. The question remains, though, what kind of impression the two reports created in the minds of their readers.*

Providence Journal   May 14, 1995

Headline:

Mentally Ill People Aren't More Violent, Study Finds

Lead: main
event findings
of study

¶2: Conse-
quences of
main event

¶3–5: Details of
main event

¶5: Detail of
how study
was
conducted

¶6: Comment
from author
of study

CHICAGO (AP)—*Mentally ill people who do not abuse alcohol or drugs are no more violent than their neighbors, a study has found.*

Mental-health advocates and former patients say the finding could help chip away at the stereotypes that have provoked unnecessary fear and driven misguided public policy for years.

Discharged mental patients with substance-abuse problems are five times as likely to commit acts of violence as people without drug problems, according to the study, published in this month's edition of the *Archives of General Psychiatry.*

Non-patients with substance abuse problems had three times the violence rate of the general population. But the violence rate was about the same for patients and non-patients who were drug-free.

The study followed 951 acute psychiatric patients in the year after their discharge in 1994 from hospitals in Pittsburgh, Kansas City and Worcester, Mass. Researchers compared the findings with a sample of 519 non-patients who lived in the same neighborhoods as the patients discharged in Pittsburgh.

John Monahan, one of the study's authors, says several recent surveys, including some conducted at Columbia University, have shown that most Americans believe mentally ill people are prone to violence.

"I think the public's fears are greatly exaggerated," said Monahan, a psychologist at the University of Virginia School of Law.

Analysis: Organization of Information in a Newspaper Report: The Inverted Pyramid

Newspaper stories report the information with the highest value first. The assumption is that busy readers, skimming the newspaper, may not read the entire news report. Accordingly, a condensed version of the most important information needs to be frontloaded, with other information following.

- ▶ **Headline:** This tells in a very brief way what the main event is (in the case of this news report, what the "study finds").

- ▶ **Lead:** The opening paragraph or two present in capsule form the most important information about the main event ("mentally ill people . . . are no more violent").

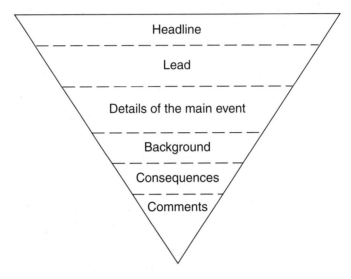

- ▶ **Details of the main event:** This provides further information on what happened, who was involved, where, how, and why.

- ▶ **Background:** Sometimes reporters will fill in background information about the main event.

- ▶ **Consequences:** This explains the larger significance of the main event (in this case, "the finding could help chip away at stereotypes").

- ▶ **Comments:** This provides insights and opinions ("'I think the public's fears are greatly exaggerated,' said Monahan").

The headline and lead always appear first. After that, the order may vary. Consider in the next news report—on the same study of violence and mental illness—how the order of information is organized.

New York Times   May 14, 1995

Studies of Mental Illness Show Links to Violence
New Finding Cites Role of Substance Abuse

By Fox Butterfield

BOSTON, May 14—After a generation of believing that the mentally ill are no more violent than other people, psychiatrists and advocates for the emotionally disturbed are wrestling with studies that show that the mentally ill may indeed be more violent in some circumstances.

Their difficulty was underscored today in a report of the latest of these studies in *The Archives of General Psychiatry*, a publication of the American Medical Association. The studies found that mental patients discharged from a hospital stay are no more violent than other members of their community, unless they have been abusing alcohol or drugs. Substance abuse increased the rates of violence by mental patients by up to five times, the study concluded, while it tripled the rate of violence by other people.

The finding about substance abuse is particularly important because the mentally ill are almost twice as likely as other people to be alcoholics or on drugs, the report said.

The study, paid for by the MacArthur Foundation, is part of a broad effort by researchers to find out why recent reports have found higher levels of violence among the mentally ill than in the general population, contradicting previous research dating from the 1950's and 1960's.

The relationship between mental illness and violence is an extremely sensitive subject because the public has long believed that the emotionally disturbed are more dangerous, despite the experts' views, and this popular perception has helped stigmatize the mentally ill.

To complicate the situation, with the closure of most state hospitals in recent years an increasing number of the mentally ill have been sent to jail or prison, where they receive little treatment, then are released only to be arrested again.

"We wanted to find some factors that distinguished which patients were at higher risk of violence, and substance abuse turned out to be a key distinction," said John Monahan, an author of the report who is a psychologist and a law professor at the University of Virginia. "We hope this will lead people not to tar everybody who is discharged from the hospital with the same brush."

The study also found that the types of violence committed by the mentally ill were largely the same that other people committed and that more than 85 percent of the violence committed by the mentally ill was directed at family members or friends, with only 14 percent of the attacks involving strangers.

"These findings clearly indicate that public fears of violence on the street by discharged patients who are strangers to them are misdirected," Professor Monahan said.

The study was conducted on 1,000 patients discharged from hospitals in Pittsburgh, Kansas City, Mo., and Worcester, Mass.

Another recent study, by Bruce Link, a professor at the Columbia University School of Public Health, found that the mentally ill are more violent if they are suffering from paranoia or from certain delusions and hallucinations.

Still another new study, by Jeffrey Swanson, an assistant professor of psychiatry at Duke University Medical Center, showed an increased risk of violence for mentally ill patients who are substance abusers and who stop taking their antipsychotic drugs, a frequent problem.

As an indication of how sensitive the issue of mental illness and violence is, the authors of the MacArthur Foundation study conducted focus groups before writing their report. "Language is important, and we wanted to cast things in the least inflammatory way," Professor Monahan said.

As a further indication of this sensitivity, the report immediately produced different reactions from the two major advocacy groups.

Mike Faenza, president of the National Mental Health Association, the nation's oldest and largest mental health organization, said: "This study's findings counter the fictional and highly stigmatizing images propagated by Hollywood movie studios and New York ad men. It is time we kill our cultural fantasy of deranged psychotic killers on the loose. The public's fear is out of time with reality."

Mr. Faenza said the report also underscored the need to "bring mental health and substance abuse treatment services together." He maintained that because of the ingrained habits of mental health professionals and the way government money is allocated, people now tend to be treated for either mental illness or for substance abuse but not jointly for both. This practice, he said, lets many patients fall through the cracks.

But Dr. E. Fuller Torrey, a psychiatrist affiliated with the National Alliance for the Mentally Ill, an advocacy group made up of family members of the emotionally disturbed, said the authors of the report had failed to draw the most important conclusion from their own data. These were data showing that mentally ill people who underwent hospitalization had a 50 percent reduction rate in violent acts in the year after their release, and people who were both mentally ill and abused drugs or alcohol had a 54 percent reduction rate in violent behavior.

"This is the first time that anyone has shown what we have long suspected, that if you treat mental illness, you can reduce the violence," said Dr. Torrey, who is executive director of the Stanley Foundation research programs in Washington.

Dr. Torrey's point was echoed in an editorial in *The Archives of General Psychiatry* by Professor Link of Columbia, who said that the most important finding in the MacArthur study is that the mentally ill tend to be violent when they are "symptomatic" in the period before hospitalization, and that after treatment, when their symptoms wane, "the risk for violence declines to the point where it is no different from the base level in the community."

Dr. Torrey is an outspoken critic of the restrictive laws against involuntary hospitalization of the mentally ill, believing that many disturbed people do not understand their disease and therefore resist attempts to treat them. This can sometimes result in untreated mentally ill people harming themselves or others.

Laurie Flynn, executive director of the National Alliance, said, "This violence is preventable." But she added that the lack of access to treatment "is a direct contributor to the criminalization problem," the growing number of mentally ill people who are sent to jail or prison rather than a clinic or hospital.

Trying not to tar every discharged mental patient with the same brush.

The situation is especially hard on family members who care for the mentally ill, Ms. Flynn said, since, as the new study found, it is relatives and friends who are most likely to be the victims of violence.

"People end up telling us it is easier to get your relative arrested than to get them treatment," she said. "It is a kind of family secret."

Dr. Torrey said he believes the amount of violence by the mentally ill has been increasing because of the closing of state hospitals and with financial pressures resulting in shorter stays for those patients who are hospitalized. Dr. Torrey estimates that the mentally ill are responsible for about 1,000 homicides a year in the United States.

But Professor Swanson said that in an earlier study he conducted in five cities, he found that the mentally ill were responsible for only about 4 percent of overall violence. Mental illness, he found, is a much smaller risk factor for violence than is being young, male, poor or addicted to alcohol or drugs.

Analysis: Framing the Story

News reports seem to be among the most straightforward forms of writing because they appear simply to inform readers. In this case, an important study was published in *The Archives of General Psychiatry* on a question of great public interest, namely the relationship between mental illness and violence, and both the Associated Press and *The New York Times* covered the story. As you can see, the two reporters' accounts of the study's findings are very similar—and yet, if you were to read just the two headlines, you might think otherwise.

It's not only the headlines that seem to create two different and perhaps divergent accounts. News reporting is never simply a matter of telling what happened. The news has to be produced—put into intelligible shape by the reporter's writing. One of the key devices reporters use to produce the news is the technique of *framing*. Notice how the headlines contribute to two quite different ways of framing the story. For the Associated Press news report, the study, as mental health advocates and former patients say, may "chip away" at "stereotypes," "unnecessary fear," and "misguided public policy." Fox Butterfield, on the other hand, frames the story by putting it in the context of an ongoing debate over the "extremely sensitive subject" of the relationship between mental illness and violence and what to do about it.

⊳ FOR CRITICAL INQUIRY

1. What was your immediate reaction when you read the two headlines? Was this reaction modified or changed as you read the two news reports?

2. Notice who is quoted in each of the news reports. How do these quotes shape the way readers are likely to understand the study? What differences, if any, do you see in the use of quotes?

3. Describe what you see as the two news reporters' purposes. To what extent are they similar? How do they differ? How would you account for these differences?

4. Work in a group with two other students. Choose a recent event that all know something about and that interests you. By yourself, write a headline and one or two opening paragraphs, just enough to frame the event. Now compare your versions. How do they differ? How is each likely to influence readers' understanding of the event?

Wikipedia

Salt-Slavery-Hypertension (SSH) Hypothesis

King John Pascual

Wikipedia is a multilingual, online encyclopedia based on open editing that has become a popular starting point for looking up information on nearly four million topics. Brown University professor of pathology and Africana studies Lundy Braun assigned her students to write a Wikipedia entry on the salt-slavery-hypertension (SSH) hypothesis they had studied in her class "Health Inequalities in Historical Perspective."

King John Pascual

BIOL 1920B

November 10, 2011

Word Count: 905 words

Salt-Slavery-Hypertension (SSH) Hypothesis

From Wikipedia, the free encyclopedia
Jump to: <u>navigation</u>, <u>search</u>

Widely popularized in the late 1980s by physician Clarence E. Grim and social scientist Thomas W. Wilson, the **Salt-Slavery-Hypertension (SSH) hypothesis** uses evolutionary theory to explain the prevalence of <u>hypertension</u>   among African Americans in the United States.[2] The hypothesis speculates that African slaves who survived the conditions of the <u>middle passage</u> (e.g. dehydration, chronic vomiting, <u>dysentery</u>, etc.) were genetically predisposed to retain salt in their bodies. Supporters of the hypothesis claim that this accounts for the high rates of blood pressure within the African American community today.[2] However, the SSH hypothesis has been subject to immense critique by the scientific community because of its historical inaccuracies and lack of valid scientific evidence.

Serge Daget, An Englishman Tastes the Sweat of an African, engraving © 1725

An Englishman Tastes the Sweat of an African

Contents

- <u>1History and background</u>
    - <u>1.1Four main points</u>
- <u>2 Critical Perspectives and Analysis</u>
- <u>3 Current Implications</u>
- <u>4 References</u>
- <u>5 Further reading</u>
- <u>6 External links</u>

\

History and Background

Within the past century, higher blood pressures have been observed among African Americans than whites in the United States. To address this health disparity, studies have sought to find genetic factors that are thought to inherently predetermine African populations to hypertension. Since the 1970s, it has been posited that African Americans must be biologically predetermined to retain sodium since they originated from hot and humid environments.[5] However, it was not until 1991 when Grim and Wilson published an article featured in the *Journal of American Medical Association* that the SSH hypothesis was placed at the forefront of the research community and general public. Their findings consisted of four main points:

(1) Salt was deficient in West Africa, which supplied most of the slaves during the Atlantic Slave Trade. [2]

(2) The naturally "fit" slaves who are more capable of retaining sodium were favored by natural selection, thus surviving the harsh dietary conditions during the voyage. [2]

(3) The effects of this evolutionary selection have loaded the gene pool of the African-American community with genes that help retain salt and water. [2]

(4) These "salt-genes" are therefore responsible for the high rates of hypertension among blacks in twentieth-century America where consumption of sodium has increased. [5]

Critical Perspectives and Analysis

Critics of the SSH hypothesis have pointed out historical flaws in Grim and Wilson's study. In an article published by the *American Journal of Public Health*, prominent historian Philip Curtin explains that salt was not at all deficient in West Africa and that in fact, most of the tropical regions near the coast had easy access to sea salt. Moreover, Curtin states, "There is no evidence that either [dehydration or salt depletion] was a significant cause of death on slave ships." Additionally, Curtin asserts that not only were the statistical figures used by Grim and Wilson incorrect and outdated but their cited sources were also not clearly specified. [2] This lack of historical legitimacy perhaps suggests that the SSH hypothesis was motivated by ideologies that echo the 19th century scientific racism and eugenics movements.

Critics from the research community have further disputed the SSH hypothesis. In a study published by the *Journal of American Heart Association*, Alan Weder and Nicholas Schork questioned the validity of the hypothesis, noting that the slave trade presented environmental pressures that were too rapid to create an evolutionary effect for such a complex disease trait (i.e. hypertension). [5] Furthermore, the logic employed in the SSH hypothesis is inherently flawed from the standpoint of basic evolutionary theory. On one hand, the SSH hypothesis relies on the idea that the scarcity of salt in West African countries has favored the selection of a uniquely African "salt-gene" through a slow evolutionary process spanning thousands of years. On another, it endorses the premise that natural selection occurred during the slave trade even though it did not span more than two centuries. Thus, the contradiction in Grim and Wilson's logic further signifies the fallacy of the SSH hypothesis.

In the 1970s, the notion that attributed the hot and humid climate of West Africa as the reason for the favorable selection of the alleged salt-gene among African populations presented yet another challenge to the SSH hypothesis. If this notion were to be true, there should be a prevalence of hypertension in West Africa, where salt has been abundant throughout history. However, recent studies have demonstrated how hypertension rates among African populations in the U.S., the Caribbean, and West Africa differ significantly. In fact, epidemiologist Dr. Richard Cooper led an international comparative study in 2005 that revealed hypertension rates being at their lowest in Nigeria and highest in Germany. [1] Thus, up to this day, there is no evidence supporting the assumption that an African "salt-gene" exists and causes African populations to be genetically predetermined for hypertension.

Current Implications

Despite the lack of scientific evidence, many still believe that the prevalence of hypertension among African Americans is biologically predetermined. Popular shows like Oprah and medical textbooks have perpetuated the SSH hypothesis as common scientific knowledge. [3] Furthermore, the appeal to racialize scientific research on the grounds of inadequate and oftentimes improper interpretation of data appears to be growing in both the general public and scientific community. For instance, BiDil, a drug aimed to reduce hypertension specifically for blacks, was approved by the FDA in 2005, [4] and a study published by *Nature Genetics* in August 2011 revealed a "novel" gene which its authors say could explain why blacks are more susceptible to asthma than other ethnic groups. [7]

Indeed, since its inception the SSH hypothesis has raised questions regarding the importance of evaluating the social determinants of disease (e.g. socioeconomic status, environmental conditions, etc.). Ultimately by adhering to the principles of biological essentialism, the SSH hypothesis stands on the verge of overlooking the urgent environmental and social factors that may have a larger influence on fundamentally addressing racial health disparities in the United States and worldwide.

References

1. ^ Richard Cooper., *et al*. "An international comparative study of blood pressure in populations of European vs. African descent". *BMC Medicine* 2005, **3:2**.
2. ^ Philip Curtin. "The Slavery Hypothesis for hypertension among African Americans". *AM J Public Health* 82:1681-1686 1992.
3. ^ Osagie Obasagie, David Winickoff. "Hypertension: What Oprah Doesn't Know,". *Los Angeles Times,* May 17, 2007.
4. ^ "Heart Failure Treatment for Black Patients, BiDil, launched". *Drug Week.,* August 5, 2005.
5. ^ http://www.jstor.org/stable/3703292?seq=3
6. ^ http://raceandgenomics.ssrc.org/Kaufman/
7. ^ http://www.huffingtonpost.com/2011/08/01/asthma-gene-african-americans_n_914811.html

Further reading

Primary sources

- Ihab Hajjar, Theodore Kitchen, "Trends in prevalence, awareness, treatment, and control of hypertension in the United States, 1988-2000," *JAMA* 290: 199-206, 2003.
- "U.S. says drug seem effective against heart failure in blacks," *New York Times* June 15, 2005
- "NAACP attacks lack of BiDil medicare coverage," *Pharma Marketletter* Feb. 1, 2007.
- Pamela Sankar and Jonathan Kahn, BiDil: Race medicine or race marketing? *Health Affairs* 11 Oct, 2005.
- Gary Puckrein, BiDil: From another vantage point, *Health Affairs*, 15 August 2007.
- Dorothy Roberts, "Is race-based medicine good for us? African American approaches to race, biomedicine, and equality," *Journal of Law, Medicine, and Ethics*, Fall 2008, 537-545.

External links

 Wikimedia Commons has media related to: ***Salt-Slavery-Hypertension Hypothesis***

- Darwinian Evolutionary Theory
- Center for Health Disparities
- American Heart Association

Analysis: Wikipedia's Core Principles

Wikipedia has three core principles—verifiability (information is based on reliable sources that readers can check for themselves), no original research (entries must cite only recognized, previously established sources), and a neutral point of view (over time, through collaborative editing, an entry should include all significant views on a topic published in reliable sources).

One of the main tasks a Wikipedia contributor faces in the case of a controversial topic like the salt-slavery-hypertension (SSH) hypothesis is how to enact these principles when the evidence weighs so overwhelmingly against the SSH hypothesis. It is not a matter of balance (by trying to add more in favor of the hypothesis) but of accuracy to the controversy and the terms of the critique of the SSH hypothesis that is at stake for the writer, King John Pascual here, to represent the current state of thought in a fair and informed manner.

⫸ **FOR CRITICAL INQUIRY** ||||||||||||||||||||||||||||||||||||||||||||||||||||||||||||||||||||||||||||||||||||||||||||||||||||||||

1. Consider how King John Pascual explains the salt-slavery-hypertension (SSH) hypothesis. Does he present a clear, if brief, explanation of the hypothesis? Are the critiques of the SSH hypothesis clearly presented? What gives these sections of the Wikipedia entry their clarity or lack of it? Do you feel the entry gives you a basic sense of the issues?

2. Consider how Pascual fashions his rhetorical stance. What does his attitude toward the SSH hypothesis and its critics seem to be? Are there places where he seems to go beyond the neutral point of view Wikipedia calls for?

3. Consider the design of the Wikipedia entry. What different types of information does it contain? What sources of information does it give you access to?

Fact Sheets

Facts About Prisons and Prisoners
The Sentencing Project
....

The Sentencing Project is a nonprofit research and advocacy organization that promotes reduced reliance on incarceration and increased use of alternatives to deal with crime. It is a nationally recognized source on criminal justice, providing data, policy analysis, and program information. Sentencing Project fact sheets, such as the one that appears here, organize a lot of information in a highly a\ccessible way. Notice how the items of information are divided into single sentences. Each has a separate focus, but, at the same time, an accumulative picture begins to emerge from the data and suggest certain conclusions. Consider how the order of information frames your understanding of the current situation of prisons and prisoners. In what sense is the design of the Sentencing Project fact sheet persuasive as well as informative?

FACTS ABOUT PRISONS AND PRISONERS

The number of people incarcerated in state and federal prisons increased by 15% from 1,316,333 to 1,518,104 between 2000 and 2010.

In addition to the more than 1.5 million people in state and federal prisons, there were 748,728 people in local jails in 2010, yielding a total incarcerated population of nearly 2.3 million.

Between 2000 and 2009, state prison populations grew at an average rate of 1.3% per year, the federal population at 4.2%, and jail populations by 2.3%.

Between 2009 and 2010, the total number of people in American prisons and jails decreased by1.1%.

1 in every 137 Americans was in prison or jail in 2010.

4,887,900 people were on probation or parole in 2010, for a total of 7,076,200 people in America under some form of criminal justice supervision.

The 2010 U.S. incarceration rate of 731 people per 100,000 population is the highest in the world.

Characteristics of People in Prison

93% of people in prison were male, 7% were female.

112,797 women were in state or federal prison in 2010.

38% of people in state or federal prisons were Black, 32% were white, and 22% were Hispanic in 2010.

1 in every 10 Black males ages 30 to 34 was in jail or prison in 2010, as were 1 in 26 Hispanic males and 1 in 61 white males in the same age group.

Black males have a 32% chance of serving time in prison at some point in their lives; Hispanic males have a 17% chance; white males have a 6% chance.

In 2010, the rate of jail or prison incarceration for Black women was 2.9 times higher than the rate for white women; the rate for Hispanic women was 1.5 times higher.

Nearly half (47%) of people incarcerated in state prisons in 2009 were convicted of non-violent drug, property, or public order crimes.

People convicted of drug offenses were 18% of state inmates in 2009 and 51% of federal prison inmates in 2010; 1 in 4 people in jail in 2002 was incarcerated for a drug offense.

Source: Bureau of Justice Statistics

1/12

1705 DeSales St. NW, 8th Floor, Washington, DC 20036 ● Tel. 202.628.0871 ●
Fax 202.628.1091 ● www.sentencingproject.org

Courtesy of The Sentencing Project. http://www.sentencingproject.org

The Sentencing Project, "Facts About Prisons and Prisoners" January 2012. From http://www .sentencingproject.org. Reprinted by permission of The Sentencing Project, Washington, DC.

National Reports

Unauthorized Immigrants: Length of Residency, Patterns of Parenthood

Paul Taylor, Mark Hugo Lopez, Jeffrey Passel, and Seth Motel, Pew Hispanic Center

··

The Pew Hispanic Center is a project of the Pew Research Center, a nonprofit and nonpartisan think tank that conducts public opinion polling and social science research on a broad range of issues, including the Internet and American life, religion and public life, global attitudes, and the press. Unauthorized Immigrants: Length of Residency, Patterns of Parenthood *was published December 1, 2011. We publish four pages of the major findings from this relatively brief report. You can find the complete report at http://www.pewhispanic.org/.*

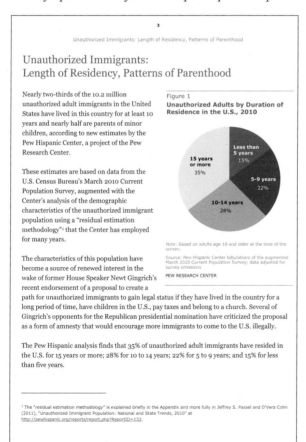

3

Unauthorized Immigrants: Length of Residency, Patterns of Parenthood

Unauthorized Immigrants: Length of Residency, Patterns of Parenthood

Nearly two-thirds of the 10.2 million unauthorized adult immigrants in the United States have lived in this country for at least 10 years and nearly half are parents of minor children, according to new estimates by the Pew Hispanic Center, a project of the Pew Research Center.

These estimates are based on data from the U.S. Census Bureau's March 2010 Current Population Survey, augmented with the Center's analysis of the demographic characteristics of the unauthorized immigrant population using a "residual estimation methodology"[1] that the Center has employed for many years.

Figure 1
Unauthorized Adults by Duration of Residence in the U.S., 2010

- Less than 5 years 15%
- 5-9 years 22%
- 10-14 years 28%
- 15 years or more 35%

Note: Based on adults age 18 and older at the time of the survey.

Source: Pew Hispanic Center tabulations of the augmented March 2010 Current Population Survey; data adjusted for survey omissions

PEW RESEARCH CENTER

The characteristics of this population have become a source of renewed interest in the wake of former House Speaker Newt Gingrich's recent endorsement of a proposal to create a path for unauthorized immigrants to gain legal status if they have lived in the country for a long period of time, have children in the U.S., pay taxes and belong to a church. Several of Gingrich's opponents for the Republican presidential nomination have criticized the proposal as a form of amnesty that would encourage more immigrants to come to the U.S. illegally.

The Pew Hispanic analysis finds that 35% of unauthorized adult immigrants have resided in the U.S. for 15 years or more; 28% for 10 to 14 years; 22% for 5 to 9 years; and 15% for less than five years.

[1] The "residual estimation methodology" is explained briefly in the Appendix and more fully in Jeffrey S. Passel and D'Vera Cohn (2011), "Unauthorized Immigrant Population: National and State Trends, 2010" at http://pewhispanic.org/reports/report.php?ReportID=133.

Pew Hispanic Center | www.pewhispanic.org

4

The share that has been in the country at least 15 years has more than doubled since 2000, when about one-in-six (16%) unauthorized adult immigrants had lived here for that duration. By the same token, the share of unauthorized adult immigrants who have lived in the country for less than five years has fallen by half during this period—from 32% in 2000 to 15% in 2010.

The rising share of unauthorized immigrants who have been in the U.S. for a long duration reflects the fact that the sharpest growth in this population occurred during the late 1990s and early 2000s—and that the inflow has slowed down significantly in recent years, as the U.S. economy has sputtered and border enforcement has tightened. It also reflects the fact that relatively few long-duration unauthorized immigrants have returned to their countries of origin.

Figure 2
Unauthorized Adults by Duration of Residence in U.S., 2000, 2005 and 2010
(%)

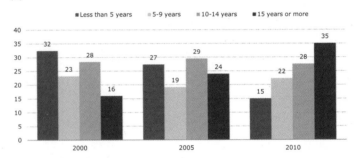

Note: Based on adults age 18 and older at the time of the survey. Percentages may not total 100% due to rounding
Source: Pew Hispanic Center tabulations of augmented March Current Population Surveys; data adjusted for survey omissions
PEW RESEARCH CENTER

Family Status

The Pew Hispanic analysis also finds that nearly half (46%) of unauthorized adult immigrants today—about 4.7 million people—are parents of minor children. By contrast, just 38% of legal immigrant adults and 29% of U.S.-born adults are parents of minor children.

Much of this disparity results from the fact that unauthorized immigrants are younger than other groups of adults in the U.S. and more likely to be in their child-bearing and child-rearing years. The median age of unauthorized immigrant adults is 36.2 years old, which is about a decade

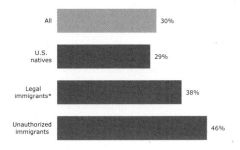

Figure 3

Share of Adults Who Are Parents of Minor Children, by Family Status and Legal Status, 2010

- All — 30%
- U.S. natives — 29%
- Legal immigrants* — 38%
- Unauthorized immigrants — 46%

Notes: Parents of minor children include the family head and spouse of families with people younger than 18.

* Includes naturalized U.S. citizens

Source: Pew Hispanic Center tabulations of the augmented March 2010 Current Population Survey; data adjusted for survey omissions

PEW RESEARCH CENTER

younger than the median age of legal immigrant adults (46.1) and U.S. native adults (46.5). The age variation accounts for 78% of the difference in the shares of unauthorized immigrants and U.S. natives who are parents.[2]

Unauthorized immigrants make up 28% of the country's foreign-born population and 3.7% of the overall population. The Pew Hispanic Center estimates that a total of 11.2 million unauthorized immigrants, including people younger than 18, live in the U.S. This figure is lower than the 2007 peak of 12 million such immigrants. The recent decrease followed a two-decade period of growth, including a rise in the population from 8.4 million in 2000.

---

[2] Of the 17.9-percentage-point difference between the number of parents with children in these two groups, 13.9 percentage points can be attributed to differences in age structure between populations. This figure is calculated by using a demographic technique called "age standardization." See Das Gupta (1993).

6

The decrease has occurred in part because of reduced flows into the U.S. among Mexicans, who constitute 58%—or 6.5 million—of the unauthorized immigrant population. About 150,000 unauthorized immigrants from Mexico came annually to the U.S. from March 2007 to March 2009, down 70% from the annual rates during the first half of the decade. As for outflow, the number of Mexican migrants who voluntarily return to Mexico has stayed somewhat steady, but removals (deportations) are on the rise. There were almost 390,000 removals (deportations) in fiscal 2010, or more than twice as many as in 2000, according to the Department of Homeland Security. About 73% of deportees in 2010 originally came from Mexico.

About 5 million unauthorized adult immigrants—49%—are in families with minor children.[3] Along with the approximately 1 million unauthorized immigrants who are children, an additional 4.5 million people younger than 18 were born in the U.S. to at least one unauthorized immigrant parent. While the population of unauthorized immigrant children has decreased from a peak of 1.6 million in 2005, the number of U.S.-born children with at least one unauthorized immigrant parent has more than doubled since 2000.

Overall, at least 9 million people are in "mixed-status" families that include at least one unauthorized adult and at least one U.S.-born child. This makes up 54% of the 16.6 million people in families with at least one unauthorized immigrant. There are 400,000 unauthorized immigrant children in such families who have U.S.-born siblings.

---

[3] "Families" are defined as adults age 18 and older who live with their minor children (i.e., younger than 18) and unmarried, "dependent" children younger than 25.

Analysis: Keeping Track of Change

Unlike the Sentencing Project, the Pew Hispanic Center is a nonadvocacy organization that does not take positions on public policy. Its mission, rather, as the Center suggests, is "to improve public understanding of the diverse Hispanic population in the United States and to chronicle Latinos' growing impact on the nation." Like other think tanks, research institutes, foundations, academic centers, and government agencies, it is involved with keeping track of changing attitudes and trends, to provide data for public deliberation and policymaking. Still, though it would certainly be out of step with its mission for the Center to take a position on what should be done about undocumented immigrants, the very questions its researchers ask and the results of its studies play a shaping role in determining how the wider public discussion takes place, what the main issues are, and how trends in the Latino population acquire significance. By striving to improve public understanding through its research, the Pew Hispanic Center also provides the themes to understand the changing realities of Latinos in the U.S.

⟫ FOR CRITICAL INQUIRY

1. Imagine you are a reporter assigned to do a news report on *Unauthorized Immigrants: Length of Residency, Patterns of Parenthood*. Write a headline and two-sentence lead paragraph. Compare your headline and lead paragraph to what your classmates have written. What do you see as the main differences and similarities? Consider how the headlines and lead paragraphs frame the information presented in the Pew report.

2. Consider the role that the pie chart and bar graphs play in presenting the research results. How do they work with the written text? Compare the visual display of information in the pie chart (Fig. 1) and the first bar graph (Fig. 2). What does each seem to emphasize? Does information appear in writing that you could represent in a visual display?

3. What is the significance of this data? Notice that the authors from Pew Hispanic Center do not draw conclusions or inferences from the information they report. Work in a group with three or four students. Identify a number of conclusions or inferences that could be drawn based on the data. These could have to do with immigration policy or understanding the experience of undocumented immigrants. You do not necessarily have to agree with the conclusions or inferences. Once you have a number to work with, consider what underlying assumptions connect these inferences to the data.

Scholarly and Popular Articles

Uncertainty and the Use of Magic

Richard B. Felson and George Gmelch

Can a Lucky Charm Get You Through Organic Chemistry?

George Gmelch and Richard Felson

George Gmelch and Richard B. Felson wrote these two articles based on their research to test Bronislaw Malinowski's theory that people use magic to relieve anxiety in situations of uncertainty. The first appeared in a leading academic journal Current Anthropology, *and the second appeared in the popular magazine* Psychology Today. *Taken together, these two articles offer a good case study of how writers translate scholarly research for a broad readership.*

Richard B. Felson and George Gmelch, "UNCERTAINTY AND THE USE OF MAGIC," *Current Anthropology* 20.3 (1979): 587–89. Copyright © 1979, Wenner-Gren Foundation for Anthropological Research. Reproduced by permission of University of Chicago Press.

Vol. 20 • No. 3 • September 1979 CURRENT ANTHROPOLOGY

Uncertainty and the Use of Magic[1]

by RICHARD B. FELSON AND GEORGE GMELCH
*Department of Sociology/Department
of Anthropology, State University of
New York at Albany, Albany, N.Y. 12222,
U.S.A. 18179*

Probably the most widely cited theory of magic is that of Malinowski (1948). Malinowski postulated that people resort to magic in situations of chance and uncertainty, where circumstances are not fully under human control. In what has become one of the most frequently cited examples of magic in primitive societies, he described the Trobriand Islanders' use of magic in fishing. On the open sea, where catches were uncertain and there was considerable danger, the islanders used a variety of magical practices. When fishing within the safety and plenty of the inner lagoon, they used none.

A number of other qualitative studies support the relationship between uncertainty and magic within modern, more scientifically oriented societies (e.g., Stouffer et al. 1949, Vogt 1952, MacNiece 1964, Gmelch 1978). The only previous quantitative test of this proposition, however, does not support Malinowski. Lewis (1963) found that the use of magic by American mothers with sick children depended on the mothers' knowledge of medicine and not on the uncertainty or danger of a particular illness. However, Lewis's use of length of illness as the measure of uncertainty is questionable.

According to Malinowski, people use magic to alleviate or reduce the anxiety created by conditions of uncertainty. Through the performance of the appropriate rituals, people "work off" the tensions aroused by fear. An alternative explanation would be that magic results from purely cognitive processes and represents an effort to produce favorable results. In other words, people believe that unknown forces—"good luck" and "bad luck"—play a role in the outcome of events and that these forces can be manipulated by magic.

This study examines these relationships using a sample of American and Irish college students. It considers the use of magic in six activities—gambling, athletics, exam-taking, illness, face-to-face interaction, and dangerous activities—in relation to the degree of uncertainty of each. It investigates the relationship between the use of magic and anxiety within each activity. Finally, it examines students' beliefs about the ability of magic to alleviate anxiety and produce favorable outcomes.

[1]We wish to thank Marcus Felson, Sharon Gmelch, and Walter P. Zenner for their comments on an earlier draft and Don Bennett, Des McCluskey, Kevin Buckley, Debbie O'Brien, and Ruth Pasquirello for their assistance in collecting the data.

Questionnaires were administered to students in sociology classes in the United States (State University of New York at Albany; $N = 270$) and in the Republic of Ireland (University College, Dublin; $N = 180$). The students in the American sample were primarily urban and from middle-class and either Catholic or Jewish background. The students in the Irish sample were predominantly Catholic, of mainly middle-class background, with as many from small towns and villages as from the city. A list of concepts and the items used to measure them is presented in table 1.

Following Malinowski, we wished to compare activities known to vary in degree of uncertainty. Since it is extremely difficult to construct objective measures of uncertainty,

TABLE 1 CONCEPTS AND QUESTIONNAIRE ITEMS USED TO MEASURE THEM

Concept	Questions Asked	Coding and Responses
Use of Magic	Do you do anything special before or during the following activities in order to give yourself luck? *(a)* when you're gambling; *(b)* when you play in a sports contest; *(c)* when taking an exam; *(d)* before an important meeting, date, or interview; *(e)* in regard to something dangerous	1. Yes 0. No Missing Data: I can't answer since I don't engage in this activity
Confidence in efficacy of magic	How certain are you that such things can bring luck?	1. Certain that they do not affect luck 2. Not at all certain 3. Somewhat certain 4. Very certain
Anxiety about activity	How much do you worry about the following? *(a)* gambling; *(b)* sports contests; *(c)* exams; *(d)* important meetings, dates, or interviews; *(e)* illness; *(f)* accidents	1. Not at all 2. A little 3. Very much Missing Data: I haven't engaged in this activity
Belief that magic reduces anxiety	Does it ever make you feel better when you do things to give yourself luck?	1. Yes 0. No Missing Data: I don't do things to give myself luck.
Uncertainty	For some things it is very certain before you start how well you'll do. For other things it is pretty unpredictable and uncertain. Rank the following in terms of certainty about the outcome you would feel before gambling; when you're ill; when you have an important meeting, date, or interview; when you play in a sports contest; when you're taking an exam.	

TABLE 2 PERCENTAGE OF RESPONDENTS WHO REPORT USING MAGIC IN ACTIVITIES VARYING IN UNCERTAINTY, CONTROLLING FOR ANXIETY

| | Anxiety | | | | | | | |
| | U.S.A. | | | | Ireland | | | |
Activity	High	Medium	Low	Total	High	Medium	Low	Total
Gambling (4.8)[a]	63	57	39	48	−[b]	65	23	33
Dangerous activities (4.4)	59	40	21	41	61	47	42	49
Exams (3.3)	45	24	−[b]	39	65	48	29	57
Sports (3.1)	67	34	19	40	36	34	19	26
Face-to-face interaction (2.9)	42	27	33	35	51	50	13	48
Illness (2.5)	40	18	16	21	39	26	10	23
Correlation with uncertainty	.64	.92	.53	.82	.64	.78	.69	.21
Probability level	.08	.01	.18	.02	.12	.03	.06	.34

[a] Mean uncertainty rank; a high rank indicates high uncertainty.
[b] Only three American students had low anxiety about exam-taking, and only one Irish student had high anxiety about gambling.

The percentage of students who use magic for each activity and at each level of anxiety is presented in table 2. For the American sample, the correlation between mean uncertainty and mean use of magic over these six activities is quite strong, whether anxiety level is controlled or not. Respondents use more magic for uncertain activities like danger and gambling than they do for more certain activities like illness and exam-taking. For the Irish sample, the overall relationship between mean uncertainty and mean use of magic is slight. However, when anxiety level is controlled, the relationship between uncertainty and magic increases substantially.

For each activity, students who experience more anxiety are more likely to use magic. Contrary to Malinowski's hypothesis, however, the uncertainty of an activity does not have a positive relationship to the amount of anxiety experienced. In fact, this relationship is negative for both samples.

Irish students use more magic than American students in four of the six activities: exam-taking, face-to-face interactions, illness, and dangerous activities. There is also a slight tendency for Americans to use more magic in gambling and sports, although the differences between the two groups are not statistically significant. Frequency distributions for

TABLE 3 PERCENTAGE OF USERS AND NON-USERS OF MAGIC REPORTING VARIOUS DEGREES OF CONFIDENCE IN THE EFFICACY OF MAGIC

Degree of Confidence	Americans			Irish		
	Users (N = 183)	Non-users (N = 81)	Total	Users (N = 183)	Non-users (N = 81)	Total
Very certain	1	1	2	11	2	9
Somewhat certain	27	12	23	31	12	26
Not at all certain	54	46	51	33	28	31
Certain it does not bring luck	18	41	25	25	58	34

degree of confidence in the efficacy of magic for the total sample and for users and nonusers of magic are presented in table 3. The table indicates very little confidence about the efficacy of magic, even among persons who use it. On the other hand, most students who use magic indicate that it often relieves their anxiety. When asked if it ever made them feel better to use magic, 76% of the Americans and 71% of the Irish who do so answered yes.

This study supports Malinowski's basic notion that people use magic in situations of uncertainty. Students reported using more magic in activities that are relatively uncertain (e.g., gambling) and less in activities that are relatively more certain (e.g., illness). It also supports Malinowski's contention that magic is used to reduce anxiety. For a given activity, the greater the anxiety the students experience, the more magic they use. Furthermore, the students indicated that using magic reduces their anxiety. The evidence, however, does not support the notion

that uncertainty results in use of magic because of the anxiety it produces. It appears instead that magic is used under conditions of uncertainty because of a belief in its ability to alter the forces of luck rather than its ability to reduce anxiety.

The fact that a significant amount of magic is used among the college students in our sample suggests that magic is not simply superstitious, irrational behavior confined to primitive peoples. Rather, magic appears to be used in various activities to produce favorable outcomes where other techniques are limited in their effectiveness. Magic is irrational, of course, if one accepts the scientific position that luck is unalterable.

Irish students reported using more magic than Americans in four of the six activities. This is not surprising, given that Ireland is a more traditional society than the United States. However, in two activities, gambling and sports, the Americans appeared to be slightly more likely to use magic than the Irish. This may be due to the fact that gambling and sports are more important and anxiety-producing for Americans.

While most students feel that magic reduces their anxiety, they do not feel as confident that it will produce favorable results. This suggests that many students are merely playing it safe. They are not sure that magic works, but they use it just in case. The cost of performing magic is small, and there is always the possibility that it may help. The lack of strong belief in the efficacy of magic may be one of the major differences between industrialized and primitive societies in the use of magic. Put simply, tribal man has faith that his magic works; modern man lacks faith but is not taking any chances.

References Cited

GMELCH, G. 1978. Baseball magic. *Human Nature* 1(8):32–39.

LEWIS, L. S. 1963. Knowledge, change, certainty, and the theory of magic. *American Journal of Sociology* 69:7–12.

MACNIECE, L. 1964. Astrology. London: Aldus Books.

MALINOWSKI, B. 1954. *Magic, science, and religion and other essays.* New York: Anchor Books.

STOUFFER, S., et al. 1949. *The American soldier.* Princeton, Princeton University Press.

VOGT, E. 1952. Water witching: An interpretation of a ritual pattern in a rural American community. *Scientific Monthly* 75:175–86.

Analysis: Testing a Theory

"Uncertainty and the Use of Magic" follows the scholarly conventions of the research article. Although Felson and Gmelch do not mark the sections of their article, as research reports often do, their report nonetheless conforms to the standard format (and may remind you of laboratory reports in science classes):

¶1–4: **Introduction.** Defines the problem to be investigated by reviewing prior research on Malinowski's theory of magic and uncertainty. Establishes the purpose of the research as testing the theory. Explains the main research questions.

¶5–6: **Methods.** Explains how researchers investigated the questions—the administration of questionnaires, the sample size, characteristics of subjects, and use of judges.

¶7–9: **Results.** Presents the results or refers to tables, without comment on the meaning or significance.

¶10–12: **Discussion.** Explains how the data relate to the central problem posed in the introduction. Often begins with the principal finding or strongest claim (e.g. "This study supports Malinowski's basic notion . . .").

¶13: **Conclusion.** Summarizes main findings and points out wider significance.

Can a Lucky Charm Get You Through Organic Chemistry?

by George Gmelch and Richard Felson

A large majority of college students employ rituals or charms to try to influence the fates, a study on two campuses now suggests. Why do they do it—and are they convinced of its efficacy as were the Trobriand Islanders?

During his stay in the South Seas in World War I, Bronislaw Malinowski observed that the Trobriand Islanders used magic in situations of danger and uncertainty, when circumstances were not fully under human control. In a classic illustration of this principle, the anthropologist compared two forms of Trobriand fishing—fishing in the inner lagoon and fishing in the open sea. In the safety of the lagoon, fish were plentiful and there was little danger; the men could rely on their knowledge and skill. On the open sea, however, fishing was dangerous and yields varied widely; to ensure safety and increase their catch, the men turned to rituals and fetishes for help. Malinowski wrote that the fishermen's magic was performed "over the canoe during its construction, carried out at the beginning and in the course of expeditions, and resorted to in moments of real danger."

Even in our technologically advanced society, we are often at the mercy of powerful, unknown forces.

How do we handle this uncertainty and unpredictability in our personal lives? Some people are fatalistic—"What will be will be." Others try to manipulate unknown forces. When they request a deity to intercede in their behalf, we call it prayer; when they attempt to influence unknown forces through ritual or the use of charms, we call it magic.

For example, when Gloria, a university secretary, has an outdoor activity planned for the day and the sun is shining, she is careful not to comment on the weather. "I think it's bad luck," she explains. "If I said it was a gorgeous day, the sky would fill up with clouds and it'd rain. I know, it's happened to me. So now I am careful not to pass any comment on the weather when I've got something planned." Gloria has a lucky number—7—and would never work for a company located on the 13th floor. She reads her horoscope in the newspaper every morning and sometimes makes a wish on the first star she sees at night. An amber glass piggy bank sits atop her dresser containing the 20 lucky pennies she has found over the years.

Mary Sue is a B+ student at the State University of New York at Albany.

George Gmelch and Richard Felson. "Can a Lucky Charm Get You Through Organic Chemistry." *Psychology Today* (December 1980): 75–77. Reprinted with permission from Psychology Today Magazine, Copyright © 1980 Sussex Publishers, LLC.

Each time she prepares for an exam, she travels 12 miles to the library of another university and sits in the same carrel to study. She once got an exceptionally high mark on a physics test after studying in that library, and ever since, she has returned.

It is perhaps surprising to some that enlightened people in an advanced society can be serious when they behave in such ways. Not long ago, we decided to investigate the use of magic among supposedly sophisticated college students. We wanted to understand why they seemed to use magic—whether their motives were similar to those of the Trobrianders and other preliterate peoples. Magic, as defined by anthropologists, refers to rituals that are meant to influence events and people but have not been proved empirically to have the desired effect. We wanted to know whether the student practitioners of magic really believed in its efficacy or were simply trying to alleviate the anxiety created by uncertain conditions by making a ritual gesture of some kind.

We distributed questionnaires on the subject to 270 students in sociology classes at the State University of New York at Albany and to 180 students at University College Dublin, in Ireland. (The choice of Irish students was a matter of convenience; one of us, Gmelch, often works in Ireland.) The students in the American sample were primarily urban and from middle-class Catholic or Jewish backgrounds. In the Irish sample, as many students came from small towns and villages as from cities; the group was predominantly Catholic and mainly middle class.

Students were asked if they did anything special to give themselves luck in each of six circumstances: when they were gambling; in a dangerous situation; taking exams; playing in a sports contest; before an important meeting, date, or interview; when they were ill. We also asked students how much they worried about each of those circumstances. In addition, we asked them how much they cared about the outcome; if using magic made them feel less anxious; and if they really believed that magic worked. We had independent judges—40 sociology students who were not included in our sample—rank the six circumstances according to how difficult it was to predict the outcome (for instance, a grade on an exam). The raters put gambling at the top of the list as entailing most uncertainty, followed by dangerous situations, exams, sports, face-to-face encounters, and, lastly, illness.

Of the 450 subjects, about 70 percent used magic. The percentage of users was about the same in the two countries: 69 percent of the Americans, 75 percent of the Irish. But larger between-nation differences were found in the circumstances under which magic was used. As the following table shows, a significantly higher proportion of the Irish employed magic in exams and face-to-face encounters, while a significantly higher percentage of

Americans used it in gambling and sports.

Situation	Americans	Irish
Gambling	48%	33%
Dangerous situations	41%	49%
Exams	39%	57%
Sports	40%	26%
Face-to-face encounters	35%	48%
Illness	21%	23%

Students used both productive magic (for example, carrying a good-luck charm to an exam), to improve achievement, and protective magic (such as crossing one's fingers), to ward off danger. Several rituals were shared by subjects of both nationalities. Asked if they had a lucky number, 43 percent of the Americans and 32 percent of the Irish said yes. Other shared practices were crossing fingers (38 percent of the Americans, 44 percent of the Irish), knocking on wood (41 percent of the Americans, 47 percent of the Irish), carrying good-luck charms (19 percent of the Americans, 13 percent of the Irish), and wearing particular clothing for luck (25 percent of the Americans, 14 percent of the Irish). Not all rituals were shared. Only the Americans—23 percent—said they walked around ladders.

Magic rituals gave students a sense of control and boosted confidence—which may have improved their performance.

Overall, the difference between the Irish and American students was not large, possibly because the uncertainties of student life are similar in the two countries. Particular kinds of rituals, such as knocking on wood, had large numbers of adherents in both countries. (It has been suggested that knocking on wood originated when men lived in huts. Supposedly, if a man was prosperous, it was important for him not to let evil gods or spirits know about it. If he knocked on the wooden walls while he spoke of his good fortune, he would cover the sound of his voice, and the gods would not hear him.)

Much student magic was associated with particular activities, for instance, exams. One young woman who was never confident that her preparation for tests was adequate believed that using a particular pen could boost her performance. "I took an economics test and afterward thought I had failed," she said. "But I got a B on the test. I knew it couldn't be me who had done that well; it must have been the pen."

In card playing, the favorite gambling activity among students, the most frequently mentioned good-luck practice was not looking at one's cards until all the cards were dealt. One student reported that he waited to look at his cards until all the other players had looked at their hands.

Athletes were among the most ardent practitioners of magic. Wearing a piece of clothing associated with a previous good performance was mentioned by both males and females. Also cited was the use of crucifixes, neck chains, and coins as good-luck charms. Some of the most elaborate personal rituals were those of male students on intercollegiate teams. Unable to attribute an exceptional performance to skill alone but hoping to repeat it in future contests, players superstitiously singled out something they had done in addition to their actual play as partially responsible for their success. That "something" might be the food they had eaten before the game, the new pair of socks or sneakers they had worn, or just about anything they had done that was out of the ordinary. Mike, a linebacker on a varsity football team, vomited and was the last player to come on the field before a game in which he made many tackles. Before each game during the remainder of the season, he forced himself to vomit and made certain he was the last to leave the locker room.

The fact that students could easily repeat the behavior they had decided was crucial to success gave them the illusion that they could influence their performance simply through repetition of that behavior. That sense of control, however groundless in reality, increased their confidence, which may have improved their performance.

To learn more about the kinds of students who practiced magic, we asked subjects whether or not, and to what degree, they believed in God, science, astrology, ESP, and the supernatural. The Irish were more likely than the Americans to believe in the supernatural (66 percent versus 50 percent), but otherwise the two student groups were similar in their beliefs.

As societies become more technologically advanced, use of magic in some activities may increase, not decrease.

In general, students had more doubt about God than about science. Approximately 90 percent claimed a belief, either strong or weak, in science, while about 80 percent said they had either a strong or a weak belief in God. Prayer was more frequent than the use of magic; for example, 39 percent of the Americans said they often prayed that things would turn out well for them, 51 percent said they occasionally prayed for favorable outcomes, and only 10 percent said they never did so. Students who used prayer tended also to use magic, suggesting that the two are related and that both may be responses to uncertainty.

Students who used magic were likely to believe in God, astrology, ESP, and the supernatural, although the relationships were not strong. Strong believers in science were just as likely as weak believers to use magic. Generally, the use of magic accompanied more practical, scientifically approved, actions. Exam magic, for instance, did not replace studying hard but supplemented it.

Despite their rational acceptance of the need to study, many students nevertheless do not accept the scientific fact that luck is random, that an outcome dependent on chance is independent of previous outcomes. Fully 27 percent of the Americans and 35 percent of the Irish agreed with the following statement: "If one has some good luck, one can expect some bad luck in the future." This implies a belief in what Piaget called "imminent justice," meaning that unknown forces will act in a just and equitable way to even things up, balancing a run of good fortune with some hard going.

Our findings confirm Malinowski's observation that people practice magic chiefly in uncertain situations. There was a statistically significant correlation between the uncertainty of an activity and the amount of magic the students used. (For the Irish, this relationship was apparent only when we controlled for anxiety, that is, when we held anxiety constant by comparing students with similar levels of anxiety.) The more uncertain the outcome, the more likely the student was to use magic. Thus, as the table on page 76 shows, more American students used magic in gambling, the activity rated most uncertain, than in exams and sports, activities with medium uncertainty. Magic was least common during illness, which had the lowest uncertainty rating. There were small to moderate correlations between the anxiety students experienced in various activities and the amount of magic they used. And, when we asked students if using magic ever made them feel better, more than 70 percent said it did. In short, magic did reduce anxiety.

This anxiety appeared to stem from the importance students attached to particular activities. As one might expect, responses to our questionnaire suggest that those students who care most about the outcome of exams, sports, or gambling feel most anxious about them and use more magic as a result.

In general, the more people care about the outcome of an activity, the more they'll use magic to "ensure" that the outcome is favorable. This leads to an interesting anomaly. As societies become more technologically advanced, people become more highly educated and, as a result, presumably less inclined to use magic. However, emphasis on achievement and success also increases with modernization. Since people seem to use more magic when they care most about the outcome of a performance, the use of magic in some activities may increase with modernization, not decrease.

We have left to last our most paradoxical finding. Although many of our subjects practiced magic, they didn't believe in it very strongly—at least not consciously. When we asked, "How certain are you that such things [magic rituals] can bring luck?" only 1 percent of the American users were "very certain." Another 27 percent answered "a little certain"; 54 percent answered "not at all certain"; and 18 percent said that they were "certain that they did not bring much luck." The comments of a 20-year-old senior illustrate the attitudes of many students. "I usually wear a certain ring and earrings every day, but I make doubly sure I wear them on the day of a test," she said. "It's not that I believe I will do poorly if I don't wear them; it's just that they were given to me by someone special, so I like to make sure I have them with me in tough situations. You could say they give me confidence."

In short, most students seem to be at least intellectually aware of the fact that magic does more to reduce their anxiety than it does to bring about favorable results. The psychoanalyst might say that belief in magic probably persists beneath the level of awareness. We prefer to say that students are just playing it safe when they practice magic. They are not sure it works, but they are not sure it doesn't, either. Since the cost of performing magic is small, they use it—just in case. This lack of strong belief in the efficacy of magic may be the major factor distinguishing practitioners of magic in industrialized societies from those in preliterate cultures. Put simply, the Trobriand fisherman had faith that his magic worked. The student with her "magic" pen lacked faith but wasn't taking any chances.

———

George Gmelch is an assistant professor of anthropology at the State University of New York at Albany

Gmelch, who was educated at Stanford University and the University of California at Santa Barbara, has done extensive research on tinkers and migrants in Ireland. He is the author and editor of four books and numerous scholarly articles and is studying the impact of return migration on small communities in Newfoundland.

Richard Felson, who earned his Ph.D. at Indiana University, is an assistant professor of sociology at the State University of New York at Albany. He has written articles on the self, social perception, and situational factors in aggression.

Analysis: Translating Scholarly Research

"Can a Lucky Charm Get You Through Organic Chemistry?" presents the same research question, methods, and results that appear in "Uncertainty and the Use of Magic," but in a way that is geared to a wider audience of readers. One of the key differences is how George Gmelch and Richard Felson provide an entry point for readers in the two articles. In the case of the scholarly article, which will be read mainly by other anthropologists, the entry point needs to be a problem that will be recognized by academic specialists as important to their field of study, and accordingly Gmelch and Felson frame the problem in terms of Malinowski's theory of magic as a response to uncertainty and whether subsequent researchers have confirmed his ideas. For nonspecialist readers, however, the authors reframe the problem in more general and personal terms—as "How do we handle this uncertainty and unpredictability in our personal lives?"—thereby providing readers with a way to identify the relevance of the research to their own lives.

⇨ FOR CRITICAL INQUIRY

1. Consider how Felson and Gmelch set up the theory they plan to test in the introduction of "Uncertainty and the Use of Magic." How do they integrate and evaluate previous research? How does this create a space for their own research? Identify a sentence or sentences that presents their purpose.

2. Consider the strategies Gmelch and Felson use in "Can a Lucky Charm Get You Through Organic Chemistry?" to translate their scholarly research for a broader audience. How do they make the presentation for specialists accessible to nonspecialists?

3. Compare your experience reading the two articles. How did you go about making sense of "Uncertainty and the Use of Magic"? What particular challenges, if any, did the scholarly article pose? What reading strategies did you use to deal with these challenges? How did your reading of "Can a Lucky Charm Get You Through Organic Chemistry?" differ from the way you read the scholarly article? What reading strategies did you use in this case?

MULTIMODAL COMPOSITION

Slide Show and Videos

Revolutionaries: Egypt's Transformers. Photographs by Platon for Human Rights Watch.

This slide show with video interviews is the result of a collaboration between Human Rights Watch and *New Yorker* staff photographer Platon to document the Egyptian revolution by photographing and interviewing key participants in order to hear their story firsthand in their own voices. Watch the slide show and listen to the interviews at www.hrw.org/features/revolutionaries-egypts-transformers. Consider what the photographs and interviews add to your understanding of events during the Tahrir Square protests. How do the written captions and interviews work together? Check out the links on the Resources page. What additional information do they make available?

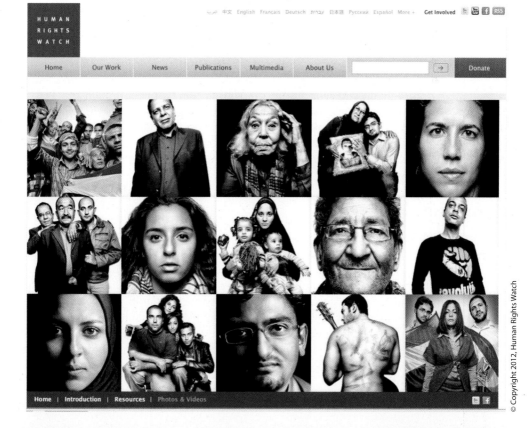

Album Notes

Grammy Award Winners

Album notes (or liner notes) range from basic recording information to more elaborate booklets with photos, concert posters, and essays in boxed sets such as James Brown's *Star Time* (1991), a four-CD career retrospective compilation that won the Grammy Award for Best Album Notes. Sometimes Grammy Award-winning liner notes appear with CDs by a single musician or group. In other cases, Grammy Award winners have written about collections that present a style of music by various artists, such as Adam Machado in 2012 for *Hear Me Howling!: Blues, Ballads & Beyond as Recorded by the San Francisco Bay by Chris Strachwitz in the 1960s* and Rob Bowman in 1996 for *The Complete Stax/Volt Soul Singles, Vol. 3: 1972–1975*.

Go to http://en.wikipedia.org/wiki/Grammy_Award_for_Best_Album_Notes to see who was nominated and who won the award over the past fifty years. Find a couple of these albums that interest you in your college or local public library. Consider the design of the liner notes—the visual style, photos, and essays. What range of information, analysis, and interpretation do they present?

FURTHER EXPLORATION

Rhetorical Analysis

Compare the Pew Hispanic Center's study *Unauthorized Immigrants: Length of Residency, Patterns of Parenthood* to Jennifer Gordon's "Workers Without Borders" in Chapter 10, pp. 311–313. Both treat the question of undocumented workers living and working in the United States, but although the Pew report is concerned with presenting research findings in an impartial way, Gordon's proposal makes an explicit argument. Analyze the rhetorical stance developed in each piece of writing. What strategies do they use to promote their credibility to readers? What do these strategies reveal about the differences between reports and proposals?

Genre Awareness

Pick a current topic. It could be obesity, video games, social networking Web sites, recent trends in eyeglass design, bhangra music, charter schools, or something else. Consider how you could present the information on the topic in at least two different modes of communication—writing (print or online), visual display of information (page, poster, brochure, and so forth), audio, video, museum exhibit, PowerPoint presentation, multimedia. What purpose would the information serve? Who would the intended readers be? What would you imagine them doing with the information? How would things vary depending on the mode of communication? Under what circumstances might one mode of communication be more appropriate than another?

WRITING ASSIGNMENT

Reports

For this assignment, design the presentation of information on a subject that interests you and that you think your intended readers have a need to know about. How much research you do will depend on time and your teacher's instructions. Here are some preliminary ideas about how to approach this assignment.

▶ **News report** on a recent event—whether on campus, in your local community, or on the national or international scene. Or you could take a recent report by a research institute like the Pew Research Center or a recent scholarly article and translate it into a news story.

▶ **Wikipedia entry:** Write a Wikipedia entry on something that has not been covered or expand a "stub" or "short article in need of expansion." Wikipedia has directions and a list of stub categories to help you get started: http://en.wikipedia.org/wiki/Wikipedia:Stub

▶ **Fact sheets** are particularly suitable if you want to introduce readers to a subject or issue they may not know much about. You could, for example, design a fact sheet on a current issue such as the "Facts About Prisons and Prisoners," to give readers a quick understanding of what is at stake concerning, say, the use of medical marijuana, U.S. military support of the Colombian government, same-sex marriage, or swine flu.

▶ **Magazine article:** Articles such as "Can a Lucky Charm Get You Through Organic Chemistry?" report on scholarly research for nonspecialist readers. You could find a recent scholarly article that interests you and translate it for a wider audience. Also see "Lost in a Smog" in Chapter 13 as a model.

▶ **Web site:** You could design a Web site to inform readers about a particular topic or issue that concerns you. You don't have to have the technical ability to put up a Web site online to design one on paper. See the directions in Chapter 18, "Web Design."

Multimodal Composition

▶ Design a slide show that reports on an event, a trend, or an artistic or cultural movement. The topic could be a major political event like Arab Spring or the Occupy movement, a cultural trend like the popularity of Swedish thrillers such as the Wallander series and *Girl with a Dragon Tattoo*, or a historic trend like the deindustrialization of rust-belt cities in the American Midwest. Consider the ratio of text to visuals. If you want, design your slide show to include interviews, as the Platon-Human Rights Watch collaboration does, even if you can't do the interviews. This can be done as a planning exercise on paper or put together as a PowerPoint presentation. See Writers' Workshop: "Vinyl Underground: Boston's In Your Ear Records Turns 30."

▶ Design the album notes for a music compilation. You can focus on the work of a particular artist or group, like James Brown or Big Star, in a career retrospective boxed set or a single CD of greatest hits. Or you can create a music anthology that concentrates on a particular trend or movement in rock, jazz, hip hop, country and western, and so on, with various artists and groups representing a distinct style or moment in time, such as rockabilly Motown, disco, or grunge. Within genres there are subgenres. For example, you can go from rock to heavy metal, to subgenres such as death metal, drone metal, speed metal, grindcore, and so on. Consider what recording information, photographs, concert posters, and other memorabilia you want to present. Check out the Web site www.albumlinernotes.com for good examples of liner notes. What visual style can you create that is somehow stylistically equivalent to the music you're presenting—what colors, typefaces, and layouts would work to produce the right look?

Invention

Identify situations that call for the kind of informative and explanatory writing featured in this chapter. Make a list of topics that interest you. Think about the information people could use and the issues that involve you and others.

Subjects	Needed Information	Issues
Torture	What constitutes torture? Does it differ from "enhanced interrogation"?	Did the United States torture detainees?
Resident assistants (RAs)	What is their role?	Should RAs be required to turn in students for drinking?
The problem of commercial overfishing	What is the scope of the problem?	What are the effects? What alternatives have been proposed?
Women in science	How many women go into scientific careers?	What limits or enables the participation of women? What programs work?

Clarifying Your Purpose and Your Readers' Need to Know

Listing information people could use and issues facing you and others helps show what gives these topics an urgency or importance that would make them worth writing about.

⟹ EXERCISE |||||||||||||||||||||||||||||||||||||||||||||||||||||||||||||||||||||||||||||||||||||||||||||||||||||

Getting Started

Pick one (or more) of the subjects of interest on your chart. Then write on each subject for five minutes or so:

1. What interests you about this subject? Why is it important to you?

2. Who are your intended readers? Why do they need information about your subject? What are they likely to know already? What should they be able to do with this information?

3. Read over what you have just written. What do you now see as the purpose of informing your readers? Do you want to help them understand something, show them how to do something, persuade them about an issue, identify something of interest, or do you have some other purpose? Assess whether this purpose is consistent with what you see as your readers' need to know. What genre appears most suitable? Why?

Background Research: Surveying the Information at Hand

Once you have determined your purpose and what your readers need to know, the next step is to assess your current state of knowledge—to determine whether the information you already have available is adequate to your purposes or whether you need to do more research.

1. Write a list of questions that cover what you think your readers need to know. Here, for example, is a list concerning the status of women in science that you can use as a model:

   ▶ What is the percentage of women in careers in science?

   ▶ What changes have taken place in this percentage over time?

   ▶ What explanations have people offered to account for these changes?

   ▶ What barriers persist in limiting women's participation?

   ▶ What, if anything, is being done to deal with these barriers?

   ▶ Are there programs that have been especially successful in encouraging women to go into science?

2. Use your list of questions to survey the information you have. Can you answer the questions with the information at hand? Is your information up to date, reliable, and authoritative? Is it relevant to your readers' needs? If you need more information, where can you get it?

3. Take into account the information you have at hand, the information you need to get, and the amount of time you have to complete this assignment. Will you be able to find what you need in the time available? If not, consider whether the scope of your project is too broad. How can you set priorities based on your sense of purpose and of what your readers need to know?

Planning

Organizing the Information

Whether you're designing a Web site or writing a fact sheet, an explanatory report, or an article, the organization of information you provide readers is crucial to the way they navigate your work. News reports have a distinctive inverted pyramid structure that presents the key information in the first paragraph or two, as you can see in "Mentally Ill People Aren't More Violent, Study Shows" and "Studies of Mental Illness Show Links to Violence." The academic article "Uncertainty and the Use of Magic" uses a standard format: Introduction, Methods, Results, and Discussion, and the Wikipedia entry has three main clusters of information—History and Background, Critical Perspectives and Analysis, Current Implications.

⟫ EXERCISE ||||||||||||||||||||||||||||||||||||||||||||||||||||||||||||||||||||||||||||||||||||||||

Organizing Your Report

To help determine how you'll organize your report, respond to the following directions:

1. Write a list of all the information you have about your topic. Make it as complete as possible.

2. What items of information can be combined? Revise your list by grouping closely related topics into clusters. If there are items that don't seem to fit, put them aside for the moment.

3. Number the revised list according to the order in which the items might appear in your report. Then label the function of each cluster of information. What will they do in the report you're planning?

4. Does any of the information you've set aside now seem to fit into your planning? What purpose will it serve?

Drafting

Introducing the Topic

Readers justifiably expect that the kind of reports featured in this chapter will cue them right away to the topic at hand. There are various ways to create this focus. Here are some options.

You can be direct and focus right away on the information you are reporting and its significance, as in "Mentally Ill People Aren't More Violent, Study Finds."

Or you could put things in historical and geographical perspective, as Daniel Pauly and Reg Watson do in "Counting the Last Fish," a *Scientific American* article on overfishing:

> Georges Bank—the patch of relatively shallow ocean just off the coast of Nova Scotia, Canada—used to teem with fish. Writings from the 17th century record that boats were often surrounded by huge schools of cod, salmon, striped bass and sturgeon. Today it

---

is a very different story. Trawlers trailing dredges the size of football fields have literally scraped the bottom clean—including supporting substrates such as sponges—along with the catch of the day. Farther up the water column, longlines and drift nets are snagging the last sharks, swordfish and tuna. The hauls of these commercially desirable species are dwindling, and sizes of individual fish being taken are getting smaller; a large number are even captured before they have time to mature. The phenomenon is not restricted to the North Atlantic but is occurring across the globe.

Or you can explain a concept, as George Gmelch and Richard Felson do in "Can a Lucky Star Get You Through Organic Chemistry?"

During his stay in the South Seas in World War I, Bronislaw Malinowski observed that the Trobriand Islanders used magic in situations of danger and uncertainty, when circumstances were not fully under human control. In a classic illustration of this principle, the anthropologist compared two forms of Trobriand fishing—fishing in the inner lagoon and fishing in the open sea. In the safety of the lagoon, fish were plentiful and there was little danger, the men could rely on their knowledge and skill. On the open sea, however, fishing was dangerous and yields varied widely; to ensure safety and increase their catch, the men turned to rituals and fetishes for help. Malinowski wrote that the fishermen's magic was performed "over the canoe during its construction, carried out at the beginning and in the course of expeditions, and resorted to in moments of real danger."

Peer Commentary

Exchange your working draft with a classmate and then answer these questions in writing:

1. Explain to the writer what you knew about the subject before you read the working draft, what you learned from reading it, and what (if anything) surprised you.

2. Explain to the writer whether you found the working draft easy to understand. Point to sections that are especially clear or interesting. Also point to any parts you found confusing.

3. What questions, if any, does the draft raise in your mind that you believe are not adequately answered? Are there points in the draft where you wanted more information from the writer? If so, explain.

4. Comment on the design. Is the purpose clear at the outset? Does the draft break the information into manageable chunks? Is the order of information easy to follow?

5. What suggestions do you have for revision?

Revising

Use the peer commentary to do a careful critical reading of your working draft.

1. Did your reader find the purpose clear?
2. Are the amount and type of information adequate? Is the information easy to understand?
3. Is the information presented in the best possible order?
4. Does the design enable your reader to move easily from point to point?

Getting the Right Order

Thinking about the order in which you present information can help you see whether one item leads to the next, what you have left out, and what you can combine.

Here are the questions on a student's working draft of a fact sheet about the herpes simplex virus:

▶ Is there a cure for herpes?

▶ How contagious is the virus?

▶ Besides the unappealing sores, does the virus pose any other health risk?

▶ What can be done to prevent it?

▶ How does herpes really spread?

▶ What about the possibility of herpes being spread by a toilet seat?

▶ How often do the symptoms recur?

▶ How is herpes treated?

▶ What can I do to prevent herpes?

After getting a peer commentary, the student revised the order by combining information, adding further information, and developing a new set of questions:

▶ What is herpes?

▶ What are the symptoms?

▶ How does it spread?

▶ What are the health risks?

▶ How is herpes treated?

▶ How can I prevent herpes?

WRITERS' WORKSHOP

Vinyl Underground: Boston's In Your Ear Records Turns 30. PowerPoint Presentation.

Stacy Yi designed this PowerPoint presentation for a class her sophomore year on Media, Mass Consumption, and Cultural Taste. The assignment asked students to report on a cultural fad or trend, taking into account why it emerged, how long it persisted, and what it morphed into. Stacy knew about hardcore vinyl fans from friends she met in the dorm. So she decided to investigate one of the largest stores for vinyl records on the East Coast.

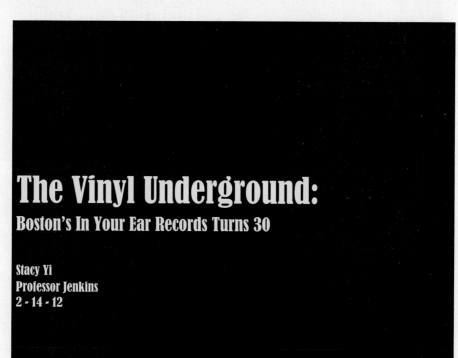

Stacy Yi, Vinyl Underground PowerPoint

A Boston institution since 1982, In Your Ear Records's  flagship store is located in the basement level of 957 Commonwealth Ave. There are two other locations, one near Harvard Square in Cambridge, and another in Warren, Rhode Island. Each is packed with CDs, tapes, turntables, posters, DVDs, and especially vinyl LPs and 45s.

Stacy Yi, Vinyl Underground PowerPoint

The mid-sized store is packed full with records. The bins are stacked deep...

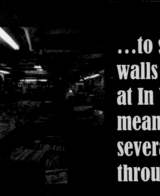

...to say nothing of the walls and aisles. Browsing at In Your Ear sometimes means reaching over several boxes just to flip through a bin.

Stacy Yi, Vinyl Underground PowerPoint

Those piles and stacks contain music of every genre. No matter what your taste, you can find something at In Your Ear.

That breadth of selection applies to media as well. What other music store still sells 8-track cassettes?

Stacy Yi, Vinyl Underground PowerPoint

"We're trying to stay behind the times," says owner Reed Lappin.

As most people increasingly turn to digital outlets for their music consumption, In Your Ear argues that there's value in the tangible artifacts of our past. You can make discoveries in these stacks that you can't make online.

In Your Ear Records is more than just a music store, it's an archive. But unlike most archives, you can take a few pieces of it home with you.

Stacy Yi, Vinyl Underground PowerPoint

Stacy's PowerPoint Reflection

In designing my In Your Ear slides I opted for simple colors and layouts, because I knew the pictures I wanted to use were busy and crowded enough. I chose the black background and yellow font as an inversion of the cover art of the Velvet Underground's first album—it connects the slides to the history of rock and roll represented by In Your Ear, and also echoes the pun in my title. The font is not exactly the same as it is on that record, but it's a close approximation. For each slide after the title card, I tried to wrap the captions around the images so that they would feel integrated, because I feel both are equal in the success of the overall text.

> **WORKSHOP QUESTIONS**

1. Consider the order of information on the slides. Notice how Stacy Yi has organized the sequence of five slides, with basic information about In Your Ear Records in the second, third, and fourth slides, and the main interpretation of the store in the fifth slide, emphasizing its style as "behind the times" and an alternative to digital music. Do you think this is the most effective order? How would it change things if the final slide came at the beginning?

2. Consider how text and visuals work together in the slide show.

3. Consider the visual design—color, typeface, and layout. Are these good choices for the topic?

REFLECTING ON YOUR WRITING

Think about how you wrote and revised the informative writing you did as this chapter's work. What did you discover along the way about informative writing that you didn't know before?

CHAPTER 9

Commentary

Commentary is a genre of writing that uses analysis and interpretation to find patterns of meaning in events, trends, and ideas. The purpose of commentary is not simply to report on things but to give readers a way to make sense of them.

This purpose should be clear if you think about the commentaries you've heard on radio and television and read in newspapers and magazines. For example, when television news commentators such as Rachel Maddow or Rush Limbaugh present their remarks, you don't see news footage on the television screen—just the commentator speaking directly to you. Thus, the focus has shifted away from the news itself to the commentator's analysis and interpretation of the news.

In contemporary society, in which new ideas emerge and trends and events occur at a dizzying pace, commentators perform several crucial functions. For one thing, they perform a *labeling* function, identifying current trends and giving readers names for these trends (for example, "metrosexuals," "outsourcing," "gentrification," "the network society"). For another, by seeking to find patterns of meaning in events, trends, and ideas, commentators call on readers to think about the *causes and consequences* of what is happening in the world today (for example, "The economic downturn has alerted average Americans to the need to cut down on spending and save more" or "The drop in reading scores results from the neglect of phonics instruction"). Finally, in the process of explaining, commentators often apportion *praise and blame*—whether of solidarity, indignant reaction, or ironic distance (for example, "No Child Left Behind has been a disastrous failure" or "It's amusing to watch the baby boomers of the psychedelic sixties tell their children not to use drugs").

Commentary is also an important genre in academic writing, where books and articles seek to provide persuasive explanations of issues in a particular field—whether it is the meaning of Hamlet's melancholia, the causes of slavery in the New World, the nature of human–computer interactions, the role of trade in Paleolithic economies, or the results of new AIDS therapies. In academic commentaries, the issues are often more technical and specialized than the issues commentators treat in the popular media. But in many respects, it is the same desire to go beyond the given facts—to find patterns of meaning, identify underlying causes, explain consequences, and make judgments—that drives academic inquiry.

Whatever the context may be, the call to write commentary grows in part out of this desire to analyze and explain what happens around us—to have satisfying accounts of our experience and to find patterns of meaning that can make the world cohere. In conversation, we routinely offer commentary on events, trends, and other people. We want to get a handle on the local scene at work, in school, in our neighborhood, and so we talk about what is going on, analyzing the motives for actions and the reasons for events. A good deal of everyday talk, in fact, serves as a kind of social analysis that shapes how we negotiate our relationships with others.

WRITING FROM EXPERIENCE

Think of a place where you routinely talk with others. It could be your workplace, the family dinner table, your dormitory, or any place you hang out. What topics come up in conversations—events, trends, ideas, people? What makes these topics of interest to the people involved? Characterize the kinds of comments people make. What role does such talk play in the particular setting? Use your findings to see if you can form any tentative generalizations about how people use conversation to find patterns of meaning and manage their lives.

READINGS

The Op-Ed Page: Contributors and Columnists

Op-ed is the shortened form of the term "opposite the editorial page" in newspaper layout. In typical page design, editorials appear on the left page, with no signature since they present the newspaper's official position, while signed commentaries from individuals appear on the right page. In turn, the op-ed page is divided between commentaries written by contributors who usually do not have any ties with the newspaper's editorial board and commentaries by regular columnists who work for the newspaper or are syndicated. Eric Liu's "Remember When Public Spaces Didn't Carry Brand Names?" and Lundy Braun's "How to Fight the New Epidemics" are examples of the first type (often called simply "op-eds"), from writers unaffiliated with the newspaper, while Paul Krugman's "Confronting the Malefactors" comes from one of the *New York Times* regular columnists.

Op-Ed

Remember When Public Spaces Didn't Carry Brand Names?
Eric Liu
....

Eric Liu has written a memoir, The Accidental Asian: Notes on a Native Speaker *(1998), and two books with Nick Hanauer on politics and civic life,* The Gardens of Democracy *(2011) and* The True Patriot *(2007). He was a speechwriter during the Bill*

Eric Liu, "Remember When Public Spaces Didn't Carry Brand Names?" *USA Today*, March 25, 1999. Reprinted by permission of the author.

Clinton presidency. His commentary on "branding" appeared as an op-ed in USA Today *in 1999.*

Opening:
*Uses example
to identify
issue

*Reveals his
perspective

*Generalizes
from example
to wider trend

¶4: * Provides
examples as
evidence of
trend

¶5–6: * Makes
qualification
and explains
his promise
about public
space

¶7–11:
*Explains
consequences
of branding

In a few weeks, when the world champion New York Yankees open their home season, will they take the field at Trump Stadium? Time Warner Park? Maybe AT&T Arena?

Chances are the park will still be called Yankee Stadium. But it won't be that way for long. Quietly, and with strikingly little protest, the Yankees have announced that they are planning to sell the "naming rights" to their Bronx homestead. By the time the 2000 season arrives, some lucky corporation may well have bought the sign outside the House that Ruth Built. And frankly, *that turns my stomach.*

It's not just that Yankee Stadium is a national treasure. It's not just that allowing the highest bidder to rename this 76-year-old icon feels like an insult—to New Yorkers, to tradition and to the memory of Yankees past, such as Joe DiMaggio. It's also that what is about to happen to Yankee Stadium is part of *a deeper, accelerating trend* in our society, the relentless branding of public spaces.

The sports world gives us *piles of examples.* San Francisco's fabled Candlestick Park is now 3Com Park. The selling of bowl names has reached sublimely ridiculous levels. (Remember the Poulan/Weed Eater Independence Bowl?) And the trend is hardly confined to sports. Branding—the conspicuous marking of places and things with corporate names and logos—is now everywhere in the civic square. Consider the public schools, some of which are flooded with advertising for merchandise and fast food. Districts around the country are raising money by making exclusive deals with Pepsi or Coke or with credit card companies or banks. In one Texas district, Dr. Pepper recently paid $3.45 million in part to plaster its logo on a high school roof to attract the attention of passengers flying in and out of Dallas. Other efforts to turn public spaces into commercial vessels are no less corrosive. Rollerblade now hawks its wares in Central Park under the banner "The Official Skate of New York City Parks." Buses in Boston and other cities don't just carry ad placards anymore; some of them have been turned into rolling billboards.

How far can this go? Over in England, the legendary white cliffs of Dover now serve as the backdrop for a laser-projected Adidas ad. Here in America, we haven't draped Mount Rushmore with a Nike "swoosh." But things are heading in that general direction.

You might say at this point, "What's the big deal? America is commercialized—get over it!" And *I admit my views may sound a bit old-fashioned.* But this isn't a matter of priggishness or personal nostalgia.

Public spaces matter. They matter because they are emblems, the physical embodiments, of a community's spirit and soul. A public space belongs to all who share in the life of a community. And it belongs to them in common, regardless of their differences in social station or political clout. Indeed, its very purpose is to preserve a realm where a person's worth or dignity doesn't depend on market valuations.

So when a shared public space, such as a park or a schoolhouse, becomes just another marketing opportunity for just another sponsor, something precious is undermined: the idea that we are equal as citizens even though we may be unequal as consumers.

What the commercialization of public spaces also does, gradually and subtly, is convert all forms of identity into brand identity.

We come to believe that without our brands, or without the right brands, we are literally and figuratively no-names. We question whether we belong in public, whether we are truly members.

We forget that there are other means, besides badges of corporate affiliation, to communicate with one another.

It could, of course, be said, with a place like Times Square in mind, that brands, logos, and slogans are now our most widely understood public language. It could be said that in this age of cultural fragmentation, the closest thing we have in common is commerce.

But is this the best vision of American life we can muster?

In the military, they worry about "mission creep." In civilian life, the problem is "market creep." And the question now is how to stem this creeping sickness. We know that there is some limit to what people will accept: a 1996 April Fools announcement that the Liberty Bell had been purchased and rechristened the "Taco Liberty Bell" provoked a storm of angry calls. Drawing the line there, though, isn't protecting an awful lot.

Maybe the renaming of Yankee Stadium will shame some legislators or zoning czars into action. *Maybe* the "corporatization" of our classrooms will spark some popular protest. *Maybe* the licensing away of Central Park will awaken us to the disappearance of public space—and to the erosion of the public idea.

Then again, *maybe not.* In which case, we'd better keep a close eye on Mount Rushmore.

Margin notes:

Ending:
Uses rhetorical question to shift to closing section

Projects possible countertendencies

Ends on note of caution

Analysis: Anticipating Readers' Thoughts

Eric Liu's commentary is typical in many respects of the kind of commentary you'll find in op-ed writing in newspapers. The tone is informal and the paragraphs are short. There is the feeling that Liu is inviting his readers to think along with him about branding public places. Notice at two key points how he seems to anticipate what readers might be thinking.

In the eighth paragraph, after he has substantiated the reality of the branding by giving a series of examples, Liu addresses readers directly and says, "You might say at this point, What's the big deal?" After acknowledging that he "may sound old-fashioned," Liu pinpoints the main issue of his commentary, namely that public spaces belong to everyone and that branding threatens to "convert all forms of identity into brand identity."

Then, in the fourteenth paragraph, Liu anticipates his readers again, this time by imagining an alternative perspective to his own, one in which brands are not so much a violation of public space but "now our most widely understood public language"—in an "age of cultural fragmentation, the closest thing we have in common."

By entertaining other points of view, Liu enhances his credibility as a reasonable person of good will, at the same time establishing the grounds for readers to join him in turning the critical focus back on branding by asking the question: "Is this the best vision of American life we can muster?"

⟫ FOR CRITICAL INQUIRY

1. Almost half of Liu's commentary—the first seven paragraphs—is devoted to establishing the reality of the branding phenomenon. As you read, when did you become aware of Liu's perspective on this trend? What cued you to Liu's point of view?

2. What exactly is Liu's argument against branding? Is there a sentence or sentences anywhere that express his main claim? What evidence does Liu offer to support his claim? What enabling assumptions connect the evidence to the claim? Are these assumptions stated explicitly or implied?

3. As noted, Liu anticipates what readers might be thinking at two key points in the commentary—at the beginnings of paragraphs 8 and 14. How does Liu handle these possible differing views? How successful do you think he is in countering or negotiating such differences?

Op-Ed

How to Fight the New Epidemics
Lundy Braun

Lundy Braun is professor of Africana studies and pathology/laboratory medicine at Brown University. Braun wrote this commentary in response to public fascination with media accounts of "killer viruses" and other epidemic diseases. Originally published in the Providence Journal *in 1995, Braun has updated her op-ed for this edition of* Call to Write.

One of the hottest topics in the news these days seems to be "killer" viruses. With the outbreak of swine flu and worries about a global pandemic, not to mention the popular accounts of epidemics of virus infection in feature films, made-for-television movies and best-selling nonfiction over the past ten years or so, the public has been captivated by the apparent power of microorganisms to sweep through towns and villages unfettered.

But hidden behind our fascination with these real and fictional epidemics is a profound feeling of betrayal, stemming from the widely held view that science had won the war against microbial infections.

The recent outbreaks have taken us by surprise, threatening our carefully nurtured sense of health and well-being. We diet, consume vitamins and exercise vigorously to

Lundy Braun PhD, "How to Fight the New Epidemics," *Providence Journal-Bulletin*, May 29, 1995. Reprinted by permission.

ward off heart disease and cancer. But infectious diseases strike in a seemingly unpredictable pattern, leaving us feeling unprotected and vulnerable. With the re-emergence of tuberculosis as a significant public health problem in the United States, cholera in Latin America, the plague epidemic in India last year and the Ebola virus infection in Zaire, HIV infection, formerly considered an isolated occurrence confined to marginalized populations, now seems a harbinger of ever more terrifying microbial agents.

Yet, the reasons for the re-emergence of infectious diseases are not particularly mysterious. In reality, infectious diseases never were conquered, and the recent epidemics are quite predictable. For centuries, infectious diseases have been the major cause of death in the developing world. Moreover, even in the developed world, successful management relies on active disease surveillance and public health policies.

In 1966, the eminent Australian immunologist Sir MacFarlane Burnet declared, "In many ways one can think of the middle of the 20th century as the end of one of the most important social revolutions in history, the virtual elimination of infectious disease as a significant factor in social life." Shared by most of the scientific community, this view is rooted in the rise of the germ theory in the late 19th and early 20th centuries that associated specific microbial agents with particular diseases.

The germ theory took hold not only because of the spectacular technical achievements represented by the isolation of the microorganisms, but also because infectious disease, once seen as divine retribution for past sins, now appeared potentially controllable. The discovery of antibiotics and the development of vaccines lent further support to this notion of control. Thus, the germ theory effectively replaced disease prevention policies based on sanitary reforms, including improvement in sewage systems and better housing conditions, which were primarily responsible for the dramatic decline in the death rates from infectious disease.

The possibility of control over these great afflictions of humankind became even more appealing in the post–World War II period when a sense of endless optimism about the future was fueled by economic expansion in industrialized countries. Unfortunately, during this period, we also began to rely exclusively on science to solve the problems of disease. Throughout this century the role of the natural and social environment in the development of disease has been largely ignored by the scientific and medical communities and policy-makers.

Yet, the obstacles to management of many infectious diseases are social as well as scientific, and disease prevention policies based exclusively on science leave us ill-prepared to respond effectively to the current epidemics.

In the case of tuberculosis, we know how the bacterium is transmitted, how it causes disease and until recently, we had drugs that were relatively effective in reducing transmission and the development of disease. Despite this wealth of medical knowledge, tuberculosis continues to thrive, primarily in marginalized groups with minimal or no access to medical care. Without a concerted effort to improve access to the health care system, tuberculosis will remain a formidable challenge irrespective of the development of new drug treatments or more effective vaccines.

In the case of AIDS, basic scientific research coupled with education, public health measures and the political will to address difficult social issues are essential to managing this epidemic.

There are many other examples of microbial diseases where the failure to integrate scientific knowledge with social programs has hampered the development of sound disease prevention policies. Cervical cancer, for example, is the second most common cause of cancer-related mortality in women worldwide. Over a decade ago, sexually transmitted human papillomaviruses were linked to this cancer. Yet years later, we still know relatively little about the mechanisms by which human papillomaviruses contribute to the development of cervical cancer. To reduce the morbidity and mortality associated with this infection we need to develop more precise ways of identifying women at increased risk of progression to cancer.

An investment in basic microbiological research will be required to answer these questions. Meantime, however, we have more than sufficient scientific information to begin to educate the population most at risk of contracting the disease, namely adolescents. Again, the failure to implement such programs is fundamentally a political issue, reflecting our reluctance as a society to deal with adolescent sexuality.

Effective management of infectious diseases is achievable. Many of the agents associated with recent outbreaks are not new microbes but rather newly recognized ones that have appeared in human populations as a consequence of social disorganization and ecological disruption. To be successful, disease-prevention policies must be based on more than technical solutions. They must be firmly rooted in an ecological perspective of disease that does not separate scientific knowledge from an understanding of the influence of the natural environment on disease and a commitment to social justice.

There are no magic bullets. We will have little impact on infectious diseases without addressing the living conditions of large segments of our society and rebuilding our public health infrastructure. In the absence of such a policy, however, future outbreaks will continue to be viewed with the mixture of fascination, fear, helplessness and misdirected social policy that has characterized our response to the recent epidemics.

Analysis: Explaining Causes and Effects

"How to Fight the New Epidemics" opens by noting the public's "fascination" when new and mysterious "killer diseases" became hot topics in the news. As you can see, Lundy Braun felt called on to address the fascination with these epidemics and the "profound feeling of betrayal" that science had not won the war against infectious diseases. For Braun, the purpose of characterizing this public mood goes beyond simply labeling a trend in the popular mind. As her commentary unfolds, readers quickly become aware that this public mood is only an occasion for her to explain the limits of the germ theory of disease and the failure of scientific and medical policy-making to take social conditions into account in preventing and controlling disease. Accordingly, Braun is asking her readers to reconsider the dominant theory of disease causation and to see that disease prevention and control relies on integrating scientific knowledge with social programs.

⇨ FOR CRITICAL INQUIRY

1. How does Braun use the hot news topic of "killer viruses" to frame her commentary?

2. Braun is addressing general readers, but she is also positioning her commentary in relation to the scientific community's understanding of modern medicine. What are the main issues involved? What are the main points of agreement and disagreement?

3. Consider how Braun uses examples of diseases such as tuberculosis and cervical cancer as evidence. How does she link these examples to specific claims? What do her enabling assumptions seem to be?

4. Do you find Braun's argument about disease causation, prevention, and control persuasive? Explain your reasoning.

Column

Confronting the Malefactors

Paul Krugman

. . . .

Paul Krugman won the 2008 Nobel Prize in economics. He is professor of economics and international affairs at Princeton University and writes two columns a week for the op-ed page at the New York Times. *"Confronting the Malefactors" is the first of several columns Krugman wrote on Occupy Wall Street in 2011.*

There's something happening here. What it is ain't exactly clear, but we may, at long last, be seeing the rise of a popular movement that, unlike the Tea Party, is angry at the right people.

When the Occupy Wall Street protests began three weeks ago, most news organizations were derisive if they deigned to mention the events at all. For example, nine days into the protests, National Public Radio had provided no coverage whatsoever.

It is, therefore, a testament to the passion of those involved that the protests not only continued but grew, eventually becoming too big to ignore. With unions and a growing number of Democrats now expressing at least qualified support for the protesters,

Occupy Wall Street is starting to look like an important event that might even eventually be seen as a turning point.

What can we say about the protests? First things first: The protesters' indictment of Wall Street as a destructive force, economically and politically, is completely right.

A weary cynicism, a belief that justice will never get served, has taken over much of our political debate—and, yes, I myself have sometimes succumbed. In the process, it has been easy to forget just how outrageous the story of our economic woes really is. So, in case you've forgotten, it was a play in three acts.

In the first act, bankers took advantage of deregulation to run wild (and pay themselves princely sums), inflating huge bubbles through reckless lending. In the second act, the bubbles burst—but bankers were bailed out by taxpayers, with remarkably few strings attached, even as ordinary workers continued to suffer the consequences of the bankers' sins. And, in the third act, bankers showed their gratitude by turning on the people who had saved them, throwing their support—and the wealth they still possessed thanks to the bailouts—behind politicians who promised to keep their taxes low and dismantle the mild regulations erected in the aftermath of the crisis.

Given this history, how can you not applaud the protesters for finally taking a stand?

Now, it's true that some of the protesters are oddly dressed or have silly-sounding slogans, which is inevitable given the open character of the events. But so what? I, at least, am a lot more offended by the sight of exquisitely tailored plutocrats, who owe their continued wealth to government guarantees, whining that President Obama has said mean things about them than I am by the sight of ragtag young people denouncing consumerism.

Bear in mind, too, that experience has made it painfully clear that men in suits not only don't have any monopoly on wisdom, they have very little wisdom to offer. When talking heads on, say, CNBC mock the protesters as unserious, remember how many serious people assured us that there was no housing bubble, that Alan Greenspan was an oracle and that budget deficits would send interest rates soaring.

A better critique of the protests is the absence of specific policy demands. It would probably be helpful if protesters could agree on at least a few main policy changes they would like to see enacted. But we shouldn't make too much of the lack of specifics. It's clear what kinds of things the Occupy Wall Street demonstrators want, and it's really the job of policy intellectuals and politicians to fill in the details.

Rich Yeselson, a veteran organizer and historian of social movements, has suggested that debt relief for working Americans become a central plank of the protests. I'll second that, because such relief, in addition to serving economic justice, could do a lot to help the economy recover. I'd suggest that protesters also demand infrastructure investment—not more tax cuts—to help create jobs. Neither proposal is going to become law in the current political climate, but the whole point of the protests is to change that political climate.

And there are real political opportunities here. Not, of course, for today's Republicans, who instinctively side with those Theodore Roosevelt dubbed "malefactors of great wealth." Mitt Romney, for example—who, by the way, probably pays less of his income in taxes than many middle-class Americans—was quick to condemn the protests as "class warfare."

But Democrats are being given what amounts to a second chance. The Obama administration squandered a lot of potential good will early on by adopting banker-friendly policies that failed to deliver economic recovery even as bankers repaid the favor by turning on the president. Now, however, Mr. Obama's party has a chance for a do-over. All it has to do is take these protests as seriously as they deserve to be taken.

And if the protests goad some politicians into doing what they should have been doing all along, Occupy Wall Street will have been a smashing success.

Analysis: Colloquial Language and Speech-Inflected Writing

Regular columnists often use colloquial language, as Paul Krugman does here in the first two sentences when he riffs on Buffalo Springfield's "For What It's Worth." Part of the work of a regular columnist is to establish an ongoing relationship with readers, and Krugman, you sense, is trying to make himself accessible, to reduce social distance between himself and readers by quoting a familiar pop song. Krugman is a highly accomplished academic, the author of many acclaimed scholarly articles, and a faculty member at an elite university. His challenge as a column writer is to find the right voice that speaks to his readers, not as an expert from on high but as a knowledgeable person who shares and is concerned about our common fate. Krugman's speech-inflected style of writing is a good way to do this.

Notice, for example, in paragraph five, when Krugman admits, "yes, I myself have sometimes succumbed" to the "weary cynicism" in today's political debate, he is weaving in and out of casual speech, starting the last sentence with the direct and blunt "So, in case you've forgotten." Later, he dismisses objections to the dress and slogans of Occupy Wall Street protesters with an abrupt "But so what?"

The "so's" and "but's" in Krugman's writing mimic the turns that happen in ordinary conversation, the give-and-take between equals trying to come to terms with the events of the day.

▷ FOR CRITICAL INQUIRY

1. Paul Krugman was one of the first newspaper columnists to come out in support of Occupy Wall Street. Trace the rhetorical moves that Krugman makes to shape the public's opinion of Occupy protesters. First, break the column into sections and label each according to what it says and what it does in the context of the overall piece of writing. What reasons does Krugman provide his readers? What assumptions would make readers more likely to share Krugman's perspective?

2. Compare Krugman's point of view on the Occupy movement to those of two other columnists at the *New York Times*, David Brooks and Gail Collins. They write their own

twice-weekly columns but also exchange views once a week at the Opinionator: Exclusive Online Commentary from the *Times*. On October 19, 2011, they engaged the question "Is Occupy Wall Street Being Overhyped?" You can read the results at http://opinionator .blogs.nytimes.com/2011/10/19/is-occupy-wall-street-being-overhyped/?ref=gailcollins

3. Read a number of Paul Krugman's columns, paying attention to how he uses colloquial language and speech-inflected writing to maintain his relationship to readers. Identify specific points where he uses these resources and others to reduce social distance and form more personal relationship with readers.

4. Along with the challenge of developing and maintaining relations with readers, Krugman also has the task of explaining economic events, trends, and ideas to a broad audience. Draw on the column here and others you find online to examine how Krugman explains complicated or technical points so laypeople can understand them.

Blog

Portraits of Thinking: An Account of a Common Laborer

Mike Rose

Mike Rose is an award-winning writer and professor of education at UCLA. The following commentary is drawn from Rose's book The Mind at Work *(2004) and appeared on Mike Rose's Blog for the first time on May 29, 2009. In the opening three paragraphs, Rose explains the purpose of the series of "portraits of thinking" featured on the blog.*

For the sixth story about cognition in action, I want to go back into history and reflect on the infamous description of a man named Schmidt, a common laborer in Frederick Winslow Taylor's 1911 *The Principles of Scientific Management*. Taylor's portrayal of Schmidt reveals an undemocratic and contradictory American attitude toward physical work, one that carries with it strong biases about intelligence. For those of you who missed the previous entries where I discuss the purpose of these portraits of thinking, I'll repeat two introductory paragraphs now. If you did read the earlier entries, you can skip right to the reflection on Schmidt, which is drawn from *The Mind at Work*.

As I've been arguing during the year of this blog's existence—and for some time before—we tend to think too narrowly about intelligence, and that narrow thinking has affected the way we judge each other, organize work, and define ability and achievement in school. We miss so much.

I hope that the portraits I offer over the next few months illustrate the majesty and surprise of intelligence, its varied manifestations, its subtlety and nuance. The play of mind around us.

*****

Following is one of the most reproduced depictions of a laborer in Western occupational literature, drawn from Taylor's *The Principles of Scientific Management*. It captures American industry's traditional separation of managerial intelligence from worker production.

Taylor was a fierce systematizer and a tireless promoter of time study and industrial efficiency. He uses an immigrant laborer named Schmidt to illustrate how even the most basic of tasks—in this case, the loading of pig iron—could be analytically broken down by the scientific manager into a series of maximally effective movements, with a resulting bonus in wages and a boom in productivity. Schmidt, Taylor claimed, jumped his rate from twelve-and-a-half tons of pig iron per day—each "pig" an oblong casting of iron weighing close to one-hundred pounds—to an astonishing tonnage of forty-seven.

Before he introduces Schmidt, Taylor sets the scene with a dispassionate analysis of the loading of pig iron at Bethlehem Steel, Schmidt's place of employment. Enter Schmidt, "a little Pennsylvania Dutchman," seemingly inexhaustible (he "trots" to and from work), frugal, in the process of building "a little house for himself." Then comes this interaction between Taylor and Schmidt:

'Schmidt, are you a high-priced man?'
'Vell, I don't know vat you mean.'
'Oh, yes, you do. What I want to know is whether you are a high-priced man or not.'
'Vell, I don't know vat you mean.'
'Oh, come now, you answer my questions. What I want to find out is whether you are a high-priced man or one of these cheap fellows here.
'What I want to find out is whether you want to earn $1.85 a day or whether you are satisfied with $1.15, just the same as all those cheap fellows are getting.'
'Did I vant $1.85 a day? Vas dot a high-priced man? Vell, yes, I vas a high-priced man.'
'Oh, you're aggravating me. Of course you want $1.85 a day—every one wants it! . . . For goodness' sake answer my questions, and don't waste any more of my time. Now come over here. You see that pile of pig iron?' . . .

Taylor badgers Schmidt for a little while longer—one wonders what Schmidt thinks of all this—and then introduces him to the supervisor who will direct his scientifically calibrated labor:

Well, if you are a high-priced man, you will do exactly as this man tells you to-morrow, from morning till night. When he tells you to pick up a pig and walk, you pick it up and you walk, and when he tells you to sit down and rest, you sit down. You do that right straight through the day. And what's more, no back talk. Now a high-priced man does just what he's told to do, and no back talk. Do you understand that? When this man tells you to walk, you walk; when he tells you to sit down, you sit down, and you don't talk back at him.

"This seems to be rather rough talk," Taylor admits, but "[w]ith a man of the mentally sluggish type of Schmidt it is appropriate and not unkind." Later, Taylor observes that

Schmidt "happened to be a man of the type of an ox . . . a man so stupid that he was unfitted to do most kinds of laboring work, even."

There's much to say about this depiction, and a number of critics, beginning with Upton Sinclair, have collectively said it: the insidious mix of scientific pretension, class and ethnic bias, and paternalism; the antagonistic management stance, the kind of authoritarian control that would lead to industrial inflexibility; the absolute gulf between managerial brains and worker brawn; the ruthlessness of full-blown industrial capitalism. All true.

In addition, though, I keep thinking of Schmidt himself, rereading Taylor's rendering, trying to imagine him beyond the borders of Taylor's page. Let us follow him through the plant, out into his world, down the road home. Though Taylor claims that a man like Schmidt "is so stupid that the word 'percentage' has no meaning to him," Taylor also tells us that Schmidt is building a house from his meager earnings. So, Schmidt had to calculate and budget, and even if he could not do formal arithmetic—we don't know if he could or couldn't—he would have to be competent in the mathematics necessary for carpentry. And for him to plan and execute even a simple structure, use hand tools effectively, solicit and coordinate aid—all this requires way more intelligence than Taylor grants him.

Taylor does not tell us if Schmidt is literate, but does note that many of the laborers "were foreigners and unable to read and write." If Schmidt were illiterate, did he develop informal literate networks to take care of personal and civic needs? We know that ethnic communities were rich in fraternal organizations that served as places of entertainment, but also as sites of political discussion and the exchange of news about the old country. Literate members would write letters, read newspapers aloud, both in their native language and English, and act as linguistic and culture brokers with mainstream institutions. The parish church or synagogue was another source of exposure to literate practices and social exchange, and, for some, a place of reflection.

Though Bethlehem Steel was not yet a site of significant union activity, labor unrest had already erupted in some sectors of steel, and discussions about safety, work conditions, and the length of the work day were in the air. Schmidt might well have heard the early rumblings about these issues and might have talked about them to others in the yard, the saloon, the neighborhood.

The point is that one cannot assume—as so many have—that the men looking back at us impassively from those photographs of the open ditch or the pouring of fiery steel, faded, blurring to silver, had no mental life, were sluggish, dull, like oxen.

Analysis: Commentary as Critical Reading

Mike Rose's intention in this blog is to rescue Schmidt from his portrayal in Frederick Winslow Taylor's *The Principles of Scientific Management*—to make his life and work intelligible from a more generous angle. To do this, Rose first briefly reviews what previous critics of Taylor, starting with Upton Sinclair, have said, thereby establishing in broad strokes the grounds for a critical reading of Taylor's treatment of Schmidt. Then, he uses clues in Taylor's portrait to imagine an alternative way of making sense of Schmidt, noting the significance of details, such as Schmidt's building his own house, that Taylor passes over. By linking these details to what we know about the richness of the social and cultural life of ethnic working-class communities in the early twentieth century, Rose locates Schmidt in his historical times. We cannot know with certainty what Schmidt was like, but Rose has fashioned a portrait of Schmidt that ascribes to him a lively mental life that is both plausible and a critical rejection of Taylor's notion of workers as dull and sluggish.

▷ FOR CRITICAL INQUIRY

1. To get more background, look up "Frederick Winslow Taylor" and "scientific management" on Wikipedia. Use this information to consider what Taylor's enabling assumptions about the nature of work and workers seem to be—and how this influences his interaction with Schmidt.

2. What alternative assumptions does Rose seem to be making in his critical reading of the encounter between Taylor and Schmidt? Where are these assumptions manifest? How do they provide the framework for an alternative understanding of Schmidt?

3. Go to Mike Rose's Blog, www.mikerosebooks.blogspot.com, and click on the "Comments" at the end of this blog entry. Describe the range of responses. What are people saying? How do they connect to this particular blog entry? What does this add to your reading of Rose's blog?

4. Find another blog on a topic that interests you. Follow the comments posted to a couple blog entries. What differences, if any, do you see between what people say in these comments and those posted on Mike Rose's Blog? What similarities? How do you account for these differences and similarities? Compare your findings to those classmates have come up with on the blogs they visited. How do you make sense of the variety of blogs and the range of commentaries bloggers put up and readers post to?

MULTIMODAL COMPOSITION

Political Cartoons and Comics: Mike Luckovich, Mike Keefe, and Tom Tomorrow

Political cartoons are a standard feature of most newspapers, many magazines, and, more recently, news and opinion Web sites. They typically rely on humor, exaggeration, and visual metaphors to expose corruption in society and the foibles of the rich and powerful in a single image that blends word and drawing. The two cartoons here come from Pulitzer Prize winners Mike Lukovich (who won in 2006 and 1995) and

Mike Keefe (who won in 2011). Notice how Lukovich comments on the Bush administration's Iraq strategy in this cartoon from 2005, using a literal corner to poke fun at the delusions of Dick Cheney and Paul Wolfowitz. Mike Keefe does something similar about a different topic—the controversial Arizona immigration law of 2010—by visualizing racial profiling.

Compare the single frame cartoon to Tom Tomorrow's *This Modern World* comic strip, where the message unfolds over time, as readers move from panel to panel. Tomorrow uses the familiar look of television news to parody the genre and the explanations of so-called experts about why terrorists attacked the World Trade Center on 9/11. For another look at parodies of television news, see Stacy Yi's rhetorical analysis of *The Daily Show* in Writers' Workshop.

Art as Social Commentary: Asma Ahmed Shikoh

Asma Ahmed Shikoh is a Pakistani artist who moved to the United States in 2002. Her art in Pakistan included paintings on the country's colonization by fast-food restaurants, such as *The Invasion*, where Ronald McDonalds overrun the streets of Karachi. (You can find this painting at Ahmed Shikoh's Web site www.asmashikoh.com.) Her more recent paintings have taken a different turn that explores the immigrant experience and her identity as a Muslim woman in the United States who has decided to wear a hijab (or head scarf). *Self Portrait—1* pictures the Statue of Liberty in a Pakistani wedding dress, while *VanWyck Blvd.* rewrites the New York City subway map in calligraphic script as an Urdu manuscript. The other two works come from a series of pictures Ahmed Shikoh made daily, using the head scarf as the central image—one hijab with a built-in iPod and the other made of Play-Doh, with Dora the Explorer figures. These four artworks are not as direct in their social commentary as *The Invasion*, but they do nonetheless seek to make sense of Ahmed Shikoh's experience by rewriting existing images.

Asma Ahmed Shikoh

Self Portrait—I

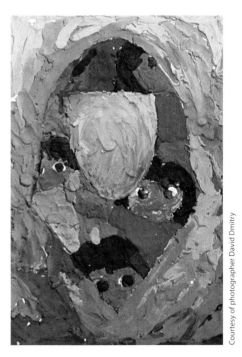

Asma Ahmed Shikoh

VanWyck Blvd

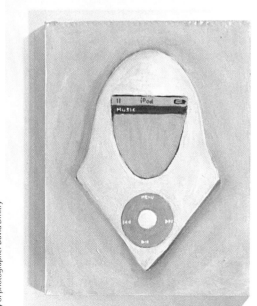

Courtesy of photographer David Dmitry

From a Group of Six Sketches

Courtesy of photographer David Dmitry

ETHICS OF WRITING

IN WHOSE INTEREST?

Commentators often seek to persuade an audience that their commentaries represent the best interests of the public and the common good. By speaking on behalf of the public, commentators play a vital role in a democracy, holding accountable those in positions of power and explaining what the public's stake is in events, trends, and ideas.

Speaking in the name of the public, however, is rarely a simple matter, and it brings with it ethical responsibilities that writers must take into account. Because commentary offers explanations, it presumes, for example, to represent other people's motives. Commentators therefore need to avoid falling into stereotyped representations of groups of people ("Gay men are promiscuous"; "Young people today don't have a social conscience"). Such stereotypes not only characterize groups unfairly but also turn these groups into "them" who are different from "us" and often present the interests of these groups as incompatible with the public interest.

Writers should be aware that speaking in the name of the public may in fact amount to speaking on behalf of some people or groups and distancing themselves from others. Writers must examine their own assumptions about who is included in the public and try to understand how the people they write about perceive themselves and their experience.

FURTHER EXPLORATION

Rhetorical Analysis

Write a rhetorical analysis of a blog and its comments, paying particular attention to how bloggers and the people who post comments on blogs construct their rhetorical stances. Consider whether they are writing as their "real name" selves or as invented online identities or as some combination. What voice do they use? How do they respond to others' comments? What differences, if any, do you see between print commentary that appears on the op-ed page of a newspaper or in a magazine and digital commentary that appears online? What significance do you see in the differences and similarities?

Genre Awareness

Compare the kind of written commentary that appears on the op-ed page of a newspaper with another genre of writing or mode of communication. You can use any of the written commentaries in this chapter (by Liu, Braun, and Rose) or you can find a commentary on another topic. For purposes of comparison you could use a visual commentary (like the political cartoons and comics, as well as Asma Ahmed Shikoh), satire such as *The Daily Show* or *The Colbert Report*, or genres of writing and visual design in advocacy campaigns or informational presentations concerned with the same issues the commentary treats. What do you see as the main similarities and differences? Consider how the written commentary and the other document are related to the place of publication or presentation where readers encounter them. How does the context (newspapers in the case of written commentaries) shape how writers design the texts and how readers use them? What do you see as the significance of the differences?

WRITING ASSIGNMENT

For this assignment, write a commentary that addresses a topic of interest to you. To help you get ideas for this assignment, consider what has called on the writers in this chapter to write commentary.

▶ **Trends:** Labeling trends gives readers a handle on what is taking place around them. Trends rely on the interpretive powers of commentators to name what's happening, thereby giving a series of events a distinct identity. The idea of "branding" in Eric Liu's commentary is a good example of how identifying and labeling trends can bring an issue into focus. There are plenty of other trends as well—body-piercing, tattooing, nostalgia for the 1980s, the growth of microbreweries, and corporate downsizing are just a few. You might write about the significance of a particular trend that is already well-known, or you can invent a new label to characterize a trend that has not been noticed before.

▶ **Policy issues:** Commentators often address issues of public policy. For example, Lundy Braun's commentary "How to Fight the New Epidemics" analyzes the causes of infectious disease and the adequacy of the "germ theory" to control disease. You might write a commentary that focuses on the causes of an issue that interests you and the implications for public policy. Accounting for why things happen is often the first step in explaining what should be done—to endorse, alter, or control the situation.

▶ **Current events:** Stories that break in the news seem to call for a swift response by commentators to shape the public's mood and its sense of issues. You might draw on a recent event to serve as the springboard for your commentary, something current that your readers are likely to know about but where the meaning is still up for grabs.

▶ **Rereading historical events:** You could comment on a historical event, as Mike Rose does when he rereads the notorious encounter between Frederick Winslow Taylor and the workman Schmidt to find new meanings. Commentators often analyze past events and point out implications that would otherwise go unnoticed. You could write a commentary about the significance of a historic event, an invention, a social movement, or an everyday occurrence.

▶ **Visual commentary:** Visual commentaries use parody to bring out the unstated logic of an event or situation. Satire and humor can be used effectively to question conventional ideas. You might write a satirical commentary that uses humor to rework existing ways of thinking. Or, if your instructor is agreeable, you might design and produce a poster, a cartoon, or a comic strip to comment on a current event, issue, or idea. Or write and perform a comic skit either as a monologue or with others.

▶ **Casebook:** A casebook brings together writings on a topic. You may have used casebooks in other courses—on the causes of World War I, say, or on interpretations of *The Scarlet Letter*. A casebook typically organizes a range of perspectives on a topic so that readers can reconstruct for themselves the context of issues surrounding the topic. This is a good project to do in groups of two or three. Pick an issue that has generated debate. It could be affirmative action, immigration, eligibility standards for college athletes, Allen Ginsberg's poetry, or any other issue that has provoked a good deal of commentary. Assemble a casebook on the issue for high school students.

First you'll need to do some library research to search newspapers and magazines for commentaries written from different positions. (Don't assume that there are just two sides—most controversies have many sides.) Select five or six commentaries that are representative of the various positions you find.

After rereading the commentaries you've selected, design your casebook in the following way:

▶ Write a brief introduction that gives readers an overview of the issue—what it is, how it began, why it is controversial—and mentions the articles you have selected.

▶ Include the readings. Before each reading, give a headnote that tells who the writer is and briefly introduces the reading. After each reading, provide discussion questions to promote thinking about it. (You can use the headnotes and discussion questions in this book as models.)

▶ At the end of the casebook, include several questions that pull together the various readings to make sure the students have understood the overall issue.

Multimodal Composition

▶ Design a political cartoon or comic strip on a recent event at the world, national, or local level. You will need to determine first your stance toward the event and the commentary you want to get across. Then consider how you can make your point visually—and what words you need.

▶ Use Asma Ahmed Shikoh's technique of rewriting such well-known images as the Statue of Liberty and the New York subway map to rewrite an image that you would like to comment on. This could be an iconic image like the Statue of Liberty, Uncle Sam, or Santa Claus. Or you could rewrite an ad, as Adbusters does. See Spoof Ads at www.adbusters.org/magazine.

Invention

As you have seen, the reading selections in this chapter offer perspectives after the fact—after events have taken place, personalities have emerged in the media, or ideas, styles, fads, and moods have started floating around in the public consciousness. The point of commentary is to name a topic, identify an important issue, and explain its significance. Commentators, in effect, are asking their readers to consider one possible way of making sense of what has happened in the past and what is going on in the present.

Naming the Topic

Corporate branding, the new epidemics, and the life of working-class communities are topics because they refer to things your readers are likely to have read about or observed in their personal experience.

Topics have names—whether those of individuals (Barack Obama, Lebron James), historical and political events (slavery, the Vietnam War), social and cultural trends (increase in two-career families, animal rights advocacy), or concepts (natural selection, Einstein's theory of relativity, the germ theory of disease). You can look up a topic and find information on it in the library. Your topic is the source of your commentary, the information whose significance you want to explore.

Background Research: Assessing Your Knowledge of the Topic

To write an effective commentary, writers often begin by assessing their knowledge of the topic they're writing about in order to make decisions about further research they might need to do. Here are some steps to help you assess your knowledge. State your topic in the form of a noun phrase (the Protestant Reformation, conversation patterns between men and women, global warming). Then, to identify what you already know and what you need to find out about the topic, respond to the following questions in writing:

1. What do you know about the topic? What is the source of your knowledge? List as many sources as you can. Which might it be helpful to reread?

2. What do you think other people know about the topic? Is it widely known, or is it likely to be of interest to a more limited readership?

3. Are there conflicting views or a range of opinion on the topic? If you're not aware of opposing views, consider whether they exist and how you could find them. If you do know, how would you describe the conflict or difference of opinion? Are there readily distinguishable sides involved? If so, do you tend to have allegiances to one side rather than the other? Explain how you align yourself to the topic and to what others have said about it.

4. Based on your answers to these questions, what further research might you do to research your topic?

Identifying the Issue

An *issue* refers to how the writer focuses attention on what he or she thinks is important about the topic. This is where the function of commentary comes in. Commentators identify issues to explain some meaningful aspect of the topic according to their own perspective.

Let's say, for example, that you want to write a commentary about video games. There are a number of issues you could use to focus your commentary.

▶ What role do video games play in identity formation?

▶ How have video games changed over time?

▶ Do video games neglect the interests of girls and women?

▶ What is public opinion about video games?

To identify an issue is also to begin explaining what it holds at stake for you and others. Why should your readers be concerned and interested? Why is the issue being raised in the first place? If you're writing about an issue that has not received attention, why has the issue been ignored and why do you want to raise it?

⟫ EXERCISE

Finding an Issue

1. Locate three readings (from newspapers, magazines, journals, or books) on the topic you are planning to write about. List as many issues as you can. You don't have to agree with the sense of the issue or be interested in writing about it just yet. The point at this stage is to get as wide a picture as possible of available issues.

2. Circle the three or four issues that interest you most. Consider what, if anything, they have in common with one another. How do they differ? Does one bring to light something that the others don't? If you notice a connection between the issues you've circled, that connection may well be worth writing about in your commentary.

3. Decide tentatively on one issue to write about. What would you say about the issue in a commentary? How does this perspective align you with some people and positions? What common ground do you share?

4. Consider the position of people who differ with you. What are the key points of difference? What objections might people have to your commentary? Are any valid? How can you use these in your commentary? What differences have to be addressed in your statement?

5. Think about the implications of your commentary. If people were persuaded by your position, what would happen? How would this be an improvement over the present condition of things? If your readers take your commentary seriously, what would you hope to achieve? Is there something you would like them to do?

Planning

Framing the Issue

Framing does two things. First, it focuses readers' attention by identifying significant features of a topic they are likely to already know something about. Framing the issue often begins with the familiar and then seeks to add a new or different angle or way of analyzing and explaining what is known.

Second, framing the issue sets up the writer to present the main point of his or her commentary. Depending on how the writer frames the issue, he or she will enter into one or another relationship to the topic and what other people have said about it.

Planning the Introduction

Commentary writers use various techniques in their introductions to name the topic and frame the issue. Here are a few:

- ▶ **Describe an event or an existing situation:** The point is to establish what is known in order to set yourself up to explain what new perspective you are going to bring to the issue. The amount of detail will depend on how familiar you think your readers will be with your topic.

- ▶ **Describe the sides of a controversy, conflict, or debate:** On issues where people differ, commentary writers often briefly sketch the opposing views to explain what they believe is at stake and to set up to their own perspective.

- ▶ **Explain the causes or origins of an issue:** Explaining the causes or origins of an issue can show readers how something came to have the importance it does, who's responsible for it, who it affects, how it's changed over time, and so forth.

- ▶ **Explain how you became aware of the issue:** Writers sometimes describe how reading, observation, or experience brought a particular issue to their attention—how something hit home for them.

- ▶ **Explain points and principles you have in common with readers:** Affirming shared values and attitudes early on in a commentary can gain consideration for your views and help set you up to introduce ideas that may diverge from the common thinking.

- ▶ **Use examples or personal anecdotes:** Beginning with an example or anecdote is a way to draw explicit connections to the larger issue by way of a specific and concrete illustration.

Planning the Ending

Endings apply the final frame to the writer's position. They give the writer the chance to have the last word, to leave readers with a closing sense of the issue and the writer's stand. Here are some ways writers design endings:

- ▶ **Point out the consequences of your position:** What would happen if your position were taken up? How would that improve the current situation?

- ▶ **Reaffirm shared values and beliefs:** What common values and beliefs does your commentary draw on? How does your position express these values and beliefs?

- ▶ **Make recommendations:** What would your commentary look like if it were carried through in practice? What concrete proposals does it lead to?

- ▶ **Call on readers to take action:** What steps can readers take, assuming they agree with you? What changes in thinking, personal habits, or public policy follow from your commentary?

Working Draft

Write a page or two as quickly as you can. Write as if you were warming up to write the "real" first draft. Begin by identifying the topic and the issue you're writing about. Explain your perspective on the issue, and quickly sketch an ending. Now you can use this writing as a discovery draft to clarify your own perspective on the issue you are writing about, to explore your own sympathies, and to understand on whose behalf you want to speak and with whom you differ. Use this draft to produce a working draft of your commentary.

Emphasizing Your Main Point and Distinguishing Your Perspective

Readers of commentary expect a writer to give them something to think about. They assume that the point of reading a commentary is not just—or even primarily—to be informed about an issue but to consider what the writer has to say about it. For this reason, it is important that the writer's main point be easy to find.

One way to make sure readers can readily see your perspective is to distinguish it from another perspective. This is a widely used technique in commentary, as we can see in Lundy Braun's "How to Fight the New Epidemics":

> To be successful, disease-prevention policies must be based on more than technical solutions. They must be firmly rooted in an ecological perspective of disease.

It's easy enough to see in this passage where Braun is coming from, in part because she shows how her perspective differs from the germ theory as a way of managing disease.

Peer Commentary

Exchange working drafts and respond in writing to these questions about your partner's draft:

1. Identify the topic of the draft. How does the writer frame the main issue? Point to a phrase or sentence. Where did you become aware of the writer's perspective? If you can't identify particular phrases or sentences, explain what you think the writer's perspective is.

2. Who is likely to agree with the writer's commentary? What beliefs and values does the commentary appeal to? Does the commentary seem to choose sides? If so, who else is on the writer's side? Who is excluded?

3. Do you share the writer's perspective on the issue? If so, does the writer make the most effective case in presenting that perspective? Can you offer suggestions about ways to improve it? If you don't share the writer's perspective, explain why. Describe your own perspective.

Revising

Read the peer remarks on your working draft. Use them to take the following questions into account:

1. Does the introduction frame the issues and forecast the main point and the direction of your commentary?

2. Is the main point located at an effective place in the commentary? How much background or context is necessary for your main point to take on significance? When it does appear, is the main point stated as clearly as possible?

3. Are details, facts, and other information about the topic clearly related to your main point? If you use examples, is it clear what point or points they are intended to illustrate?

4. Do your explanations develop the main point of the commentary, or do they raise other issues? If they do, is this intended on your part, or are you starting to jump from issue to issue? Can you point out the connection between issues so that readers will be able to follow your line of thought?

5. Does the ending offer a satisfying sense of closure? Will readers find it easy to see how you arrived at your final point? Does the ending help to emphasize the main point or lesson of the commentary?

Maintaining a Reasonable Tone

Commentary offers writers the opportunity to stake out a position on issues they are passionate about. Commentators often want to make sense of things because they are invested and believe there is really something that matters. For this reason, commentators pay attention to the tone of their writing so that their readers, whether they share the writer's perspective or not, will at least take the commentary seriously as a reasonable effort to explain and analyze.

Notice the differences between the two drafts of a commentary on how born-again Christians are portrayed in the media.

First Version

I am so sick of the way born-again Christians are portrayed in the media. What's wrong with people? Do they think all born-agains are narrow-minded, Bible-waving bigots like the ones portrayed in the Steve Martin movie *Leap of Faith*? Is the desire for sensationalism so strong that the media have to make every born-again a Bible-waving fanatic who chains herself to abortion-clinic doors and supports the madmen who shoot the doctors that perform abortions? It is so unfair to focus on the extremist fringe and ignore all the normal people who are born-again Christians.

Revised Version

The film *Leap of Faith* raises troubling questions about how born-again Christians are portrayed in the media. Steve Martin plays a television evangelist whose goofy grin turns into a rapturous and demented smile when the fat, sweaty men and women in his congregation start rolling on the floor and speaking in tongues. The sexual pleasure Martin's character gets is meant to show how repressed he was in the first place and how church service is a substitute for a healthy sexual life. But the fact is this movie is only one example of the way that born-again Christians are portrayed in the media. America's most popular image of a born-again Christian is a narrow-minded, Bible-waving bigot who doesn't know how to have fun.

WRITERS' WORKSHOP

Stacy Yi. "Where More Americans Get Their News . . . Than Probably Should": Rhetorical Analysis of *The Daily Show*

Stacy Yi wrote this rhetorical analysis in her first-year writing class. It was an ungraded exploratory writing assignment that called on students to do a short (500-word) analysis of the use of parody in political or social commentary. Students picked their own examples to examine how parody deliberately copies or imitates a style or a work in a satirical way to open a new perspective.

One of the slogans Comedy Central uses to advertise "The Daily Show with Jon Stewart" is "Where More Americans Get Their News . . . Than Probably Should." The self-deprecating humor of the line suits the show's tone, but it also reveals much about how "The Daily Show" functions as social and political commentary. By employing and subverting the conventions of typical network news broadcasts, the producers of "The Daily Show" fuse the form and content of their analysis and commentary, appearing to be that which they are actively critiquing.

Nearly every aspect of a "Daily Show" broadcast can be traced back to the tradition of nightly news programs, and cable news in particular. The show begins with martial-sounding strings and trumpets introducing the theme song as slick, swirling graphics fill the screen, eventually revealing a brightly lit set that features a desk, illuminated world map, and a backdrop that appears to be just monitors piled on monitors. Jon Stewart, in the role of lead anchor, begins by introducing the top news stories, usually with attendant video clips. Often in the second segment one or more of the Daily Show correspondents join Stewart, or contribute pre-taped stories. Finally, Stewart introduces a guest and conducts a short interview. The mechanics of news broadcasts are reproduced faithfully, right down to the sign-off motto, "here it is, your moment of Zen."

But those mechanics are put in place only to be corrupted. Within seconds the theme song shifts into a raucous guitar anthem (written by punk legend Bob Mould), and Stewart doesn't maintain the objective anchorman persona for very long. He critiques the stories he "reports", usually by pointing out the absurdity and hypocrisy of the media figures featured in the video clips. In the process of crafting that analysis Stewart slips into set-up/punchline structures and characters, tactics familiar to him from his career as a stand-up comedian. And the Daily Show correspondents themselves inhabit personas that are caricatures (but barely) of broadcast journalists. All of this subversion, which relies on an informed audience's understanding the conventions of television news, provides the show with a meta edge that isn't as easily found in the Opinion page of a newspaper. By embodying everything they reject, Stewart and company are then able to step outside of it and demonstrate, through a visceral example, why it must be rejected.

That movement between parody and commentary can make it difficult to categorize what "The Daily Show", and Jon Stewart in particular, does. Critics and fans alike seem inclined to label Stewart a journalist, or commentator for his part, Stewart maintains that he's just a comedian and entertainer who chose politics and media as his targets. But why can't it be both? By embedding commentary in comedy, "The Daily Show" is able to reach a wider, and younger, audience than might otherwise engage in politics and social critique.

REFLECTING ON YOUR WRITING

Use the following questions to interview someone who has recently written a commentary. It could be a classmate, but also consider interviewing columnists of your student or local newspaper.

1. What prompted you to write the commentary?
2. How did you decide to establish the focus of the piece?
3. What conflicts, if any, did you experience when you wrote it?

Compare the writer's experience writing the commentary with your own.

P roposals put forth plans of action that seek to persuade readers they should be implemented. Like commentary, proposals involve analyzing issues and clarifying differences. But proposals focus more centrally on defining problems and proposing solutions.

This difference between commentaries and proposals is not an absolute one but a matter of emphasis. After all, the perspectives writers make available in commentaries have consequences for solving problems. Whether or not writers of commentaries make it explicit, their perspectives often imply certain policies, courses of action, and ways of living. The difference is proposals emphasize this dimension. The focus of attention shifts from an explanation of the writer's understanding to what can be done.

Let's look at a situation that might call for a proposal. A local community group thinks that a vacant lot the city owns could be converted into a neighborhood park. The group knows there's strong support for local parks among city residents and municipal officials. But it also knows that the city's resources are limited, so any proposal involving spending would need ample justification—to show that the proposed park would solve a problem of some urgency. So the group might show that, compared to other areas of the city, the neighborhood lacks recreational facilities. Or, if the lot has given rise to other problems—for example, as a site for drug dealing—the group might argue that a park could simultaneously solve that problem.

In its proposal, the group would need to show that the proposed solution will have the intended effects. If the group claims drug dealing is part of the problem, then its proposal needs to explain exactly how turning the lot into a park can get rid of the dealers. But this isn't enough. The group would also need to show that the solution deals with the problem in the best, most appropriate way, given the alternatives available and the needs and values of the people affected (perhaps drug dealing could be dealt with more cheaply and effectively through increased police surveillance; perhaps the lot is too small to serve all age groups, and the neighborhood and city would be better off expanding a park in an adjoining neighborhood).

A proposal that is both capable of solving the problem and suitable for doing so is said to be *feasible*. To have a chance of being implemented, a proposal needs to establish that it passes the *feasibility test*—that its solution will have the intended effects and that it fits the situation.

Proposals typically require research. The community group proposing the park could strengthen its case by showing that the proposed park fits the needs of the neighborhood, given the age and interests of its residents. This information could be obtained by surveying households, as could specifics about the kinds of recreational facilities to include in the park.

Proposals must convince readers—to fund a project, implement a solution, or change a policy. Proposals are a form of persuasive writing, and clear statements of problems and solutions, demonstrations of feasibility, documentation through research, and careful organization all help make a proposal persuasive to readers.

WRITING FROM EXPERIENCE

In our daily lives, we are constantly making proposals. Analyze one such proposal by describing an instance in which you encountered a situation, defined it as a problem, and proposed a solution. Explain the steps you followed to define the problem, consider alternatives, anticipate objections, and formulate a feasible solution—even though you probably did not experience the problem solving you engaged in as a series of steps. Looking back on this experience, what made your solution successful or unsuccessful? Were there any unforeseen consequences?

READINGS

Workers Without Borders
Jennifer Gordon

....

Jennifer Gordon is professor of labor and immigration law at Fordham Law School. This proposal appeared in the New York Times *on March 10, 2009.*

AMERICANS are hardly in the mood to welcome new immigrants. The last thing we need, the reasoning goes, is more competition for increasingly scarce jobs. But the need for immigration reform is more urgent than ever. The current system hurts wages and working conditions—for everyone.

Today, millions of undocumented immigrants accept whatever wage is offered. They don't protest out of fear of being fired or deported. A few hundred thousand guest workers, brought in for seasonal and agricultural jobs, know that asserting their rights could result in a swift flight home. This system traps migrants in bad jobs and ends up lowering wages all around.

The solution lies in greater mobility for migrants and a new emphasis on workers' rights. If migrants could move between jobs, they would be free to expose abusive employers. They would flow to regions with a shortage of workers, and would also be able to return to their home countries when the outlook there brightened, or if jobs dried up here.

Imagine if the United States began admitting migrants on the condition that they join a network of workers' organizations here and in their home countries—a sort of transnational union. Migrants could work here legally. They could take jobs anywhere in the country and stay as long as they liked. But they would have to promise to report employers that violated labor laws. They could lose their visas by breaking that promise.

This plan, which I call Transnational Labor Citizenship, would give employers access to many more workers on fair terms. It would give people from countries like Mexico greater opportunities to earn the remittances upon which their families and economies rely. It would address the inconsistency and inhumanity of policies that support free trade in goods and jobs but bar the free movement of people.

How could we make this happen? Congress could certainly mandate the change. If that seems unlikely, we could start with a bilateral labor migration agreement with a country like Mexico, making membership in a transnational workers' organization and a commitment to uphold workplace laws a requirement for Mexicans to obtain work here.

We might try a smaller pilot project involving a single union in an industry like residential construction or agriculture. One model would be the Farm Labor Organizing Committee's guest worker union, which protects migrant agricultural workers on some North Carolina farms. The union provides representation and benefits wherever the workers are. It has organizers near North Carolina's tobacco and cucumber fields, and an office in Mexico, where the laborers return home for the winter.

Migrant mobility has been tried with success in the European Union. When the Union expanded in 2004 to include eight Eastern European countries, workers in Western Europe feared a flood of job seekers who would drive down wages. In Britain, for example, the volume of newcomers from countries like Poland was staggering. Instead of the prediction of roughly 50,000 migrants in four years, more than a million arrived.

Yet, as far as economists can tell, the influx did not take a serious toll on native workers' wages or employment. (Of course, what happens in the global downturn remains to be seen.) Migrants who were not trapped in exploitative jobs flocked to areas that needed workers and shunned the intense competition of big cities. And when job opportunities grew in Poland or shrank in Britain, fully half went home again.

To be sure, Europe's approach has its problems. Some migrants were cheated on their wages and worked in unsafe conditions. This illustrates that mobility alone is not enough. We also need good workplace protections, and effective support to realize them.

Unions could play a key role in rights enforcement if they embraced migrants as potential members, becoming for the first time truly transnational institutions. And government could partner with workers' organizations. Recently, the New York Department of Labor announced that it had begun to work with immigrant centers and unions to catch violators. This is a promising example of a new alliance to protect the rights of both immigrants and native-born workers.

Like it or not, until we address the vast inequalities across the globe, those who want to migrate will find a way. Despite stepped-up enforcement at the borders, hundreds of thousands of immigrants still come illegally to the United States every year. Raids terrorize immigrants but do not make them go home. Instead, rigid quotas, harsh immigration laws and heavy-handed enforcement lock people in. As the recession deepens, undocumented immigrants will hunker down more. They may work less, for worse pay, but they will be terrified to go home out of fear they can never return.

The United States needs an open and fair system, not a holding pen. The best way forward is to create an immigration system with protection for all workers at its core.

Analysis: Developing a Solution

Jennifer Gordon's proposal for a transnational organization of workers without borders starts with a problem that many Americans will recognize immediately—namely that undocumented workers are providing the labor for employers in the United States in agriculture, construction, gardening, hotels, restaurants, meat packing, manufacturing, and other industries. She doesn't spend much time laying out the problem, aside from noting it "traps migrants in bad jobs and ends up lowering wages all around." Her focus rather is on the solution and how to implement it. To make her case for migrant mobility, she cites the experience of the European Union. This is meant to be reassuring in that the influx of migrant workers did not lower native workers' wages or limit their employment. But in a key rhetorical move, she also concedes problems, in that some workers "were cheated on their wages and worked in unsafe conditions." Notice how this sets her up to make a refinement in her proposal by saying that workplace protection, as well as mobility, is a crucial part of her proposal.

> FOR CRITICAL INQUIRY

1. Anyone making a proposal has to consider the ratio between defining the problem (and its urgency for action) and the proposed solution. Consider how Jennifer Gordon does this. What does she assume about her readers in doing so?

2. Identify the reasons Gordon offers for her proposal. What unstated enabling assumptions is she making?

3. What objections might one make to Gordon's proposal? How do you think she would respond?

Proposal for Funding

Poets of Place (POP!)

Sarah Ehrich and Meredith Jordan

....

Sarah Ehrich and Meredith Jordan were creative writing students in Writing, Literature & Publishing's M.F.A. program when they wrote this proposal for grant funding from the Graduate Student Association. They were successful in securing the grant, and POP! took place in the summer of 2011.

POETS OF PLACE (POP!)
Instructors: Sarah Ehrich, Meredith Jordan

Description of Project

The overriding theme guiding Poets of Place (POP!) is the meaningful interaction between inside/outside—inside and outside the classroom, inside and outside of our communities, inside and outside of ourselves.

POP! will be a free, part-time summer poetry-writing program for Boston Public School teenagers. We will meet twice weekly for 1.5 and 3 hours each meeting over the month of July, dividing our time between the classroom—where we will navigate poetic craft through lessons and workshops—and the field—where we will explore Boston neighborhoods, using primary and sensory research as the material for exploring our theme and for writing poems.

The meetings will work toward and culminate in a **Final Project/Event** open to the public at the end of the month. At this event, students will showcase the work they have done through sharing their poems. They will be a leading force involved in all aspects of the event—from planning to emcee-ing to performing. We also plan to have an established, local poet to participate in the event and visit one of our sessions.

Rationale

At the core of the program is the belief that creative expression builds *confidence* and gives students a means to engage with and think deeply about the interplay of their external and internal experience.

POP! will operate on the principle that environment plays a key part in shaping individual and communal identities and that being aware of the complex interaction between our surroundings and ourselves is an important step on the way to *self-understanding, critical thinking* and becoming a *community leader.*

In addition, POP! is in part a response to the continued separation between schools and neighborhood communities in Boston. The public schools, serving predominantly black and Latino students[1], are facing a budgetary crisis. In the "Redesign and Reinvest" plan, the City of Boston plans to shut down or merge 18 public schools to save money; this plan highlights the further division between schools and geographical community. Through POP!, students will explore this separation and how to be an engaged *leader* in their communities.

Like Emerson's recent initiative, EmersonWrites, the Saturday creative writing workshops offered to high school students during the school year, POP! will break down divisions in Boston, reaching out to its own surrounding communities and connecting Boston Public Schools with Emerson College. In this way, POP! will contribute to the larger goal of increasing the number of Boston students who graduate from college, a priority of Mayor Menino's administration. POP! will give students a *college setting* experience in order to make higher learning a realizable goal.

Outcomes

▶ *Confidence* and *Self-Understanding:* Legitimizing creative and personal voice through exploratory creative writing exercises.

▶ *Critical Thinking:* Using field research, exploratory writing, classroom discussion, and revision to analyze the theme of inside/outside.

▶ *Community Leadership:* Exploring and understanding communities in Boston and sharing new knowledge through organizing and implementing the Final Event.

▶ *College Mind-Set:* Exposure to a college setting and personal investment in education and learning through a creative project.

Logistics
Students and Recruitment

▶ *10 students from Boston Public Schools:*
Through connections with students participating in EmersonWrites, and school visits in late May, we plan to recruit 10 dedicated students. We will have an online application that will include a writing sample and statement of interest. In just under three weeks of recruiting, EmersonWrites was able to enroll 40 students. In the same amount of time, we will be able to meet our enrollment goal.

---

[1]According to the BPS website, the breakdown is as follows: Hispanic (39%), Black (37%), White (13%), Asian (9%), Other/Multiracial (2%). 74% of BPS students are eligible to receive free & reduced-price meals in school (65% free, 9% reduced).

▶ *Rising Sophomores and Juniors:*
The sophomore and junior years in high school are important in terms of thinking about college. To address our goal of college mind-set, we will target this age-group.

Classroom

▶ *Emerson Setting:*
Wednesday evenings from 5:30–7:00, we will meet in an Emerson classroom. Students will be exposed to a college setting.

We will also have one Monday evening session for a debriefing after excursion #3 and final event preparation.

▶ *Lessons and Exploratory Writing:*
In the classroom portion of the program, students will gain knowledge in poetic craft and will be given time to write, share and revise their work. They will also take part in analytic classroom discussion to engage deeply with our theme.

Field Work

▶ *Saturday Excursions:*
Over three Saturdays from 11:00–2:00pm, we will explore three different communities in Boston. We will spend our lunch hour (1:00–2:00) eating at a neighborhood restaurant, discussing the excursion, and writing.

▶ *Introduction to Research:*
Students will learn how to gather sensory data and conduct primary research to inform our conversation and writing about inside/outside.

Final Project/Event

▶ *Community Leadership:*
Students will be involved in all aspects of organizing and implementing the final event. It will be a chance for them to share their discoveries with their communities and others.

▶ The Final Event will take place Wednesday evening (7/27), from 6:00–8:00pm.

▶ We will rent a community space (art gallery, local restaurant, or performance venue) to hold a poetry reading showcasing the students' work.

▶ An established poet from the Boston community will also be present at the event and share some of his or her work.

▶ The students may ask family and friends to attend the event, bringing together members from varying communities throughout Boston.

▶ A final magazine combining the students' work will be on display and copies will be available.

Curriculum Outline/Calendar:

Wednesday, 7/6	Introduction to course theme, goals and final event.
	Lesson: Inspiration and Tone
	Why we are moved to write and how we communicate that inner impulse.
	Writing Exercise and Workshop #1
Saturday, 7/9	Excursion #1
	Chinatown: gate, public park, and writing/restaurant.
Wednesday, 7/13	Debrief after excursion #1
	Lesson: Imagery and Figurative Language
	How to bring meaningful sensory experience to the page.
	Visit from established poet who will be reading at the final event.
	Writing Exercise and Workshop #2
Saturday, 7/16	Excursion #2
	Jamaica Plain: comparing different T-stops and writing/restaurant.
Wednesday, 7/ 20	Debrief after excursion #2
	Lesson: Shape of the Poem and Revision
	What different forms does poetry take and why? What are some revision exercises to improve drafts of poems?
	Revision Exercise and Revision Workshop
Saturday, 7/ 23	Excursion #3
	East Boston: public park and writing/restaurant.
Monday, 7/25	Debrief after excursion #3
	Final event preparation.
Wednesday, 7/27	Final Event

Credentials and Professional Development

Sarah Ehrich:

My most important professional pursuits have been working with teenagers. After college, I spent two years as a full-time tutor and teaching assistant at Match Charter High School in Boston. After, I worked for another two years as an Admissions Counselor at Brandeis University, guiding teenagers and their families through the college application process. Currently, I work as a writing tutor at a Boston Public School, Snowden International, and co-teach a poetry course with EmersonWrites.

These experiences have exposed me to the persistent problem of the achievement gap in this country and have instilled in me a passion for using writing as a means to giving students fundamental tools for success. I have both tutored students for MCAS (Massachusetts Comprehensive Assessment System) and taught them poetry, and I discovered the latter led to significant gains in confidence, self-awareness, investment in learning and critical thinking.

Teaching teenagers through POP! is a means to continue working toward the positive results I have seen in programs like EmersonWrites.

Meredith Jordan:

My previous teaching and mentorship experience qualifies me to be an instructor for POP! As an undergraduate, I took part in the teaching program titled the Young Poet's Society. For this creative writing enrichment program, I prepared 90-minute lesson plans for sixth and seventh grade students. After presenting a lesson on figurative language and the mechanics of poetry, I engaged the students in creative writing exercises. POP! would follow a similar format balancing a lesson with time to creatively write. I was also fortunate to become a peer mentor for the Honor Fraternity Phi Sigma Pi (PSP) during my time as an undergraduate. As the initiate advisor for PSP, I was responsible for coordinating service events for as class of 21 students where the students gained leadership skills and reached out to the community. At Emerson, I took the WR600 teaching class, which gave me concrete ideas on classroom management and lesson plan ideas. As part of my graduate fellowship, I worked with Professor Pablo Medina and reviewed his students' papers for a fiction course during the Spring 2011 semester. This gave me experience evaluating students' work.

This program will give me valuable teaching experience that will further my career goal to become a teacher of creative writing. I will gain skills in curriculum development in planning the coursework and classroom leadership as I manage a classroom of ten high school students. This project also furthers my fundamental belief the creative expression is important to learning and vital way for young people to express themselves.

POP! BUDGET

Expense Type		Cost
Recruitment Costs	Flyers (50 color copies)	$20.00
	Transportation to BPS locations (5-8 school visits)	$40.00
Supplies and Materials	Notebooks (1 per student)	$20.00
	Pens and Dry Erase Markers	$15.00
	Printing for Workshop and Handouts (6 classes)	$60.00
Saturday Excursions	Transportation (12 people, 3 excursions)	$145.00
	Lunch (10 students and 2 instructors, 3 excursions)	$360.00
Final Event	Venue	$300.00
	Refreshments	$150.00
	Rentals (microphone, video camera, projector)	$200.00
Magazine	50 magazines at $6 each with color cover	$300.00
	Total	**$1,610.00**

Analysis: Making Purposes Visible

In some instances, such as Jennifer Gordon's "Workers Without Borders," proposals appear in the form of an essay. In other instances, however, such as Sarah Ehrich and Meredith Jordan's Poets of Place (POP!), proposal writers use widely recognized conventions to make their purposes visible to a funding agency—in this case arranging the proposal into sections that describe the proposed activity, explain its rationale, and present the projected outcomes. Here the writers are attempting initially to persuade readers that their proposal has a worthy goal and meets a real need. Then, as readers turn to the following sections on logistics and the day-by-day breakdown of activities, they can judge for themselves whether the design of the proposed project is capable of promoting the outcomes just designated.

FOR CRITICAL INQUIRY

1. Consider the case Sarah Ehrich and Meredith Jordan make on behalf of their summer poetry project. Notice in particular the order of supporting points in the Rationale section. What does the principle of organization seem to be? Why have they arranged things in this order? What effect does the order of ideas have on readers? Does the Rationale section seem to set up the Outcomes section?

2. How do the next three sections—Logistics, Curriculum Outline/Calendar, and Credentials and Professional Development—relate to the Rationale and Outcomes sections? Do they seem a logical extension?

3. Compare the POP! proposal to the Proposal for a Campus Coffee House in the Writers' Workshop section at the end of the chapter. Notice the coffee house proposal labels main sections Problem and Solution instead of Description, Rationale, and Outcomes. What effect does this have on readers? What other differences do you see?

Research Proposal

Training Fighters, Making Men:
A Study of Amateur Boxers and Trainers

Stacy Yi

Stacy Yi wrote this proposal for a class on urban ethnography that called on her to design a research project based on fieldwork.

Background

Significant research has been devoted to the sport of boxing, the majority of which has concerned itself with the economic achievements and careers of professional fighters (Dudley, 2002; Wacquant, 1998; Early, 1996; Hare, 1971; Weinberg & Arond, 1957). Yet the sport of boxing is pursued not only by professional pugilists but also by amateur and recreational boxers, for whom economic success and fame are not necessarily the primary motivation. Rather, for a substantial number of athletes, boxing affords a set of possibilities that may not be available elsewhere. In a time of deindustrialization, changing social circumstances, and transformation of urban space, pugilism may enable the formation of identity accessible in few other social spaces. With declining employment opportunities, especially for inner-city men of color, the workplace is not always available as a site for young men to construct masculine selves. Thus, the boxing gym may offer one of the last social realms for the construction of identity, the expression of masculinity, and the negotiation of violence and aggression.

Objectives

Mention the terms "manly art" and "sweet science of bruising," or merely the word boxing, and gender is implicit. Yet in order to understand the forms of masculinity implicit in the sport, gender must be analyzed explicitly. The research I propose examines the formation of identity in a boxing gym to understand how competitive amateur fighters use the culture of training and bodily discipline to create forms of masculinity. Michel Foucault suggests that discipline is a form of power that takes the body as its object; in institutions such as prisons, schools, the military, and, as I would contend, the gym, bodies are manipulated, trained, and thus transformed (Foucault, 1977). I would like to understand how the discipline demanded in the gym facilitates the production and transformation of masculinities and attendant forms of incorporated identity[1] (Connerton, 1989).

Understanding the formation of identity requires apprehending the social relations cultivated in the boxing gym. For this reason, my research examines the relationships developed between trainers and their boxers. Coaches and fighters characterize their relationships as those of life mentoring and deep social trust rather than as merely athletic. As coaches consider it their responsibility to provide both athletic and life guidance, I would like to understand the experiences that inform and shape the advice they impart and how they disseminate such information. Many trainers have, in their pasts, participated in criminal activity, been incarcerated, and engaged in a process of rehabilitation. I would like to discern how trainers simultaneously coach their athletes and discourage them from partaking in similar criminal activity. Thus my project seeks to examine the effect trainer-knowledge has on their athletes in relation to crime and life choices.

Focusing on trainers and amateur athletes, my specific research questions are: (1) what identities are created and performed in the boxing gym? (2) how do trainer-amateur boxer

---

[1] In his work How Societies Remember, Paul Connerton makes the distinction between "assigned" and "incorporated" identities. Whereas assigned identities are largely non-negotiable, incorporated identities, such as forms of masculinity, are those individuals seek to produce or attempt to transform (Connerton, 1989).

relationships factor in identity formation ? (3) how do trainers influence life choices and train their boxers in extra-athletic ways?

Research Plan and Methodological Approaches

My research will be conducted at Harry's East Side Gym. To examine the process by which identity is constructed and social relations between trainers and their athletes forged, I will employ two methods: participant observation and interviewing. Participant observation will allow me to document the patterns of social interaction in Harry's East Side Gym and to examine the multiple ways identity is formed and trainer guidance delivered (Emerson, Fretz, & Shaw, 1995). Interviewing will allow me to investigate the dynamics of the relationships among boxing, identity formation, masculine selfhood, and life choices.

Participant Observation. Over the course of one year, I will follow a group of 25–30 amateur athletes, who train for the Golden Gloves of New York City, the most prestigious annual amateur event in boxing, and their trainers. I will recruit my sample based upon 5 trainers with whom I have established a close working relationship and who have agreed to collaborate with me. I plan to observe these athletes and their mentors beginning in September 2003, when training typically commences, and through the course of the tournament, which runs January through May. I also plan to observe the group after the tournament has finished—over the summer months—to study how the fighters use the gym and interact with their trainers when competition is not imminent. Over this year, I will examine the mundane daily activities and regimens of boxers and their trainers in the gym five days a week. I will also accompany them to the tournament in order to observe their extraordinary experiences of competition, talking with them before and after the fights. As they prepare for the Golden Gloves, I plan to analyze the social relations between the amateurs and their trainers, examining how homosocial bonding develops and shapes the process of training. I plan to study how the athlete-coach relationship emerges and influences the decisions boxers make about labor, leisure, and crime.

Interviewing. In addition to participant observation, I will also conduct 25–30 extensive, open-ended interviews with the amateur boxers and their trainers. One goal of the interviews is to identify the range of recurring themes associated with identity, mentoring, violence, and life choices. These interviews will focus on the meanings that informants attach to their participation in the sport, the range of experiences they have had with boxing, and the alternatives boxing may offer to street crime. In structuring and conducting these interviews, I am particularly interested in fighters' own expectations of training and competition: why they became involved and how they assess their progress. Of crucial importance is how they conceptualize violence and corporeal harm in the sport and how they envision their participation in this dynamic of physical conflict. I will also examine the connections between their activities in the gym and other aspects of their lives, such as labor, leisure, education, and family.

Based upon these open-ended interviews, I will then re-interview the group of boxers and trainers with a structured battery of questions about the factors involved in their senses of identity, their connection with boxing and with the mentor-mentee relationship. I will standardize my list of questions in order to facilitate a comparison of my respondents' answers. Together, these methods will enable an understanding of how identity and masculinity are formed, contested, or perhaps exposed as unstable. They will also provide an elucidation of how trainers intervene, inform and shape this process.

References

Connerton, P. (1989). *How societies remember.* New York: Cambridge University Press.

Dudley, J. (2002). Inside and outside the ring: Manhood, race, and art in the literary imagination. *College Literature*, 29, 53–82.

Early, G. (1996). Mike's brilliant career. *Transition*, 71, 46–59.

Emerson, R. M., Fretz, R. I., & Shaw, L. L. (1995). *Writing Ethnographic Fieldnotes.* Chicago: University of Chicago Press.

Foucault, M. (1977). *Discipline and punish: The birth of the prison.* New York: Pantheon Books.

Hare, N. (1971). A study of the black fighter. *Black Scholar*, 3, 2–8. *Slavery to Freedom.* New York: Oxford University Press.

Wacquant, L. (1998). A fleshpeddler at work: Power, pain, and profit in the prizefighting economy. *Theory and Society*, 27, 1–42.

Weinberg, S. K., & Arond, H. (1952). The occupational culture of the boxer. *American Journal of Sociology*, 57, 460–469.

Analysis: Research Proposals

Research proposals are similar in many respects to other types of proposals, whether to change a policy or improve a service. The same task of defining a problem and then proposing a satisfactory solution is common to all. What distinguishes a research proposal is that the problem is one of understanding something—the structure of DNA, the effects of asbestos on the health of South African miners, or the legacy of slavery in the United States—and the solution is to design a workable research plan to investigate the subject and produce new insights. Most research proposals seek to persuade the reader about the merit of the research and the researcher's ability to carry it out.

The research question or questions in a proposal are crucial. As you can see in this proposal, the research plan follows from the questions Stacy Yi wants to answer. Explaining the central research questions accomplishes two things in the proposal. First, it tells readers why the research is meaningful. Second, it enables them to judge whether the proposed plan of action is in fact well-suited to answer the questions.

FOR CRITICAL INQUIRY

1. Consider the first two sections of "Training Fighters, Making Men." How does the Background section identify a neglected area of study? How does the Objectives section raise specific questions about amateur boxers?

2. Evaluate the match between the research questions and the research plan in the proposal. Does the research plan seem capable of providing answers to the questions each of the fieldwork proposals raises? Why or why not?

3. How does the discussion of methodological approaches relate to the research plan and the research question? How does it add (or does it) to the persuasiveness of the research proposal?

Petitions

Tell Apple: Stop Slavery Practices at Foxconn's Manufactories
Monica Balmelli

Support and Pass the California Dream Act
California Dream Network

Petitions are an indispensable part of a democratic society, offering citizens the means to express their views and call for changes in public policy. You might think of petitions as a sub-genre of proposals. The two petitions in this section provide good examples of how individuals and advocacy groups use petitions to propose change—to call on people to understand the urgency of their proposals and to give support by joining others in signing a petition.

The first petition "Tell Apple: Stop Slavery Practices at Foxconn's Manufactories" was written by an individual, Monica Balmelli, and posted on the progressive Web site for online petitions Change.org. This petition calls for a change in labor policy at the Chinese plants of a major Apple supplier. You can read Monica Balmelli's explanation "Why This Is Important" to understand the issues involved. You can read the report that Balmelli refers to, "Foxconn and Apple Fail to Fulfill Promises: Predicaments of Workers After the Suicides," at Students & Scholars Against Corporate Misbehaviour Web site www.sacom.hk.

The second comes from the successful campaign of the California Dream Network to pass two acts of legislation, AB130 and AB131, guaranteeing that undocumented students in the California state system of higher education can receive private and public financial aid. Both these bills were passed, and this selection opens with a brief explanation from the California Dream Network "How We Won."

© Leila La Très Sage

Tell Apple: Stop Slavery Practices at Foxconn's Manufactories

Why This Is Important

I'm a music lover. So when Apple introduced the first iPod, I eagerly bought one. Several years later, I also bought an iPhone and an iPad. I love Apple so these were easy purchases. But when I learned about the suicides and slavery conditions at the Apple factories in China, I rethought my purchases, and started doing some research about these allegations.

Foxconn is the manufactory of Apple Inc. in China where workers are subjected to unlawful and dehumanizing working conditions. According to Students & Scholars Against Corporate Misbehaviour (SACOM), workers are often forced to work 6–7 days a week, resulting in a monthly overtime 2–3 times over the legal limit. Many times these employees are enclosed and forced to work overtime until they reach their daily productivity goal. Furthermore, when this goal is not met, the workers are at the mercy of the abuse of the managers, which is so brutal that Foxconn has been forced to acknowledge this problem.

Even more disturbing are the suicides where exhausted workers jump out the factory windows. There have been reports that Foxconn employed counselors in order to support the workers with the intensive work pressured to avoid more suicides during labor hours. Additionally, I found some reports that jumping nets were placed outside windows.

There were also reports of unsafe exposure to dangerous chemicals and operation of machines without proper training and safety procedures, which often result in injuries that are not compensated.

Due to their low wages, workers are forced to live inside the factory. Sometimes these dorms are not only partially built, but they also lack electricity and water; and rooms are shared by 5–20 people. However, most damaging is the restriction on workers of forming unions and selecting their representatives in order to advocate for better working and living conditions.

SACOM has been evaluating and monitoring Apple promises for years now, but little or no improvement for these workers has been achieved. I have attached some of their reports and video in this petition.

As a longtime Apple consumer, I feel responsible for supporting a product at such a high human cost. My Apple products are a big part of my life, but at what cost? I want to buy products made with dignity, not out of suicides and exploitation.

For that reason, I'm asking you to join me and tell Apple Inc. and Foxconn to stop this corporation malpractice. We want to see the workers in a safe work environment according to law, with all the requirements that a human being needs in order to be healthy and safe and to live a worthy life.

The Petition

We the undersigned are asking Apple Inc. to provide a safe, healthy, and worthy work environment for the employees at Foxconn manufactories.

As much as we, the consumers, like Apple products, we are not willing to compromise the dignity of other human beings. We are aware that the employees at Foxconn are forced to work long hours that exceed the legal overtime in China, and even without a meal and a break in order to meet the daily production goal. We are also aware of the abuse that the employees are subject by the managers in order to meet the expected production target. Furthermore, workers are exposed to dangerous chemicals, and operate machines without proper training and safety procedures, which unfortunately often results in injuries that are not compensated.

Another issue is the low wages, which force workers to live in dormitories that in most cases are not adapted for a decent and comfortable living. In many factories, the dorms are partly built, restricted from washing clothes, and electricity and water are limited.

For this reasons, we are asking Apple to remedy the labor conditions at Foxconn by:

1. Allowing workers to have a break and lunchtime, as the law labor requires in China.
2. Allowing workers to select representatives and organize unions according the Trade Union Law in China.
3. Providing compensation due to injuries and rights violations to workers.
4. Allowing an independent third party to monitor Foxconn labor policies.

As customers of Apple Inc., the quality of your products is equally important as the treatment of the workers at your overseas manufactories. Here in the USA, Apple plants and offices have outstanding working conditions, and we would like to see that vision transferred to the manufactories in China by eliminating the slavery sweatshops conditions. Therefore, we are advocating for collaboration between Apple and Foxconn in order to meet the goals above.

For the last years, Apple has delivered the best technology, but now it is time to deliver the best lawful work environment for the employees at Foxconn, whom after all, are the ones that have made all this success possible for the company by manufacturing quality products.

Sincerely,

[Your name]

Support and Pass the California Dream Act

How We Won

Oct 10, 2011

Every year, about 65,000 undocumented students graduate from U.S. high schools and 40 percent of them reside in California. But in California, those students were blocked from accessing financial aid to further their studies—something that resulted in thousands of would-be college graduates not furthering their educations. Now, thanks to more than 12,400 supporters who signed a petition, made calls, and demanded equal access to education in California, the state will see thousands and thousands of new graduates each year.

The full California DREAM Act ensures that undocumented students in the state can apply for and receive private and public financial aid. From the beginning, the bill faced enormous hurdles, as misinformation flowed, the bill was tied up in committee and seemed like it wouldn't reach the floor for a vote in time, and, finally, lingered on the governor's desk as it awaited a signature.

But students from the California Dream Network mobilized around the petition, organized personal deliveries around the state, and encouraged supporters to make daily calls to legislators and the governor to make sure that the dreams of so many Californians would not be overlooked. It worked: On October 8, 2011, Gov. Jerry Brown signed AB 131, the final half of the California Dream Network, into law!

The Petition

Greetings,

We, the undersigned, urge the State Legislature and Governor Brown to support equal access to higher education for all students and pass the California Dream Act (AB 130 and AB131).

Every year, approximately 65,000 undocumented students graduate from high schools across the nation with 40 percent of them residing in the state of California. A significant number of these hard-working immigrant youth are student body presidents, honor students, dynamic community leaders, outstanding athletes, and aspiring professionals who desire to pursue and complete a higher education and contribute back to their communities. However, due to their immigration status undocumented students are unable to apply and receive state or federal financial aid and thus cannot pursue their educational goals at their full potential.

Both, AB 130 and AB 131 would ensure that California's investment in the education of immigrant youth continues beyond K–12 by granting hard-working undocumented

---

youth the opportunity to pursue and achieve their higher educational goals and thus create a more educated, innovative and competitive workforce. AB 130 would allow students that meet in-state tuition requirements to apply and receive scholarships derived from non-state funds at their respective colleges or universities. AB 131 would go one step further by allowing eligible students to apply and receive financial aid at California public colleges and universities. The types of financial aid these students would be eligible for include Cal Grants, Institutional Student Aid, and Board of Governors Fee Waiver.

The California Dream Act has enjoyed broad support in the past and reached the Governor's desk only to be vetoed in four different occasions: 2006, 2007, 2008, and 2010. We urge you to take leadership and support immigrant youth to ensure the economic prosperity and future of California by signing the CA Dream Act into law in 2011.

The CA Dream Act has gained support from different faith groups, businesses, chambers of commerce, and community organizations such as the Greater Los Angeles Chamber of Commerce, the San Francisco Chamber of Commerce, CHIRLA, the Archdiocese of Los Angeles, ACLU, the University of California, and the California Federation of Teachers only to name a few.

Undocumented students are some of the most hard-working and brightest students in the nation who aspire to become teachers, engineers, politicians, doctors, and productive members of our society. At a time when the economic projections for the state of California suggest that by 2025, two of every five jobs will require a college graduate, we must ensure that all California students have equal access to higher education. It is in the best interest of our state's economy and future and that of the country to have an educated workforce to provide the innovation and leadership necessary to keep California at the forefront of the global economy and maintain its historic tradition as a national leader in enacting progressive legislation.

I strongly urge the State Legislature and Governor Brown to show leadership on this issue, and support and immediately pass the California Dream Act (AB 130 and AB 131) in 2011.

[Your name]

Analysis: The Signer's Identity

One interesting difference between the two petitions is the identity the petition makes available to the signer. Each petition, in a sense, offers a shared sense of common endeavor with the other signers. In "Tell Apple: Stop Slavery Practices at Foxconn's Manufactories," signers are identified in a general sense as consumers and in particular as Apple users and lovers. This enables a certain appeal on the part of signers for Apple to match the quality of its design and production with quality working conditions for the people who make the high-quality products. "Support and Pass the California Dream Act," on the other hand, opens by identifying signers simply as "we, the undersigned." Who this "we" amounts to becomes clearer a bit later when the petition lists the many business, religious, civic, legal, community, and educational groups and institutions that support the act—projecting a strong sense of bipartisan support that cuts across political lines. Notice how the "we" is further modified in the next to last paragraph, when it is represented in terms of "our society" and "our state's economy and future"—how signers, in effect, come together in their concern that California remain "at the forefront of the global economy."

⇨ FOR CRITICAL INQUIRY

1. Consider how the background statement written by Monica Balmelli, "Why This Is Important," sets up the call to sign the petition "Tell Apple: Stop Slavery Practices at Foxconn's Manufactories." Identify the reasons Balmelli gives for signing the petition. Identify which of these reasons appear in the petition itself. Compare the appeal Balmelli makes to readers to sign the petition to the appeal in the petition to Apple. Explain the differences and similarities.

2. Identify how undocumented students are portrayed in the "Support and Pass the California Dream Act" petition. Notice, for example, the term "hard-working" appears three times. What is the California Dream Network, the advocacy group that wrote the petition, trying to accomplish by this portrayal? How does this picture of undocumented students relate to other themes in the petition?

3. Compare the rhetorical situations that the petitions seem to be responding to. How is the call to write, the urgency of the petition, defined in each case? Can you imagine other ways of presenting the call to write? How do the two petitions respond? What do you see as interesting differences and similarities?

ETHICS OF WRITING

PROBLEMS AND CONFLICTS

Understanding the situations that confront us in everyday life and in public affairs as problems that can be solved is a powerful way of making reality appear to be more manageable. Once you have defined a problem, it then becomes possible to think in terms of a solution.

It's important to recognize that problems don't just pop up out of the blue. They take shape according to the way people define them based on the urgencies they are feeling. In turn, depending on how the problem is defined, particular solutions seem more— or less—logical than others. Formulating a problem invariably means positioning yourself in relation to what others think and believe—aligning yourself with particular values and beliefs and distancing yourself from others.

Problems, in other words, grow out of underlying differences and conflicts about values and beliefs which can lead to very different statements of the problem and thus to different proposed solutions. At the same time, defining social situations strictly as problems can paper over long-term conflicts and differences, causing experts and professionals to be culturally insensitive to the lay people they serve and, unthinkingly, impose their own values and beliefs in the name of solving problems.

MULTIMODAL COMPOSITION

Web Site: Forgive Student Loan Debt to Stimulate the Economy

The Web site for Robert Applebaum's campaign Forgive Student Loan Debt is built around the proposal that calls on President Obama and Congress to abolish student loan debt as a means of economic stimulus. "Free us of our obligations to repay our out-of-control student loan debt," the proposal says, "and we, the hardworking, middle-class Americans who drive this economy will spend those extra dollars now." As you can see by browsing around the Web site, the basic appeal of the proposal appears repeatedly: ending student debt repayment is not just a bailout for one group but benefits everyone by spurring economic growth. Notice how the Web site is constructed of links that take readers to multiple genres and subgenres of writing (including proposal, FAQs, petition, blog, news stories, and reading lists), multiple media platforms (such as Facebook, Tumblr, and YouTube), and multiple modalities (from writing to audio and video, to T-shirts). Printed flyers like this one are standard features in advocacy campaigns of all sorts, combining, in this example, text and the campaign logo. Notice how it adds another dimension by offering tear-off tabs at the bottom with the campaign's URL.

Posters: Health Advocacy Campaigns

Since the 1964 Surgeon General's Report on Smoking and Health made the dangers of smoking widely known, organizations such as the American Lung Association and Centers for Disease Control have combined visual and verbal resources in public health posters that call on people to stop smoking or to not start in the first place. The challenge these anti-smoking campaigns have faced over the years is the relentless marketing of cigarettes by tobacco companies and the images of glamour, masculinity, sophistication, and pleasure that have been associated in the media and popular culture with smoking. To be persuasive, anti-smoking posters have to redefine the cultural meaning of smoking and the identities cigarette ads offer to smokers—to provide positive alternative images of nonsmokers. For background, go to "Visual Culture and Public Health Posters" at the U.S. National Library of Medicine Web site http://www.nlm.nih.gov/exhibition /visualculture/index.html and click on "Anti-Smoking Campaigns."

Consider how the four anti-smoking posters have created rhetorical stances that invite readers/viewers to take on identities as nonsmokers. Begin by examining the appeal of cigarette advertising. Cigarette ads from the past can be found easily online by Googling "cigarette advertising history" and hitting Images. Consider the four ads presented here and how they counter the allure of smoking. To what extent do they use fear of the dangers of smoking? To what extent do they project positive benefits of not smoking? How do the posters combine brief passages of written text with visual images to form one message?

U.S. National Library of Medicine/National Institutes of Health

Dejé de Fumar poster reproduced with permission. © 2012 American Lung Association. www.Lung.org

American Lung Association.

California Department of Public Health

FURTHER EXPLORATION

Rhetorical Analysis

Analyze the argument in one (or more) of the proposals in this chapter. Pay particular attention to the enabling assumptions that connect the claim (the writer's proposal) and the evidence. Consider how the shape of the writer's argument is likely to influence readers' evaluations of whether the proposal is feasible or not.

Genre Awareness

Think of a current problem—campus-wide, local, national, or international. Imagine a feasible solution to the problem. You could write a formal proposal to solve the problem, as the students who proposed a campus coffee house did—see the Writers' Workshop section, later in this chapter. Let's assume you're really serious about getting your proposal implemented. What other genres of writing might you use to publicize your proposal?

WRITING ASSIGNMENT

For this assignment, write a proposal that formulates a problem and offers a solution. Think of an existing situation that calls for attention, whether it is on campus or at the local, national, or international level. Something may be wrong that needs to be changed. Something may be lacking that needs to be added. Something worthwhile may not be working properly and therefore needs to be improved. Or it may be that a situation needs to be redefined in order to find new approaches and solutions.

Proposals can be group projects or done individually. Here are some possibilities:

▶ **Public policy proposals:** These range from op-ed pieces in newspapers, like Jennifer Gordon's "Workers Without Borders," to petitions and legislation that propose to do things such as change immigration laws, recognize gay and lesbian relationships, require a balanced budget, or devise a national health care plan.

▶ **Proposals for new or improved services:** Proposals call on government agencies, professional associations, educational institutions, and private foundations to provide new or improved services—for example in health care, education, and recreation. Sarah Ehrich and Meredith Jordan's proposal for a summer poetry program for Boston Public School teenagers and "Proposal for a Campus Coffee House" (see Writers' Workshop) are good examples of this type of proposal. You might write a proposal based on a situation you see on campus—to improve residential life, food service, social climate, advising, or academic programs. Or you may want to write a proposal for new or improved services in your local community or at the state or federal level.

▶ **Research proposals:** Stacy Yi's "Training Fighters, Making Men" offers an example of a research proposal. You might draw on one of the classes you're taking right now to write a research proposal. What is an interesting and important problem or issue that has emerged in readings, lectures, and discussions? How would you go about researching it?

Multimodal Composition

▶ Design a Web site for an advocacy campaign by an existing organization or one that you make up. Create a name and a logo for the campaign; include the goals and strategy of the campaign, its audience, and the types of written and visual material needed to carry out the campaign. The forgive student loan debt and anti-smoking campaigns in this chapter offer examples.

▶ Design a poster that promotes healthy behaviors, such as the anti-smoking messages. Consider the limits of "just say no" campaigns. Is it realistic to abolish a particular behavior or should you design messages calling on people to better manage risk in terms of diet, drinking, sexual behavior, drugs, and so on? How can you do this by linking an image and a catchy phrase or two?

Invention

To think about proposals you might write, work through the following exercises. Your proposal may well grow out of a situation you are currently in, or it may stem from an experience you have had in the recent past.

1. Start by taking an inventory of the issues around you that might call for a solution. Begin by thinking small and local. What groups, clubs, teams, or other organizations do you belong to? What issues face these groups? What issues face students at your college or university?

2. Now broaden your thinking to national and international issues. What do you see as real problems? Which problems do you care enough about to spend time researching and proposing a solution to? Who might listen to you? What is the best forum for getting people to hear your proposal?

3. Once you have created your list of possibilities, narrow it down to the three most promising options, beginning with the ones you care most about or that have the potential to make your life (or that of others) markedly better.

4. Decide tentatively on the audience. Who can realistically make changes happen? To whom do you have realistic access? With whom do you have credibility? Create a list of possible audiences and consider the implications each audience holds for the successful implementation of your proposal. Your definition of the problem may change depending on your audience. Do these shifts in definition hold any consequences for you or for those you are trying to help?

Background Research: Formulating the Problem

By formulating problems, writers take situations that already exist and point out what aspects call for urgent attention and action. In this sense, problem formulation is always in part an interpretation—a way of establishing the relevance of a problem to readers.

Illegal drugs are a good example of how problems can be defined in a number of ways. Some would say, for example, the problem is that illegal drug trade results in police corruption and powerful underworld drug cartels. Others would argue that drugs are causing social decay and destroying the moral fiber of a generation of American young people. Still others would hold that Americans and drug laws haven't distinguished adequately between recreational drugs like marijuana and addictive drugs like heroin and cocaine. In the following chart, notice how different problem formulation leads to different proposals.

Issue	Illegal drug use		
Problem	Underworld drug trade	Social decay	Need for redefinition
Proposed Solution	Step up war against major drug dealers.	Educate and create jobs programs.	Decriminalize marijuana.
	Cut off drugs at point of distribution.	Eliminate conditions of drug use, such as poverty and hopelessness.	Make legal distinctions that recognize differences among drugs (recreational versus addictive).

Use the chart as a guide to analyze an existing situation by breaking it down into a number of problems and solutions. You will probably not be able to address in one proposal all the aspects of the situation that you identify as problems. In fact, you may find that the proposed solutions suggested by the various problems are contradictory or mutually exclusive.

Assessing Alternatives

Once you have identified a number of possible solutions to the problems you've defined, you can then assess the relative strengths and weaknesses of proposals. One way to do this is to test the feasibility of proposed solutions—their capability and suitability to solve problems. Again this can be done by using a chart:

Problem	What policy on international drug trade should the government follow?	
Proposed Solution	Legalize drug trade under state control.	Step up the war against international drug trade.
Capability	Unknown. Costs and benefits uncertain. Would require considerable administration. What about possible black market?	Could reduce amount of illegal drugs to enter the U.S. However, very costly to have widespread effect. What about domestic trade?
Suitability	Politically unpopular. Voters would interpret as a state endorsement of drug use.	Foreign policy implications must be carefully considered.

Planning

Relative Emphasis on the Problem and the Solution

In proposals, the amount of space devoted to formulating the problem and to explaining the solution may vary considerably, depending on the writer's situation and purposes. Look, for example, at the relative emphasis on the problem and on the solution in Stacy Yi's research proposal "Training Fighters, Making Men" and in Jennifer Gordon's "Workers Without Borders."

"Training Fighters, Making Men"

¶1: Gives background

¶2–5: States objectives of study and research questions (the problem)

¶6–10: Presents research plan and methods (the solution)

¶9: Indicates significance of research

Notice in this case that 50 percent of the proposal (¶1–5) is concerned with formulating the problem in the Background and Objectives sections, while the second half of the proposal (¶6–10) consists of explaining the solution in the Research Plan.

This makes sense, for a research proposal needs to indicate how a researcher plans to answer her research question. On the other hand, Jennifer Gordon devotes only the first two paragraphs (out of 13 total) to formulating the problem and the rest to presenting a solution (in ¶3–13)

Developing a Working Outline

Review the writing and thinking you've done so far. Use the following guidelines to sketch a working outline of your proposal. The guidelines indicate the main issues that writers typically address to design persuasive proposals.

1. **State the problem:** Decide how readily readers will recognize the problem and how much agreement already exists about how to solve it. Your first task is to establish the relevance of the problem to your intended audience. Who does the problem affect? What makes it urgent? What will happen if the problem is not addressed?

2. **Describe the solution:** Because effective proposals present both general goals that appeal to shared values and attitudes and the specific solution to be accomplished, you need to state the goals you have identified and then state clearly how and why your proposed solution will work. Describe the solution and the steps needed to implement it. Decide on the level of detail required to give readers the necessary information to evaluate your proposal.

3. **Explain reasons:** Identify the best reasons in support of your proposal. Consider the available alternatives and to what length you need to address them. Finally, think about what counterarguments are likely to arise and to what length you need to deal with them.

4. **Ending:** Some proposals have short endings that reinforce the main point. Others, such as the advertisements commonly found in magazines and newspapers, end by calling on readers to do something.

Working Draft

Use the working outline you have developed to write a draft of your proposal.

Matching Problems and Solutions

Perhaps the most important feature of a persuasive proposal is the match between the problem as the writer defines it and the solution as the writer describes and explains it. Unless the two fit together in a logical and compelling way, readers are unlikely to have confidence in the proposal.

Proposal writers often link solutions to problems in two ways—in terms of long-term goals and specific objectives. Long-term goals project a vision of what the proposed solution can do over time, whereas specific objectives tell who is going to do what, when they are going to do it, what the projected results will be, and (in some instances) how the results will be measured.

As you design your proposal, consider how you can effectively present your goals and objectives. Your goals will give readers a sense of your values and offer common ground as the basis for readers' support, and your objectives will help convince readers you have a concrete plan of action that can succeed.

Peer Commentary

Once you have written a draft proposal, exchange drafts with a classmate. If you are working in a group, exchange drafts among groups. Write a commentary to the draft, using the following guidelines.

1. How does the proposal establish the need for something to be done—by defining a problem, describing a situation, using an example, providing facts and background information? Is the need for action convincing? Who is likely to recognize and want to address the main issue of the proposal? Who might feel excluded? Is there any way to include more potential supporters?

2. Where does the proposal first appear? Is it clear and easy to find? Put the proposal in your own words. If you cannot readily paraphrase it, explain why. What are the long-term goals? What are the specific objectives of the proposal? Is it clear who is going to do what, when, how much, and (if appropriate) how the results will be evaluated? Do you think the proposal will have the results intended? Why or why not? What other results might occur?

3. What reasons are offered on behalf of the proposal? Do you find these reasons persuasive? Why or why not? Are these the best reasons available? What other reasons might the writer use?

4. Does the solution appear to be feasible? Why or why not? Does the writer need to include more information to make the proposal seem more feasible? What would it take to convince you that this proposal would work?

5. Is the proposal addressed to an appropriate audience? Can the audience do anything to support the actions suggested in the proposal? If not, can you suggest a more appropriate audience? If so, does the way the proposal is written seem suitable for that audience? Point to specific places in the text that need revision. What kinds of changes would make the proposal work better for the audience?

Revising

Now that you have received feedback on your proposal, you can make the revisions you think are necessary—to make sure that the solution you propose follows logically and persuasively from the problem as you have defined it. To help you assess the relationship between your problem formulation and the solution you propose, consider this early draft of the problem and solution sections of the "Proposal for a Campus Coffee House."

Notice two things. First, this proposal devotes approximately equal space to the problem and to the solution. Second, the early draft does not clearly separate the problem statement from the solution statement. In fact, as you can see, the problem is initially defined as the lack of a solution—a logical confusion that will make readers conclude that the reasoning is circular (the reason we need X is because we don't have it), which is not likely to be very persuasive. To see how the writer straightened out the relationship between problems and solutions, compare this early draft to the revised version that appears in Writers' Workshop.

Early Draft

The Problem: Drinking on Campus

The absence of an alcohol-free social life has become a major problem at Warehouse State. Because there are no alternatives, campus social life is dominated by the fraternities, whose parties make alcohol easily available to minors. Off campus, local bars that feature live bands are popular with students, and underage students have little difficulty obtaining and using fake IDs.

The Student Counseling Center currently counsels students with drinking problems and has recently instituted a peer counselor program to educate students about the risks of drinking. Such programs, however, will be limited and largely reactive unless there are alcohol-free alternatives to social life on campus.

The Solution: Campus Coffee House

The Student Management Club proposes to operate a campus coffee house with live entertainment on Friday and Saturday nights in order to provide an alcohol-free social environment on campus for 200 students (capacity of auxiliary dining room in Morgan Commons when set up cabaret-style).

Such a campus coffee house would have a number of benefits. It would help stop the high levels of drinking on campus by both legal and underage students (Martinez & Johnson, 2010), as well as the "binge drinking" that has increased the number of students admitted to the student infirmary for excessive drinking by almost 50% in the last four years. It would serve as a public endorsement of alcohol-free social life, enhance student culture by providing low-cost alcohol-free entertainment on campus, and support current ongoing alcohol abuse treatment and prevention programs.

WRITERS' WORKSHOP

A group of three students wrote the following "Proposal for a Campus Coffee House" in response to an assignment in a business writing class that called on students to produce a collaboratively written proposal to deal with a campus problem. Their commentary on the decisions they made formulating problems and solutions and designing the format appears after the proposal.

PROPOSAL

Proposal for a Campus Coffee House

To meet the problem of excessive drinking on campus, we propose that a coffee house, open on Friday and Saturday nights with live entertainment, be established in the auxiliary dining room in Morgan Commons and operated by the Student Management Club to provide an alcohol-free alternative to undergraduate social life.

The Problem: Drinking on Campus

A recent study by the Student Health Center indicates high levels of drinking by undergraduates on campus (Martinez & Johnson, 2010). Both legal and underage students drink frequently (Fig. 1). They also increasingly engage in unhealthy "binge

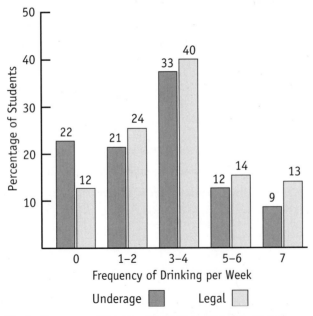

Fig. 1   Frequency of Drinking Per Week, Underage and Legal

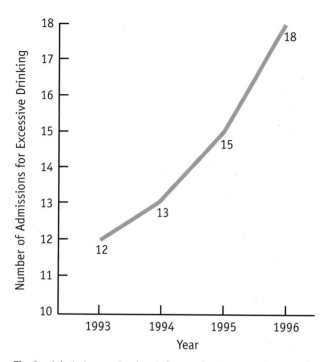

Fig. 2   Admissions to Student Infirmary for Excessive Drinking

drinking" to the point of unconsciousness. The number of students admitted to the student infirmary for excessive drinking has increased almost 50% in the past four years (Fig. 2). These patterns of drinking conform to those observed in a recent national study (Dollenmayer, 2008). Like many other colleges and universities, Warehouse State is faced with a serious student drinking problem (Weiss, 2007).

Currently there are few alternatives for students seeking an alcohol-free social life. Campus social life is dominated by the fraternities, whose parties make alcohol easily available to minors. Off campus, local bars that feature live bands are popular with students, and underage students have little difficulty obtaining and using fake IDs.

The Solution: Campus Coffee House

The Student Management Club proposes to operate a campus coffee house with live entertainment on Friday and Saturday nights in order to provide an alcohol-free social environment on campus for 200 students (capacity of auxiliary dining room in Morgan Commons when set up cabaret-style).

Such a campus coffee house would have a number of benefits. It would serve as a public endorsement of alcohol-free social life, enhance student culture by providing low-cost alcohol-free entertainment on campus, and support current ongoing alcohol abuse treatment and prevention programs. The Student Counseling Center currently counsels students with drinking problems and has recently instituted a promising peer counselor program to educate students about the risks of drinking. Such programs, however, will be limited and largely reactive unless there are alcohol-free alternatives to social life on campus.

Organizational Capability

The Student Management Club has the experience and expertise needed to run the proposed coffee house. Since 1991, it has successfully run a coffee counter in Adams Union, open five days a week from 8 to 3:30. Management majors are interested in expanding their work into the areas of arts programming and publicity.

Budget

The proposed campus coffee house will require initial funding of $1,250 to begin operations. See cost breakdown in Table 1, Initial Expenditure. We believe, however, that such expenditures are one-time only and that the campus coffee house should become self-supporting. See projected budget in Table 2.

TABLE 1 INITIAL EXPENDITURES

Supplies (mugs, plates, spoons, forks, paper products, etc.)	$ 750
Coffee, tea, milk, pastries	250
Publicity	250
Total	$1,250

TABLE 2 PROJECTED BUDGET

Per evening of operation			
Income		Expenses	
(estimated)	$400	Entertainment (band or singer)	$100.00
		Staff (2 persons, 5 hrs each @$5.35)	53.50
		Supplies	75.00
		Food	100.00
		Publicity	25.00
		Total	$353.50

References

Dollenmayer, L. C. (2008). Patterns of alcohol use among American college students. *Journal of the American Medical Association*, 275(16), 223–229.

Martinez, M., & Johnson, R. (2010). Alcohol use and campus social life. Livingston, NM: Student Health Center, Warehouse State University.

Weiss, I. (2007, December 2). Drinking deaths prompt concern on campus. *New York Times*, pp. 1, 7.

Writers' Commentary

Following are excerpts from a group meeting, which the participants taped. Here are some passages from the transcript where the three group members, Kathy, Andrea, and Bruce, talk about why they got involved in the coffee house project and how they went about writing the proposal.

KATHY: One of the things that has been interesting about working in this group is that the members come to it from different perspectives. Andrea and I see the coffee house more as a crusade against drinking, which we've watched do a lot of damage to some people we know. So that's a pretty big motivation to get involved, to provide alternatives. Bruce, I think, is into it more out of his interest in folk music and running coffee houses.

BRUCE: Yeah, I mean I do support the idea of having alcohol-free alternative places for students to go. That makes sense to me. But, I agree, definitely. My main thing is arts programming and administration, that whole business. If I can, that's what I want to do when I graduate.

Some of that came up when we were trying to think of reasons for the coffee house, and I was into how it would help promote the arts on campus. We ended up not using that stuff.

ANDREA: Right, but I think Kathy and I became more aware of how we had to make sure the proposal didn't sound moralistic. Remember at first we defined the problem as "drinking on campus" and only later changed it to "excessive drinking." We wanted the proposal to sound positive—that a coffee house would enhance student life.

BRUCE: Exactly. We didn't want it to sound like punishment. And you're right, the proposal doesn't really come out against drinking as the problem but against excessive drinking, binge drinking. I mean alcohol is legal for people over 21. Besides it's unrealistic to think a campus coffee house or anything else for that matter is going to end drinking on campus.

ANDREA: Another thing I felt we tried to do in the proposal was link the coffee house concept to other campus anti-drinking programs. I thought we did a pretty good job of listing benefits in the solution section.

▷ WORKSHOP QUESTIONS

1. Consider how well the proposed solution matches the problem defined in this proposal. Is the problem well defined and substantiated by adequate evidence? Does the proposed solution seem to offer a feasible approach to excessive drinking on campus? Are there other important factors the writers have not taken into account?

2. The writers, as you may have noticed, are reasonably concerned that their proposal not sound moralistic, even though Kathy and Andrea were initially interested in the idea because of their strong feelings about drinking. Do you think they have been successful in presenting their proposal as a "positive" step to "enhance student life"? If so, what is it about the proposal that creates this impression? If not, why?

3. Imagine that you are on a campus committee that reviews proposals and decides which ones to support. There are more worthy proposals than there are funds available, so you will have to make some hard decisions. The proposal for a campus coffee house is one of the finalists, and the committee plans to meet each group of proposers before making its decision. Draw up a list of questions you would ask Kathy, Andrea, and Bruce to help you make a decision.

REFLECTING ON YOUR WRITING

If you did a group proposal, when you have finished, hold a meeting to look back and evaluate the experience of working together.

1. Explore the reasons each member was drawn to the problem the proposal addresses. To what extent do these reasons overlap? How are they distinct from each other? How did they combine in the group? What influence did this have on writing the proposal?

2. Describe how the group went about writing the proposal. What parts went smoothly? What problems, if any, did the group have? How did individual members and the group deal with problems in the writing?

If you wrote an individual proposal, ask similar questions: What called you to the problem you address? What made it important or urgent? How did you go about writing the proposal? What was easy about it? What problems, if any, did you have? How did you deal with these problems?

CHAPTER 11

343-347
348-365

Reviews

Reviews take place informally all the time in everyday life. Is the psychology course you're taking any good? Is the latest Jay-Z album worth buying? Where's a good place to get a cheap meal? People turn to reviews when they are called on to evaluate something, to make a critical judgment of its qualities, whether it is a class, a music CD, an employee's performance, or a government program.

A standard place to find reviews is in the arts section of newspapers and magazines—reviews of books, music, film, video games, art, architecture, television, and dance. Newspapers in print and online versions, along with other Web sites, also feature reviews of consumer products and restaurants and travel sections that consider tourist attractions and vacation spots, often with tips on what to see and do and where to stay. In turn, readers use reviews in a variety of ways: to get information, to get advice from experts, and to compare their judgments to the reviewer's.

You've probably written book reviews in school. Sometimes students think the point of book reviews is to prove to teachers they've read the book, but it's important to understand the role that reviewing plays in academic work. Like newspapers and magazines, scholarly journals feature reviews that assess the contribution of new books to a field of study. Just as key, though, is the way scholars and researchers are persistently reviewing the literature in their field to frame their own intellectual projects and explain the significance of their work. One of the standard features of an academic article is a literature review that locates the work being presented in relation to previous work, whether by applying an established concept to a new case, tackling a neglected topic, or offering a counterinterpretation.

At the center of all these reviews are the criteria used to make evaluations. The criteria reviewers use may be explicit or implicit. *Consumer Reports*, for example, uses explicit criteria based on quantitative data. Often, however, the criteria are far less explicit. In arts reviews, for example, readers must frequently figure out the criteria from the critic's discussion and analysis of the film, rock show, or photography exhibit.

Whether readers find a review persuasive will depend to a large extent on whether they believe the criteria used are justifiable. At times, readers may accept the criteria

People are going to disagree

used and yet not agree with how the criteria are applied. In other cases of evaluation, people disagree not because they apply shared criteria in different ways but because their criteria of evaluation differ altogether. In a heterogeneous society such as our own, it is virtually inevitable that people's evaluations—whether in politics, academic work, the arts, or other areas—and the criteria and assumptions that underlie them will differ in interesting, sometimes trying, and always significant ways.

WRITING FROM EXPERIENCE

How do you and the people you know find out about movies, CDs, television shows, live music, books and magazines, restaurants, plays, dance performances, concerts, and Web sites? Do you read reviews that appear in newspapers, magazines, or online? How often do you hear and make use of informal, word-of-mouth reviews from family, friends, or coworkers? Think of a discussion you had in which people's evaluations differed. What was being reviewed? What did people say? Why did their evaluations differ? Did they seem to be using the same criteria but applying them differently, or were they using different criteria? How did the discussion end? Did anyone modify his or her views?

READINGS

Film Reviews

The Girl with the Dragon Tattoo

David Denby (New Yorker) and Peter Travers (Rolling Stone)

....

These reviews appeared in December 2011, when the long-anticipated American version of Stieg Larsson's The Girl with the Dragon Tattoo *opened in movie theaters, starring Rooney Mara in the role of the cyberpunk heroine/hacker Lisbeth Salander. David Denby has been a film critic at* The New Yorker *since 1998 and Peter Travers at* Rolling Stone *since 1989. Pairing their reviews enables us to examine how evaluation can differ among the leading film critics. The Metacritic score appears with each review. See below for more on rating systems.*

© Columbia Pictures/Photofest

David Denby's Review
Metacritic score: 90

You can't take your eyes off Rooney Mara as the notorious Lisbeth Salander, in the American movie version of Stieg Larsson's "The Girl with the Dragon Tattoo" (opening December 21st). Slender, sheathed in black leather, with short ebony hair standing up in a tuft, her fingers poking out of black woollen gloves as they skitter across a laptop keyboard, Mara (who played Mark Zuckerberg's girlfriend at the beginning of "The Social Network") cuts through scene after scene like a swift, dark blade. Salander is a twenty-four-year-old hacker with many piercings, of herself and of others. She's both antisocial and intensely sexual—vulnerable and often abused but overequipped to take revenge. She lives in an aura of violence. Salander obviously accounts for a big part of the success of Larsson's crime novels—both men and women are turned on by her—and Mara makes every scene that she appears in jump. She strips off and climbs right onto Daniel Craig, as Mikael Blomkvist, the investigative journalist who takes Salander on as a partner, and whom she makes her lover. Craig looks a little surprised. In this movie, he is modest, quiet, even rather recessive. It's Mara's shot at stardom, and he lets her have it.

Much of the movie is set on a private island controlled by the Vanger clan, a wealthy Swedish industrial family peopled with criminals, perverts, solitaries, exiles, dead Nazis, and a grieving old man, Henrik Vanger (Christopher Plummer), who has never got over the disappearance of his grandniece, forty years earlier. In one last attempt to find her, he hires Blomkvist, who has been temporarily discredited in a libel suit, and sets him up as an investigator on the island, a place that no American one-per-cent family would ever dream of owning. It's way up north, windy, snowy, and treacherously beautiful; once you cross the bridge to this enclave, you enter an icy hell. Blomkvist and Salander, warming each other, conduct their investigation from the island, hacking into whatever files they need; they leave only when they have to, with Mara, head down in the wind, tearing around Sweden on a motorcycle like—well, like a bat out of hell. The movie zips ahead, in short, spiky scenes punctuated by skillfully edited montages of digitized photographs and newspaper articles. David Fincher, who directed the picture (working with Steven Zaillian's screenplay), moves at a much faster pace than he did in "Zodiac," his 2007 movie about a murder investigation. In "Zodiac," every time a piece of evidence trembles into view, it quickly recedes again. That movie is an expression of philosophical despair: the truth can never be known. "Dragon Tattoo" says the opposite: it celebrates deduction, high-end detective work—what Edgar Allan Poe called "ratiocination." Everything can be known if you look long and hard enough, especially if you have no scruples about hacking into people's bank accounts, e-mails, and business records. Salander is a criminal, but she's our criminal.

At heart, of course, the material is pulpy and sensational. The Vanger men committed atrocious crimes against women in the past, and Salander, who is a ward of the state, is twice brutalized by a smarmy social worker who controls her money. There are certainly lurid moments, but I wouldn't say that Fincher exploits the material. When Salander is raped, the scene registers as a horror; it's prolonged and discomforting. And her revenge, however justified, and however much it may amuse the audience, is another horror. This is a bleak but mesmerizing piece of filmmaking; it offers a glancing, chilled view of a world in which brief moments of loyalty flicker between repeated acts of betrayal.

Peter Travers' Review
Metacritic score: 63

Something's missing. I felt it last month when I initially saw the American film version of *The Girl With the Dragon Tattoo*, the first in the bestselling Millennium trilogy by the late Swedish author Stieg Larsson. On second viewing, I still feel a letdown. How could I not? David Fincher, the director of a handful of films I revere, from *Fight Club, Seven, Panic Room* and *Zodiac* to last year's masterful *The Social Network*, is at the helm. From him, expectations are high for a transgressive take on the book's search for a serial killer of women. From him, we get—what?—a faithful adaptation that brings the dazzle but shortchanges on the daring.

Fincher chose well in Rooney Mara (she's unforgettable dumping Jesse Eisenberg's Mark Zuckerberg in the opening scene of *The Social Network*). Mara is astonishing as Lisbeth Salander, the pierced, bisexual, tattooed twentysomething hacker who teams up with journalist Mikael Blomkvist (a curiously wan Daniel Craig) to unearth secrets in the family of Henrik Vanger (Christopher Plummer), an industrialist who thinks his grandniece, Harriet, was murdered 40 years ago.

Fincher and cinematographer Jeff Cronenweth capture the chill of Vanger's private island and the despicable family tree of Nazis, killers and incestuous pervs. Unlike the juicy pulp of Niels Arden Oplev's 2009 Swedish adaptation, with a fierce Noomi Rapace as Lisbeth, Fincher's *Girl* is elegantly austere, as though the material merited an artful gaze instead of crass energy.

Girl moves in fits and starts as if screenwriter Steve Zaillian felt no minor character unworthy of a share in the film's two hours and 40 minutes. Though the actors give their all, notably Stellan Skarsgård as the brother of the missing Harriet and Joely Richardson as an estranged relative, the film hangs back when you want it to come out swinging. Only Mara lets it bleed. Her defensive, bruised-animal performance inexorably draws you in. Lisbeth is a hunter of male predators, and her takedown of her rapist guardian

(Yorick van Wageningen) is justifiably graphic. But what pulls her toward Mikael? Craig's distant, self-amused performance offers no clues. Editors Kirk Baxter and Angus Wall excel at crosscutting between Lisbeth and Mikael, separately investigating the case with orgasmic relish. But when the two hook up in Mikael's cabin and Lisbeth strips to jump his bones, the expected sparks—sexual and soulful—never materialize. The thrumming score by Trent Reznor and Atticus Ross, along with a slashing opening-credit scene in which Reznor and Karen O rework Led Zeppelin's "Immigrant Song," promise a fire the film fails to stoke. Even the altered ending gives no offense. Fincher's *Girl* is gloriously rendered but too impersonal to leave a mark.

Analysis: Agreements and Disagreements

Although their overall evaluations of *The Girl with the Dragon Tattoo* differ significantly—27 points according to Metacritic's scoring—David Denby and Peter Travers agree that Rooney Mara is "astonishing" (Travers) as Lisbeth Salander, making "every scene that she appears in jump" (Denby). For Travers, however, "something's missing," as he says in a wonderfully direct opening sentence. You can see there are things Travers admires about the film, but he keeps coming back to the sentiment in the opening line, leading to the final judgment: "Fincher's Girl is gloriously rendered but too impersonal to leave a mark." In contrast, Denby has praise for the film as a whole—the acting, cinematography, editing, and direction. Notice how he sets up his final judgment by opening the last paragraph with a concession—"At heart, of course, the material is pulpy and sensational"—only to turn these characteristics of the film into part of its success as a "bleak but mesmerizing piece of filmmaking."

▷ FOR CRITICAL INQUIRY

1. Consider the organization of David Denby's review. When did you become aware that it is a positive review? What cues did you pick up? Examine how you became aware of the reasons for Denby's positive evaluation of the film. Where do they appear in the review? Are the reasons stated explicitly or implied?

2. What exactly does Peter Travers think is missing from the American version of *The Girl with the Dragon Tattoo*? Identify words and phrases in his review that provide supporting evidence for his judgment of the film. What assumptions does Travers seem to be making about what films need to be successful? Are these stated explicitly or implied?

3. Watch *The Girl with the Dragon Tattoo*, even if you have seen it before. As you watch, keep Denby and Travers in the back of your mind, paying attention to what they would like or not like in the film. After viewing the film, locate your own evaluation of the film in relation to Denby and Travers. Do you find yourself aligned with one of the film critics? How would you distinguish your views from one or the other or both? Do they seem to use the same criteria you use to evaluate the film? How would you explain the points on which you agree or disagree with the two film critics?

4. Metacritic is in the business of converting reviews into quantitative scores. Do they seem accurate? How did they influence your reading of the two reviews?

List

2012 List of Banished Words
Lake Superior State University

....

The Lake Superior State University annual list of banished words uses the conventions of year-end best or most notable lists in a way that is light-hearted and serious at the same time. Consider how the authors of the list have pulled this off: What is the appeal of the list to readers? What interesting questions about language does it raise? Why is it funny? Consider also, in a broader sense, the function that annual lists of best films or jazz albums or compact cars play in the culture. Work in a group with three or four other students. Gather a number of best-of-the-year lists from any field. What features do they have in common? How do they vary? How do people use the lists—in the same or different ways? Who puts the lists together? What gives the lists authority and credibility?

Lake Superior State University released its 37th annual List of Words Banished from the Queen's English for Misuse, Overuse and General Uselessness, an amazing list that is bound to generate some blowback.

"Worn-out words and phrases are the new normal this year, but with some shared sacrifice, we can clean up the language and win the future," said an LSSU representative.

LSSU wordsmiths emerged from their man cave long enough to release the new list, something the school has done since 1976.

"With the addition of this year's nominations, the list of words and phrases banished over the years has become ginormous."

Former LSSU Public Relations Director Bill Rabe and friends created "word banishment" in 1975 at a New Year's Eve party and released the first list on New Year's Day. Since then, LSSU has received tens of thousands of nominations for the list, which includes words and phrases from marketing, media, education, politics, technology and more.

Thank you in advance for reading!

Amazing

Received the most nominations. LSSU was surprised at the number of nominations this year for "amazing" and surprised to find that it hadn't been included on the list in the past. Many nominators mentioned over-use on television when they sent their entries, mentioning "reality" TV, Martha Stewart and Anderson Cooper. It seemed to bother people everywhere, as nominations were sent from around the US and Canada

---

Lake Superior State University "2012 List of Banished Words." (http://www.lssu.edu/banished/current.php). Reprinted with permission.

and some from overseas, including Israel, England and Scotland. A Facebook page—"Overuse of the Word Amazing"—threatened to change its title to "Occupy LSSU" if 'amazing' escaped banishment this year . . .

"It's amazing that you haven't added that word to your list over the years. Totally, absolutely, really amazing. Not quite astounding, but still amazing." Charles Attardi, Astoria, NY

"Although I am extremely happy to no longer hear the word 'awesome' used incorrectly and way too often, it appears to me it is quickly being replaced with 'amazing.' Pay attention and you will no doubt be amazingly surprised to find that I am right." Gregory Scott, Palm Springs, Calif.

"People use 'amazing' for anything that is nice or heartwarming. In other words, for things that are not amazing." Gitel Hesselberg, Haifa, Israel

"Every talk show uses this word at least two times every five minutes. Hair is not 'amazing.' Shoes are not 'amazing.' There are any number of adjectives that are far more descriptive. I saw Martha Stewart use the word 'amazing' six times in the first five minutes of her television show. Help!" Martha Waszak, Lansing, Mich.

"Banish it for blatant overuse and incorrect use . . . to stop my head from exploding." Paul Crutchfield, Norwich, Norfolk, UK

"The word which once aptly described the process of birth is now used to describe such trivial things as toast, or the color of a shirt." JP, Comox, British Columbia, Canada

"Anderson Cooper used it three times recently in the opening 45 seconds of his program. My teeth grate, my hackles rise and even my dog is getting annoyed at this senseless overuse. I don't even like 'Amazing Grace' anymore." Sarah Howley, Kalamazoo, Michigan

"The word has been overused to describe things only slightly better than mundane. I blame Martha Stewart because to her, EVERYTHING is amazing! It has lost its 'wow factor' and has reached 'epic' proportions of use. It's gone 'viral,' I say! 'I'm just sayin'!'" Alyce-Mae Alexander, Maitland, Florida

Baby Bump

Although nominated by many over the years, this phrase came in as a close second to "amazing" this year.

"This is a phrase we need to finally give birth to, then send on its way." Mary Sturgeon, Vancouver, British Columbia, Canada

"I'm tired of a pregnancy being reduced to a celebrity accessory. Or worse, when less-than-six-pack abs are suspected of being one." Afton, Portland, Oregon

"I am so sick of that phrase! It makes pregnancy sound like some fun and in-style thing to do, not a serious choice made by (at the very least) the woman carrying the child." Susan, Takoma Park, Maryland

"Why can't we just use the old tried-and-true 'pregnant?' I never heard anyone complain about that description." Eric, Poca, West Virginia.

Shared Sacrifice

"Usually used by a politician who wants other people to share in the sacrifice so he/she doesn't have to." Scott Urbanowski, Kentwood, Michigan

Occupy

"'Occupy Wall Street' grew to become Occupy 'insert name of your city here' all over the country. It should be banished because of the media overuse and now people use it all the time, i.e. 'I guess we will occupy your office and have the meeting there.' 'We are headed to Grandma's house—Occupy Thanksgiving is under way.'" Bill Drewes, Rochester Hills, Michigan

"It has been overused and abused even to promote Black Friday shopping." Grant Barnett, Palmdale, California

"Why couldn't they have used a more palatable kind, like pecan or peach?" Bob Forrest, Tempe, Arizona

Blowback

Sometimes exchanged with "pushback" to mean resistance.

"'Blowback' is used by corporate (types) to mean 'reaction,' when the word 'reaction' would have been more than sufficient. Example: 'If we send out the press release, how should we handle the blowback from the community?'" John, Los Angeles, California

Man Cave

"Overused by television home design and home buying shows, has trickled down to sit-coms, commercials, and now has to be endured during interactions with real estate people, neighbors and co-workers." Jim, Flagstaff, Arizona

"It is not just over-used, it is offensive to we males who do not wish to hunker (another awful word, often misused) down in a room filled with stuffed animal heads, an unnecessarily large flat-screen TV and Hooters memorabilia. Not every man wants a recliner the size of a 1941 Packard that has a cooler in each arm and a holster for the remote. So please, assign 'man cave' to the lexicographic scrap heap where it so rightly belongs." David Hollis, Hubbardsville, New York

The New Normal

"The phrase is often used to justify bad trends in society and to convince people that they are powerless to slow or to reverse those trends. This serves to reduce participation in the political process and to foster cynicism about the ability of government to improve people's lives. Sometimes the phrase is applied to the erosion of civil liberties. More often, it is used to describe the sorry state of the U.S. economy. Often hosts on TV news channels use the phrase shortly before introducing some self-help guru who gives glib advice to the unemployed and other people having financial difficulties." Robert Brown, Raleigh, North Carolina

Pet Parent

"Can a human being truly be a parent to a different species? Do pet 'owners' not love their pets as much as pet 'parents' do? Are we equating pet ownership with slave holding? This cloyingly correct term is capable of raising my blood sugar." Lynn Ouellette, Buffalo, New York

Win the Future

A political phrase worn wherever you look—to the left (President Obama) or the right (Newt Gingrich).

"On its very face, it's an empty, meaningless phrase. It basically says that anyone who opposes anything meant to 'win the future' must want to 'lose the future,' which is highly unlikely. But, hey, you may already be a winner." Jim Eisenmann, Madison, Wisconsin

Trickeration

"Why? Why? Why? This one seems to be the flavor du jour for football analysts. What's wrong with 'trick' or 'trickery?' No doubt, next year's model will be 'trickerationism.'" Gene Bering, Seminole, Texas

"A made-up word used by football analysts to describe a trick play. Sounds unintelligent. Perhaps they've had a few too many concussions in the football world to notice." Carrie Hansen, Grayling, Michigan

Ginormous

"No need to make a gigantic (idiot) out of yourself trying to find an enormous word for 'big.'" Coulombe, Sanford, Florida

"This combination of gigantic and enormous makes the hair stand up on the back of my neck every time I hear it. Each utterance reminds me of the high school drop-out that first used this offensive word in my presence." Gina Bua, Vancouver, Washington

"This word is just a made-up combination of two words. Either word is sufficient, but the combination just sounds ridiculous." Jason, Andover, Maine

Thank You in Advance

"Usually followed by 'for your cooperation,' this is a condescending and challenging way to say, 'Since I already thanked you, you have to do this.'" Mike Cloran, Cincinnati, Ohio

Diamond Dancers: The Sparkly World of Van Halen (*New Yorker*)

Sasha Frere-Jones

....

Sasha Frere-Jones is the pop music critic at the New Yorker, *where this review appeared in the March 19, 2012, issue.*

POP MUSIC

DIAMOND DANCERS

The sparkly world of Van Halen.

BY SASHA FRERE-JONES

David Lee Roth sings the band's hits, but Eddie Van Halen's guitar makes them art.

The careers of older pop acts often match those of actors. There are the Robert De Niros, charismatic innovators who change the common technique and then settle into an unchallenging winter phase. (Think the Rolling Stones.) There are the Tommy Lee Joneses, who gain range and intensity with age. (Leonard Cohen comes to mind.) And there are the Matthew Brodericks, who thrive on their youthful bounce and then, abruptly, look their age. Van Halen, which has returned with its original vocalist, David Lee Roth, for an extended tour and its first album with him since 1984, is trying valiantly not to be among the latter.

The band's name, and nerve center, comes from the guitarist Eddie Van Halen and his brother Alex, the drummer, who started playing together in Pasadena, in the mid-seventies. Joined by Roth and the bassist Michael Anthony, Van Halen began performing multiple shows per night around Southern California. Despite its image as a prototypical hard-rock band, and the effect it has had on thousands of grimacing musicians, the band is an anomaly in an aggressive cohort. The two engines of its output are Roth's exceedingly direct approach to hedonistic lyrics and Eddie Van Halen's unique guitar tone, which he calls "the brown sound." When a song is called "Dance the Night Away," it is about dancing the night away. When a song is called "Beautiful Girls," it's about beautiful girls. Van Halen's guitar achieves a similar kind of lightness, albeit with all the complexity and shading that Roth's lyrics oppose.

In keeping with a California tradition of tinkering in the garage, Van Halen extensively modified his guitars, many of them Fender Stratocasters. He dipped his pickups in surfboard wax to reduce feedback and boiled his strings to stretch them. To facilitate his finger-tapping technique, he holds his pick between his thumb and his middle finger, freeing his index finger to bang on the frets. His sound isn't much like the blunt, crunchy presence heard in a lot of hard rock and metal, and it's not like that heard in many blues-based bands, where a guitarist often adds color by turning a tube amplifier way up, to create natural distortion. Van Halen's manipulations give him an unexpectedly gentle version of loud, more gas than flame, more shimmer than glare.

The band's hit "Dance the Night Away," from 1979, embodies its contradictory impulses. The song begins with a syncopated cowbell, less macho blast than block-party invitation, and moves easily into Van Halen's springy, fractured chords, which sound half arpeggiated and half strummed, as if he couldn't play it straight when it was possible to illuminate the notes from all sides. His playing is exactly as sparkly as Roth's vests and jumpsuits. In the chorus, the band deploys its secret weapon: harmony vocals as sweet as any bubblegum pop from the sixties, heavily indebted to Anthony, who usually sang the highest of three parts. "Dance the Night Away" is exuberant pop that has been classified as hard rock only by dint of the guitar's prominence. Darkness, doubt, and mystery are useless here. (In the documentary film "The Van Halen Story," the group's longtime bodyguard Eddie Anderson said that one of Roth's job requirements for him was that he be able to roller-skate.)

In 1984, the band began to splinter under the weight of Roth's ego, Eddie Van Halen's drinking, and the challenge

Victor Melamed

of being one of the biggest and most cheerful rock bands in the world. That year, the group logged its only No. 1 hit, "Jump," an atypical track driven by keyboards and an elemental video that played on MTV constantly. But Roth left the band, and the shaggy, nondescript singer Sammy Hagar joined up for four surprisingly successful albums. Roth returned to the fold for a brief tour in 2007, and now the fans have what they want (except for Anthony, who was replaced in 2006 by Eddie's son, Wolfgang).

How much of the original bounce has Van Halen retained? For better or worse, the band hasn't left the past behind. Five of the tracks on the new album, "A Different Kind of Truth," are versions of songs that were first recorded in 1976. The guitars have a generic feel, satisfying and thick, but without Van Halen's elusive, rippling hues. The band's fearless embrace of entertainment is still a tonic, however. The lusty talk is in place, the harmony vocals settle over the proceedings like a protective membrane, and there are no attempts to pull off things that Van Halen can't pull off. "Tattoo" is about tattoos. "She's the Woman" is about a woman.

At Madison Square Garden, two weeks ago, the band confronted its catalogue and a live audience. The latter were a generous lot, few below the age of forty and many accompanied by at least one faithful fellow-Halenite. (Roth dedicated the set to a fan named Nick, who was attending his four-hundredth Van Halen show.)

At certain points, amid the sensate joy of hearing the brown sound fill a large room, I thought the band's showbiz mandate might sink the performance. The Van Halens play roughly as well as they need to, but Diamond Dave had set the bar too high the first time. On the band's 1984 world tour, Roth would open the show by tossing a bottle of Jack Daniel's offstage and doing a flying kick-split, legs at three and nine, off the drum riser. In 2012, there is a miniature parquet dance floor placed downstage center and dusted with talcum. Wearing what looked like a cross between toe shoes and white canvas sneakers, Roth was able to slide and shuffle around on this surface, with very few kicks or jumps.

Roth hasn't gone sober, as Van Halen has, but he's managed to retain his remarkably fit body. At the Garden, he wore the outfits of a circus ringmaster: skintight tuxedo pants, an aquamarine metallic hoodie, and various jackets, none of them matte. His moves now have a weird echo of Bob Fosse routines. He slides and then stops suddenly, and then scissors his feet as if to start some variant of salsa dancing. His movements took him farther backward, to vaudeville, as if he had become the tummler he once only referenced.

It was the Van Halens who kept the show going, though they would have been lost without Roth doing his best Roth impersonation. Eddie Van Halen opted for a look more casual than that of most of the audience members: a striped T-shirt, jeans, and hiking boots. When Roth decided to shout rather than sing, or forgot the words (as he did during a forgettable new number called "Chinatown"), Eddie and Wolfgang were there with backup that functioned, for much of the show, as lead vocals. Which isn't to say that this version of Van Halen would make for a bad birthday present. The band sticks with the hits, and brings nothing distracting to the celebration. It's just that nobody in the room is levitating. (You do get to watch footage of Roth on a farm with his sheepdogs.)

The only thing close to transcendence was Eddie Van Halen's moment alone onstage. Sitting on the drum riser, with his guitar on one leg, Van Halen played "Eruption," from the band's début album, a solo guitar piece that probably can't be matched for pure peacock swagger. Before "Eruption," Van Halen's technique of fretting with one hand and tapping the fretboard with the other, which creates an almost mechanical blur of notes, was unknown to most pop listeners. The song seemed outlandish in 1978; now it sounds like rock guitar-playing as it's always been, carefully shaped and slightly fragile. Van Halen wove in "Cathedral," from the 1982 album "Diver Down," another solo guitar piece that is mostly executed with twists of the volume knob, creating soft swells of sound, a cloudy approach that has little of "Eruption" 's hyperactive chatter. When he was done, the evening of jokes and self-deprecating patter had receded, and something different hung in the air. It wasn't necessarily rock. It was Eddie. ♦

Analysis: Capturing a Career and a Live Performance

Sasha Frere-Jones's review of Van Halen was occasioned by the reunion of band members Eddie and Alex Van Halen and the group's original vocalist David Lee Roth, the release of a new CD *A Different Kind of Truth,* and a concert appearance at Madison Square Garden. This convergence of events established a rhetorical situation that called for coming to terms with the band's career, which started in 1972 and took off to stardom with its first hits in 1978. Most of all, the situation seemed to highlight the challenge facing aging pop stars: "How much of the original bounce has Van Halen retained?" The first part of the review puts the group's career in perspective, and the second section provides a close look at the band in live performance—and a measured evaluation of their lasting power.

⟫ FOR CRITICAL INQUIRY

1. Consider the comparison between older rock stars and older actors that Sasha Frere-Jones sets up in the opening paragraph. How does this establish the terms of the review's significance? What does it put at stake for readers?

2. Frere-Jones gives a quick overview of the band's history. What function does this perform in the review?

3. Reread the second section of the review that focuses on the band's live performance. What does Frere-Jones notice about the band playing live? How is this different or similar to what he writes about the group's recorded music?

4. Consider the effect of the final paragraph—from its opening line, "The only thing close to transcendence was Eddie Van Halen's moment alone onstage," to the closing line, "It was Eddie." What takes place in between that moves readers from the beginning to the end of the paragraph? What lasting impression do you think Frere-Jones wants to have on readers?

Notice Review

The Roots. *Undun.* *** 1/2 Stars

Michael Walsh

Notice reviews, like this one from the Boston Phoenix, *are brief assessments of new music releases, films, video games, art exhibits, and so on. Notice reviews often use rating systems that award stars (or some other symbol).*

The year was 1999, and the Roots were entering a cool-kids club thanks to the release of *Things Fall Apart*. You can probably rattle off the names of their fellow travelers: Black Star, D'Angelo, Common, et al. Perhaps foremost though, was producer J Dilla. Questlove once praised the late great's drum programming as "musically drunk and sober at the same time." And 12 years later, we have the Roots 13th studio album, their most fully realized effort since *Things* and the first to pay proper respect to Jay, who died in 2006. There's a concept here: a gangbanger's life story told in reverse. But the "concept" is almost irrelevant. Despite the album's discordant tendencies, MC Black Thought comes as brutish as ever, and their now-standard cast of collaborators (P.O.R.N. and Dice Raw) sound more at ease over these lanky beats than they did on more combustible previous efforts. It's uncertain if *Undun* will ever be hailed as a "classic," given the malleability of

---

Michael Walsh. "The Roots. Undun." *Boston Phoenix.* Dec. 14, 2011. Reprinted by permission.

that term amongst hip-hop heads. But at the tail end of a year in which mixtapes have usurped full-lengths—in terms of both quality and press coverage—its satisfying unity is a rebuke to the disposability of the blogosphere.

Music Review

Run the World: A Global View of Women's Place at the Top of the Pops (*Flaunt*)
Daphne Carr

Daphne Carr is an academic, music writer, and editor of the Best Music Writing series who got started in the riot grrrl zine community in the 1990s. She published Pretty Hate Machine *(2011), on the Nine Inch Nails album of that title. This review appeared in the online and very hip* Flaunt.

If the 1990s were the decade of women in rock, then the 2000s were the decade of women everywhere taking the lead in musical spheres. Exemplified by that transnational rogue M.I.A., the new feminine pop star tended to be from the global south—or at least repping it—and produced music intensely hybrid in genre and pop in orientation.

This isn't a top-down or bottom-up trend: it's more like a global shift in recognition for the powerful "weirdness" of female musicians and songwriters. This shift towards the freakier side of pop can be witnessed within the self-styled exotics of Ukrainian tech-folkie

Photo by Derrick Belcham

Julianna Barwick (USA)

Daphne Carr, "Run the World: A Global View of Women's Place at the Top of the Pops." *Flaunt.com*. http://flaunt.com/columns/118/run-world-global-view-women%E2%80%99s-place-top-pops. Reprinted by permission of Daphne Carr.

Kazety (Czech Republic)

Ruslana, the New Zealand dolly queen Kimbra, and the increasingly abstract tracks of Beyoncé. Even Lady Gaga, in her queer radicalist and blonded melting pot white-girl thing, borrows heavily from the sound trash of Europe rather than its highs.

Remember when women got stuck on the hook? The U.S. millennial shift from hip hop to hip hop/R&B was a good one for women with Mary J. and Lauryn Hill paving the way for the kind of crossover that became de rigueur in the 2000s. The blurred genre lines may have been a contributing factor to the rise of Nicki Minaj, a true MC who ruled the summer with the R&B structured "Super Bass," which even featured a hook by another woman (co-songwriter Ester Dean). The unintended consequence is a resurgence of interest in women rappers, both contemporary and historical (check Peanut Butter Wolf's excellent Ladies First mixtape if you're missing MC Lyte in your life). Meanwhile, French-Chilean Ana Tijoux has quietly become the Spanish language's best female MC with the her nods to early-'90s hip hop, making fresh sounds from vintage Native Tongues styles, showing how misguided are Simon Reynolds' ears (eyes?) when in his recent book Retromania he argues that the presence of the past killed pop progress in the 2000s. Where riot-grrl bible Girls To the Front might have documented gender-balanced punk gigs, now the concept of "girls to the front" also means moving to the forefront of sonic innovation.

One of the things I noticed right away when coaching bands at the Willie Mae Rock Camp for Girls in Brooklyn is that kids don't understand or care about genre rules. Instruments, lyrics, and structures are all free spaces until some jerk comes in to tell them they're doing it "wrong." That's why we use rock as verb and encourage girls to go with whatever weird lineup and weirder song ideas they might have. Turns out the traditional band is a historical anomaly, and a peek onto Pitchfork's listings show weirdoes from Gang Gang Dance, Zola Jesus, and Julianna Barwick pushing past the boredom of rock's rigid four-piece confines and making great pop-sensed tunes outside any construct. Check out Chile's Dadalú or the Czech Republic's Kazety for similarly deconstructed "post-rock" pop that still has the feral punk energy so beloved underground while going to territories thus unnamed.

And as for the bleaker domains of our world—places where women aren't allowed to drive, let alone rock—let's finish this celebration with a listen to ladies behind the unfallen in the "Arab Spring." Iran has had a thriving dance music scene of exile and underground electro, some of which includes female lead vocals of various sexy persuasions. This wouldn't be unusual except that women's public singing has been illegal since the 1970s, and in late August 2011 the Iranian government banned the use of all classical Persian love poetry in song, finding epic poet Nizami Ganjavi's 12th-century references to "finding a place to be alone" too steamy. So goes the politics of pleasure for the group 25 Band, a duo of Tamin and A-Del who sound like every night of my life at Twilo (or perhaps Will.i.am's interior monologue in Farsi), having to uproot and find themselves a new home in the more hedonistic Dubai.

So you can only imagine the situation of Salome, the country's first actively releasing female rapper and graffiti artist. She took her name from reading Oscar Wilde and considers the idea of women being oppressed in Iran to be a Western cliché. Meanwhile, the government has called rap a form of satanism and prohibits most of its official circulation. Instead, the genre lives on the internet. Salome sounds just how you'd expect an amateur artist to sound: out of tune, badly tracked, oddly produced, not very hip. It's bedroom pop, done as best she can by a woman who can't legally sing in public. But these days, women can sing from their bedrooms to the world. And once they break free or get out of the bedrooms, well . . . We all know who runs the (pop) world, don't we?

Analysis: Marking Trends

One role of music reviewers is to notice trends, to pay attention not just to singles and albums but to emerging tendencies, fashions, scenes, and styles. In fact, reviewers are often responsible for naming new trends and getting them wider acknowledgment. Daphne Carr's "Run the World" is a good example of a review that does this, proclaiming the 2000s "the decade of women everywhere taking the lead in musical spheres." Notice that Carr is as much a sponsor, advocate, and participant in this trend—"the global shift in recognition for the powerful 'weirdness' of female musicians and songwriters"—as a reviewer evaluating it from the sidelines. There is nothing inappropriate about this. Reviewers are paid to be partisan, to make judgments that say this new artistic, literary, or musical movement is important. Reviewers by definition are involved in shaping opinion, whether it's in the pages of mass circulation magazines like the *New Yorker* and *Rolling Stone*, where the reviews of *The Girl with the Dragon Tattoo* appeared, or in smaller hip places like *Flaunt*, where Carr's "Run the World" was published.

⟴ FOR CRITICAL INQUIRY ‖‖‖

1. Daphne Carr is arguing that women are not just present in rock, as the riot grrrl movement of the 1990s made clear, but "taking the lead" globally. To make this case, Carr gives examples of female musicians from all over the world who may not be well-known in the United States. Do some research on the musicians listed in Carr's review of women in pop music. You'll find places online you can listen to tracks, and many of the women are on YouTube. Notice the musical styles are various and wide ranging. What, if anything, holds the musicians together? What is the "powerful 'weirdness'" Carr refers to on the part of "female musicians and songwriters"?

2. List other trends, fashions, scenes, and styles in music. Look first for the obvious—for well-recognized genres and subgenres such as doom metal, freak folk, or gangsta rap. What individual musicians and bands would you put in the category? What generalization about the style would you make? Next, see whether you can identify trends that have not been named yet or are just emerging. Which musicians would you include? How would you characterize the style? What significance does it have for the pop music scene in general?

3. Compare Carr's review of women in rock to Sasha Frere-Jones's review of Van Halen. How does Frere-Jones's focus on a single band differ from Carr's more sweeping overview of the women's music scene? How do the questions and evaluations from each reviewer differ or overlap? What does each approach bring to light?

Design Review

Graphic Designers Are Ruining the Web

John Naughton

· ·

John Naughton is professor of the public understanding of technology at the Open University in the United Kingdom. He writes regularly about the Internet for the Guardian, *the* Observer, *and other periodicals.*

What happens when you click on a weblink? Here's one answer: a request goes from your computer to a server identified by the URL of the desired link. The server then locates the webpage in its files and sends it back to your browser, which then displays it on your screen. Simple.

Well, the process was indeed like that once—a very long time ago. In the beginning, webpages were simple pages of text marked up with some tags that would enable a

---

browser to display them correctly. But that meant that the browser, not the designer, controlled how a page would look to the user, and there's nothing that infuriates designers more than having someone (or something) determine the appearance of their work. So they embarked on a long, vigorous and ultimately successful campaign to exert the same kind of detailed control over the appearance of webpages as they did on their print counterparts—right down to the last pixel.

This had several consequences. Webpages began to look more attractive and, in some cases, became more user-friendly. They had pictures, video components, animations and colourful type in attractive fonts, and were easier on the eye than the staid, unimaginative pages of the early web. They began to resemble, in fact, pages in print magazines. And in order to make this possible, webpages ceased to be static text-objects fetched from a file store; instead, the server assembled each page on the fly, collecting its various graphic and other components from their various locations, and dispatching the whole caboodle in a stream to your browser, which then assembled them for your delectation.

All of which was nice and dandy. But there was a downside: webpages began to put on weight. Over the last decade, the size of web pages (measured in kilobytes) has more than septupled. From 2003 to 2011, the average web page grew from 93.7kB to over 679kB.

You can see this for yourself by switching on the "view status" bar in your browser; this will tell you how many discrete items go into making up a page. I've just looked at a few representative samples. The *BBC News* front page had 115 items; the online version of the *Daily Mail* had a whopping 344 and *ITV.com* had 116. *Direct.gov* had 71 while *YouTube* and *Wikipedia*, in contrast, came in much slimmer at 26 and 15 respectively.

Driving Demand for Broadband

Whether you view this as a good thing or not depends on where you sit in the digital ecosystem. Aesthetes (and graphic design agencies) drool over the elegance of pages whose look and feel is determined down to the last pixel. Engineers fume at the appalling waste of bandwidth involved in shipping 679kB of data to communicate perhaps 5kB of information. Photographers love the way their high-resolution images are now viewable on Flickr and Picasa. Futurists (and broadband suppliers) rejoice that this epidemic of obese webpages is driving a demand for faster (and more profitable) broadband contracts and point to the fact that communications bandwidth is increasing at a rate even faster than processing power.

Personally, I'm a minimalist: I value content more highly than aesthetics. The websites and pages that I like tend to be as underdesigned as they are cognitively loaded. Take for example, the home page of Peter Norvig, who is Google's director of research. In design terms it would make any graphic designer reach for the sickbag. And yet it's highly functional, loads in a flash and contains tons of wonderful stuff—such as his memorable demolition of the PowerPoint mentality in which he imagines how Abraham Lincoln's Gettysburg Address would look as a "presentation". Or his hilarious spoof of Einstein's "annual performance review" for 1905, the year in which he published the five papers that changed physics for ever. (Einstein, you may recall, was a humble patent clerk in Berne at the time.)

But in addition to these plums, Norvig's site is full of links to fantastically useful resources—such as the open source code that accompanies his textbooks. And it's as easy to navigate as anything produced by a web-design agency for £100 000 [$175,000] plus an annual service contract.

Sites like his remind one that the web is not just about shopping or LOLcats but is the most wonderful storehouse of information and knowledge that humanity has ever possessed.

Think of it as the Library of Alexandria on steroids. And remember that it's as accessible to someone in Africa on the end of a flaky internet connection as it is to a Virgin subscriber in Notting Hill who gets 50MB per second on a good day.

Analysis: Criteria of Judgment

This review differs from others in this chapter. It doesn't deal with a single work, like the reviews of *The Girl with the Dragon Tattoo,* or promote a trend, like Daphne Carr's global overview of women in pop music. Instead, it focuses more on its own criteria of judgment, applied to the visual design of Web sites. John Naughton's column in the *Guardian (UK)* isn't identified specifically as a review, in the way reviews of the new Play Station Vita or iPhone appear in the tech section of the *Guardian* and many other newspapers. Rather, it uses a key element of the review—the criteria of judgment—to make an argument against "obese webpages" and in favor of a minimalist look that uses less bandwidth per kB of information.

⇨ FOR CRITICAL INQUIRY

1. Consider the shape of John Naughton's argument. First, he explains how webpages are drawing on more and more items. Then, he labels these webpages "obese" and in need of losing weight, so they will use less bandwidth and look more like the slim webpages he favors. Notice how he incorporates in passing the perspectives of graphic designers and photographers, acknowledging people's feelings about webpages depends on where they are located in the digital ecosystem. How does he locate himself in this regard? What assumptions does he make that connect the increase in webpage size to his plea for minimalism?

2. Naughton presents Peter Norvig's homepage as an example of the minimalism he prefers. Visit Norvig's home page www.norvig.com and click on some links. What was your response initially to its "underdesigned" look? What is your evaluation of the Web site after checking it out in more detail?

3. Use Naughton's criteria of judgment about webpages to develop your own. Find a Web site you think is very well designed and one that isn't. Use these choices to examine what is central to your evaluation. Compare your criteria of judgment to those of your classmates, taking into account the assumptions enabling the evaluations. You might work together in small groups or in the class as a whole to create a list of best and worst webpages, to illustrate the evaluations you have worked out with others.

MULTIMODAL COMPOSITION

Rating System: Metacritic

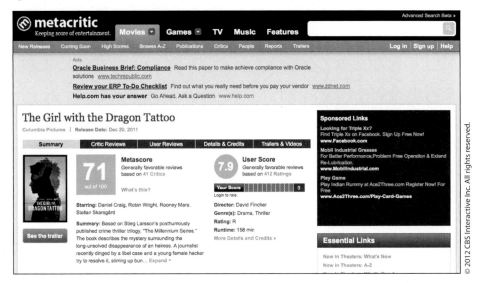

Rating systems of all kinds—from Roger Ebert's thumbs-up or thumbs-down, to *Consumer Reports,* to the BCS weekly college football poll—are a common feature online and in print.

As you can see on its logo, Metacritic's mission is "keeping score of entertainment." Metacritic.com collates reviews of movies, video games, music albums, DVDs, and television shows according to a 100-point scale. Some reviews, such as the notice review of the Roots' *Undun,* from the *Boston Phoenix,* use their own rating system, whether alphabetic grades or stars based on a five-star scale. In other cases, where reviews don't use a rating system, Metacritic converts the text into a number, taking into account the judgment and tone of the review. Metacritic also weights reviews, giving greater influence to reviews that appear in major publications. You can learn more about the controversies surrounding Metacritic's scoring system by visiting the Wikipedia entry.

Check out Metacritic. Consider, for example, how the three and a half stars Michael Walsh gave *Undun* are converted into a score of 88, helping make the Roots' album the second best-reviewed of 2011, at least according to Metacritic.

Field Guide: *The Stray Shopping Carts of Eastern North America: A Guide to Field Identification*

The Stray Shopping Cart Project uses the features of a familiar genre—the field guide of birds, plants, animals, and so on—to classify stray shopping carts into "false strays" and "true strays." What started as a Web site has turned into a book, *The Stray Shopping Carts of Eastern North America: A Guide to Field Identification*—a parody of the genre of field guides that uses and exposes the systems of identification and classification that guides rely upon. Go to www.strayshoppingcart.com and visit the page "Understanding the System" for the project's explanation of its classification scheme and terminology.

Gather a number of field guides to examine in class. Depending on your instructor's directions, you could open this up to other guides—travel, hiking, restaurants, museums, and so on. In any case, consider how they classify and organize information, who their intended readers are, and what purposes they serve. How do the guides integrate text and visuals? Based on this examination, develop a working definition of field and other types of guides as a genre of writing.

↘ CONCEPTS / TERMINOLOGY

SOURCE

Any business that uses shopping carts in a conventional manner.

CLOSED SOURCE: A SOURCE that has gone out of business.

SOURCE AGENTS: Employees or subcontractors of the SOURCE who collect and return stray carts.

CLASS A: FALSE STRAYS

1) A shopping cart that while on the SOURCE lot is diverted from its primary function, damaged, or otherwise rendered useless.

2) A shopping cart that appears to be a stray cart but that is ultimately returned to service in the SOURCE from which it originated.

CLASS B: TRUE STRAYS

1) A cart that will not be returned to the SOURCE from which it originated.

2) CLASS B: TRUE STRAY TYPES may be used as secondary designations for CLASS A: FALSE STRAY specimens.

TYPES

The subdivisions of CLASSES A and B.
(There are currently 11 CLASS A TYPES and 22 CLASS B TYPES included in the System.)

SPECIMEN

A cart that has been photographically documented and assigned a single or multiple TYPE designations.

ICONS

The subdivisions of CLASSES A and B, abbreviated by using the CLASS letter alone with the TYPE number.	A green CLASS B TYPE icon with a brown border represents a secondary CLASS B TYPE designation.	SOURCE UNKNOWN	DESIGNATION RETAINED

When an image contains multiple carts and there is no notation indicating otherwise, the TYPE designations should be assumed to refer to all carts in the image.

GAP SPACES

Vacant lots, ditches, spaces between buildings, behind buildings, under bridges and overpasses, and all manner of vacant GAPS between properties, public or private.

8 / INTRODUCTION

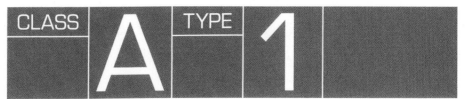

CLOSE FALSE

→ A cart found at the edge of the SOURCE parking lot or within a two-block radius.

→ Often found in ditches, on median strips, and on grassy areas adjacent to the SOURCE parking lot.

→ A/1 carts are often subject to acts of B/12 SIMPLE VANDALISM.

This specimen was found just beyond the edge of its native SOURCE lot.

16 / CLASS A: FALSE STRAYS

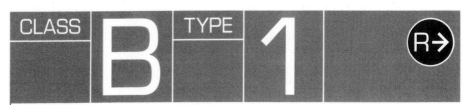

OPEN TRUE

→ A cart situated on a street or sidewalk, or in a park or parking lot, outside of a two-block SOURCE radius.

→ Impossible to differentiate from A/9 REMOTE FALSE.

→ All TRUE STRAY carts theoretically transition through and retain the B/1 designation, thus all CLASS B TYPES are B/1 OPEN TRUE.

This specimen was found four miles from its SOURCE of origin.

30 / CLASS B: TRUE STRAYS

ETHICS OF WRITING

REVIEWING AS A PARTISAN ACTIVITY

Reviewers are by no means neutral observers. On the contrary, they are in the business of being partisan. After all, even the more quantitative and objective reviews, such as the product ratings in *Consumer Reports*, require that criteria for evaluation be chosen and weighted.

Reviewers have a responsibility to their readers because something of consequence is at stake: a consumer wants to spend money on the best available product; an employer wants to know which workers to promote; a business or government agency needs to know what changes in the system are needed. For precisely this reason, reviewers have a responsibility to those whose products and performances are being reviewed. Even if unfair, negative reviews can kill a play or sidetrack an artist's career.

As you begin considering what kind of review you might write, these issues of partisanship and responsibility will inevitably arise. On whose behalf will you be writing? What are the potential consequences of the evaluations you will make? What responsibilities does this bring to you as a reviewer?

FURTHER EXPLORATIONS

Rhetorical Analysis

Pick one or two of the reviews in this chapter. Identify the main criteria of evaluation. Notice how criteria of evaluation express enabling assumptions. Explain how the criteria enable the reviewer to connect the evidence provided to the review's central claim. Consider how widely shared the criteria of evaluation are likely to be on the readers' part. What does the reviewer's assumption seem to be? Does the reviewer appear to assume that the criteria can be taken for granted as something most readers already believe, or do the criteria require explanation and justification?

Genre Awareness

John Naughton's "Graphic Designers Are Ruining the Web" might be classified as a commentary or a review. That is, it seems to have elements of both. The same might be said of Daphne Carr's "Run the World." Compare the two, examining how much emphasis there is in each on the function of review and on the function of commentary. To what extent do you find elements of one genre incorporated into another in other reading selections in this chapter or elsewhere in the book? Find an example of a piece of writing you could call a blurred genre, where the influence of more than one genre is involved in making the meaning of the text.

WRITING ASSIGNMENT

Review

Write a review. Pick something to review that you know well or that you find interesting and would like to learn more about. You will write this review for a particular group of readers, so you might target a particular publication, such as a student or local newspaper or one of the national magazines. This will help you anticipate what your readers already know, what they value, and what criteria they accept as a basis of evaluation.

The subject of your review can be drawn from many spheres of life. Here are some common types of reviews:

▶ **Media:** Television programs, radio shows, movies, and musical recordings are all possible subjects for reviews. You could write a review essay of a film or CD and also a notice review—and then reflect on the differences.

▶ **Live performances:** Attend a musical concert, a play, or a club with live music and write a review of the performance.

▶ **The Web:** As the Internet grows more crowded, people can use help finding which sites are worth visiting and which are not. Gather an assortment of related Web sites and write a comparative review of them. Or just focus on one site and review it in depth.

▶ **Exhibits:** Local museums, on and off campus, may be featuring special art, historical, or scientific exhibits that you could review.

▶ **Books:** You could review a best-seller, a recent book in an academic field that interests you, a controversial book, a book that is particularly popular with college students, or an older book that invites a revisit.

▶ **Sports:** Write a preview of an upcoming season of a college or professional sport, or make a prediction about an important game.

▶ **Leisure and entertainment:** Write a restaurant review, a guide to entertainment on campus, or an evaluation of backpacking routes you have taken. Visit historical places, local parks, or parts of a city, and write a review of what they have to offer.

▶ **Education:** Write a review of a course you have taken, a textbook, or a program you have been involved in (such as an orientation for first-year students or a summer program).

▶ **Paired reviews:** Work with a partner to write paired reviews that offer differing judgments about a CD, movie, upcoming sports event, or who is going to win an Academy Award.

▶ **Greatest or best lists:** You could list the top ten (or twenty-five or hundred) rap songs, punk bands, teenage movies, game shows, actresses, hockey players, or presidents, and explain your criteria of evaluation. Some lists focus on the best of the year, whereas others identify the all-time greatest.

► **Course review:** Work together as a class to review your writing course. The review will require planning questions and methods, conducting research, compiling and analyzing the information obtained, and finally evaluating the course based on that information. Here is a procedure, which you may want to modify, depending on the size of your class and the scope of your review:

1. Establish criteria for evaluating the course.

2. Make a list of questions to give you information related to the criteria you're using.

3. With your questions in mind, decide how you will get answers. You could use surveys, written evaluations, interviews, or discussion groups. Decide which methods would be practical as well as most useful for getting the information you need.

4. Conduct the research and compile the results. How you compile results will, of course, depend on the method of gathering information you used. For example, survey responses can be tallied, whereas interviews would have to be analyzed.

5. Interpret the results of your research and prepare a review based on this analysis.

Multimodal Composition

► Design a rating system for reviewing consumer products, musical recordings, movies, restaurants, or some other product or service.

► Use the Stray Shopping Cart Project as an invitation to imagine how you might identify and classify other previously neglected things in a field guide.

Invention

Exploring Your Topic

To get started thinking about your topic and how you might approach it in a review, assess what you already know and what further information you need.

> ⤷ **EXERCISE** ||||||||||||||||||||||||||||||||||||||||||||||||||||||||||||||||||||||||||||||||||||||||

Assessing What You Know

A common feature of reviews is to explain how a particular book, film, or recording fits into a larger body of work ("*London Calling* is the Clash masterpiece that pulls together the range of musical sources in their earlier work") or a particular genre ("James Ellroy's *LA Confidential* belongs on the same shelf as the great *noir* novels of Dashiell Hammett, Raymond Chandler, and Jim Thompson"). Such explanations help readers see the significance of the work in question and establish the credentials of the reviewer as a knowledgeable person. Here are some questions to identify background information you can use in your review:

▶ What do you know about the author of the book, the director of the film, the composer or musical leader? What other works do you know by the same person? How is this work like or different from those other works?

▶ How would you describe the genre of the work? What do you know about the history of the genre? What other examples can you think of?

▶ What is the critical evaluation of the writer, director, or composer? Do you know of reviews, articles, or books on your subject? Do the critics and reviewers seem to agree, or are there debates, differences, or controversies? If so, what's at stake?

Establishing Criteria of Evaluation

Criteria are the standards critics and reviewers use to justify their evaluations. They can be described as the enabling assumptions by which reviewers link their claim (the movie was good, bad, disappointing, sensationalistic, and so on) to the available evidence (the movie itself). In some circumstances, you will need to explain the criteria, as Peter Travers does in his review of *The Girl with the Dragon Tattoo* when he calls the film "a faithful adaptation that brings the dazzle but shortchanges on the daring." In others, you can assume readers will share your criteria, as in Daphne Carr's review of women in rock: "Check out Chile's Dadalú or the Czech Republic's Kazety for similarly deconstructed 'post-rock' pop that still has the feral punk energy so beloved underground while going to territories thus unnamed."

▷ EXERCISE |||||||||||||||||||||||||||||||||||||||||||||||||||||||||||||||||||||||||||||||||||||||||||||||||||||||

Identifying Criteria

To identify criteria that may help you in your evaluation, respond to the following questions.

▶ What is a particularly good example of the type of item you are reviewing? What qualities make it good?

▶ What makes a particularly bad example? Don't simply write the opposite of the "good" qualities listed above. Instead, think of several bad examples, and identify what made them stand out as inferior.

▶ Find three or four sample reviews. What criteria do reviewers use in their evaluations? To what extent are these different from or similar to the criteria in the good and bad examples you've chosen? What is the significance of these differences and similarities?

Assessing Your Criteria

To assess how you might apply the criteria you have identified, consider these questions:

▶ Write down a series of assertions you want to make about what you are reviewing. Use this form of sentence: "X is significant because Y" or "What made X a great movie is Y."

▶ Analyze the assertions. What criteria are you applying in each instance? Do you think readers are likely to accept these criteria as reasonable ones? Why or why not?

▶ How might people apply the same criteria but come up with a different evaluation? Are there criteria of evaluation people might use that differ from those you use? How would these criteria influence a reviewer's evaluation?

Planning

Considering the Relation Between Description and Evaluation

One issue reviewers face is how much they need to describe what they are reviewing. How much detail should you give? Should you summarize the plot of the movie or book? If so, where and in what detail? How can you best combine such description with your evaluation?

Answers to these questions will depend in part on what your readers are likely to know about the topic. Their level of familiarity will shape how much you are called on to provide as background information and description.

These are very real considerations. At the same time, however, it is important to see description and evaluation not as separate writing strategies that require separate space in a review but as strategies that are related to each other.

In this regard, consider the second paragraph in David Denby's review of *The Girl with a Dragon Tattoo*, where he begins by summarizing:

> Much of the movie is set on a private island controlled by the Vanger clan, a wealthy Swedish industrial family peopled with criminals, perverts, solitaries, exiles, dead Nazis, and a grieving old man, Henrik Vanger (Christopher Plummer), who has never got over the disappearance of his grandniece, forty years earlier. In one last attempt to find her, he hires Blomkvist, who has been temporarily discredited in a libel suit, and sets him up as an investigator on the island, a place that no American one-per-cent family would ever dream of owning. It's way up north, windy, snowy, and treacherously beautiful; once you cross the bridge to this enclave, you enter an icy hell. Blomkvist and Salander, warming each other, conduct their investigation from the island, hacking into whatever files they need; they leave only when they have to, with Mara, head down in the wind, tearing around Sweden on a motorcycle like—well, like a bat out of hell.

Then, Denby shifts to a more analytical and evaluative stance, explaining how the movie works and why it succeeds:

> The movie zips ahead, in short, spiky scenes punctuated by skillfully edited montages of digitized photographs and newspaper articles. David Fincher, who directed the picture (working with Steven Zaillian's screenplay), moves at a much faster pace than he did in "Zodiac," his 2007 movie about a murder investigation. In "Zodiac," every time a piece of evidence trembles into view, it quickly recedes again. That movie is an expression of philosophical despair: the truth can never be known. "Dragon Tattoo" says the opposite: it celebrates deduction, high-end detective work—what Edgar Allan Poe called "ratiocination." Everything can be known if you look long and hard enough, especially if you have no scruples about hacking into people's bank accounts, e-mails, and business records. Salander is a criminal, but she's our criminal.

Using Comparison and Contrast

Reviewers use comparison and contrast to put what they are reviewing in perspective, by seeing how it stacks up to something similar—whether it is other work of the same kind or other work by the same artist.

Notice, for example, how in the paragraph above David Denby compares *The Girl with the Dragon Tattoo* to an earlier film *Zodiac* by the same director David Fincher, to point out pacing as one of the recent film's strengths. Peter Travers, on the other hand, uses comparison, in this case between the 2011 American version and the 2009 Swedish one, to point out a weakness: "Unlike the juicy pulp of Niels Arden Oplev's 2009 Swedish adaptation, with a fierce Noomi Rapace as Lisbeth, Fincher's *Girl* is elegantly austere, as though the material merited an artful gaze instead of crass energy."

Working Draft

Use the writing you have already done to get started. Consider how your opening can characterize what you're reviewing and make your evaluation clear to readers. Reviewers do not necessarily point out the criteria of judgment they are using. Nonetheless, to engage your readers, you need to make sure the criteria are easy to identify, even if they are only implied. Consider, too, how you can weave description and other background information into your review. Are there comparisons and contrasts worth making?

Distinguishing Your Views

Sometimes, reviewers not only evaluate a work or performance; they also locate the evaluation in relation to evaluations others have made. Doing so enables them to distinguish their views from what others have said or written and thereby clarify exactly where they are coming from and what criteria they are using.

Take, for example, Jon Pareles's review of Coldplay's third album *X&Y* in 2005, "The Case Against Coldplay":

> Clearly Coldplay is beloved: by moony high school girls and their solace-seeking parents, by hip hop producers who sample its rich instrumental sounds and by emo rockers who admire Chris Martin's heart-on-sleeve lyrics. The band emanates good intentions, from Mr. Martin's political statements to lyrics insisting on its own benevolence. Coldplay is admired by everyone—everyone except me.

Pareles's stance is contentious, but it is certainly clear. In other cases, rather than going head on with others, reviewers will emphasize what others have neglected or downplayed:

> Reviewers have justifiably noted how sinister John Travolta is in *The Taking of Pelham 1 2 3* but missed the sly self-effacing sense of humor he brings to the role.

Peer Commentary

Exchange the working draft of your review with a classmate. Respond to the following questions in writing:

▶ Is the subject defined clearly? Does the review give the reader enough details and background information to understand the reviewer's evaluation? Are there things you wanted to know that the writer left out? Are there things the writer mentions but that you would like to know more about?

▶ Does the reviewer's evaluation come across clearly? As you read the draft, where did you become aware of the reviewer's evaluation? Point to the sentence or passage. Do you understand what the reviewer's criteria are? Do they need to be stated more clearly? Are they reasonable criteria? Are there other criteria you think the writer should take into account?

▶ Does the review seem balanced? How does the reviewer combine description and evaluation? Does the reviewer talk about good and bad points, positive and negative aspects? Is the tone appropriate?

▶ Does the reviewer use comparisons? If so, where and for what purposes?

▶ What suggestions would you make to strengthen the review?

Revising

Use the peer responses to revise your working draft. Consider these issues:

▶ Do you bring the work or performance into focus for your readers by using strategies such as describing it, characterizing what type or genre it is, explaining how it is similar to or differs from others of its kind, and providing adequate background information?

▶ Is your evaluation clear and easy to understand, or are you hedging in one way or another?

▶ Does it make sense in your review to engage what others have already written or said about the work or performance? If so, how can you distinguish your own perspective from others'?

▶ Do you attend to both good and bad points, positive and negative features? Remember, being balanced does not mean being objective or neutral. To make an evaluation you have to commit yourself and explain how, given the good and the bad, you have made a judgment based on criteria.

Options for Meaningful Endings

The ending of your review should do more than just summarize what you have already said. Look at the ending as an opportunity to leave your readers with something further to think about regarding the significance of the work or performance you've reviewed.

Notice, for example, the strategy for ending that Stacy Yi uses in her working draft "More Than Just Burnouts," a review of Donna Gaines's book *Teenage Wasteland* (the full text appears in Writers' Workshop, below). In this case, Stacy ends her review by indicating who would be interested in the book and why.

Working Draft

In conclusion, I believe this is an important book that should be read by anyone interested in finding out more about the "gritty underside of white teen life in the suburbs" (cover notes). Compared to the sensationalistic stories in the press that blame teenage suicide on drugs or heavy metal, Donna Gaines has taken the time to listen—and to hear what the kids have to say.

The strategy Stacy Yi has chosen, of course, is not the only possible way to end her review meaningfully. Here are two other strategies reviewers commonly draw on.

▶ Anticipate a possible objection.

   Some readers may think that Donna Gaines identifies too much with the "burnouts"—and that her research is thereby "contaminated" by her personal allegiances. Gaines's partisanship, however, gives the book its unique authority. By gaining the trust of Bergenfield's heavy metal kids, Gaines is able to give their side of things and to show how they make sense of their world. After reading *Teenage Wasteland*, it's hard not to think these kids need an advocate who can speak on their behalf.

▶ Connect to a larger context of issues.

   Youth-bashing has become a popular spectator sport in recent years, and events such as the school shootings in Littleton, Colorado, and elsewhere have fueled adult fears and anxieties about teenagers. Perhaps the most important achievement of *Teenage Wasteland* is that it cuts through the moral panic and the sensationalistic stories in the press and on TV about young people. Instead, Gaines gives us an understanding of how alienated teenagers experience their lives.

WRITERS' WORKSHOP

Stacy Yi. "More Than Just Burnouts: Book Review of Donna Gaines's Teenage Wasteland"

Written for a sociology course on youth culture, the following is a working draft of a review of Donna Gaines's book *Teenage Wasteland*. The assignment was to draft a four-page review that evaluated the book, to exchange it with a classmate for peer commentary, and to revise. Stacy Yi had a number of concerns she wanted her partner to address in the peer commentary. Here's the note she wrote:

> I'm worried that I spend too much time summarizing the book and not enough explaining my evaluation of it. What do you think? Do I say too much about the author and the book's contents? Is my evaluation clear to you? Do you think I give enough explanation of why I liked the book so much? Any other suggestions are also appreciated. Thanks.

As you read, keep in mind what Stacy asked her partner. When you finish reading the working draft, consider how you would respond.

WORKING DRAFT

Youth culture. Teenagers have devised many different ways of growing up. From jocks and preps to neo-Beatnik and hip-hop kids, most high schools contain a range of distinctive social groupings. In *Teenage Wasteland*, Donna Gaines looks at a group of "burnouts" and heavy metal teens in suburban New Jersey, the "dead end" working-class kids who are alienated from school and community. The opening paragraphs explain the situation that led Gaines to write this book:

> When I heard about the suicide pact it grabbed me in the solar plexus. I looked at the pictures of the kids and their friends. I read what reporters said. I was sitting in my garden apartment looking out on Long Island's Jericho Turnpike thinking maybe this is how the world ends, with the last generation bowing out first.
>
> In Bergenfield, New Jersey, on the morning of March 11, 1987, the bodies of four teenagers were discovered inside a 1977 Chevrolet Camaro. The car, which belonged to Thomas Olton, was parked in an unused garage in the Foster Village garden apartment complex, behind the Foster Village Shopping Center. Two sisters, Lisa and Cheryl Burress, and their friends, Thomas Rizzo and Thomas Olton, had died of carbon monoxide poisoning. (3)

The remainder of the introduction reveals the rationale and research plan for Gaines's investigation of the suicides. What began as an assignment for the *Village Voice*, for which Gaines writes regularly, eventually became her doctoral work as well as the book in review.

Besides providing more details about the instigating event, the Bergenfield suicide pact, the introductory pages also provide autobiographical details about the author which are essential to understanding Gaines's devotion to her task, as well as her informed frame of reference. Gaines, too, in many ways, was a "burnout." She describes her growing up years and habits. She explains that "like many of [her] peers, [she] spent a lot of [her] adulthood recovering from a personal history of substance abuse, family trauma, school failure, and arrests" (4). To put this life behind her, Gaines turned to social work, first as a "big sister" with junior high students in Brooklyn and then as a helper on a suicide prevention hotline. After becoming a

New York State certified social worker, Gaines worked in the special adoptions and youth services divisions and as a street worker providing services for troubled teens. Eventually she moved into research and program evaluation and finally returned to school to complete her doctorate in sociology.

In the introduction, Gaines also explains the need for the book. Initially, she was reluctant to write about suicidal teens because she felt that "if I couldn't help them, I didn't want to bother them" (6). She did not like the idea of turning vulnerable people like the Bergenfield teens into "research subjects" by getting them to trust her with their secrets. Despite these qualms, however, she did decide to go to Bergenfield and ultimately spent two years hanging out with the "burnouts" and "dropouts" of suburban New Jersey, talking to them about heavy metal music, Satanism, work, school, the future, and many other things. Gaines was angry because these teens had been classified by adults as "losers" and never allowed to tell their side of the story. The press had explained the suicides as the result of the individual problems of troubled teens and failed to see, as Gaines does so clearly in her book, how the suicides "symbolized a tragic defeat for young people" (6) and a wider pattern of alienation.

Teenage Wasteland reveals the sense of sadness among the teens in Bergenfield. "By nineteen," Gaines writes, "you've hit the brick wall and you really need something. Because there is nothing to do here and there is nowhere to go" (78). Young people hanging out seems to annoy and even frighten adults. Nevertheless, for these teens, there does not seem to be anything else to do. According to Gaines, they have been neglected by society for so long, experienced so much lack of care in so many ways, that they see no alternatives. They see no hope for anything better.

The only "ticket out" these teens see is to be like Jon Bon Jovi or Keith Richards. The chance of becoming a rock star, of course, is one in a million. The dream breaks down, the kids realize their limitations, and they feel they have run out of choices for the future. There seem to be no alternatives to their bleak situations:

> At the bottom are kids with poor basic skills, short attention spans, limited emotional investment in the future. Also poor housing, poor nutrition, bad schooling, bad lives. And in their bad jobs they will face careers of unsatisfying part-time work, low pay, no benefits, and no opportunity for advancement.

There are the few possibilities offered by a relative—a coveted place in a union, a chance to join a small family business in a service trade, a spot in a small shop. In my neighborhood, kids dream of making a good score on the cop tests, working up from hostess to waitress. Most hang out in limbo hoping to get called for a job in the sheriff's department, or the parks, or sanitation. They're on all the lists, although they know the odds for getting called are slim. The lists are frozen, the screening process is endless. (155)

According to Gaines, these are "America's invisible classes," the "unseen and unheard . . . legions of young people who now serve the baby boom and others, in fancy eateries, video stores, and supermarkets" (157). Given this situation, it is no surprise that Bergenfield's teens turn to Satanism and heavy metal to give them a sense of power and a refuge in a world over which they feel they have no control. There are no good jobs, and the social programs for these teens only label them as "troubled" or "deviant" or "burnouts" and do not work.

One truly fascinating part of the book involves Gaines's etymology of the term "burnout." Besides providing at least twenty-five synonyms for the term, she also explains its evolution. Furthermore, she differentiates between "burnouts" and "dirtbags"—a subtle yet significant distinction. Her discussion of how these terms reflect teens feeling "powerless, useless, and ineffectual" is, in itself, powerful, useful, and effectual in helping readers understand the deep sense of alienation afflicting the "teenage wasteland."

In conclusion, I believe this is an important book that should be read by anyone interested in finding out more about the "gritty underside of white teen life in the suburbs" (cover notes). Compared to the sensationalistic stories in the press that blame teenage suicide on drugs or heavy metal, Donna Gaines has taken the time to listen—and to hear what the kids have to say.

⇨ WORKSHOP QUESTIONS

1. In her note to her partner, Stacy Yi raises a number of issues about her working draft. One of these concerns the amount of description and evaluation that appear in the draft. She seems worried that she spends too much time summarizing the book and talking about the author and not enough on evaluation. How would you respond to this concern? What suggestions would you offer?

2. It is obvious that Stacy admires *Teenage Wasteland*, but she raises the question of whether the criteria of evaluation she uses come across clearly enough. Reread the draft and mark those passages that make an evaluation or imply one. What seem to be the criteria Stacy uses in each case? If the criteria are not stated explicitly, express in your own words what they seem to be. What advice would you give Stacy about presenting her criteria of evaluation more explicitly?

3. In the third paragraph, Stacy compares the treatment of the Bergenfield suicide pact by the press to Gaines's treatment in *Teenage Wasteland*. What is the point of this comparison? Do you think Stacy could do more with it? If so, how could the comparison be extended and strengthened? Do other comparisons appear in the draft? If so, are they effective, or could they use more work? Are there other comparisons you can think of that Stacy might use?

REFLECTING ON YOUR WRITING

The assignments throughout the chapter have put you in the role of a reviewer and shown how you might evaluate a performance, a program, or a policy. For your portfolio, shift focus to discuss how you have been reviewed by others—by teachers in school, supervisors at work, judges at performances, and peer commentators in your writing course.

First, give a little background on your experiences of being evaluated in and out of school. What were the circumstances of the evaluations? Why were you being evaluated? What criteria were used? What was your response to the evaluations? Were these experiences helpful to you? Explain why or why not.

Second, use this background to reconstruct your attitude toward evaluation when you entered your writing course. Has your attitude changed? Why or why not? What has been the effect on you as a writer, a student, and a person of receiving reviews from both your teacher and your peers? What differences, if any, do you see between teachers' and peers' evaluations? What suggestions would you offer for improving the process of evaluation in your writing course?

CHAPTER 12

Multigenre Writing

Publicity, Advocacy Campaigns, & Social Movements

The final chapter in Part 2 presents a multigenre writing assignment that calls on you to design a group of print and new media texts that work together toward a common rhetorical goal.

You will have to determine the rhetorical situation and the nature of your response. Here are three possible ways to frame your response:

▶ You could be largely informative in purpose, to publicize an issue of concern (such as bullying) or a cause (such as preserving a historic building) or to announce an event, such as a concert, a film series, a museum exhibit, or a symposium of speakers. The motive of **publicity** is to inform people, but it is not a neutral rhetorical stance. Rather, publicity notifies people about what is happening, explaining and educating with the aim of raising awareness and shaping the climate of public opinion.

▶ An **advocacy campaign** is a more engaged response because it seeks not just to enlighten people but also to persuade them to act, to join with others in calling for change. Advocacy campaigns often focus on a single issue—such as legalizing medical marijuana, providing affordable housing, saving an endangered species, or forgiving student loan debt.

▶ A social, political, artistic, or cultural **movement** is broader than a campaign. A movement may consist of a number of organizations. For example, the Sierra Club, Greenpeace, the Rainforest Alliance, Friends of the Earth, the Wilderness Society, and other international, national, and local groups make up the environmental movement worldwide, forming coalitions and initiating advocacy campaigns. Political movements like Occupy or the Arab Spring seem to appear spontaneously at the grassroots level, with looser organizational connections but a strong sense of solidarity and popular participation. Cultural and artistic movements, like the Beats, punks, Riot Grrrls, or hip-hop, articulate new identities, styles, and sensibilities, often along generational lines, as young people come to terms with their moment in history.

Differences in scope and motive among publicity, advocacy campaigns, and social movements are important to understand as you sort out your own rhetorical purposes. But it is also important to see that publicity, advocacy campaigns, and social movements are not mutually exclusive categories. Rather, they overlap and intertwine. The rhetorical task is to see what they make possible in a multigenre writing project and how you can use their various capacities to approach this assignment.

Multigenre writing projects are a good way to pull together and reflect on what you've learned in Part 2 about genres of writing, rhetorical analysis, and the design of multimodal compositions. This chapter presents a multigenre writing assignment that gives you lots of space to come to terms with a rhetorical situation that calls for understanding and action. To help you plan your work, we look at some samples of multigenre writing projects, their motives, and the means of communication they employ.

UNDERSTANDING PUBLICITY

Publicity seeks to engage the public's attention in a world that is already oversaturated with print and electronic messages. The task, accordingly, is to design messages that are memorable, attention structures that will stay with readers, shaping their perceptions and understanding of the topic or issue at hand. Here are two examples of publicity that are meant to promote public interest and participation—a film series and a transnational art exhibit.

Classic Film Noir: Designing and Publicizing the Fall Film Series at Warehouse State

A group of students at Warehouse State decided they wanted to design a film series that featured film noir classics from the 1940s and 1950s. This involved research on

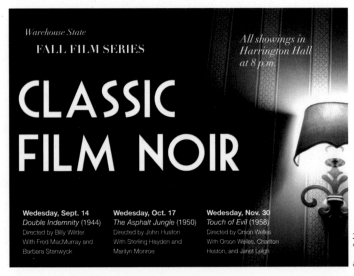

Steve Schirra

film noir, its characteristic features, and its cultural context, as well as decisions about which films to show.

To publicize the film series, the Warehouse State group designed the following items:

▶ A **poster** advertising the film series and establishing a visual style for the rest of the publicity.

▶ A **program** for the film series, using the same visual style as the poster, that included an introductory essay on the history and style of film noir and individual essays on each film, its director, and its critical reception.

▶ A **Web site** that incorporated the essays from the program along with links to other sources of information about film noir.

⊃ **FOR CRITICAL INQUIRY** ||||||||||||||||||||||||||||||||||||||||||||||||||||||||||||||||||||||||||||||||

Publicity and Visual Style

Consider the visual style of the poster. How does it seek to invoke the mood of film noir? If you're not familiar with the genre, do some research on film noir, its themes, and cinematic look.

Proyecto Boston-Medellin: Bilingual Press Release for *Mujeres: Medellin/Women: Medellin*

Mujeres: Medellin/Women: Medellin was a transnational exhibition of four emerging Colombian women artists and a simultaneous live broadcast between Boston and Medellin. The project linked Tamera Marko's first-year multilingual writing class at Emerson College to students and faculty at Universidad Nacionale de Colombia, with Emerson students writing grant proposals, editing artist statements, and publicizing the exhibit in English and Spanish, as you can see from the two press releases:

Press Package: October 17, 2011
Contact Tamera Marko   Phone 619 808 9462   Email tamera_marko@emerson.edu

Emerson College & La Universidad Nacional de Colombia present

Proyecto Boston-Medellín 2011
MUJERES: Medellín / WOMEN: Medellín
EXHIBIT Oct. 26, 2011 • 4-8pm • Bill Bordy Theater
Free & open to the public

If you type "Mujer" + "Medellín" in Google, most of the first 15 pages direct us as browsers worldwide to prostitution, mail-order brides and sex tours. In this exhibition, we seek to complicate these representations of women in Medellín by including diverse social, cultural, and physical contexts in which women build the city of Medellín. This exhibition features photographs, video, written word and an interactive multi-media living room installation made by and about women who are Medellín's community leaders, mothers and daughters, actors in armed conflict and peace workers in this city that has suffered successive cycles of violence. More than 120 Emerson students in First Year Research Writing classes collaborated with PBM exhibits' young emerging artists via Facebook and video-conference to bring the *art* and the *artists* to this exhibit.

This exhibit will debut in a **simultaneous live broadcast in two cities**: Boston and Medellín. The artists will be in Boston to meet and greet the public and discuss their art. The artists' families, colleagues, teachers, community members, and protagonists in the artists' documentaries and photographs, as well as other artists, scholars and city residents will be at the AULA Internacional in Medellín. We will be able to interact with each other at both exhibits via live video conference broadcast.

About the Artists In 1991, when the United States was bombing Baghdad—when these women artists were babies— their home Medellín was the most violent city in the world. They were in elementary school when bombs were exploding throughout their city. They also went about their daily lives of school, friends, birthdays, and holidays. Now they are young emerging artists and students at the Universidad Nacional de Colombia in Medellín. Their art seeks to understand, re-frame, remember, and reinvent themselves and their city. This is their debut in the United States.

About the Directors Tamera Marko has Ph.D. in Latin American History and is currently Assistant Director of the First Year Writing Program at Emerson College. Dr. Marko is also the Director of the Duke University's Duke Engage Program in Medellin with her partner Jota Samper. She has published articles on social mobility in the Americas and her work with PBM has garnered international recognition and has won various awards within the academic community. Jota Samper has a Master's Degree in the Department of Design and Urban Planning (DUSP) at MIT, where he is now a Ph.D. candidate. He has worked has an architect and artist in the last 15 years in 6 countries, including Colombia, the United States, Mexico, Brazil, India, and France. He is a native of Medellín, Colombia.

More info about the artists, behind-the-scenes production, or to schedule an artist to speak to your class, see: http://rw121emersonmedellin.blogspot.com Contact: tamera_marko@emerson.edu 619 808 9462

Press Package: October 17, 2011
Contact Tamera Marko   Phone 619 808 9462   Email tamera_marko@emerson.edu

Emerson College & La Universidad Nacional de Colombia apresenta

Proyecto Boston-Medellín 2011
MUJERES: Medellín / WOMEN: Medellín
EXPOSICION 26 de octubre de 2011 • 4-8pm • Bill Bordy Theater
Gratis y abierto al público

Si tú buscas "Mujer" + "Medellín" en Google, las primeras 15 páginas se refieren en su mayoría a prostitución, esposas por correo y turismo sexual. En nuestra exposición deseamos ampliar la representación del papel de la mujer en el contexto social, cultural y físico en que ellas construyen nuestra ciudad. Nuestra exhibición incluye: fotografía, videos, palabras escritas de y sobre mujeres de Medellín: líderes comunitarias, madres y hijas, actores en el conflicto armado y constructoras de paz en una ciudad que ha sufrido sucesivos ciclos de violencia.

Esta exposición hará su lancamiento en una transmisión simultánea en vivo en dos ciudades: Boston y Medellín. Las artistas estarán en Boston para conocer y saludar al público y hablar de su arte. Las familias, colegas, profesores, miembros de la comunidad y las protagonistas en los documentales y fotografías de las artistas, así como otros artistas, académicos y habitantes de la ciudad será en el Aula Internacional de Medellín. Nosotros serámos capaces de interactuar unos con otros, en los dos exposiciones en Boston y en Medellín a través de transmisión en vivo de video conferencia.

Las Artistas: En 1991, cuando Los Estados Unidos fue atentando Bagdad—cuando estas mujeres artistas eran bebés—su natal Medellín fue la ciudad más violenta del mundo. Estaban en la escuela primaria cuando estaban explotando bombas a lo largo de su ciudad. También pasaron sobre su vida cotidiana de la escuela, amigos, cumpleaños y fiestas. Ahora son jóvenes artistas y estudiantes de la Universidad Nacional de Colombia en Medellín. Su arte busca comprender, recordar y reinventarse a sí mismos y a su ciudad. Este es su *debut* en los Estados Unidos.

Más información sobre las artistas, producción detrás de las cámaras, o para programar una artista para hablar con su clase: **http://rw121emersonmedellin.blogspot.com** / tamera_marko@emerson.edu
Tel: 619 808 9462

Publicity and Rhetorical Stance

Consider the rhetorical stance the press releases establishes. It contains some basic information about the art exhibit, but it also situates itself in relation to the public's understanding of Medellin. What understanding does it seek to promote? What reasons does it offer readers to attend the exhibit?

AN INVENTORY OF GENRES

The chapters in Part 2 of *Call to Write* include genres of writing that often appear as publicity or in advocacy campaigns and social movements.

▶ Occupy posters (Chapter 2)

▶ Meth Science Not Stigma: Open Letter to the Media; Open Letter to Chancellor Linda P. B. Katehi; Letters to the Editor; Occupy the Boardroom Letter-Writing Campaign; Doctors Without Borders Letter of Appeal (Chapter 6)

▶ Jewish Voice for Peace postcards (Chapter 7)

▶ Sentencing Project Fact Sheets; Human Rights Watch Slide Show and Videos (Chapter 8)

▶ Op-ed: How to Fight the New Epidemics; Political Cartoons and Comics; Art as Social Commentary (Chapter 9)

▶ Proposal for Funding; Petitions: Tell Apple: Stop Slavery Practices at Foxconn's Manufactories and Support and Pass the California Dream Act; Forgive Student Loan Debt Web site; Health Advocacy posters (Chapter 10)

Your publicity, campaign, or movement is likely to differ in focus, but these examples can be useful as models of various genres of writing.

ANALYZING ADVOCACY CAMPAIGNS

A good way to plan a multigenre writing project is to investigate how various organizations have set up advocacy campaigns and the types of print and new media writing they employ to get their message across.

Caring Across Generations: Press Kit

Caring Across Generations (CAG) is a campaign for quality long-term care for older adults, the disabled, and others who need it and for support of quality jobs, decent working conditions, and career advancement for caregivers. A press kit is a standard feature of public relations used by businesses, musicians, writers, filmmakers, and

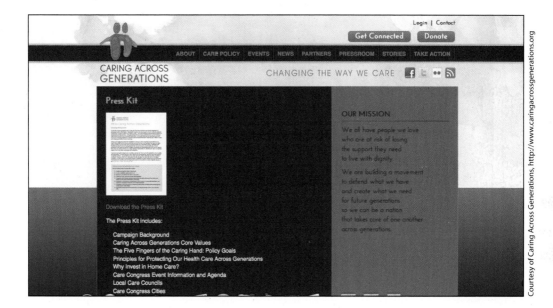

other artists to launch new products, CDs, books, or films or to announce mergers, concert tours, or other news. Press kits typically consist of background information ("backgrounder"), fact sheets, frequently asked questions, a press release, photos, and sometimes video and live music.

➢ FOR CRITICAL INQUIRY

Press Kits and Advocacy Campaigns

Check out CAG's press kit at www.caringacrossgenerations.org/pressroom/press-kit to see how advocacy groups use press kits to publicize their campaigns. Consider the various types of writing included in the press kit. How does the press kit explain the need for a campaign? How does the press kit seek to influence readers? How does the material in the press kit go together? How would you describe the rhetorical stance (the ethos, pathos, and logos) of the press kit in particular and the campaign in general? What role does the press kit play in the campaign?

Jobs with Justice: Social Media

Jobs with Justice is a national network of unions, religious groups, community organizations, and student activists that fights on behalf of working people for economic justice and a better social future. A striking new feature of advocacy groups like Jobs with Justice is the use of social media to disseminate information, influence public opinion, organize coalitions, promote solidarity, and coordinate events and activities. It is now pretty much taken for granted that organizations like Jobs with Justice, Human Rights Watch, and Greenpeace will have an active presence on Facebook, Twitter, Flickr, and YouTube.

Courtesy of Jobs With Justice, http://www.jwj.org/

▷ FOR CRITICAL INQUIRY

Advocacy Campaigns and Facebook

Visit Jobs with Justice's Facebook page www.facebook.com/jobswithjustice. What do you find? How is the page organized? Categorize the various types of material that appear. What does their function seem to be? What identity and purpose does Jobs with Justice project on Facebook?

MAKING SENSE OF SOCIAL, POLITICAL, ARTISTIC, AND CULTURAL MOVEMENTS

Social, political, artistic, and cultural movements are often known by declarations, statements of purpose, manifestos, or mission statements that define the movement's aims and serve as a rallying-point and source of identification for its supporters. Consider the opening lines of two famous political documents:

> When in the Course of human Events, it becomes necessary for one People to dissolve the Political Bands which have connected them to another, and to assume among the Powers of the Earth, the separate and equal Station to which the Laws of Nature and of Nature's God entitle them, a decent Respect to the Opinions of Mankind requires that they should declare the causes which impel them to the Separation.

> —Thomas Jefferson, Declaration of Independence

A spectre is haunting Europe—the spectre of Communism.

—Karl Marx and Frederick Engels, *Manifesto of the Communist Party*

Notice how the tone and rhetorical stance differ. Jefferson emphasizes the need "in Respect to the Opinions of Mankind" to explain why the American colonies were compelled to declare independence from England, and he projects a tone of reasonableness. Marx and Engels are more direct, casting communism as a danger to the ruling classes in Europe, and their tone is threatening.

The different stances make sense in the circumstances. Jefferson and the American revolutionists sought support from European allies and the conscience of public opinion. Marx and Engels, on the other hand, cast communism as an unreconciled menace to the old order, a dramatic break with the past. The closing lines of the *Manifesto* project a new identity for working people: "Let the ruling classes tremble at a Communistic revolution. The proletarians have nothing to lose but their chains. They have a world to win. WORKINGMEN OF ALL COUNTRIES, UNITE!"

In the next two sections, we present more recent examples of statements of purpose and manifestos.

Occupy Providence: Statement of Purpose

Randall Rose

....

The way that Occupy Providence chose its statement of purpose (sometimes called a "mission statement") provides insight into the Occupy movement and its emphasis on popular participation and democratic decision making. Occupy Providence supporters posted mission statements online, and the top vote-getters were submitted to the General Assembly, where the statements were discussed and a final, revised version adopted. Below are the four top vote-getters, followed by the revised version that became Occupy Providence's official statement of purpose.

From: Randall Rose rrose@pobox.com

Date: Fri, Oct 21, 2011 at 3:44 PMSubject: Mission statement vote results

To: occupy-providence@googlegroups.com

In the online mission statement votes, 52 votes were cast. One version got 9 votes and three others were tied for second place with 5 votes each. We are submitting the top 4 vote-getters to the General Assembly tonight and will have printed copies of them to pass out. We had planned to give only the 3 most popular ones to the GA, but several versions were tied for second place.

Randall Rose, "Occupy Providence Mission Statement." Reprinted by permission of Randall Rose.

Here are the complete voting results, starting with the most popular versions. When several versions were tied, I've shown them in alphabetical order.

The Following Version Received 9 Votes Out of 52

Occupy Providence is a movement of the 99%. Inspired by people's occupations spreading rapidly across the globe, we occupy to bear witness to the savage inequality and fundamental injustice of a system that places profit over people, hatred over humanity, and oppression over liberation. We occupy to build a movement capable of shaking the foundations of this system, and of creating a new society within the shell of the old.

The Following Version Received 5 Votes Out of 52

Occupy Providence is a gathering of people who seek to exercise their rights to freedom of speech and peaceful assembly in order to publicly protest gross financial and social inequalities taking place in the United States. We will maintain a physical presence in Providence's Burnside Park, to show support and solidarity with "Occupy" movements across our nation and worldwide. We seek to give voice to the majority of Americans, who have not been adequately represented in our flawed political process, by means of a truly democratic General Assembly. Our indefinite occupation is to be non-violent, non-destructive, non-discriminatory, harassment- and substance- free. Occupy Providence welcomes all people regardless of race, gender, orientation, ethnicity, age, religious views, sexual orientation, and political views.

The Following Version Received 5 Votes Out of 52

Occupy Providence is a non-violent democratic assembly comprised of individuals who find that the current socioeconomic order of our society has become intolerable.

The rapidly increasing gap between the wealthy and the poor, combined with a structurally flawed political system that amplifies the power of the elite, has effectively silenced the voices of the 99%. For far too long, we common citizens have stood idly by waiting for these issues to resolve themselves, but we can wait no longer.

Occupy Providence welcomes people of every race, gender, ethnicity, age, religion, sexual orientation, and political position. Discrimination and hate speech have no place in our organization, for Occupy Providence is based on radical inclusivity. We gather as a mosaic of beliefs, ideas and morals, determined to speak our minds equally and freely in order to come to a consensus through the democratic processes our so-called political representatives have long since forsaken.

Occupy Providence stands in solidarity with Occupy Wall St. and all of the other Occupy Movements across the world that are currently serving as vehicles for social and economic change. We are Occupy Providence and we are nothing more than the megaphones of the 99%. We will be heard.

*Occupy Providence, as an organization, is not aligned with any political affiliation, though our individual members may be. Any political view shared by an individual member is strictly the view of that individual.

The Following Version Received 5 Votes Out of 52

We the people of Occupy Providence, inspired by the fervor and progress of our sister-Occupy movements and protests around the world, raise our voice against injustice and in support of the well-being and fair treatment of all people. We are a grassroots community of people from all over Rhode Island, with widely-varying backgrounds and belief systems, who welcome anyone to join us with open arms.

America's government was founded on the promise that it would protect the rights and the interests of the people. This promise has been broken. Large corporations and certain individuals have been allowed to use their massive wealth to gain undue control over the American political system, ultimately to the detriment of the economic security of hundreds of millions of people. We will tolerate such gross corruption no longer.

The occupation of Burnside Park, which commenced October 15th, 2011, is the first of many non-violent actions we will take to inspire change at all levels of our community, from local residents across the entire world. Through our democratic decision making process, we provide platform and strength for the voices of the 99%. As we claim our space in the park, we provide a visual reminder that we are too many to be ignored any longer. And through further direct action, we will continue the process of educating our fellow human beings, and returning the power to the hands of the people, where it belongs.

Occupy Providence Official Statement of Purpose [approved by General Assembly, October 24, 2011]

Occupy Providence is a gathering of people who seek to exercise their right to freedom of speech and peaceful assembly, inspired by people's occupations spreading rapidly across the globe. We occupy to demonstrate an alternative to the fundamental inequality and injustice of a system which places profit over people and oppression over liberation. We seek to give voice to the 99%—the majority of Americans, who have not been adequately represented in our flawed political process—by means of a truly democratic General Assembly. We believe in developing a society that is truly of, by and for the people. Our indefinite occupation is non-violent, non-destructive, non-discriminatory and harassment-free. Occupy Providence welcomes all people regardless of race, gender, sexual orientation, gender expression, ethnicity, age, level of ability, legal status, religious views or position on the political spectrum. We work towards organizing a movement capable of overcoming an unjust system and forming a new society within the shell of the old.

⏩ FOR CRITICAL INQUIRY

Crafting a Statement of Purpose

Consider what the four top vote-getters share in common and how they differ. How does the official statement of purpose approved by the General Assembly integrate elements from the four statements? What does it leave out? What reasons can you imagine motivated Occupy supporters to make these decisions?

Riot Grrrl Manifesto

Kathleen Hanna

• •

The Riot Grrrl movement emerged in the early 1990s out of the punk, grunge, and hardcore music scenes, with a do-it-yourself ethic and a powerful feminist sensibility. Bands such as Bikini Kill, Bratmobile, and Heavens to Betsy defined the Riot Grrrl sound, and a new wave

of homemade 'zines such as Revolution Girls Style Now *and* Bikini Kill *gave voice to the Riot Grrrl consciousness. Kathleen Hanna, the lead singer and songwriter of the band Bikini Kill, wrote the Riot Grrrl Manifesto, which appeared in* Bikini Kill *in 1991.*

BECAUSE us girls crave records and books and fanzines that speak to US that WE feel included in and can understand in our own ways.

BECAUSE we wanna make it easier for girls to see/hear each other's work so that we can share strategies and criticize-applaud each other.

BECAUSE we must take over the means of production in order to create our own meanings.

BECAUSE viewing our work as being connected to our girlfriends-politics-real lives is essential if we are gonna figure out how we are doing impacts, reflects, perpetuates, or DISRUPTS the status quo.

BECAUSE we recognize fantasies of Instant Macho Gun Revolution as impractical lies meant to keep us simply dreaming instead of becoming our dreams AND THUS seek to create revolution in our own lives every single day by envisioning and creating alternatives to the bullshit christian capitalist way of doing things.

BECAUSE we want and need to encourage and be encouraged in the face of all our own insecurities, in the face of beergutboyrock that tells us we can't play our instruments, in the face of "authorities" who say our bands/zines/etc are the worst in the US and

BECAUSE we don't wanna assimilate to someone else's (boy) standards of what is or isn't good or cool.

BECAUSE we are unwilling to falter under claims that we are reactionary "reverse sexists" AND NOT THE TRUEPUNKROCKSOULCRUSADERS THAT WE KNOW we really are.

BECAUSE we know that life is much more than physical survival and are patently aware that the punk rock "you can do anything" idea is crucial to the coming angry grrrl rock revolution which seeks to save the psychic and cultural lives of girls and women everywhere, according to their own terms, not ours.

BECAUSE we are interested in creating non-hierarchical ways of being AND making music, friends, and scenes based on communication + understanding, instead of competition + good/bad categorizations.

BECAUSE doing/reading/seeing/hearing cool things that validate and challenge us can help us gain the strength and sense of community that we need in order to figure out how bullshit like racism, able-bodieism, ageism, speciesism, classism, thinism, sexism, anti-semitism and heterosexism figures in our own lives.

BECAUSE we see fostering and supporting girl scenes and girl artists of all kinds as integral to this process.

BECAUSE we hate capitalism in all its forms and see our main goal as sharing information and staying alive, instead of making profits or being cool according to traditional standards.

BECAUSE we are angry at a society that tells us Girl = Dumb, Girl = Bad, Girl = Weak.

BECAUSE we are unwilling to let our real and valid anger be diffused and/or turned against us via the internalization of sexism as witnessed in girl/girl jealousism and self defeating girltype behaviors.

BECAUSE I believe with my wholeheartmindbody that girls constitute a revolutionary soul force that can, and will change the world for real.

⊃ FOR CRITICAL INQUIRY

Manifestos and New Identities

Manifestos give voice to new identities, new styles in music, fashion, and visual design, and new ways of being in the world. Consider what the Riot Grrrl Manifesto is seeking to accomplish and the particular consciousness it is trying to put into words. (You may want to do some research on Riot Grrrls and listen to some of the music that came out of the movement.) Notice how the manifesto is organized by a sequence of statements that begin with "BECAUSE." This gives the manifesto a strong sense of urgency in explaining the reasons behind the Riot Grrrl movement. Just as Thomas Jefferson felt compelled to give reasons to explain why the American colonists declared independence from England, Kathleen Hanna's Riot Grrrl Manifesto wants to explain the urgent need for a Riot Grrrl movement. What is the basis of new identities in the Riot Grrrl Manifesto? What does the Riot Grrrl Manifesto distance itself from? What is the vision of the future it projects?

WRITING ASSIGNMENT

Writing Assignment

This writing assignment asks you to put together what you have learned about various genres of writing in order to imagine how individual print and new media texts can be designed as part of a larger multigenre writing project. This can be an individual or group assignment, depending on your teacher's directions. Here are some guidelines to take into account:

1. Identify a rhetorical situation where there is something at stake for you, some sense of exigency that calls on you to respond—that makes you want to inform others, raise awareness, advocate for change, articulate new identities, or establish new forms of cultural or artistic or political expression. Consider your purposes and the various possibilities available to frame your response.

2. Determine what research you need to do. This is likely to include research on the issue, cause, or event you're writing about. You should also become familiar with the styles and rhetorical possibilities of publicity, advocacy campaigns, and social, political, artistic, or cultural movements by researching some examples, depending on the focus of your project.

3. Identify your audience. Consider the complexity of your audience—whether there are primary and secondary audiences or audiences that do not yet exist that your writing seeks to call into being.

4. Decide how to represent the results of your research. What genres of print and new media are best suited for this project? What combination of genres and what means of communication are most fitting?

REFLECTING ON YOUR WRITING

To come to terms with the work you've done on this multigenre writing assignment, write a reflection. Here are some things you might take into account:

▶ **Rhetorical situation.** How did you (and classmates if this was a group assignment) identify the call to write? What motivated you to take on a particular issue or topic?

▶ **Rhetorical stance.** Explain how you decided on your particular orientation toward the issue or topic. What were you trying to accomplish? How did you fashion a voice in the writing you did?

▶ **Audience.** Who did you address in this project? Was there more than one audience involved in your considerations? If so, who was your primary audience? Were there secondary audiences?

▶ **Genre choices.** Explain the genres you chose for this assignment. Why did they seem appropriate? How do they go together? What did you learn by examining possible models for your project? Did you modify them for your own purposes? Explain your decisions.

▶ **Final evaluation.** Looking back on the work you've done, consider how well you accomplished what you set out to do. What do you think works well or not so well in your conception of the project and in the execution of its individual parts? What would you do differently?

PART 3

Writing and Research Projects

INTRODUCTION: DOING RESEARCH AND THE NEED TO KNOW

People do research all the time, perhaps without even being aware of it.

▶ High school students do research to decide which colleges to apply to. People looking for a new car may consult *Consumer Reports* or talk to friends. If you are planning a vacation, you might look at travel guides.

▶ Researchers in the workplace do marketing surveys, product development, and productivity studies. Professional fields like law and medicine are defined in many respects by the kind of research practitioners in those fields do to deal with clients' legal situations or to diagnose patients' conditions and recommend treatment.

▶ Public opinion polling has become a common feature of politics and journalism. Advocacy and public interest groups conduct research on questions that matter to them—whether it's the impact of hydrofracking for natural gas on the environment, inequalities in income and wealth, or drunken driving.

▶ Research defines the fields of study in academia—from literature and philosophy to mass communication, to chemical engineering—as well as the work students do in their various courses: critical essays, term papers, lab reports, case studies, book reviews, design proposals, and so on.

▶ Writers of all sorts do research—investigative reporters breaking a newspaper story on the treatment of detainees at Abu Ghraib prison; freelance writers preparing a magazine article for *Natural History* on changes in the migratory patterns of caribou in Alaska; or novelists researching Southern California in the 1950s, to write a noir thriller set in Hollywood.

One thing these examples have in common is that they are all motivated by the need to know. In each case, something is calling on a person or a group of people to do research—to get the information needed, to investigate a problem, to provide a new way of seeing things.

Researchers in different fields, of course, have different ways of asking questions and different ways of answering them. Take the AIDS epidemic, for example. Biomedical researchers ask questions about the nature of the human immunodeficiency virus (HIV) and about treatment that can alter the course of infection, whereas psychologists, sociologists, and anthropologists have studied the effect of AIDS on the identities of HIV-negative gay men, the benefits and drawbacks of needle-exchange programs, and the role of the sex industry in the transmission of the virus. Economists calculate the financial impact of AIDS, and researchers in literary and film studies examine the representations of AIDS in fiction and movies.

The following chapters focus for the most part on academic research, the kind of assignments you are likely to get in college courses. Chapter 13 presents examples of research writing and explains how to organize a research project. Chapter 14 discusses how to work with sources, and Chapter 15 provides a guide to print, electronic, and other sources. Chapter 16 discusses field research and includes a sample field report.

Doing Research

Critical Essays, Research Papers, and Magazine Articles

In college classes, the call to do research comes from teachers, in the form of a writing assignment. Accordingly, whatever the assignment or field of study may be, it's worth beginning with what faculty are looking for when they ask students to do research.

In the first part of this chapter, we'll examine faculty expectations about research projects and present examples of two familiar writing assignments that call on students to work with sources: the five-page critical essay and the ten- to fifteen-page or longer research paper. We also include a magazine article written by a student for *Scientific American* as an example of a multimodal composition that might be assigned in a writing or journalism class.

In the second part of the chapter, we'll take an overview of the research process and follow one student, Amira Patel, as she designs and carries out a research project in an American history course.

WHAT IS FACULTY LOOKING FOR? UNDERSTANDING ACADEMIC WRITING

Faculty assign short critical essays (say, five to seven pages) and longer research papers (ten to fifteen pages or more) because they want students to act like members of a field of study, whether drama critics, literary scholars, design theorists, or historians. Those writing assignments call on the students to participate in the ongoing discussion of key issues, problems, and questions and to position themselves in relation to what experts in the field have already said. Faculty know, of course, that students are novices in the field. But that's why faculty ask students to gain some experience in engaging with topics and themes in a field of study.

To understand critical essays and research papers as genres of academic writing, it helps to consider these faculty expectations:

▶ **Faculty expect you to work with your sources**—to create an interplay of perspectives and interpretations instead of just summarizing what the authorities have said. For example, it's not enough to report on the French Revolution in 1789 (to prove to your instructor that you've done research). The real question is, what have historians said about the French Revolution, how do these interpretations differ, and why?

▶ **Faculty expect you to identify the central discussions, debates, and controversies in a field**—and to use them to locate your own thinking in relation to what the authorities have said. In academic writing, it is rare that problems or issues have been settled. Usually, there are discussions, debates, and controversies taking place, in which scholars argue for a particular interpretation or way of understanding the matter at hand. Your task as a researcher is to understand these ongoing controversies and figure out where you stand in relation to them.

▶ **Faculty expect you to create your own research space.** A critical essay or research paper does not simply convey information from reliable sources. It uses these sources to establish a problem or issue that has significance. Even in cases where an instructor assigns the problem or issue to examine, it's still up to you to explain why and how this question is worth investigating and what makes it meaningful.

SAMPLE STUDENT PAPERS FOR ANALYSIS

In the two examples of student writing that follow, we look more closely at how students have responded to these faculty expectations. The first paper is a critical essay, which uses Modern Language Association (MLA) citation form. The second paper uses American Psychological Association (APA) style.

Critical Essay in MLA Format

Stacy Yi wrote this critical essay "Jigsaw Falling Into Place?: Radiohead and the Tip-Jar Model" when she was a sophomore for a mass communication course in media and culture. The assignment called on students to identify and analyze a recent event or trend in the media that illustrates changing patterns of content distribution in the digital era.

Yi   1

Stacy Yi

Professor Watkins

Media & Culture

5 April 2010

Jigsaw Falling Into Place?:

Radiohead and the Tip-Jar Model

Late in the afternoon of October 3, 2007 I faced a decision that was much more difficult than I'd anticipated: how much did I want to pay for a digital download of Radiohead's seventh album, *In Rainbows*? It should've been easy; the download was offered by the band itself on its website, not a third party linked to through Napster or The Pirate Bay, and the price was given only by the text "it's up to you." Unlike the music I'd downloaded for free in the past, all without the artist's permission, *In Rainbows* came with no embedded moral problem. The band didn't seem to mind if I opted to pay nothing. Eventually I settled on $6, entered my payment information, received my download, and sat back to enjoy the album, but I wondered about the other thousands, and eventually millions, of fans like me, specifically about how they viewed this sudden influx of responsibility and the decisions it led them to make.

Uses a personal anecdote to introduce the issue of the essay

I wasn't the only one with questions. Editorials in newspapers and on websites, blog postings and attendant comment sections, and conversations with friends all asked what this experiment would mean for music retail and digital sales, copyright law, and the stability of the industry's conventions. Everyone who took interest in the situation seems to believe, whether they side with or against the band's decision, that Radiohead changed the conversation about content distribution, one that extends beyond music to other media. Would this be the first wave in a gradual rewriting of the industry's rules, or was the band merely exercising its sizable economic muscles in a one-shot deal?

Generalizes from personal experience to raise the central question

Many of those commentators compared Radiohead's sales plan for *In Rainbows* to the tip jar on the counter of the local coffee shop. The comparison isn't quite parallel because tips are generally given for quality service that accompanies an already-purchased product. In Radiohead's case, however, the product and service are one and the same (at least until *In Rainbows* was released in the stores, months

Introduces model

Qualifies its applicability

later, on TBD Records.) That fits with Greg Kot's observation, from *Ripped: How the Wired Generation Revolutionized Music*, that the band wanted only "to leak its own album, give fans a taste of the new music, and invite them to buy the sonically superior physical product once it became available in a few months" (1). Using an online tip jar for digital sales, then, is not necessarily the best way to make money, but an effective means of promoting a product to be sold later at a fixed rate.

Explains one thing the model brings to light

Although Radiohead aren't the first to use the tip-jar model of sales, their particular tip jar perhaps did have the widest reach, which may have influenced the success of the experiment. "[Radiohead] seems more interested in getting the new album into as many hands as possible, and doing so legally … but [the band] has no trouble selling out venues, and … its [sic] still in its prime for CD sales," says the editorial page of the *L.A. Times*. If Radiohead's status as a high-profile, top-selling international act is partly responsible for raising sales figures, then the tip-jar model might only change that small segment of the industry that can command such attention. Ayala Ben-Yehuda of *Billboard* puts it succinctly in her article "Networth": "online fan-funding efforts certainly sound like a grass-roots and democratic way to launch a career, but the few bands that can actually motivate enough fans to make donations to their recording effort probably don't need the help."

Considers a limitation of the model

Musician Kim Gordon of the band Sonic Youth agrees, arguing "we're not in that position either. We might not have been able to put out a record for another couple of years if we'd done it ourselves: it's a lot of work. And it takes away from the actual making music" (qtd. in Peschek 5). Gordon's emphasis of production and creation over distribution not only implicitly critiques Radiohead's artistic decisions, it also rebuffs the notion that large-scale change is possible in the music industry. If the tip-jar distribution model is too complicated for a band of limited resources (even a comparatively successful, long-lived band like Sonic Youth), then the changes that will come as traditional music retail shifts towards a greater online presence will be cosmetic; the advantages presented by the internet will only reinforce a sales model that relies on record labels and distributors to do the work that might otherwise detract from the quality of music produced.

Explains the limits

Examines model in another context

However, the tip-jar model has been widely adopted on the Internet and factors significantly in various proposals for refiguring online news content to recoup lost profits. Some critics argue that clicking on sponsored ads while visiting a favorite website is the same as tipping, while companies like TipJar, LLC, and TipJoy offer tip-collection services for companies and bloggers eager to earn more direct revenue than that offered by ad sales. The programming is relatively simple to integrate into any content outlet, and though the logistics required to distribute an album's worth of mp3s are likely more complex than those involved in offering a 500-word editorial, it's not difficult to imagine a young band, writer, cartoonist, or activist publishing content and earning enough through donations to at least partially subsidize further work. In fact, this sounds much like the "grassroots and democratic way to launch a career" that Ben-Yehuda describes. Furthermore, the social factors that inform the value of those donations may shift the conversation from launching a career to something much larger.

Draws implications of the model

Economists have long held that opting to pay any amount of money for a good when a "free-ride" is possible is impure altruism, and even though the motives behind such giving may not be enlightened, they are no less valid. "Social pressure, guilt, sympathy, or simply a desire for a 'warm-glow' may play important roles in the decisions of agents," says economist James Andreoni, and those influences impact our understanding of what a donation means (464). The positive feelings that come from doing something generally considered good can be seen in Viviana A. Zelizer's concept of special monies, which recognizes that "extraeconomic factors systematically constrain and shape" the uses, users, allocation, control, and sources of money (351). Unlike the rational, "all-purpose" value of money, which is the same in any context, a tip, as a form of "special money," can have a different value, or even a different function, depending on the context. From this perspective, the viability of the tip-jar model is determined by the specific relationship between consumer and producer or provider rather than by general guidelines set by an artist, a company, or even the industry. This seems especially true online, where the fragmentation and specialization of those groups defies blanket solutions and plans.

Introduces a concept ("special monies") to analyze how tip-jar model works

In other words, a tip given to a freelance blogger or an unsigned local musician is essentially different from one given to the *Boston Globe* or Radiohead in that the stakes behind the former are far greater than those of the latter. The social forces motivating people to tip accessible, independent artists are likely to encourage continued giving, particularly when an online tipper's warm-glow feelings stem from a perceived responsibility to the artist's continued content production. The tip feels more "necessary" because the audience has entered into a more direct relationship with the artist, and the online tip becomes not only an investment in the future output of an artist but also a means for the audience to actually participate in production, to become part of the machinery that's responsible for the eventual album, book, or design. Eduardo Porter, in a *New York Times* editorial published shortly after *In Rainbows'* release, extrapolated that participation to include not just the creation of new content, or even a new means of production, but perhaps of a new economy itself (1).

Explains potential consequences

Established bands like Radiohead and Nine Inch Nails (who offered a variation on the tip-jar model with *Ghosts I-IV* in 2008) rose to prominence on the established economy. For them, "pay what you will" schemes are a useful promotional tool, a means of self-sufficiency in the shadow of large corporations, and an interesting experiment. And while that independence is likely satisfying, it isn't likely to create Porter's new economy. That will be left to the artists, publishers, and others toiling unknown in bedrooms and classrooms, pushing exposure via social-networking profiles to the limit, and whatever audience is willing to follow them into a new system of exchange. The first true tip-jar success story seems likely to describe a community effort, the kind often absent from the myth of the individual artist.

Ends by drawing a distinction between "established" and "unknown" artists to suggest where change based on tip-jar model is likely to occur

The hesitation noted by several voices in the debate is reasonable, particularly as the question of what value, monetary or otherwise, any given consumer will place on a song, album, or entire catalog remains nebulous and somewhat intimidating. Radiohead's gambit may not have been the call to revolt as some had hoped, but it may still contain the DNA for a change to come some years from now.

Yi   5

Works Cited

Andreoni, James. "Impure Altruism and Donations to Public Goods: A Theory of Warm-Glow Giving." *The Economic Journal* 100.401 (1990): 464–477. Print.

Ben-Yehuda, Ayala. "The Indies Issue: Networth." *Billboard* 28 June 2008. *LexisNexis.* Web. 18 Oct. 2009.

Kot, Greg. "Radiohead Reinvents Itself—An Except from 'Ripped: How the Wired Generation Revolutionized Music." *Chicagotribune.com* The Chicago Tribune, 17 May 2009. Web. 16 Oct. 2009.

"Pay What You Want For Radiohead." Editorial. *Los Angeles Times* 2 Oct. 2007. Web. 30 Oct. 2009.

Peschek, David. "Youth Movement." *The Guardian* 5 June 2009. Web. 16 Oct. 2009.

Porter, Eduardo. "Radiohead's Warm Glow." Editorial. *New York Times* 14 Oct. 2007. Web. 16 Oct. 2009.

Zelizer, Viviana A. "The Social Meaning of Money: 'Special Monies.'" *The American Journal of Sociology.* 95.2 (1989): 342–377. Print.

Analysis: Working with a Model

One of the interesting features of Stacy Yi's critical essay is her use of a model—the tip-jar model that a number of commentators suggested—to examine Radiohead's "pay what you will scheme" and to draw out its implications not only for the music industry but for online content distribution more generally. Notice that Stacy does not apply the tip-jar model rigidly. Rather, she uses it flexibly to bring to light certain aspects of online content distribution and the relationship between artists and audience. It's a matter of testing how useful the tip-jar model is in explaining recent trends in the media.

⊳ FOR CRITICAL INQUIRY

1. Consider how Stacy Yi sets up the context of issues in the opening paragraphs of her essay. How does she move from a personal anecdote to the central question of her essay?

2. Consider how Yi develops the tip-jar model in the essay. How does she integrate her sources to examine what the tip jar can and cannot explain? Pick one or two passages where she has effectively created an interplay of her sources and the tip-jar model. How does this interplay contribute to the essay overall? Are there other passages where she is less successful in working with her sources? Explain your answer.

3. Consider the ending of the essay. What is the final point Yi is making? Does it seem to flow logically from the discussion in the rest of the essay?

Research Paper in APA Format

Andy Mgwanna wrote this research paper in Introduction to Criminal Justice. As you read, consider how Andy establishes the purpose of the paper and how he uses his research as evidence.

The Prison Privatization Debate:

The Need for a New Focus

Andy Mgwanna

Warehouse State

November 20, 2011

Abstract

The dramatic increase in the privatization of prisons has sparked controversy about the ethics, economics, and administration of prisons-for-profit. This paper examines the arguments made for and against the privatization of prisons and prison services. Proponents argue that privatization provides low-cost, high-quality prisons, saving taxpayers money and generating profits. Opponents question the costs and quality of privately run prisons and argue that profits and incarceration are not compatible. Others, however, have suggested that the prisons-for-profit debate has reached an impasse and the terms of discussion about prison policy need to include a stronger emphasis on rehabilitation and recidivism.

In 1976, the state of Florida hired a private company to operate the Weaversville Intensive Treatment Unit for Juvenile Delinquents. In 1982, the state privatized a second facility, the Okeechobee School for Boys (Young, 2006, p. 12). Several years later, federal, state, and local governments began privatizing a range of prison services and entire correctional facilities in order to cut costs and accommodate a rapidly expanding number of inmates. This recent wave of privatization in corrections can mean several things. First, it can mean that private companies contract with local, state, and federal governments to provide such services in public prisons as medical care, counseling, mental health, and drug treatment, education and vocational training, laundry and food services, and staff training. Second, privatization can mean that prison labor is contracted out to private companies such as Chevron, Victoria Secret, and Best Western who hire prisoners to enter data, make products, and take telephone reservations (Davis, 2003, p. 102).

Third, privatization can mean that a private company owns and operates a correctional facility as a for-profit enterprise.

Almost as soon as the ink from these new contracts had dried, a heated debate about the ethics, economics, and administration of prisons-for-profit erupted. In this paper, I examine the debate about privatization of prisons and prison services in order to identify the issues it raises for prison policy. First I provide some background on privatization. Second, I investigate the arguments for private prisons and the arguments against private prisons. Finally, I suggest that the debate about privatization has reached an impasse and needs to be broadened to include a stronger emphasis on rehabilitation and recidivism.

Background on the Privatization of Prisons and Prison Services

Privatization dates back to the mid-1800s when private companies were given contracts to run Louisiana's first prison, Auburn Prison, Sing Sing in New York, and San Quentin in California. As the use of private companies to run jails and prisons increased, a number of groups protested. Businesses and labor advocates objected to the free labor many private prisons contracted out because it was unfair competition. Reformers cited whippings, malnourishment, overwork, and overcrowding as evidence of prisoner abuses in private facilities. By the end of the nineteenth century, states had largely stopped using private companies and assumed full management of correctional facilities themselves (Young, 2006).

By the mid 1980s, however, federal, state, and local governments once again were allowing private companies to run their jails, prisons, and detention centers. Smith (2007) attributes this decision to the intersection of the "ideological imperatives of the free market; the huge increase in the number of prisoners; and the concomitant increase in imprisonment costs" (p. 4). The American Federation of State, County, and Municipal Employees (AFSCME) (2000), the largest public service employees union in the country, which counts prison employees among its members, says that the trend of privatization at the end of the twentieth century can be attributed to Thomas Beasley, the Tennessee Republican Party chairman, who founded the Corrections Corporation of America (CCA) in 1983, with help from Jack Massy, who started Kentucky Fried Chicken. Since the CCA's inception and with help from Wall Street firms such as Goldman Sachs and Merrill Lynch, the private prison industry has expanded dramatically in scope (Parenti 1999, p. 14).

Today private companies operate juvenile detention centers, county jails, work farms, state and federal prisons, and INS holding camps all over the United States. The Corrections Corporation is the largest private prison operator. In 2003, it managed 58,732 beds in 59 jails, detention centers, and prisons in 20 states and the District of Columbia. One third of CCA's revenue comes from the federal government, while the remaining two thirds come from state and local government. The CCA's largest clients are Wisconsin, Georgia, Texas, Tennessee, Florida, and Oklahoma. Although the CCA tried to operate facilities overseas, after a series of setbacks, it now works primarily in the United States. It is the sixth largest prison system in the United States with only Texas, California, the Federal Bureau of Prisons, New York, and Florida managing more prisoners (Smith, 2007, p. 9). The CCA owns 49% of U.S. prison beds under private operation, while Wackenhut Corrections, an offshoot of the Wackenhut Corporation, a private security and investigation firm founded by former FBI agent George Wackenhut, controls 21% (Lyon, 2007).

Arguments for Prison Privatization

Proponents of privatization present two main points when they argue that private companies can maintain low-cost and high-quality prisons and prison services while generating a profit for investors. First, they argue that private prisons offer significant savings over government-run prisons. Segal (2005) reviewed 23 articles by government officials and academics and found that private prisons are, on average, 10 to 15% cheaper than government prisons. Taxpayers are also saved the expenses and risk of building new facilities. Tabarrok (2004) says private prisons offer 15 to 25% savings on construction and 10 to 15% on administration. These savings, in turn, pressure public prisons to lower their costs. He writes:

States with a greater share of prisoners in private prisons have lower costs of housing public prisoners. Perhaps more tellingly, from 1999 through 2001, states without any private prisons saw per-prisoner costs increase by 18.9 percent, but in states where the public prisons competed with private prisons, cost increases were much lower, only 8.1 percent. (p. 6)

Another economic reason supporters offer for privatization is that although most prisoners come from urban areas, many new prisons are located in rural areas, providing jobs where there are few employment opportunities (Huling, 2002, p. 98). And finally, according to Joel (2004), wages earned by staff in private prisons are equal to or higher than those earned in public prisons (p. 5).

Second, proponents of privatization point to the high quality of private prisons. Segal (2005) cites four reasons why quality in private prisons matches or exceeds the quality in public prisons. First, the results of six independent studies, which focused specifically on quality, indicate that private prisons are equal to if not better than government prisons. Second, 44% of private prisons have been accredited by the American Correctional Association, which provides standards for quality, management, and maintenance, while only 10% of government prisons have been accredited (see fig. 1). Third, almost all contracts with private prisons are renewed. Fourth, no private facilities have been placed under court order for issues of quality.

Others argue that high standards within private prisons are likely to be maintained and even improved upon as more companies enter the market. Frequent rebidding will likely force companies to maintain high quality in order to retain contracts. To preempt the argument that the economic goals of running a prison for profit conflict with the operational objectives, which is providing services, Joel (2004) writes:

The contracting process significantly reduces such dangers. Contractors must abide by state laws, regulations, and policies and are held accountable for fulfilling these obligations. If the state is dissatisfied, it can refuse to renew the contract. Some states, such as New Mexico and Tennessee, also include termination clauses within contracts in the event a contractor provides inadequate services. In addition, contractors are watched very closely by the courts, the

Prison Privatization Debate 5

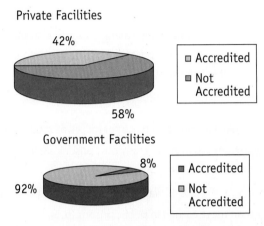

Private Facilities

42%

- Accredited
- Not Accredited

58%

Government Facilities

8%

- Accredited
- Not Accredited

92%

Fig. 1   Facilities with ACA accreditation, from "Prison Privatization and the Use of Incarceration."

press, civil-rights groups, and prison-reform groups. Such close scrutiny forces the contractor to maintain adequate standards. (p. 5)

Arguments Against Prison Privatization

Those who oppose prison privatizations are a heterogeneous group, and they oppose privatization for several reasons: ethical, financial, and administrative. Those who oppose prison privatization on ethical grounds argue that punishment and profit are not compatible (Smith, 2007). Fundamentally the goal of for-profit corporations is to make as much money as possible, and in the case of prisons, profits depend on people being incarcerated. Accordingly, AFSCE (2000) objects to privatization on the grounds that it allows private companies to profit from crime. Along similar lines, Mattera, Khan, and Nathan (2003) note that the "existence of an industry based on incarceration for profit creates a commercial incentive in favor of government policies that keep more people behind bars for longer periods of time" (p. 15).

Second, opponents assert that private prisons do not save money. AFSCME (2000) asserts that there is no indication that private prisons demonstrate cost savings, while The Sentencing Project (2004) found little evidence that prison privatization resulted in significant public savings. An earlier study by the General Accounting

Office (GAO) in 1996, which found that private and public correctional facilities cost the same amount of money (Parenti, 1999, p. 154). In addition, the finances of private prisons are often in disarray. Mattera, Khan, and Nathan (2003) point out that CCA nearly went bankrupt in the 1990s after borrowing $1 billion to build speculative prisons and undergoing a troubled corporate restructuring. In 2000, the CCA's chief executives lost his job, and the company settled a series of lawsuits from shareholders to the tune of $120 million. CCA today "is weighed down by debt. It also continues to face weak demand for new private prisons at the state and local level" (Mattera, Khan, and Nathan, 2003, p. 21). Wackenhut has not fared much better. The corporation has been charged with squeezing money out of rehabilitation programs, counseling, and literacy courses. In 1995, for example, investigators accused Wackenhut of diverting almost three quarters of a million dollars from a drug treatment program in a Texas facility. Opponents also argue that whatever money may be saved in private prisons is the result of the low wages and substandard benefits staff are given (AFSCME, 2000). In discussing the CCA, Mattera, Khan, and Nathan (2003) write:

> The CCA has sought to depress its labor costs by keeping wages low and by denying its employees traditional (defined-benefit) pension plans. There have been reports of understaffing and high rates of turnover at some of its facilities. For example, the annual turnover rates at several CCA facilities in Tennessee have been more than 60 percent. (p. 16)

Third, opponents of private prison facilities charge that CCA and other private companies poorly manage their facilities, allowing prisoner abuse, violence, medical maltreatment, and escapes (Lock Up Private Prisons, 1999). Mattera, Khan, and Nathan (2003) found that CCA routinely failed to give prisoners adequate medical care, create an environment where inmates were safe from harm—both from other prisoners and from correctional staff—and control the drug activities of both prisoners and CCA employees. Further, as Parenti (1999) shows, in a 15-month period, the privately-operated Northeast Ohio Correctional Center in Youngstown, Ohio experienced six escapes, 44 assaults, 16 stabbings, and two murders (p. 234). At the same time, prisoners have protested and rioted against substandard conditions. In 1995, North

Carolinian prisoners, who were living in overcrowded conditions in a Tennessee prison, burnt their dorms in a several-hour riot (Parenti, 1999, p. 173).

Sexual abuse has been one of the chief allegations against Wackenhut. In 1999, Wackenhut lost a $12 million a year contract with Texas after several correctional officers were indicted for having sexual relations with female prisoners. Wackenhut fired five guards in a work-release facility in Fort Lauderdale, Florida, after learning they were having sex with inmates. After the U.S. Justice Department found Wackenhut subjected inmates to "excessive abuse and neglect," the state of Louisiana reassumed operations of a juvenile prison (The Sentencing Project 2004).

CCA and other private prison companies have been plagued by escapes and inadvertent releases of violent inmates. Greene (2002) writes that 37 inmates escaped custody from private prisons in 1999 alone (p. 97). Mattera, Khan, and Nathan (2003) estimate that at least a dozen inmates have been mistakenly released from custody (p. 25). In some situations, the mistakes are administrative. For example, after one month of operation, an employee at the David L. Moss Criminal Justice Center permitted an inmate to post bond after registering the wrong offense. But in other situations, CCA employees have been fooled by inmates passing as other prisoners, who are eligible for release. Some prisoners are never recaptured. At the same time, important security positions in a facility in Georgia went unfilled for 8-hour shifts 20 times in one month (Lock Up Private Prisons, 1999).

After chronicling dozens of incidents of abuse, violence, and murder in private prisons, Greene (2002) summarizes the case of opponents of prison privatization:

> Industry executives will tell you that the prison management disasters catalogued here are just isolated events, confined to a handful of underperforming facilities. But evidence is mounting that a number of key structural deficiencies—high staff turnover, defective classification and security procedures, inadequate program services —are found in many private prisons. (p. 112)

Conclusion: A New Focus?

The debate between supporters and opponents of private prisons and the privatization of prison services has reached a stalemate. Supporters argue that

Prison Privatization Debate 8

well-documented studies of financial savings demonstrate the logic of the market and the superiority of privatization. Opponents argue that privatization amounts to an abdication of government responsibility that has produced systematic abuses. As we have seen, the sides in the debate are deeply divided by their assumptions and beliefs. A problem with this impasse, as O'Brien (2006) suggests, is that the key issues of rehabilitation and recidivism, which have significant implications for the cost of the prison industrial complex, have been lost in a polarized debate. O'Brien (2006) argues that rather than becoming bogged down in the pros and cons of privatization, we should focus on incentives to both private and public prisons to prevent recidivism:

> If private competition can find the keys to making young offenders become productive citizens rather than career criminals, government will save far more money than the typical 10 to 25 percent savings now found with privatization. Two out of three released convicts are now rearrested. Preventing a young offender from coming back for 20 years can save $400,000 per head (at $20,000 per year in incarceration expenses).

O'Brien (2006) helps to redefine the debate about privatization by shifting the measure of success from short-term financial savings to the long-term outcomes of prisoners. This should please opponents of privatization because it makes rehabilitation, instead of profits, the central function of the prison system. At the same time, such a redefinition should please supporters of privatization because it does not give up on private competition but rather challenges for-profit prisons to develop guidelines and programs that promote rehabilitation and thereby reduce long-term recidivism. In any case, by focusing on outcomes rather than ownership, O'Brien (2006) offers at least a starting point to move beyond the current impasse.

References

American Federation of State, County and Municipal Employees (2000). The evidence is clear, crime shouldn't pay. Retrieved from http://www.afscme.org/private/evidtc.htm

Davis, A.Y. (2003). *Are prisons obsolete?* New York: Seven Stories.

Greene, J.A. (2002). Entrepreneurial corrections: Incarceration as a business. In M. Mauer and M. Chesney-Lind (Eds.). *Invisible punishment: The collateral consequences of mass imprisonment* (pp. 95–113). New York: New York Press.

Huling, T. (2002). Building a prison economy in a rural area. In M. Mauer and M. Chesney-Lind (Eds.), *Invisible punishment: The collateral consequences of mass imprisonment* (pp. 197–213). New York: New York Press.

Joel, D. (2004, May 24). A guide to prison privatization. The Heritage Foundation. Retrieved from http://www.heritage.org/Research/Crime/BG650.cfm

Lock up private prisons: Chronic problems demonstrate why incarceration should be left to the state. (1999, October 6). *The Atlanta Constitution* 6 Oct. 1999. Retrieved from http://lexis-nexis.com

Lyon, J. (2007, February 3). Open debate needed over private sector impact on prison system. *The Financial Times*. Retrieved from http://lexis-nexis.com

Mattera, P., Khan, M., & Nathan, S. (2003). Corrections corporation of America: A critical look at its first twenty years. *A report by the grassroots/Leadership, the corporate research project of good jobs first, and prison privatisation international*. Retrieved from www.soros.org/initiatives/justice/articles_publications/cca_20 _years_20031201/CCA_Report.pdf

O'Brien, T. (2006, January 26) Letter to the editor. *The Washington Post*. Retrieved from http://lexis-nexis.com

Parenti, C. (1999). *Lockdown America: Police and prisons in the age of crisis*. New York: Verso.

Segal, G. (2002). Corporate corrections? Frequently asked questions about prison privatization. The Reason Foundation. Retrieved from http://www.reason.org /corrections/faq_private_prisons.shtml

Sentencing Project (2004). *Prison privatization and the use of incarceration*. Retrieved from http://www.sentencingproject.org/pdfs/1053.pdf

Smith, P. (2007). Private prisons: Profits of crime. *Covert Action Quarterly*. Retrieved from http://mediafilter.org/caq/Prison.html

Tabarrok, A. (2004, November 23). Private prisons have public benefits. *Pasadena Star News*. Retrieved from http://lexis-nexis.com

Young, M. T. (2006, January 27). Prison privatization: Possibilities and approaches to the privatization of prisoner security and services. *Criminal Justice Working Papers*. Retrieved from www.law.stanford.edu/programs/academic /criminaljustice/workingpapers/MTafollaYoung_05.pdf

Analysis: Finding a Place in a Debate

Andy Mgwanna establishes the purpose of his research paper at the end of the second paragraph, when he says that he will (1) give background information on prison privatization, (2) analyze the positions for and against, and (3) explain how the debate has reached an impasse. Notice how the paper builds toward the conclusion it has already anticipated in the introductory section.

¶1–2: Introduction

Establishes trend toward privatization

Defines privatization

Explains purpose of the paper

¶3–7: Background on the Privatization of Prisons and Prison Services

Provides reasons for the emergence of privatization

Explains the scope of privatization

¶8–10: Arguments for Prison Privatization

Economic

Quality

¶11–16: Arguments Against Prison Privatization

Ethical

Economic

Administrative

¶17–18: Conclusion: A New Focus?

Concludes debate has reached an impasse

Suggests a way to refocus

As you can see, one of the important features of this paper is that it does not simply describe the debate about privatization but presents a position on it. Readers may sense that the writer sympathizes with one side in the debate. Opponents of privatization, after all, get twice the space as supporters. However, Mgwanna's main point is that the pro–con debate itself has reached an impasse and that the terms of the debate need to be changed. And in this way, he goes beyond merely reporting research findings to draw an arguable conclusion about the prison privatization debate.

⇨ FOR CRITICAL INQUIRY

1. A question readers are entitled to ask about a research paper is whether its conclusions are justified by the evidence presented. Explain the conclusion Andy Mgwanna reaches at the end of the paper. Consider whether the background section and analysis of the privatization debate provide adequate grounds to draw such a conclusion. When you first read the conclusion, did Mgwanna's position seem adequately prepared for?

2. One feature of this paper is that it promises to give a balanced account of the privatization debate. Consider how the writer goes about that in the sections for and against prison privatization. Does the analysis of the debate seem to be a fair and accurate one? Explain your answer by pointing to particular passages in the two sections.

3. How does Mgwanna use his sources? Pick passages in the paper to analyze what the writer is seeking to accomplish by citing sources from his research. Try to identify at least three distinct purposes his sources are meant to serve.

CHECKLIST FOR MLA AND APA STYLE

The two main styles of citation and manuscript preparation in academic research were developed by the Modern Language Association (MLA) and the American Psychological Association (APA). You can find details in Chapter 14, "Working with Sources," about using each style to set up in-text citations and Works Cited or References pages. Here is information about manuscript preparation.

Features Common to Both MLA and APA Style

▶ Manuscript should be double-spaced, including block quotations and Works Cited or References pages. Do not add extra spacing.

▶ Format a one-inch margin all around—top and bottom, left and right.

▶ Indent five spaces to begin a paragraph.

▶ Use ragged right margins.

▶ Don't end the line at the bottom of a page with a hyphen.

▶ Number pages consecutively, including Works Cited or References pages.

Special Features Called for by MLA Style

▶ Unless your teacher tells you to, do not include a separate cover sheet. Type the following information, double-spaced, at the top left corner of the manuscript, in this order: your name, your professor's name, course number, and date. Double-space and center the title of your paper. Follow conventional rules of capitalizing words in a title. Don't use quotation marks, italics, boldface, underlining, all capitals, or showy fonts. Double-space and begin the text.

▶ Insert page numbers in the upper right corner, flush with the right margin, one-half inch from the top of the page. Precede the page number with your last name. Begin the text one inch from the top.

▶ Begin your bibliography on a separate page, titled "Works Cited." Center the title one inch from the top, without any quotation marks, underlining, boldface, or italics. Include in the Works Cited only those works you have cited in the text of the paper. It is not a comprehensive bibliography (you may have used other works which are not cited).

Special Features Called for by APA Style

▶ Unless your teacher directs otherwise, use a separate cover page. Center your title approximately one-third from the top of the page. Type the title double-spaced if it has more than one line. Follow usual capitalization conventions. Don't use all caps, boldface, quotation marks, underlining, or italics. Double-space and type your name. Double-space again and type the course number, and then, following another double space, type the date.

▶ On the page immediately following the cover sheet, include a one-paragraph "Abstract" of no more than 120 words that summarizes the content of your paper.

▶ Begin the text on the third page. Don't repeat the title. Number all the pages, beginning with the cover sheet as page 1 and the Abstract as page 2. Type a running head (the first two or three words of the title) before the page number.

▶ APA style research papers are much more likely than MLA style papers to use section headings. Some research papers use the conventional headings—"Introduction," "Methods," "Results," and "Discussion"—but others use headings based on the content of the paper.

▶ Begin your References section on a separate page, following the text. Center the word "References" one inch from the top, without any underlining, italics, quotes, boldface, or other special treatment.

MULTIMODAL COMPOSITION

Magazine Article: Michael E. Crouch, "Lost in a Smog"

Magazine articles rely on research but present it in ways that differ from academic writing. Michael E. Crouch wrote "Lost in a Smog" for a sophomore-level science writing class, using the audience, writing style, and page layout of *Scientific American* to design this article. It provides a good example to investigate the differences and similarities between magazine and academic writing.

Bettman/Corbis

Lost in a SMOG

By Michael E. Crouch

TRAFALGAR SQUARE [above] thickly shrouded in the Great Smog of 1952. Similarly, the Canary Wharf skyline [right] obscured by a blue cloud of ozone during the heat wave of summer 2003. Even 50 years after the environmental disaster, London's skies are susceptible to choking smogs that pose serious health threats to its citizens.

The nights come on fast during a London December, but when the sun was not visible by midday on December 6, 1952, something was obviously wrong. This was no solar eclipse; the combination of a harsh cold front and a city's dependency on coal produced the greatest peace-time disaster in London's long history: a cloud of thick, impenetrable pollution that covered the city and everything within a 20-mile radius for three days.

Provoked by a particularly harsh winter, a large portion of London's 8.3 million citizens fired up their coal stoves and hid away in the warmth of their homes to avoid the bitter cold. Their reaction to the chilly weather was intuitive; the unfortunate outcome was not. Millions of chimneys unleashed sooty, sulphurous smoke, a by-product of coal-burning, into the atmosphere. A weak winter sun, the cold front, and low winds gave the smoke nowhere to go. A well-intentioned population had no idea about the disaster they were in the process of unleashing.

When the Londoners emerged, the sight was – well, there was no sight. Visibility had dropped to near zero, and the air was thick with acrid coal smoke. The sun could scarcely penetrate the massive cloud of haze, a condition with which Londoners were all too familiar. So frequent were the hazes that in 1905, Dr. HA Des Vouex created the term 'smog,' a word combined of 'smoke' and 'fog,' two of London's most common wintertime occurrences. Most smogs proved only an inconvenience, and a scant few even approached the death tolls seen in 1952. The Great Smog, however, was suffocating, and for a few harrowing days, London found itself completely enveloped in its pollutants.

When the smog had cleared on December 9, the people of London saw more than they were ready to. The death toll was disturbingly high: nearly 4,000 Londoners had succumbed to the elements of the deadly poison and its after-effects from December 5 until Christmas. In one week alone, 4,703 people met their ends, though in truth, not all of those who died that week expired because of the smog. In 1951, the number of Londoners who had died in the same time span equaled 1,852 people, mean-

Michael Fresco/Rex USA

ing that the death toll was up by more than 150% in 1952. The smog-related deaths did not cease with the exit of the cloud. Two recent publications in *Environmental Health Perspectives*, one by Michelle L. Bell and Devra Lee Davis and the other from Andrew Hunt and a team of researchers, suggest that lingering effects of the smog killed more than 8,000 Londoners within the next year. In all, they contend the Great Smog claimed approximately 12,000 lives.

What bearing does this have on the lives of 8 million Londoners today? A trio of Clean Air Acts, the first of which the British government passed in 1956 as a response to the Great Smog of 1952, has insured that London's skies are free from the excess sulfur dioxide (SO_2) and particulate matter that accompanied coal burning. The three laws instituted smokeless zones around London – effectively stopping the use of coal domestically – and forced industries to utilize large smoke stacks so that pollution would be released higher in the air and more easily dispersed by the wind. Furthermore, coal itself – replaced by cleaner burning fuels – is no longer such a popular source of heat and energy in the famed city. Knowing all this, one might be tempted to write off disasters like the Great Smog and insist that they cannot happen today. Doing so, however, would be a grave mistake.

Today coal-burning chimneys pollute the skies above London much less frequently, but motor-vehicle emissions pump out air toxins that are just as harmful, if not worse. Millions of cars and buses add to a wealth of air pollution, much of which is nearly invisible. Coal smoke contributed mainly sulfur dioxide (SO_2) and particulate matter (PM) to the atmosphere; motor vehicles pump out carbon monoxide (CO), nitrogen dioxide (NO_2), and PM. This deadly mix, a poisonous cocktail that can lead to the creation of harmful ground-level ozone (O_3), kills thousands of Londoners prematurely every year. To say that skies above London are in the clear just because they are seldom overcast with a sickening mixture of smoke and fog is to ignore the fact that the city, and much of the rest of the world, has a lot to learn about air pollution.

Microscopic Killers

THESE DAYS, it is widely understood that inhaling smog or smoke is a health risk, yet few actually understand why this is. Still fewer even know what smog is, whether it is the smog that enveloped London in 1952 or the smog that we are more familiar with in the 21st century. Understanding these facts is an important step in learning that modern air pollution, too, presents a serious threat.

Smogs that killed prior to 1952 were not without precedence in London, but most posed smaller health risks

The days of oppressive killer smogs are gone, but pollution lingers on in a new form

than the Great Smog. Londoners died with great frequency during the smogs of December 1813, January 1880, February 1882, December 1891, December 1892 (1,000 dead), and November 1948 (700-800 dead). Smogs continued to plague London even after 1952 and the passage of the first Clean Air Act, which created for the first time in London smokeless zones where only clean fuels could be burned. The last large-scale smog occurred in 1962 and claimed 750 lives. Inferring from these disasters, it seems simple to think polluted air could kill, but how does it do so?

Let us look to 1952 for an example. Precipitating the disaster, fog formed. On December 5, the air near the ground was thick with moisture, and the ground itself was cool. The two conditions together caused condensation, and all the water vapor that formed settled onto unseen dust particles that always inhabit the air, thus creating the relatively harmless condition of fog. The naturally occurring fog trapped in its midst all the coal smoke released from countless London chimneys. Aided by the winter sun, which could neither warm the air enough to get it moving nor penetrate the smog to shed light on the dismal situation, the pollution became even thicker between December 6 and December 8. Visibility was at times only a few meters; at others, pedestrians could not even see their feet. The air, thick and humid, was an irritant to both the eyes and respiratory systems of Londoners.

Coal smoke fills the air with acids containing free ions of hydrogen. These ions can create acid rain that is strong enough to kill plants. Today one can still see the remnants of the acidic smogs of London on the city's older buildings, a shade darker than they were when the architects of the past built them.

The unpleasant smog reeked havoc on the throats and lungs of Londoners. In humans, the acid irritates the throat and bronchial tubes, causing them to become inflamed and produce excess mucus. Thusly, smog adversely affects those with existing lung and heart conditions. Cases of asthma, pneumonia, bronchitis, and tuberculosis all flare up under these conditions. As one would imagine, the dead in London were comprised mostly of the people afflicted with these conditions, the elderly, and the very young. The smog also hit hard those with heart disease. Inhaling mostly coal smoke limited the amount of oxygen they took into their systems, and many died because of low levels of the compound in their blood.

Several new studies suggest that the Great Smog also affected the long-term health of those who lived through it. Along with releasing sulfur dioxide, coal smoke burns off small, sooty particles covered in moisture, called PM. Michelle L. Bell of Johns Hopkins Bloomberg School of Public Heath and Devra Lee Davis, acclaimed author and a researcher at Carnegie Mellon University, suggest that "the true scope and scale of the health effects linked with London's lethal smog extended over a longer period than originally estimated." The team, which waded through and analyzed piles of 50-year-old data to come to its conclusions, contends that illnesses in January and February of 1953 had a strong correlation to both the sulfur dioxide and PM levels during the Great Smog. Bell and Davis believe this correlation means that the excess deaths were due to a lagged effect of exposure to PM.

Picking up where Bell and Davis' research left off, Andrew Hunt and a team of researchers from the State University of New York Upstate Medical University and the Royal London Hospital studied archived lung tissues from 16 Londoners who perished in the Great Smog in order to determine how PM affected their deaths. The team found high concentrations of PM in the tissue samples. Particu-

Overview/Troubling Pollutants

- Recent reviews of London's Great of Smog of 1952 indicate that particulate matter (PM) can have both severe short and long-term effects on the human cardiac and respiratory systems.
- Coal smoke is no longer the most dangerous toxin that occupies London's air. Motor vehicles are the main source of pollution in the modern day capital. Their toxins do as much, if not more, harm to humans as coal smoke does.
- Although PM and sulfur dioxide levels in London are lower than they were 50 years ago, carbon monoxide, nitrogen dioxide, and ground-level ozone levels are now much higher. It is estimated that, along with PM, these three chemical compounds cause 1,600 to 2,000 Londoners to die prematurely every year.

CHANGE OF SEASONS

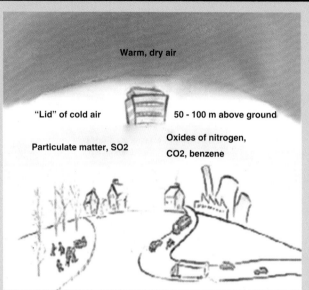

Warm, dry air

"Lid" of cold air   50 - 100 m above ground

Particulate matter, SO2   Oxides of nitrogen, CO2, benzene

Summer Smog (Below)

While London must now endure summer smogs, or photochemical smogs, they are not alone in such an experience. Virtually every urban area in the world has to deal with this sort of pollution thanks to the advent and proliferation of the automobile.

Summer smogs, unlike their winter counterparts, contain very little smoke, so the term smog is somewhat misleading. However, the mixture of pollutants in summer smogs varies greatly; seven ingredients make up a summer smog: ozone, carbon monoxide, nitrogen dioxide, hydrocarbons, lead, PM and sulfur dioxide. Hydrocarbons – of which VOC are a subgroup – react with the sun's solar energy and nitrogen dioxide to produce ozone. As is the case in the winter, the formation of smog is aided by low winds. When the sun is not visible, summer smog is not a problem.

Winter Smog (Above)

London particulars, another phrase for the city's frequently occurring smogs, are a part of the mystique of London, but they are by no means particular to the capital city. Donora, Pennsylvania, saw 20 of its residents die and nearly half of its population of 14,000 became ill when a smog settled overhead in October 1948. In December 1930, over 60 residents of the Meuse Valley in Belgium succumbed to a five-day smog.

How did all these disasters occur? They begin with the arrival of an anticyclone, a weather system marked by low wind speeds and moist air near ground level. Colder air remains further up in the atmosphere while warmer air stays near the ground, allowing the cooler earth to cause condensation-forming fog. Any pollutants released into the air mingle with the fog, trapped in place by the anticyclone's high pressure. Thick smog then slowly poisons anyone unfortunate enough to be lost amidst its cloudy form.

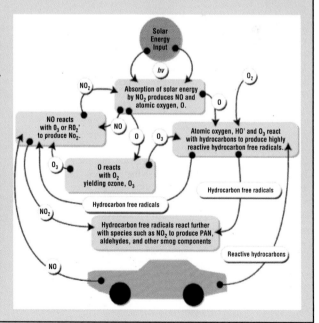

Solar Energy Input

hv

NO_2

O_2

Absorption of solar energy by NO_2 produces NO and atomic oxygen, O.

O

NO reacts with O_3 or RO_2' to produce No_2.

NO

O O_3

Atomic oxygen, HO' and O_3 react with hydrocarbons to produce highly reactive hydrocarbon free radicals.

O_3

O reacts with O_2 yielding ozone, O_3

Hydrocarbon free radicals

NO_2

Hydrocarbon free radicals

Hydrocarbon free radicals react further with species such as NO_2 to produce PAN, aldehydes, and other smog components

Reactive hydrocarbons

NO

COVER-UPS AND BLUNDERS

ONLY AFTER A GREAT push from the public and the media did the British government decide to take action to curb more smog disasters. Even then, the official reaction was lukewarm at best. "Today everybody

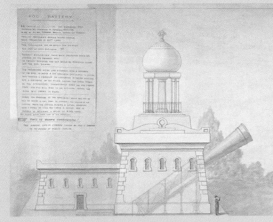

Guildhall Library, London

A PROPOSAL for an air cannon that would blast away London's pollution woes.

expects the government to solve every problem. It is a symptom of the welfare state. For some reason or another 'smog' has captured the imagination of the press and people…. Ridiculous as it appears, I suggest we form a committee. We cannot do very much, but we can be seen to be very busy, and that's half the battle nowadays," wrote Harold Macmillan, then Minister of Housing, in a secret memo shortly after the Great Smog of 1952. Unfortunately, his attitude was typical of most government officials of the time.

England had mounted a war debt of over £31 billion, and the government was hesitant to add new expenditures to its budget. Britain took drastic measures, such as the selling of horsemeat for food, to overcome its deficit. Most shocking, however, is that the country sold all its cleaner-burning coal to foreign industries in order to make a larger profit. Those inside the country received the leftovers: sooty coal whose smoke filled the London sky for five days in 1952.

Actions originally taken by the government to battle the fog were wholly ineffective. The National Health Service distributed over three

late matter inhabited two different areas of the lung tissues: those associated with short-term storage (lung airways) and those associated with long-term storage (situated around the vessels and bronchioles of the lung and in the lymph nodes). Carbonaceous PM, synonymous with the combustion of coal and diesel fuel, was found in both retention compartments, suggesting that the people of London were not only hit hard by the Great Smog, but they were exposed to these kinds of PM over long periods of time.

Neither group purports to know exactly how PM causes deaths. A plethora of studies since the early 1990s, however, have tried to establish the link. Among the many possibilities are that PM causes decreased red blood-cell counts, increased blood viscosity, heart rate changes, increased arrhythmias, and increased defibril-

lator discharges. None of these hypotheses have been established. All that is known is that in smog incidents, elevated PM concentration is highly correlated with increased death rates. Understanding of the PM problem is crucial to populated cities where pollution levels are much higher than those found here in America.

A New Danger

THANKS TO the first Clean Air Act, homes in London can no longer burn coal as a means to generate heat. Londoners instead turned to the cleaner systems of electric and gas-powered heating. Thus, the days of oppressive killer smogs are gone, but pollution lingers in a new form. The vehicles that Londoners rely on are slowly poisoning the city's air.

Diesel fuel, when burned, gives off nearly the same carbonaceous PM that coal burning does. The trucks, buses, and taxis that rely on this fuel spit out cancer-causing chemicals, such as benzo-a-pyrenes, while they transport citizens and goods about the city.

These vehicles and others also subject the city to carbon monoxide. Carbon monoxide is undetectable by humans, being both colorless

THE AUTHOR

MICHAEL E. CROUCH is in his final year of study at Worcester Polytechnic Institute in Massachusetts, where he majors in Technical, Scientific, and Professional Communication. This article is a portion of his MQP, the WPI senior project, which he is completing abroad in the city of London. Crouch has written about health communication on the Internet and researched ancient Near Eastern artifacts for the Higgins Armory Museum of Worcester, MA.

million face masks made of gauze to the people of London. The masks did nothing to prevent the harmful effects of the smog, something Health Minister Iain Macleod knew even before the NHS gave them out. One American tobacco company offered to donate to the British government 100,000 masks that employed a filtering technique designed for cigarettes. The ministers refused the offer in order to curb advertising.

London had a history of eccentric fixes to its smog problem. A plan from 1925 proposed that several giant air cannons be placed around the city. When smog rolled in, the cannons would fire several blasts of powerful winds until the acrid haze was dispersed. Nothing like this was ever constructed. London post-1952 had no shortage of these unique "solutions." Anti-fog lozenges gave the consumer a false sense of security against the poisonous air. Fog flares, designed to guide buses through the premature darkness that smogs brought during the day, proved that the government had no hope – or perhaps no intention – of preventing more deadly clouds of pollution.

When none of these solutions proved helpful, government officials, eager to take the onus off themselves, explained that 5,655 of the deaths which occurred in the months following the Great Smog were due to a bout of influenza. This explanation was widely accepted until 2001, when Michelle Bell and Devra L. Davis published their study of the fatalities. In order for the number of reported influenza deaths to fit the average number of people who succumb to the disease (0.2%), almost one in every three Londoners would have to have contracted the illness. There is simply no evidence that such a widespread epidemic occurred.

There is no telling whether the British government could have saved lives if they had taken action against London's pollution problems sooner than it did. Four major smog events took place between 1956 and 1962, killing another 2,700 people. Not until 1956 did the Clean Air Act put an end to coal burning in homes and some industrial settings. Perhaps legislation in 1952 could have prevented some of these later disasters; perhaps not. What is clear is that a government must tackle the issue of pollution and environmental health in order to better the lives of its citizens.

and odorless. When inhaled, the gas attaches itself to human red blood cells, preventing the distribution of carbon monoxide and oxygen to and from the lungs. A large amount of carbon monoxide can lead to asphyxiation, the consequence of sitting in an idling car without proper ventilation for too long.

Another byproduct of fuel combustion, nitrogen dioxide is visible as reddish-brown gas and has a pungent and irritating acrid odor. Nitrogen dioxide, like coal smoke, is associated with acid rain. In humans, it can aggravate cases of asthma and other lung conditions.

Though it is directly attributed to automobiles, ground-level ozone is not emitted from any vehicle. Instead, nitrogen dioxide reacts with Volatile Organic Compounds (VOC) – organic chemicals commonly found in household cleaners and some fuels – and sunlight to form the gas, which in its pure form is bluish and has a penetrating odor. Studies have shown ozone at ground level to be harmful to those with lung ailments, and it has the ability to damage crops and forests. Some believe it also causes asthma.

The combination of these three gases and PM makes air hazardous to breath and prematurely kills between 1,600 to 2,000 Londoners every year. Surges in the levels of these pollutants send people to hospitals with respiratory ailments in great numbers. This is no surprise as England's relaxed standards on motor vehicle emissions means that the country has higher concentrations of carbon monoxide, nitrogen dioxide, and ground-level ozone than the US and many countries in Europe.

London has begun to experience more smog in the summertime. Increased global warming and automobile emissions are combining to make summers unbearable on the historically cold island. The summer of 2003 saw the first ever temperatures above 100° F in England. The season's harsh sun not only caused heat exhaustion, but also increased ozone levels in the air, creating a deadly trio of extreme heat, humidity, and smog. An estimated 2,045 people died from exposure to all three. Clearly, problems with pollution are not over for England, and much still needs addressing.

A Grim Future

IF LONDONERS have anything to look forward to in the next century, it is that their winters will likely become warmer, and the feared smogs that accompany the season will be a thing of the past. That may be where the hope ends, though. Projections suggest that global warming will increase summertime temperatures, too. High temperatures could consistently reach 100° F and above. Summer smogs, the air full of ozone, would be the new concern for Londoners.

Other predictions foretell a future much less desirable. A group of scientists who make up the Intergovernmental Panel on Climate Change (IPCC) have predicted that the combination of global warming and pollution will prove so overwhelming by the year 2100 that the entire northern hemisphere will be enveloped in an impenetrable smog. Summon up what it would be like to live the title to Devra Davis' acclaimed book, *When Smoke Ran Like Water*. Much of the population would have to escape to the southern hemisphere, as the north would no longer be hospitable to animals or plants.

This horrible scenario is, of course, only a prediction. Whether or not it will come to pass remains to be seen. The world has nearly ten decades to prevent or prepare for this outcome. In the meantime, most countries are moving forward with stricter air pollution regulations.

The search for a new fuel source to power automobiles is surging forward. London already has three hydrogen-powered buses in its fleet. With no carbon in their fuel source,

the buses produce much less pollution. Other buses in the city are being retrofitted with pollution filtering devices to bring down PM and nitrogen dioxide emissions.

Instead of pushing expensive cars with alternative fuel systems onto its citizens, London is trying to promote a better public transportation system. City officials also encourage Londoners to use their vehicles only when necessary, such as when going to work. The campaign has been successful; the last year has seen a 30 percent increase in the number of cyclists in the city.

Despite the many attempts to clean up London's historically polluted air, both the government and the public have much to do in order to prevent more smog disasters. If no one takes action on this issue, Londoners may want to start hoping that their government plans to join the US in occupying the moon within the next century because instead of premature darkness, their city could be experiencing perpetual darkness. SA

MORE TO EXPLORE

The Big Smoke: A History of Air Pollution in London since Medieval Times. Peter Brimblecombe. Methuen, 1987.

Toxicologic and Epidemiologic Clues from the Characterization of the 1952 London Smog Fine Particulate Matter in Archival Autopsy Lung Tissues. Andrew Hunt, Jerrold L. Abraham, Bret Judson, and Colin L. Berry in *Environmental Health Perspectives*, Vol. 111, No. 9, pages 1209-1214; July 2003.

When Smoke Ran Like Water: Tales of Environmental Deception and the Battle Against Pollution. Devra Lee Davis. Basic Books, 2002.

London Air Quality Network Homepage: **www.erg.kcl.ac.uk/london/asp/home.asp**

Analysis: Information Design

Research-based magazine articles, such as those that appear in *Scientific American, Natural History, Smithsonian,* and so on, tend to differ from academic research writing by relying much more extensively on the visual display of information. Notice how the page layout of Michael E. Crouch's "Lost in a Smog" employs photos with captions, old illustrations, diagrams, sidebars and information boxes, and a list of bulleted points. Notice that the magazine article also uses color in a way that contrasts with the black-and-white look of most academic writing, whether in scholarly journals or student papers.

⅀ FOR CRITICAL INQUIRY

1. How do the photos on the first page of Michael E. Crouch's "Lost in a Smog" help you visualize the topic he's writing about?

2. Crouch's article is divided into four sections. Describe the function each section seems intended to perform. Do you think the order of information works well?

3. What do the diagram "Change of Season," the sidebar "Cover-Ups and Blunders," and the "Overview" information box add to Crouch's presentation of information? Notice how they are colorized, using screens. What does this add to the information design?

4. Consider how Crouch handles his sources, by quotes and other references within the article and a "More to Explore" reading list at the end of the chapter. How does this compare to the handling of sources typical of MLA-style and APA-style research writing? How do these differences in citation express differences in audience and the relation between writers and readers?

THE RESEARCH PROCESS: AN OVERVIEW

In this section, we'll be following Amira Patel as she works on a research paper for her American immigration history course. First, we present an overview of the research process—to identify the main steps in responding to the call to write a research paper and some of the key tasks involved at each point.

▶ **Defining a research question:** Do preliminary research to get an overview of your topic. Start to focus your reading to develop a research question. Evaluate your research question and revise or modify it if necessary. Write a proposal to clarify the purpose of your research.

▶ **Finding sources:** Use your library's card catalog, indexes, bibliographies, and other databases to identify print and electronic sources. Browse sites on the Internet. Keep a working bibliography.

▶ **Evaluating sources:** Take notes. Photocopy sources. Assess the relevance and credibility of the sources. Look for assumptions and biases. Keep an open mind. Be prepared to revise or modify your own thinking in light of what you've read.

▶ **Making an argument:** Take into account all you have read. Determine where you stand in debates and controversies. Develop an argument that answers your research question.

▶ **Planning and drafting:** Develop a working outline of your paper. Start drafting. Reread sources and find additional information as needed. Revise or modify your outline if necessary.

Defining a Research Question

Research depends in part on knowing what you are looking for. This will depend, of course, on the research assignment. In some cases, the assignment will provide specific directions; in others, it will be open-ended. If you have questions about what the assignment is calling on you to do, make sure you consult with your instructor.

Here is the research assignment Amira Patel was given in her American immigration history course.

> The final writing assignment of this course is a term paper, 12 to 15 pages, that researches any topic of your interest in American immigration history, 1880 to present. You should begin by clearly defining your research question and writing a proposal. The paper should establish the importance of the problem you are researching and offer an interpretation. You should not simply report what happened or summarize what you have read. You are expected to read sources from the period you have chosen along with scholarly accounts.

Analyzing the Assignment

Analyzing the assignment means identifying what it is calling on you to do so that you can clarify your own purposes and determine how you will work with your sources. Some assignments provide the purpose for you—for example, to explain why or why not Willie Loman is a tragic hero in *Death of a Salesman*. In other cases, you'll have to figure out what you need to do and what your stance will be in relation to the context of issues, the sources, and your readers.

Here are some common ways that researchers position themselves:

▶ **To provide an overview of the current thinking of experts:** The purpose is largely informative—to report on what experts in the field think about an important issue. You might, for example, explain the current views of experts on the extinction of dinosaurs or report on the latest results of drug treatment of HIV-positive people.

▶ **To analyze the arguments in a controversy:** The purpose is to explain the positions people have taken in a current debate. This goes beyond just reporting on what the experts think, to analyzing how they differ and what their enabling assumptions are. You might, for example, analyze the positions experts have taken in regard to the prosecution of pregnant women for doing harm to their fetuses by drinking or taking drugs.

▶ **To position your own interpretation in relation to what others have said:** In this case, the purpose is not simply to explain how and why the experts differ but also to put forward your own analysis and interpretation. You might, for example, examine the causes of a resurgence of tuberculosis or the consequences of deregulation in the telecommunications industry, explaining how your thinking relates to the views of others—how and why it differs, how and why it shares common ground.

▶ **To take a stand on a controversy:** Here the emphasis is on the consequences of analysis and interpretation. You might argue, for example, that there should (or should not) be salary caps for companies that receive federal bailout funds. Or you could argue that the United States should (or should not) adopt more stringent limits on commercial fishing in the North Atlantic.

Following a Research Path: Analyzing the Assignment

Amira's First Reaction

This is exactly what I was afraid of. I hate these kind of open-ended writing assignments where the teacher doesn't give you any idea of what you should write about. I have no idea.

Amira's Reaction after Talking to Other Students

Okay, I have calmed down a little. I know I've got to get an angle on the assignment. What we were reading about American nativism and negative attitudes toward immigrants between 1880 and 1920 was interesting to me. Maybe I can find something in that. It seems like the important thing is to find a good research question and then explain how to answer it.

Preliminary Research

Sometimes you know right away what you want to research. In other cases, especially when the topic you're researching is new to you, you'll need to do some preliminary research to develop a research question. The following sources offer good places to start:

▶ **The Web:** Google can help you identify useful Web sites and other online sources. The quality and reliability of Wikipedia pages varies, but the best ones offer good background information and links.

▶ **Encyclopedias:** You can find an overview of many topics in general and specialized encyclopedias. See the list of general and specialized encyclopedias in Chapter 15.

▶ **Recent books:** Skim a recent book on your topic, looking in particular at its introduction, to see how the writer describes the issues the book addresses. Check the bibliography for further sources.

▶ **Recent articles:** Find a recent article in a scholarly journal or a popular magazine on your topic. Read the article, noticing what question or questions the writer poses and (in the case of academic articles) what sources are listed in the references.

▶ **Classmates, librarians, teaching assistants, faculty members:** Talk to other people who know something about your topic and the current questions people are asking about it. They can help you understand what the issues are and what sources you might look for.

Your preliminary research should give you ideas about the way others have approached the topic you're interested in, the kinds of questions they raise, and the differences of opinion and interpretation that divide them. This research should also help you identify other books and articles on the subject that you may want to consult.

Following a Research Path: Preliminary Research

Amira's Reflections on Getting Started

I thought I'd see what I could find about nativism on the Web and if that would give me any ideas about the paper.

I used "American Nativism" as a key word on Google, and after looking at a couple of sites that didn't seem that helpful, I found the Wikipedia page and a pdf "Cycles of Nativism in U.S. History." I read these and learned that nativism was wider than just 1880 to 1920. Both talked about the English Only movement as a kind of nativism that surfaced in the 1990s. Maybe I should use that as my topic. I think I'd rather do something about recent immigration.

Next, I typed in "English Only" and found a lot of information on English Only at James Crawford's "Language Policy Web Site and Emporium." Crawford seems to be a pretty prominent writer about language issues, and the site has articles and sections of his books. It also links to the website of the Institute of Language and Education Policy, which has more on English Only.

By this point, I was beginning to feel I had found a good topic in "English Only." I just wasn't sure what my research question should be.

Developing a Research Question

Once you've done some preliminary research, answer the following questions to refine your own sense of the research question you want to investigate:

1. What questions, issues, and problems appear repeatedly? Why do people think they are important?
2. Are there arguments, debates, or controversies that appear in what you've read? What positions have others taken? What seems to be at stake in these arguments? Do you find yourself siding with some people and disagreeing with others?

3. Is there some aspect of your topic that people don't seem to pay much attention to? Why do you think this is so? Are they neglecting questions or issues that could provide a good focus for research?

4. Given what you've read so far, what questions, issues, arguments, and controversies do you find most interesting? What, in your view, makes them important?

Following a Research Path: Defining the Research Question

Amira's Further Thoughts about a Research Question

It's interesting that so many Americans in the 1990s started thinking English should be the official language and that bilingual education should be banned. It's almost as though the whole English Only thing just came out of the blue, when organizations like US English started getting together and sponsoring legislation to make English the official language. But that can't be true. There's got to be some reason it happened in the 1990s, when so many new immigrants from Asia and Latin America were coming into the country.

Writing a Proposal

Some teachers ask students to write a proposal that defines the purpose of their research and indicates their research plan. Even if your teacher does not require a proposal, writing one can be a useful exercise to help you clarify your purpose.

A research proposal typically does three things:

1. Identifies the general topic or problem of the research and explains its significance.
2. Presents the specific issue and the research question you are addressing.
3. Sketches briefly the research plan, indicating how it will answer the research question.

Following a Research Path: Writing a Proposal

Amira's Research Proposal

American nativism goes back as far as the Alien and Sedition Acts of 1798 and anti-Catholic agitation in the 1830s and 1840s, directed toward recent immigrants from Ireland. According to many historians, the period of 1880 to 1920 witnessed virulent outbursts of nativism against the waves of new immigrants arriving in the United States. It seems that every time large numbers of people immigrate to this country, American nativism arises. For my research project, I am interested in American attitudes toward the new immigrants who have been coming to the United States since the 1990s, from Asia, Central and Latin America, and the Caribbean. I plan to focus specifically on the English Only movement as a response to this immigration. The question I'm research- ing asks why American nativism emerged in this form in the 1990s. My plan is to do some background research on earlier forms of nativism but to focus mainly on what the English Only movement is and what it believes. I will also research the conditions in the country in the 1990s so I can explain how this movement took root.

FINDING SOURCES

Once you have established a direction for your research project, the next step is in-depth research. You will find detailed information on a wide range of research sources in Chapter 15, "A Guide to Print, Electronic, and Other Sources." In this section, we look first at what the Web and the library have to offer you as a researcher. Then we follow Amira on her research path.

The Web and the Library: What They Offer Research Projects

Part of doing research is understanding what you can expect from the various sources available and which are considered credible for academic research projects. Let's look at what the Web and your college library can offer.

What the Web Is Good For

Web pages such as the Wikipedia entry on American nativism and "Cycles of American Nativism" can offer general background information and useful bibliogra- phy, but they are not considered authoritative scholarly sources in their own right. Most teachers would question a research paper that relied very heavily on them.

The Web is very good for getting public documents, reports, studies, and policy statements from government agencies, professional associations, universities, and nonprofits. It is very good at answering specific questions (if, say, you want to know how many people immigrated to the United States between 1965 and 1990 or how many households speak Spanish as the first language). It's also good for finding information about institutions or organizations such as U.S. English, to see how it presents itself and the case for English Only.

You may find sources such as James Crawford's Language Emporium that can be considered credible and authoritative. Crawford is widely recognized as an impor- tant writer on language policy, and so the articles and the sections of his books at the Web site are good sources for academic research. You may find such reliable sources at Web sites associated with universities, museums, research institutes, or other organizations. But you can't count on it.

Conclusions: Use the Web for background and specific information. Don't expect to write a research paper based exclusively or primarily on Web sources. The Web can be complementary to library research, but it can't substitute for it.

What the Library Is Good For

College and university libraries provide a number of ways to find appropriate scholarly and popular books and articles, in both print and electronic form.

Searchable library catalogs can be used to make subject searches that will identify books on a particular topic in the library's holdings. Some books may be available in electronic form.

Searchable online databases and library subscription services such as JSTOR, Project Muse, PubMed, and LexisNexis can identify articles on your topic in scholarly journals, popular magazines, and newspapers, with access to abstracts or the complete text. Note, however, that not all scholarly and popular periodicals are included in these services. For this reason, don't count on finding all the readings you need online. It's quite likely you will need to look up articles in print form in the library stacks.

In fact, it can be rewarding to browse the shelves where books and journals on your topic are kept. Use the call number of a book that looks promising and see what other books are nearby. (You can also do this on many online library catalogs.)

Finally, libraries have knowledgeable librarians who can answer your questions and help guide you in the research process.

Conclusions: Expect that even with the best available online databases and library subscription services, you will not be able to find all the books and articles you need online. Plan to make use of the library in person. Browse the stacks. Consult with librarians.

How to Identify Relevant Sources

How you read depends on your purposes and where you are in the research process. Once you have identified a research question, you are probably reading to gather information and to understand what others have said about the question you're investigating. As you're reading a source, ask yourself how relevant it is for your research question:

▶ Does it provide useful background information?

▶ Does it review previous research on the question?

▶ Could it help explain differences of opinion on the question?

▶ Can you use it as supporting evidence for your analysis and interpretations?

▶ Does it present evidence or ideas that run counter to your perspective? How should you take these into account?

Keeping a Working Bibliography

As you identify key research sources, make sure you take down the information you need to find the source as well as the information you'll need for your Works Cited or References section.

Books: Include the complete name of the author(s) and any editor or translator; the title and subtitle of the book; the place of publication, name of publisher, and date of publication.

Articles: Include complete name of the author(s); title and subtitle of the article; periodical name, volume and issues numbers, date, and page numbers; name of electronic database and date of access (if applicable).

Online sources: Include author's name (if available); title of the work; title of the overall Web site; publisher or sponsor of the site (if available); date work was published on the site (if available); date of access; URL.

Following a Research Path: Finding Relevant Sources

Let's look at Amira's notes as she looks for useful sources.

Using the Library Catalog

I already had the title of some books from browsing the Web, but I wanted to do a systematic search of the university library.

First, I tried "English Only movement" as a subject heading but only got three books. When I looked up one of them, <u>Nativism Reborn</u>?, I noticed the catalog entry listed other subjects: "Language policy—United States," "English language—Political aspects," and "English language—Social aspects—United States." I tried all these, and the best by far was "Language policy—United States." It turned up 33 references. I printed the search and headed for the stacks.

Using Electronic Databases: Readers' Guide Abstracts

I had used Readers' Guide Abstracts in high school, and I know they list a lot of popular magazines. I wanted to get a sense of what people were saying about English only legislation in the 1990s. I used English-Only as a keyword and set dates from 1990 to 2000. That turned up 26 helpful sources that included abstracts.

Finding Full-Text Articles Through Electronic Databases

I knew the library had full-text subscription services, but I had never used them before. So I asked a librarian where to start, and he suggested Academic Search Premier and JSTOR. Each works a little differently and what you get depends on the keywords you use. Sometimes it's overwhelming, and I had to sort through a lot to find what I was looking for on the English Only movement of the 1990s but I did find a number of really helpful articles.

Finding Immigration Statistics

As I got deeper into my research, I realized that the English Only movement emerged as immigration to the United States increased after the immigration law changed in 1965. I wanted to get some statistics on the patterns of immigration—where people came from, how many there were, where they settled. I remembered looking at the U.S. Citizenship and Immigration Services Web site when I was getting started, so I decided to go back and see what they had. I found the Office of Immigration Statistics that had the information I was looking for.

EVALUATING SOURCES

As you continue your research, keep in mind that you can't accept what your sources say at face value. Here are some considerations to keep in mind:

▶ Is the date the work was published appropriate to your purposes? In many cases, the most recent source is the most authoritative. At the same time, it may be appropriate to read older work that is acknowledged as important. In Amira's case, it makes sense to read sources from the period she is investigating, the 1990s, when the English Only movement emerged.

▶ What credibility does the writer have? Is he or she acknowledged as an authority?

▶ What is the writer's point of view? What are his or her political allegiances?

▶ Is the publication or press in which the source appears of good reputation? What is its editorial slant?

Following a Research Path: Annotated Bibliography

Amira kept an annotated bibliography with a full citation of the source, a summary of key points, selected quotes, and her own notes evaluating the source and identifying further questions for her research.

Selection from Amira's Annotated Bibliography

"No Official Language: Federal Court Strikes Down Arizona's English-Only Law."
Time *19 Feb. 1990: 82.*

Explains that federal court struck down a very restrictive official English law requiring all state and local governments to conduct their business in English only. Reverses state court that upheld the constitutional amendment known as Article 28 (or sometimes called Proposition 106) adopted as voter initiative in 1988. Federal judge Paul Rosenblatt ruled the law violates the First Amendment.

Notes: This is helpful for my time line. Looks like this English-Only law has a long history with appeals that go up to Supreme Court in 1997 and 1999. Persistence of English Only forces is very interesting here. I need to find out who is behind the appeals. Another constitutional amendment was passed in 2006.

O'Beirne, Kate. "English as the Official Language of the U.S. and Bilingual Education." National Review 1 July 1996:21.

Cites opinion polls:

▶ In a 1996 Gallup Poll, 82% favored making English the official language.

▶ A 1993 poll by the Tarrance Group found 78% of registered voters favored official English laws and over 60% favored it strongly.

▶ A 1993 poll by the *San Francisco Chronicle* found that 90% of Filipinos, 78% of Chinese, and nearly 70% of Latino immigrants in California favored official English.

Gives details on the Republican Party position on official English and bilingual education, ballots, and health care. Argues that given popular support for official English, Republicans should take stronger stand.

Key quote: "We must stop the practice of multilingual education as a means of instilling ethnic pride or as a therapy for low self-esteem, or out of elitist guilt over a culture built on the tradition of the west." Bob Dole, in a speech to the American Legion.

Notes: Great find. *National Review* is an important conservative magazine, and Kate O'Beirne seems to be a prominent conservative commentator. Helps explain ideas of English Only movement. Check *San Francisco Chronicle* poll. I may need to explain high support of official English among immigrant groups. May be a sign of desire to assimilate and could be used to argue that official English is unnecessary.

MAKING AN ARGUMENT

Doing research is learning new things and encountering new perspectives. Research involves you in a conversation with other people, who may influence what you think and believe. Stay open to these influences. It's not unusual for researchers to modify their initial ideas in light of what they find in their research.

At the same time, you need to assess what you've been reading so that you can make your own argument about the issues you've been examining. Here are some questions to help you determine the argument you want to make:

▶ What sources have made the strongest impression on you, whether you agree with them or not?

▶ How have your sources influenced your thinking? Do you see your research question in the same way as when you started researching? What changes have occurred?

▶ What new perspectives or questions have you encountered? How do you plan to deal with them?

▶ Given all this, how can you put an argument together?

Following a Research Path: Making an Argument

Amira's Statement of Purpose

A lot of what I've read about the English Only movement (like James Crawford's *Hold Your Tongue* and Raymond Tatalovich's *Nativism Reborn?*) sees it as an anti-immigrant backlash. The articles I've read by supporters of English Only don't come right out and say they are anti-immigrant, but they do talk about how the U.S. is losing its national identity because of immigration and multiculturalism. They use terms like "balkanization" to create the impression that America is fragmenting into separate ethnic groups. They seem to think that the English language can hold everything together.

The feeling I get is that people are afraid that they are going to be overwhelmed by Spanish-speaking immigrants, if not now, then in the near future. Crawford's idea of "Hispanophobia" makes a lot of sense to me as a way to explain the English Only movement. That's what I think I want to say in my paper.

PLANNING AND DRAFTING YOUR PROJECT

There's always more to read, and it may seem that the research process could continue indefinitely. In certain respects, of course, this is true. Individuals have devoted their lives to research and never really reached the end of what they could learn. That's why deadlines are so useful—to remind writers that they need to emerge from the research process and start writing.

An important point here is that you need to make sure you're not using research to procrastinate and avoid writing. As already mentioned, when you're reading and evaluating your sources, you should also be making tentative plans about how to use these materials in your paper. Moreover, you can begin drafting well before you end your research. In fact, many researchers find that drafting helps them refine the focus of their research and directs them to issues they need to investigate further. To put it another way, you don't have to stop your research when you begin writing. But you do have to begin writing.

Following a Research Path: Making an Outline

Amira's First Outline

Set up the issue of English Only

> background information on states with English Only laws
> public opinion polls
> emergence of U.S. English and English first in the 1990s
> present basic positions and arguments of English Only

State purpose of paper: to explain the emergence of English

> Only movement in the 1990s as "Hispanophobia" resulting from new patterns of immigration and cultural anxiety

Historical background

> relation of language policy and nativism/Americanization
> Anti-Irish literacy requirements for voting (1850s)
> American Protective Association's campaign vs. German-language instruction in parochial schools (1880s)
> U.S. Bureau of Americanization (early 1900s)

1965 Immigration Reform Act

> ended racial quotas
> "new immigration"
> demographic shifts increase in Latino population

Analysis of English Only movement

> familiar sources of nativism in the 1990s:
> economic stagnation (California)
> widening gap between rich and poor
> distrust of public institutions
> breakdown of community

"Hispanophobia" in California and the Southwest

> historical roots
> present manifestations
> explain focus on language as symbol of imagined lost community

A CLOSING NOTE

As you can see from Amira Patel's sketch of her outline for her research paper on the English Only movement, she has listed topics and points of analysis that will be central to drafting her paper. Her task now is to begin writing so that she can see how the information and ideas from her research connect to each other.

You'll no doubt reach a similar point in your own research—when it's time to start writing. Remember that you know a lot by this point. You will have information, evidence, and arguments from others that may not be widely available to your readers. Don't assume that just because you know something, everyone else must know it too. You're the authority who is immersed in the topic and issues of your research, and it's your job to explain how it all fits together. Keep in mind what your purpose is in writing your research paper. To what extent do you need to inform, explain, evaluate, or argue about the issues that have come up in your research? What sources are likely to persuade your readers to take your point of view seriously? How can you make the best use of what you've found in the research process?

In the next chapter, we look at some of the options for incorporating your sources into critical essays and research papers.

CHAPTER 14

Working with Sources

As noted already, academic writing does more than simply present the results of research. More importantly, it shows how the writer's research grows out of issues and problems in a particular field of study, and it explains the significance of the research to this ongoing discussion. Integrating and citing sources in a research paper lets your readers know how your work fits into a larger conversation.

Students sometimes think that using sources weakens their writing—that readers will think the important ideas in a paper come from others instead of from them. In college, however, readers expect writers to use and acknowledge sources. Readers want to understand what others have said about the issue you've researched, who has influenced your thinking, and how you stand in relation to the analyses, interpretations, and arguments others have offered. In fact, these expectations define in many respects what it means to work with sources.

In this chapter, we look first at some of the ways academic researchers work with their sources. Next, we present information on what plagiarism is and how to avoid it by properly integrating your sources. Finally, we cover how to document your sources in MLA and APA formats.

WORKING WITH SOURCES TO ANSWER YOUR RESEARCH QUESTION

In academic writing, you want to demonstrate how you are using your sources to create a meaningful answer to your research question. Here are some of the common ways to work with sources in college:

▶ **To support a position, analysis, or interpretation:** In "You Are Being Lied to About Pirates," the columnist Johann Hari draws on the work of historian Marcus Rediker to make the point that pirates "have never been quite who we think they are." Notice how Hari integrates a phrase from Rediker into the last sentence of this paragraph:

Pirates were the first people to rebel against this world. They mutinied—and created a different way of working on the seas. Once they had a ship, the pirates elected their captains, and made all their decisions collectively, without torture. They shared their bounty out in what Rediker calls "one of the most egalitarian plans for the disposition of resources to be found anywhere in the eighteenth century."

▶ **To assess the uses and limits of an analysis or interpretation:** In "Uncertainty and Uses of Magic, " researchers Richard B. Felson and George Gmelch take as their task testing Bronislaw Malinowski's theory of magic.

According to Malinowski, people use magic to alleviate or reduce the anxiety created by conditions of uncertainty. Through the performance of the appropriate rituals, people "work off" the tensions aroused by fear. An alternative explanation would be that magic results from purely cognitive processes and represents an effort to produce favorable results. In other words, people believe that unknown forces—"good luck" and "bad luck"—play a role in the outcome of events and that these forces can be manipulated by magic.

This study examines these relationships using a sample of American and Irish college students.

▶ **To apply a concept to a new case or situation:** In "Radiohead and the Tip-Jar Model," Stacy Yi uses the notion of the "tip jar" to analyze Radiohead's online release of *In Rainbows* with the price of "it's up to you":

Many of those commentators compared Radiohead's sales plan for *In Rainbows* to the tip jar on the counter of the local coffee shop. The comparison isn't quite parallel because tips are generally given for quality service that accompanies an already-purchased product. In Radiohead's case, however, the product and service are one and the same (at least until *In Rainbows* was released in the stores, months later, on TBD Records.) That fits with Greg Kot's observation, from *Ripped: How the Wired Generation Revolutionized Music*, that the band wanted only "to leak its own album, give fans a taste of the new music, and invite them to buy the sonically superior physical product once it became available in a few months" (1). Using an online tip jar for digital sales, then, is not necessarily the best way to make money, but an effective means of promoting a product to be sold later at a fixed rate.

▶ **To change the terms of a debate:** In his research paper, "The Prison Privatization Debate: The Need for a New Focus," Andy Mgwanna shows how the arguments for and against the privatization of prisons have reached an impasse. Then he explains what has been neglected by the debate and points to a new focus:

A problem with this impasse, as O'Brien (2006) suggests, is that the key issues of rehabilitation and recidivism, which have significant implications for the cost of the prison industrial complex, have been lost in a polarized debate. O'Brien (2006) argues that rather than becoming bogged down in the pros and cons of privatization, we should focus on incentives to both private and public prisons to prevent recidivism.

▶ **To uncover an enabling assumption and its consequences:** In "How to Fight the New Epidemics," Lundy Braun first cites a well-known scientist to establish the dominant view of infectious diseases:

In 1966, the eminent Australian immunologist Sir MacFarlane Burnet declared, "In many ways one can think of the middle of the 20th Century as the end of one of the most important social revolutions in history, the virtual elimination of infectious disease as a significant factor in social life." Shared by most of the scientific community, this view is rooted in the rise of the germ theory in the late 19th and early 20th centuries that associated specific microbial agents with particular diseases.

▶ Then she explains the consequences of the germ theory's assumptions about disease causation:

Thus, the germ theory effectively replaced disease prevention policies based on sanitary reforms, including improvement in sewage systems and better housing conditions, which were primarily responsible for the dramatic decline in the death rates from infectious disease.

WHAT IS PLAGIARISM?

Plagiarism is taking the words or ideas of someone else and presenting them as your own, without properly acknowledging their source in another's work. There are different ways in which plagiarism occurs.

Cheating

Buying a research paper, paying someone else to write a paper for you, or turning in someone's old paper is academic dishonesty, plain and simple, and is obviously intentional.

Copying

Reproducing sentences or passages from a book or article without citation may be intentional or may be due to a lack of understanding how properly to acknowledge sources.

Copying Patterns

Plagiarism includes copying sentence structures, even if you change some of the words.

You can see how copying patterns works in a recent example, where Kaavya Viswanathan says that she "accidentally borrowed" sections from *Sloppy Firsts*, a book by Megan McCafferty, for her novel *How Opal Mehta Got Kissed, Got Wild, and Got a Life.* Because of the plagiarism, her publishers withdrew the novel. Below are the examples of similar passages in the two books.

McCafferty's novel, page 7:	Viswanathan's novel, page 14:
"Bridget is my age and lives across the street. For the first twelve years of my life, these qualifications were all I needed in a best friend. But that was before Bridget's braces came off and her boyfriend Burke got on, before Hope and I met in our seventh grade Honors classes."	"Priscilla was my age and lived two blocks away. For the first fifteen years of my life, those were the only qualifications I needed in a best friend. We had bonded over our mutual fascination with the abacus in a playgroup for gifted kids. But that was before freshman year, when Priscilla's glasses came off, and the first in a long string of boyfriends came on."
McCafferty, page 6:	**Viswanathan, page 39:**
"Sabrina was the brainy Angel. Yet another example of how every girl had to be one or the other: Pretty or smart."	"Moneypenny was the brainy female character. Yet another example of how every girl had to be one or the other: smart or pretty."

Failure to Cite Properly

The most common form of unintentional plagiarism results from not understanding how to use and cite sources properly. For this reason, to avoid plagiarism you need to be aware of the conventions of citation and the various options you have in integrating sources into your writing.

Avoiding Plagiarism: How to Cite Properly

Here is a passage from Alan M. Kraut's chapter "Plagues and Prejudice: Nativism's Construction of Disease in Nineteenth- and Twentieth-Century New York" that appears on page 67 in *Hives of Sickness: Public Health and Epidemics in New York City*, the type of source you're likely to be working with in academic writing:

> As early as the 1830s, Irish immigrants who lived in rundown shanties and tenements along New York's rivers were being blamed for importing the cholera epidemic (from which they suffered disproportionately). Fear of cholera, especially after the epidemic of 1832, stimulated public demand for inspection of emigrants prior to departure.

Soon, those who left from Western European ports began to receive an exam from a physician employed by the country of departure, lest shiploads of emigrants be annihilated by cholera during the voyage.

WHAT DO I HAVE TO CITE?

A reliable rule of thumb is that you should cite the source of any information, analysis, interpretation, or argument that is not common knowledge. It is common knowledge, for example, that William Shakespeare was a playwright in Elizabethan England, the Earth travels around the sun, and Darwin formulated the theory of natural selection. This is information so widely known that it doesn't really belong to anyone. On the other hand, a literary critic's interpretation of Hamlet, an analysis of how Darwin developed his idea of natural selection, or an argument about the consequences of climate change is not considered common knowledge because it belongs to a particular person or group.

Problem 1: Copying and Failing to Cite Properly

Notice the following student-written passage plagiarizes (probably unintentionally) by copying sentences and failing to identify the source.

▌ COPIED PHRASES ARE HIGHLIGHTED

During the 1830s, there was widespread concern about the danger of cholera being brought to the United States by immigrants. Prime suspects were the Irish, **who lived in rundown shanties and tenements along New York's rivers** and who suffered a high rate of cholera. Following the cholera epidemic of 1832, public pressure mounted to examine emigrants before they left Europe. Physicians hired by the European countries inspected departing passengers, **lest shiploads of emigrants be annihilated by cholera during the voyage.**

▌ REVISED VERSION

According to Alan M. Kraut, during the 1830s, there was widespread concern about the danger of cholera being brought to the United States by immigrants. Prime suspects were the Irish, "who lived in rundown shanties and tenements along New York's rivers" and who suffered a high rate of cholera. Following the cholera epidemic of 1832, public pressure mounted to examine emigrants before they left Europe. Physicians hired by the European countries inspected departing passengers, "lest shiploads of emigrants be annihilated by cholera during the voyage" (67).

Notice how the revised version (1) turns the source "on" by attributing the ideas to the author ("According to Alan M. Kraut") and then turns it "off" with the page citation (67) at the end of the passage, and (2) carefully puts direct quotes in quotation marks.

Problem 2: Copying Sentence Structure and Failing to Cite Properly

Notice in this example how the student copies sentence structure and does not cite the source of the ideas.

Alan M. Kraut (original source)	**Student**
Soon, those who left from Western European ports began to receive an exam from a physician employed by the country of departure, lest shiploads of emigrants be annihilated by cholera during the voyage.	Before long, those departing from Western European ports were examined by doctors hired by the country of departure, so that boatloads of emigrants would not die from cholera during the trip.

▌ REVISED VERSION

Following the cholera epidemic of 1832, public pressure mounted to examine emigrants before they left Europe. Physicians in European ports of departure inspected passengers in an effort to prevent the spread of cholera (Kraut 67).

Notice how the revised version (1) integrates ideas into the student's own sentence structure, and (2) includes citation of the author's name and the page number at the end of sentence.

Options for Integrating Sources

The three basic methods of integrating sources are *paraphrasing, summarizing,* and *quoting.* Whichever you use, be sure to cite properly. Turn your source "on" by citing the author with a phrase like "According to Alan M. Kraut" or "Kraut points out" and "off" by citing the page number in parentheses. When you do not identify the author with one of these phrases, include the author's last name and the page number (Kraut 67).

Paraphrasing means restating in your own words and sentence structure. A paraphrase is typically about the same length as the original and is used when you want to explain the details in the original source:

According to Alan M. Kraut, during the 1830s, there was widespread concern about the danger of cholera being brought to the United States by immigrants. Prime suspects were the Irish, who suffered a high rate of cholera. Following the cholera epidemic of 1832, public pressure mounted to examine emigrants before they left

Europe. In order to prevent devastating outbreaks of disease onboard the ships, physicians hired by the European countries inspected departing passengers (67).

Summarizing means selecting main ideas from the original and presenting them in your own words and sentence structure. Summaries range from a sentence to a paragraph or more, depending on the amount of detail you need. Notice, in this example, how details are omitted to emphasize a single point:

During the 1830s the fear that immigrants were bringing cholera with them to the United States led to health inspections of departing passengers in the European ports (Kraut 67).

Quoting means duplicating the exact words as they appear in the original. In general, use direct quotations selectively. Quotations are best suited when you want to capture something in the original you would lose by paraphrasing, or when a direct quotation from an expert will lend authority. Short quotes, even a key word or phrase, are often more effective than longer ones.

Short Quotations

Words

Writers typically quote single words to emphasize important points and represent key concepts in their discussion. Often the quoted word is a term that someone has coined for analytical purposes, as in these two instances:

The ceremonial suspension of normal identities by World Wrestling Federation stars offers spectators a way to participate in what Victor Turner calls a "liminal" moment, when ordinary time and everyday human affairs come briefly to a halt and the extraordinary takes over.

Stuart Hall's notion of "encoding/decoding" in media communication enables us to see how messages are transformed as they circulate from production to reception.

Notice in these two examples that the key terms *liminal* and *encoding/decoding* appear in quotes and that in each case the author is noted. There are no page numbers, however, because the terms appear throughout the original sources, which are then acknowledged in Works Cited.

Phrases

You can integrate phrases as elements in sentences of your own construction:

Alan M. Kraut explains how the growing fear that immigrants were bringing cholera to the United States "stimulated public demand for inspection of emigrants prior to departure" from Europe (67).

Sentences

You can use a complete sentence or two from your source:

> According to Alan M. Kraut, "Fear of cholera, especially after the epidemic of 1832, stimulated public demand for inspection of emigrants prior to departure" (67).

Long Quotations

Use an indented block for long quotations. MLA identifies long quotations as more than four lines, whereas APA uses forty words. Indent one inch (or ten spaces) from the left margin if you are using MLA style, or a half-inch (or five spaces) from the left margin if you are using APA style, and in both cases double-space the passage, with no extra space above or below the block. Using this block form tells readers that the material is quoted directly from the original, so you don't need quotation marks. The page citation goes in parentheses after the punctuation at the end of the quote. The example below uses MLA style—indenting ten spaces to form the block. For single paragraphs or portions of a paragraph, do not indent the first line. If you quote two or more paragraphs, indent three additional spaces (one-quarter inch) at the beginning of each successive paragraph.

> Public health historian Alan M. Kraut points out how Americans have long viewed immigrants as carriers of disease:
>
> > As early as the 1830s, Irish immigrants who lived in rundown shanties and tenements along New York's rivers were being blamed for importing the cholera epidemic (from which they suffered disproportionately). Fear of cholera, especially after the epidemic of 1832, stimulated public demand for inspection of emigrants prior to departure. Soon, those who left from western European ports began to receive an exam from a physician employed by the country of departure, lest shiploads of emigrants be annihilated by cholera during the voyage. (67)

Fitting Quotations to Your Sentences

Under certain circumstances, you may modify the material you're quoting. The two basic techniques for modifying the original passage are ellipses and brackets. You use ellipses to omit something in the original and brackets to add or change something. Here are examples of typical uses of each.

Ellipses

Use ellipses when you want to omit part of the original passage. If you are omitting material in the middle of a sentence, use a set of three spaced periods, with a space before and after.

> "As early as the 1830s," Alan M. Kraut notes, "Irish immigrants . . . were being blamed for importing the cholera epidemic" (67).

When you quote single words or phrases, you don't need to use ellipses because readers can see you're quoting only part of a passage. If the material you're omitting occurs between sentences, include a fourth period to mark the end of the first sentence.

Alan M. Kraut notes similarities between the official response to cholera, polio, and tuberculosis in the nineteenth and early twentieth centuries and to AIDS in the 1990s:

> In the early 1990s, the federal government continued to pursue institutional means of epidemic control to stop AIDS at the border, a means that stigmatizes immigrants of all nationalities. . . . As in earlier crises, the federal government had sought to use exclusion to control the epidemic; immigrants were subjected to mandatory testing for no clear epidemiological reason other than foreign birth. (83)

Brackets

Brackets are used to make small changes in the original passage so that it fits grammatically into your sentences.

According to Alan M. Kraut, the federal government's use of mandatory AIDS testing repeats a pattern that can be found in earlier public health crises, "stigmatiz[ing] immigrants of all nationalities" (83).

Brackets can also be used to add clarifying material.

▌ ORIGINAL

Wealthy New York City merchants and uptown landowners, who in the early 1850s proposed the creation of Central Park, hoped to create a refined setting for their own socializing. But seeking to establish the public value of their project, they also invoked the language of the English sanitary reformers and claimed the park would improve the health and morals of the city's working people.

(Alan M. Kraut, "Plagues and Prejudice," p. 57)

▌ USE OF BRACKETS

Alan M. Kraut shows how the proposal to create Central Park drew on themes from the public health movement: "seeking to establish the public value of their project, they [wealthy New York City merchants and uptown landowners] also invoked the language of the English sanitary reformers and claimed the park would improve the health and morals of the city's working people" (57).

Quotations within Quotations

The passage you want to quote may at times contain quoted material. If the passage is long enough to use block form, then keep the quotation marks as they are in the original. If, however, you are going to incorporate a quotation that includes a quotation into your own sentence, then change the double quotation marks in the original into single quotation marks.

▌ ORIGINAL

Against this backdrop of economic depression, the physician and city inspector John Griscom launched a new phase of sanitary reform in his 1842 report when he singled out "the crowded conditions, with insufficient ventilation" of dwellings as "first among the most serious causes of disordered public health."

Alan M. Kraut, "Plagues and Prejudice," p. 54

▌ QUOTATION WITHIN A QUOTATION

Alan M. Kraut claims that "John Griscom launched a new phase of sanitary reform in his 1842 report when he singled out the crowded conditions, with insufficient ventilation 'of dwellings as first among the most serious causes of disordered public health' " (54).

CHECKLIST FOR USING QUOTES EFFECTIVELY

The following questions offer further guidelines as you review your work and consider needed revisions.

Do You Need the Quote?

Quoted material should be chosen carefully to advance the line of thinking in a research project. It should emphasize main ideas, not just be used decoratively or as proof that you've read a number of sources.

The plot of *Wuthering Heights* puts the death of the heroine in the middle of the novel. Although she has died in childbirth, Catherine Earnshaw relentlessly haunts Heathcliff until eighteen years later he too finally rests by her side in a grave "on the edge of the churchyard" (Frank 219).

The quoted phrase does not really contain an idea that matters to the discussion. Quotes like this one should be scrutinized closely to see if they are needed.

Is It Clear Where Sources Start and Stop?

One of the keys to avoiding plagiarism is marking clearly where quoted material starts and stops. In the example below, notice how the first two quotes—the high-lighted sentence and phrase—seem to be floating in the paragraph, and how the in-text citation (219) confusingly appears before the writer has finished quoting from the source.

> *Wuthering Heights* uses subtle psychological portrayals of its main characters, Catherine Earnshaw and Heathcliff, to turn them into mythic figures. **"They are driven, tormented, violent lovers, and there are no wedding bells for them in the final chapter."** In the grip of a titanic passion, their love can only be real-ized in death. Before his death, Heathcliff arranges to have the sides of his and Catherine's adjoining coffins dismantled **"so that in death they might finally achieve the consummation of their love" (219).** This is the "perfect and irrevocable union," Katherine Frank says, "which had tormented and eluded them when they were alive."

All the quoted material is from Katherine Frank's book *A Chainless Soul*, but read-ers have to guess the source of the first two quotes. This problem is easily fixed, as you can see by the highlighted revisions:

> *Wuthering Heights* uses subtle psychological portrayals of its main characters, Catherine Earnshaw and Heathcliff, to turn them into mythic figures. "They are driven, tormented, violent lovers," **Katherine Frank says,** "and there are no wed-ding bells for them in the final chapter." In the grip of a titanic passion, their love can only be realized in death. Before his death, Heathcliff arranges to have the sides of his and Catherine's adjoining coffins dismantled "so that in death they might finally achieve the consummation of their love." **According to Frank,** this is the "perfect and irrevocable union—which had tormented and eluded them when they were alive" (219).

Are Sources Used Purposefully or Just Strung Together?

Make sure your sources are set up so that readers can see how each quoted and para-phrased idea fits into your writing. Sources that are strung together, as in the follow-ing example, resemble research notes transcribed directly into a paper. As you can see, the writing seems to ramble from quote to quote without any sense of purposeful direction:

> The musical label "soul" is associated with Motown and Memphis in the 1960s, but the term has been in use much longer. According to gospel singer Mahalia Jackson, "What some people call 'the blues singing feeling' is expressed by the Church of God in Christ. … The basic thing is soul feeling. The same in blues as in spirituals. And also with gospel music. It is soul music" (qtd. in Ricks 139). "Soul assumes a shared experience, a relationship with the listener . . . where the singer confirms and works out the feelings of the audience. In this sense, it remains sacramental" (qtd. in Guralnick 3). "As professions, blues singing and preaching seem to be closely linked in both the rural or small town settings and in the urban ghettos" (Keil 143). Nonetheless, "Ray Charles's transformation of dignified gospel standards into cries of secular ecstasy came in for a good deal of criticism at first, mostly from the pulpit" (Guralnick 2).

A revision of this paragraph would require unpacking each quote by explaining the ideas and connecting them to the main points in the paper. Each quote may need its own paragraph, or the writer might combine two or more quotes in a paragraph. In any case, the quotes need space to breathe.

Do You Provide Commentary Where It Is Needed?

Quotes don't speak for themselves. As you've just seen in the example with the string of quotes, you need to connect your sources to the main points in your paper so that readers can see how and why the sources are significant. Your commentary is crucial to making these connections explicit. In the following example, notice how the quote leaves us hanging because it is not followed up by commentary from the writer:

> *Wuthering Heights* is partially based on the Gothic tradition, a quasi-horror writing that features haunting imagery, desolate landscapes, and supernatural encounters. Bronte draws on the Gothic to turn her main characters, Catherine Earnshaw and Heathcliff, into mythic figures in the grip of a titanic passion. Catherine marries Edgar Linton, and Heathcliff marries Edgar's sister Isabella, but these marriages have no impact on Catherine and Heathcliff's passionate love. Nor does death. Although she dies in childbirth in the middle of the novel, Catherine relentlessly haunts

Heathcliff until eighteen years later he too finally rests by her side. As Katherine Frank explains:

> Before he dies, Heathcliff makes a ghoulish arrangement with the sexton to knock out the adjoining sides of his own and Catherine's coffins so that in death they might finally achieve the consummation of their love—a perfect and irrevocable union—which had tormented and eluded them when they were alive. (219)

In earlier Gothic novels, the central narrative is often approached by way of a frame tale that uses diaries, letters, and other documents, which are transcribed or edited by the narrator. Similarly, the reader approaches the narrative of *Wuthering Heights* via an outsider, Lockwood.

A few lines of commentary from the writer would not only consolidate the point in the paragraph but also set up a smoother transition into the next paragraph, as shown in the example that follows.

> … the consummation of their love—a perfect and irrevocable union— which had tormented and eluded them when they were alive (219).
> In true Gothic style, Bronte blurs the line between life and death to create an imaginary world of haunted and uncontrollable passions.
>
> This imaginary world is typically both verified and kept at a mysterious distance in Gothic novels by a frame tale that uses diaries, letters, and other documents, which are transcribed or …

DOCUMENTING SOURCES: MLA AND APA STYLE

The two main styles of citation—MLA and APA—use parenthetical citations within the text. Information about the source is included in the text and keyed to a list of sources at the end of the paper—*Works Cited* in MLA style and *References* in APA. The information called for by MLA and APA in the parenthetical citation differs somewhat. MLA uses author and page, whereas APA uses author, year, and page.

The following pages describe MLA and APA systems for citing sources within the text and for listing sources at the end of the paper. For further information, you can consult *MLA Handbook for Writers of Research Papers* (7th ed., 2009) or the MLA Web site www.mla.org, and *Publication Manual of the American Psychological Association* (6th ed., 2009) or the APA Web site on documenting electronic sources www.apastyle .org/apa-stylhelp.aspx.

IN-TEXT CITATIONS

The following list shows how MLA and APA styles set up parenthetical in-text citations for many types of sources.

Sources with One Author

In many instances, you cite the author in the sentence that uses the source material.

MLA

According to Daniel J. Czitrom, following the Civil War, there appeared the "first rush of literature on the pathology of mass communication, with which we are so familiar today" (19).

Note that you do not repeat the author's name when you give the page number at the end of the quotation.

APA

According to Daniel J. Czitrom (1982), following the Civil War, there appeared the "first rush of literature on the pathology of mass communication, with which we are so familiar today" (p. 19).

Note that in APA style, the date of publication appears immediately after the author's name.

If you don't cite the author in the sentence, then use these forms:

MLA

Following the Civil War, there appeared the "first rush of literature on the pathology of mass communication, with which we are so familiar today" (Czitrom 19).

MLA style notes the author and the page number, with no punctuation in between and no "p." before the page.

APA

Following the Civil War, there appeared the "first rush of literature on the pathology of mass communication, with which we are so familiar today" (Czitrom, 1982, p. 19).

APA style includes the author's name, the date of publication, and the page number, with commas in between and "p." before the page number.

Notice that for both MLA and APA styles, the final period comes after the citation.

MLA

> Following the Civil War, there appeared the "first rush of literature on the pathology of mass communication, with which we are so familiar today" (Czitrom, *Media* 19).

When you have more than one source by an author, MLA style uses the author's name, a shortened version of the title (the full title is *Media and the American Mind: From Morse to McLuhan*), and the page number.

APA

> Following the Civil War, there appeared the "first rush of literature on the pathology of mass communication, with which we are so familiar today" (Czitrom, 1982, p. 19).

APA style remains the same because the work is already noted by the year. However, if you are citing in APA style more than one work published by an author in the same year, add a letter to the date (1982a, 1982b), and key these to your references at the end of the paper. For example, if you cited a second work Czitrom published in 1982, the first work would be cited as:

> (Czitrom, 1982a, p. 19)

and the second would look like this:

> (Czitrom, 1982b, p. 43)

Sources with Multiple Authors

MLA and APA use different systems to cite sources having more than one author.

MLA

If the work has two or three authors, cite all:

> Despite the claims made for it, literacy "is not in itself a panacea for social inequity" (Lunsford, Moglen, and Slevin 2).

If the work has more than three authors, use the first author's name followed by "et al."

> What we know of Indian cultures prior to 1700 has mostly been gleaned from the evidence of various artifacts, such as pottery, weapons, and stories passed down from generation to generation (Lauter et al. 5).

APA

If the source you are citing has two authors, include both last names in the reference, separated by an ampersand (&).

Nigeria home-video movies "are turning out the Nigerian story in a no-holds-barred fashion which leaves no room for anybody to hide" (Ofeiman & Kelani, 2005, p. 245).

For sources with three to five authors, list all of the authors' last names the first time you cite the source, separating each name by a comma and putting an ampersand before the final name.

Despite the claims made for it, literacy "is not in itself a panacea for social inequity" (Lunsford, Moglen, & Slevin, 1990, p. 2).

For subsequent citations, include simply the last name of the first author followed by "et al." and the year and the page. If a source has six or more authors, use the last name of the first author and "et al." in every citation:

Despite the claims made for it, literacy "is not in itself a panacea for social inequity" (Lunsford et al., 1990, p. 2).

Sources with No Author Listed

If no author is listed on the work, both MLA and APA use a shortened version of the title.

MLA

A 1996 study found that men who frequent prostitutes or have many sexual partners may increase their wives' risk of cervical cancer ("Man's Sex Life").

Note that if your source appears on a single page, MLA does not require you to list the page number.

APA

A 1996 study found that men who frequent prostitutes or have many sexual partners may increase their wives' risk of cervical cancer ("Man's Sex Life," 1996, p. 15).

The MLA and APA citations use a shortened version of the title of the article, "Man's Sex Life and Cancer in Wife Linked."

Online Sources

Sources you have accessed through a Web site, online periodical, or online database are handled in much the same way as print sources.

MLA

Hurricane Katrina revealed "some of the blank spots and overlooked inequities in race relations that were shocking to many whites but lived realities for most blacks" (Carpenter 2).

If no author is listed, use the title of the document. If the document has numbered paragraphs rather than pages, use the number following a comma and the abbreviation par. (e.g., McKenzie, par. 4). For documents with no numbered pages or paragraphs, no number is listed.

APA

Hurricane Katrina revealed "some of the blank spots and overlooked inequities in race relations that were shocking to many whites but lived realities for most blacks" (Carpenter, 2006, p. 2).

If no date of publication is given, use "n.d." If no author is listed, use a shortened version of the title. When there are no page numbers, use paragraph numbers to document quotes:

The marketing of race-specific drugs such as Bi-Dil has raised "troubling questions about the reinstitution of race as a biological category in medicine" ("Return of Race," n.d., para. 4).

Indirect Quotations

For cases where you want to quote something that appeared as a quote in one of your sources, use "qtd. in" (MLA) or "cited in" (APA). In the following two examples, the writer is quoting the blues musician Son House from an interview that appeared originally in Pete Welding's book *The Living Blues* and then was quoted by Greil Marcus in his book *Mystery Train.*

MLA

"He sold his soul to the devil to get to play like that," House told blues historian Pete Welding (qtd. in Marcus 32).

APA

"He sold his soul to the devil to get to play like that," House told blues historian Pete Welding (cited in Marcus, 1975, p. 32).

WORKS CITED (MLA) AND REFERENCES (APA)

Every source that appears in the text should be listed in a separate section at the end of your paper. Don't include works that you read but did not cite. MLA calls the list "Works Cited," whereas APA uses "References." Both systems alphabetize by author's last name or the first word in the title of a work with no author.

Books

Here is the basic format for MLA and APA. Notice how they differ.

MLA

> Hedges, Chris. *Empire of Illusion*. New York: Nation Books, 2009. Print.

MLA style uses the complete first name of the author, capitalizes major words in the title, lists the date at the end of the citation, and indents the second line five spaces. The period following the book title is not underlined or italicized. In MLA style, use the abbreviation "UP" for university presses, as in Columbia UP. MLA style gives the publication medium, Print or Web.

APA

> Hedges, C. (2009). *Empire of illusion*. New York: Nation Books.

APA style uses the author's first initial, lists the date right after the author's name, capitalizes only the first word in the title and after a colon (plus any proper nouns), spells out "University Press," and indents the second line five spaces.

> Both systems double-space the text throughout.

Notice in the examples that the place of publication is well-known. In these cases, don't add the state. In APA citations where the place of publication is not well-known, do add the state: for example, "Thousand Oaks, CA: Sage."

Two Listings by One Author

MLA

> Gilroy, Paul. *Postcolonial Melancholia*. New York: Columbia UP, 2005. Print.
> ---. *"There Ain't No Black in the Union Jack": The Cultural Politics of Race and Nation*. Chicago: U of Chicago P, 1987. Print.

When you're listing two or more works by the same author, use alphabetical order according to title. For the second title, type three hyphens and a period in place of the author's name.

APA

> Gilroy, P. (1987). *"There ain't no black in the Union Jack": The cultural politics of race and nation*. Chicago: University of Chicago Press.
> Gilroy, P. (2005). *Postcolonial melancholia*. New York: Columbia University Press. 530–533.

APA style uses chronological order to list works, beginning with the earliest. When an author has more than one work published in the same year, list them in alphabetical order by title, and add lowercase letters to the year—e.g., 1977a, 1977b:

> Gould, S. J. (1977a). *Ontogeny and phylogeny*. Cambridge, U.K.: Cambridge University Press.
> Gould, S. J. (1977b). Sociobiology: The art of storytelling. *New Scientist, 80*, 530–533.

Books with Multiple Authors

MLA

For two or three authors, list them in the order in which they appear on the book's title page. Invert only the first author's name.

> Current, Richard Nelson, Marcia Ewing Current, and Loie Fuller. *Goddess of Light*. Boston: Northeastern UP, 1997. Print.

If there are more than three authors, you may list them all or list only the first author followed by "et al."

> Anderson, Daniel, Bret Benjamin, Christopher Busiel, and Bill Parades-Holt. *Teaching On-Line: Internet Research, Conversation, and Composition*. New York: Harper, 1996. Print.

or

> Anderson, Daniel, et al. *Teaching On-Line: Internet Research, Conversation, and Composition*. New York: HarperCollins, 1996. Print.

APA

For works with two to six authors, list the authors in the order in which they appear on the title page, using last name and initials. Use an ampersand before the last author's name.

> Anderson, D., Benjamin, B., Busiel, C., & Parades-Holt, B. (1996). *Teaching online: Internet research, conversation, and composition*. New York: HarperCollins.

Books by a Corporate Author or Organization

Give the name of the corporate or organizational author as it appears on the title page.

MLA

> NOW Legal Defense and Educational Fund. *Facts on Reproductive Rights: A Resource Manual*. New York: NOW Legal Defense and Educational Fund, 2004. Print.

APA

> NOW Legal Defense and Educational Fund. (2004). *Facts on reproductive rights: A resource manual*. New York: Author.

Books by an Anonymous Author

In MLA style, if no author is listed or the author is anonymous, begin with the title of the publication.

MLA

> *Primary Colors: A Novel of Politics*. New York: Random, 1996. Print.

APA

> *Primary colors: A novel of politics*. (1996). New York: Random House.

In APA style, begin the entry with the title if no author is listed. If a work's author is designated as "Anonymous," however, use the word *Anonymous* at the beginning of the entry.

An Edition of an Original Work

MLA

> Melville, Herman. *Moby-Dick*. 1851. Ed. Alfred Kazin. Boston: Houghton, 1956. Print.

APA

> Melville, H. (1956). *Moby-Dick* (A. Kazin, Ed.). Boston: Houghton Mifflin. (Original work published 1851).

An Introduction, Preface, Foreword, or Afterword

MLA

> Kazin, Alfred. Introduction. *Moby-Dick*. By Herman Melville. Ed. Alfred Kazin. Boston: Houghton, 1956. v-xiv. Print.

APA

> Kazin, A. (1956). Introduction. In H. Melville, *Moby-Dick* (A. Kazin, Ed.) (pp. v–xiv). Boston: Houghton Mifflin.

Edited Collections

MLA

> Grumet, Robert S., ed. *Northeastern Indian Lives*. Amherst: U of Massachusetts P, 1996. Print.

APA

> Grumet, R. S. (Ed.). (1996). *Northeastern Indian Lives*. Amherst: University of Massachusetts Press.

Works in Collections and Anthologies

MLA

Fitzgerald, F. Scott. "Bernice Bobs Her Hair." *The Short Stories of F. Scott Fitzgerald: A New Collection.* Ed. Matthew J. Bruccoli. New York: Scribner, 1989. 25-47. Print.

Ochs, Donovan J. "Cicero's Rhetorical Theory." *A Synoptic History of Classical Rhetoric.* Ed. James J. Murphy. Davis: Hermagoras, 1983. 90-150. Print.

APA

Fitzgerald, F. (1989). Bernice bobs her hair. In M. J. Bruccoli (Ed.), *The short stories of F. Scott Fitzgerald: A new collection.* (pp. 25–47). New York: Scribner.

Ochs, D. J. (1983). Cicero's rhetorical theory. In J. J. Murphy (Ed.), *A synoptic history of classical rhetoric* (pp. 90–150). Davis, CA: Hermagoras.

Translations

MLA

Sartre, Jean-Paul. *The Age of Reason.* Trans. Eric Sutton. New York: Bantam, 1959. Print.

APA

Sartre, J. P. (1959). *The age of reason.* (E. Sutton, Trans.). New York: Bantam Books.

Books in a Later Edition

MLA

Woloch, Nancy. *Women and the American Experience.* 3rd ed. New York: McGraw-Hill, 1999. Print.

APA

Woloch, N. (1999). *Women and the American experience* (3rd ed.). New York: McGraw-Hill.

Dictionary Entries and Encyclopedia Articles

MLA

"Australia." *The Concise Columbia Encyclopedia.* 3rd ed. 1995. Print.

"Freeze-etching." *Merriam-Webster's Collegiate Dictionary.* 11th ed. 2003. Print.

Jolliffe, David A. "Genre." *Encyclopedia of Rhetoric and Composition.* Ed. Theresa Enos. New York: Garland, 1996. Print.

In MLA style, for familiar reference works such as *Merriam-Webster's Collegiate Dictionary* and *The Concise Columbia Encyclopedia,* you can omit listing the editors and publication information. For less familiar or more specialized sources, however, you should include all the information. Page numbers are not needed as long as the work is arranged alphabetically.

APA

> Australia. (1995). *The concise Columbia encyclopedia* (3rd ed.). New York: Columbia University Press.
>
> Freeze-etching. (2003). *Merriam-Webster's collegiate dictio*nary (11th ed.). Springfield, MA: Merriam Webster.
>
> Jolliffe, D. A. (1996). Genre. In Theresa Enos (Ed.), *Encyclopedia of rhetoric and composition*. New York: Garland.

Government Documents

MLA

> United States. Dept. of Commerce. International Trade Administration. *A Guide to Financing Exports.* Washington: GPO, 2005. Print.

APA

> Department of Commerce, International Trade Administration. (2005). *A guide to financing exports* (Monthly Catalog No. 85024488). Washington, DC: U.S. Government Printing Office.

APA includes the catalog number of the publication.

Unpublished Doctoral Dissertations

MLA

> Barrett, Faith Priscilla. "Letters to the World: Emily Dickinson and the Lyric Address." Diss. U of California, 2000. Print.

APA

> Barrett, F. P. (2000). *Letters to the world: Emily Dickinson and the lyric address.* Unpublished doctoral dissertation, University of California, Berkeley.

Articles in Print Periodicals

Here are examples of the basic MLA and APA formats for listing articles that appear in print periodicals such as scholarly journals, magazines, and newspapers. See the next section on Online Sources if you have accessed an article through an online periodical Web site or database.

MLA

> Bangeni, Bongi, and Rochelle Kapp. "Identities in Transition: Shifting Conceptions of Home among 'Black' South African University Students." *African Studies Review* 48.3 (2005): 110-31. Print.

MLA style uses the author's full name, marks article titles by using quotation marks and capitalization, and lists both volume (48) and issue (3) numbers for journals, no matter whether there is continuous pagination or not. Notice that MLA separates page numbers with a hyphen and shortens the second number, 110–31.

APA

> Bangeni, B., & Kapp, R. (2005). Identities in transition: Shifting conceptions of home among "black" South African university students. *African Studies Review, 48* (3), 110–131

APA style uses abbreviations for first and middle names, and the date follows the author's name. APA does not use quotation marks or capitalization for article titles (except for the first word of the title and any subtitle, and any proper nouns and proper adjectives). In APA style, the name of the journal, the volume number (48), and the comma that follows it are all italicized, and the issue number is included in parentheses (3) for journals that page issues separately. Notice that APA uses an en dash to separate page numbers and does not shorten the second number.

For journals with continuous pagination, drop the issue number:

> Lu, M-Z. (2006). Living-English work. *College English, 68,* 605–618.

Magazine Articles

The first two examples show how to list magazines that appear monthly or bimonthly and weekly or biweekly. The third example is an article without an author listed.

MLA

> Kelly, Kevin. "The New Socialism." *Wired* June 2009: 116-121. Print.
> "Pleas from Prison." *Newsweek* 24 Nov. 1997: 44. Print.
> Grossman, David. "The Age of Genius." *New Yorker* 8 June 2009: 66-77. Print.

APA

> Kelly, K. (2009, June). The new socialism. *Wired,* 116–121.
> Pleas from prison. (1997, November 24). *Newsweek* 44.
> Grossman, D. (2009, June 8). The age of genius. *The New Yorker,* 66–77.

Notice that APA style capitalizes "the" in the title of magazines and newspapers such as *The New Yorker* and *The Nation*, whereas MLA style does not include a capital "the" in the title of the *New Yorker* or the *Nation*.

Newspaper Articles

MLA

"AMA Plans Seal of Approval for Physicians." *Providence Journal-Bulletin* 19 Nov. 1997: A5. Print.

Wangsness, Lisa. "Lobbyist at Center of Healthcare Overhaul." *Boston Globe* 30 June 2009: A12. Print.

Notice that MLA style lists day, month, and year in that order, with no punctuation.

APA

AMA plans seal of approval for physicians. (1997, November 19). *The Providence Journal-Bulletin*, A5.

Wangsness, L. (2009, June 30). Lobbyist at center of healthcare overhaul. *The Boston Globe*, A12.

Notice that APA style lists year, followed by a comma, then month and day.

Editorial

MLA

"Lessons from Prudhoe Bay." Editorial. *New York Times* 6 Aug. 2006: A30. Print.

APA

Lessons from Prudhoe Bay [Editorial]. (2006, August 6). *The New York Times*, A30.

Review

MLA

Schwarz, Benjamin. "Land of Hope and Glory." Rev. of *Golden Dreams: California In an Age of Abundance, 1950-1963*, by Kevin Starr. *The Atlantic* July/August 2009: 113-115. Print.

APA

Schwarz, B. (2009, July/August). *Land of hope and glory* [Review of the book *Golden dreams: California in an age of abundance, 1950–1963*]. *The Atlantic*, 113–115.

If there is no author listed for the review, begin with the title of the review. If there is no title, use "Rev. of *Title*" for MLA format and "[Review of the book *Title*]" for APA. In this case, alphabetize under the title of the book being reviewed.

Letter to the Editor

MLA

Jenkins, John. Letter. *Dallas Morning News* 18 June 2009: A12. Print.

APA

Jenkins, J. (2009, June 18). [Letter to the editor]. *Dallas Morning News*, A12.

Online Sources

For online sources, such as articles accessed through online periodicals or databases and Web sites, MLA and APA guidelines call for much of the same information you use for print sources, such as document title and author's name (if it is available). In addition, both MLA and APA also call for the date of publication or update for online sources, if it is available.

MLA style calls for the date you retrieved an online source, but it does not require listing the URL for online sources unless the reader would not be able to locate the resource through a Web search for the title or author, or if the publisher requires it.

APA style includes retrieval information, but not the date of retrieval unless the source is likely to change, as on Wikis.

Articles in Newspapers and Magazines

MLA

Robison, Clay. "Word Doesn't Travel Fast on Perry Trips." *Houston Chronicle.* Houston Chronicle, 29 Oct. 2007. Web. 15 May 2012.

Schiff, Stacy. "Know It All: Can Wikipedia Conquer Expertise?" *New Yorker.* New Yorker, 24 July 2006. Web. 1 July 2011.

MLA style includes author and title, then both the name of the online periodical in italics and the publisher—followed by date of publication, the medium of publication, and the date of retrieval.

APA

Robinson, C. (2007, October 29). Word doesn't travel fast on Perry trips. *The Houston Chronicle.* Retrieved from http://www.chron.com/CDA/archives/

Schiff, S. (2006, 24 July 26). Know it all: Can Wikipedia conquer expertise? *The New Yorker.* Retrieved from http://www.newyorker.com/archive/2006/07/31/060731fa_fact.

APA style includes author, date of publication, title, publication, and URL. If the URL continues to a second line, try to break at a backslash.

Articles in Scholarly Journals

MLA

> Rodriguez-Alegria, Enrique. "Eating Like an Indian: Negotiating Social Relations in the Spanish Colonies." *Current Anthropology* 46.3 (2005): 253-78. Web. 29 Sept. 2012.

APA

> Rodriguez-Alegria, E. (2005). Eating like an Indian: Negotiating social relations in the Spanish colonies. *Current Anthropology, 46* (3), 253–278. doi: 10.1876/cuan.2005.0987.

APA recommends using a DOI (digital object identifier) if available. DOIs are designed to be stable, long-term links to online articles in scholarly journals. Many publications now include them, but not all. If there is no DOI, use the URL instead when you list retrieval information.

Online Books and Reports

MLA

> Wendell, Barrett. *English Composition*. Cambridge, MA: Charles Scribner, 1891. Google Book Search. Web. 14 Sept. 2012.

APA

> Harrison Rips Foundation. (2000). *Creating underdevelopment: Capital flight and the case for debt reduction in South Africa*. Retrieved from http://www.ripsfoundation.org /southafrica.report.html.

Online-Only Publications and Scholarly Projects

MLA

> Foster, George. "Language Policy in Namibia." *Southern African Review* 7.1 (2004): n. pag. Web. 2 July 2012.
> Baxter, Bruce, ed. *The Robert Creeley Online Archive*. Warehouse State College, n.d. Web. 2 Dec. 2011.

APA

> Foster, G. (2004). Language policy in Namibia. *Southern African Review, 7* (1). Retrieved from http://www.soafricanreview.org.
> Baxter, B. (Ed.). (n.d.) *The Robert Creeley Online Archive*. Retrieved from http://www.wsc .edu/cholsonarchives/html.

Notice how "n. pag." (no pagination) appears in MLA style for online publications that do not use page numbers and how "n.d." (no date) appears in both MLA and APA style when no date of publication or update is available.

Web Sites

MLA

> Crawford, James. *Language Policy Web Site & Emporium*. n.d. Web. 14 Oct. 2012. http://www.languagepolicy.net/.
>
> *Kheel Center for Labor-Management Documentation and Archives*. 2009. Cornell University School of Industrial and Labor Relations. Web. 14 July 2012.
>
> *U.S. English Only*. Home page. 19 Jan. 2009. Web. 8 Feb. 2012.

The order of information for MLA: Name of author, creator, or site owner, if available; title of document, if named; title of Web site, if distinct from title of document; date of last posting, if available; name of any institution or organization associated with the date; medium of publication (Web) date of retrieval; URL enclosed in angle brackets < >, if necessary.

In the first example above, no posting date is given, only the date of retrieval. The second example includes both posting and retrieval dates. Notice in the "U.S. English Only" example, where the Web site is not titled, you add the description "home page" without underlining or putting it in quotes.

APA

> Crawford, J. (n.d.). *Language policy web site and emporium*. Retrieved from http://www.languagepolicy.net.
>
> Kheel Center for labor-management documentation and archives. (2009). Retrieved from Cornell University School of Industrial and Labor Relations Web site: http://digitalcommons.ilr.cornell.edu/kheel/.

The order of information for APA: Name of author, creator, or site owner, if available; date of last posting; title of document, if named; and URL in one sentence, without using angle brackets or a period at the end.

As is true with print sources, APA uses an initial for an author's first and middle names and capitalizes only the first word in a document title and the first word following a colon. Notice in the second example that you use "n.d." (no date) if there is no date of posting available.

Web Sites: Secondary Pages

MLA

> de Ferranti, David. "Innovative Financing Options and the Fight against Global Poverty: What's New and What Next?" *Brookings Institute*. July 2006. Web. 29 July 2012.
>
> "The Triangle Factory Fire." *Kheel Center for Labor-Management Documentation and Archives*. 24 Mar. 2007. Cornell University School of Industrial and Labor Relations. Web. 14 Oct 2011. http://www.ilr.cornell.edu/trianglefire/.

Notice that the URL links to the Web page cited, not to the home page of the Kheel Center.

APA

> de Ferranti, D. (2006, July). *Innovative financing options and the fight against global poverty: What's new and what next?* Retrieved from the Brookings Institute Web site: http://www.brookings.edu/papers/2006/07development_ferranti.aspx.
>
> The triangle factory fire. (2005, March 24). Retrieved from Cornell University of Industrial and Labor Relations, Kheel Center for Labor-Management Documentation and Archives Web site: http://www.ilr.cornell.edu/trianglefire/.

Notice that the Brookings Institute and the Kheel Center Web sites are included in the retrieval statement.

Blogs

MLA

> *Off the Dribble.* New York Times, 30 Dec. 2011. Web. 2 Jan. 2012.
>
> Gerstner, Joanne C. "Spurs Prepare to Close Out Jazz." *Off the Dribble.* New York Times, 7 May 2012. Web. 15 May 2012.

Notice the first entry refers to the entire blog, whereas the second refers to a specific blog entry. The name of the sponsor or publisher appears after the name of the blog.

APA

> Gerstner, J. C. (2012, May 7). Spurs prepare to close out Jazz [Web log post]. Retrieved from http://offthedribble.blogs.nytimes.com/.

Note that APA style includes Web log post (or Web log comment) in brackets, but not the title of the blog or the sponsor.

Wiki

MLA

> "Drone Metal." Wikipedia. Wikimedia Foundation. 21 Feb. 2012. Web. 7 May 2012.

APA

> "Drone Metal." (2012, February 21). In *Wikipedia.* Retrieved May 7, 2012 from http://en.wikipedia.org/wiki/Drone_metal.

Online Posting to Electronic Forum

MLA

> Michael, Toni. "George W. Bush—The Legacy." Online posting. *Table Talk.* 1 Aug. 2008. Web. 15 Nov. 2011.

Marshall, Richard. "The Political Economy of Cancer Research." Online posting. *H-Net List on the History of Science, Medicine, and Technology* 21 Apr. 2003. Web. 28 Sept. 2012.

APA

Michael, T. (2008, August 1). George W. Bush—the legacy. Message posted to Table Talk, archived at http://tabletalk.salon.com/webx?14@@.773d395b/50.

In general, only cite in References those postings that have been archived and thus can be retrieved. See note on APA in next section.

Email

MLA

Wheeler, Anne C. Message to the author. 25 Feb. 2012. E-mail.

Dever, Elizabeth. "Re: Eddie Vetter's Conversion." Message to the author. 4 May 2012. E-mail.

For email, list the title (if there is one) from the email's subject heading.

APA

APA style treats email, as well as any nonarchived postings on electronic forums, as a nonretrievable source. Cite emails and other nonretrievable sources in the text as personal communications, but do not list them in the References section. For example:

Medical historians have challenged Elaine Showalter's view of chronic fatigue syndrome (L. Braun, personal communication, February 25, 2012).

Miscellaneous Sources

Films or Video Recordings

MLA

Citizen Kane. Screenplay by Orson Welles. Dir. Orson Welles. RKO, 1941. Film.

No Country for Old Men. Dir. Joel Coen and Ethan Coen. Perf. Josh Brolin, Javier Bardem, Tommy Lee Jones. Paramount, 2008. DVD.

APA

Nolan, C. (Director). (2008). *The Dark Knight* [DVD]. Hollywood: Warner Bros.

Welles, O. (Writer-Director). (1941). *Citizen Kane* [Film]. Hollywood: RKO.

The amount of information to include about films and videocassettes depends on how you have used the source. In addition to title and director, you may cite the writer and performers as well.

Television and Radio Programs

MLA

"Tuskegee Experiment." *Nova*. WGBH, Boston. 4 April 2012. Television.

APA

Tuskegee experiment. (2012, April 4). *Nova* Boston: WGBH.

Records, Tapes, and CDs

MLA

Ellington, Duke. *The Far East Suite*. Bluebird, 1995. CD.

Verdi, Giuseppe. *La Traviata*. London Symphony Orchestra. Cond. Carlo Rizzi. Teldec, 1992. CD.

White Stripes. *Get Behind Me Satan*. V2, 2005. CD.

APA

Ellington, D. (Composer). (1995). *The far east suite* [Record]. New York: Bluebird.

Verdi, G. (Composer). (1992). *La Traviata* [With C. Rizzi conducting the London Symphony Orchestra] [CD]. New York: Teldec.

White Stripes. (2005). *Get behind me Satan* [CD]. New York: V2.

Interviews

MLA

Haraway, Donna. "Writing, Literacy, and Technology: Toward a Cyborg Literature." By Gary A. Olson. *Women Writing Culture*. Ed. Gary A. Olson and Elaine Hirsch. Albany: SUNY, 1995. 45-77. Print.

Press, Karen. Personal interview. 27 Apr 2012.

Sole, Kelwyn. Interview by Anita Amirault. *Cape Town Poetry Newsletter* 20 Mar. 2001: 30-34. Print.

MLA cites interviews by listing the person being interviewed first and then the interviewer. Note that the first two interviews are published and the third is unpublished.

APA

> Amirault, A. (2001, March 20). Interview with Kelwyn Sole. *Cape Town Poet Newsletter,* 30–34.
>
> Olson, G. A. (1995). Writing, literacy, and technology: Toward a cyborg literature [Interview with Donna Haraway]. In G. A. Olson & E. Hirsch (Eds.), *Women writing culture* (pp. 45–77). Albany: State University of New York.

APA lists the name of the interviewer first and then puts information on the interview in brackets. APA does not list unpublished interviews in references but cites them only in parenthetical citations in the text: (K. Press, personal interview, April 27, 2003).

Lecture or Speech

MLA

> Kern, David. "Recent Trends in Occupational Medicine." Memorial Hospital, Pawtucket, RI. 2 Oct. 2011. Address.

APA

> Kern, D. (2011, October 2). Recent trends in occupational medicine. Paper presented at Memorial Hospital, Pawtucket, RI.

CHAPTER 15

A Guide to Print, Electronic, and Other Sources

For most research projects, your college library is the main source of information, and you can count on spending a good part of your research time reading and analyzing books, articles, and newspapers (although your research question may also lead you to conduct field research—which is treated in the next chapter).

A lot of what you need is available online, through electronic databases like JSTOR, LexisNexis, and Academic Search Premier. In addition, you can access a world of information and ideas on the Web, ranging from serious scholarly discussion to wildly opinionated debates of questionable value.

In addition, depending on your research project, you may find yourself doing research at live performances and museums or by watching the media. In any case, doing research is a matter of knowing your way around print, electronic, and other sources and understanding how they differ in terms of credibility and authority.

TYPES OF PRINT SOURCES

Books

Books can be sorted into three main types:

▶ **Scholarly books**, published by university or academic presses and written by faculty and other researchers, are meant to contribute to a field of knowledge. They have gone through a careful review by peer readers who are knowledgeable about the field and editors. At the time they're published, scholarly books should be up to date in terms of the issues they engage and the literature in the field they've reviewed. For these reasons, scholarly books have a high degree of credibility, especially among academics, and will likely be seen as respectable sources for any research project. (You still need, of course, to analyze the claims, evidence, and assumptions in a scholarly book and to assess its relevance to your research.)

▶ **Trade books** are published by commercial presses, such as Penguin or Free Press, and written by journalists, professional writers, and scholars seeking a broader audience. Intended for the general public, trade books can range considerably in quality and credibility. Some are well researched, even though they may be documented in an informal way, and written by highly reputable authors, whereas others may be rush jobs to capitalize on some event in the news. For these reasons, you need to assess the authority and credibility of trade books on an individual basis.

▶ **Other books** from religious and political presses, nonprofits and professional associations, trade unions, and research institutes can be valuable sources, depending on your research process. Some religious and political presses (e.g., Maryknoll, Monthly Review, South End) have good reputations and reliable editorial practices. Research institutes (sometimes called "think tanks") like the Pew Center and the Brookings Institution issue books, pamphlets, and reports that are credible. Other presses can be fly-by-night and have much sketchier reputations. Make sure you know the organization behind the press.

Periodicals

Here are six different types of periodicals and a quick look at what they cover.

▶ **Scholarly journals** (e.g., *American Sociological Review, Rhetoric Society Quarterly, New England Journal of Medicine*) contain recent research by scholars in the field written for other scholars. Articles are subjected to a rigorous review process by peer readers and the journal editor, so they have a high degree of credibility and authority.

▶ **Popular magazines**, such as *Rolling Stone, Glamour, Sports Illustrated*, and *Wired*, focus on a particular market niche—whether music, young women, sports fans, or computer enthusiasts. Others, such as *Discover, Smithsonian*, and *Natural History*, popularize topics in a range of fields for interested readers. Some popular magazines like *People* and *Us* feature mainly lightweight articles about celebrities, whereas others, such as *Scientific American*, contain serious articles written by reputable writers for the educated public.

▶ **Public affairs magazines** (e.g., *New Republic, The Nation, Atlantic Monthly*) publish highly reputable and well-researched articles, often by well-known writers, on topics of current interest to their audience of educated readers. Some public affairs magazines have a partisan political perspective (e.g., *National Review* is conservative, and *In These Times* is left-liberal). Others feature a range of perspectives. Public affairs magazines can be helpful in acquiring background information and a sense of the issues about current events.

▶ **Newsmagazines** such as *Newsweek, Time,* and *U.S. News and World Report* come out weekly, with news reports and commentaries on current events. Written by experienced journalists, the articles in newsmagazines can help you understand recent and past events in detail—and the editorials and commentaries give you a sense of the climate of public opinion. They can be a good supplement to your research, but should not be the main source.

▶ **Newspapers** such as the *New York Times, Wall Street Journal,* and *Washington Post* cover national and international news, along with the latest in science, business, sports, culture, and the arts. These national newspapers have highly credible reputations and are good sources for background, especially if you're researching a historical topic. Local newspapers can provide useful information on local events, past and present.

▶ **Trade magazines,** for example, *Advertising Age, PC Computing,* and *Farm Journal,* focus on a particular profession or industry, with articles written by industry experts for others in the field. These magazines can give you a good sense of how a profession or industry sees an issue—and thereby can be a helpful supplement to your research, depending on what your research project is.

THE LIBRARY

Your college library is likely to be your main source for books and periodicals. Many college libraries offer workshops on doing research and how to use the various research sources. Check with your library to see what programs and services it offers students.

The Library Catalog

You can search most online library catalogs by author, title, periodical, subject heading, or keyword. A note on the last two:

▶ *Subject headings* are normally based on the Library of Congress Subject Headings (LCSH), a reference source that lists the standard subject headings used in catalogs and indexes. Consult the LCSH to identify subject headings that are relevant to your research. Notice also that book entries in online catalogs include related subject headings. Once you find books that look useful, you can use the subject headings listed.

▶ *Keywords* include words that appear in the author's name, book title, subject heading, and in some cases a summary or abstract. Keyword searches can be useful because they don't depend on preestablished subject headings (but do include them). Keyword searches also allow you to combine several keywords to give your search more focus.

If you don't find relevant books using subject headings or keywords, consult with a reference librarian. He or she can help you refine your search—and can point you to other resources the library has that you'll find helpful.

Reference Books

Your library is likely to have a range of reference books that will be useful to your research. These may be available in print or electronic form.

▶ *General and specialized encyclopedias* help you get started on a research project and provide key information as your research deepens. General encyclopedias, such as *Collier's Encyclopedia* or the *Encyclopedia Britannica*, provide overviews on a topic, but specialized encyclopedias, such as the *Encyclopedia of Philosophy* or the *Women's Studies Encyclopedia*, give more in-depth and scholarly treatments of a subject.

▶ *Bibliographies* list books and articles published on particular subjects and fields of study. Some are annotated, with brief descriptions and sometimes evaluations of the entries. You can search for bibliographies by adding the term *bibliography* or *annotated bibliography* to a keyword search. Ask a reference librarian what bibliographies your library has that may be relevant to your research.

▶ *Disciplinary guides and companions*, such as the *Cambridge Companion to Postcolonial Literary Studies* or the *Harvard Guide to American History*, give you overviews of a field of study by respected scholars. They also include important bibliographical information on important work in a particular discipline.

▶ *Other reference works* include atlases, almanacs, yearbooks, biographical and historical dictionaries, and handbooks. You can browse the reference section to see what your library has available. Ask a reference librarian to help you identify the reference relevant to your research.

Electronic Databases

There are literally hundreds of searchable electronic databases that provide continually updated lists of newspaper, magazine, and scholarly journal articles, often with the full text available as pdfs.

▶ *General databases* are portals to a collection of databases. These include Academic Search Premier, LexisNexis (with access to laws, statutes, legal opinions, and global news sources) and LexisNexis Academic, and ProQuest (with access to periodical articles).

▶ *Subject-specific databases* focus on areas of study. These include ERIC (an education database), PubMed (on medical research), MLA International Bibliography (on literary criticism), and PsycINFO (on psychology research).

Part of the trick of research is identifying the most relevant database for your purposes. Most libraries have an index of databases with descriptions of their contents. Reference librarians will help you get started using the most appropriate databases for your research and give you helpful suggestions about how to search them. (Also see the section "How to Use Keywords" below for tips on effective searching techniques.) These electronic databases are library subscription services; availability varies from library to library. In addition, as of March 2012, Google Books had scanned over 20 million books, which can be searched through Google by clicking Books, to find information and sample chapters for in-copyright books and downloadable full-text versions of public domain and out-of-copyright books.

SEARCHING THE WORLD WIDE WEB

Everyone knows the World Wide Web is filled with information from all manner of sources. Some of these are appropriate for academic research projects, but others are not. When you use a popular search engine such as Google, MSN Search, or Yahoo!, pay attention to whether you land at a reputable Web site, one that is sponsored by a credible individual, group, or institution (a university, library, research institute, government agency, foundation, nonprofit, or news service). Advocacy groups and corporations put up a good deal of information on the Web, much of which can be useful to a research project, but make sure you take into account their perspective and interests. Google Scholar can be useful in locating academic sources, but it is not a substitute for the academic databases your college or university library is likely to have available.

How to Use Keywords

The secret to using electronic databases and Web search engines is to find the right keyword or combination of keywords. This will typically take some experimenting. Adding modifiers will help you find what you need. For example, if you're researching Elvis Presley's first recordings at the Sun studios in 1954, you'll get a more focused search on Google if you use *Elvis Presley Sun sessions* rather than just *Elvis Presley*. Reference librarians will help you identify keywords that work for your research project.

Reference librarians will also help you use advanced search options that are offered by many databases and search engines, as well as command terms and characters (called Boolean operators) to refine your search and narrow the hits you get. Boolean operators differ among databases and search engines. Here are some of the most commonly used:

> ▶ **Quotation marks or AND or + limit your search by connecting terms.**
> Google connects terms automatically, but in other cases entering *Elvis Presley Sun sessions* or *Elvis Presley AND Sun sessions* or *Elvis Presley + Sun sessions* will limit the number of hits.

▶ **NOT or—also limits your search by eliminating material.** Let's say you want to find information on concussions in professional sports aside from football. In this case, enter *concussion AND professional sports NOT football* (or–*football*).

▶ **OR expands your search.** If you are searching for material on the abolition of capital punishment in Russia before the Soviet Union fell in 1989, enter *death penalty AND abolish AND Russia OR Soviet Union.*

GOVERNMENT PUBLICATIONS

The U.S. government publishes massive amounts of information annually, largely through the Government Printing Office (GPO). You can search the catalog of government publications at http://catalog.gpo.gov/F?RN=263462424.

The Library of Congress offers access to an enormous range of government and library resources at www.loc.gov/index.html, including Thomas (after Thomas Jefferson) with legislative information, databases on Congress, current bills, public laws, committee information, online version of the Congressional Record, and other current and historical documents at http://thomas.loc.gov.

Many government agencies have their own Web sites, including the Bureau of the Census at www.census.gov, which has a vast amount of statistical and demographic data.

OTHER SOURCES

Attending events and performances such as lectures, seminars, readings, plays, and concerts; visiting museums; and watching films, videos, and television or listening to the radio and recorded music are all important forms of research. Depending on the nature of your research, these activities provide information and perspectives to supplement your work with print and electronic sources. Or they can be the main focus of your research. This section briefly explains what performances, museums, and the media offer to researchers.

Performances and Events

Your college may sponsor lectures, readings, or seminars that bring noted speakers to campus. Attending such events provides you with information that you couldn't find elsewhere and gives you the opportunity to question the speaker. In addition, college or local theaters and music and dance companies may stage plays and concerts related to your research. Attending such live performances can deepen your understanding, say, of a Shakespeare play, a Verdi opera, or a style of jazz, folk, or popular music—and offer a useful supplement to reading about the topic or listening to recordings. In all these instances, taking notes is probably the most appropriate research strategy.

On the other hand, performances may themselves provide the focus for your research. You might, for example, want to research what takes place at a Metallica concert or a poetry reading in a local bookstore. In cases such as these, you'll likely draw on observation and perhaps interviews, as well as reading pertinent sources or listening to recordings.

Museums

Visiting art, science, natural history, and history museums can provide you with a wealth of information to enhance your research. Depending on your topic, you can see in person paintings, sculpture, or photographs pertinent to your research; artifacts and displays from a historical period you're investigating; or scientific exhibits. Some museums as well as historical societies have special collections and archives that offer research sources unavailable elsewhere. Again, note taking is probably the research strategy you'll use.

Museums can also be the focus of a research project. Museum studies is a relatively new field that covers the subject of who visits museums, why, and what they do. By reading some of the literature in this field, you can frame questions to answer with field research methods—observation, interviews, and questionnaires.

Media

Documentary films, television and radio programs, and music and spoken-word recordings can be good sources of information to add to the print and electronic sources you're using.

At the same time, films, television, radio, or recorded music are valuable sources for studying the media and mass communication. For example, if you want to investigate the issue of violence in children's television shows, you may want to watch a variety of children's programs in order to count the incidences of violence and identify the types of violence depicted. Or you could analyze television commercials to see how men and women are depicted and what, if any, gender stereotypes are perpetuated. In this type of research, it can be quite helpful to tape television or radio programs so that you can return to them in the course of your inquiry.

CHAPTER 16

Fieldwork and the Research Report

Not all research is conducted in the library. In fact, the library may be just a starting point, providing an overview of your topic and the background information you need in order to undertake field research. Field research includes observations, interviews, and questionnaires.

Researchers turn to these methods of inquiry when they have questions that can't be addressed solely on the basis of print or electronic sources. Here are some examples of research topics and the fieldwork they might lead to:

▶ To determine whether a shopping mall in the area should enforce a curfew for teenagers, you observe the mall on weekend nights to see what danger or nuisance, if any, teenagers pose.

▶ To understand the effects of state-mandated testing on classroom teachers, a student in an education course decides to interview ten sixth-grade teachers whose classes will be taking the test.

▶ To find out how much the undergraduates at their college drink each week, a group of students designs and administers an anonymous questionnaire.

As you can see from these examples, the kind of field research you do and how extensive it will be depend on the questions with which you begin, as well as the amount of time you have. Field research can be time consuming, but it can also give you information and insights that you could not get in any other way.

In this chapter, we'll look first at the genre of the research report. Next, we consider how researchers design fieldwork. Finally, we discuss how researchers work in the field and three common methods they use—observation, interviews, and questionnaires.

ETHICS OF RESEARCH

INFORMED CONSENT

Informed consent means that a person who is asked to participate in a research study has adequate information about its purpose and methods to make a voluntary decision about whether he or she will take part. If you are asking people to be interviewed or to fill out a questionnaire, you need to explain what your research is about, why you're doing it, and what you plan to do with the results. As a rule, you should guarantee your research subjects' anonymity by not referring to them by name or by using a pseudonym. In some instances, such as oral histories or interviews with public figures, it may be appropriate to use people's real names. Most colleges and universities have Institutional Review Boards that can give you more information about obtaining informed consent.

UNDERSTANDING THE GENRE: RESEARCH REPORTS

The research report is the primary means of communication that natural and social scientists, engineers, computer scientists, and other researchers use to present their findings. Academic journals in a range of fields—from biochemistry and astronomy to sociology and psychology—are filled with articles reporting research that employs various methods of investigation. (See "Uncertainty and the Use of Magic" by Richard B. Felson and George Gmelch, in Chapter 8, pages 259–264, for a scholarly research report.)

A research report is really quite simple and fairly standardized in its form. If you have ever done a lab report in a science class, you're already familiar with its parts: Introduction, Literature review, Methods, Results, Discussion, and Conclusions.

To see how these sections work in an actual research paper, let's look at "Food Sources in South Providence," a research report that Luis Ramirez wrote for a field research assignment in the sociology course "Hunger in America." As you read, notice how each section functions within the report.

Food Sources in South Providence

Luis Ramirez

Introduction

Establishes a general problem

The economic downturn that started in 2008, combined with reductions in state social programs, has made <u>access to food a growing source of concern for low-income individuals and families in Rhode Island</u>. The unemployment rate in Rhode Island increased from 7.1 percent in April 2008 to 11.1 percent in April 2009, the highest in New England and the second highest in the nation (Kaiser Family Foundation, 2009). Moreover, Rhode Island was the only state in New England to experience a decline in median wages between 2000 and 2006; it has the ninth least affordable rents in the country; and social programs for low-income families such as cash assistance through the RI Works Program, housing subsidies, medical care, and child care have been slashed (Brewster, 2008). The convergence of these factors has put a good deal of stress on individual and family budgets. Forty-six percent of Rhode Islanders who seek food assistance through the Rhode Island Community Food Bank network of pantries choose between paying for food and paying for utilities. An additional 32 percent choose between food and medicine or medical care (Rhode Island Community Food Bank, 2009). One of the results is that hunger in Rhode Island has grown from affecting 1 out of 10 households in 1998 to affecting 1 out of 8 households today (Nord and Hopwood, 2008).

Introduces the specific question that the research addresses

Given the state of the economy and a shrinking safety net, <u>it is crucial to understand how low-income individuals and families secure food to meet their household's dietary needs</u>. With the elimination or restriction of public assistance programs, dependence on non-commercial food sources that low-income families use to evade hunger may increase to buffer the cuts and loss of benefits. Non-commercial food sources can be divided into four categories: 1) public assistance programs, 2) home production, 3) emergency relief, and 4) gifts (see Table 1).

Describes prior research

A <u>good deal of research on people's diets</u> has focused on measuring food intake and its nutritional quality by such methods as the "twenty-four hour recall,"

Food Sources 2

the "food frequency" checklist, the "seven day diet record," and direct weighing and measuring of daily meals (Pelto, Jerome, & Kandel, 1980). Other researchers have attempted to develop indicators to assess hunger (Physicians Task Force on Hunger in America, 1985; Radimer, Olson, & Campbell, 1990). These studies have been useful in providing information about general patterns of food use, diet, nutrition, and the prevalence of hunger. What these studies do not include, however, is information about how people actually acquire their food.

Creates a research space by indicating a gap in prior research

More recently, researchers have examined how low income individuals and families use supplemental sources of income beyond public assistance programs and wages to make ends meet (Rank & Hirschl, 1995; Edin & Lein, 1997). These researchers have found that the benefits allocated from food stamps and public assistance are not enough to meet basic needs, despite recipients' attempts to budget and stretch their limited resources. The purpose of this study is to determine whether this is the case with low-income families in South Providence and the extent to which they depend on non-commercial food sources to provide for basic needs.

Describes recent research

Proposes to extend recent research

TABLE 1 NONCOMMERCIAL FOOD SOURCES

Table 1 gives details of noncommercial food services

1. Public assistance	Food stamps
	AFDC
	Special Supplemental Feeding Program for Women, Infants, and Children (WIC)
	School breakfast and lunch programs
2. Home production	Private and community gardens
	Gathering food (nuts, berries, herbs, greens, etc.) in public parks
	Fishing
3. Emergency food relief	Churches
	Community centers
	Food banks
4. Gifts	Familial networks
	Friends and neighbors

Methods

A questionnaire on how people acquire their food was administered to thirty low-income individuals who use the services of South Providence Neighborhood Ministries (SPNM). SPNM is a not-for-profit community center which provides a range of services such as emergency food relief, clothing and utility assistance, English as a Second Language classes, tutoring programs, sewing lessons, public health programs, and so on. The questionnaire was administered, with the informed consent of participants, in January and February 2009.

The demographic characteristics of the study population are summarized in Table 2. Of the 30 participants, 28 (93.3%) were women and two (6.6%) were men. Twenty were Latino (66.7%), five (16.7%) African American, three (10%) Southeast

TABLE 2 DEMOGRAPHIC CHARACTERISTICS OF STUDY POPULATION

	Number	Percentage
Age		
Younger than 18	1	3.3
18–30	6	20
31–50	18	60
51+	5	16.7
Marital Status		
Married	8	2.7
Not Married	27	73.3
Ethnicity		
Latino/Hispanic	20	66.7
African American	5	16.7
Southeast Asian	3	10
African	2	6.7
Work		
Employed	6	20
Unemployed	24	80

Food Sources   4

Asian, and two (6.7%) African. Six (20%) worked full or part-time, while 24 (80%) were unemployed.

Results

Presents data from research without commenting

This study found that the participants draw on a number of non-commercial food sources to meet their families' dietary needs. As Table 3 illustrates, the majority participated in public assistance programs of one type or another, including RI Works Program (56.7%), food stamps (66.7%), WIC (50%), school lunch programs (84.2%), and school breakfast programs (78.9%).

TABLE 3   NUMBER AND PERCENTAGE OF HOUSEHOLDS USING PUBLIC ASSISTANCE PROGRAMS

	Number	Percentage
AFDC		
yes	17	56.7
no	13	43.3
Food Stamps		
yes	20	66.7
no	10	33.3
WIC		
yes	15	50
no	15	50
School Lunch		
yes	16	84.2
no	3	15.8
School Breakfast Program		
yes	15	78.9
no	4	21.1

As shown in Table 4, a number of participants fish for food (26.7%), grow food (30%), and gather food in public parks and other places (20%).

**TABLE 4 NUMBER AND PERCENTAGE OF HOUSEHOLDS ENGAGING IN
VARIOUS FORMS OF HOME PRODUCTION (FISHING FOR FOOD,
GROWING FOOD, GATHERING FOOD)**

	Number	Percentage
Fishing		
yes	8	26.7
no	22	73.3
Growing		
yes	9	30
no	24	70
Gathering		
yes	6	20
no	24	80

Table 5 shows the number of participants who use emergency food relief and family networks to acquire food. The vast majority of study participants use food pantries and other emergency food distribution centers (97.6%). Nineteen (65.5%) say they visit on a regular basis about once a month, and ten (34.5%) say they go sporadically. Eleven people (44%) eat at a relative's house at least once a month, and six people (24%) feed relatives at least once a month.

Discussion

Identifies most important finding

The <u>most significant results</u> of this study are the extent to which participants use a range of food sources to meet their basic needs. These results appear to confirm the findings of Rank and Hirschl, and Edin and Lein that neither public assistance nor low-paying jobs provide people with sufficient resources to make ends meet. <u>My study found</u> that benefits from RI Works Program and food stamps are not enough to meet a family's dietary needs. Therefore, supplemental sources, such as fishing, food production, food gathering, emergency food relief, and family food sharing are important sources of food for many low-income people.

Food Sources   6

TABLE 5 NUMBER AND PERCENTAGE OF HOUSEHOLDS WHO UTILIZE EMERGENCY RELIEF AND FAMILIAL NETWORKS

	Number	Percentage
Emergency Relief		
yes	29	97.6
no	1	3.3
Feed Relatives Often		
yes	6	24.0
no	19	76.0
Are Fed by Relatives Often		
yes	11	44.0
no	14	56.0

Explains possible implications of the study results

The study results also suggest that at least some people who are eligible for public assistance do not choose it as a food option. One participant said that he does not like to use government programs and would rather use emergency food relief because the people are "nicer" and "not as condescending." It may be that food pantries are no longer temporary and infrequent means of meeting people's household food needs. Rather, people may be using food pantries as a regular strategy to feed their families, particularly at the end of the month when benefits from RI Works Program and food stamps run out.

Conclusion

Note tentative language "suggest," "may," "perhaps"

Perhaps the most troubling aspect of this study is that low-income people were already using many means of acquiring food, in addition to public assistance programs, before the economic downturn and the shrinking safety net, and that this reliance, if anything, is likely [to] increase. The number of working poor households served by food pantries has grown from 25 percent in 1997 and 29 percent in 2001 to 32 percent in 2009, at the same time the number of households that use pantries and receive food stamps has decreased from 49 percent in 1997 and 46 percent in 2001 to 36 percent in 2009 (Rhode Island Community Food Bank, 2009). These figures suggest that emergency food relief sources such as food pantries will continue to be under growing pressure to serve their clients. Familial networks are also vulnerable, as those who are currently feeding other family members lose food support through RI Works Program, food stamps, and SSI.

References

Brewster, K. (2008, September). Rhode Island's shrinking safety net. Paper presented at the Women Ending Hunger conference, Providence, RI.

Edin, K., & Lein, L. (1997). Work, welfare, and single mothers' economic survival strategies. *American Sociological Review*, 61, 253–266.

Kaiser Family Foundation. Rhode Island unemployment rate (seasonally adjusted), 2008–2009 (2009). Retrieved from http://www.statehealthfacts.org/23&cat=1&rgn=41

Nord, M. & Hopwood, H. (2009). A comparison of household food security in Canada and the United States. (Economic Research Report No. ERR-67). Washington, D.C.: United States Department of Agriculture.

Pelto, G. H., Jerome, N. W., & Kandel, R. G. (1980). Methodological issues in nutritional anthropology. In N. W. Jerome, R. G. Kandel, & G. H. Pelto (Eds.), *Nutritional anthropology: Approaches to diet and culture* (pp. 27–59). New York: Redgrave.

Physicians Task Force on Hunger in America (1985). *Hunger in America: The growing epidemic*. Boston: Harvard University School of Public Health.

Radimer, K. L., Olson, C. M., & Campbell, C. C. (1990). Development of indicators to assess hunger. *Journal of Nutrition*, 120, 1544–48.

Rhode Island Community Food Bank (2009). Statistics. Retrieved from www.rifoodbank.org/matriarch/MultiPiecePage.asp_Q_PageID_E_31_A_PageName_E_StatsThermometerGraphic

Rank, H., & Hirschl, R. (1995). *Eating agendas*. New York: Basic Books.

…enre

…he roles they play in this and many other
…enre works in a fuller sense, we need to take

…troduction establishes the purpose of the
…ical moves:

…low-income individuals and families access-
…downturn and reduced social programs.

… of understanding how low-income people
…ey rely on noncommercial sources.

…le's diets by citing sources from the literature.
…ating a gap in previous research.

…and proposes to extend it by examining how
…c needs.

…letermining the extent to which low-income
…rely on noncommercial food sources.

…luction is a relatively complex passage that
…establish a general problem and then to cre-
…ion by showing how the proposed research
…n can be extended. This Introduction offers a
…rs justify their research question by explain-
…it fits into a body of prior work.

…at first glance may seem straightforward, as
…e was administered and presents the demo-
…The underlying question that the Methods
…well equipped the proposed method is to
…e learn that the questionnaire asked thirty
…ey acquired their food. The study population
…ight have included a bit more explanation of
…to gather the needed information.

… note about the Results section. First, the
…ar without any comment on their meaning
…e key features of research reports: the data
…rpreted. For students who are used to writ-
…claim followed by supporting evidence, the
…d. But the logic here is that of displaying the
…commenting on it. In keeping with this logic
is the second feature to note, namely, that the complete data are displayed
visually in tables and main points summarized in the text.

▶ **Discussion:** Instead of discussing the results point by point as they appear in the Results section, discussion sections typically begin with the most important finding of the research and explain how it relates to the central research question. That takes place here in the first paragraph. Notice, too, that the interpretations of the results use such tempered terms as "appear to confirm" and "suggest." (No researcher would claim that the results prove anything definitively. There is always room for further research and new questions.)

▶ **Conclusion:** The conclusion draws out a major implication of the study by emphasizing the growing reliance on food pantries and familial networks. It doesn't propose a solution, for the study is a research report, but the issues it identifies are of potential significance to policy makers concerned about food security.

⇗ WORKING TOGETHER

Analyzing a Research Article

1. Work in a group of three or four. Find a short article that reports research in an academic journal such as *Current Anthropology, American Journal of Public Health,* or *American Journal of Sociology.*

2. Analyze the introduction (and literature review if it's a separate section). Pay particular attention to how the article establishes the general problem or topic, how it defines the research question, and how it relates that question to prior work.

3. Use the rhetorical moves in the analysis of "Food Sources in South Providence" to see how the introduction creates a research space.

DESIGNING A FIELD RESEARCH PROJECT

You can use the discussion of the research report genre as a way to start thinking about how to design a field research project. Many of the key considerations you'll need to take into account have already been raised. Here are some questions to help you use your knowledge of the genre to plan your research:

▶ What is the general problem or issue that you want to investigate? You might be interested, say, in the experience of Iraq veterans, the Poetry Slam scene, the problem of cheating, or the role of fraternities and sororities at your college.

▶ What background information is available on the problem or issue? What specific research has already been done? What questions have guided that research?

▶ How can you use background information and previous research to help you carve out a research space to develop a significant question? Are there gaps in the research?

▶ Is there research you could extend? Perhaps there are studies of student attitudes toward cheating and toward fraternities and sororities that could be updated. On the other hand, there may be lots of writing on Poetry Slams but little or no research.

▶ What research method or combination of methods best fits your research question?

Writing a Proposal

A proposal can serve as the first draft of the Introduction to your research report by explaining:

▶ What the general problem or issue is

▶ What the specific question you're asking about the problem or issue is

▶ How the main question you're trying to answer relates to previous work

▶ Why the particular method you're planning to use is an appropriate research strategy for answering the question

▶ How you plan to conduct the research

▶ What you think the significance of the results might be

OBSERVATION

Observation has an important advantage over other research methods: it gives you direct access to people's behavior. Let's say you've done some background research on how men and women interact in conversations, and you want to test some of the findings in the published literature. You might decide to see whether students at your college follow the pattern described by Deborah Tannen in *You Just Don't Understand*—that men interrupt more during conversations and are less likely than women to use questions to elicit comments from others. Interviewing or surveying wouldn't give you very reliable information, because even if people were willing to be honest about how they behave in conversations, it's not likely that they could be accurate. In contrast, by going to the school dining hall over a period of several days, you could observe what men and women in fact do when they talk and what conversational patterns emerge.

The Process of Observation

Planning

The following questions can help guide your planning. You can use them to write a proposal that explains the role of observation in your research plan (see "Writing a Proposal," above).

▶ Why does the line of research you're pursuing call for observation? What research question or questions are you addressing?

THREE CONSIDERATIONS TO TAKE INTO ACCOUNT WHEN YOU DO OBSERVATIONS

1. Recognize that you'll be observing a limited group and making a limited number of observations. Your findings may confirm or dispute what you've read, or they may suggest new questions and lines of research. Be aware, however, that although your results are valid for the group you observed, the group itself may not be representative of all the students at your college, not to mention all men and women. So when you generalize on the basis of your observations, acknowledge the scope of your research and ensure that the claims you make take these limits into account.

2. Take into account, too, the fact that your presence can have an effect on what you observe. People sometimes behave differently when they know they're being watched. They may clown around, try to make themselves look good, or otherwise act in relation to the observer. The best way to deal with this fact is to conduct multiple observations. In many cases, people being observed will get used to the presence of the observer over time.

3. Finally, be aware of the assumptions you bring to the observations—both when you are conducting the research and when you are analyzing the results. All researchers, of course, operate from a point of view, so there's no reason to think you can be a neutral bystander just recording what happens. For this reason, however, there is a very real danger that you will record in your observations only what you expected to see. Observers' assumptions can cause them to miss, ignore, or suppress important events. Being conscious of your own assumptions can help keep you open to things you had not anticipated.

▶ How exactly can observations help you answer your research question?

▶ What kinds of observations would be most useful? Whom and what do you want to observe? What are the best times and places for these observations? How many observations should you do?

▶ What should your observations focus on? What exactly do you want to record in your field notes? What method or methods will you use to record your observations?

You may need to request permission to observe, as well as permission to use any recording devices.

Conducting Observations

When you arrive at the place where you'll do your observation, look for a vantage point where you will be able to see what's going on and yet won't be obtrusive. Consider whether you want to move periodically from one spot to another to get a number of different perspectives on the activity or place you're observing. Make sure any equipment you've brought—camera or tape recorder—is ready to use.

Researchers typically develop their own system of taking field notes. Nonetheless, a few suggestions may be helpful. Begin by writing down the basic facts: the date, time, and place. Keep your notes on one side of the page. Depending on your research questions, here are some things to consider:

▶ **The setting:** Describe the overall size, shape, and layout. You may want to sketch it or draw a diagram. Note details—both what they are and how they are arranged. Pay attention to sounds and smells, as well as to what you can see.

▶ **The people:** Note the number of people. What are they doing? Describe their activities, movement, and behavior. What are they wearing? Note ages, race, nationality, and gender. How do they relate to one another? Record overheard conversation, using quotation marks.

▶ **Your response:** As you observe, note anything that is surprising, puzzling, or unusual. Note also your own feelings and reactions, as well as any new ideas or questions that arise.

Analyzing Your Notes

After you've finished your observation, read through your notes carefully and, if you want, type them up, adding related points that you remember. Then make sure you analyze your notes from the standpoint of your research questions:

▶ What patterns emerge from your notes? What are your main findings? What, if anything, surprised you?

▶ What research questions do your notes address? What issues remain to be addressed?

▶ Do your observations confirm what you have read? How would you explain any discrepancies?

▶ What should your next step be? Should you go back to the library? Should you conduct further observations? If further observations are needed, what form should they take?

⟩ FIELDWORK PRACTICE ||||||||||||||||||||||||||||||||||||||||||||||||||||||||||||||||||||||||||||||||||||||

Observation

After getting their permission, observe the dinnertime conversation and interaction of your family or a group of friends, taking notes on your observations. When you are finished, read through your notes, considering what they reveal about the patterns of interaction you observed. Then answer the following questions:

1. Do you think your presence as an observer had an effect on what people said and did?

2. How difficult is it to observe and keep notes? What, if anything, could you do to make the process easier?

3. What did you expect to happen at dinner? How did these assumptions influence your observations? Were some things you observed unexpected? Do you think your assumptions caused you to miss anything? Were there certain things you chose not to include in your notes? Why?

4. What tentative conclusions do you think are legitimate to draw from your observations?

INTERVIEWS

As noted in Chapter 6, "Profiles," interviews are often an essential part of capturing the personality and opinions of the person being profiled. Interviews, of course, are not limited to profiles; they have a range of uses. Here are three common situations in which researchers can make good use of interviews, either as the main basis of a research project or a component.

▶ **Interviews with experts:** Interviewing an expert on anorexia, the 1980s loft jazz scene in New York City, the current status of the cod fishing industry, or virtually any topic you're researching can provide you with up-to-date information and analysis, as well as a deepened understanding of the issues involved in these topics—and can make a significant contribution to a research project. In such cases, interviewing an expert offers a source of information that supplements print or electronic sources.

▶ **Interviews with key participants:** Interviews can do more than just supplement your research. In some cases, interviewing takes on a central role in a research project, especially in research on contemporary issues where it makes sense to talk to the people involved. Suppose you are planning to research the role of public libraries in relation to recent immigrants. You would certainly want to see what's been written about the topic, but you could also interview librarians at neighborhood branches who work with, say, Russian Jews, Southeast Asians, Haitians, or Latinos. In turn, these interviews could lead to further interviews with recent immigrants, as well as community organizations, to get their perspective on what libraries are doing and might do. The research paper you write would quite likely feature prominently the information you'd gathered from these interviews as the main source of data, with print and electronic sources providing background and context for your research.

▶ **Oral histories:** Interviews with people who participated in significant historical events can provide a useful focus for research. To understand the event from the perspective of a rank-and-file worker, you might interview a trade unionist who participated in a significant strike. Or to understand the origins of the New Right on college campuses in the early 1960s, you might interview someone who was involved in the founding of Young Americans for Freedom. Interviews such as these are often called oral histories because they are the spoken accounts of important historical moments, based on people's memories of their lived experience. For this type of research, you need, of course, to look at what historians have said—both to generate questions before the interview and to relate the oral history to professional accounts after the interview as part of the written presentation of your research.

As you can see, the type of interviewing you do depends largely on the kind of research question you're raising and the sources it leads you to.

The Interview Process

Planning

The following considerations can help you get started on planning interviews. You can use these considerations to write a proposal that explains how the interviews fit into your research design (see "Writing a Proposal," on page 483).

▶ **Background research:** The first step, as in any research, is to get an over-view and basic information about your topic. At this point, you are likely to be formulating questions to guide your research. Consider how interviewing can help you answer these questions. What do you hope to find out?

▶ **Choosing interview subjects:** The nature of your research question should suggest appropriate subjects to interview. Does it make sense to interview an expert on the topic? Or does your research seem to call for interviews with people involved in the subject you're investigating? Are the people you're considering likely to provide the information you're looking for?

▶ **Preparing interview questions:** Use the notes from your background research to prepare interview questions. Interviewers normally use open questions to get their subjects talking—phrasing questions so that the natural answer is a "yes" or a "no" generally leads to a dead end. How open, of course, depends on your research question and your subject. If you are interviewing an expert, your questions should be precise and seek specific information ("Estimates vary on the number of cod in the North Atlantic. Can you give me your view?"). For oral histories, on the other hand, questions often begin at a general level ("Tell me what it was like growing up in Oklahoma") but become more specific ("Do you recall when and why your family decided to migrate to California?"). When you have come up with a list of questions, organize them so that one question leads logically to the next.

▶ **Considering the types of interviews:** The in-person, face-to-face interview is probably the best-known type of interview, but there are alternatives you may want or need to consider. The "Four Types of Interviews" box summa-rizes four possibilities, their advantages and disadvantages.

Setting Up the Interview

Whether the person you plan to interview is a stranger, a friend, or a relative, you'll need to set up the interview. Generally, this means writing a letter or mak-ing a telephone call, both to ask for permission and to set a time (or a deadline in the case of an interview by mail). Introduce yourself and your purpose. Be honest about what you are doing—many busy people are happy to help students with assignments. However, be prepared to be turned down. Sometimes busy people are just that—busy. If someone seems too busy to meet with you in person, ask whether you could interview him or her by telephone, mail, or email—or whether

FOUR TYPES OF INTERVIEWS

- **In-person interviews:** In-person interviews have some significant advantages over the other types. Often, when answering your question, the person you are interviewing may take the conversation in a new direction. Although at times this means you'll need to guide the conversation politely back to your topic, sometimes the new direction is one that you hadn't thought of and would like to explore. At other times, you may realize that your questions aren't working and that to get the information you need, you'll have to revise and supplement them on the spur of the moment.

  Some researchers prefer to take handwritten notes during in-person interviews. Doing so, however, poses certain difficulties. Responses to your questions may be long, and you may not be able to write fast enough. And devoting all your attention to note taking makes it harder to think about what the person is saying and harder to guide the interview by choosing the next question or formulating a new one. For these reasons, many researchers use a tape recorder. But be flexible about using one. Most people don't mind, and the tape recorder will simply fade into the background. But some people are bothered by it and might not be as open as they would be if you took notes. If you feel the disadvantages of tape recording are outweighing the advantages, be prepared to change methods.

- **Telephone interviews:** Telephone interviews are similar to in-person interviews. Both enable you to be flexible in your questioning. However, some people may find telephone interviews a bit more difficult to manage because rapport may not emerge as easily as in an in-person interview.

  A speakerphone is useful if you've been given permission to record the conversation. Even if you haven't, a speakerphone makes it easier for you to take notes.

- **Email interviews:** Sometimes you might prefer or may have to conduct your interview by email. You might, for example, want to interview someone who isn't willing or able to schedule an in-person or telephone interview but who has no objection to answering questions. One advantage of email interviews is that they provide you with a written record. On the other hand, it may be difficult to follow up on interesting ideas or to clarify points. Phrasing and organization of questions are especially crucial in mail or email interviews because you can't adjust your line of questioning as you can in an in-person or telephone interview.

- **Online interviews:** Interviews can also be conducted online. Real-time synchronous communication sites, such as IRCs (Internet Relay Chat), MUDs (multi-user domains), and MOOs (MUD object oriented), allow computer users from around the world to "talk" to each other in writing in real time.

  Like email interviews, online interviews help simplify note taking by recording the conversations. Make sure, however, that you are familiar with the technology necessary to record the interview—you don't want to lose all of your hard work.

the person knows someone else you could interview. Above all, be polite. Be sure to schedule the interview far enough in advance of your due date to allow you to follow up with more questions or with further research if the interview leads to areas you had not previously considered. For in-person or telephone interviews that you want to record, ask at this point for permission to record. If it's appropriate, ask the person you're interviewing whether there is anything you should read before the interview.

Conducting an In-Person or Telephone Interview

For in-person and telephone interviews, the interview itself is a crucial moment in your research. To get an in-person interview off on the right foot, arrive promptly. Make sure that you dress appropriately and that you bring your questions, tape recorder (if you have permission to record the interview), a pad and pens, and any other materials you might need. For telephone interviews, make sure you call at the time agreed upon.

Because in-person and telephone interviews are really conversations, the results you get will depend in part on your flexibility as a listener and a questioner. The person you're interviewing will be looking to you for guidance, and it is quite likely that you'll be faced with choices during the interview. Let's say you are interviewing someone about why she attends your college. She says, "I came because they've got a really good computer science program, I got a good financial aid package, and I didn't want to go very far from home. You know what I mean?" Then she pauses, looking at you for direction. You've got a choice to make about which thread to follow—the student's academic interests, her financial situation, or her desire to stay near home.

After the Interview

Especially with in-person and telephone interviews, plan time immediately afterward to review the results of the interview and to make further notes. Transcribe your tape, if you recorded the interview, or print out hard copies of email or online interviews. Make sure that you've noted direct quotations and that you've written down pertinent information about the interview (such as the time, date, and location).

Analyzing the Transcript

Material from an interview can be used in many different ways in a research project. It can be central to the final report or can provide supplementary quotations and statistics. The ideas you had ahead of time about how you would use the interview might be changed by the interview or by other aspects of your research process. To help you understand what use to make of the interview, write responses to these questions:

▶ What are the most important things you learned? List what seem to be the main points.

▶ What, if anything, surprised you? Why?

▶ What does the interview contribute to your understanding of your research question? How does the information relate to what you've already learned about your topic? If information, opinion, and point of view differ, how do you account for this?

► What questions does the interview raise for further research? What sources does it suggest you use?

A Final Note on Interviews

Be sure to thank the people you interview. (A note or email message is a nice touch.) When you've finished your paper, send them a copy along with a letter or email thanking them again.

⏵ FIELDWORK PRACTICE |||||||||||||||||||||||||||||||||||||||||||||||||||||||||||||||||||||||||||||||||||||||||

Interviewing

Work with a partner. Interview your partner about why he or she decided to attend your college. Before the interview, think about the questions you want to ask, how you want to conduct the interview—in person, by telephone, online, or via email—and how you want to keep track of what's said. After the interview, write a paragraph or two about the experience. What sorts of questions were most effective? Did any ideas and topics come up that you had not expected? What decisions did you make during the interview about threads to follow in the conversation? What were the advantages and disadvantages of the interview method you chose? What problems did you experience in recording information?

Compare your response to the interview process with those of classmates. What generalizations can you, as a class, draw about interviewing?

QUESTIONNAIRES

Questionnaires are similar to interviews, except that they obtain responses from a number of people by using questionnaires. They can target a particular group of people—to find out, for example, why students at your college have chosen to major in biomedical engineering or why employees at a particular company do or don't participate in community service activities. Or they can examine the beliefs and opinions of the "general public," as is the case with those conducted by political pollsters and market researchers on everything from people's sexual habits to their religious beliefs, to their product preferences.

Although interview questions are generally open, questionnaires tend to use more "closed" questions, such as true/false, yes/no, checklists, ranking, and preference scales. In this sense, they sacrifice the depth of information to be gotten about one person for the breadth of data about many people.

Deciding whether you should design and distribute a questionnaire depends largely on what you're trying to find out. If, for example, you've read some research on the television viewing habits of college students and want to find out whether students at your school fit the patterns described, it makes sense to ask many students about their habits rather than to interview three or four. The results you get are liable to give you a more accurate picture. At any rate, as a way to start, write a proposal that explains your research project and why a survey is the best method (see "Writing a Proposal," on page 483).

The Process of Designing and Conducting a Questionnaire

If a questionnaire seems appropriate to your research project, you'll need to decide who your subjects are, prepare the questionnaire, distribute it, and then compile and analyze the results.

Getting Background Information

Designing a questionnaire is similar to designing an interview. Namely, you'll begin by researching your topic to get an overview and background information. Then you'll determine whether a questionnaire is the most appropriate method for addressing your research question: Does it make sense to gather information on the opinions and habits of a number of people instead of talking to a few in depth or doing another form of research? At this point, before you expend the time and effort it takes to design and conduct a questionnaire, make sure that a questionnaire is likely to provide you with the information you're seeking.

Selecting Participants

To be sure that they can generalize from the results of their questionnaires, professional researchers try to obtain responses from a representative sample of the population they're investigating. If, for example, you're surveying employees of a company or students who major in bioengineering, it should be easy enough to send questionnaires to all of them. In other cases, however, you may need to choose people within the population at random.

For example, if you're studying the students' opinions of a first-year writing program, you could get a random sample by surveying every tenth person on the class lists. But even in that case, you would have to make sure that your responses were representative of the actual population in the classes and reflected their demographic composition. You might have to modify the distribution of your questionnaire to guarantee it reached a representative sample—men, women, blacks, whites, Latinos, Asians, traditional-age students, and returning students.

If your results were to be meaningful, you'd also need to include enough participants to give your survey credibility. Keep in mind that regardless of how you conducted your survey, not everyone would participate. In fact, as pollsters are well aware, it's generally necessary to survey many more people than you expect to receive responses from. Often, as few as 10 percent of the surveys mailed out are returned. A good rule of thumb is to aim for 40 percent, and if you don't get it the first time, do multiple distributions.

When you wrote up your findings, any generalizations based on your questionnaire should be limited to the population your survey represented (you should not, for example, generalize about American voters as a whole based on a survey of students at your college). You would need to be sure to discuss any potentially relevant information on survey participants, such as information on age, gender, or occupation.

ETHICS OF RESEARCH

LOADED QUESTIONS

Public opinion polls are a fixture in American politics. Most political candidates, the two major political parties, and many other political organizations and advocacy groups use opinion polls to understand the public's mood and to shape policy. In fact, at times political polls can go beyond simply providing information that will play an active role in the formation of public policy. In political debates, the results of opinion polls are often used to buttress the position of one side or the other. Because opinion polls have become such an important part of political life, there is the temptation to use them in a partisan way.

Take, for example, a poll conducted by advocates of casino gambling in Rhode Island to determine the degree of public support. The main question in the poll—"Would you approve a casino if it would reduce your property taxes and improve education?"—is clearly a loaded one because it stacks the deck with casino proponents' arguments. As political pollster Darrell West noted, the "corollary question from an anti-gambling perspective" might read, "Would you support a casino if you thought it would raise crime rates and increase the level of gambling addiction?"

Not surprisingly, a majority of people polled favored casino gambling when the question was framed in terms of casino revenues reducing taxes and improving education. However, when the question was posed in an unbiased way—"Do you favor or oppose the construction of a gambling casino?"—the results were quite different. Fifty-three percent opposed the casino, 42 percent supported it, and 5 percent had no opinion.

Designing the Questionnaire

The results of your survey will depend to a large extent on the questions you ask. Here are some considerations to take into account in designing a questionnaire:

1. Include a short introduction that explains the purpose of the survey and what you will do with the results. Point out that survey participants' opinions are important. Ask them to complete the survey, and give them an estimate of the time it will take to do so.

2. Make sure the questions you ask are focused on the information you need for your research. It's tempting to ask all sorts of things you're curious about. The results can be interesting, to be sure, but asking more questions than you actually need can reduce your response rate. In general, keep the questionnaire brief in order to maximize returns.

3. Design the questionnaire so that it is easy to read. The visual design should suggest that it won't take long to fill out. Don't crowd questions together to save space. And leave plenty of space for open questions, reminding survey respondents that they can write on the back.

4. At the end of the questionnaire, include a thank-you and explain where or to whom it should be returned.

Types of Questions

Questions can take the form of checklists, yes/no questions, categories, ranking scales, and open questions. Each type of question works somewhat differently from the others. Usually you will want to combine several types to give you the particular information you need. You also need to consider the most effective and logical order to present the questions. Questionnaires typically begin with the least complicated or most general questions and end with open-ended questions.

Here are examples of the most common types of questions designed for a research project investigating whether the political attitudes and involvement of students at the researcher's college support or refute claims in the published literature that students today are generally apathetic when it comes to politics.

CHECKLIST

Which of these political activities have you participated in? Please check all that apply.

_____ voted in national election

_____ voted in state or local election

_____ campaigned for a candidate

_____ worked for a political party

_____ attended a political rally or demonstration

_____ belonged to a political organization or advocacy group

_____ other (specify): _____

Yes/No Questions

Are you a registered voter?

_____ Yes

_____ No

Categories

How would you describe your political views?

_____ left wing

_____ liberal

_____ moderate

_____ conservative

_____ right wing

_____ none of the above/don't know

Ranking Scales

Please rank the following items according to their importance as national priorities. (Use 1 for the highest priority, 7 for the lowest.)

_____ strengthening the economy

_____ reducing crime

_____ balancing the budget

_____ improving education

_____ improving the health care system

_____ improving race relations

_____ reducing poverty

Lickert Scale

[Lickert scale questionnaire items gauge the degree of agreement with particular statements of opinion. Researchers typically design a sequence of such items.]

Please indicate the degree to which you agree or disagree with the following statements. Enter the number that best expresses your view on each item.

1—Strongly agree

2—Agree

3—Not Sure

4—Disagree

5—Strongly Disagree

_____ It is important to be well informed about current political events.

_____ There's no point in getting involved in politics because individuals can have little influence.

_____ Voting in elections is a responsibility, not just a right.

_____ The political system is controlled by politicians and lobbyists.

Open-Ended Questions

[Open-ended questions call for brief responses. Such questions are more time consuming and difficult to tabulate than closed questions, but they can often yield information that other types of questions will not.]

What, if anything, has motivated you to be interested in political affairs?

_____

_____

_____

What, if anything, has posed obstacles to your being interested in political affairs?

_____

_____

_____

After you've prepared your questionnaire, try it out on a few people. Do their answers tell you what you wanted to know? Based on these answers, have you covered all the issues and have you phrased your questions well? If you see any problems, revise your questionnaire. Now is the time to get it right—before you administer it to a lot of people.

Conducting the Survey

Your questionnaire can be distributed in various ways: in person, by mail, by telephone, or online through listservs, newsgroups, or Web sites. Your choice of how to conduct the survey will depend on your choice of a sample population, your deadline, and your resources (mail surveys, for example, can be quite expensive because you'll need to provide stamped, self-addressed envelopes).

Compiling, Analyzing, and Presenting Results

Compiling results amounts to tallying up the answers to each question. This is a fairly straightforward procedure for closed questions such as checklist, yes/no, multiple-choice, and ranking and Lickert-scale items. For open questions, you might write down key words or phrases that emerge in the responses and tally the number of times these (or similar) words or phrases occur. Keep a list of answers that seem of special interest to use in your research report as quotations.

Researchers present the results of closed questions in the form of percentages in the text of their reports. In addition, you may want to design tables or other visual displays of your results to complement the written report.

Remember that your results do not speak for themselves. You must analyze and explain how they are significant to your research project. The following questions can help you begin such an analysis:

▶ What patterns emerge from responses to individual questions? What patterns emerge from responses across questions?

▶ How would you explain these patterns? Try to think of two or more explanations, even if they appear to be contradictory or mutually exclusive.

▶ What is the significance of these explanations for your research? If the explanations seem contradictory, can you think of ways to reconcile them? If not, on what grounds would you choose one or the other?

▶ What tentative claims might you make based on your analysis of the results? How would you justify such claims?

⊃ FIELDWORK PRACTICE ||||||||||||||||||||||||||||||||||||||||||||||||||||||||||||||||||||||||||||||||||||

Conducting a Survey

Work in a group of three or four. Your task is to design a pilot questionnaire to determine student opinion about some aspect of the academic program or student services at your college. You could focus on, say, advising, orientation for new students, required first-year courses, tutoring, or anything else that interests you. Begin by listing the kind of information that you want to get. Then write five to ten questions that seem likely to give you this information. Test your questionnaire by administering it to ten to fifteen classmates. Once you've gotten their responses, evaluate your survey:

1. Did you get the information you were looking for?

2. Is each of the questions worded in such a way that it provides the information you anticipated?

3. Should you word any of the questions differently to obtain the information you're seeking? Should you delete any of the questions or add new ones?

4. Explain your answers.

5. Compare your group's experience with that of other groups. What conclusions can you draw about questionnaire design?

PART 4

Delivery: Presenting Your Work

INTRODUCTION: DELIVERING THE MESSAGE

Whether you are designing the manuscript of a critical essay or research paper, a fund-raising letter, a brochure, a Web site, or a PowerPoint presentation, the visual appearance of your work carries meanings and has its own rhetorical effects.

There are three main reasons to learn more about the visual design of page and screen and how the delivery of messages embodies writers' and designers' purposes:

▶ **To establish credibility with readers:** The reader's first impression of a print text or computer screen is likely to be influenced by its visual appearance. A sloppy manuscript or a Web site that's hard to navigate will raise doubts about the credibility of the person who prepared it. This in turn can undermine the rhetorical effectiveness of the message, no matter how interesting or insightful the content might be. Design is a means to establish the writer's ethos—by presenting the writer and the message as credible and authoritative.

▶ **To enhance readability:** One of the marks of effective page and screen design is that readers find the content easy to follow. Writers use visual cues such as paragraph breaks, white space, headings, and bulleted lists, whereas Web designers are concerned with the amount and size of text on a screen, the relationship between text and graphics, and the navigability of a Web site. In either case, the goal is to enable the reader to concentrate on the message by carefully designing its presentation.

▶ **To assist in planning:** As you have seen in earlier chapters, many genres of writing, such as letters, public documents, reports, and proposals have a typical "look" that makes them immediately recognizable. The visual design of print and electronic documents also provides a scaffolding to help writers and designers organize and present their messages.

In the following chapters, you will find more information on how to design effective documents of various sorts. Chapter 17, "Visual Design," explores some of the purposes of visual communication and offers suggestions about designing such familiar documents as flyers, newsletters, and brochures. Chapter 18, "Web Design," offers a basic introduction to the rhetoric and design features of Web sites, while Chapter 19, "PowerPoint Presentations," looks at how you can plan effective talks and use visuals such as PowerPoint.

CHAPTER 17

Visual Design

Learning to write means learning how to design a range of print and digital texts—everything from academic papers, reports, and résumés to flyers, brochures, newsletters, posters, and Web sites. At one time, writers passed along typed manuscripts to designers who turned them into print pages by choosing typefaces, doing page layout, and adding illustrations. Today, there is often little difference between writing and designing pages. It's a continuous process of desktop publishing as writers decide which fonts to use, add images, and design the look of the page as they are composing.

Writers today are just as likely to be writing for screens, tablets, and e-readers as for the print page. What Gunther Kress calls the "centuries-long dominance of writing" is giving way to "the new dominance of the image." In the past, images typically served to illustrate written texts that narrated information. Today, images increasingly are the primary vehicle for displaying information. Rather than the continuous writing of the book, readers now often encounter in magazines and Web sites chunks of written text that fit into the image space of the print and electronic page as visual design elements. In short, the visual proportions of writing are changing, as text and images take on new ratios, to make new compositions.

In this chapter, we begin by exploring what these changes look like visually. Then we consider how visual design is used for purposes of identification, information, and persuasion. Finally, we will see how you can create effective page designs and use type to enhance your message.

THE LOGIC OF WRITING AND THE LOGIC OF THE IMAGE

What Gunther Kress calls the "logic of writing" produces pages that invite readers to follow the written text as the main focus of their attention. The goal of visual design is to involve readers in what writers have to say, and any images or visual displays of information are subordinate to the writing and are meant to illustrate its main themes and important ideas. Graphic designers sometimes use the term "quiet pages" to refer to such readerly designs, like the following:

Ben Austen, "The Last Tower: The Decline and Fall of Public Housing." *Harper's*, May 2012

As you can see, the image on the opening page of the article is clearly secondary to the writing, with just a caption "Photograph of 1230 N. Burling © Paul D'Amato" at bottom right to identify the photo. More photos appear in the rest of the article to help readers visualize people and places, but they are secondary to the writing.

The "logic of the image," on the other hand, designs pages that are meant to display information visually—whether alone or accompanied by written text. Images are meant to stand on their own by combining words and graphics rather than illustrating information and ideas that appear in the written text. In this sense, the logic of the image joins reading and seeing together in a single act, whereas the logic of writing separates reading and seeing as independent complementary acts. Consider, for example, the design of the information at the top of the two pages from a *National Geographic* article "The Gulf of Oil" on the BP oil spill of April 2010. Notice how many separate items of information there are and how you decode the display of information.

REPORT

THE LAST TOWER

The decline and fall of public housing
By Ben Austen

Forty years ago, when U.S. cities began abandoning high-rise public housing, blasting crews would fill a tower with explosives and in a few monumental booms all would be reduced to rubble and rolling clouds of dust. It was as swift as it was symbolic. Now the demolitions are done by wrecking ball and crane, and the buildings are brought down bit by bit over months. This gradual dismantling seemed especially ill suited to the felling, in March 2011, of the last remaining tower at Cabrini-Green. Described almost unfailingly as "infamous" or "notorious," this Chicago housing project had come to embody a nightmare vision of public housing, the ungovernable inner-city horrors that many believe arise when too many poor black folk are stacked atop one another in too little space. For the end of Cabrini-Green, I imagined something grandiose and purifying—the dropping of a bomb or, as in *Candyman*, the 1992 slasher film set in Cabrini's dark wasteland, a giant exorcising bonfire. Instead, as I watched, a crane with steel teeth powered up and ripped into a fifth-floor unit, causing several feet of prefabricated façade to crumble like old chalk. Water sprayed from inside the crane's jaws to reduce dust.

Ben Austen is a contributing editor of Harper's Magazine. His article "Southern Culture on the Skids" appeared in the October 2010 issue.

The fifteen-story high-rise was known by its address, 1230 N. Burling. Already stripped of every window, door, appliance, and cabinet, the monolith was like a giant dresser

without drawers. The teeth tore off another hunk of the exterior, revealing the words I NEED MONEY painted in green and gold across an inside wall.

Chicago was once home to the second-largest stock of public housing in the nation, with nearly 43,000 units and a population in the hundreds of thousands. Since the mid-1990s, though, the city has torn down eighty-two public-housing high-rises citywide, including Cabrini's twenty-four towers. In 2000, the city named the ongoing purge the Plan for Transformation, a $1.5 billion, ten-year venture that would leave the city with just

15,000 new or renovated public-housing family units, plus an additional 10,000 for senior citizens. Like many other U.S. cities, Chicago wanted to shift from managing public housing to become instead what the Chicago Housing Authority (CHA) called "a facilitator of housing opportunities." The tenants of condemned projects were given government-issued vouchers to rent apartments in the private market, or were moved into rehabbed public housing farther from the city center, or wound up leaving subsidized housing altogether.

The centerpiece of the plan, though, was an effort to replace the former projects with buildings where those paying the market rate for their units and those whose rents were subsidized would live side by side. Since 1995, when the federal government rescinded a rule that required one-to-one replacement of any public-housing units demolished, the U.S. Department of Housing and Urban Development has awarded billions of dollars to cities nationwide to topple housing projects and build in their stead these mixed-income developments.

During his twenty-two years as Chicago's mayor, Richard M. Daley had moved Lake Shore Drive and created Millennium Park, but he believed the Plan for Transformation represented his most sweeping effort to reshape the city's landscape. Daley proclaimed

Photograph of 1230 N. Burling © Paul D'Amato

"The Gulf of Oil." *National Geographic*, October 2010

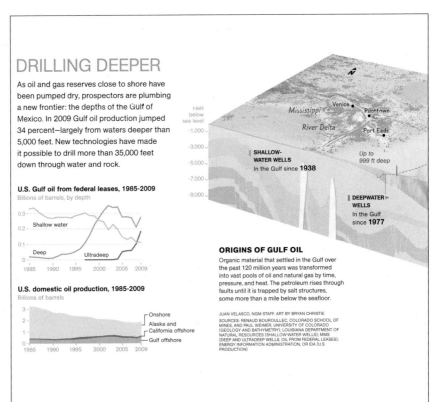

DRILLING DEEPER

As oil and gas reserves close to shore have been pumped dry, prospectors are plumbing a new frontier: the depths of the Gulf of Mexico. In 2009 Gulf oil production jumped 34 percent—largely from waters deeper than 5,000 feet. New technologies have made it possible to drill more than 35,000 feet down through water and rock.

U.S. Gulf oil from federal leases, 1985-2009
Billions of barrels, by depth

U.S. domestic oil production, 1985-2009
Billions of barrels

ORIGINS OF GULF OIL

Organic material that settled in the Gulf over the past 120 million years was transformed into vast pools of oil and natural gas by time, pressure, and heat. The petroleum rises through faults until it is trapped by salt structures, some more than a mile below the seafloor.

JUAN VELASCO, NGM STAFF. ART BY BRYAN CHRISTIE
SOURCES: RENAUD BOUROULLEC, COLORADO SCHOOL OF MINES, AND PAUL WEIMER, UNIVERSITY OF COLORADO (GEOLOGY AND BATHYMETRY); LOUISIANA DEPARTMENT OF NATURAL RESOURCES (SHALLOW-WATER WELLS); MMS (DEEP AND ULTRADEEP WELLS, OIL FROM FEDERAL LEASES); ENERGY INFORMATION ADMINISTRATION, OR EIA (U.S. PRODUCTION)

its cement job. It failed to circulate heavy drilling mud outside the casing before cementing, a practice that helps the cement cure properly. It didn't put in enough centralizers—devices that ensure that the cement forms a complete seal around the casing. And it failed to run a test to see if the cement had bonded properly. Finally, just before the accident, BP replaced the heavy drilling mud in the well with much lighter seawater, as it prepared to finish and disconnect the rig from the well. BP declined to comment on these matters, citing the ongoing investigation.

All these decisions may have been perfectly legal, and they surely saved BP time and money—yet each increased the risk of a blowout. On the night of April 20, investigators suspect, a large gas bubble somehow infiltrated the casing, perhaps through gaps in the cement, and shot straight up. The blowout preventer should have stopped that powerful kick at the seafloor; its heavy hydraulic rams were supposed to shear the drill pipe like a soda straw, blocking the upward surge and protecting the rig above. But that fail-safe device had itself been beset by leaks and maintenance problems. When a geyser of drilling mud erupted onto the rig, all attempts to activate the blowout preventer failed.

The way BP drilled the Macondo well surprised Magne Ognedal, director general of the Petroleum Safety Authority Norway (PSA). The Norwegians have drilled high-temperature, high-pressure wells on their shallow continental shelf for decades, he said in a telephone interview, and haven't had a catastrophic blowout

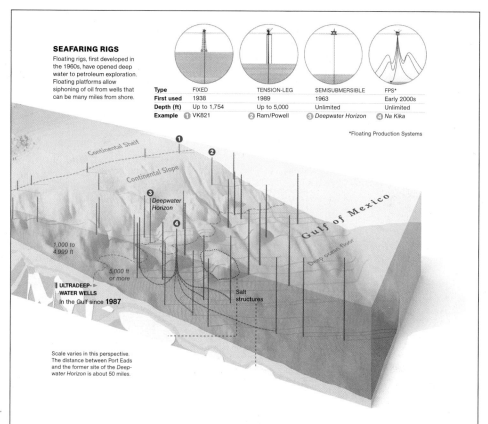

SEAFARING RIGS

Floating rigs, first developed in the 1960s, have opened deep water to petroleum exploration. Floating platforms allow siphoning of oil from wells that can be many miles from shore.

Type	FIXED	TENSION-LEG	SEMISUBMERSIBLE	FPS*
First used	1938	1989	1963	Early 2000s
Depth (ft)	Up to 1,754	Up to 5,000	Unlimited	Unlimited
Example	① VK821	② Ram/Powell	③ *Deepwater Horizon*	④ Na Kika

*Floating Production Systems

Continental Shelf

Continental Slope

① ② ③ *Deepwater Horizon* ④

Gulf of Mexico

Deep ocean floor

1,000 to 4,999 ft

5,000 ft or more

Salt structures

▌ ULTRADEEP-WATER WELLS
In the Gulf since **1987**

Scale varies in this perspective. The distance between Port Eads and the former site of the *Deepwater Horizon* is about 50 miles.

since 1985. After that incident, the PSA and the industry instituted a number of best practices for drilling exploration wells. These include riserless drilling from stations on the seafloor, which prevents oil and gas from flowing directly to a rig; starting a well with a small pilot hole through the sediment, which makes it easier to handle gas kicks; having a remote-controlled backup system for activating the blowout preventers; and most important, never allowing fewer than two barriers between the reservoir and the seafloor.

"The decisions [BP] made when they had indications that the well was not stable, the decision to have one long pipe, the decision to have only six centralizers instead of 21 to create the best possible cement job—some of these things

were very surprising to us here," says Ognedal.

The roots of those decisions lie in BP's corporate history, says Robert Bea, a University of California, Berkeley expert in both technological disasters and offshore engineering. BP hired Bea in 2001 for advice on problems it faced after it took over the U.S. oil companies Amoco and ARCO. One problem, Bea says, was a loss of core competence: After the merger BP forced thousands of older, experienced oil field workers into early retirement. That decision, which made the company more dependent on contractors for engineering expertise, was a key ingredient in BP's "recipe for disaster," Bea says. Only a few of the 126 crew members on the *Deepwater Horizon* worked directly for BP.

The drilling operation itself was regulated by

THE GULF OF OIL   47

⚡ FOR CRITICAL INQUIRY ||||||||||||||||||||||||||||||||||||||||||||||||||||||||||||||||||||||||||||

Understanding the Logic of Writing and the Logic of the Image

1. Notice how you decode the words, images, and color of the Sentencing Project's "Felons and Voting Rights." How do you put the three together? Pay attention to where your eyes go. Compare this act of reading and seeing to reading just written words on the page.

■ Kentucky and Virginia prohibit almost all ex-felons from voting

□&□ 35 states ban those on probation or parole for felonles from voting

□ 13 states allow those on probation and parole to vote

■ Maine and Vermont allow even incarcerated felons to vote

□ 9 states further restrict voting for ex-felons depending on the crime, or in Nebraska, for a two-year waiting period.

Sentencing Project. "Felons and Voting Rights"

2. The Plant is a net-zero energy vertical farm and food business operation currently in the process of development in a former meat-packing plant in an old industrial neighborhood in Chicago. This diagram visualizes the various systems that will work together in The Plant:

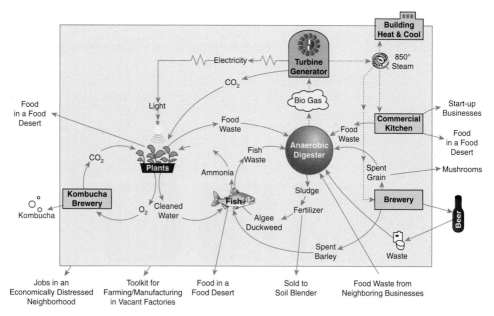

Reprinted by permission of The Plant/Plant Chicago, NFP. www.plantchicago.com.

Visit the Web site of The Plant at www.plantchicago.com. Consider what you learn about The Plant according to the "logic of writing" compared to "the logic of the image." You'll find a video feature titled "How the Plant Works." Check this out and compare it to the diagram reproduced here.

3. Textbooks at every level, from elementary school through college, are turning increasingly to the visual display of information (the "logic of the image"). Compare a recent textbook for an introductory college course in biology, economics, history, or other field to an older textbook that was published before 1980. Consider to what extent each relies on the "logic of writing" compared to the "logic of the image."

HOW VISUAL DESIGN EMBODIES PURPOSES

In this section, we consider how visual forms embody designers' purposes in three ways:

▶ Identification

▶ Information

▶ Persuasion

Identification

A primary function of visual design is to identify things, places, publications, and organizations. Street and building signs, posters, flags, logos, trademarks, letterheads, package labels, and mastheads on newspapers and magazines are some of the typical visual forms used for identification.

One well-known example of designing for purposes of identification is the signage system the United States Department of Transportation commissioned the American Institute of Graphic Arts (AIGA) to create for transportation facilities and international events. Graphic designers Roger Cook and Don Shanosky designed thirty-four symbol signs in 1974, to which sixteen additional images were added in 1979. The remarkable clarity and legibility of these now iconic images provided a means of visual communication to bridge language barriers and cultural differences.

United States Department of Transportation

Signs. United States Department of Transportation. Roger Cook and Don Shanosky

You will no doubt recognize immediately many or all of the eighteen signs from the AIGA system of graphic identification reproduced here. Consider how the designers distilled complex messages into simple and consistent visual forms.

Logos are another instance of designing for purposes of identification. Bill Marsh is the graphic editor of the Week in Review section of the Sunday *New York Times,* where this piece on logo redesign appeared on May 31, 2009.

IDEAS & TRENDS

Warmer, Fuzzier: The Refreshed Logo

By BILL MARSH

THE WORLD ECONOMY is in mid-swan dive. Wallets are in lockdown. So how does a company get people to feel just a little bit better about buying more stuff? (And perhaps burnish a brand that has taken some public relations lumps?)

Behold the new breed of corporate logo — non-threatening, reassuring, playful, even child-like. Not emblems of distant behemoths, but faces of friends.

"A logo is to a company what a face is to a person," said Michel Tuan Pham, a professor of marketing at Columbia Business School. "It's hard to memorize facts about a person when you only know their name but you haven't seen their face." So logos remind consumers about companies' traits and pluck at emotions, "the glue that ties all the information about the brand name together," Mr. Pham said.

The economy, environment, image repair — new logos may address all of these. They are also meant to stand out in a crowd, but there are striking similarities among recent redesigns.

TONED-DOWN TYPE   Bold, block capital letters are out. Their replacements are mostly or entirely lower case, softening the stern voice of corporate authority to something more like an informal chat.

"Logos have become less official-looking and more conversational," said

Patti Williams, a professor of marketing at the University of Pennsylvania's Wharton School. "They're not yelling. They're inviting. They're more neighborly."

Blogs and e-mail, Ms. Williams said, may be encouraging a quieter, calmer, lower-case branding vernacular. Who isn't tired of screeds that assault the reader via THE CAPS LOCK KEY?

Here are two remakes:

Wal-Mart before  and after

Kraft before  and after

Letterforms are lighter and rounder — an extended family of homogenized fonts that would be comfortable on a local newsletter or generic Web page.

FRIENDLY FLOURISHES   Kraft Foods has joined Amazon.com and Hasbro, all represented by logos that smile. And to further lighten the corporate mood, whimsy in the form of sprigs and bursts has been appended to several big brands.

Wal-Mart's old mark was navy blue, but it felt Red State. The company has

been under heavy attack for its labor and environmental practices, bruising its brand in bluer quarters.

A major image overhaul is under way, and a new logo is starting to appear across the country. The military-style Wal-Mart star has given way to a yellow twinkle that punctuates a new message: this is a company that cares, with fast and friendly service and a fresh, innovative outlook, according to Linda Blakley, a Wal-Mart spokeswoman.

HAPPIER COLORS   "The economy is the No. 1 influence this year," said John H. Bredenfoerder, a color expert and design director at Landor Associates, the brand-consulting company that produced the new Cheer detergent emblem. Amid all the gloom, he said, "people need a little joy in their lives." Cue the new logos: electric blue type with accents in school bus yellow, red, purple, orange and green.

Last year's top influence, green for sustainability, remains; leaves still sprout across the corporate landscape.

Mr. Bredenfoerder said that blue was also gaining as a stand-in for the environment (think of earth's blue orb as seen from space, or clear blue waters) as well as for fresh optimism. But please, make it a joyful sky blue — not dark, corporate-titan navy.

Signs of Change

THEN

WAL★MART

KRAFT

now

Walmart ☀

kraft foods ☀
Make today delicious

With little fanfare, **Wal-Mart** began replacing its commanding all-capitals logo with lighter blue text in September, punctuated by what the company calls a "spark."

The food giant **Kraft** unveiled a new corporate identity, with a smile and "flavor burst," in February. Its old racetrack-shaped, block-capitals emblem remains on packaging.

Analyzing Logos

1. Consider how Marsh sets up the context of logo redesign. What is the rhetorical situation? Where is the call to redesign coming from? How do the three redesign features—"toned-down type," "friendly flourishes," and "happier colors"—affect the identity of the brand?

2. The National Aeronautics and Space Administration (NASA) logo has an interesting history. The logo on the left (called the "meatball") was the official insignia 1959–1982 and 1992-present, while the logo on the right (called the "worm") was used 1975–1992.

NASA

   Do a search for online sources with opinions and analysis of NASA's changing logos. What seems to be at stake for graphic designers and others? What assumptions about design do you see in comparisons of the two logos?

3. Bring to class three or four similar items you can buy in a grocery store. They could be jars of spaghetti sauce, bottles of spring water, packages of laundry detergent, or whatever. How does the design of the packaging—the brand name, logo, color of the label, fonts, shape of the product, or anything else that's notable—seek to create an identity for its product that distinguishes it from other products of its type?

Information

The purpose of information design is not simply to add visual interest to documents that are primarily verbal but to help readers visualize important processes, trends, and relationships. Notice how the visual display of information enhances the appearance of the page and makes the information easier to process.

orem ipsum dolor sit amet, vilputate consectetuer adipiscing elit, sed diam nonummy nibh euismod ipsum duis autem

CURRENT SNOOZE ALARM SALES

in vulputate velit esse molestie consequat, vel illum dolor e eu feugiat nulla facilisis at vero eros et acc umsan et iusto odio dignissim qui blandit pr aesent luptatum zzril delenit augue duis dolo re te feugait nulla facili. Lorem ipum dolor sit amet, consectuer adipiscing elit, sed diam

YEAR	$ UNTIS SOLD	$ RETAIL
1965	1,100	$ 12,000
1970	65,000	430,000
1975	220,000	2,800,000
1980	673,000	5,900,000
1985	1,220,000	11,670,000

nonummy nibh euismod tincidunt ut laoreet dolore magna aliquam erat volutpat dolore te feugait nulla facilisi. Duis autem vel eumle iriure dolor te feugait. aliquip ex ea commodo conse quat. Duis autem vel eum iriure dolor in hen drerit in vulputate velit esse molestie nulla facili sis at Lorem ipsum dolor sit amet, vilputate consectetuer adipiscing elit, sed diam nonummy nibh e dio dignissim qui blandit pr aesent luptatum zzril delenit augue duis dolo re te feugait nulla facilisi. Lorem ipum dolor sit amet, consectuer

Lorem ipsum dolor sit amet, vilputate consectetuer adipiscing elit, sed diam nonummy nibh euismod ipsum duor in hendrerit in vulputate velit esse molestie cois at vero eros et

PROJECTED TARDISNOOZ SALES

Lorem ipsum dolor sit amet, vilputate consectetuer adipiscing elit, sed diam nonummy nibh euismod ipsum duis autem vel eum iriure dolor in hendrerit in vulputate velit esse molestie consequat, vel illum dolor e eu feugiat nulla facilisis at vero eros et acc umsan et iusto odio dignissim qui blandit pr aesent luptatum zzril delenit augue duis

PROJECTED TARDISNOOZ SALES

YEAR	$ UNITS PROJECTED		$ RETAIL
1990	34,100		$ 430,000
1991	81,000		970,000
1992	239,000	(Break-even)	2,400,000
1993	310,000		3,700,000
1994	228,000	(Recession Projected)	2,200,000
1995	426,000		4,450,000

Lorem ipsum dolor sit amet, vilputate consectetuer adipiscing elit, sed diam nonummy nibh euismod ipsum duis autem vel eum iriure dolor in hendrerit

orem ipsum dolor sit amet, vilputate consectetuer adipiscing elit, sed diam no

CURRENT SNOOZE ALARM SALES

in vulputate velit esse molestie consequat, vel illum dolor e eu feugiat nulla facilisis at vero eros et acc u qui blandit pr aesent luptae feugait nulla facit, scing elit, sed diam

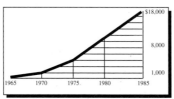

nonummy nibh euismod tincidunt ut laoreet dolore magna aliquam erat volutpat dolore te feugait nulla facilisi. Duis autem vel eumle iriure dolor te feugait. aliquip ex ea commodo conse quat. io dignissim qui blandit pr aesent luptatu

Lorem ipsum dolor sit amet, vilputate consectetuer adipiscing elit, sed diam nonummy nibh euismod ipsum duor in hendrerit in vulputate velit esse molestie cois at vero eros et Lorem ipsum dolor sit amet, vilputate consectetuer adipiscing elit, sed Diam nonummy nibh euismod ipsum duis autem vel eum iriure dolor in hendrerit in vulputate velit esse molestie co nulla facilisis at vero eros et acc umsan et iusto odio dignissim qui blandit pr aesent luptatum zzril delenit augue duis

PROJECTED TARDISNOOZ SALES

Lorem ipsum dolor sit amet, vilputate consectetuer adipiscing elit, sed diam nonummy nibh euismod ipsum duor in hendrerit in vulputate velit esse molestie cois at vero eros et

Cengage Learning

The visual display of information can be divided into three categories: textual, representational, and numerical.

Textual Graphics

Textual graphics organize and display information to emphasize key points and supplement the main text.

- ► **Sidebars and information boxes** add additional information to the main text and visual interest to the page layout. (See Mike Crouch's "Lost in a Smog" in Chapter 13 for examples.)

- ► **Tables** organize and display information that enables readers to make comparisons. (See Luis Ramirez's "Food Sources in South Providence" in Chapter 16 for examples.)

- ► **Time lines** represent change over time.

- ► **Flowcharts and organizational charts** show processes, functions, and relationships.

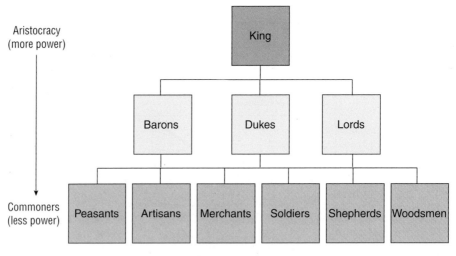

Organizational Chart

Graphic Representation of Timeline for Reporting of Cases

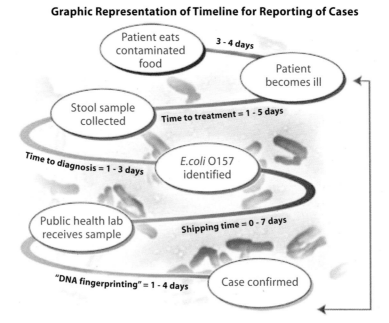

Timeline for Reporting of *E. coli* Cases. Centers for Disease Control.

Representational Graphics

Representational graphics use pictures to orient readers in time and space and to illustrate processes, relationships, and events.

▶ **Photographs, drawings, and other illustrations** enable readers to visualize the content of the written text.

▶ **Maps** often use color coding to help readers visualize the relative location of events or the distribution of a phenomenon.

▶ **Diagrams** use simplified representations to help readers visualize how processes take place.

ISRAEL ZONES & SETTLEMENTS

- Israeli settlements within occupied territories
- Israeli-occupied areas
- Palestinian home-rule areas
- UN, UNDOF, and DMZ zones*

LEBANON

UN Zone

Tyre

UN Zone

Israeli-held "security zone"

Qiryat* Shemona

UNDOF Zone

Al Qunaytirah

1949 Armistice Line

Nahariyya

DMZ

Golan Heights

Acre

Sea of Galilee

Mediterranean

Haifa

Tiberias

SYRIA

Nazareth

DMZ

Sea

I S R A E L

Irbid

1949 Armistice Line

Hadera

Jenin

Netanya

Jarash

Herzliyya

Nablus

1967 Cease-Fire Line

Petah Tiqwa

Tel Aviv-Jaffa

West Bank

Rishon LeZiyyon

Amman

Ramla

Ramallah

Jericho

Ashdod

No Man's Land

Jerusalem

River

Ashqelon

Bethlehem

Ma'daba

Qiryat Gat

Gaza

Erez

Hebron

Dead Sea

JORDAN

Gaza Strip

Deir el Balah

1950 Armistice Line

1949 Armistice Line

Khan Yunas

Beersheba (Be'er Sheva')

Al Qatranah

I S R A E L

Al Karak

Dimona

Sedom

Safi

1949 Armistice Line

Nizzana

N

0 10 20 30 40 km

0 10 20 30 mi

EGYPT (Sinai)

Mizpé Ramon

*UNDOF : UN Disengagement Observer Force
DMZ : Demilitarized Zone

Unayzah

© MAPS.com/CORBIS

Notice how the color coding on this map enables readers to visualize the extent of Israeli settlement in occupied areas of Palestine.

Numerical Graphics

Numerical graphics put the primary focus on quantitative data instead of words or diagrams. Numerical graphics enable writers to analyze the data they are working with and to represent trends and relationships.

▶ **Tables** are probably the simplest form of numerical graphic. Although tables have the lowest visual interest of numerical graphics, they are useful when you have large amounts of information you want to organize and display in a logical and orderly way. (See tables in Richard B. Felsen and George Gmelch's "Uncertainty and the Use of Magic," Chapter 8.)

▶ **Line graphs** are used to show variation in the quantity of something over a period of time. By charting the number of cases on the vertical axis and the period of time on the horizontal axis, writers can establish trends. (See line graphs on pages 515–516.)

▶ **Pie charts** divide the whole of something into its parts, displaying the individual items that make up 100 percent of the whole. Pie charts help readers see the relative weight or importance of each slice in relation to the others. For this reason, many graphic designers agree that to avoid clutter and ensure readability, pie charts should use no more than seven or eight slices.

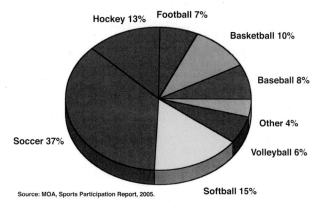

More Than One-Third of Anchorage's Sports Participation Are Soccer Players

Hockey 13%   Football 7%   Basketball 10%   Baseball 8%   Other 4%   Volleyball 6%   Softball 15%   Soccer 37%

Source: MOA, Sports Participation Report, 2005.

Pie Chart

▶ **Bar charts** enable writers to compare data and to emphasize contrasts among two or more items over time. Bar charts run along the horizontal axis from left to right. **Column charts** serve the same function as bar charts but run along the vertical axis, from down to up.

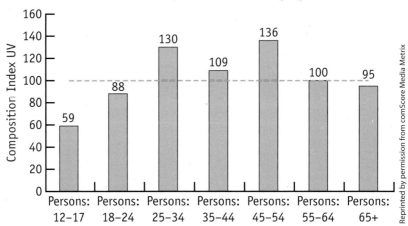

Column Chart

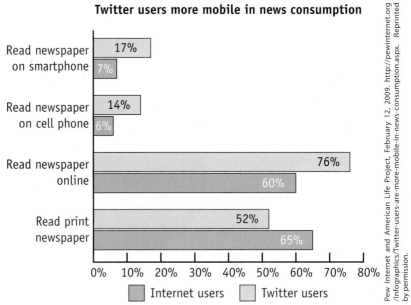

Bar Chart

ETHICS OF INFORMATION DESIGN

DATA DISTORTION

The information design expert Edward R. Tufte says that inept and misleading graphics are widespread in part because visual designers believe that statistical data are boring to readers and in need of jazzing up. As Tufte shows, however, instead of making the data livelier, graphic effects often misrepresent or exaggerate the meaning of the data.

Notice in the illustration below, that the numerical increase in "Fuel Economy Standards for Autos" from 1978 to 1985 is 53 percent—from 18 to 27.5 miles per gallon. As represented, however, the increase from the line representing 1978 standards, which is 0.6 inches, to the line representing 1985 standards, which is 5.3 inches, amounts to 783 percent—a huge distortion of the facts. Moreover, by departing from the usual order of listing dates on an axis—either bottom to top or left to right—the new standards seem to be surging directly at us, exaggerating their effect.

Tufte redesigned this display of information with a simple graph so that the size of the graphic matched the size of the data. As you can see, instead of the dramatic, ever increasing change presented in the original, Tufte's redesign shows that the new standards start gradually, double the rate between 1980 and 1983, and then flatten out—a pattern disguised in the original display. Notice, finally, how the redesign includes a simple comparison of the expected average mileage of all cars on the road to the new car standards, another clarifying item of information missing from the original.

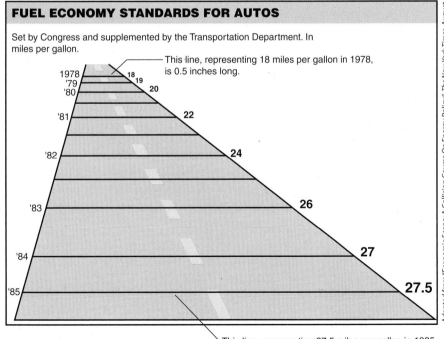

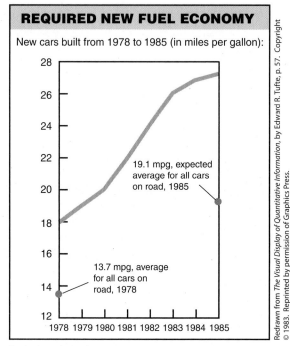

Redesigned graph

✑ FOR CRITICAL INQUIRY

Analyzing Visual Display of Information

1. Look through some recent issues of magazines and newspapers to find three examples of the visual display of information to bring to class. Be prepared to explain how (or whether) your examples organize and display information in a way that complements the written text. Does the size of the graphic match the size of the data? If not, what is the effect?

2. The following situations present clusters of information that can be represented in visual form. In each case, decide whether a line graph, a bar chart, or a pie chart is the best choice to convey the information to readers. Make a sketch of your choice to display this information.

   a. You are preparing the annual report for a community service organization at your college. Part of your task is to explain how the organization has spent the annual budget of $7,500 it receives from the college. Expenditures are the following: $1,500 for printing leaflets, brochures, and the quarterly newsletter; $1,000 for speakers' fees; $500 for a workshop for members; $2,500 to send five members to a national conference on community service; $1,750 for donations to local community organizations; and $250 for refreshments at meetings.

   b. Biology classes at your college are in high demand. No new faculty have been hired nor have any new courses been offered in the past ten years. With the rapid increase of biology majors, classes are overenrolled. In some cases, even majors can't register for the courses they need. You want to make the case that your college needs to hire more biology faculty and offer more courses. Here are the numbers of biology majors enrolled at the beginning of each academic year from 2004 to 2012: 2000—125; 2004—132; 2005—114; 2006—154; 2007—158; 2008—176; 2009—212; 2010—256; 2011—301; 2012—333.

c. You are working for your college's office of alumni affairs and you are involved in a campaign to increase alumni donations. No one has ever researched whether donations vary depending on the major of alumni. To help plan the campaign, you are asked to find out how donation differs according to the major of alumni. You decide to look first at alumni who graduated between 1985 and 1994 and have established their careers. Here is the number of alumni who graduated in the ten-year period and the donations they gave in 2007 arranged by type of major: social sciences, 1,300 graduates—$158,000; humanities, 1,680 graduates—$98,000; business, 2,180 graduates—$326,000; engineering, 940 graduates—$126,000; sciences, 1,020 graduates—$112,00; fine arts, 720 graduates—$48,000; nursing and allied health, 680 graduates—$54,000.

3. In a group with two or three other students, choose one of the reading selections that appear in another chapter. Design a visual display of information to emphasize a main point, trend, relationship, or process in the reading. Be prepared to explain your design.

Courtesy of Men Can Stop Rape/www.mencanstoprape.org

Persuasion

You don't have to look very far to see how visual design is used for purposes of persuasion. Advertising, public service announcements, and advocacy campaigns contend for our visual attention.

Persuasion can address its readers in a number of ways. The famous Uncle Sam army recruitment poster of World War I, for example, took a direct approach to readers, staring them straight in the eye to deliver its command message: "I Want You." A British recruitment poster from the same era took a more indirect approach, putting readers in the role of spectators looking into a living room after the war where children ask their father, "Daddy, what did YOU do in the Great War?"

Notice, on the other hand, how the poster from Men Can Stop Rape appeals not to shame but to positive self-image.

Analyzing Persuasion in Visual Design

1. Find a number of advertisements, public service announcements, or other forms of publicity that integrate words and images into a visual design. Try to get as wide a range as possible. Bring five or six to class. Work in a group with two or three other students. Pay attention to how each visual design addresses you as a reader-viewer. Is it direct address, where you feel someone is talking to you? Or are you positioned in the role of a spectator? Consider how these approaches—direct and indirect—embody the designer's purposes and the persuasive effects.

2. Use the same group of materials. This time analyze how seeing and reading work together and separately in the way you make sense of the message. What are the images you see? What are the words you read? How do they go together to form a message?

VISUAL DESIGN: FOUR BASIC PRINCIPLES

In this section we look at four basic principles that apply to virtually any document you may be called on to design. Each principle emphasizes a particular aspect of design, but all four overlap and mutually reinforce each other.

▶ **Group similar items together:** Grouping similar items creates visual units of attention on the page and thereby helps readers organize and remember information.

▶ **Align visual elements:** Alignment refers to the placement of visual elements on the page—whether you center them or align them left or right. Alignment enables readers to connect the visual elements on the page.

▶ **Use repetition and contrast to create consistent visual patterns:** *Repetition* unifies disparate visual elements and cues readers to where they can expect certain types of information to appear. *Contrast* is a way to emphasize certain visual elements—to make them stand out.

▶ **Add visual interest:** Visual design can follow the first three principles and still be a bit boring. Adding visual interest will not only make readers more likely to pay attention to your message. It also enhances your credibility as someone who knows how to make a sophisticated and stylish presentation.

Use the Four Principles to Redesign Documents

To see what the four principles look like in practice, here are examples of using them to redesign a résumé and a flyer.

Redesigning a Résumé

Groupings of information don't stand out

Alignment is inconsistent—some headings are centered, some flush left

No clear pattern established by repetition and contrast

Martha Smith
143 Oakland Avenue
Philadelphia, PA 19122
(215) 555-2000

Education

Bachelor of Arts in English
Temple University, 1999

Experience

Journalism internship—*Philadelphia Inquirer*
1998–1999
> Covered and wrote by-lined articles on school board meetings
> Researched sex education K–12 for special report
> Assisted editor in preparing special education supplement

Public Relations Assistant—Trinity Repertory Theater, Camden, NJ
1997–1998
> Wrote advertising copy and designed promotional brochures
> Conducted focus groups
> Prepared instructional materials for Theater in the Schools

Writing Center Tutor—Temple University
1996–1999
> Tutored students on wide range of writing assignments
> Worked with international students
> Trained new tutors

Entertainment Editor—*Temple Daily* News
1997–1998
> Planned and assigned music, art, drama, and film reviews
> Edited reviews
> Led staff meetings

Related Skills
> Written and spoken fluency in Spanish, reading ability in French
> Feature Writing, Graphic Design, Editing, Photojournalism

Achievements/Activities:
> Dean's list (every semester)
> Member of Sigma Tau Delta, International English Honor Society
> Secretary of Amnesty International, Temple University chapter
> Varsity cross-country and indoor and outdoor track

References: Available upon request

Résumé (original)

Groupings are more distinct

Visual elements are aligned in a consistent pattern

Use of rules and boldface creates a pattern by repetition

Use of bold-face and sans-serif headings creates a pattern by contrast

MARTHA SMITH

143 Oakland Avenue
Philadelphia, PA 19122
(215) 555-2000

Education

1999   Bachelor of Arts in English
         Temple University

Experience

1998–1999   **Journalism internship** at *Philadelphia Inquirer.* Covered and wrote by-lined articles on school board meetings. Researched sex education K-12 for special report. Assisted editor in preparing special education supplement.

1997–1998   **Public Relations Assistant** at Trinity Theater, Camden, NJ. Wrote advertising copy and designed promotional brochures. Conducted focus groups. Prepared instructional materials for theater in the Schools.

1996–1999   **Writing Center Tutor** at Temple University. Tutored students on wide range of writing assignments. Worked with international students. Trained new tutors

1997–98   **Entertainment Editor** at *Temple Daily News.* Planned and assigned music, art, drama and film reviews. Edited reviews. Led staff meetings

Related Skills

Written and Spoken fluency in Spanish, reading ability in French. Coursework in feature writing, graphic design, design, editing, and photo-journalism.

Achievements/Activities

Dean's list (every semester)
Member of Sigma Tau Delta, International English Honor Society, Secretary of Amnesty International, Temple University chapter, Varsity cross-country, and indoor and outdoor track

References available upon request

Résumé (redesign)

Redesigning a Flyer

Centered layout makes visual elements "float" on the page

No consistent color scheme

No clear pattern of information design

Flyer (original)

Groups visual elements

Aligns visual elements

Creates coherent visual pattern by grouping

Creates contrast by reverse lettering

Uses consistent color scheme

Creates visual interest

Flyer (redesign)

WORKING WITH TYPE

In the age of the personal computer, writers have access to literally hundreds of type fonts and can change their size and underline, italicize, or make them boldface with the click of a mouse. The vast range of possibilities now available, however, can be overwhelming. Writers need to understand what their options are in using type and what kinds of effect their design decisions are likely to have on readers. Here are some basic suggestions about working with type:

▶ **Use white space as an active element in design:** White space is not simply the empty places on a page where no writing or visuals appear. White space plays an active role in creating the visual structure of a document and the relationship among its parts. Notice, for example, how white space makes headings more or less prominent by creating a hierarchy of levels:

Level 1 heading (for titles)

xxxxxxxxxxxxxxxxxxxxxxxxxxxxxxxxxxxxxxxxxxxxxxxxxxxxxxxxxxxxxxxxxx
xxxxxxxxxxxxxxxxxxxxxxxxxxxxxxxxxxxxxxxxxxxxxxxxxxxxxxxxxxxxxxxxxx
xxxxxxxxxxxxxxxxxxxxxxxxxxxxxxxxxxx.

Level 2 heading (on separate line)

xxxxxxxxxxxxxxxxxxxxxxxxxxxxxxxxxxxxxxxxxxxxxxxxxxxxxxxxxxxxxxxxxxx
xxxxxxxxxxxxxxxxxxxxxxxxxxxxxxxxxxxxxxxxxxxxxxxxxxxxxxxxxxxxxxxxxxx
xxxxxxxxxxxxxxxxxxxxxxxxxxxxxxxxxxxxxxxxxxxxxxxxxxxxxxxxxxxxxxxxxxx
xxxxxxxxxxxxxxxxxxxxxxxxxxxxxxxxxxxxxxxxxxxxxxxxxxxxxxxxxxxxxxxxxxx
xxxxxxxxxxxxxxxxxxxxxxxxxxxxxxxx.

Level 3 heading (with text following) xxxxxxxxxxxxxxxxxxxxxxxxxxxxxxxxxxxxx
xxxxxx xxxxxxxxxxxxxxxxxxxxxxxxxxxxxxxxxxxxxxxxxxxxxxxxxxxxxxxxxx xxxx
xxxxxxxxxxxxxxxxxxxxxxxxxxxxxxxxxxxxxxxxxxxxxxxxxxxxxxxxxxxxxxx xxxxxx
xxxxxxxxxxxxxxxxxxxxxxxxxxxxxxxxxxxxxxxxxxxxxxxxxxxxxxxxxxxxxxxxxxx
xxxxxxxxxxxxxxxxxxxxxxxxxxxxxxxxxxxxxxxxxxxxxxxxxxxxxxxxxxxxxxxx.

▶ **Use leading appropriately:** Leading is the typographer's term for the white space that appears above and below a line of type. The basic guideline is that you need more leading—more space above and below type—when lines of print are long, less when they're short. A research paper, for example, is easier to read if it's double-spaced. On the other hand, in newsletters and other documents with columns, it's better to use less leading.

Column A

For shorter lines, as in newsletters and other documents with columns, use less leading. If there's too much white space, readers' eyes can drift when they leave one line and look for the start of the next.

Column B

For shorter lines, as in newsletters and other documents with columns, use less leading. If there's too much white space, readers' eyes can drift when they leave one line and look for the start of the next.

Notice the difference between Column A and Column B:

▶ **Use uppercase and lowercase:** In general, the combination of uppercase and lowercase letters is easier to read than all uppercase.

THIS IS BECAUSE UPPERCASE (OR CAPITAL) LETTERS ARE UNIFORM IN SIZE, MAKING THEM MORE DIFFICULT TO RECOGNIZE THAN LOWERCASE LETTERS, ESPECIALLY ON COMPUTER SCREENS OR SINGLE-SPACED OR ITALICIZED.

The combination of uppercase and lowercase uses more white space, produces more visual variety, and thereby helps the eye track the lines of print.

▶ **Use appropriate typeface and fonts:** Typeface and fonts refer to the design of letters, numbers, and other characters. There are thousands of typefaces available. The visual appearance of typeface contributes to the personality or character of your document. Part of working with type is choosing the typeface that creates the right image and thereby sends the appropriate message to your readers.

Serif and Sans-Serif Typefaces

Typefaces are normally divided into two groups—serif and sans serif. Serif typefaces include horizontal lines—or serifs—added to the major strokes of a letter or a character such as a number. Sans-serif typefaces, by contrast, do not have serifs. Notice the difference:

Serif	Sans-Serif
Century	Geneva
Palatino	Arial
Times	Helvetica

The typical use and stylistic impact of the typefaces vary considerably. Serif typefaces are more traditional, conservative, and formal in appearance. By contrast, sans-serif typefaces offer a more contemporary, progressive, and informal look. Accordingly, serif is often used for longer pieces of writing, such as novels and textbooks. It is also the best bet for college papers. The horizontal lines make serif easier to read, especially in dense passages, because they guide the reader's eyes from left to right across the page. On the other hand, technical writers often use sans-serif for user's manuals and other documents because it evokes a more modern, high-tech look.

#occupy Art Exhibit, Yellow Peril Gallery, Providence, RI

Marcel McVay

Consider the design choices in this poster for the art exhibit #occupy—grouping, alignment, repetition/contrast, and visual interest. Take into account the choice of color and typefaces as well. Does the poster seem to be visually unified? What visual message does it convey?

CHAPTER 18

Web Design

This chapter presents a basic introduction to Web design. It doesn't explain the technical side of composing Web pages or putting them up on a server. That's beyond the scope of this book. Rather, we look at the rhetorical purposes and design principles of Web sites.

This chapter can be used in a variety of ways. According to your instructor's directions, you can read it to learn more about the design of Web sites, or you can use it to plan your own Web site. Whether you actually construct a Web site will depend in part on your instructor, your technical expertise, and the time and technical resources available. One option is to plan the Web site on paper as an exercise or writing assignment.

THE RHETORICAL PURPOSES OF WEB DESIGN

To examine what calls on individuals and organizations to design Web sites, we use the same three purposes as in Chapter 17, "Visual Design"—identification, information, and persuasion—to see how Web sites embody their designers' purposes and how these purposes sometimes overlap.

Identification: Coco Fusco's Web Site

Coco Fusco is an art critic and performance artist. Her Web site contains a good deal of information and is at least implicitly persuasive in advertising her publications and videos. Still, the main purpose of the Web site is to project her identity as an artist and a cultural provocateur who raises questions about U.S. treatment of detainees, the effects on women workers of a globalized economy, immigration, and the dynamics of race, ethnicity, and gender in politics, culture, and art.

Information: Image Archive on the American Eugenics Movement

The "Image Archive on the American Eugenics Movement" is a good example of an informational Web site developed by an academic or research institution, in this case the Cold Spring Harbor Laboratory, which was an important center of eugenics research from 1910–1940, at the height of the American eugenics movement, and its now thoroughly discredited attempt to breed better humans by keeping racial and ethnic groups apart and sterilizing the "unfit."

Persuasion: Amnesty International

Amnesty International is devoted to defending human rights worldwide. The Amnesty International Web site is typical of advocacy group sites. It offers lots of information in the form of reports and news updates, but it is also frankly partisan in its attempts to influence public opinion and get people involved in Amnesty International campaigns.

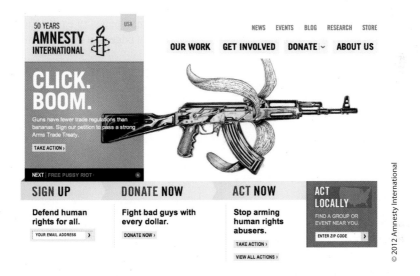

⇗ FOR CRITICAL INQUIRY

1. Visit Coco Fusco's Web site, www.thing.net/~cocofusco. Consider how it works as a home page that projects the image and identity of Fusco as a critic and performer. What dominant impression does it create about Coco Fusco and her works? How is this identity amplified by other pages in the Web site? Considering the range of performance, video, and photographic projects Fusco has been involved in, how would you explain her identity and her works?

2. Start with the Project Overview page at the "Image Archive on the American Eugenics Movement" at http://www.eugenicsarchive.org/eugenics/list2.pl to understand the purpose of the Web site. Browse the site. How does the information it makes available fulfill the Web site's purpose? How is the Web site organized? Who might use it?

3. Visit Amnesty International's Web site, www.amnesty.org. How does the site establish its credibility? What information does it provide? What does it call on visitors to do?

4. Now compare your experience visiting the three Web sites. How do the sites make their purposes clear? What features of the Web sites did you find particularly effective, useful, instructional, or entertaining? Were there features that didn't seem to work well? What generalizations might you draw about how visitors experience Web sites? What criteria can you begin to develop about what makes an effective Web site?

THE STRUCTURE OF WEB DESIGN

The structure of a Web site determines how pages are linked to each other and how visitors are thereby able to move from page to page. Web sites can have a **deep structure**, where visitors must click through a series of pages to get from the home page to a more remote destination.

In other cases, the Web site may have a **shallow structure**, where the home page presents enough options so that visitors can get to any destination in the site with only a click or two.

A **hypertext structure**, on the other hand, links pages to each other so that visitors can take different routes to get from the home page to a destination.

⊳ EXERCISE ||||||||||||||||||||||||||||||||||||||||||||||||||||||||||||||||||||||||||||||||||||||||||||||

Analyzing Web Structure

Work in a group of three or four. Analyze the structure of one of the three Web sites featured earlier in the chapter, a Web site that appears elsewhere in this book, or one that interests your

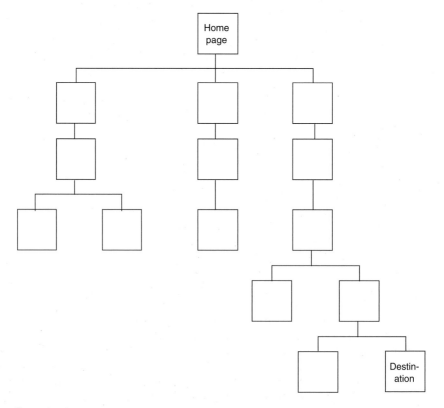

Deep structure

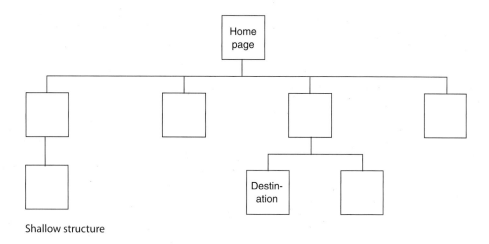

Shallow structure

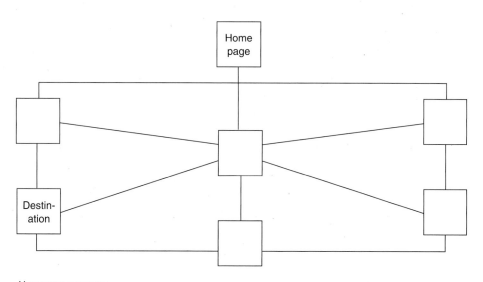

Hypertext structure

group. Design a chart that shows how the pages are linked to each other, using the charts of deep, shallow, and hypertext structures as models. Consider how well the structure fits the purpose of the Web site and how easily you were able to move about the site. If time permits, your instructor may ask groups to present their findings and the class as a whole to draw conclusions about effective structures of Web design.

THE VISUAL DESIGN OF WEB SITES

All the principles presented in Chapter 17, "Visual Design," apply to Web sites as much as to printed material. Here are some visual design considerations to take into account when you're planning a Web site:

▶ **Establish a consistent visual theme:** Home pages typically give an overview of the Web site by identifying its purpose and providing navigation tools. Just as important is that home pages also send a visual message about the site. Establishing a visual theme on the home page is crucial to the unity of a Web site and its credibility. Web designers consider how their choice of logo, images, background color, and font can best embody the site's purposes. As in other kinds of visual design, repetition and consistency are critical factors. Well-designed Web sites often use an identifying logo or header, the same background color, and the same placement of navigation tools on each page to create a consistent visual theme.

▶ **Make the navigation tools obvious and easy to use:** The navigation tools on a home page amount to a virtual table of contents that gives an overview of the Web site. Visitors should be able to see at a glance the main topics, even if the pages listed as navigation tools contain further links. There are various ways to set up navigation tools. You can use a navigation bar, icons, or buttons. In any case, keep the design, color, and placement consistent throughout the site. Visitors find it reassuring, for example, when the navigation tools are present on each page as a sidebar or at the top of the page. That helps them know where they are in the site and enables them to get back to the home page without clicking the back button on the browser. It's also helpful on longer pages to include a navigation bar at the bottom of the page so visitors don't have to scroll back to the top.

▶ **Resist clutter:** It can be tempting, particularly if you have the technical ability, to load up a Web site with such "bells and whistles" as animation, busy backgrounds, lurid colors, and lots of graphics. The danger, however, is that cluttering the page with extraneous material creates a chaotic effect. Visitors become impatient rather quickly if the Web page they're trying to read is jam packed, even if they are interested in the material. Whatever appears on the page should follow from the purpose of the Web site and not be simply decorative. Use white space creatively, as noted in Chapter 17, to enhance your design and focus the visitor's attention.

▶ **Create manageable chunks of information:** Despite the new and exciting multimedia features such as graphics, video, and sound, written text remains the key element of many Web sites. At the same time, using written text effectively is one of the major challenges of Web design because of the size of most people's computer screens and their reluctance to scroll through a long document or read a written text that sprawls all the way across the page. (If they're really interested, they'll print it and read the hard copy.) This means that if you want people to read the pages on a Web site, you have to break up the written text into manageable chunks that can fit easily on a screen or require minimal scrolling. In many ways, this is a new approach to writing, which we'll look at more in the next section.

WRITING ASSIGNMENT

Planning a Web Site

In this assignment, you encounter some of the decisions Web designers face in planning a Web site. As you'll see, they are similar in many respects to the decisions you've made in planning other kinds of writing. But, as just mentioned, there are also some important differences between writing print material and writing for the computer screen that you must take into account.

Identifying the Call to Write

Planning a Web site begins, as other types of writing do, by identifying a call to write and clarifying your purposes. There are various situations that might call on you to design a Web site. You might believe there is an urgent issue on your campus, in your local community, or on the national or international scene. You might decide there is something people need to know about, or you may want to persuade them about your point of view. Or you may feel the desire to express yourself. As you've seen, Web design can embody the various and sometimes overlapping purposes of identification, information, and persuasion.

Here are some questions you might ask yourself at this point:

1. Why and how is a Web site a fitting response to the call to write? What can you do in a Web site that you can't do in other genres of writing?

2. What do you see as the main purpose of the Web site?

3. What personality and visual look do you imagine the Web site projecting?

Understanding Your Audience

One of the answers you may have given about choosing a Web site instead of another genre of writing is that it gives you a particular kind of access that connects you to readers online.

To help you plan your Web site, it's worth exploring that connection to online readers, the people who visit your Web site:

1. Who do you imagine will visit your Web site? Are you planning the Web site for a specialized audience or for a more general one? What attitudes and knowledge about the topic of your Web site do you think your intended visitors will have?

2. How will the design of the Web site indicate who your target audience is? Will your intended audience see that it's a site they would be interested in?

3. What do you want visitors to do when they get to the Web site? Is your purpose to have them navigate around your site, or do you plan to provide them with links to related Web sites?

Understanding the Genre

As already noted, one of the key differences between Web sites and many other genres of writing is that Web sites break up information into manageable chunks that can fit on the screen. Instead of giving readers written texts to read linearly, from beginning to end, Web sites link chunks of information together and give visitors navigation tools to determine their own paths from page to page. In this way, Web sites can create layers of information.

Designing Web Structure

Work through the following steps to design the structure of your Web site:

1. List as many topics as you can, taking into account what you think visitors need or want to know. Combine topics that overlap or are repetitive. Imagine that each topic represents a separate Web page. The Web site you're designing might have anywhere from ten to twenty pages, including the home page. If you decide to include links to other Web sites, you can design a "Links" page or incorporate the links on your own pages where appropriate.

2. Select the topics you want to include on the Web site, and write each topic on a separate note card. Make sure to designate one note card for the home page.

3. Now arrange the note cards to try out designs for your Web site. Put the home page at the top as the entry point. Experiment with various arrangements of information. What topics should appear as navigation tools on the home page? What additional topics should be linked to these pages?

4. Draw a chart of the tentative structure of the Web site you're planning.

Drafting and Revising

Using your Web structure chart as a guide, write drafts of the individual Web pages. If you find some of the pages are too long, you may need to create new linked pages and revise the structure of the Web site. On the other hand, you may find you can combine planned pages into one. Whatever the case, each page should present a manageable chunk of information that is easy to read on the computer screen and has a sensible place in the structure of your Web design.

REFLECTING ON YOUR WRITING

If you have created a Web site to put up on a server or designed a series of Web pages on paper, it's worth considering at this point how composing for the Web compares to composing for print media. What do you see as the main differences and similarities?

CHAPTER 19

PowerPoint Presentations

Oral presentations that use PowerPoint or more recent presentation software such as Prezi are standard features of the workplace, public affairs, and the academy. Planning a presentation has much in common with planning a piece of writing, but there are some key differences as well. Understanding these differences helps you use your knowledge of planning written texts to design presentations that use PowerPoint. Here, we first consider these differences, and then discuss how you can plan, rehearse, and deliver an effective presentation.

UNDERSTANDING THE DIFFERENCES BETWEEN WRITTEN AND ORAL PRESENTATIONS

Depending on the occasion and the speaker's purposes, oral presentations pursue the same goals as written texts do: to inform, analyze, explain, and persuade. With a written presentation, however, readers have a text in front of them to refer to. They can read at their own pace—and reread sections as many times as necessary.

In oral presentations, however, listeners have to grasp the presenter's meanings as he or she is speaking. PowerPoint slides are helpful in focusing listeners on the speaker's message, but still there is no going back to an earlier section, as readers can do with written texts. The words evaporate as they are spoken, and the slides change. In addition, research on adult attention spans indicate that even the most interested listeners can focus on a presentation for only twenty minutes or so (although the same person could read for a longer duration).

What's important is to understand that oral presentations put special demands on speakers to hold their audience's attention and enable them to follow the talk and understand its main points.

DEVELOPING AN ORAL PRESENTATION

For our purposes here, we'll look at developing an oral presentation to give in one of your classes. These guidelines, however, are applicable to other situations that call on you to give an oral presentation.

Preliminary Considerations

Consider how much time you have for your presentation. Listeners appreciate oral presentations that hold to their time limit. Such presentations require careful planning and rehearsal. Underprepared oral presentations tend to ramble in ways that listeners will find distracting.

Consider also how you will deliver the oral presentation. There is nothing quite so dull as speakers who read a paper to listeners, often with their heads down and eyes on the written text. Effective oral presentations are spoken, and preparation and rehearsal are the best way for you to establish eye contact with your listeners and give them the feeling you are speaking to them.

Some speakers write out their presentations and then memorize them. This can be risky, however, especially if you have a memory lapse during the presentation. A safer way is to develop an outline of main points and use it to practice until you can deliver your presentation without hesitation. If you're using PowerPoint slides, they can serve as a kind of outline to keep you on track.

Planning the Oral Presentation

Identifying the Call to Write

Consider what makes the topic of your presentation interesting, important, controversial, or amusing. What do your listeners have to gain? Do you want to inform them, explain a concept, define a problem and propose a solution, evaluate a work or performance, advocate a point of view, or align yourself with others in a controversy?

Defining Your Audience

Who are your listeners? What interests do they have in the material you're presenting? What level of knowledge do they have about the topic? What do they need to know? How do you strike a balance between the needs of your instructor and your classmates?

Planning the Introduction

Introductions in oral presentations have two main purposes.

▶ First, they introduce the topic, and you need to do this in a way that will suggest its significance and promote listeners' interest in what you have to say. An amusing anecdote, a telling example, a telling fact or statistic, or a controversial statement by an authority on the topic are possible opening strategies.

▶ Second, the introduction helps listeners follow your presentation by forecasting its organization as well as its content. At the beginning, tell your listeners what the purpose of your presentation is, and provide them with an overview of its structure and the main points you'll be covering. PowerPoint slides are particularly helpful to listeners in this regard, so they can visualize where the talk is going and stay oriented as it develops.

Arranging Your Material

A consistent scheme of organization is key to making your presentation easy to follow. Depending on your material, you could use a chronological, topical, or problem-and-solution type of organization.

Provide explicit transitions so that listeners can see how the parts of your presentation are related. For example, you might say, "Now that we've seen the scope of the problem of homelessness, we turn to three proposals to deal with it." Help your listeners keep the "big picture" in mind by connecting the main points and omitting extraneous details. Some details may be interesting in their own right, but if they don't help lead your listeners through the main points of the material you're presenting, then you should resist the temptation to include them.

Planning the Ending

Cue your listeners that you are ending by saying something like "In closing, I want to emphasize. . ." or "To review the key points. . . ." At the same time, you want to conclude with something more than a mere summary—such as an especially apt example that illustrates the crux of your talk, a troubling question that remains, or research that needs to be done. End on a strong note. Nothing undermines an ending like a nervous giggle or a shrug and "I guess that's it."

Being Prepared for Questions

One of the advantages of oral presentations is that the audience is present and can respond immediately with questions and comments. If your instructor wants a period of questions and responses after the presentation, pause for a moment after your ending, and then say, for example, "I'd be happy to try to answer any questions you might have." If you are not sure you understand a question, ask the person who raised it for clarification. If you don't know the answer to a question, don't fake it or act defensively. Just say you don't know.

DESIGNING POWERPOINT SLIDES

PowerPoint slides not only offer a way to hold listeners' attention and help them remember key points but also help you plan your presentation because the design of slides enables you to distill your material into its most essential elements. Think of visuals not as secondary sources to illustrate information at various points in the presentation but as a visualization of the structure of the presentation and each of its main points. If you've done a good job of designing your visuals, your audience should be able to grasp the main points of your presentation from reading the visuals you show.

Here are some suggestions for designing PowerPoint slides:

Designing Visuals

▶ **Design a slide for each main point in your presentation:** Once you have determined the main points in the presentation, write them out in a list. Now you can begin to consider how best to represent each point visually. In some cases, the visual will consist of an outline or key phrases. In other cases, the visuals may be a table, graph, or other type of illustration.

▶ **Keep text as concise as possible:** Slides with text should give the audience enough information to coordinate easily with what you are saying. Long or dense passages of text will distract the audience from the spoken presentation.

▶ **Use tables, graphs, or other illustrations selectively and accurately:** You may well want to reproduce visuals directly from sources you've read, or you may design your own representation of information. Your selection should be keyed to the main points in your presentation. In either case, make sure your visuals render the information accurately—and that they provide your audience with a label of the information being presented and cite its source.

▶ **Use large type, clear fonts, and an appropriate color scheme:** Fourteen- to 24-point type size will usually give an easily readable projection on a PowerPoint presentation, depending on the size of the room where you'll be speaking. Don't use more than two different fonts (such as Times New Roman and Helvetica) or more than two different styles (such as bold and italic) on a single slide. In general, use dark type on a light background. Light text on a dark background looks attractive but may not be easily readable, especially in a room with the lights on. Your visuals should have a clean and professional look. Avoid a visual presentation that will appear busy or unserious.

Using Visual Aids in a Presentation

▶ **Use the slides, but don't just read them:** As mentioned earlier, each slide should be linked to a key point in your presentation. Your audience can read the slide. Your task is to make the connection between what's on the slide and the line of thought in your presentation. You can refer to keywords and terms on the slide, but don't just read it verbatim.

▶ **Don't stand between your audience and the slide.** Your audience should be able to see both you and the screen where the slide is projected.

▶ **Look at your audience, not at the slide.** Maintaining eye contact with your audience is an important way of holding their attention and involving them in the presentation. You want them to feel that you are talking to them—not to the visual you are showing.

▶ **If appropriate, use a pointer to direct attention.** You can use either an old-fashioned pointer or a laser highlighter to stress particular aspects of a slide.

For more on PowerPoint, see Edward R. Tufte's "PowerPoint Is Evil" and Ellen Lupton's "Dos and Don'ts of PowerPoint" at the end of the chapter.

REHEARSING YOUR PRESENTATION

Even if you know your material well, you could undermine all your work unless you rehearse. No matter how intelligent the speaker, an audience will associate long pauses, mumbling, failure to make eye contact, awkward transitions, or fumbling with visual aids as evidence of the presenter's lack of familiarity with the topic and lack of planning. To make sure you don't send the wrong message, you've got to practice.

In fact, rehearsing your presentation is not just something you do once you've finished preparing it. Rehearsing is an important way of developing and revising what you've got on paper. In many cases, it's only when a speaker practices that he or she becomes aware that more information is needed in a section of the talk or that the proper emphasis on main points isn't coming through effectively.

To get the most out of rehearsing, you need an audience. Some speakers practice in front of a mirror, but a person (or even better, a group of people) can provide you with kinds of feedback that may not occur to you. Or you may be able to record your presentation with a video camera, so that you can review it to determine what changes are called for. However you rehearse, though, you need some criteria to evaluate the presentation. Here are some suggestions about what to look for:

GUIDELINES FOR EVALUATING ORAL PRESENTATIONS

- Is the purpose of the presentation clear from the start?
- Is the presentation easy to follow? Do listeners know where they are at each point along the way?
- Do major points receive proper emphasize? Do they stand out clearly?
- Does the speaker use variation in tone, pitch, and loudness to emphasize major points? A monotone puts listeners to sleep, but verbal emphasis at inappropriate points will throw listeners off.
- Is the pace of the presentation appropriate? Too fast a pace makes an audience think the speaker is rushing through just to get it done, whereas going too slow can make them start to squirm.
- Does the speaker maintain effective eye contact with listeners?
- Does the speaker handle the visuals smoothly and effectively? Are the visuals well coordinated with the presentation? Are they easy to read?
- Does the speaker use gestures and body language effectively during the presentation?
- Does the presentation stay within the time allotted?

Answers to these questions give you important information about how you need to change your presentation. Make sure you give yourself time to practice the revised version.

FURTHER THOUGHTS ON POWERPOINT

We present Edward R. Tufte's essay "PowerPoint Is Evil" and slides from Ellen Lupton's "PowerPoint Dos and Don'ts" to examine in greater depth the meaning and style of PowerPoint presentations. Edward R. Tufte is professor emeritus of political science, computer science and statistics, and graphic design at Yale University. He is also the author, designer, and publisher of three highly influential books on information design, The Visual Display of Quantitative Information *(1983),* Envisioning Information *(1990),* Visual Explanation *(1997), and* Beautiful Evidence *(2006). Ellen Lupton is a leading graphic designer, teacher, and theorist whose books include* Thinking with Type *(2004),* D.I.Y.: Design It Yourself *(2006), and* Graphic Design: The New Basics *(2008) You can find a pdf of the PowerPoint slides at www.elupton.com/index.php?id=52.*

PowerPoint Is Evil
Power Corrupts.
PowerPoint Corrupts Absolutely.

Genevieve Lang

Imagine a widely used and expensive prescription drug that promised to make us beautiful but didn't. Instead the drug had frequent, serious side effects: It induced stupidity, turned everyone into bores, wasted time, and degraded the quality and credibility of communication. These side effects would rightly lead to a worldwide product recall.

Edward R. Tufte , "PowerPoint is Evil." Reprinted by permission, Edward R. Tufte, *The Cognitive Style of PowerPoint* (Cheshire, CT: Graphics Press, 2003), as appeared in *Wired Magazine*, September 2003.

Yet slideware—computer programs for presentations—is everywhere: in corporate America, in government bureaucracies, even in our schools. Several hundred million copies of Microsoft PowerPoint are churning out trillions of slides each year. Slideware may help speakers outline their talks, but convenience for the speaker can be punishing to both content and audience. The standard PowerPoint presentation elevates format over content, betraying an attitude of commercialism that turns everything into a sales pitch.

Of course, data-driven meetings are nothing new. Years before today's slideware, presentations at companies such as IBM and in the military used bullet lists shown by overhead projectors. But the format has become ubiquitous under PowerPoint, which was created in 1984 and later acquired by Microsoft. PowerPoint's pushy style seeks to set up a speaker's dominance over the audience. The speaker, after all, is making power points with bullets to followers. Could any metaphor be worse? Voicemail menu systems? Billboards? Television? Stalin?

Particularly disturbing is the adoption of the PowerPoint cognitive style in our schools. Rather than learning to write a report using sentences, children are being taught how to formulate client pitches and infomercials. Elementary school PowerPoint exercises (as seen in teacher guides and in student work posted on the Internet) typically consist of 10 to 20 words and a piece of clip art on each slide in a presentation of three to six slides—a total of perhaps 80 words (15 seconds of silent reading) for a week of work. Students would be better off if the schools simply closed down on those days and everyone went to the Exploratorium or wrote an illustrated essay explaining something.

In a business setting, a PowerPoint slide typically shows 40 words, which is about eight seconds' worth of silent reading material. With so little information per slide, many, many slides are needed. Audiences consequently endure a relentless sequentiality, one damn slide after another. When information is stacked in time, it is difficult to understand context and evaluate relationships. Visual reasoning usually works more effectively when relevant information is shown side by side. Often, the more intense the detail, the greater the clarity and understanding. This is especially so for statistical data, where the fundamental analytical act is to make comparisons.

Consider an important and intriguing table of survival rates for those with cancer relative to those without cancer for the same time period. Some 196 numbers and 57 words describe survival rates and their standard errors for 24 cancers.

Applying the PowerPoint templates to this nice, straightforward table yields an analytical disaster. The data explodes into six separate chaotic slides, consuming 2.9 times the area of the table. Everything is wrong with these smarmy, incoherent graphs: the encoded legends, the meaningless color, the logo-type branding. They are uncomparative, indifferent to content and evidence, and so data-starved as to be almost pointless.

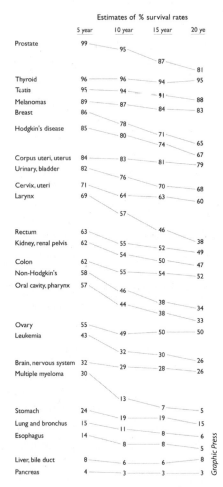

GOOD. A traditional table: rich, informative, clear.

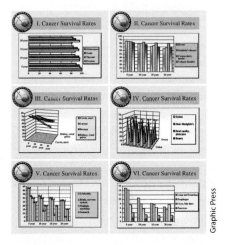

BAD. PowerPoint chartjunk: smarmy, chaotic, incoherent.

Chartjunk is a clear sign of statistical stupidity. Poking a finger into the eye of thought, these data graphics would turn into a nasty travesty if used for a serious purpose, such as helping cancer patients assess their survival chances. To sell a product that messes up data with such systematic intensity, Microsoft abandons any pretense of statistical integrity and reasoning. Presentations largely stand or fall on the quality, relevance, and integrity of the content. If your numbers are boring, then you've got the wrong numbers. If your words or images are not on point, making them dance in color won't make them relevant. Audience boredom is usually a content failure, not a decoration failure.

At a minimum, a presentation format should do no harm. Yet the PowerPoint style routinely disrupts, dominates, and trivializes content. Thus PowerPoint presentations too often resemble a school play—very loud, very slow, and very simple.

The practical conclusions are clear. PowerPoint is a competent slide manager and projector. But rather than supplementing a presentation, it has become a substitute for it. Such misuse ignores the most important rule of speaking: Respect your audience.

PowerPoint Dos and Don'ts

Ellen Lupton

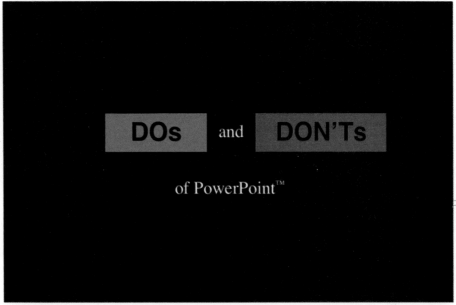

Ellen Lupton, *PowerPoint Dos* and *Don'ts*, from www.designwritingresearch.org. Reprinted by permission of Ellen Lupton.

DO Break up your text into manageable chunks.

Respect your audience.

Write less. Use more space.

Reprinted by permission of Ellen Lupton

THIS IS TOO MUCH TEXT

PowerPoint has become a ubiquitous medium of business communication. At sales meetings, training seminars, and conferences, the audience has come to expect a PowerPoint slide show with every talk. This is not necessarily a good thing. Not only do people expect PowerPoint, they also expect it to be dull. PowerPoint has become associated with puffed-up presentations by paid consultants, corny "interactive" discussions led by professional facilitators, and any dull event where you get a free pencil. The fact is, everyone should learn PowerPoint. But you need to learn to use it well, and you need to know when not to use it at all.

Reprinted by permission of Ellen Lupton

BULLETS ARE NOT ENOUGH

• PowerPoint has become a ubiquitous medium of business communication.
• At sales meetings, training seminars, and conferences, the audience has come to expect a PowerPoint slide show.
• This is not necessarily a good thing.
• Not only do people expect PowerPoint, they expect it to be dull.
• PowerPoint has become associated with puffed-up presentations by paid consultants, corny "interactive" discussions led by professional facilitators, and any dull event where you get a free pencil.
• The fact is, everyone should learn PowerPoint.
• But you need to learn to use it well, and you need to know when not to use it at all.

Reprinted by permission of Ellen Lupton

WRITE LESS

USE MORE SPACE

Reprinted by permission of Ellen Lupton

DON'T Use design elements to create "interest."

If your content is boring, design can't save you.

EXCITING BACKGROUND. DULL CONTENT.

● PowerPoint has become a ubiquitous medium of business communication.
● At sales meetings, training seminars, and conferences, the audience has come to expect a PowerPoint slide show.
● This is not necessarily a good thing.
● Not only do people expect PowerPoint, they expect it to be dull.
● PowerPoint has become associated with puffed-up presentations by paid consultants, corny "interactive" discussions led by professional facilitators, and any dull event where you get a free pencil.
● The fact is, everyone should learn PowerPoint.
● But you need to learn to use it well, and you need to know when not to use it at all.

DO Use design elements to build or emphasize content.

Colors, boxes, bullets, and font variations CAN make your presentation more clear and meaningful.

Reprinted by permission of Ellen Lupton

USE A HIERARCHY OF FONT SIZES AND SHORT BULLET POINTS

People expect PowerPoint during

- puffed-up presentations by paid consultants
- corny meetings led by professional facilitators
- any event where you get a free pencil

Reprinted by permission of Ellen Lupton

DON'T Use preprogrammed presentation designs.

A little design is a dangerous thing.

These preprogrammed designs are just distracting.

Reprinted by permission of Ellen Lupton

This is called Ribbons.

It's inspired by Victoria's Secret.

Reprinted by permission of Ellen Lupton

This is called Blush.

It's inspired by the Ladies Underwear department at WalMart.

CHOOSE A BLANK PRESENTATION

AND AN EMPTY SCREEN

AND BUILD YOUR OWN SHOW!

Examining PowerPoint

1. Edward R. Tufte says that PowerPoint has a particular "cognitive style" that is "disturbing" in schools. How would you define the "cognitive style" Tufte is pointing to? What does he see as the problem? How do the examples of "good" and "bad" PowerPoint design illustrate Tufte's point?

2. Compare Tufte's sense of "good" and "bad" PowerPoint design to Ellen Lupton's "Dos and Don'ts of PowerPoint." Do they seem to share similar assumptions about information design? What do you see as main similarities and differences?

3. Consider Tufte's assertion that "PowerPoint's pushy style seeks to set up the speaker's dominance over the audience." Explain what Tufte is getting at. Take into account how he reinforces his point with the visual satire of the "totalitarian impact of presentation software."

4. Use Tufte's ideas, Lupton's advice, and your own sense of what PowerPoint does well and not so well to design your own examples of "good" and "bad" PowerPoint slides. Imagine you are making a presentation to your class on a topic you know a lot about. Explain what makes the "good" slides "good" and the "bad" slides "bad."

PART 5

Writers at Work

INTRODUCTION: UNDERSTANDING THE WRITING PROCESS

No two writers compose in the same way, and an individual may work in different ways on different writing tasks. Nonetheless, there are predictable elements in a writing project that can be listed:

▶ **Invention:** Developing an approach to the topic and to readers, assessing purpose, doing research, choosing the appropriate genre.

▶ **Planning:** Designing the arrangement of material, finding an appropriate pattern of organization.

▶ **Drafting:** Creating a working draft, getting ideas down on paper.

▶ **Peer commentary:** Getting feedback from others, seeing the working draft through the reader's eyes.

▶ **Revising:** Rereading the working draft, clarifying purpose and organization, connecting the parts.

▶ **Manuscript preparation:** Designing, editing, and proofreading a document.

Because of the way the elements of writing have been listed, you may think that they constitute a series of steps you can follow. If you look at how writers work, however, you'll see that they may well manage these elements in quite different ways. Some writers like to start drafting before they develop a clear plan, whereas others would not think of drafting without a carefully developed outline.

Nor are the elements necessarily separate from each other. Some people revise as they draft, working carefully over each section before going on to the next, whereas others write quickly and then think about needed revisions. Nor do writers spend the same amount of time on each of the elements. Depending on the writing task and their own writing habits, writers learn how to manage the elements in ways that work for them.

Writing can be exhilarating, but it can be aggravating too. You can probably think of times when writing seemed to pour out, leading you to previously unsuspected ideas and precisely the right way of saying things. On the other hand, you may have had moments when you couldn't begin a writing task or got stuck in the middle. The way to get to the source of such difficulties is to think about how you are managing the elements of your writing task. Are you spending your time doing what needs to be done to get the writing task completed? Should you be revising and editing passages that you may eventually discard? Is this keeping you from figuring out how (or whether) the passage connects to other points? If you see your draft diverge from your outline, should you follow it or go back and revise your plan? When you're stuck in the middle of a draft, do you need to turn to invention—to read more or talk to others?

Answers to these questions will vary, of course, depending on the writing task and your own habits as a writer. The point is that experienced writers learn to ask such questions in order to get their bearings, especially when the writing is not going well, to see where they stand in putting a piece of writing together and what they need to do next.

⟩⟩ REFLECTING ON YOUR WRITING

How You Managed a Writing Task

Think of a writing task you completed recently, in school or out of school. Analyze how you managed the task. To do this, consider the following questions:

1. What called on you to write? Describe how you defined the writing task. How did you establish your purpose? What did your exploration of the topic involve? How did you imagine your readers and the relationship you wanted to establish with them? What genre did you choose? Did you talk to others about your ideas?

2. Explain how you planned the writing. How much planning did you do? When did you plan, and what form did it take?

3. Describe how you drafted. When did you begin? How much invention and planning did you do before you started drafting?

4. Describe what feedback, if any, you received on your draft. What was the effect of this feedback?

5. What kinds of revisions did you make? When did you revise—during drafting, after you had a complete working draft, at various points?

6. What final form did the writing take? Were any considerations of document design involved? Did you edit and proofread the final version?

Now look back over your answers to these questions. What conclusions can you draw about how you managed the elements of the writing process in this instance? What, if anything, would you do differently if you had to do the task again?

CHAPTER 20

Case Study of a Writing Assignment

To see how a student writer manages a writing task and how writers and readers can work together effectively, we follow a student, Katie DiMartile, preparing a paper for a popular culture course.

INVENTION

Understanding the Call to Write

It may be difficult to get started on a writing project if you are uncertain about the call to write and the kind of writing task it presents. You may not be clear, for example, about what an assignment in one of your courses is calling on you to do. If you feel shaky about the purpose of a writing assignment, other students in the class probably do too. Of course, you could talk to the teacher, but you may also want to collaborate with classmates to clarify the purpose of the assignment and develop an approach to it.

Here is the writing assignment Katie DiMartile was given in Introduction to American Popular Culture.

WRITING ASSIGNMENT

Introduction to American Popular Culture

Roadside memorials, sometimes in the form of crosses, wreathes, or flowers, line America's roads at the sites of fatal car accidents. Because many of these memorials feature crosses or other religious symbols, many people object to their placement on public land. However, such memorials are also a part of important cultural traditions to many people. The controversy over roadside memorials has resulted in a

© David Bacon/Alamy

lively public debate over whether or not such memorials should be permitted on our nation's roadsides. After reading two short articles on the controversy, write a short (2-page, 500 word) essay in which you take a position on whether or not roadside memorials should be banned. You will need to defend your position by explaining your reasons for supporting or countering a particular perspective in order to persuade your audience to take up your position.

⇨ FOR CRITICAL INQUIRY ||||||||||||||||||||||||||||||||||||||||||||||||||||||||||||||||||||||||||||||||||||||||

Analyzing a Writing Assignment

Work with two or three classmates to analyze the Introduction to American Popular Culture writing assignment and to determine what it is calling on students do. The following guidelines can be used for virtually any writing assignment.

Guidelines for Analyzing Writing Assignments

1. Look for key words in the assignment—such as *describe, summarize, explain, analyze, take a position,* or *evaluate critically.* Discuss what these terms might mean in relation to the material you're being asked to write about and the goals and focus of the course.

2. Consider what information you need to do the assignment successfully. Where can you get this information? Does the assignment call for additional research, or is it based on class readings and discussion? Are there things you know or have learned in other classes that might prove useful?

3. Look for any special directions the assignment provides about the form of writing. Does it call for a specific genre (such as a report, a proposal, or a review)? Does it call for documentation? Consider the assigned length. What is it possible to do well within these limits?

After your group has answered these questions, compare your response to those of other groups. At this point, what advice would you give Katie as she begins the assignment?

Understanding Readers

Another difficulty in getting started on a writing task may be uncertainty about what interests readers. Sometimes writers believe that if they have thought of something, everyone else must have too. Underestimating the importance of their own ideas, they feel reluctant to express them. One way to test your ideas is to discuss them with other people. That way you not only reassure yourself that your ideas are valid but also begin to formulate a plan for approaching your readers.

Talking out the ideas you have for a paper is a good way to understand your readers. Here are some guidelines for doing this, followed by a transcript of Katie's discussion with her classmate Tyler.

Guidelines for Understanding Your Readers

1. Find a willing listener, describe your writing task, and then tell your listener what you are thinking of writing about and what you are thinking of saying about it.

2. Ask your listener what she already knows about your subject, what she would like to know about it, and whether she has ideas or information you could use in your writing.

Transcript of Katie's Discussion with Tyler

KATIE: I've got to write this paper for my pop culture course on roadside memorials. I have to say whether or not I think they should be banned. I never knew there was so much to consider. There is a lot of debate about these memorials.

TYLER: Sounds cool. I've seen those memorials before around my hometown, but I never knew that there was a debate about them. So what are you going to say?

KATIE: Well, that's the problem. A lot of people oppose the memorials because they are shaped like crosses or other religious symbols. Religion is such a touchy subject. I don't feel comfortable writing about it. I thought I could maybe say something about how the memorials are important because they remind people to be safe on the road. That's definitely what happened when some friends of mine put up a memorial for someone at my school who died in a car accident. Every time I saw it, I would slow down or at least think about being more attentive. But I'm worried this is too obvious. What do you think? Does that sound interesting?

TYLER: Oh yeah. I've had the same experience. Even if there are plenty of other signs telling me to slow down or be careful, those memorials really make you think about how important it is to be safe.

KATIE: I kind of also want to say something about how they give the victim's family some closure. I mean, it seems like in all the debates people seem to lose track of the fact we are talking about someone's loved one losing their life.

TYLER: That does seem important. And I think you are right that people seem to get too caught up in the controversy to think about this on an emotional level.

KATIE: You really think so? I mean, do you think I can do something here? My teacher has to like it, you know.

TYLER: That goes without saying. I think you have a couple of solid reasons why these memorials should be allowed on our roadways. Now you just have to get it on paper.

KATIE: I hope so. Thanks, Tyler. I better get to work.

Exploring the Topic

At a certain point, writers need to get some ideas down on paper, even if the writing is of a preliminary sort. One way to start is to do exploratory writing, in which you're tentatively working out the focus and direction of your paper. If you want someone to look at your exploratory writing, use the guidelines below. Make sure that the person who reads your writing understands that it is an initial attempt to discover what you want to say.

Guidelines for Responding to Exploratory Writing

▶ Ask your reader to circle or underline key phrases and interesting ideas, whether or not they seem to be the main point of the writing.

▶ Ask your reader to tell you whether there seem to be, implied or lurking just off the page, ideas that you could develop.

After thinking about her conversation with Tyler, Katie decided to do some exploratory writing. Below are her writing and the response from her friend Kevin.

Katie's Exploratory Writing

I remember during my freshman year of high school, my friend lost his brother in a car accident. My friend maintained a small memorial at the site and I went with him a couple of times to lay down some fresh flowers. I know that the memorial was really important to my friend in coping with the loss of his brother. Also, whenever I drove by the memorial, it really made me think about how driving is such a big responsibility. I could never go past that spot without checking my speed or becoming more alert.

Kevin's Response

I really like how you were able to draw on your own experience [of] a roadside memorial and the impact it had on you and your friend. However, I think you need to be careful with how you write about this experience. As I understand it, your assignment is an analytical and persuasive one, not just a personal essay about your experience. Maybe you could explain more clearly why the memorial was so important to your friend. How can you generalize that to explain why memorials should be allowed in all cases? Maybe you could find a way of connecting how the memorial affected your friend and how it affected you to come up with a main point.

Planning

When using discussions with others about their ideas for a writing project, writers need to develop a plan for their writing to highlight the main point and provide supporting evidence.

After Katie talked to Tyler and got a response to her exploratory writing from Kevin, she mulled over the results. She knew it was time to use this information to plan her essay. Tyler and Kevin helped her see that she needed to write an analytical essay that made a central claim and backed it up with evidence. A personal essay that focused on her feelings about her family was not the kind of writing called for by the assignment.

At this point, she worked by herself, developing her main idea and arranging reasons to support it. She sketched the following brief outline so that she could begin drafting.

Katie's Brief Outline

Introduction

Begin with other ways our country memorializes tragedy

Explanation of roadside memorials and the controversy surrounding them

Claim: roadside memorials gives a sense of closure to victim's loved ones and cautions
    other drivers

Body

Give reasons why this is so

Example of friend's memorial for his brother

Reminds drivers to slow down

Memorials are more difficult to ignore than regular road signs

Ending

Human aspect more important than the controversy

Regulations for what memorials look like?

Drafting

Any plan a writer develops needs to be tested by writing a working draft. Outlines, sketches, or other kinds of preliminary planning tell you only so much. To see where your ideas are going, you must commit them to paper.

After she sketched a brief outline, Katie wrote a working draft. As you can see, she used ideas and suggestions from Tyler and Kevin. But, as is the case in individual writing projects, she worked independently to write the draft. Here is what she came up with.

Katie's Working Draft

Our culture has always made a point of remembering the dead. For example, in Washington D.C. there is the Tomb of the Unknown Soldier, the Vietnam Memorial, and many others. Additionally, there are memorials at Columbine, Ground Zero, Oklahoma City, and Virginia Tech honoring those who lost their lives in those tragedies. With all of these memorials already in place one would think that remembering victims of car accidents would be acceptable, but there are people who oppose them. In a country that usually respects and honors the dead, it is surprising that there be a controversy over something as simple as roadside crosses. A roadside memorial to those who died in a car accidents give the loved ones of the deceased closure and serve as a warning to other drivers.

When someone is killed unexpectedly in a car accident, loved ones are left with a tragic loss. Coping with such a dramatic loss can be hard and going to the site and seeing the memorial gives the family closure. By putting a cross, or another symbol, at the site of a fatal car accident the victim is being remembered. One of my friends lost his brother in a car accident during our freshman year of high school. I went with him several times during that year to put flowers at the sight of his brother's accident. Keeping these roadside memorials up helps the families get through the grieving process.

As more people are on the roads these memorials don't just serve as ways to remember the deceased, they act as warning signs for other drivers. As you're driving down the road and you see a little white cross you almost always check your speed and become more aware of your surroundings. People can blow off speed limit and other warning signs because they see them all the time. But when you see a small cross you know someone actually lost their life, they didn't just get a speeding ticket. Roadside memorials make the danger of driving much more real, and therefore make drivers more cautious when they're behind the wheel.

Proposals to ban roadside memorials ignore the important functions they serve. First of all, the memorials provide a place for the loved ones of the victims of car accidents to go to mourn. Being able to commemorate the deceased in this way can help provide closure to such an incomprehensible tragedy. Furthermore, when other drivers see these memorials out on the road, they are reminded to slow down and be more attentive. Roadside memorials can bring something positive to the tragedy by helping others be safer. These functions are too important to be overlooked by those who would see roadside memorials banned. Perhaps the best way to compromise between the different sides of this controversy is to enforce regulations on the form of such memorials.

Peer Commentary

A working draft means just that—a draft to work on by getting feedback and figuring out what kinds of revisions are called for. To get the most useful kind of feedback to a working draft, make sure your readers know they're looking at a work in progress, not a final draft.

There are different kinds of commentary you get from readers at this point. Your readers:

▶ *Describe* the writer's strategy.

▶ *Analyze* the organization of the essay.

▶ *Evaluate* the argument.

Each kind of commentary provides different information to help you plan revisions. Sometimes you want just one kind of commentary; at other times, you want more than one.

The following sections describe the different kinds of feedback, explain their purposes, and provide guidelines. After each, there is an example of the type of peer commentary in response to Katie's working draft.

Describe the Writer's Strategy

A good first step in getting feedback on a working draft is to ask your reader to suspend judgment for a moment and instead to analyze the function of each paragraph in your working draft—how the paragraphs support the main point and how they are connected to each other. In this way, a reader can give you a blueprint of what you have written. This helps you see how (or whether) the parts fit together. You can use this information to decide how well your paragraphs play the roles you intended for them (or whether they perform some other function). This is also a good basis for the following two types of commentary, in which readers analyze the organization and evaluate the ideas of a working draft.

Guidelines for Describing the Writer's Strategy

▶ What is the writer's main point? Identify the sentence or sentences that express the main point. If you don't find such a sentence, write your own version of what you think the main point is.

▶ Write a statement about each paragraph that explains the function it performs and how it fits into the organization of the working draft. Use words that describe function, such as *describes, explains, gives reasons, proposes,* or *compares.*

Sample Description of Katie's Draft

Main point: Roadside memorials should not be banned.

¶ **1:** Starts with a broad view of the main problem, then questions the controversy before introducing reasons for support.

¶ **2:** Further explains one of the reasons introduced in the first paragraph. Generalizes from a personal experience to support the point.

¶ **3:** Elaborates on an idea introduced in the first paragraph. Describes scenario that serves as an example to support the idea.

¶ **4:** Summarizes main points and proposes a solution.

Analyze the Organization

Sometimes, in the struggle to get your ideas down on paper, you may lose perspective on how effectively you've organized them. For this reason, it is helpful to ask someone to analyze the presentation of your main idea and examine the supporting evidence.

Again, ask readers to put aside their personal responses to your ideas. Explain that you want them to focus instead on the organization of what you have written. If they have already described the function of paragraphs in the draft, they use that description as the basis of their **analysis**.

Guidelines for Analyzing the Organization

1. What is the main point of the draft? Is it clear and easy to find? Does the introduction help readers anticipate where the draft is going?

2. Do the following paragraphs develop the main point, or do they seem to develop some other point? Is it easy to tell how the paragraphs relate to the main point, or do they need to be connected more explicitly to it?

3. Is each of the paragraphs well focused, or do some of them seem to have several ideas contending for the reader's attention? If a paragraph needs more focus, how could this be achieved?

4. Within the supporting paragraphs, do some points seem to need more development? Are there points that don't belong at all?

5. Is the ending or conclusion effective? Does it provide a sense of closure?

Sample Analysis of the Organization of Katie's Draft

I like the opening because your examples are powerful and make the reader sympathetic. You do a good job of starting general and then focusing in more specifically on the essay question. However, I wasn't totally clear on the main point. You imply that you believe that these memorials should be permitted, but you do not actually state so until the beginning of the last paragraph. I think you could use a clinching statement at the end of the first paragraph that states this main point so that it is really clear.

In ¶ 2, you give an example that illustrates the problem. But the example doesn't help support your claim. You say that your friend's brother was a victim and you describe going to the memorial, but I think you could explain how exactly the memorial helped your friend. Expand on how this personal example connects to the main claim of the paragraph and supports your idea.

¶ 3 explains how roadside memorials can serve as warning signs to other drivers. I like the theory you propose, but I think you should emphasize the point that traditional road signs don't have the same impact on drivers as the memorials. This could help clarify what you mean by "memorials make the danger of driving much more real."

Finally, in ¶ 4 you summarize your main points again and begin to develop a possible solution to the problem. I would focus more on the compromise you suggest instead of summing up what you have already said.

Evaluate the Argument

Although the first two kinds of commentary ask readers to set aside their evaluation of your ideas, sometimes you really want to know what they think. This is especially likely if you're making an argument or dealing with a controversial topic. For this kind of peer commentary in particular, you'll find it helpful to have more than one reader and to discuss with each reader the comments he or she makes. In this way, you have the opportunity to see how your ideas relate to other points of view and to understand the enabling assumptions you and others bring to the issue. This helps you make decisions about how to clarify your own position and handle differing views as you revise.

Guidelines for Evaluating the Argument

1. Analyze the parts of the argument. What is the claim or main point of the working draft? What supporting evidence is provided? What enabling assumptions connect the evidence to the claim?

2. Do you agree with the essay's main point? Do you accept the essay's assumptions? Explain why.

3. *If you disagree* with the essay's main point or do not accept one or more of its assumptions, what position would you take on the issue yourself? How would you support your position? What assumptions would you make? How would you refute the main point of the essay? What alternative perspectives does the draft need to take into account?

4. *If you agree* with the essay's position, explain why. Do you think the essay makes the best possible argument supporting it? How would you strengthen it? What would you change, add, or omit? Why?

Discuss the responses with your readers. If you disagree, the idea is not to argue about who is right, but to keep talking to understand why your positions differ and what assumptions might have led you to take differing positions.

Sample Evaluations of the Argument in Katie's Draft

Commentary 1

Katie, your main claim seems [to be] that you support the roadside memorials and think they are important, and you support this idea by talking about how the different ways in which these memorials help people. The reasons you give are that they help families of victims grieve and that they caution other drivers to be safe. You seem to think that the good these memorials do is more important than whatever reasons people have for wanting to see them banned.

I can definitely see what you mean. I think these memorials could be beneficial to both mourners and other drivers. But I don't really see how anyone would disagree with the argument you have crafted without also knowing the reasons people are against them in the first place. I think you could provide more motivation for the essay by explaining the controversy in more depth. Maybe if you clarified why some people are against these memorials in the first place, then your own reasons for supporting them would have more of an impact.

Commentary 2

[Analysis of the parts of the argument is similar to Response 1.]

I don't know if I totally agree with your assumption that the way these memorials help the community is more important than the fact that they could infringe on peoples' rights. A lot of these memorials are shaped like crosses and I don't think it's right to put religious symbols on public property. I think you have a lot of good points about the potential good these memorials can do, but how would you answer to people who think like me? I think it would be worth at least acknowledging the other side so that you seem well-informed about the issue.

The only other thing is the final paragraph. You seem to mostly repeat the main points that you have already made in the essay. Maybe there's some way you could expand on the solution you propose or point out the larger problems or consequences.

Discuss the commentaries with your readers. You might disagree with them, but the idea is not to argue about who is right but to keep talking in order to understand why your positions differ and what assumptions might have led you to take differing positions.

Revising

Writing isn't a precise science with right and wrong answers, and neither is talking about written work in progress. When others comment on your writing, each person has his or her own responses, insights, and suggestions. At times you'll get differing suggestions about what to do with your working draft, as is the case with the two commentaries on Katie's working draft. This doesn't necessarily mean that one reader has seen the true problem in your writing and the other has missed it altogether. By telling you the effect your writing has on each of them, both readers are giving you information to work with.

It's important to understand why readers have responded to your writing as they did. Try to imagine their point of view and what in your writing might have prompted their response. Peer commentary doesn't provide writers with a set of directions they can carry out mechanically. Rather, they must analyze and interpret their readers' responses.

Here are some guidelines for revising, followed by Katie's commentary about how she made use of the peer commentary she received on her working draft.

Guidelines for Revising

1. What do your readers see as the main point of your draft? Is that the main idea you intended? If your readers have identified your main point, do they offer suggestions to make it come across more clearly? If you think they missed your main point, consider why this is so. Do you need to revise the sentence or sentences that express your central point?

2. Do your readers see how the evidence you supply supports your main point? If so, do they offer suggestions about strengthening the evidence you're using to back up your main claim? If not, does this mean you need to revise your main point or revise the supporting evidence?

3. What do your readers think you assume to connect your evidence to your main claim? Is this what you had in mind? If not, how can you change the relationship between your claim and the evidence you provide?

4. If your readers agree with your essay's position, why is this so? Do they think you make the best possible case? If they disagree, consider their positions and the assumptions they are making. Do they offer alternative perspectives you could use?

5. Do you provide a meaningful ending that points out an important consequence or implication of your argument?

Katie's Thoughts on Her Peer Commentaries

As I began to write this paper, I wasn't really sure about the topic. I couldn't think of things to say and that frustrated me. All of the suggestions you made will really help me improve the essay. I realized it was a mistake not to state my main point at the end of paragraph 1. In fact, I never really said what my main point was at all. My supporting material needed to be developed. I wasn't really explaining the examples that I gave in paragraphs 2 and 3. I also needed an ending that did more than repeat what I had already written.

Notice in Katie's revisions of her working draft how she uses ideas from the two commentaries to plan a revision. First, we present two paragraphs from the working draft, with Katie's annotated plans for revision. This is followed by the final draft.

DiMartile 1

Katie DiMartile

American Pop Culture

Prof. Brown

November 14, 2008

Roadside Memorials

Our culture has always made a point of remembering the dead. For example, in Washington D.C. there is the Tomb of the Unknown Soldier, the Vietnam Memorial, and many others. Additionally, there are memorials at Columbine, Ground Zero, Oklahoma City, and Virginia Tech honoring those who lost their lives in those tragedies. While all these memorials are accepted by the public without question, roadside memorials, small monuments marking the sites of fatal car accidents, are plagued by controversy. Some argue that such memorials should be banned because they often

DiMartile 2

contain religious symbols that should not be displayed on public property. Others think that the memorials could distract drivers and become safety hazards. However, such proposals to ban roadside memorials ignore the important functions they serve.

One important function that roadside memorials serve is that they can help the victim's loved ones get through the grieving process. When someone is killed unexpectedly in a car accident, loved ones are left with a tragic loss. Coping with such a dramatic loss can be hard and going to the site and seeing the memorial gives the family closure. By putting a cross, or another symbol, at the site of a fatal car accident the victim is being remembered. One of my friends lost his brother in a car accident during our freshman year of high school. I went with him several times during that year to put flowers at the site of his brother's accident. More than visiting his brother's grave or talking to his family, visiting the memorial seemed to bring my friend peace. I believe standing where his brother lost his life helped my friend feel closer to him.

Roadside memorials are not just important to families or loved ones, but they can act as warning signs to other drivers. Roadside memorials make the danger of driving much more real because they remind drivers of the serious consequences of reckless behavior on the road. When I drive down the road and see a memorial it reminds me to check my speed and become more aware of my surroundings. It is easy to ignore speed limit and other warning signs because they are so familiar. But when you see a small cross you know someone actually lost their life, they didn't just get a speeding ticket.

Perhaps the best way to compromise between the different sides of the controversy over roadside memorials is to enforce regulations on the form of these monuments. Memorials could feature pictures of the deceased or meaningful personal items instead of religious symbols. There could be rules for where memorials could be safely erected. Such regulations would still allow roadside memorials to provide important services to loved ones and drivers while also respecting the views of others and maintaining proper safety.

Final Touches

Collaboration on a piece of writing includes working on the final touches. Copy editors routinely edit the manuscripts of even the most famous writers, making suggestions about words, phrases, sentences, or passages that might be unclear, awkward, or grammatically incorrect. Then proofreaders carefully review the final draft for any misspellings, missing words, typos, or other flaws.

Directions for Editing

Ask the person editing your manuscript to look for any words, phrases, sentences, or passages that need to be changed. The person can do this in one of two ways: he or she can simply underline or circle problems, write a brief note of explanation in the margin when necessary, and let you make the changes; or he or she can go ahead and make tentative changes for you to consider. Your teacher will let you know which method to follow.

Sample Editing

Notice the editing suggestion here to stay consistent with the personal example in ¶ 3 by using first person instead of "you."

Sentence in Katie's Revised Draft:

As you're driving down the road and you see a little white cross you almost always check your speed and become more aware of your surroundings.

Final Version:

When I drive down the road and see a memorial, it reminds me to check my speed and become more aware of my surroundings.

Directions for Proofreading

The person proofreading your final copy can underline or circle grammatical errors, usage problems, typos, and misspellings, and let you make the final corrections. Or she or he can supply the corrections. Again, it's up to your teacher which method to follow.

TALKING TO TEACHERS

Much of what has been said here about how writers and readers collaborate also applies to talking about your writing with teachers. There may be times, for example, when you have trouble figuring out a writing assignment. You may be confused about the suggestions you've received in peer commentaries, or you may not fully understand the teacher's comments. In such situations, you might request a conference with your teacher.

Talking about writing with teachers is most productive if you prepare ahead of time. If you want to discuss a writing assignment, reread the directions carefully and prepare questions on what isn't clear to you about the assignment. If you want to talk about the feedback you've gotten from peers, reread their commentaries and bring them with you to the conference. If you want to talk about a paper that has already been graded, make sure you read it over carefully, paying particular attention to the teacher's comments.

In any case, have realistic expectations about what could happen at the conference. Don't expect your teacher to change your grade or give you a formula for completing the assignment. The point of the conference is for you to understand what your teacher is looking for in a piece of writing.

GOING TO THE WRITING CENTER

One of the best places to talk about writing is a writing center, where you can meet and discuss your writing with people who are interested in the writing process and in how students develop as writers. Find out whether your college has a writing center. If so, it will be listed in the campus directory, and your writing teacher will know about its hours and procedures.

Sometimes students think the writing center is only for those with serious writing problems, but that is not the case. Students of all abilities can benefit from talking to writing tutors. Whether the people who staff the writing center at your college are undergraduates, graduate students, or professional tutors, they are experienced writers who like to talk about writing.

If your campus has a writing center, make an appointment to interview one of the tutors. Ask what kinds of services the center provides and what insights into college writing the tutor offers. Even better, take a writing assignment you're working on or a paper that's already been graded to serve as the basis for a conversation with the tutor.

CHAPTER 21

Working Together

Collaborative Writing Projects

Working on collaborative writing projects differs in important respects from working with others on individual writing projects. In the case of individual writing projects, the final result belongs to you; you are accountable for it and you get the bulk of the credit, even though the writing reflects the input of others. Collaborative writing, on the other hand, aims for a collective outcome produced jointly by a team of people with shared responsibility for the results.

Consider, for example, how a group of three students worked together on a research project in an environmental studies course. Their task was to create a map of the sidewalk shade trees the city had planted and maintained in the downtown area over the years and to make recommendations about where new trees should be planted. After they had surveyed the downtown area, sketched a preliminary map, and made tentative decisions about where new trees should go, they gave each member a section of the report to draft. One wrote the background. One reported their findings. The third student wrote the recommendation section. Once the drafts were finished, the group met to consider what revisions were needed to produce a final report. One student made these changes, and the other two members created the maps.

When individuals work together on collaborative writing projects, they manage the writing task in various ways, depending on the nature of the task and the decisions the group makes. Sometimes, as in the example above, individuals each write separate sections, which are then compiled into a single document and edited for uniformity of style. At other times, they may work together so closely in planning, drafting, and revising a document that it becomes impossible to distinguish one person's work from another's. In still other cases, the group works together planning and doing research, one individual does the drafting, and then the group works together again to plan revisions.

There is no single best way to work on collaborative writing projects. Experienced writers learn when it makes sense to produce a collaboratively written document and which writing strategy the situation seems to call for.

Although collaborative writing projects differ, each of them reveals one of the most important benefits of working together—namely that the final written product is based on the collective judgment of a group of people. When a group works well together, the resulting energy and involvement lead to writing that goes beyond what anyone in the group could have produced alone.

Successful collaborative writing depends on organization, meetings, and constant communication. This chapter looks at how groups produce effective collaborative writing. The first section offers some general guidelines about working in groups. The second section considers how groups manage a collaborative writing project from start to finish. The final section presents further writing suggestions for groups.

▷ WORKING TOGETHER ||||||||||||||||||||||||||||||||||||||||||||||||||||||||||||||||||||||||||||||||||

Exploring Experience

Form a group with three or four other students. Have each student describe an experience in which he or she worked together with other people. The experience can be positive or negative, and it need not involve writing. After everyone has described an experience, try to reach a consensus, even if you agree to disagree, about what makes group work successful or unsuccessful.

COLLABORATIVE WRITING

Guidelines for Collaborating in Groups

Any group of people working together on a project face certain issues, and a group collaborating on a writing project is no exception. The following guidelines are meant to keep a group running smoothly and to forestall some common problems.

Recognize That Group Members Need to Get Acquainted and That Groups Take Time to Form

People entering new groups sometimes make snap judgments without getting to know the other people or giving the group time to form and develop. Initial impressions are rarely reliable indicators of how a group will be. Like individuals, groups have life histories, and one of the most awkward and difficult moments is getting started. Group members may be nervous, defensive, or overly assertive. It takes some time for people to get to know one another and to develop a sense of connectedness to the group.

Clarify Group Purposes and Individual Roles

Much of the initial discomfort and anxiety has to do with uncertainty about what the purpose of the group is and what people's roles in the group will be. Group members need to define their collective task and develop a plan to carry it out. That way, members understand what to expect and how the group operates.

Recognize That Members Bring Different Styles to the Group

As you have seen, individual styles of composing vary considerably. The same is true of individuals' styles of working in groups. For example, individuals differ in the way they approach problems. Some like to spend a lot of time formulating problems, exploring the complexities, contradictions, and nuances of a situation. Others want to define problems quickly and then spend their time figuring out how to solve them. By the same token, people have different styles of interacting in groups. Some like to develop their ideas by talking, whereas others prefer to decide what they think before speaking. Successful groups learn to incorporate the strengths of all these styles, making sure that even the most reticent members participate.

Recognize That You May Not Play the Same Role in Every Group

In some instances, you may be the group leader, but in other instances you have to play the role of mediator, helping members negotiate their differences; or critic, questioning the others' ideas; or timekeeper, prompting the group to stick to deadlines. You may play different roles in the same group from meeting to meeting or even within a meeting. For a group to be successful, members must be willing and able to respond flexibly to the work at hand.

Monitor Group Progress and Reassess Goals and Procedures

It's helpful to step back periodically to take stock of what has been accomplished and what remains to be done. Groups also need to look at their own internal workings to see whether the procedures they have set up are effective and to ensure that everyone is participating.

Quickly Address Problems in Group Dynamics

Problems arise in group work. Some members may dominate and talk too much. Others may withdraw and not contribute. Still others may fail to carry out assigned tasks. If a group avoids confronting these problems, the problems only get worse. Remember, the point of raising a problem is not to blame individuals but to promote an understanding about what's expected of each person and what the group can do to encourage everyone's participation.

Encourage Differences of Opinion

One of the things that makes groups productive is the different perspectives individual members bring to group work. In fact, groups of like-minded people who share basic assumptions are often not as creative as groups where there are differences among members. At the same time, group members may think that they can't bring up ideas or feelings because to do so would threaten group harmony. Sometimes it's difficult to take a position that diverges from what other members of the group think and believe. But groups are not forms of social organization to enforce conformity;

they are working bodies that need to consider all the available options and points of view. For this reason, groups should encourage the discussion of differences and look at conflicting viewpoints.

HOW TO WORK TOGETHER ON COLLABORATIVE WRITING PROJECTS

Because collaborative writing differs from individual writing, it is worth looking at each step involved in working on a joint project.

Organizing the Group

One of the keys to collaborative writing is getting off to a good start. You need to decide on the size of the group, its composition, what to do at your first meeting, and how to share the labor.

Group Size

For many collaborative writing projects in college classes, a group of three or four is often the best size. A smaller size—only two students—doesn't offer the group as many resources, and anything larger than four could create problems in managing the work with so many involved.

Of course, there can be exceptions. For example, your teacher may decide to do a collaborative project involving the entire class—developing a Web home page for the class or a Web site devoted to a particular topic, with everyone's participation.

Group Composition

Some teachers like to put groups together themselves. Others like to give students input into the group they are in. If the teacher puts the groups together, it's a good idea to ask each student whether there is someone in class he or she particularly wants to work with or particularly wants to avoid working with. It can help, too, to take schedules into account and match students who have free time in common when they can meet.

The First Meeting

The first meeting should focus on the basics:

1. Exchange phone numbers, email addresses, campus box numbers, and the best times to reach group members.
2. If possible, establish a listserv of group members on the campus network.
3. Identify the best times for meetings.
4. Agree on some basic procedures for running meetings. For example, do you want a group coordinator to lead meetings? If so, will one person serve

throughout the project, or will you rotate that position? How do you plan to keep records of meetings? Will you have a recorder for the project, or rotate? How long will each meeting last? Who is responsible for developing the agenda?

Division of Labor, or Integrated Team?

Some groups approach collaborative projects by developing a division of labor that assigns particular tasks to group members who complete them individually and then bring the results back to the group. This has been the traditional model for collaborative work in business, industry, and government. It is an efficient method of work, especially when groups are composed of highly skilled members. Its limitations are that weak group members can affect the quality of the overall work and that some group members may lose sight of the overall project because they are so caught up in their own specialized work.

More recently, groups have begun to explore an integrated approach in which the members all work together through each stage of the project. An integrated-team approach involves members more fully in the work and helps them maintain an overall view of the project's goals and progress. But it also takes more time—that must be devoted to meetings and, often, to developing good working relationships among members.

These two models of group work are not mutually exclusive. In fact, many groups function along integrated-team lines when they are planning and reviewing work, but also farm out particular tasks to individuals or subgroups. So you need to discuss and develop some basic guidelines on group functioning.

Organizing the Project

The Proposal

The first task is to decide what the project is and what its goals are. One of the best ways to do this is to write a proposal. Your teacher is the logical audience for your proposal. If you are doing a project with an on- or off-campus group, members of that group should also receive your proposal.

Proposals should include:

▶ **A statement of purpose:** Define the topic or issue you are working on. Explain why it is important or significant. What have others said about it? State what you plan to do and explain why.

▶ **A description of methods:** Explain how you plan to go about the project. What research do you need to do? How will you do it?

▶ **A plan for managing the work:** Explain what roles group members will play and what skills they bring to the task.

▶ **A task breakdown chart:** A task breakdown (or Gantt) chart shows the tasks involved and their scheduling. Such a chart is especially useful for planning collaborative projects because it shows how tasks relate to each other.

Task Breakdown Chart

Task Week ending	Sept. 12 19 26	Oct. 3 10 17 24 31	Nov. 7 14 21 28	Dec. 5 12 19

1. Gather preliminary info., contact agency

2. Proposal draft–revise final–review, edit

3. Progress report

4. Research on food programs

5. Interviews with people served by agency

6. Brochure design get photos graphics

7. Progress report

8. Write text

9. Print brochure take to agency feedback revision

10. Final version

Once the group is up and running, it needs to figure out how to stay on track—how to keep the work moving ahead and how to deal effectively with problems as they arise.

Incorporating a calendar into your task breakdown chart is one way to stay oriented. Two other ways are to run productive meetings and to write interim progress reports.

Productive Meetings

Group meetings are productive when they get work done, address issues and conflicts, and keep group members accountable. Although failing to meet can cause group members to feel disconnected, meeting for no reason can be just as demoralizing. For meetings to be productive, there must be a real agenda and work that needs to be done. One way to set an agenda is to agree at the end of each meeting what will be accomplished before the next meeting, and by whom. That way the agenda grows out of the progress of the project, and group members are kept accountable. If problems in group functioning come up, they should be addressed immediately at the next meeting.

Progress Reports

Progress reports are another way to enhance group members' accountability—both to one another and to their teacher. They serve to chart the development of a project at regular intervals. On your task breakdown chart, include one or two progress reports that follow the completion of major parts of the project:

- ▶ **Tasks completed:** Describe with details what you have done.

- ▶ **Tasks in progress:** Be specific about what you are doing, and give completion dates.

- ▶ **Tasks scheduled:** Describe briefly tasks you haven't yet started, including any not originally entered on the task breakdown chart.

- ▶ **Issues, problems, obstacles:** Explain how these emerged and how your group is dealing with them.

In some cases, teachers may ask groups for oral as well as written progress reports. This is a good way for everyone in class to see what the other groups are doing.

Confidential Self-Evaluation

In addition to requiring group progress reports, some teachers also like to ask individual students to assess how their group has been functioning and what their role in it has been. These self-evaluations are confidential and directed only to the teacher. They can be useful in helping the teacher anticipate when groups are having difficulties or personality problems. They are also useful to individual students because they offer an occasion to reflect on the experience of group work and what it means to them as writers, learners, and persons.

Drafting, Revising, and Editing

One thing that often surprises students working in groups for the first time is finding out that they have already started to draft their document from the moment they began to put their proposal together.

For many writing tasks, the final document draws and expands on what is in the proposal—explaining why the issue or problem is important, what others have said about it, what the group has learned about it, and what recommendations the group has to make.

But whatever the writing task happens to be, groups have to make decisions about how to handle drafting, revising, and editing collaboratively written documents. Here are some possible approaches. Your group must decide which one best suits your purposes.

▶ Members draft individual sections. The group compiles the sections and revises together.

▶ One person writes a draft. The group revises together.

▶ Members draft individual sections. One person compiles the sections and revises the document.

With any of these approaches, a final editing should be done by an individual or by the group.

However you decide to organize drafting, revising, and editing, make sure everyone contributes to the final document. The draft does not become final until everyone has signed off on it.

Collaborative drafting and revising can raise sensitive issues about individual writing styles and abilities. Some people are protective of their writing and defensive when it is criticized or revised. Be aware of this. If you think other group members are either trying to impose their own style or are feeling discouraged, bring these matters to everyone's attention, and try to sort them out before you continue on the writing task.

Giving Credit

Some teachers ask collaborative writing groups to preface their final document with an acknowledgments page that explains who should get credit for what in the overall project. You should also acknowledge anyone outside your group who helped you on the project.

Final Presentation

The final presentation of a collaborative project takes place when the document reaches its intended destination—whether it's the teacher, the Web, a politician or government official, or a community organization. You may want to schedule an oral presentation to go along with the delivery of the document.

Online Collaboration

The new electronic communication technologies have created new ways for groups to work together, even when their members are far apart. It's no longer necessary to meet face to face to have the kind of exchange that gives a joint project energy and creativity. With the nearly instantaneous transmission of documents, commentary, and conversation, collaborators can now stay in touch, confer, argue, and refine their ideas with an immediacy that was unimaginable in the past.

Of course, group members don't need to be halfway around the world from each other to take advantage of the new technologies. Here are some good ways of how to use these technologies in collaborative writing projects:

▶ **Stay in touch with group members.** Ongoing communication among group members is one of the keys to successful group work. Setting up a listserv on email can help members to stay in touch in and out of class.

▶ **Consult with people everywhere.** Through email, newsgroups, and Web sites, your group can contact a wide range of people who are knowledgeable about your topic—to ask questions, get information, and try out ideas. Online communication is much quicker and simpler than letters or phone calls.

▶ **Share working drafts.** To put together a successful collaboratively written document, coauthors need easy access to one another's working drafts. Drafts can be shared in ways that range from downloading files on email to state-of-the-art hypertext authoring systems.

▶ **Confer on drafts.** Online conferences make it easy for all group members to have input on drafts. New methods include "real-time" synchronous conferences facilitated by networking software.

REFLECTING ON YOUR WRITING

Consider a collaborative writing task you have completed. Explain why the particular situation seemed to call for a collaboratively written document instead of an individually written one. How did your group go about organizing and managing the writing task? What role or roles did you play in the group? What problems or issues did you confront, and how did you handle them? What was the result of the group's work? From your own perspective, what do you see as the main differences between collaborative and individual writing? What do you see as the benefits and limits of each?

CHAPTER 22

Writing Portfolios

Assembling a portfolio offers the opportunity to reflect on your writing and consider the motives that have animated your writing projects and the decisions you have made to realize your aims. Putting a portfolio together involves a critical reading of your own writing, in much the same way that you engage the work of other writers when writing critical essays, book reviews, or peer commentaries. A portfolio provides the occasion to come to terms with your writing over a period of time, to identify patterns in your development as a writer and to assess the strengths and weaknesses in the body of work you have produced.

In most cases, the purpose of a portfolio is to select a few pieces from a larger body of work in order to demonstrate a particular focus, skill, or growth over time. Depending on the situation, a portfolio might also include a reflective letter to the reader that assesses the collected work and shorter individual notes to introduce each piece of writing in the portfolio.

In this chapter, we look briefly at some common types of portfolios. Then we present some sections from the portfolio that Stacy Yi designed to present her work as a writer during her first year in college, as examples of various components that might be included in a portfolio.

COMMON TYPES OF PORTFOLIOS

The purpose and design of portfolios vary according to the rhetorical situations that call on writers to assemble them. Here are three common types:

A Portfolio for a Single Course or Assignment

A teacher might ask a student to compile a portfolio of work completed in a single writing course, or even a single writing assignment, in order to demonstrate growth or mastery of skills. This kind of portfolio might include early brainstorming exercises, exploratory and working drafts, peer reviews and writer's responses, and final drafts, to illustrate how the student revised his or her approach to the assignment and how successful those revisions were. Such a portfolio often takes a case study approach, in which the writer examines closely the history of one or more assignments, providing a reflective commentary to explain the motive of a piece of writing; how it formed in response to a rhetorical situation; the choices the writer made during the writing project; and how well, in retrospect, the writer believes the aim of the writing project was realized.

A Capstone Portfolio

Other teachers, or perhaps even an entire writing program or department, might ask for a capstone portfolio, which presents revised, final drafts from several courses during a semester or academic year, or even across multiple years of study. The purpose of a capstone portfolio is to examine work over time, to identify how a writer has changed and developed by taking on the rhetorical demands of a variety of writing tasks. As you will see in a moment, Stacy Yi's portfolio was designed to present and reflect on the writing she did in her first year in college—in two required composition courses as well as in two other courses she took.

A Professional Portfolio

It is common for professionals of all sorts—graphic designers, writers, artists, journalists, architects, teachers, interior decorators, contractors, and fashion designers—to assemble portfolios of their best and most distinctive work. Professional portfolios make a person's accomplishments available to potential clients as well as to hiring committees and prospective employers. This type of portfolio is meant to showcase an individual's most fully realized work, focusing on specific skills and capabilities. A professional portfolio typically includes only final, polished pieces of writing. It does not have the same emphasis on the process of composing or the decisions a writer makes that are found in case studies and capstone portfolios.

Print and Electronic Portfolios

Electronic portfolios enable writers, visual designers, and professionals in general to showcase a broader range of their work in slide shows, videos, interviews, and other multimodal compositions that include sound, images, moving pictures, and links to other sources of information. Many professional writers—poets, novelists, and nonfiction writers—have their own Web sites, featuring samples of their work along with reviews, biography, live interviews and readings, and other information.

Electronic portfolios are convenient in making work widely available on the Web; they can be burned on CDs to make a permanent copy; and they are easy to update. At the same time, it's worth noting that although print portfolios are more limited in what they can contain, they bring with them a special kind of attention and a reading space that is quite different from the experience of reading online. In a sense, it is what print portfolios lack—the constant choices readers have online, the multiple reading paths and links to other pages—that promotes a particular type of sustained focus and concentration as readers turn from one page to the next. It's a quieter, less busy experience of reading that may provide the best context for others to encounter your writing.

Stacy Yi's Capstone Portfolio

Stacy Yi assembled a first-year capstone portfolio that included writing from her two required composition courses, WR101 and WR102, and from a media and culture course and a sociology class on youth culture. This is the table of contents of her portfolio:

- ▶ A reflective letter.

- ▶ "iComics." Position paper. WR101. See pp. 84–87 for Stacy's first draft, peer review, and her writer's response.

- ▶ "Radiohead and the Tip Jar Model." Critical essay. CM151: Media and Culture. See pp. 397–401.

- ▶ "A Lawyer's Crusade Against Tobacco." Profile. WR102. See p. 237 for the early draft and the revision of the introduction.

- ▶ "More Than Just Burnouts: A Review of Donna Gaines' *Teenage Wasteland*." Book review. SOC201: Youth Culture. See draft and writer's reflection on pp. 373–375.

- ▶ "Revising Somali Pirates: A Rhetorical Analysis of 'You Are Being Lied to About Pirates' by Johann Hari," "A Very Edgy Ad: Phonak Hearing Aids," and "Where More Americans Get Their News . . . Than Probably Should: *The Daily Show*." Rhetorical analysis. WR102. See pp. 58–60, 239–240, and 308–309.

- ▶ A note on peer reviewing.

A Reflective Letter

A reflective letter in a capstone portfolio will typically discuss the choices you made in designing your portfolio, explain your development as a writer and the role of writing in your life, evaluate strengths and weaknesses in your writing, and discuss your experience as a writer and as a person in your writing class. The letter should provide readers with a sense of who you are. It might also indicate where you see yourself going next in developing your writing.

Stacy Yi's reflective letter introduces a capstone portfolio that collects written work in her first year in college from across the curriculum. She addresses the reader directly, and from the beginning establishes a fairly casual tone for her reflection. Notice that Stacy draws on not only her college experiences, but also her prior history with writing as a high school student in order to contextualize the work presented in the portfolio and, simultaneously, to make a claim about the evolution of her attitude toward writing.

Dear Professor Morrison, Interested Readers, et al.

Thank you for taking the time to read my first-year writing portfolio. As you make your way through my work, I trust that you'll find my earlier efforts are less successful, whereas the later entries are somewhat more complex and, at the very least, interesting. I think that's the kind of growth you'd expect to see in any writing student's portfolio. What I hope you'll also notice, and that I feel is more interesting, is a change in attitude about what "good" writing looks like and what texts can do overall. To better explain this, I should give you a bit of background.

In high school I was always a good student and, specifically, a good writer. I made good grades and scored highly on the written portions of standardized tests, wrote for the school newspaper, contributed to the school's annual writing anthology, and was praised by my teachers for my abilities. And so as an incoming freshman, I felt I knew how to write and that any introductory writing course would be at best a refresher and at worst a waste of time. I know many of my friends felt the same way.

But over the course of the semester, I realized that the kind of writing I was good at in high school was only one kind of several and that the skills that went into writing a good AP English essay were not necessarily the same skills required to petition an administrator to allow a controversial figure to speak on campus or to write a profile of an anti-smoking activist. For example, consider my earliest work in the portfolio—"iComics," a position paper about digital comics that I wrote in my fall semester composition course. Constructing an argument is a rhetorical technique I was familiar with prior to taking my first year writing courses. However, I was less familiar with the idea of fully engaging other writers and using their thinking to better position my own. My peer reviewer noticed this and gave me some good suggestions for revision. At this point in the year, I was still using sources in a limited way to back up my own opinion or prove to the teacher that I did enough research.

Later, in my second semester "Media and Culture" course, I wrote an essay about Radiohead and the digital release of their album *In Rainbows* that I think reflects a greater sensitivity to the discourse I chose to engage with. Rather than taking a position early on and finding sources to support it, I first worked through the thoughts and opinions of other writers from a variety of disciplines, including music criticism and economics. Finally, I gave my assessment of the situation, but left the conclusion open to different points of view. This is an approach I never would have considered in high school, where placing a thesis anywhere but in the introductory paragraph is heresy. I think this reflects a more complex manner of working with other writers' texts, where I'm not just using them to support my point but entering into a conversation with them and finding my own place to speak.

An important way my view of writing expanded was the result of writing in different genres over the year. I began to understand that there is not just one way to write—that there are many more kinds of writing than thesis and support papers. I have chosen two examples to illustrate my encounters with a range of genres, including one that was new to me, the profile, and one, the book review, that was familiar but that I had to rethink from the days of book reports in junior high and high school. Doing the profile showed me that some genres make a point but in a different way than thesis and support papers. It took me a little while to understand that the point was not to make some statement about issues but to bring the person to life. With the book review, I knew I couldn't rely on just summarizing the main ideas, as I had done for the most part in high school, but I wasn't totally sure what college-level book reviews looked like. So I decided I should do some research, and I looked up book reviews in sociology journals to see how they approached books.

Along similar lines, I'm also including two short rhetorical analyses we did as ungraded homework. I was surprised by how much I enjoyed doing these. I consider myself good at analyzing literature in English classes, but I had never analyzed other forms of communication, like newspaper columns, ads, and a TV show. This was another way my view of writing expanded. I started to see that writing isn't just about rules and following the form but can involve a lot of deep analysis of how writers try to involve readers in the meaning of a text.

This expansive notion of writing can only grow, as I can't imagine ever again feeling comfortable saying that I "know" writing. It's more accurate now to say that I know *about* writing, and I look forward to discovering even more about it, in and out of school.

Sincerely,

Stacy Yi

Introductory Notes to Individual Pieces of Writing

Stacy's reflective letter gives an overview of what she learned about writing in her first year in college and uses individual writing assignments as evidence. You may want to include shorter introductory notes to individual pieces of writing to cue readers to look at specific features of the writing or to keep a particular point in mind.

Introduction. Re: "iComics." Position Paper. WR101

I will admit to at first not entirely understanding the peer review I received for this assignment. My partner wanted me to include a quote from the other side of the debate, to give that part of the essay more legitimacy and therefore make my counterargument stronger. I found that strange, because I thought including more information about the side I was arguing against would make my text too balanced and maybe muddle my own position. But as I read my partner's draft, and workshopped a few others in class, I realized that hijacking the discourse and keeping information from readers is not the way to conduct argument. By spending time trying to understand my peer partner's comments rather than just dismissing them, I ended up with a much stronger and more complex essay.

Introduction. Re: "A Lawyer's Crusade Against Tobacco." Profile. WR102

Revising my profile was probably the most difficult task I faced in my introductory writing courses. I was accustomed to writing about people through a historical lens, beginning with the earliest information you could gather and writing up to the present. To be honest, that's the kind of writing I developed after doing interviews, because the easiest thing is to take all of that information and just narrate it in chronological order. It's more challenging instead to take the interview and think about what I learned about the subject by conducting it and which details that I didn't write down might actually be worth mentioning. The final draft is far more interesting because it includes more of my own thinking.

Introduction. Re: "More Than Just Burnouts: A Review of Donna Gaines'
Teenage Wasteland." Book review. SOC201: Youth Culture

I've included this book review in my portfolio, even though it wasn't an assignment
in one of my writing classes, because I liked how it turned out, and to show that the
skills I developed in those writing classes transfer to other classrooms. In this case,
my sociology professor asked us to pick a book from a list of seminal texts and write
a review, so I selected *Teenage Wasteland* (because the title reminded me of two of
my favorite things, the Who and T.S. Eliot). I liked the book, but it seemed pointless
to just say, "You should read it." The material was very heavy and seemed to warrant
a more complex response. So after doing a little research and genre analysis, which
involved reading other academic book reviews in sociology journals, I decided I had
to explain what the book was about, how it fit into the discourse, and then offer my
specific opinion about the significance of Gaines' approach to teenage culture. That's
a more complicated, but ultimately more satisfying, task than just summarizing and
making a recommendation.

Introduction. Re: "Revising Somali Pirates: A Rhetorical Analysis of 'You Are
Being Lied to About Pirates' by Johann Hari," "A Very Edgy Ad: Phonak Hearing
Aids," and "Where More Americans Get Their News . . . Than Probably Should:
The Daily Show." Rhetorical analysis. WR102

Writing *The Daily Show* rhetorical analysis was one of my favorite assignments
because it meant I could stream entire weeks' worth of episodes in one sitting and
call it research. And writing about the show was easy because I've been watching it
for as long as I can remember, so I feel like I know it as a text inside out. Sometimes
it's difficult to write about the things you love because all you want to say is how
much you love it and the *why* gets mixed up. But in this case, I felt I was able to
articulate why and still express my appreciation for Jon Stewart at the same time.

Analyzing the Phonak ad, however, was more difficult but just as interesting.
When I first saw the ad, I thought it was kind of funny, but I didn't know exactly what
I could say besides that. Plus, the ad has comparatively little content compared to
the entire run of *The Daily Show*, and so I had to work to extract meaning from every

little bit. What I realized is that if I used the basic rhetorical appeals—ethos, pathos, and logos—I could actually come up with a pretty interesting analysis of how the ad constructs this weirdly edgy rhetorical stance.

And this takes me to the first rhetorical analysis we did at the start of the term. I had no idea what rhetorical analysis meant. What I realized is that I could analyze literature, but I was reading articles and newspaper columns for their content. It was pretty interesting to see that you could analyze other types of writing too.

A Note on Peer Reviewing

Writing peer reviews was somewhat easier for me than it was for some of my peers, at least initially. When we wrote our first peer review, one of my classmates objected, telling the instructor he didn't feel justified critiquing someone else's writing while he was still learning to write. I interjected and told the class that even though we weren't professionals, we all still had enough experience as writers to know what worked and didn't work. I learned this from my creative writing workshop in high school. And although I still believe that is true, my early peer reviews were more like a list of trouble spots, without much helpful commentary or solutions offered. I knew enough to identify what I didn't like about my partner's writing but wasn't necessarily able to explain what in particular wasn't working and how to address it. I was already confident as a critic, but going through the peer review taught me skills that could back that confidence up.

Miscellaneous

Depending on your teacher's instructions, you may include a miscellany of writing done in or out of classes—letters, notes, email, blogs, poetry, fiction, leaflets, flyers, and so on. Introduce these writings by explaining what called on you to write them and how they differ from the other writing in your portfolio.

PART 6

Guide to Editing

INTRODUCTION: WHY WRITERS EDIT

Editing is the final step in preparing a print or digital document. There are two good reasons for editing:

▶ One is that readers invariably form judgments depending on how well writers handle the conventions of standard English usage. For better or worse, language differences of all sorts—typos, grammatical errors, punctuation mistakes, misspelled words, and stylistic lapses—can make a bad impression on readers and undermine a writer's credibility.

▶ A second reason is that sentences are basic units of meaning that express relationships among ideas. Writers edit not just to make sure that their sentences are grammatically correct but also to clarify what they are trying to say.

For these reasons, experienced writers think of editing as more than just avoiding errors. Editing involves working with sentences to make a piece of writing persuasive to readers.

In this guide to editing, we look at how writers work with sentences. The guide is divided into five parts:

▶ First, we consider some of the basic strategies writers use in composing sentences.

▶ Second, we present editing techniques to enhance the clarity, emphasis, and variety in sentences.

▶ Third, we review ten common sentence problems, along with editing strategies for correcting them.

▶ Fourth, we look at some typical editing issues that arise for second-language writers.

▶ Fifth, we examine some logical fallacies.

COMPOSING SENTENCES

Consider this series of sentences:

Shipmasters sought to maximize profits. They crammed into their holds as many immigrants as possible. Shipboard illness was quite common. Mortality was common too. Typhus ravaged tightly packed passengers to the New World. So did diarrhea.

Obviously there is something wrong with the way this passage reads. Not only are the sentences choppy, but they also fail to link key elements to each other so that readers can see the relationship of ideas. Here is a passage from Alan M. Kraut's "Plagues and Prejudice," a chapter on American attitudes toward immigrants and disease that appears in *Hives of Sickness: Public Health and Epidemics in New York City*. (We have added boldface to key words showing relationship.) Notice how he combines elements together to form a pattern of meaning:

> **Because** shipmasters sought to maximize profits by cramming into their holds as many immigrants as possible, shipboard illness **and** mortality were quite common.
>
> Typhus **and** diarrhea ravaged tightly packed passengers to the New World.

Coordination and Subordination

The techniques Kraut uses to form a pattern of meaning are coordination and subordination.

Coordination

Coordination links two or more clauses, or word groups that contain a subject and verb, in a way that emphasizes their relatively equal weight in a sentence. Notice how the following sentences can be combined by coordination:

> No one showed up for the concert.
>
> The band put on their uniforms.
>
> They picked up their instruments.
>
> The band played the opening tune right on time.
>
> > No one showed up for the concert, **but** the band put on their uniforms, picked up their instruments, and played the opening tune right on time.
>
> or
>
> > No one showed up for the concert; **nonetheless**, the band put on their uniforms, picked up their instruments, and played the opening tune right on time.

Notice how much easier it is now for readers to grasp the relationships among the actions described in the original sentences. The first clause ("no one showed up") is balanced in relationship to the second clause about the band, with each receiving relatively equal weight and thereby relatively equal attention on the reader's part. The nature of the relationship, moreover, is emphasized by **but** and **nonetheless**. Finally, by including the verbs **put**, **picked**, and **played** in a sequence, the sentence now makes it easier for readers to see how they form a series of continuous actions.

Subordination

Subordination enables writers to show how some clauses in a sentence modify, qualify, or comment on the main clause. Here's a version that uses subordination instead of coordination:

> **Even though** no one showed up for the concert, the band put on their uniforms, picked up their instruments, and played the opening tune right on time.

Here the use of subordination focuses readers' attention more emphatically on the band, and the fact that no one showed up is now represented as the circumstance in which the band acted.

Or you could change the emphasis altogether:

Because they had already put on their uniforms and picked up their instruments, the

band played the opening tune right on time, **even though** no one showed up to hear

them.

Writers use coordination and subordination in passages of writing to avoid the monotony of simple sentences and to guide the reader to the relationships and points of emphasis that are important to the writer's meaning.

▷ WORKING TOGETHER |||||||||||||||||||||||||||||||||||||||||||||||||||||||||||||||||||||||||||||||||||||||

Using Coordination and Subordination

The following is a passage from a history textbook about the 1994 inauguration of Nelson Mandela as the president of South Africa, following the end of apartheid and the first democratic elections in the country's history. The passage has been rewritten to eliminate coordination and subordination as much as possible. Notice how choppy it is. Your task is to revise the passage by using coordination and subordination to combine elements so that the sentences better express key relationships and points of emphasis.

Nelson Mandela was inaugurated as president. Thabo Mbeki and F.W. de Klerk were inaugurated as deputy presidents. The inauguration took place in the amphitheatre of the Union Building in Pretoria. It took place on May 10, 1994. It was a brilliant autumn day. It was a colorful ceremony. It was witnessed by many foreign and local dignitaries. There was a new, richly symbolic national flag. There was singing at appropriate moments of the *Die Stem* and *Nkosi sikeli' iAfrika*. These were later woven into a single anthem. It was widely hailed as one of the greatest acts of national reconciliation in modern times. It was a fitting prelude to the difficult tasks which lay ahead.

(Adapted from Rodney Davenport and Christopher Saunders, *South Africa: A Modern History*)

Follow these steps:

1. First, do a revision of the passage on your own.
2. Next, work with two or three other students. Compare the revisions. Where do they differ? At this point, don't argue about better or worse versions. Instead, consider each group member's reasons for the revisions he or she has made.
3. Once you have gone through the whole passage this way, go back to the beginning, and working together as a group, see whether you can agree on a revision.

4. Compare the revision your group has done to the revisions of other groups. Again, locate differences and consider the reasons why groups have revised in different ways. Then see whether the groups can agree on one revised version.

Modification

Subjects and verbs are the heart of a sentence, and combining them enables writers to express actions and represent states of being. In many instances, however, subject and verb, by themselves, cannot perform the work a writer wants a sentence to do. Writers use *modification* to add meaning to their sentences to clarify the relationship of ideas and to add needed details and specific information. We've just seen how one clause can modify another clause. Let's add to this by seeing how words and phrases modify in some sentences from Jerald Walker's essay "Before Grief," which appears in Chapter 2, pp. 39–42:

▶ **Single words: adjectives and adverbs.** Sometimes modification amounts to adding adjectives to nouns, as in "There was a **dazzling child** vocalist with a **pink gangster** hat." Imagine how little interest and key information this sentence would have without the adjectives—"There was a vocalist with a hat." Likewise, adverbs modify verbs, adding to their meaning, as in "All of these points were argued **compellingly** but a little too **loudly**."

▶ **Phrases.** Phrases are word groups that do not have a subject and verb. Notice how phrases modify first the "child vocalist" and then the "hat":

There was a dazzling child vocalist

⌐ with a pink gangster hat

⌐ slicing toward one eye

The Architecture of Sentences

Sentences can establish complex structures of meaning through coordination, subordination, and modification. To see the relationship of the parts of sentences, we can diagram them along horizontal and vertical axes. By locating the main clause farthest to the left, we can see the phrases and clauses that modify it as we move to the right. And we can also see the phrases or clauses that modify the modifiers at another step to the right. The vertical axis (up and down) enables us to visualize the accumulating depth and detail in the sentence. Adding arrows shows how the clauses and phrases connect. What we end up with is a sense of the space a sentence occupies and an architecture of how the sentence is constructed.

Though my siblings and I were only having fun,

↑

messing around,

⌐ for Michael,

↓

this was serious business, this was *work*—[the two main clauses]

↑ ↑

like performing was work for James Brown,

/

the man whose style he had already mastered,

↑

like performing was work for Smokey Robinson,

↑

the man whose soul he had already cloned.

⇨ WORKING TOGETHER |||||||||||||||||||||||||||||||||||||||||||||||||||||||||||||||||||||||||||||||||||||||||||||||||||||||||||||||

Diagramming the Architecture of Sentences

1. Working together with two or three other students, diagram the following sentences from Gretel Ehrlich's essay "The Solace of Open Spaces" as the sentence from Jerald Walker's "Before Grief" has been diagrammed, locating the main clause to the left, then arranging the modifying phrases and clauses to the right. Add arrows to show how phrases and clauses are linked.

    Seventy-five years ago, when travel was by buckboard or horseback, cowboys who were temporarily out of work rode the grub line—drifting from ranch to ranch, mending fences or milking cows, and receiving in exchange a bed and meals. Gossip and messages traveled this slow circuit with them, creating an intimacy between ranchers who were three and four weeks' ride apart.

2. Work with two or three other students to diagram the opening sentence of Walker's "Before Grief." This is a paragraph-long sentence that uses parallelism in a series of phrases and clauses divided by semicolons that all begin with "before." Notice that these "before" statements start simple and become more complex as they lead to the main clause, "There was a dazzling child vocalist." Once you've completed the diagram and can visualize the architecture of this long sentence, consider how it directs the reader's attention.

Active and Passive Voice

You may have heard the advice that writers should, whenever possible, use active instead of passive voice. There is a good deal of truth to this advice. *Active voice* in many cases makes sentences easier to read because it follows the natural order of events in which somebody does something, by making the actor into the subject of the sentence. Compare these sentences:

Passive Voice

The ability to write well has traditionally been included as one of the goals of a college education.

Active Voice

Educators, parents, and employers have traditionally included the ability to write well as one of the goals of a college education.

Notice that in the first version you can't tell who includes the ability to write well as one of the goals of a college education; therefore, the significance of the sentence is hard to evaluate. An action is going on, but no one is performing it. In the second version, the writer puts the actors in the subject position and thereby makes it easier for the reader to understand and evaluate what the sentence is saying.

Many sentences can be switched from the passive to active voice with little difficulty, and usually with a gain in clarity and emphasis.

Passive Voice

The teacher said that the essays we wrote last week would be returned to us.

[Who's returning the essays?]

Active Voice

The teacher said he would return the essays we wrote last week.

[The teacher is.]

Passive Voice

The dog was run over by a car that was driven by a man who was drunk.

[Unnecessarily wordy]

Active Voice

The drunk driver ran over the dog.

[Simpler]

In these sentences, as you can see, using the active voice not only makes the sentences easier to read but also more clearly assigns responsibility to the actor who performs the action. Passive voice is used widely in government and business to avoid designating responsibility:

Bombs were dropped on civilian targets for the third day in a row.

The Smith family was denied housing assistance.

The workforce was reduced to enhance the company's competitive position in the market.

On the other hand, there are some instances in which the passive voice makes sense, depending on where you want the emphasis in a sentence to fall. Compare these sentences:

Passive Voice

In 1938, the former Bolshevik leader Leon Trotsky was murdered by Stalinist goons. This murder brought to a close Trotsky's tragic struggle against the consolidation of Stalin's one-man rule in the Soviet Union.

Active Voice

In 1938, Stalinist goons murdered the former Bolshevik leader Leon Trotsky. By eliminating Trotsky, Stalin took another step toward consolidating his one-man rule in the Soviet Union.

Notice that the first sentence begins a topic chain by focusing on Trotsky's murder, whereas the second does the same by focusing on Stalin as the murderer. In this case, the decision whether to use active or passive depends on how the writer plans to develop the paragraph.

⌘ WORKING TOGETHER |||||||||||||||||||||||||||||||||||||||||||||||||||||||||||||||||||||||||||

Choosing Active and Passive Voice

Notice in the following passage that the verbs are in boldface. In some, but not all, of the sentences, the use of active and passive voice has been altered from what appears in the original version.

> Love **is believed** by Americans to be the basis for enduring relationships. A 1970 survey **found** that the ideal of two people sharing a life and home together **was held** by 96 percent of all Americans. When the same question **was asked** in 1980, the same percentage agreed. Yet when a national sample **was asked** in 1978 whether "most couples getting married today expect to remain married for the rest of their lives," no **was said** by 60 percent.

(Adapted from Robert N. Bellah et al., *Habits of the Heart*)

1. Working together in groups of three or four, identify the verbs as active or passive.

2. Then consider whether active or passive voice is more suited in the context of the sentence and passage. What changes in voice would you make? Which verbs would you leave as they are? How would you explain your choices?

3. Once you have completed your work, compare the results to what other groups have done.

Diction and the Use of Jargon

Diction refers to the word choices a writer makes in composing sentences. These choices give a piece of writing its particular tone of voice—formal, informal, or something in between. As a rule of thumb, it's helpful to think of diction as a way of adjusting your choice of words to your purpose and to your readers' needs.

For example, the diction in the following sentence is too informal for a college paper:

> The deal about *Moby-Dick* is that America's heaviest word-slinger, Mr. Herman Melville, uses that awesome white whale to pose some really bold questions about the nature of reality.

A more appropriate sense of word choice might lead to something like this:

> In *Moby-Dick*, Melville uses the white whale to pose searching questions about the nature of reality.

On the other hand, you can veer too far in the direction of a formal style, and your word choice can come off sounding inflated (and a bit silly):

> In his magisterial work *Moby-Dick*, our master literary helmsman Herman Melville uses the white leviathan of the watery depths to pose profound and eternally perplexing questions about the nature of reality.

The term *jargon* refers to the specialized language a group or profession uses to accomplish its purposes. Because it is specialized, jargon by definition excludes some people. The following sentences, for example, may be difficult for many ordinary readers to understand:

> The novel feature of the structure is the manner in which the two chains are held together by the purine and pyrimidine bases.
>
> (James Watson and Francis Crick, "A Structure for Deoxyribose Nucleic Acid")

> To give a text an Author is to impose a limit on that text, to furnish it with a final signified, to close the writing.
>
> (Roland Barthes, "The Death of the Author")

Yet people actively involved in science and in literary theory will immediately recognize the terminology used. In fact, they would not be able to do their work without such jargon. So if jargon seems impenetrable to outsiders, it seems an essential tool of the trade to insiders—to use in agreed-on ways such concepts as *purine* and *pyrimidine*, *Author* and *signified*.

That doesn't mean that jargon is forever closed off to all but an initiated few. One of the points of a college education is to gain access to the specialized vocabularies and ways of using words that characterize the various fields of study. From this perspective, there is no reason you should not use technical terms when you are writing within a community of specialists. To speak and write in that vernacular is a sign of membership.

For example, if you were writing to a friend or general reader, you probably wouldn't write:

> The migration of birds proceeds southward every winter.

It sounds stuffy and uses a noun—*migration*—to name the main action in the sentence. You'd probably write instead:

> Birds migrate south in the winter.

But if you were writing a paper in a course on animal behavior, the following sentence might well be appropriate:

> The annual winter migration of certain bird species follows well-determined flight
>
> paths to the southern hemisphere.

Using the abstract noun—*migration*—as the subject (instead of the birds who do the migrating) makes sense in this case because the concept of "migration" and its connection to "flight paths" is the focus of the sentence.

Academic and professional jargon rely heavily on *nominalization*—nouns that are created from other words by adding *-tion, -ity, -ness, -ance, -ment,* and *-ism*. As you can see from the example, *migration*—the nominalized form of the verb *migrate*—enables us to see the idea of birds' seasonal movement as the focus of the sentence. In this case, nominalization provides a concept to think with.

In other cases, however, nominalization just clogs up sentences by making things sound more complicated than they actually are. Often called overnominalization, this style is widespread in the professions, government, and business. For example, this sentence,

> The recent investigation of the staff's observance of personal wellness habits pro-
>
> vides indication of a marked reduction in the consumption of tobacco products and
>
> alcoholic beverages.

could be revised to read:

> According to a recent study, the staff are smoking and drinking less.

⇨ WORKING TOGETHER ||||||||||||||||||||||||||||||||||||||||||||||||||||||||||||||||||||||||||||||||||

Analyzing Jargon

The following two paragraphs come from the writer and editor Malcolm Cowley's essay "Sociological Habit Patterns in Linguistic Transmogrification," in which he pokes fun at inflated and jargon-laden prose. The first paragraph is a sample of sociological writing. The second is Cowley's translation of the passage into a plain and straightforward style.

Original

In effect, it was hypothesized that certain physical data categories including housing types and densities, land use characteristics, and ecological location constitute a scalable content area. This could be called a continuum of residential desirability. Likewise, it was hypothesized that several social data categories, describing the same census tracts, and referring generally to the social stratification of the city, would also be scalable. This scale would be called a continuum of socio-economic status. Thirdly, it was hypothesized that there would be a high positive correlation between the scale types on each continuum.

Malcolm Cowley's Translation

Rich people live in big houses set further apart than those of poor people. By looking at an aerial photograph of any American city, we can distinguish the richer from the poorer neighborhoods.

1. Working together in groups of three or four, read the two paragraphs and determine how Cowley has translated the original passage. Consider carefully what he has gained in his translation and whether anything has been lost. Don't just assume that Cowley's version is better.

2. Explain for whom it is better and on what terms it is better. Can you think of other ways to translate the passage that would be appropriate for a particular audience?

3. Explain your response and compare it to the responses of the other groups.

ETHICS OF WRITING

DOUBLESPEAK

The use of jargon to exclude, obfuscate, and mystify readers is often called "doublespeak." This style of writing typically uses not only passive voice (to evade responsibility) and overnominalization (to make the simple sound complex) but also euphemisms that avoid saying what things really are. The town dump, for example, becomes a "sanitary land fill," bad handwriting becomes "deficient grapho-motor skills," and students taking courses over television are called "low-residency students." A good deal of doublespeak, of course, comes from writers who are simply trying to sound as though they belong in a particular profession, government agency, or corporate position—and who do not intend to deceive their readers. The problem, though, is that the style of doublespeak, with its evasions and inflated language, is misleading. When government agencies refer to budget cuts as "advanced downward adjustments" or employers call strikebreakers "replacement workers," you can be sure they aren't trying to tell you the whole truth.

EDITING SENTENCES

Editing involves working with sentences and sequences of sentences to enhance their clarity, emphasis, and variety. In this section, we look at editing strategies writers use for these purposes.

Editing for Clarity

Two common problems that interfere with the clarity of sentences are wordiness and vagueness. In the following sections, you'll find examples of each problem and strategies for editing.

Wordiness

Wordiness means what it says: Too many words are used to express what the writer has to say. Here are some wordy sentences, followed by revised versions.

Original

As far as I have been able to tell, after doing thorough research on the matter, I conclude that the kind of popular music being broadcast today—whether rap, alternative, grunge, or metal—does not hold up to the music people used to hear when they were listening to the underground radio stations of the late sixties.

Edited

The popular music on the radio today—whether rap, alternative, grunge, or metal—does not hold up well compared to the music underground radio stations played in the late sixties.

Original

There can be little question, in my opinion, that it is a well-established fact that at least a sizeable number of students drink to the point of inebriation.

Edited

Everyone knows many students get drunk.

Vagueness

Words are *vague* when they don't convey with adequate precision and specificity what the writer is trying to say. Take this sentence, for example.

Original

My roommate is a weird guy who does strange things sometimes.

From what is available to us, it is difficult to tell exactly what the writer means by "weird" or what the "strange things" might be. Clearly the writer is trying to convey an impression of his roommate, but we don't have enough information to know what he means or whether his sense of "weird" and "strange" matches our own. Here's how the writer could eliminate vagueness:

Edited

My roommate studies a lot. He rarely parties during the week and never starts the weekend like the rest of us do by draining a keg on Thursday night.

Those two sentences would certainly clear things up, though as readers we may or may not see the roommate's behavior as "weird."

In most cases of vagueness, editing is largely a matter of unpacking the actual meaning that is lurking behind the use of vague words like *weird* and *strange*. There are a number of other adjectives writers sometimes fall into using on early drafts— *awful, fantastic, great, marvelous, nice, peculiar, terrific,* and *wonderful.*

In other instances, writers use words such as *aspect, factor,* or *situation* when they could be much more specific.

Original

Some aspects of the movie were lame, but in general the dramatic situation was terrific.

Edited

Despite some overly talky scenes, the dramatic tension will keep viewers engrossed in the film.

As this revision shows, specific words and phrases enhance the clarity of a sentence.

Editing for Emphasis

Editing for emphasis is a way of directing your readers' attention to the most important parts of a sentence. Writers know that the places of greatest emphasis are the beginning and the end of a sentence, so they structure their sentences accordingly, locating less important information in the middle. You can edit sentences for emphasis by paying attention to the following:

- ▶ Word order
- ▶ The use of parallelism and emphatic repetition
- ▶ The use of climactic order

Emphatic Word Order

Make use of readers' tendencies to focus on the opening and closing of sentences. Notice how the most important material in the following example is buried in the middle of the sentence.

Original

With its headquarters in Washington, D.C., the National Breast Cancer Coalition, which is an advocacy group promoting research and treatment of breast cancer, was founded in 1992.

Edited

Founded in 1992, the National Breast Cancer Coalition, an advocacy group based in Washington, D.C., promotes research and treatment of breast cancer.

Parallelism and Repetition

Parallelism and repetition are useful techniques for creating emphasis in a sentence by focusing the reader's attention on key elements. Notice in the following well-known line how parallel phrases emphasize the main points:

… and that government **of the people, by the people**, and **for the people** shall not perish from the earth.

(Abraham Lincoln, "Gettysburg Address")

Writers can also use parallel sentences to create emphasis, as in these examples:

Ask not what your country can do for you; **ask what** you can do for your country.

(John F. Kennedy, "Inaugural Address")

You have read the horrifying stories. **You have seen** the gruesome pictures. **You have heard** of the unspeakable atrocities.

(Doctors Without Borders, "Letter of Appeal")

As you can see from these examples, the effective use of parallelism depends on the repetition of grammatical elements. In some cases, writers enhance emphasis by repeating key words and phrases, as in this example:

I said that it was intended that you should **perish** in the ghetto, **perish** by **never being allowed** to go behind the white man's definitions, **by never being allowed** to spell your proper name.

(James Baldwin, "My Dungeon Shook")

When you edit, look for opportunities to create emphasis by using parallelism and repetition. Notice, for example, how the first example lacks emphasis, and the second example emphasizes key elements.

Hypothetical Draft Version

To increase the odds that more lives will be saved, we need to send surgeons, anesthetists, doctors, and nurses. Surgical kits are important to provide. Also antibiotics are necessary.

Actual Final Draft Version

Every surgeon, anesthetist, doctor, and nurse that we can send, every surgical kit that we can provide, every antibiotic we will administer increases the odds that more lives will be saved.

(Doctors Without Borders, "Letter of Appeal")

Climactic Order

Climactic order moves to a climax at the end of a sentence by reserving the final position for an especially important idea. Descriptive phrases and clauses create suspense that is resolved only toward the end of the sentence. Notice how the following sentences can be combined to create climactic word order. Here is a series of statements:

The Puritans were virtuous, hardworking, and pious. Schoolbooks idealize the Puritans as a "hardy band" of no-nonsense patriarchs. They were disciplined. They razed the forest and brought order to the New World. Occasionally, though, they would wander off after some fancy clothes, or rendezvous in the woods with the town prostitute.

Ishmael Reed's Published Version

Virtuous, hardworking, pious, even though they occasionally would wander off after some fancy clothes, or rendezvous in the woods with the town prostitute, the Puritans are idealized in our schoolbooks as a "hardy band" of no-nonsense patriarchs whose discipline razed the forest and brought order to the New World.

(Ishmael Reed, "America: The Multinational Society")

Editing for Variety

If all the sentences in a series are similar in length, type, and structure, the writing is likely to get monotonous and to lack any sense of rhythm. The strategies for enhancing emphasis that you have just reviewed tend to produce greater variety among sentences. In this section, we look at two other editing strategies for increasing variety by (1) varying sentence length and (2) adding an element of surprise.

Sentence Length

Varying sentence length effectively depends on understanding the roles that sentences of different lengths can play in a passage of writing. Short sentences are particularly useful for emphasis and dramatic contrast. Longer sentences enable you to establish relationships among the ideas in a sentence and to add rhythmic variation. Middle-length sentences typically do the main work in a passage of writing, providing description and explanation. The trick is to find effective combinations of all three. Notice in the following edited version how combining some sentences and compressing others provides greater variety of sentence length and thereby enhances the message in the passage.

Hypothetical First-Draft Version

There was a time when people wanted to keep the peace and the crockery intact at the dinner table. They held to a strict dinner-table rule. The rule was never to argue about politics or religion. I don't know how well it worked in American dining rooms. It worked pretty well in school, where we dealt with religion by not arguing about it.

Children came out of diverse homes. They carved up the turf in their neighborhoods. They turned the playgrounds into religious battlefields. But intolerance wasn't tolerated in the common ground of the public classroom.

Actual Final Draft Version

There was a time when people who wanted to keep the peace and keep the crockery intact held to a strict dinner-table rule: Never argue about politics or religion. I don't know how well it worked in American dining rooms, but it worked pretty well in our schools. We dealt with religion by not arguing about it.

Children who came out of diverse homes might carve up the turf of their neighborhood and turn the playgrounds into a religious battlefield, but the public classroom was common ground. Intolerance wasn't tolerated.

(Ellen Goodman, "Religion in the Textbooks")

Surprise

Another way of adding variety to your sentences is to put in new information or a twist of thought at the end. Changing direction at the end of a sentence can be effective if it is used sparingly, to create dramatic effects and set up transitions to the next sentence or paragraph. Here are some examples of sentences that use this technique.

When I left the Buffalo Bill Historical Center I was full of moral outrage, an indignation so intense it made me almost sick, though it was pleasurable, too, as such emotions usually are.

(Jane Tompkins, "At the Buffalo Bill Museum")

Thus the American Center of PEN, the organization of novelists, poets, essayists, editors, and publishers, finds it necessary to distribute each year a poster entitled "Writers in Prison." This poster, which is very large, simply lists the writers who are currently locked in cells or insane asylums or torture chambers in various countries around the world—who are by their being and profession threats to the security of political regimes.

(E. L. Doctorow, "False Documents")

PROOFREADING SENTENCES: TEN COMMON PROBLEMS

The final editing writers do is to proofread their manuscripts to identify and correct any errors that may remain. Of course, writers often eliminate sentence-level problems as they revise and edit to clarify their meaning. But there is still the necessary final step of careful proofreading to make sure that the writing is grammatically correct, observes the conventions of standard usage, and contains no misspelled words.

Proofreading differs from the kind of editing you've just reviewed that focuses on enhancing the clarity and emphasis of sentences and passages. In contrast, its purpose is to make sure everything is technically correct. For this reason, when you are proofreading, it helps not to read for the content or meaning of the writing but instead to concentrate exclusively on recognizing grammatical or spelling errors. Some writers like to begin at the end of a manuscript, proofreading the last sentence first and then working backward, looking carefully at each sentence. Others place a rule or blank piece of paper under the line they are proofreading to focus their attention.

In this section, we review ten common problems that you should watch for when you are proofreading your writing.

1. Sentence Fragments

We look at sentence fragments first because they are the sentence-level errors readers consider the most serious. College faculty and professionals are more likely to notice sentence fragments than other errors and to base judgments about a writer's abilities on them. There is no grammatical reason why sentence fragments are worse than other errors, but their impact on readers does seem to be strong and to undermine confidence in the writer. For this reason, it is key to find and correct sentence fragments.

A sentence fragment is easy to define: it is a part of a sentence presented as a complete sentence. Notice in the following sentence how a fragment occurs when a sentence part is detached and made to stand on its own.

Original

I have not been happy. Since my family moved to a new neighborhood miles away from my friends.

Edited

I have not been happy since my family moved to a new neighborhood miles away from my friends.

Editing Strategy: Connect the detached part.

In the following example, an incomplete sentence part stands alone.

Original

Basketball fans have been arguing for years about whether the Boston Celtics or the Los Angeles Lakers were the team of the 1980s. Which is an argument no one will ever finally resolve.

Edited

Basketball fans have been arguing for years whether the Boston Celtics or the Los Angeles Lakers were the team of the 1980s. No one will ever finally resolve this argument.

Editing Strategy: Make the detached part into a complete sentence.

Sometimes verbs that modify nouns are taken to be the main verb in a sentence, thereby creating a fragment.

Original

The committee charged with deciding which plants to close and which employees to lay off.

Edited

The committee was charged with deciding which plants to close and which employees to lay off.

Editing Strategy: Change the modifier *charged* into the verb *was charged*.

Or:

Edited

The committee charged with deciding which plants to close and which employees to lay off will present their recommendations next week.

Editing Strategy: Keep the modifier and add a main verb.

ETHICS OF WRITING

USING NONSEXIST AND NONDISCRIMINATORY LANGUAGE

The way people use certain words reflects and shapes attitudes about social groups and the roles of men and women. For example, to refer to women as "the ladies," "the girls," or "the weaker sex" conveys the attitude that women are not equal to men; it thereby perpetuates the subordination of women, whether intended or not. Similarly, to emphasize a woman's appearance conveys the attitude that women (but not men) should be judged by their looks and what they wear. It is easy enough, for instance, to see the inappropriateness of writing this:

IBM president George Smith, looking elegant in a charcoal pinstriped Armani suit set off by platinum cuff links and British handmade calfskin shoes, spoke to financial reporters about the company's third-quarter economic report.

So, using the same standard, it treats women unfairly to write:

Executive director of the Modern Language Association, Hazel Sims, looking elegant in a muted plaid suit, set off by silk scarf and alligator heels, testified before Congress yesterday about proposed cuts in the National Endowment for the Humanities.

By the same token, to identify a woman as wife or mother when she is appearing in a professional role conveys the attitude that women's identities are based on these domestic roles instead of the roles they play in public life. It seems ludicrous to write this:

IBM president George Smith, married for thirty-three years to high school sweetheart Wanda Smith, and devoted father of four, spoke to financial reporters about the company's third-quarter economic report.

So, using the same standard, it is inappropriate to write:

Executive director of the Modern Language Association, Hazel Sims, married for eighteen years to successful oral surgeon Ralph Moriconi, and mother of two teenage girls, testified before Congress yesterday about proposed cuts in the National Endowment for the Humanities.

It is also the case that certain words and phrases convey attitudes about racial, ethnic, and other social groups. For example, African Americans are no longer referred to as *colored people* or *Negroes*, terms that carry a history of segregation and racial oppression with them and reinforce stereotypes about racial inequality. Moreover, the older terms deny African Americans the right to determine their own collective identity and the terms by which they will be known. Similarly, people from Central and South America are increasingly using

the terms *Latina* and *Latino* to replace the older term *Hispanic*. And many gays and lesbians prefer those designations to the older term *homosexual*.

To write responsibly means to be sensitive to the ways in which language can perpetuate stereotypes and exclude and insult people. Here are some guidelines for using nonsexist and nondiscriminatory language:

1. Replace masculine nouns with more inclusive words when you are referring to people in general. To use masculine terms when you are talking about both sexes suggests that men are the standard by which human beings are known. There are available alternatives that are more inclusive.

Example	Alternative
mankind	humanity, human beings, people
the best man	the best person, the best man or woman
manmade	synthetic, manufactured, crafted
the common man	the average person, ordinary people
forefathers	ancestors

2. Replace masculine pronouns when you are referring to people in general. Here are some strategies.

Original

Each taxpayer must file his annual federal return by April 15.

Edited by changing to plural

Taxpayers must file their annual federal returns by April 15.

Edited by eliminating unnecessary gender reference

Each taxpayer must file an annual federal return by April 15.

PART 6 GUIDE TO EDITING

Edited by using *he or she, his or her*

Each taxpayer must file his or her annual federal return by April 15.

(*Note:* Use this last strategy sparingly and avoid *s/he* or *his/her* forms.)

3. Use nongendered terms to refer to occupations and social roles. Otherwise, it will seem that certain jobs and roles are reserved for men.

Example	Alternative
chairman	chair, chairperson
congressman	representative, member of congress
coed	student, first-year
freshman	student
mailman	mail carrier
fireman	firefighter
policeman	police officer
newsman	journalist, reporter
salesman	sales representative, sales clerk

4. Replace language that reinforces stereotypes or perpetuates discriminatory attitudes. The responsible approach is to find language that is inclusive and avoids offending.

Original

The public library should provide literacy programs for foreigners who don't speak English.

Edited

The public library should provide programs for recent immigrants who don't speak English.

Original

The abnormal sexual orientation of homosexuals makes some straight people feel uncomfortable.

Edited

The sexual orientation of gays and lesbians makes some straight people feel uncomfortable.

Original

White trash families have started to move into the neighborhood where I grew up.

Edited

Poor working-class families have started to move into the neighborhood where I grew up.

2. Comma Splices and Fused Sentences

Comma splices join two complete sentences together by using a comma. Fused sentences join complete sentences together without using any punctuation. The same editing strategies work in either case—separate the sentences, use a conjunction (*and, or, but, for, nor, so, yet*), use a semicolon, or subordinate one sentence to the other.

Comma Splice

Original

At seven in the evening, the City Council members filed into the auditorium to begin the meeting, however the mayor was not there because he had been arrested that afternoon for taking bribes.

Edited

At seven in the evening, the City Council members filed into the auditorium to begin the meeting. However, the mayor was not there because he had been arrested that afternoon for taking bribes.

Editing Strategy: Separate into two sentences. *However*, by itself, is not a conjunction and therefore cannot join two sentences together.

Or:

Edited

At seven in the evening, the City Council members filed into the auditorium to begin the meeting; however, the mayor was not there because he had been arrested that afternoon for taking bribes.

Editing Strategy: Use a semicolon to join the sentences.

Fused Sentence

Original

The Basque language spoken in parts of France and Spain puzzles linguists it appears to be unrelated to other European languages.

Edited

The Basque language spoken in parts of France and Spain puzzles linguists, for it appears to be unrelated to other European languages.

Editing Strategy: Use a conjunction—*for*—to join the sentences.

Or:

Edited

The Basque language spoken in parts of France and Spain puzzles linguists because it appears to be unrelated to other European languages.

Editing Strategy: Subordinate one sentence to the other.

3. Subject-Verb Agreement

Subjects and verbs need to agree in number. Singular verbs go with singular subjects, and plural verbs go with plural subjects.

Subject-verb disagreement is unlikely in a sentence such as this one:

Bill and Jim consider football the most important thing in life.

But when a subject is separated from its verb by an intervening phrase or clause, writers sometimes lose track of agreement, as in this sentence.

Bill and Jim, who have been competing all season for the starting position as quarterback, considers football the most important thing in life.

Note: When a phrase beginning with *along with, as well as, together with*, or in *addition to* follows the subject, it does not become part of the subject and does not make a singular subject plural.

Bill, along with his best friend Jim, was competing for the starting position as quarterback.

The best editing strategy in sentences like these is to ignore the intervening phrase in order to concentrate on the subject of the sentence and its agreement with the verb. Here is another example of how intervening phrases can cause confusion.

Original

The behavior of their children sometimes drive parents crazy.

Edited

The behavior of their children sometimes drives parents crazy.

Editing Strategy: Don't mistake *children*, which is part of a prepositional phrase, for the subject simply because it is closer to the verb than the actual subject *behavior*.

Collective nouns refer to groups of people, things, or animals—*team, staff, family, herd, audience,* or *tribe.* When the collective noun acts as a single unit, use a singular verb:

The team has achieved its greatest victory.

But when members of the group act as individuals or are referred to as such in the sentence, use a plural verb:

The faculty were praised for their many accomplishments.

4. Verb Shift

Watch for shifts in verb tense that are inconsistent and illogical.

Original

Jane and Margot went to the party last Friday, but when they saw it was a drunken mess, they decide to leave.

Edited

Jane and Margot went to the party last Friday, but when they saw it was a drunken mess, they decided to leave.

Editing Strategy: Keep the tense of *decided* consistent with the time of the action—in the past, last Friday.

When you are writing about events in a work of literature, a film, or a television show, use the present tense consistently.

Original

Hamlet clearly agonizes about whether he should take his fate into his own hands. As he said: "To be or not to be. That is the question."

Edited

Hamlet clearly agonizes about whether he should take his fate into his own hands. As he says: "To be or not to be. That is the question."

Editing Strategy: Note that Hamlet is not a person who spoke at some time in the past. He is a character in a play. Put what he does and says in the present tense.

If you are writing about a writer or artist who lived in the past, treat what he or she did accordingly.

Shakespeare wrote his plays to be performed. He was not writing literature. He was working as the playwright of a theater company to put plays on stage. The written versions came later.

5. Pronoun Agreement

Just as subjects have to agree with their verbs, so pronouns have to agree with their *antecedents* (the word a pronoun stands for). In many sentences, the relationship between pronouns and antecedents is easy to see:

Jane always drinks milk with her meals.

Jim drinks milk with his meals too.

Things can become confusing when the antecedent of the pronoun is a collective noun. When the collective noun acts as a single unit, use a singular pronoun:

The Northwood Unified School District always serves milk in its breakfast program.

When you emphasize the individual actions of group members, use a plural pronoun:

The staff left their hotel rooms and gathered together in the lobby.

6. Pronoun Reference

It is important not only for pronouns to agree in number with their antecedents but to make it easy for readers to see how they refer to a particular antecedent. Watch for instances in which the reference of a pronoun to its antecedent is ambiguous.

Original

After fertilizing the flower beds and pruning the dead branches from the apple tree, I watered them thoroughly.

Edited

After fertilizing the flower beds and pruning the dead branches from the apple tree, I watered the beds thoroughly.

Editing Strategy: Eliminate the ambiguous reference (did you water the beds, the dead branches, or both?) by substituting a noun for the ambiguous pronoun.

Or a pronoun can be used so vaguely that readers will find it difficult to see what the pronoun refers to.

Original

Workers are laid off, corporations are relocating their plants in other countries; nevertheless, profits and executive salaries are soaring. This is why people are so angry at corporate America.

Edited

Recent trends in industry have caused a popular uproar against corporate America: workers are laid off, corporations are relocating their plants in other countries; nevertheless, profits and executive salaries are soaring.

Editing Strategy: Provide a name, *recent trends in industry*, for what *this* means in the original sentence. Notice that the edited sentence clarifies a question readers might have about the original sentence, namely does *this* refer to all or just some of what appears in the preceding sentence.

7. Modifiers

Modifiers can be tricky at times. Dangling modifiers, misplaced modifiers, and disruptive modifiers can cause confusion for readers.

Dangling Modifier

Original

Driving home from work today, a cat dashed in front of my car and was nearly run over.

Edited

When I was driving home from work today, a cat dashed in front of my car, and I nearly ran it over.

Edited

When I was driving home from work today, I nearly ran over a cat that dashed in front of my car.

Editing Strategy: Cats can't drive cars, which is what the original sentence implies. Eliminate the dangling modifier by using a clause rather than a phrase that modifies the noun that appears next to it.

Misplaced Modifier

Original

I found an old Duke Ellington album in the record store that I have wanted to buy for years.

Edited

In the record store, I found an old Duke Ellington album that I have wanted to buy for years.

Editing Strategy: Presumably it is the Duke Ellington record the writer wants to buy—not the record store. Move the modifier closer to the word it modifies.

Disruptive Modifier

Original

Some politicians, even though reliable scientific studies have demonstrated the dangers of secondhand tobacco smoke, still minimize the health risks.

Edited

Even though reliable scientific studies have demonstrated the dangers of secondhand tobacco smoke, some politicians still minimize the health risks.

Editing Strategy: Relocate the modifying phrase so that subject and verb are closer together.

8. Mixed Construction

Mixed construction refers to sentences that start out having one sentence structure but shift to another. This will cause readers to do a double take.

Original

Because even the most experienced writers make grammatical errors means all writers need to edit carefully.

Edited

Because even the most experienced writers make grammatical errors, all writers need to edit carefully.

Editing Strategy: Separate the mixed parts of the sentence into two complete sentences joined by a conjunction.

Original

When Dwight Howard made both free throws is why the game went into overtime.

Edited

When Dwight Howard made both free throws, the game went into overtime.

Editing Strategy: Combine the mixed parts by subordinating one to the other.

9. Faulty Predication

Faulty predication occurs when the second part of a sentence comments on or defines a topic different from the topic presented at the beginning of the sentence.

Original

Maria's love of opera wanted to go to Juilliard for voice training.

Edited

Because of her love of opera, Maria wanted to go to Juilliard for voice training.

Editing Strategy: A "love of opera" can't want to go to Juilliard. Maria does.

Original

Nationalism is when people identify emotionally with their country.

Edited

Nationalism is a sentiment that arises when people identify emotionally with their country.

Edited

Nationalist sentiments arise when people identify emotionally with their country.

Editing Strategies: *Is when* is a nonstandard construction writers sometimes use to define terms. The abstract term *nationalism* needs to be defined by another term or set of terms.

10. Parallelism

When you have a series of items, make sure they appear in parallel form.

Original

A backpacking trip requires the proper equipment, to be physically fit, and that you know about the wilderness.

Edited

A backpacking trip requires the proper equipment, physical fitness, and knowledge about the wilderness.

Edited

A backpacking trip requires that you have the proper equipment, that you are physically fit, and that you know about the wilderness.

Editing Strategies: Both edited versions put the items in parallel order. The first is more succinct, with its focus on noun phrases, whereas the second focuses more on the reader.

Original

The New York Knicks want to draft a power forward who can rebound, with strong defensive skills, and who can score.

Edited

The New York Knicks want to draft a power forward who can rebound, play strong defense, and score.

Editing Strategy: Here the edited version creates a parallel sequence of verbs and drops the repetition of who can.

TEN COMMON PROBLEMS FOR SECOND-LANGUAGE WRITERS

In this section, we look at ten editing problems that second-language writers of English often encounter.

1. Subject/Pronoun Repetition

In some languages pronouns repeat the subject. In English, however, this repetition is not permitted.

Original

Celia Cruz she is one of the most famous Cuban singers.

Edited

Celia Cruz is one of the most famous Cuban singers.

Original

The person who did the most to encourage me in school he was my grandfather.

Edited

The person who did the most to encourage me in school was my grandfather.

2. Articles

Deciding when to use the indefinite articles *a* and *an* or the definite article *the* can pose some problems. There are general guidelines you can follow for proper, count, and noncount nouns.

Singular and Plural Proper Nouns

A proper noun is the capitalized name of a specific person, place, group, or thing. Singular proper nouns rarely use an article. On the other hand, plural proper nouns usually do.

Original (Singular)

The Disney World is a popular tourist attraction.

Edited

Disney World is a popular tourist attraction.

Original (Plural)

Himalayas are the youngest of the world's mountain chains.

Edited

The Himalayas are the youngest of the world's mountain chains.

Singular and Plural Count Nouns

Count nouns refer to people and things that can be counted—one baseball player, two automobiles, several friends, many tomatoes. As a general rule, use *a* or *an* before a singular count noun when it refers to something in general:

Original

Modern kitchen needs a dishwasher, microwave, and food processor.

Edited

A modern kitchen needs a dishwasher, microwave, and food processor.

But use *the* when you are referring to a specific thing:

Original

A kitchen in our apartment has a dishwasher, microwave, and food processor.

Edited

The kitchen in our apartment has a dishwasher, microwave, and food processor.

For plural count nouns, use no article when you refer to something in general:

Computers are changing the way people communicate.

But use *the* when you are referring to specific things:

The computers in the campus center are broken.

Noncount Nouns

Noncount nouns name things or ideas that cannot be counted: electricity, silver, steel, happiness, laughter, childhood. Noncount nouns use either no article or *the*. They never take the article *a* or *an*. Use no article when the noncount refers to something general:

Original

The silver is a precious metal.

A childhood is one of life's special moments.

Edited

Silver is a precious metal.

Childhood is one of life's special moments.

But use *the* for specific noncount nouns.

Original

Silver in the bracelet was tarnished.

Childhood of Charles Dickens was a difficult time.

Edited

The silver in the bracelet was tarnished.

The childhood of Charles Dickens was a difficult time.

3. This, That, These, and Those

This, that, these, and *those* are sometimes called *demonstrative adjectives* or *demonstrative pronouns* because they point to something specific. *This* and *that* are singular. *These* and *those* are plural. Make sure they agree in number with the nouns they modify.

Original

This shoes are too big.

Those shirt is too small.

Edited

These shoes are too big.

That shirt is too small.

4. Adjectives

The use of adjectives in English differs from their use in some other languages. Here we look at the form and sequence of adjectives.

Adjective Form

Unlike some other languages, English never requires that adjectives take a plural form to agree with the nouns they modify.

Original

Their garden is famous for its beautifuls roses.

Edited

Their garden is famous for its beautiful roses.

Adjective Sequence

Using more than one adjective in a sequence to modify a noun can be confusing. Should you write "the green expensive new Chevrolet minivan" or "the expensive new green Chevrolet minivan"? The following list explains the order in which adjectives normally appear:

Amount:	a/an, the, that, four, several, many, a few
Quality:	good, bad, beautiful, ugly, expensive, cheap
Physical description:	large, small, tall, short, round, square, flat
Age:	young, old, new
Color:	green, blue, white, black
Origin:	German, French, Mexican, Brazilian, Vietnamese, Chinese
Material:	wood, plastic, chrome, fiberglass, ceramic
Noun used as an adjective:	Chevrolet, television (as in television program), football (as in football game)

Using this order, you can make up new sequences. For example:

Four beautiful old Vietnamese ceramic vases

A few ugly yellow plastic ashtrays

5. Prepositions: *At, On, In*

At, on, and *in* are prepositions that designate time and location.

Time

Use *at* for a specific time:

Our class meets at 9:00.

I was born at 5:00 A.M.

We eat lunch at noon.

Use *on* for days and dates:

Our class meets on Mondays and Thursdays.

I was born on April 21.

Use *in* for months, years, seasons, and times during the day (morning, afternoon, evening):

Our class begins in August.

I was born in 1982.

We eat dinner in the evening.

Location

Use *at* for specific addresses, named locations, general locations, or locations that involve a particular activity:

I live at 158 South Maple Street.

We plan to study at Savuth's apartment.

Jorge and Clara are at work.

The movie theater is at the mall.

Use *on* for names of streets, modes of transportation, floors of buildings, pages, and tracts of private land:

I live on South Maple Street.

She arrived in this country on a plane.

Our class is on the tenth floor of the Armadillo Building.

You can find that poem on page 452.

The hiking trail is on the Mohunk Nature Preserve.

Use *in* for the names of geographical areas of land—cities, states, countries, continents—or enclosed areas:

I was born in Bangkok.

Our college is in South Dakota.

Melissa studied in Costa Rica for a year.

Can I leave my books in your room?

6. Participles: -*ing* and -*ed* Endings

Present (-*ing*) and past (-*ed*) participles can be confusing at times. Use the present form (-*ing*) to describe when someone or something produces a result:

The movie was boring, but it has a surprising end.

My roommate has some annoying habits I don't want to mention.

Use the past (-*ed*) form to describe how someone or something experiences such results:

Bored by most of the movie, I was surprised by its end.

I am annoyed by some of my roommate's habits.

7. Present Tense: Third-Person -s Endings

Check present tense verbs to make sure you add an -s or -es ending to third-person singular verbs:

Original

Maria often write to her mother in the Dominican Republic.

Edited

Maria often writes to her mother in the Dominican Republic.

But notice that with plural nouns and verbs the -s ending goes at the end of the noun:

Original

The two Dominican students often writes to their families.

Edited

The two Dominican students often write to their families.

8. Auxiliary Verbs: Do, Does, Did and Have, Has, Had

When you use the auxiliary verbs *do, does*, and *did*, the base form of the main verb always follows. *Have, has*, and *had* are always followed by the past participle (*-ed*) form:

Original

They did not helped their friend.

Gong Li has wanting to visit her family in China.

Edited

They did not help their friend.

Gong Li has wanted to visit her family in China.

9. Conditional (If) Clauses

Using *if* clauses enables a writer to state a condition and then in the main clause to describe the result. There are, however, a number of possible outcomes that can be indicated in the main clause. This section shows how the specific meanings vary depending on the verb tense you choose for the main clause. Notice the differences if the condition is (1) true in the present, (2) untrue or contrary to fact in the present, and (3) untrue or contrary to fact in the past:

If Clauses: True in the Present

If the condition is generally or habitually true:

If Clause	Result Clause
If I study hard,	I get good grades.
(*If* + subject + present tense)	(subject + present tense verb)

If Clauses: True in the Future as a One-Time Event

If I study hard,	I will get good grades.
(*If* + subject + present tense)	(subject + future tense verb)

If Clauses: Possibly True in the Present as a One-Time Event

If I study hard,	I might (may, could, should) get good grades.
(*If* + subject + present tense)	(subject + modal + base form)

If Clauses: Untrue in the Present

If I studied hard,	I would (could, might) get good grades.
(*If* + subject + past tense)	(subject + *would, could, might* + base form)

If Clauses: Untrue in the Past

If I had studied hard,	I would (could, might) have gotten good grades. (subject + *would, could, might* + *have* + past participle)
(*If* + subject + past perfect)	

10. Idiomatic Two- and Three-Word Verbs

A number of verbs change their meanings by adding a preposition or an adverb. If you are not certain about the use of idiomatic verbs, it's best to consult an English dictionary for second-language writers or ask a native speaker. Here are a few examples.

ran into someone means "encountered a person by chance."

ran away from somewhere means "fled or escaped."

ran over a curb, person, cat, or *dog* means "drive a car (or other vehicle) over."

ran up a bill means "spent a lot of money."

look into means "investigate."

look out for means "watch carefully."

LOGICAL FALLACIES

A logical fallacy is a flaw in reasoning that weakens the legitimacy of a writer's argument. Statements that contain logical fallacies nevertheless can appear to be plausible and may have persuasive effects. Logical fallacies are sometimes meant intentionally to distort the issues and mislead readers. (Advertising and political campaigns offer examples here.) But at other times, logical fallacies appear not because the writer intends to deceive readers but because she or he has misstated the point. As you will see, this can be a matter of oversimplification, poor word choice, and unclear connections among the parts of a statement.

Faulty Cause-and-Effect Relationship

This problem in reasoning mistakes a sequence of events for a causal relationship. It assumes that because one event happened after another, the first event caused the second.

> Children and adolescents who play violent video games are more prone to antisocial behavior.

This statement may be true, but it is hard to accept on its own terms. Readers would be justified to think the writer needs at least (1) to explain why and how playing violent video games leads to antisocial behavior (do people automatically imitate what they see on video games?) and (2) to account for all those children and adolescents who play violent video games and are not prone to antisocial behavior. All cause-and-effect arguments should be analyzed carefully to make sure A in fact does arguably cause B. After all, in this case, the cause and effect could run in the opposite direction—that is, it might be that children and adolescents already "prone to antisocial behavior" are drawn to playing violent video games. Or it could be that some third factor is responsible for both.

False Analogy

Analogies are based on comparisons. To tell readers, for example, that the evolution of biological species resembles a branching tree can be useful and clarifying. In false analogies, the writer assumes that because things resemble each other in certain respects, conclusions about one thing can automatically be applied to the other.

> The war in Afghanistan has gotten us into the same quagmire the government blundered into in Vietnam.

The writer's assumption that the situation in Afghanistan is identical to that in Vietnam is not a safe one. To be sure, both cases raise the question of U.S. military intervention. But the statement ignores many dissimilarities that the writer would need to take into account in order to make a persuasive argument that U.S. military presence in Afghanistan will necessarily lead to the same quagmire as the one that occurred in Vietnam.

Slippery Slope

In this type of reasoning, a writer predicts a chain of events that is inevitable and quite often catastrophic. The *slippery slope* argument is often used to argue that an opponent's proposal will have disastrous consequences, unforeseen by its advocates.

> If we decriminalize marijuana, people who smoke pot as a recreational drug will start experimenting with heroin, and in no time we'll have a nation of junkies.

The writer assumes a disastrous chain of events will eventuate as the inevitable consequence of the first step—decriminalizing marijuana. Critical readers will not be persuaded by such a sweeping scenario unless the writer can explain why and how the chain of events is going to unfold in the way described.

Red Herring

A *red herring* is something that is thrown into an argument to distract readers from the real issues.

> The argument that women in the military should take part in combat just as their male counterparts do sounds fair in principle but actually violates one of the most fundamental laws of nature—the division of labor between men and women. People who do not recognize this law are most likely to be homosexuals, and they are probably the prime violators of the laws of nature in America today.

The writer begins with a position that is reasonable, whether you agree with it or not. But the second sentence does not follow logically. Worse, it takes off in a whole other direction to attack people with whom the writer differs.

Ad Populum

Ad populum means "to the people." It refers to arguments that seek to mobilize readers' biases and prejudices instead of using principled reasoning.

> We need to limit the number of immigrants admitted into the United States annually. They are taking jobs away from real Americans. Go to your local convenience store and see whether you can understand the English the employees are speaking. Koreans, Indians, Pakistanis, Russians. It's out of control. How would you like your daughter or sister to marry one of these people?

The writer takes the controversial issue of immigration and begins by arguing that the United States needs a new policy. But then instead of explaining why, the writer launches off on a line of scare tactics to evoke fears of foreigners.

Ad Hominem

Ad hominem means literally "to the person" and refers to personal attacks on an opponent rather than rational debate on the issues.

> Councilman Roberts voted against needed increases in school aid. That's no surprise.
> After all, he sends his children to private school and doesn't care about public educa-
> tion. He's just another rich guy who drives a Mercedes, wears Armani suits, and eats at
> the most expensive restaurants every chance he gets.

Councilman Roberts may have used bad judgment to oppose school aid. At least, this writer thinks so. And the fact that he sends his children to private school may help explain what his priorities are and why he voted as he did. So up to a certain point, it may be principled and useful to look at an opponent's personal situation and motives in order to cast doubt on his credibility. But the car Roberts drives, the clothes he buys, and the kinds of restaurants he eats in don't really fit the line of reasoning developed here.

Bandwagon Appeal

The *bandwagon appeal* tries to persuade us on the grounds that everyone already believes in an idea or holds a particular view or supports a certain policy. The reason we should "join the bandwagon" in these cases does not have to do with the rational merits of an argument but with the fact that everyone else is already on board.

> Isn't the fact that Budweiser is the best-selling American-made beer proof enough?
> How could so many satisfied customers be wrong?

Advertising relies a good deal on the bandwagon appeal, playing in part on people's anxieties about being left out. Notice in this case how the argument seeks to replace independent judgment with a sense of belonging to a group of "satisfied customers."

Begging the Question

Arguments *beg the question* when they assume as a given what in fact they are supposedly trying to prove. This line of reasoning is sometimes called circular reasoning because it tries to support an assertion with the assertion itself.

> We need to institute a policy of mandatory registration of handguns because it is
> up to the government to make sure it has complete records of exactly who owns
> handguns.

Because "registering handguns" actually means "keeping complete records of who owns guns," the argument really says, "We should register handguns because we should register handguns."

Either/Or

Either/or reasoning turns issues into false dilemmas by oversimplifying things, making it appear that there are only two polarized positions.

> Either you support a free-market, free-enterprise system like the one we have in the
>
> United States, or you are an enemy of democracy.

Notice two things here. First, the argument makes it seem that there are only two possible positions—for or against a free-market, free-enterprise system—thereby reducing the complexity of the situation drastically. Second, not only is the dilemma posed a false one, but the term used in opposition to support of a free-market system—"enemy of democracy"—is itself inaccurate because it falsely conflates capitalism and democracy as the same.

⟫ WORKING TOGETHER ||||||||||||||||||||||||||||||||||||||||||||||||||||||||||||||||||||||||||||||||||||||||||

Logical Fallacies

1. Working in a group with two or three other students, choose five of the fallacies presented above, and write an example of each kind of argument. One or two sentences are likely to be enough. Do not label the arguments you write according to type of fallacy.

2. Exchange the written examples with another group. Discuss the five arguments the other group wrote. What seems to be the problem in reasoning with each argument? What would it take to put the argument on more solid ground? What revisions or new support would you suggest for each argument?

Index

Note: **Boldfaced** page numbers indicate illustrations.

GUIDE TO READING SELECTIONS

Readings found within the text are listed here by theme.